Acknowledgements

Those well versed in reading between the lines of an author's acknowledge-
ments will know that these brief lists of debts incurred sometimes have their
own codes, not dissimilar to those of broadsheet obituary columns. Thus, the
heat rises as one moves from the rather impersonal thanks to funders, librar-
ies, and archives, through the warmer expressions of gratitude to colleagues
and friends, to the final statements of devotion to loved ones whose tireless
forbearance is what really made everything else possible. I don't propose to
buck the trend here, but the danger is that the book itself comes to resemble
something born out of adversity, a creation that only just made it. This is not
quite how the making of *Fight or Flight* seems to me. For one thing, it's had
a very long gestation as the product of two decades of teaching university
students. For another, it's as much the result of reading the work of others as
of archival research in France, Francophone Africa, the United States, and
Britain. Most of all, it's been a pleasure to write. For all of that, I thank—I
hope not too impersonally—my students, my fellow historians, and Luciana
O'Flaherty, Matthew Cotton, Emma Barber, and Miranda Bethell at Oxford
University Press.

The Leverhulme Trust helped make the final writing of the book so
enjoyable by funding a Senior Research Fellowship between 2009 and 2012.
This, too, merits real warmth and more than a single sentence, but I hope
the trustees will find the book some sort of recompense for their support.
Archivists and librarians at the various institutions cited in the notes and
bibliography were, without exception, welcoming and accommodating.
Andrew Barros, Talbot Imlay, and Peter Jackson, Canadians with sharp eyes
for the paradoxes of Franco-British relations, helped me think through my
ideas. So, too, did David Anderson, Martin Alexander, Liz Buettner, Alison
Carrol, Georg Deutsch, Claire Eldridge, Martin Evans, Chris Goscha, Jim
House, Sam Kalman, Simon Kitson, Fabian Klose, Mary Lewis, Fred Logevall,
Patricia Lorcin, Neil MacMaster, Joe Maiolo, Philip Murphy, Natalya Vince,
and Mathilde von Bülow. In Paris, Raphaëlle Branche, Emmanuel Blanchard,

Jean-François Klein, Emmanuelle Sibeud, and Sylvie Thénault have guided me through the complexities of French colonial affairs.

Stacey Hynd, Justin Jones, and Andrew Thompson, colleagues in global and imperial history at Exeter University, read chapter drafts, providing vital help along the way. Another, Richard Toye, went through the entire type-script, a typically generous act for which I'm very grateful. My mother was equally kind, scrutinizing several chapters and reminding me what is—and isn't—a verb. If the book makes sense, it is in no small measure down to her. Thanks to Chouie, a small cat with a big miaow, for enforcing the tea breaks. More than anyone else, Suzy made the whole thing possible—and makes everything worth it.

FIGHT OR FLIGHT

FIGHT OR FLIGHT

BRITAIN, FRANCE, AND THEIR ROADS FROM EMPIRE

MARTIN THOMAS

OXFORD
UNIVERSITY PRESS

OXFORD
UNIVERSITY PRESS

Great Clarendon Street, Oxford, OX2 6DP,
United Kingdom

Oxford University Press is a department of the University of Oxford.
It furthers the University's objective of excellence in research, scholarship,
and education by publishing worldwide. Oxford is a registered trade mark of
Oxford University Press in the UK and in certain other countries

Published in the United States of America by Oxford University Press
198 Madison Avenue, New York, NY 10016, United States of America

British Library Cataloguing in Publication Data

Data available

Library of Congress Control Number: 2013937985

ISBN 978–0–19–969827–1

Printed in Great Britain by
Clays Ltd, St Ives plc

Contents

List of Illustrations

List of Maps

Preface

On the morning of 1 November 1954, an Algerian baker gathered his family together to share some important news. A little-known revolutionary movement calling itself the *Front de Libération Nationale*, or FLN, had mounted over fifty coordinated attacks against public buildings, police stations, and communications centres throughout the French colony. Writing almost half a century later, the baker's daughter, Louisette Ighilahriz, recalled her father's words. 'It's the end of humiliation,' he said.[1] Louisette soon proved her devotion to the FLN cause. Using the pseudonym 'Lila' she couriered weapons and scraps of intelligence to fellow militants, her secret cargo sometimes hidden inside bread baked by her father. But it was in the summer of 1957, during the final weeks of the notorious Battle of Algiers, that her life changed for ever. She and a group of fellow combatants were ambushed by French parachutists near Chebli, a town just south of the capital. She was shot and wounded, the prelude to years of imprisonment. A story of anti-colonial commitment, of bravery, of deprivation, Louisette Ighilahriz's Algerian war would come to the French public's attention for a different reason entirely. Writing in *Le Monde* on 20 July 2000, she revealed what her parachutist captors had done to her. A harrowing autobiographical account published ten months later went further still.

As summer turned to autumn 1957 Ighilahriz lay bandaged and in plaster in the Algiers Mustapha hospital. There, she was injected with the 'truth drug' Pentothal. She said nothing. Still bed-ridden, she was then transferred to one of the city's army interrogation centres. Frustrated by her defiance, a parachutist captain took charge of proceedings. He cut her bandages with a bayonet. He prodded at her wounds. Then he raped her 'with all sorts of objects'.[2] The torture continued over days, weeks, months. And, as the audible screams of her

---

1. Louisette Ighilahriz, *Algérienne* (Paris: Fayard, 2001), 46; also cited in Allison Drew, *We are no longer in France: Communists in Colonial Algeria* (Manchester University Press, 2014), ch. 7.
2. Marnia Lazreg, *Torture and the Twilight of Empire: From Algiers to Baghdad* (Princeton University Press, 2008), 161, citing Ighilahriz, *Algérienne*, 98–104.

fellow detainees proved, it had become the army's way of doing things.[3] More than four decades later Ighilahriz explained that she was writing about her experiences to remind French society that, for Algerians like her, the road from empire was travelled via a war of immeasurable cruelty.[4] Her book sold well. But another, published almost simultaneously, sold better. Written by Paul Aussaresses, a senior army intelligence officer and a colleague of Ighilahriz's tormentor, it was a shockingly frank and apparently remorseless account of how torture, death squads, and summary killings were integral to the work of the security forces in Algeria.[5] The logic of Aussaresses's account was straightforward: if France wanted to keep its empire, activities like this were necessary.[6]

These histories of people disfigured by violence and violation, of minds warped by colonial conflict, are bound up with the ways in which a large colonial empire came to an end. Theirs are stories of fight and flight. Of fights between opposing ideas of authority and legitimacy, one imperial, the other rooted in local demands for greater freedom. Of eventual flight as colonial authorities either negotiated their way out or packed up and left in *de facto* surrender to their local opponents. The examples above relate to Algeria, a French-ruled territory. But equally troubling accounts have emerged from Britain's colonial record.[7] In some places—not just Algeria but, as we shall see, India, Palestine, Kenya, and Vietnam, among others—the societal disruption involved was immense. In others, violence between colonial authorities and presumptive national movements was less pronounced. Sometimes it was virtually absent. This book examines why. In narrative terms, it is a story of how the British and French empires ended. In analytical terms, it is a comparative account of why they ended in particular ways. Above all, it is an exploration of a kind of cognitive dissonance, a collective disconnect between attitudes and worldviews so different that, for some, empire was worth defending at all costs while, for others, it was either manifestly indefensible or increasingly irrelevant. Finally, the book examines an

---

3. For discussion of rape as a weapon of war, see Raphaëlle Branche, Isabelle Delpha, John Horne, Pieter Lagrou, Daniel Palmieri, and Fabrice Virgili, 'Writing the history of rape in wartime', in Branche and Virgili, eds, *Rape in Wartime* (Basingstoke: Palgrave-Macmillan, 2012), 1–16.
4. Ighilahriz, *Algérienne*, cover material.
5. Général Paul Aussaresses, *Services Spéciaux: Algérie, 1955–1957* (Paris: Perrin, 2001).
6. Lazreg, *Torture*, 1, 141.
7. From Kenya and Palestine especially: for very recent accounts, see Huw Bennett *Fighting the Mau Mau: The British Army and Counter-Insurgency in the Kenya Emergency* (Cambridge University Press, 2012); Matthew Hughes, 'From law and order to pacification: Britain's suppression of the Arab Revolt in Palestine, 1936–39', *Journal of Palestine Studies*, 39:2 (2010), 6–22.

accelerating rate of historical change, one that would see these once mighty empires brought down within two or three generations—in historical terms, the blink of an epochal eye.

By the end of the 1950s, only a few years after Louisette Ighilahriz began her struggle, the French and British empires were approaching dissolution. 1960. The year that marked John F. Kennedy's election, a widening Sino-Soviet split, and the first commercially available contraceptive pill, was also the 'year of Africa'. It was so called because seventeen African countries achieved independence from their European rulers. Some, including the vast tropical domains of the former Belgian Congo, descended into revolutionary turmoil. But most, including fourteen former French colonies below the Sahara, took their place on the world stage relatively peacefully.[8] Africa's newly independent states played an integral part in securing a landmark commitment from the United Nations later that same year. The UN General Assembly's Resolution on the Granting of Independence to Colonial Countries and Peoples, affirmed that self-determination—understood, in this case, as the freely declared will of the majority within a colonial territory—conferred the right to sovereign statehood.[9]

Passed on 14 December 1960, this Resolution 1514 rejected the proposition that inadequate political or economic preparations by a colonial power could justify any delays in conceding national independence. Having lost the arguments that the UN had no authority to interfere in 'internal' colonial affairs and that the colonial nationalist groups vying for power were either unrepresentative, dangerous, or both, the final weapon left to Britain and France as imperial powers—namely, that their remaining African possessions could not yet stand on their own feet—was kicked away.[10] Writing four years later in October 1964, Vivien Beamon, a member of America's National Council of Negro Women, captured the mood among her fellow activists: 'Independence in Africa . . . helped stimulate our civil rights movement, which in turn has helped stimulate civil rights movements in Southern Rhodesia, Mozambique, and South Africa. Everything ties together.'[11] The days of white colonial domination were numbered. Or so it seemed.

8. Tony Chafer and Alexander Keese, eds, *Francophone Africa at Fifty* (Manchester University Press, 2013).

9. Brad Simpson, 'The United States and the curious history of self-determination', *DH*, 36:4 (2012), 681.

10. DDF, 1960, vol. II, no. 308, 'Note de la Direction d'Afrique-Levant, fin décembre 1960'.

11. Quoted in Brenda Gayle Plummer, *In Search of Power: African Americans in the Era of Decolonization, 1956–1974* (Cambridge University Press, 2013), 86.

One would be forgiven for thinking that the end of empire, the onward march of decolonization, the acclamation of civil rights, and the emergence of a fiercely independent 'Third World', were, by then, generally recognized phenomena. Yet, slant the historical lens differently and the picture is transformed. What the sociologist Julian Go has called the 'blurry continuum' between formal imperial rule and informal influence or control would remain a marker of relationships between numerous former colonies and their erstwhile European rulers.[12] In other places colonialism refused to die. Several of Africa's largest and most populous countries—Algeria, South Africa, Southern Rhodesia, Angola, and Mozambique—were still caught in the vice-like grip of racially discriminatory regimes. Some were close to rebellion, others already wracked by political violence.[13] In Washington, US State Department officials noted ominously that, across Africa, black majority populations confronted privileged white settler communities 'across a sea of developing hate'.[14]

The apparent disintegration of European empire into racially coloured violence was far from unique. In Southeast Asia, two conflicts whose recent ancestry was predominantly colonial were about to explode. The first, between Kennedy's America and Communist North Vietnam, was demographically and environmentally devastating for the victorious Vietnamese, internationally and culturally debilitating for the United States. The second, between formerly British-governed Malaysia and once Dutch-ruled Indonesia, became the prelude to the mass killing and ruthless authoritarianism of President Suharto's Indonesian military regime. France and Britain were, in different ways, instrumental to each of these conflicts. Yet the French presence in Vietnam formally ended in 1954 and Britain finally handed over power in Malaysia six years after that. France had fought and lost in Vietnam. Britain, ostensibly at least, had fought and won in Malaya. What did these contrasting trajectories signify?

Certainly by 1960 Britain and France, Europe's predominant imperial powers over the preceding two centuries, were in general, if not quite total, colonial retreat. The rulers of both countries still treated certain lines in the

---

12. Julian Go, *Patterns of Empire: The British and American Empires, 1688 to the Present* (Cambridge University Press, 2011), 11.
13. The Zimbabwean case is especially instructive: see Heike L. Schmidt, *Colonialism and Violence in Zimbabwe: A History of Suffering* (Oxford: James Currey, 2013).
14. Ryan M. Irwin, 'A wind of change? White redoubt and the postcolonial moment, 1960–1963', *DH*, 33:5 (2009), 898, 907–8, quotation at 915.

sand or, more often, their garrison outposts in warmer seas, as sacrosanct. The French dismissed them as 'the confetti of empire', but some of these places—Hong Kong, Aden, Cyprus, Djibouti, New Caledonia—were anything but ephemeral to the global systems of imperial power that shaped them.[15] For all that, Europe's former colonial giants were picking fewer imperial fights than in previous decades. And their preference for flight, for negotiated pull-outs, became clearer as the 1960s wore on. Why had these global empires shrunk so quickly—over the course of a generation spanning the twenty years since the end of the Second World War? Or, to reverse the lens again, why did it take fully two decades (indeed, much longer) before the rulers of empire acknowledged that the game was up, that colonies and colonialism were becoming indefensible strategically, politically, ethically? Probing these questions a little further, perhaps the hardest problem to solve is why wars and violence erupted in some colonies in the throes of decolonization but not in others. What, in other words, configured the paths towards fight or flight? Why were some blocked and others cleared? The following chapters offer some answers.

15. Robert Aldrich, 'When did decolonization end? France and the ending of empire', in Alfred W. McCoy, Josep M. Fradera, and Stephen Jacobson, eds, *Endless Empire: Spain's Retreat, Europe's Eclipse, America's Decline* (Madison, WI: University of Wisconsin Press, 2012), 222.

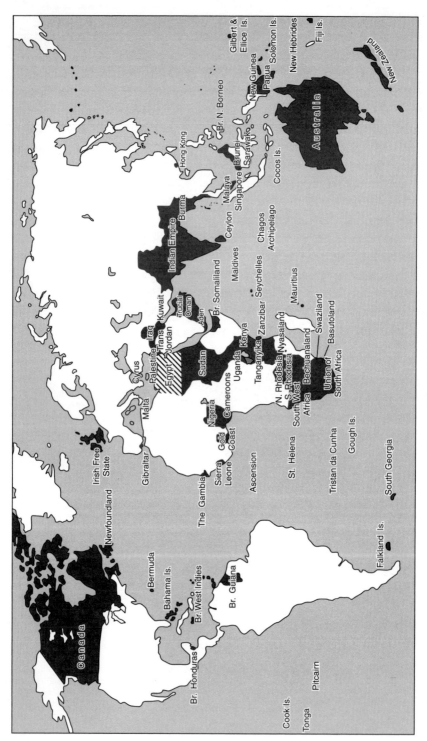

Map 1. The British Empire.

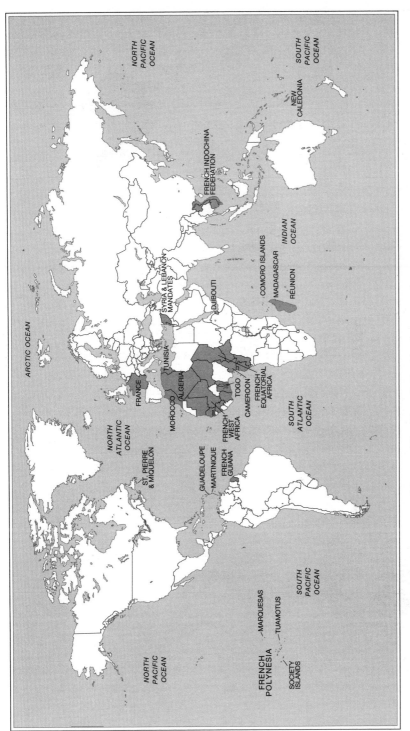

Map 2. The French Empire between the wars.

Introducing *Fight or Flight*

In May 2010 *Hors-la-loi (Outside the Law)*, a high-budget film about three Algerian brothers caught up in their country's violent struggle for colonial independence from France, premiered at the Cannes Film Festival. Rachid Bouchareb, the film's director, was soon embroiled in a peculiarly French storm of media controversy, one that, while overtly intellectual, quickly became politicized and highly emotive. At issue was his depiction of a 1945 Algerian uprising which was used to justify the massacre of thousands of civilians by colonial security forces and French settler vigilantes.[1] French-born and of Algerian descent, Bouchareb in his previous film, *Indigènes (Days of Glory)*, had tackled the vital contribution made by North African soldiers to the French Army's campaigning in Europe during the final years of the Second World War. This was something that the authorities in Paris proved reluctant to acknowledge either at the time or since. But *Hors-la-loi* went further. Bouchareb turned post-war France from a country shaped by its wartime resistance to Nazi occupation into a colonialist regime whose viciousness provoked desperate—and legitimate—resistance by persecuted Algerians. So stark was this juxtaposition that the director was accused by the French Defence Ministry, by Gaullist parliamentarians, and by elements within the French press of playing fast and loose with history.[2] Others disagreed. *Hors-la-loi* figured among the nominees for 'Best foreign language film' at America's Academy Awards later in 2010.

Arguments over the depiction of an especially violent episode in France's recent colonial past offer an entry-point to the issues discussed in this book. For, if *Hors-la-loi* was anything, it was a study of why those living under colonialism took up arms against an imperial regime that refused to give ground. It was a cinematic depiction of the choices inherent in 'fight or flight'. What, then, does this seemingly simple phrase actually imply?

The search for answers might take us back to the early nineteenth century. Reflecting on the features of violence between states, Prussia's foremost strategic theorist Carl von Clausewitz identified certain variables whose interaction determined the probability, intensity, and outcome of armed conflicts. One of these was the extent of popular support for war and the degree to which different sections of the public were personally engaged by it. Another was the clarity with which politicians defined what was being fought for. Clearly defined goals and commensurately higher levels of public support assisted the achievement of strategic objectives.[3] These objectives might be military victory or, telescoping forward to the cases examined in this book, the continuation or termination of colonial rule.

Clausewitz was writing well over a century before what is loosely identified as the era of decolonization between 1945 and 1975—during which Britain and France, along with fellow European imperialists the Netherlands, Belgium, Italy, and Portugal, lost or surrendered sovereign control over the bulk of their once-dependent territories. Nor was he discussing colonial conflict, although memories of Napoleonic colonization in German-speaking Europe were surely fresh in his memory.[4] Yet Clausewitz's insights provide a fitting starting point for discussion for two reasons. One is that wars of decolonization were generally characterized by massive mobilization of colonial populations against their European rulers (the 'stronger levels of support' that Clausewitz identified as critical) alongside only limited engagement—public or military—by the colonial power.[5] The other is that British and French colonial authorities professed the need, not just to defeat their armed opponents, but to address the grievances of their civilian backers. Although not always expressed with Clausewitz-like precision, the 'defined goals' of colonial officialdom in situations of armed revolt connected the achievement of military objectives to the subsequent implementation of socio-political reforms. This is where the challenge lay.

The more we unpick these two apparently basic points, the more the policies of colonial government reveal fundamental dichotomies. As we shall see, the form and extent of popular engagement in contested decolonization—whether for it or against it—was something to which politicians in Britain and France responded very differently in the two decades following the Second World War's end. Equally, while responses to violent colonial disorder supposedly combined the firm hand of military intervention with soothing promises of political concessions, only belatedly, if at all, did colonial authorities treat their opponents as credible negotiating partners, still less as legitimate ones.[6] More often than not, this reluctance proved to be a dreadful mistake.

This book, then, begins from the proposition that wars of decolonization were not somehow unavoidable. Most were deliberately chosen. What follows is a history of these paths to violence, of armed conflict, its incidence and its avoidance, in the end of the British and French Empires during the mid to late twentieth century. The story is told in three ways. First, in comparing French and British approaches to the challenges of anti-colonial opposition, I try to explain why conflict was prevented or promoted in particular times and places. If Britain is perceived to have escaped from empire without 'serious shock', France did not.[7] Are these presumptions correct? Second, the book compares experiences of decolonization region by region, albeit predominantly in Asia and Africa. The third comparison is between those whose opposition to colonial rule drove them to violence and those for whom it did not. Those individuals who decided to take up arms against colonial domination were typically resisting something they found intolerable. But relatively few burned the bridge to eventual dialogue. Their decisions about resistance or accommodation were also inter-connected. The outbreak of fighting or decisions to negotiate in one territory influenced other colonized peoples contemplating their own paths to freedom. Putting these comparisons together, the fundamental question that faces us is why violent politics predominated in some places and not in others. My suggestion is that, in most situations, this issue turned on the choices made by the imperial powers and their opponents about resisting the end of empire or negotiating it, about fight or flight.

Some might see antecedents to this story, whether in the classical period or in other, more recent historical times. In the late eighteenth century France and Britain had each surrendered the North American domains of their first empires after fighting ineffectually to keep them. French losses in Canada during the Seven Years War of 1756–63 and the American Revolution of the 1770s were portents of later decolonization. The first was bound up with the greater strategic resources of an imperial rival—Britain. The second was the consequence of a settler rebellion against imperious rule from London. And following each defeat, the geopolitical focus of empire shifted elsewhere—in Britain's case, initially to South Asia; rather later in the French case, to the African continent. This is where the sheer magnitude of modern colonialism begins to distinguish it. Over 450 million people in Asia and Africa fell under European colonial rule between the 1830s and the treaty settlements that carved up the Ottoman Middle East following the First World War.[8] After the end of the Second, the figure climbed to almost a billion. This massive growth in numbers, as much the consequence of population increases and improving life expectancy as of geographical extensions to imperial power, was thrown into sharp reverse in the twenty years after 1945. By the end of the 1960s fewer than fifty million souls remained European colonial subjects and only Portugal clung on to the bulk of its overseas territories. The process involved is usually described as decolonization.[9] Although historians can agree on the terminology, they differ sharply about the principal causal factors as work.

Imperial historians, as their name implies, have tended to focus on empires' collapsing institutional structures, changes in administrative practice, shifting European public and political attitudes, and the consequent adoption of colonial reforms. Reinvigorated in recent years by closer attention to empire cultures and the networks of communication and migration that spread them, imperial history remains primarily European in focus, its foremost concern being to explain modern European empire as a historical phenomenon. Historians of Africa, Asia, and the Caribbean pursue different approaches, although these, too, are grounded in the primacy of their regional interests. For them, studying the end of empire must begin with the people most affected by it—not so much European publics as populations in the developing world for whom decolonization was imminent, proximate, and visceral. This focus on the global 'south' as the source of revolutionary transformation echoes the 'Third Worldism' that dominated new left thinking in the 1960s and 1970s. But, as a historical methodology, it implies something else: not an ideological stance, but rather, as Mark Philip Bradley puts it, a pre-eminent concern with the experiences of the colonized, not the colonizers. 'In this view, independence was not so much given as taken, and anticolonial actors and their construction of post-colonial states and society become central elements of the story.'[10]

The distinction between these two approaches should not be overdrawn. Since the mid 1990s scholars of empire and area studies specialists have converged, for the most part accepting that imperialism cannot be reduced to one-way traffic, whether European or otherwise. Empire is now studied in more imaginative ways that reject the old binaries of European 'metropole' and colonial 'periphery' in favour of more complex interlocking relationships built on cultural transmission, economic inter-dependence, and shared—albeit opposing—histories of colonialism. One of the achievements of this more integrated new imperial history has been to explain how politicians and publics came to adopt 'imperialist' outlooks. The apparent oddity of an avowedly liberal parliamentary democracy in Britain and a relatively egalitarian, liberal republic in France each possessing vast colonial empires was always more apparent than real. In Britain, certain strands of liberalism and imperialism walked hand in hand. In France, the republican commitment to liberty and the revolutionary values of 1789 was used to reframe colonial domination as culturally educative and socially beneficial, a civilizing process that would bring genuine emancipation to other, less fortunate societies.[11] Meanwhile, France's status as the 'eldest daughter' of the Catholic Church suggested that France was duty-bound to its self-proclaimed task 'of freeing the indigenous colonized peoples from savagery and ignorance'.[12]

For most of the nineteenth century and much of the twentieth, the one constant in British and French international politics was the exploitation of non-European ethnic groups through authoritarian systems of political control that denied equivalent civil rights, economic entitlements, and citizenship status to whites and non-whites. Reduced to their absolute essence, varieties of imperial rule invariably replicated these and other forms of discrimination.[13] Colonial dominion, whatever the official policy monikers applied to it—among them, indirect rule, diarchy (in India), and 'preparation for self-government' in the British case; assimilationism, associationism, or integrationism in the French case—was followed, eventually, by the struggle against decolonization.[14] The expansion and ultimate contraction of empire, as well as the strategic networks, economic relationships, and cultural affiliations that underpinned it framed the canvas on which the global presence of Britain and France was drawn. The colonial dimension of this picture may, at times, have been less vivid than other aspects of international affairs, from inter-state conflict to the construction of alliance systems, even the internal consolidation of the French Republic itself. But empire was always there.

It might appear self-evident that the history of empire cannot be either European or non-European—it has to be both. But the real point is this: interpretations of colonialism now concentrate on these conjunctures, on the intersections between European imperial ideas and practices and non-European responses to them. And in the generation after 1945 the practices and the responses changed more dramatically than ever before, bringing European colonial rule to its knees.

Trying to bring the methods of imperial history together with those of other historical fields, the following chapters look both beyond the purely political, 'high policy' decisions of British and French governments and their colonial administrations, and beyond the nationalist parties, insurgent groups, and social movements that opposed them. Decolonization, as we shall see, was sometimes driven by other pressures. Economic change in post-war Europe and the wider world altered patterns of trade. Levels of industrialization increased. Colonial towns and cities mushroomed, often chaotically. And customary forms of agriculture struggled to survive. Each of these transformations bore directly on the relevance and viability of continuing imperial rule. Social changes were equally significant. To take only two examples, the emancipation of French women in 1944 and the increasing secularization of British and French society altered the terms in which the defence of empire was articulated and the constituencies to which imperialists and anti-imperialists appealed.

Finally, cultural change, too, impacted on decolonization. Between the book's starting point in the era of the First World War and its endpoint in the 1970s French and British families, communities, and civil society groups became less hierarchical and less deferential. The 'banal imperialism' characteristic of French and, even more so, of British society in the early twentieth century, an acceptance of empire so ingrained in everything from early-years education to media reportage, leisure, sport, and family connections that it passed almost unnoticed, became less reliable as a political indicator as the post-war decades rolled forward.[15] The end of deference—to political authority at least—was also implicit in the mounting pressure for decolonization within colonial societies. Meanwhile, in the imperial mother countries and their dependencies, improving living standards and the development of mass consumerism transformed basic ideas about wants and needs, duty, and sacrifice. An amalgam of these and other economic, social, and cultural factors refashioned political cultures in Britain, France, and their empires, shaping fight or flight choices and the ways they were understood by politicians and publics.

It is worth recalling that these choices, often amounting to the pursuit of war, were rarely articulated or understood in moral terms. Perhaps one reason why is that long-standing colonial problems, unlike particular episodes, especially those with a scandalous flavour, did not always register highly in the wider political cultures of Britain or France. A danger for anyone enthralled by the history of empire and processes of decolonization is that we assume the political actors and public audiences of the day shared the same fascination. How misguided this can be. One has only to recall Winston Churchill's disdainful, if disarming, comment as France's war in Indochina entered its final stages in 1953: 'I have lived seventy-eight years without hearing of bloody places like Cambodia.'[16] Tragically, all too often such 'bloody places' appeared fleetingly on the radar of western commentators, and normally only in response to social crises that were read as affirmation of their benighted status beyond the pale of the normative standards of western civilization. If the history of empire has one justification above all, it is surely to remind us that those normative standards dripping with disapproval of colonial backwardness produced some of the most savage violence, gross iniquity, and chronic upheavals of our recent past.

The historian, trying to be true to source material and historical context, needs to bear these factors in mind. There is plenty in the chapters to come that one might be tempted to condemn. That is a judgement best left to the reader on the basis of the evidence presented. As David Anderson, a historian of Kenya, has suggested, there is little analytic purpose and no real scholarly value in trying to measure which colonial power was cruellest by counting the dead from colonial wars, repression, and other forms of violence. Wherever possible, we need to know who such victims were, and how many there were. But a comparative history of decolonization should not be some polemical 'league table' of barbarity.[17] It should, rather, try to explain why recourse to extreme violence seemed not only logical, but defensible, even ethically imperative, to those who authorized or performed it.[18] Colonial fights, as we will see, were never reducible to the crass simplicities of struggles for 'hearts and minds' in which imperial powers strove to win some sort of popularity contest against their anti-colonial opponents. For one thing, wars of decolonization, while never described in these terms at the time, were characterized by ruthless methods of population control, not by the kid-gloves treatment supposedly integral to 'hearts and minds' counter-insurgency.[19] For another thing, the fact that security forces' resort to violence was often meant to be exemplary did not imply that it was kept within narrow limits. At one extreme such 'exemplary' actions involved deliberate counter-terror designed to intimidate local populations; at another, the material affirmation of western technological supremacy through bombardment of recalcitrant 'rebel zones', often from the air.[20] Recourse to violence against civilian populations whose material improvement and cultural elevation was, in theory at least, a first principle of empire exposed the hollowness of colonial promises and affirmed the underlying weakness of imperial authority.[21]

It is worth pausing a moment to consider the nature of this weakness. The widespread assumption that colonial conflicts were highly 'asymmetric', or heavily lop-sided, in the military and economic resources that imperial powers and their insurgent opponents could bring to bear is deeply misleading. Britain and France, it is true, had the means to divert professional military forces and advanced technologies to fight against decolonization. But they rarely did so. Colonial counter-insurgency, when fought over long periods, typically involved large numbers of police, paramilitaries, and locally-recruited 'loyalist' forces all of whom used fairly traditional weaponry to do their killing. Deployment of professional troops or young national servicemen to colonial wars certainly took place, but, with the notable exception of French Indochina and, even more so, French Algeria, it usually involved thousands, not tens of thousands of European soldiers. Again these two French conflicts give the lie to an otherwise general rule that wars of decolonization did not require 'total' mobilization of metropolitan political, economic, or cultural resources. For the populations of post-war Britain and France, violent disorder somewhere in their empire was perennial, a part of the imperial soundtrack, not an abrupt change of tune. The result was to normalize rebellion and violence as aspects of the wider process of holding or, eventually, losing an empire. Even colonial defeats were, in John Horne's words, 'partial' for British and French society insofar as they involved no fear of occupation, no surrender of domestic territory, no loss of basic rights.[22]

Even if the stakes were lower for Britain and France than the 'struggles for survival' of 1914–18 and 1939–45, empire defeats could still generate venomous politics and endless recrimination. And for the colonial populations directly involved, colonial warfare was neither remote nor 'low intensity'. It was threatening, divisive, devastating. Civilian casualties, whether relative to military losses or in terms of overall population, could be staggeringly high. Public engagement was greater too. The Vietnamese path to victory in 1954 was traceable in sustained popular mobilization. The triumph of Algeria's FLN was grounded in strict enforcement of popular compliance. Elsewhere the success of anti-colonial nationalists was built upon less violent forms of political action—outflanking rivals, repeating a clear message, winning over the young and taking control of the apparatus of local administration. In these non-violent cases, as in their violent counterparts, any asymmetry was reversed: it was the colonial power, not the colonial population that seemed poorly equipped to meet the challenge.

Another point to emphasize from the outset is that neither the British nor the French empires were unitary, coherent, or closed territorial polities.

Rather, they were multifarious systems that included formal colonial administration and control in some places, more informal (even invisible) networks of strategic, economic, and cultural predominance in others. Even
territories that were clearly run as colonies—in the British case, Nigeria,
Jamaica or Burma for instance; in the French case, Senegal, Guadeloupe, or
Cochin-China (southern Vietnam)—on closer inspection defy such generic
classification. Nigeria was the exemplar of 'indirect rule', yet its northern
and southern provinces were administered very differently. Jamaica, a British
colony to be sure, fell within a US sphere of Caribbean influence during
and after the Second World War. Burma was ruled as an off-shoot of British
India by the Raj administration in Delhi until 1937. It then came under
Colonial Office control for only four years until the shock of foreign invasion made Burma the strategic epicentre of British efforts to halt Japan's
advance through mainland Asia.

On the French side, Senegal, the departure point for French incursion
into the Sene-Gambian Valley, retained a complex form of dual administration that reflected its past importance as the commercial centre of French
slaving in West Africa. Thus, the so-called *originaires*, those born inside Senegal's original 'four communes' of Saint Louis, Dakar, Rufisque, and Gorée
island, enjoyed French citizenship and, from 1916, voting rights that were
denied to their fellow Senegalese in the colony's interior. Guadeloupe was
another colony with origins in early modern slavery and the commercial
attractions of sugar and rum. Like its near-neighbour Martinique, it was
reinvented as an overseas *département* in 1946, a transition that, on paper at
least, replaced the hierarchical architecture of colonial administration with
the more horizontal bureaucracy of French local government. Finally,
Cochin-China and its steamy capital, Saigon, was another hub for wider
colonial penetration, this time north and westwards through Vietnam, Laos,
and Cambodia. Cochin-China was ruled colonially as part of a larger Indochina federation in which more mixed systems of 'royal protectorate' survived elsewhere. And the entire composite federation was redesigned
immediately after the Second World War in a bid to conceal its imperial
foundations. None of these territories, nor the changes in administrative
status they underwent were anomalous. The more one looks beneath the
veneer of colonial rule, the more idiosyncrasies appear.

So can any generalizations be made? In broad terms, economic considerations weighed more heavily in British than French decolonization.
Conversely, domestic political division features more prominently in the

French case than the British. In this sense, the value attached to gradualism and compromise in British political culture was strikingly different to French traditions of protest and intolerance of low-performing coalition administrations. These traditions, although elusive and vaguely stereotypical, did surface in the contrasting official rhetoric that peppered the British and French roads from empire. If the traffic lights of British decolonization tended to oscillate between amber and green, their French equivalents sometimes stuck on red. Where British governmental statements were often placatory, understated and, it must be said, misleading, declarations of French governmental intent were usually framed in a more confrontational language of triumph or defeat.[23] It seems appropriate then to begin our story by investigating the colonial dimensions to a shared Franco-British victory. This takes us to the year 1918.

I

Imperial Zenith?
The Victors' Empires after
the First World War

'In no single theatre are we strong enough.' So lamented Field Marshal Sir Henry Wilson, the austere, thin-faced Ulsterman who, as Chief of the Imperial General Staff in May 1920, held the ultimate responsibility for the strategic defence of the British Empire. The list of danger zones he identified was a long one. Ireland in the grip of civil war; Germany unbowed and resentful; Turkey determined to recover lost ground; Egypt seething in the aftermath of failed revolution; Palestine, its future in British hands uncertain; Iraq reeling from northern and southern rebellions; Persia, wavering between British and Soviet influence; India wracked by food riots and nationalist ferment; even the home waters of the British Isles less defensible than they once were.[1] Yet surely Britain, the old imperial lion, had just won a war with the help of its loyal overseas subjects.

Along with France, the other imperial giant, the British were only now dividing the war's colonial spoils in the Middle East and Africa. Why, then, was Wilson's imperial forecast so gloomy?

The basic reason was simple. Neither at this point, nor in the decades that followed, did British (or, as we shall see, French) political and military decision-makers match the pace of colonial change or predict its course. This was not some sort of collective lapse of judgement. Few on the eve of war in 1914 could have foreseen the scale of colonial problems immediately after it. Admittedly, some challenges were unsurprising. Rebellion in Ireland had been stewing for decades. Yet its eruption, first into an Anglo-Irish confrontation, then into civil war sent shock waves throughout the British Isles and the wider Empire. Wartime French governments also predicted—indeed

Figure 1. 'The Empire Needs Men!' The metaphor of imperial family—and British seniority—deployed in First World War recruitment.

exaggerated—the potential for wartime dissent in their turbulent North African territories, especially after Ottoman Turkey, a largely Muslim country, entered the war against the Allies in October 1914.[2] But disorders in other places—British-ruled Ceylon or the federation of French West Africa for instance—were unforeseen. Like their European overseers, colonial societies were rocked by the war's insatiable appetite for new blood.

Anti-conscription protests, expressions of desperation more than organized revolts, spread through French North and West Africa between 1915 and 1917. The call-up system assigned quotas to local notables or chiefs, whose job it became to ensure that sufficient draftees appeared before regimental recruiters. The cycle would then repeat itself a few months later. These recurrent call-ups disrupted agricultural production and sapped people's respect for their customary rulers. Recruiters' methods seemed arbitrary. Often they were brutal too. Families confronted painful choices over which young family members could be spared.[3] Here the fight or flight dilemma took human form. Thousands of young Africans both in this World War and the next escaped 'paying the blood tax' by fleeing across colonial frontiers from French into British territory, or vice versa.[4] Politicians and generals who had expected that mobilization of colonial resources and, more particularly, manpower would help win the war were compelled, briefly, to pause.[5] The social destabilization caused by colonial conscription was not confined to French Africa. Even the most ardent enthusiasts for the employment of Indian, Canadian, Algerian, or West African troops on the Western Front did not expect that these men would die in their tens of thousands over four years of trench warfare. By 1917 imperial governors throughout both empires expressed mounting unease over the destabilization caused by such losses.[6]

A post-war crisis of empire

Still more unanticipated were the extraneous pressures that Europe's imperial masters would face after 1918, ironically, as direct costs of victory. Few predicted that two of the most dangerous challengers to British and French imperial power would be Japan and Italy. Both were erstwhile allies of '14–'18 dissatisfied with their limited share of the spoils.[7] Fewer still foretold the coming reorientation in American diplomacy, economics, and outlook. Veteran politicians and seasoned diplomats in London and Paris indulged the attachment of the US President Woodrow Wilson to open diplomacy, international conflict regulation, and ethnic self-determination as ways to prevent future war in Europe.[8] But none of them welcomed the extension of 'Wilsonian' ideas to the non-European world.[9]

As the new Mandate frontiers shown in Map 3 were imposed between the Arab territories formerly ruled by the Turks, favoured clients were selected among local elites to help consolidate the presence of the new imperial masters from Britain and France. In the process, older, more malleable conceptions of civic identity among the populations of former Ottoman provinces from Syria, through Palestine to Iraq, were supplanted by harsher, inflexible assertions of communal difference. Ethnic identities became reified and increasingly politicized, used as a marker of inclusion or exclusion by

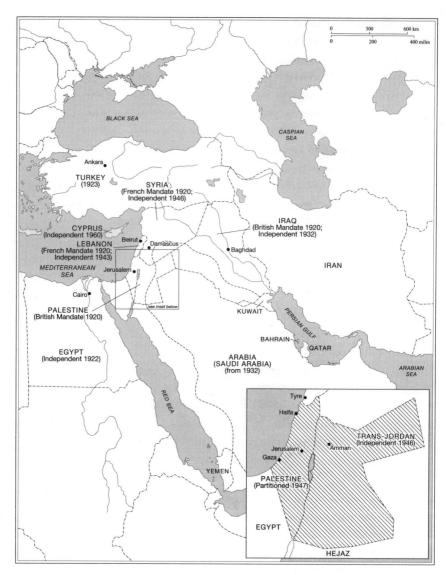

Map 3. Middle East Mandates.

hardliners on all sides of the Middle East's new ethno-politics. In Syria, for example, identifying oneself as Sunni, Druze, Alawite, or Christian acquired a stronger political significance.[10] The notion that, by the early 1920s, social identities would become ossified into fixed categories might have seemed outlandish to the subjects of erstwhile Ottoman dependencies only years before. So, too, for British and French imperial administrators the idea that an international regulatory authority—the League of Nations—might set limits to planned territorial acquisitions and monitor their standards of colonial governance would have appeared ludicrous a decade earlier.[11]

Perhaps even more important, the full implications of British and French emergence from the war as financial dependents of the United States were barely understood after the conflict, let alone before it. Fateful post-war decisions were made in London and Paris that pegged sterling and the franc at high tradable values tied to a new 'gold standard'. The resultant inflated value of each currency created huge financial problems, not just domestically but imperially too.[12] As always, questions of money and empire remained interlocked. Few colonies were unaffected by the fortunes of the British and French economies. The ups and downs of metropolitan currencies, export industries, and employment markets reverberated through colonial territories in the decade between the end of World War I and the Wall Street Crash in October 1929. The depression then brought these connections into even starker relief.[13]

As Robert Boyce puts it, the inter-war period's most remarkable feature was the simultaneous disintegration of the international political system and the international economic system.[14] The consequences of this double-edged collapse would become clearer once the depression of 1929–35 brought its two constituent elements crashing together in the rise of economic nationalism, fascist militarism, and a new arms race with a terrifying impetus of its own.[15] Refracted within colonial territories, the 'deglobalizing' of international trade after 1930 was felt in calamitous falls in commodity prices, real-terms inflation, and declining purchasing power.[16] Hard lives got harder still. For colonial subjects the depression was primarily experienced in terms of the affordability of food. In pockets of colonial Africa and much of southern Asia poverty diets deteriorated into chronic malnourishment.[17]

The intersection between colonial food costs, deteriorating public health, and social disorder was evident before the depression of course. There were food riots in southern India in 1918.[18] In Dakar, in Senegal, French West Africa's federal capital, bubonic plague, the second outbreak in five years, killed over 700 in 1919. The spread of infection was facilitated by problems associated with chronic poverty, especially overcrowding and poor hygiene.[19] Well into the inter-war period particular lethal epidemics retained their association with specific colonial regions—cholera in India, sleeping sickness in the Congo Basin, yellow fever in Indochina. Politically, the most salient feature of the crisis of empire in the decade prior to the 1929 crash was the emergence of organized opposition movements, often the forerunners of the nationalist groups against which British and French colonial security forces would struggle for years to come. In 1919 Britain's service chiefs, thrown off balance by the developing civil war in Ireland, fretted that the empire's expanded frontiers could not be held.[20] Post-war demobilization made matters worse. Colonial ex-servicemen, especially the hundreds of thousands from the Indian subcontinent, seemed a volatile constituency sure to be targeted by anti-British agitators inside and outside the empire.[21] During 1918 and 1919 former soldiers were central to economic protests and ugly race riots from Liverpool to Kingston, Jamaica, making a mockery of presumed imperial unity in Britain's victorious Empire.[22]

The allied coalition had often enunciated contradictory war aims. But their central message was that ethnic self-determination offered the best route to the long-term stabilization of states and the relations between them.[23] This was a message enthusiastically taken up by politicians, public intellectuals, and other elite actors in the colonial world. Sa'd Zaghlul, spokesman of Egyptian nationalism, Shakib Arslan, a Druze parliamentarian from Syria, India's Bal Gangadhar Tilak, and a boyish Nguyen Ai Quoc (later to adopt the *nomme de guerre* Ho Chi Minh) all petitioned the peace-makers in Paris for limited reforms that would concede greater equality to the elite social groups they represented.[24] Without exception, their claims were rejected. Independent 'nation-states' were not set to arise from the ashes of former colonies; the League of Nations was not about to protect the rights—national or individual—of colonial peoples.[25] British public pressure for it to do so, articulated through the League of Nations Union, was yet to register.[26] In several dependencies, not least British India, the disappointments of the so-called 'Wilsonian moment' were keenly felt.[27] This is a reference to President Woodrow Wilson, whose pressure for funda-mental changes in the way international relations were conducted had, briefly, promised some redistribution of wealth and power in colonial territories. In practice, the 'moment' in question proved fleeting. But the nationalist genie was out of the bottle.[28]

Egypt's administrative elite of *effendiyya*, Palestinian share-croppers, Saigon's silk-farmers, and Caribbean cane-cutters: all clashed with colonial security forces, turning workplace protests into acts of rebellion. Those driven to protest by poverty, discrimination, or both, found common cause with local politicians, often from more elite backgrounds, who demanded basic rights and, ultimately, nationhood for their communities.[29] Uprisings, repression, and the devastating impact of severe economic crisis made large parts of the British and French Empires from Jamaica to Indochina virtually ungovernable by 1939.[30] In these locales, the advent of another world war did not catalyse pressure for withdrawal; it merely contained pre-existing opposition for a few more years. So this chapter's core argument is simple. Understanding the end of empire should not begin with the consequences of the Second World War but with the colonial crises that prefigured it. Fight or flight was a reality decades before 1945.

New territories and threats to Britain's Empire

Colonial representatives hopeful that the Great War might usher in fundamental changes in the way the British and French empires were run were quickly disillusioned, something that seems sadly predictable in hindsight. Particularly so when one considers the way territorial redistribution of former Ottoman territories in the Middle East was handled by the two victorious imperial powers. The acquisitive instincts of British and French post-war governments were nowhere more apparent than in their squabbling over the carcass of the Ottoman Empire. In a diary entry in October 1918 the Cabinet Secretary Maurice Hankey recorded the improvisation and mistrust in inter-allied discussions about the choicest morsels of territory. On the 3rd he noted the fury in the War Cabinet after it emerged that the Foreign Secretary A.J. Balfour had promised the French that the horse-trading embodied in the 1916 Sykes-Picot agreement would stand. France would 'get' an enlarged Syria, probably including the oil-bearing region of Iraqi Mosul. The Prime Minister Lloyd George would have none of it. He was determined to revoke the Sykes-Picot accords in order to secure an enlarged Palestine for Britain and the incorporation of the Mosul *vilayet* into a British-ruled Mesopotamia (Iraq). He even devised 'a subtle dodge' to invite the United States to govern Palestine and Syria. This, he thought, might scare the French into conceding a British-run Palestine in order to safeguard France's toehold in the Levant.[31]

With such convoluted scheming it was hardly surprising that in the unsettled Middle Eastern political climate after 1918 differing British and French calculations about the wisdom of supporting the Hashemite dynasty

poisoned relations between the two imperial powers.[32] The Hashemite King
Feisal established an independent, populist regime in Syria in late 1918, and
figured among those that lobbied the Versailles peacemakers a year later.[33] It
was to no avail. After a brief military showdown outside Damascus Feisal's
Syrian government was evicted by the French military administration that
took charge of the country as a League of Nations 'mandate' territory in
July 1920.[34] Britain, by contrast, stuck with monarchical figureheads, identifying loyalist communities that might serve them. Feisal seized the opportunity to relocate to Iraq. His brother Abdullah was installed as Emir of
another British mandate—Transjordan.[35] As these arrangements suggest,
Britain emerged with vastly increased Middle Eastern assets and commitments, next to which French acquisition of mandates over Syria and its
splinter state, Lebanon, seemed almost modest.[36] Thus a paradox: the destabilization of the British and the French empires between 1914 and 1923 did
not preclude their expansion. Both reached their largest physical extent in
the early 1920s.

Home-grown opposition to empire struggled to make itself felt in inter-
war Britain. The anti-imperialist sympathies of liberal critics, missionary
groups, members of the Fabian Colonial Bureau, or rank-and-file supporters
of the Labour party and the TUC were narrowly circumscribed. For one
thing, it was widely presumed that political reforms and material improvements to colonial life were best accomplished with British sponsorship, an
assumption reinforced by the Colonial Office rhetoric of 'trusteeship',
which recast imperial rule as being guided as much by ethical concerns as
by profit or strategic advantage. For another thing, tough economic conditions at home sapped enthusiasm for any imperial spending or loosening of
trade privileges liable to affect British prosperity or working-class pockets
adversely.[37] Imperial loyalty remained an unspoken certainty among British Ministers of every political stripe between the wars, but the extent of
ministerial enthusiasm for, and interest in, empire varied sharply. For the
Colonial Secretary Leo Amery, child of the Raj and perhaps Britain's most
fervently imperialist parliamentarian, his colleagues in Stanley Baldwin's
second Conservative government were a shocking disappointment.[38] Reflecting on the past twelve months on New Year's Eve 1928, he confided his
thoughts to his diary: 'I have felt myself very much estranged from most of
my colleagues in the Cabinet. I cannot help feeling that they understand
nothing about the Empire, and some of them are acquiring a definitely
anti-Dominion complex.'[39]

As Amery discerned, an inter-war crisis of empire was real enough, its aftershocks linked to a wider global crisis triggered by the war's messy aftermath.[40] Europe's two imperial giants were bloated with colonial territory but perilously short of the ready money and powerful allies needed to digest it. Britain's imperial 'world system', as explained by John Darwin, required certain pre-conditions, first to facilitate its expansion in the nineteenth century, next to sustain it through the early twentieth, and, finally, to permit its recovery after the upheavals of the Second World War. Among these was a relatively passive East Asia. It is arguable whether this was ever achievable. It was certainly absent from the mid-1920s onwards. Closer to home, a balance of European continental forces proved equally unattainable until the Cold War imposed an artificial but enduring stasis on European boundaries after 1945. Elsewhere, the benevolent strength of North American partners—Canada and, above all, the United States—offered more constant assurance. Some French and British leaders—French premier Georges Clemenceau at the start of the inter-war period, Britain's Neville Chamberlain at the end of it—treated America disdainfully.[41] But US goodwill ebbed and flowed within a narrow tidal range, and helped keep British imperial power afloat most of the time. US anti-imperialism should not be overplayed. A cherished myth of America's history after 1776, it was belied by the facts. America remained a prominent Southeast Asian imperialist between the wars and a commercial rival for colonial markets elsewhere.[42] The Suez crisis of 1956 proved that Washington's whip-hand packed a killer punch, but anti-imperial US interventionism remained the exception and not the rule.

Unfriendly towards the western empires after the 1917 Revolution, Soviet Russia was also more quiescent towards capitalist imperialism than British and French doomsayers imagined.[43] During and after the Russian Civil War the more empire-minded of Britain's strategic planners identified Cold War-style Soviet threats to Britain's presence in Asia. The Conservative Foreign Secretary, and former Indian Viceroy, Lord Curzon took these anxieties furthest, but he was never alone.[44] In December 1924 the General Staff warned of Soviet pressure on a northern Asian tier of British imperial interests that traced an arc from the Shanghai international settlement through India's North-West frontier and Afghanistan to northern Iran and Kurdish Iraq.[45] It must have seemed oddly familiar to politicians and soldiers who built their careers in the age of Victorian high imperialism. But there was a new aspect. Fear of Communism introduced an ideological edge to the old Great Game of vying for imperial supremacy in central and eastern Asia. No

longer a straightforward competition for clients, markets, and territory, the
Game was now dominated by intangible, transnational factors. The spectre of
Tsarist bayonets was replaced by the spread of new ideologies and hostile
propaganda that were harder to monitor and deter.[46] Among the strategic
planners accustomed to this kind of global geo-politics, the Russian menace
to colonial rule was no longer simply conceived in terms of military incursion but of Comintern-sponsored internal sedition as well.[47] Fears of a subversive anti-colonial 'enemy within' encouraged the creation of additional
secret service and special branch agencies throughout the empire.[48] But for
other grand strategists in government, British imperial defence policy
retained its Oceanic flavour. Summarizing the problems of protecting the
British Empire in June 1926, the chiefs of staff framed the problem in global
maritime terms:

> Scattered over the globe in every continent and sea, peopled by races of
> every colour and in widely differing stages of civilisation, the component
> parts of the Empire have this much in common from the point of view of
> defence, that, with occasional and insignificant exceptions they are able to
> maintain order with their own resources supplemented in some cases by
> Imperial garrisons maintained for strategical reasons. But for any larger
> emergency requiring mutual support or co-operation they are dependent on
> the sea communications which unite them. If these communications are
> closed they become liable to defeat in detail. Moreover, the Mother Country,
> the central arsenal and reserve for the whole Empire, is dependent for the
> essentials of life on the maintenance of a network of sea communications
> extending not only to the territories of the Empire, but to every part of the
> world. The maintenance of these sea communications, therefore, is the first
> principle of our system of Imperial Defence.[49]

Imprinted with the Admiralty's dominance of Britain's inter-war military
establishment, here were the essentials of 'empire-mindedness', 'blue water
imperialism', defence of free trade, and the enduring myths of British plucky
'Island race' history rolled into one.[50]

The French Empire after 1918

To talk in similar terms of a French 'world system' would be misleading.
France attached prime significance to European affairs—and dangers—not
to global ones. Contrasting interests in oil provide some indication of this.

France, like Britain, devoted unprecedented attention to securing oil supplies during the 1920s. New interests were acquired in Iraq, Poland, and Romania, and oil exploration continued in its colonies of Algeria and Madagascar. Unlike Britain, however, French oil needs were comparatively small. French industry consumed 1.2 million tons in 1923 next to Britain's five million. The disparity was largely explained by the larger size of Britain's oil-fired merchant navy. With fewer oceanic commitments, French governments also opted for tighter regulation of the domestic oil market to maintain stocks and dampen fluctuations in fuel prices in preference to massive investment in overseas drilling.[51] The motor of French imperialism was not oil-driven.

Nor was it propelled by settlers. With no equivalents of Britain's Dominions, there were not enough French-born whites living in the empire to challenge the fixation on continental matters. As if to underline the point, one of the largest francophone migrant diasporas—the French Canadians of Quebec—were governed as part of a British Dominion, not a French one. Substantially self-governing, the Dominions' dominant Anglo-identities were shaped by nineteenth-century migration and complex networks of familial, cultural, and economic ties.[52] Canada, Australia, New Zealand, and, more problematically, South Africa and the Rhodesias were major political actors in their own right, as much making the British world system as being made by it.[53] On paper at least, from 1926 Canada, Australia, New Zealand, and South Africa enjoyed 'equal status' with Britain as associates in an emerging Commonwealth. In practice, it was years before these new arrangements were fully enacted. The scale of white settlement in these societies makes it difficult to see them as early models of a successful Anglophone 'flight' strategy, of a gradual and more or less amicable loosening of British imperial control.[54] Fiercely proud of their nation-building achievements, the white Dominions remained, to varying degrees, culturally deferential and economically and strategically tied to Britain until the 1950s. Although formally self-governing, the Dominions' enduring sense of Britishness signified not just a positive cultural choice but some degree of imperial attachment as well.[55]

France, of course, had its white enclaves overseas, from the Caribbean territories to the settler-dominated cities of North-West Africa. The administrative buildings and residential apartments of Tunis, Algiers, Oran, and—fastest growing of them all—Casablanca, put one more in mind of Marseilles than Marrakech.[56] But even Algeria, 'made French' to the extent that it was constitutionally subsumed into a metropolitan super-structure of regional *départements* and Interior Ministry oversight, remained stubbornly

foreign, exotic, and, on occasion, hostile. Fictional writing by French Algerian settlers, which attracted a wide readership in inter-war France, played
on these traits. Algeria's settlers—or *colons*—were still looked upon, and
considered themselves to be, a race apart, a rugged, hybridized community
accustomed to adversity and contemptuous of the woolly idealism of metropolitan imperialists.[57]

With no large, self-governing territories to accommodate, the French
Empire's rulers were, by inclination, centralizers aspiring to greater colonial uniformity. To achieve this, they were keener than their British counterparts to export metropolitan ideas, practices, and cultural norms to
dependent societies.[58] Overseas territories were, for them, integral to a
French 'empire nation-state'. Built on republican ideals and dedicated to
the closer integration between motherland and empire, this was more a
politico-cultural project than an economic reality sustained by domestic
financial investment and multi-continental white settlement. A world system it was not, but a vehicle for the promotion of an idealized brand of
'Frenchness' it certainly was.

French colonial administration was elevated to the status of a doctrine
because of its cultural emphasis on changing the beliefs, habits, and associational life of subject peoples. The principal weapon in the colonial armoury
was the French language, command of which was an obvious marker of an
individual's successful 'assimilation' to French standards of probity and politics.
Potentially all-embracing, this doctrine of 'assimilationism' in fact remained
highly exclusive.[59] Advanced education, which required money, connections,
or both, was one route to citizenship—the official imprimatur of Frenchness.
Accidents of birth, especially a French-born father, were another.[60] For the
majority who secured it after 1918, citizenship came as a reward for sacrifice:
either a professional career in the military or active service in the Great War.
Assimilation, then, came with undeclared economic requirements, a heavy
gender bias, and a pronounced martial flavour. All three were at odds with the
egalitarian rhetoric used to justify it.[61]

We would thus be ill-advised to think of French colonialism as qualita-
tively unique insofar as its declared cultural objective of integrating—or
assimilating—dependent societies with France remained substantially unfulfilled. Equally, we should resist the temptation to be dismissive. To its many
supporters at home and, indeed, in the colonies, the French empire differed
from its British equivalent because its *raison d'être* was the betterment of
dependent peoples. The lives of colonial citizens, an elite minority, were

bound to be enhanced thanks to their complete immersion in French values. Meanwhile, the mass of colonial subjects, despite being confined to a lesser status, would still profit from seeing and hearing French administration, language, and cultural practices performed around them. France's imperial training grounds were the classroom, the magistrate's office, the midwifery clinic, and the colonial army recruitment centre. The African, Asian, and Afro-Caribbean peoples who passed through these places as schoolchildren, as property owners, as mothers, or as soldiers were stepping up the rungs of the assimilation ladder to the lofty heights of citizenship of the Republic.[62] In the two sub-Saharan federations that spanned West and Equatorial Africa as well as in the other great French imperial federation, Indochina, colonial rule was of sufficiently long standing to have produced thousands of young men (numbers of women were significantly smaller) who had reached the top of the ladder. Those who climbed up through military service could reasonably expect post-war civilian employment, perhaps as policemen, or postal employees. But the smaller numbers that had undergone French secondary or even higher education craved access to more sought-after positions: in the professions, in local or even national government. Most would be disappointed.[63]

The consequent alienation of these *évolués* (literally, 'the [culturally] evolved') in francophone black Africa and French Vietnam was critical to the emergence of two distinct strands of opposition to colonialism. The first was primarily cultural, a reassertion of the vitality of indigenous arts, linguistic forms, and associational life denigrated by French colonial educators and administrators. The second was more conventionally political: the rejection of assimilationist rhetoric as an elaborate sham and a turn towards integral anti-colonial nationalism. The former strand was exemplified by the negritude movement, which emerged among a select group of black African and Antillean students, writers, and political activists in inter-war Paris. Theirs was a predominantly literary, humanistic opposition, often militant in tone but never violent in practice. Writers like the Martiniquan poet Aimé Césaire stressed the distinctiveness and intrinsic value of African cultures and the specificity of black historical experience of European enslavement and persecution. Yet they also acknowledged the utility of a continued relationship with France.[64] The greater radicalism of the latter strand was personified by Ho Chi Minh. Along with several co-founders of the Indochinese Communist Party (ICP) between 1918 and 1930 he made the journey from Paris-based student *évolué* dressed in suit and tie to Marxist outlaw in peasant attire.[65] Proponents of socialist modernization, these first-generation Vietnamese Communists lambasted colonialism's stultifying effects. Colonial citizens were condemned to be subordinate, ersatz copies of the real thing. And French administrators absolved themselves of responsibility for the poor majority of their colonial subjects by claiming that social inequalities were endemic and unchangeable.[66]

Ho and his colleagues had touched a nerve. Advocates of assimilation confronted two dilemmas between the wars. One was that its limited achievements became harder to conceal. The other was that the policy was no longer in vogue among bureaucrats or politicians. During and immediately after the First World War administrators in the French colonial federations proclaimed their conversion from assimilationist ideals to a more pragmatic and less disruptive style of governance, dubbed associationism.[67] Closer to British ideas of indirect rule in its selective accommodation with local customs and cultures, associationism was less republican and radical than politically and socially conservative. In a complete role reversal, during the inter-war years official colonial rhetoric venerated traditional hierarchy, customary law, and the authenticity of peasant life.[68] Where assimilationism sought to re-engineer colonial societies, associationism preserved them as if in a museum. One of its more obvious by-products was to marginalize the *évolués* whose acquisition of French citizenship had been a key justification for 'assimilation'.[69] Traditional authority figures— Ivorian chiefs, Senegalese sufi brotherhoods, Vietnamese mandarins and village headmen, once derided as obstacles to the spread of republican civic virtues, were reinvented as guarantors of social stability and authentic representatives of local opinion.

French colonial 'fights' over the next thirty years typically began with efforts by *évolué* groups to challenge the consequent rigidities of associationism. The techniques of these early opponents varied, although the issues at stake still centred on political rights—admission to citizenship, access to administrative posts, and a wider colonial franchise. Some *évolués*, like the leaders of Vietnam's early Communists, despaired of compromise and began organizing labour protests, army mutinies, and peasant rebellion.[70] But most chose other, peaceful routes of protest. A common tactic was to highlight the enduring cultural dynamism of colonized societies despite the stifling impact of French cultural dominance which silenced eloquent voices, denied economic opportunity, and withheld basic rights.[71] The negritude movement, in particular, disparaged combat, preferring to engage in cultural warfare. Their core argument was simple. The colonial turn towards associationism was a lie. Far from respecting local culture, association presumed that African societies were inferior and inert. The doctrine encouraged venality among the privileged and demanded obedience from the rest.[72]

Supporters of associationism were undaunted. Their air of confidence mirrored the changes taking place in the training of the inter-war generation of colonial service appointees. A quiet revolution was occurring in the colonial academy. For almost four centuries between France's early colonial acquisitions in the sixteenth century and the consolidation of the 'second' French colonial empire with nineteenth-century conquests in Africa and Indochina, imperial bureaucracy was an adjunct to the administration of the French Navy (or 'Marine'). Notoriously hostile to republicanism, navy bureaucrats, often of aristocratic or *haut bourgeois* background, were staunch conservatives in colonial affairs.[73] The idea of a specialist colonial service was long resisted and a discrete Ministry of Colonies was only established in March 1894. For decades afterwards, this Ministry, often identified by its Paris location in the rue Oudinot, remained a backwater. On occasion, powerful Ministers, such as Théophile Delcassé (in the mid 1890s), Georges Leygues (1906 to 1909), and Marius Moutet (1936–38) injected vigour to the rue Oudinot. In general terms, though, the Ministry administered rather than governed.

French decision-making

For much of the early twentieth century, policy-making remained the preserve of a loose coalition of empire interest groups, misleadingly labelled the 'colonial party'. Headed by senior parliamentarians such as Eugène Étienne (before 1914) and Albert Sarraut (after 1918), the colonial party accommodated provincial chambers of commerce, Paris bankers, geographical societies, missionary groups, and senior civil servants. Some were animated by republican conviction, a few by religion; some by specialist academic interest, others by the strategic potential of imperial territories. Most of the bureaucrats and businessmen involved were modernizers. Most of the missionaries, servants of God's Empire, not of France's, were the opposite, equating 'modernity' with secularism and decadence.[74] Yet somehow they all advanced imperial interests. Commerce was especially well represented. Provincial businesses, traders, and shippers with ties to particular colonial markets lobbied for their pet causes. Port cities had much to gain. Built on the Atlantic slave trade, Bordeaux still traded heavily with black Africa. Merchants in Marseilles favoured links with the Maghreb and Middle East. Silk magnates in Lyons relied on assured, cheap supplies from Lebanon and Vietnam much as the Lancashire textile industry depended on Indian cotton.[75]

High finance was less prominent within the colonial party, except in the lucrative field of French colonial banking, which expanded rapidly after the First World War. Other French speculators looked beyond colonial frontiers for better returns on capital invested abroad. Tsarist Russia was much favoured before 1914; the new states of Eastern Europe more so after the holders of Russian stock lost their shirts in October 1917. Some imperial projects did attract Paris money. The transport sector was a favoured recipient; so was southern Vietnam's rubber industry.[76] Rubber profits made Cochin-China the highest earning French colony per franc invested by the hugely influential Bank of Indochina in the 1920s.[77] Railway projects such as an arterial Vietnamese line and inter-city networks in North Africa were the subject of major inter-war loan issues.[78] So, too, were colonial air routes and their accompanying infrastructure, which often came with the promise of additional state subsidy. But the Paris Bourse was no City of London when it came to less glossy, day-to-day matters of empire investment and trade.[79]

With so many rival interests to accommodate, the colonial party could be cacophonous. It was, though, a supremely successful lobby group because its leading members understood the Third Republic's institutional dynamics. The colonial party set the course of long-term imperial expansion because its members could mobilize Paris bureaucracy, the Catholic orders, employers' groups, the major banks and, above all, the National Assembly to advance empire interests.[80] Rue Oudinot personnel and the short-lived coalition governments that were the Third Republic's trademark bent to its wishes.

Colonial party supporters were interested in results. They were less concerned with colonial doctrine. Nor were imperialist attachments identifiable with any particular political party of the late Third Republic. All professed loyalty to the Empire; even the Communists, who talked of colonial 'nations in formation' under French guidance. But none were sufficiently enthused by it to put imperial claims at the heart of their manifestos.[81] Inter-war associationism emerged instead from the confluence of three factors. First was the professionalization of the colonial service. Second was the growing popularity of the social sciences within French academia. And third was the belief shared by bureaucrats and social scientists that ethnography was a uniquely colonial discipline with scientific precepts that would enable officials, not just to administer dependent peoples but to understand them.[82]

Those individuals who personified all three elements were best placed to put the new thinking into practice. Leading ethnographers boasted extensive colonial experience. Perhaps the most influential, Maurice Delafosse, was a former director of political affairs in the federal government of French West Africa. Another West Africa veteran, Henri Labouret, made ethnography integral to the curriculum of the École Coloniale, the college for trainee empire administrators on the avenue de l'Observatoire in Paris. Delafosse and Labouret persuaded other long-serving officials in French Africa that ethnology and its close cousin social anthropology were bedrocks of successful colonial government.[83] Their chief disciple was Georges Hardy, appointed to head the École Coloniale in 1926.[84] Hardy's innovation was to marry these 'colonial sciences' with practical courses of instruction— a programme of associationist ideas translatable into administrative practice. Officials trained in Hardy's methods venerated ethnographic 'fieldwork' as a prerequisite for sound policy choices. It was not that simple. Ethnography came loaded with presumptions and prejudices in regard to colonized societies and their limited ability to cope with economic modernization. Industrial diversification, urbanization, and the spread of waged labour were thus interpreted as socially destabilizing, even morally wrong. Puritanical, ascetic Islam was dangerous and 'un-African'; heterodox Sufism more malleable and tolerant.[85] Party politics and European-style jury trial, both predicated on adversarial argument, were, according to Hardy's graduates, too much for African minds to handle.[86] Needs and wants were better articulated through traditional means—customary law (although officials remained hazy about what this was), chiefly courts, and village elders.[87] Scientific colonialism, in other words, revealed as much about its practitioners' beliefs as about those of their colonial subjects.

The number of anthropologists roaming colonial Africa was much smaller than the ranks of agronomists, medical specialists, and engineers that filled the colonial administrations after the Second World War. But the anthropologists were perhaps more influential in determining the actions of governments.[88] Specialist officials pointed to ethnographic findings about 'tribal custom', local 'folklore', and 'authentic tradition' to justify colonial tutelage as a work of social conservation.[89] No matter that the sheen of academic objectivity legitimized policies that typecast Africans in particular ways, consigning them to a pre-modern status in which industrialization, advanced education, and gender equality became foreign-borne ills to be avoided.[90] Others see baser motives in this 'politics of retraditionalization'.[91] Stripped of assimilation's cultural baggage about remaking colonial societies in the French image, associationism was a turn towards low-cost, high-extraction administration.[92] At its heart was the 'bargain of collaboration' with local elites—the chiefs, mandarins, and village elders who made the system work. The bargain preserved their titles and limited legal and tax-raising powers. They upheld rural order and furnished the authorities with revenue, labour, and military recruits in return.

It also stored up problems in the longer term. Just as the gap between what assimilation claimed and what it delivered frustrated *évolués'* groups, so the bargains with favoured conservative elites that made association work in practice stirred resentment among those who got nothing from the deal. The fault with both doctrines lay in their underlying selectivity more than the ways they were enacted. Imperial rule was neither dictatorial nor hegemonic; there was scope for contestation from the lowest levels of administrative interaction between officials and local peoples to the higher reaches of colonial policy-making. This basic truth applied in the British as in the French empire. Europeans set the tone for administrative, legal, commercial, and religious practice, but colonial bureaucrats, magistrates, traders, and missionaries were rarely able to impose their will without fear of contradiction. French African and Indochinese territories were governed with a more pronounced military presence than neighbouring British dependencies, but the same collaborative propositions applied.[93] Cooperation between imperial representatives, local elites, and other indigenous auxiliaries were everywhere to be found.[94] Stripped of its rhetorical justifications and doctrinal labels, empire was a system of endless reciprocal arrangements in which insiders, of all ethnicities and creeds, accrued substantial rewards at the expense of the excluded.

The system's long-term dangers were just as severe in the British Empire as they were in the French. Literacy opened doors to alternate political futures: the thoughts of Gandhi, Marcus Garvey, or Marx as well as new strains of pan-Islamist or pan-Africanist thought. In British-ruled Sudan, for instance, nationalist opposition coalesced among the educated young officials trained as staffers for regional government after the First World War. By 1919 Cairo was a pole of attraction for anti-Western opinion throughout the Arab world. Alarmed by this development, the British administration in

Khartoum embarked on a policy of 'Sudanization'. National dress became de rigueur. Arabic-speaking, Muslim Sudanese of high social rank displaced Egyptians and Lebanese within the *effendiyya* class that performed most clerical tasks from tax collection to property registration.[95] By selecting future Sudanese administrators at Khartoum's elite Gordon College along lines of language, ethnicity, religion, class, and gender, College staff reinforced the social structures of the pre-colonial period. It was these educated northerners who first articulated clear ideas of the Sudanese nation as a unitary whole with Khartoum as its capital, and colonial provinces plus the vast southern hinterland as its subordinate parts. In the words of Heather Sharkey, these young northern Sudanese became 'imperialism's most intimate enemies, making colonial rule a reality while hoping to see it undone'.[96] Educated southerners, the product of Christian missionary schools, were, by contrast, frozen out of what would be an Arab-dominated and Arabic-speaking post-colonial state.

Repression and violence in the French Empire

Sudan presents the clearest inter-war example of a short-term administrative expedient with unforeseen long-term consequences. In other places colonial violence played a bigger part in determining future political developments. The First World War peace settlements came less than a generation after the concentration camps of Spanish Cuba and the South African War or, more infamously still, General Lothar von Trotha's campaign of extermination against the Herero and Nama of German South West Africa. And there were few indications that the ultra-violence of 'pacification'—in Rudyard Kipling's formulation, the 'savage wars of peace'—was a thing of the past. During the First World War colonial uprisings in the British Empire (Ireland, Ceylon, Egypt, Waziristan, Iraq) and in the French (Algeria, Niger, Indochina, Morocco) were ruthlessly put down, often by troops acclimatized to exceptionally brutal methods and high casualty rates by their own wartime experiences.[97]

So it was in the three principal inter-war uprisings in the French Empire: in Morocco and Syria during 1925, and in rural northern Vietnam between 1930 and 1932. Morocco's Rif War originated in a post-war challenge by Berber clan groups against Spanish and French occupation of the country's northern margins.[98] Fighting between Spanish colonial forces and the foremost Riffian tribal confederations began in 1920. From 12 April 1925, what had been a Spanish–Riffian war became a predominantly French–Riffian one. Three *harkas* of Riffian forces, together close to 5,000 strong, traversed the boundary separating the Spanish and French Moroccan protectorates. Scores of French garrison blockhouses were overrun within days.[99] This was not improvised rebellion but, in Marshal Philippe Pétain's words, a war fought against 'the most powerful and best armed enemy we have ever encountered in colonial operations'.[100]

The French Premier Paul Painlevé told his fellow Senators on 2 July 1925 that the French in Morocco were victims of an unprovoked attack, poor reward for the benefits of modernization and political stability conferred elsewhere by protectorate government.[101] He overlooked a critical decision taken by Louis-Hubert Lyautey's French Moroccan administration a year earlier. French military advance into the Ouergha River Valley, centre of the Rif's wheat production, threatened to close off food and water supplies to the area's dominant clans.[102] The unprovoked 'invasion' of French territory was, in fact, a reoccupation of essential Riffian farmland recently seized by the Protectorate authorities.[103] With so much at stake, fighting intensified over the summer. By mid October French official casualty figures recorded 2,176 soldiers killed and 8,297 wounded. Many were North and West African colonial troops. These were the heaviest French military losses since the Armistice and the Rif War would remain the largest engagement by French colonial forces between the wars. With the campaign draining the French Treasury of almost a billion francs, Painlevé's ministers wanted the war won quickly. Lyautey's despairing efforts to salvage some measure of collaboration with the Riffians came to nothing.[104] Pétain replaced him in Rabat, bringing two additional army corps and the promise of quick victory. A metropolitan army General relatively unfamiliar with imperial soldiering, Pétain began his autumn offensive in late September. Almost 160,000 French troops took part, advancing along the northern Rif frontier.[105] That autumn Pétain's forces brought the tactics of the Western Front—artillery barrages, mustard gas, and infantry assaults—to bear against Riffian clansmen and women.[106] The resultant defeat and exile of Mohammed Ben Abdel Krim el-Khattabi was less of a turning point than the means chosen to achieve it. Misleadingly described by Painlevé's government as a 'police operation', the Rif War pointed the way towards the fight strategies adopted by successive French administrations over coming decades to crush anti-colonial opposition.

It was only weeks before the invocation of new leadership, the injection of extra resources, and unrestrained use of overwhelming firepower in Morocco was repeated in French Syria. There, too, the escalatory dynamics of asymmetric colonial repression were equally apparent.[107] By December 1925, what had started as a local rebellion among the Druze population of southern Syria against an overbearing French military governor had triggered urban uprisings in Syria's three largest provincial towns: Homs, Hama, and Aleppo.[108] Violence in the countryside was more arbitrary. French irregular forces, substantially composed of Circassian and Kurdish units, destroyed villages and executed men suspected of assisting the rebels. Reprisal killings and the display of corpses in acts of intimidation became commonplace.[109]

The capital, Damascus, also experienced the full ferocity of pacification after Druze insurgents infiltrated the city's southern districts. In August 1925 barbed wire and checkpoints went up around the city. These were intended both to keep rebel forces out and to assist security force dragnets against supporters of prominent Damascene families linked to a newly-established nationalist group, the Syrian People's Party.[110] Mass arrests disrupted the Party's networks but failed to contain the trickle of rebel fighters into the capital. In the pre-dawn hours of 18 October around forty Druze fighters led by Hasan al-Kharrat entered the city's Shaghur quarter. A police station was set ablaze; troops caught unawares in local brothels were killed. A larger Druze column, joined by scores of Damascene sympathizers, joined the rampage later in the day. The high commissioner's converted city residence, the 'Azm Palace, was comprehensively looted. Although tanks and roving columns worked their way towards the rebel force, uncertainty persisted about its size. That evening, General Maurice Gamelin, who would lead the army into the battle for France in 1940, ordered the shelling of the city's most rebellious districts. Aircraft joined the assault. Civilians, including large numbers of European residents, fled in terror or hid in basements. Certain that rebels were hiding among the tenements but unwilling to send troops in to conduct house-by-house searches, Gamelin stepped up the pressure. The next morning, artillery fired high explosive shells across a wide arc that included the city centre.[111] Whole swathes of the capital were in ruins by the time city dignitaries negotiated a ceasefire. The Damascus municipality counted 1,416 dead, among them 336 women and children.[112]

Such indiscriminate shelling was shocking proof that the minimum force maxims identified with Lyautey's former Moroccan administration were discredited. France's premier imperial general returned to France to end his

Figure 2. Peace restored? Marshal Lyautey hosts the visit of the Duke and Duchess of York to the Paris Colonial Exhibition in Vincennes. (The Duke is on the Duchess's right.)

career in a largely honorific role, notably as titular organizer of the enormous Paris Colonial Exhibition that opened in Vincennes in May 1931.

Lyautey's military successors were never open to compromise. Faced with a powerful incursion, Gamelin in Syria, like Pétain in Morocco, chose devastating force, an option as recklessly inappropriate in the densely-populated inner suburbs of Damascus as it was in the Riffian highlands. Theirs was a policy of annihilation. By the time the much reinforced Levant army moved in to crush the remaining pockets of Syrian resistance in the Jabal Druze and elsewhere in August 1926, the revolt's original causes were overshadowed by the violence deployed to stamp it out.[113] Misguided French efforts to modernize the rural economy and restructure provincial administration contrary to the wishes of local notables might have been remedied.[114] Instead, over 100,000 were left homeless, the agricultural economy thrown into recession, and any prospect of dialogue with emergent Syrian nationalism destroyed.[115] Perhaps most significantly, the 'Great Revolt' passed into popular memory as a heroic lost cause, providing a banner around which otherwise disparate Syrian nationalists could rally in defiance of the French Mandate for the next twenty years.

Nor was there any sign of security force restraint in Indochina, witness to some of the colonial world's most staggering political violence throughout a tempestuous century of French rule. The causes, costs, and consequences of these clashes have generated an impressive literature.[116] Connections have also been made between the flashpoints of inter-war dissent in French-ruled Vietnam during the early 1930s and the outbreak of the Indochina War in 1946. An army mutiny at Yen Bay, a garrison 160 kilometres northwest of Hanoi, and a more sustained peasant uprising between May 1930 and September 1931 in the central Vietnamese provinces of Nghe-An and Ha-Tinh, known retrospectively as the Nghe-Tinh soviet movement, have each been read as indicators of a militant nationalism partly inspired by Vietnamese cultural renovation, partly by Communist ideology.[117] The local severity of the Depression also played its part. Communist leader Ho Chi Minh and Phan Bội Châu, founder of the Duy Tân Hôi (Vietnam Reformation Society) and his country's leading nationalist exile, were each natives of Nghe-An.[118] Poverty nourished Nghe-An's radical tradition. Poor and densely populated, the provincial capital, Vinh, and its outlying farming districts were acutely susceptible to adverse changes in the region's agricultural market. A combination of low-yield land, drought conditions, and repeated harvest failure caused widespread peasant malnutrition.[119] But these economic factors were ignored by the colonial administration, which treated dissent almost as an environmental condition, something intrinsic to Vietnam and its people, rather than a phenomenon generated by the political economy of colonialism.[120] Depicting Vietnam as inherently lawless absolved the authorities of responsibility for social unrest and it normalized the resort to harsh repression within a society allegedly accustomed to the language of violence: legal distinctions between the killing of civilians and the eradication of insurgents collapsed.[121]

Guided by local militiamen, Foreign Legion units led the crackdown after Yen Bay.[122] Their prime targets were the supporters of two main groups: Vietnam's nationalist party, the Việt Nam Quôc Dân Dang (VNQDD) and its new rival, the Indochinese Communist Party (ICP). In practice, army violence was arbitrary and judicial retribution severe. On 17 June 1930 thirteen VNQDD members, including party leader Nguyen Thai Hoc, were escorted to Yen Bay for execution by guillotine.[123] The event was concealed from public view to minimize the risk of creating martyrs to the nationalist cause.[124] But the French Communist Party newspaper, *L'Humanité*, broke ranks. It reproduced the statements made by the condemned and graphically recounted their struggling as Foreign Legionnaires forced the men onto the chopping block. Literally decapitated, the VNQDD declined as a political force, leaving the way open for Communist resurgence in the later 1930s. The executed VNQDD leaders did not figure within official casualty figures for the nine-month period, February to October 1930, which listed 345 rebels killed, 124 wounded, and 429 arrested. Government forces, by contrast, came away unscathed.[125]

On 10 April 1930, several weeks after the original mutiny at Yen Bay, the Chamber of Deputies finally debated the situation in Indochina. Socialist Deputy Marius Moutet dominated the proceedings. A Lyons lawyer and a committed pacifist, Moutet was an eloquent critic of judicial abuses in the empire. Outside Parliament he used his position within the League for the Rights of Man (*La Ligue des Droits de l'Homme*, LDH), the most influential human rights lobby in France, and its associated committee for the defence of political prisoners, to condemn French actions in northern Vietnam.[126] Moutet's preoccupation with colonial affairs was unusual among LDH members, whose journal described colonial subjects in pejorative, sometimes racist terms.[127] Queasy about colonial oppression, the League still defended republican imperialism as a force for good.[128]

So Moutet's was rather a lone voice. He railed against the mockery of French justice as the colonial authorities imposed control, pointing out that a specially-convened criminal commission in Tonkin (Vietnam's northernmost territory) passed fifty-two death sentences on Yen Bay mutineers. Another special criminal court in Saigon handed down an additional thirty-four death sentences in under twenty-four hours.[129] Only the poet Louis Aragon, a founder of the surrealist movement and an organizer of the militantly anti-colonial 'Red Front', was as vociferous in denouncing this fight strategy run wild.[130] For all their efforts, few beyond the margins of the extreme left and Paris Bohemia seemed to be listening.

Step forward five years to Fascist Italy's invasion of Haile Selassie's Ethiopia in late 1935. It was then that sixteen members of the *Académie Française*,

France's most prestigious academic body, issued an 'Intellectuals' manifesto for the defence of the West'. The signatories were all authoritarian right-wingers. Among them were Charles Maurras, father-figure of the ultra-rightist 'Leagues' like the *Croix de feu* (Cross of fire), whose members took to the streets in their thousands during in the 1930s, and Robert Brasillach, a future collaborationist executed for treason in 1945. Their 1935 manifesto was an unabashed defence of European colonial domination. It mocked 'a false legal universalism which sets the superior and the inferior, the civilized person and the barbarian, on the same equal footing'. The 'Intellectuals' manifesto' provoked outrage from French liberals, Moutet and his LDH colleagues among them. But the fact remained that less than five years before the Second World War the 'right' of European nations to rule 'lesser' societies remained dogmatically self-evident to other prominent French commentators.[131]

Repression and violence in the British Empire

To a degree, British inter-war techniques of repression mirrored those of France. General Reginald Dyer's decision to order imperial troops to fire on hundreds of civilian protesters at Amritsar on 13 April 1919 confirms that extreme state violence was by no means confined to French colonies.[132] General Dyer conceived his task in Amritsar as a military operation against a hostile population in 'enemy territory'.[133] It was a view that won him considerable support in Britain, where his defenders maintained that his unscrupulousness stamped out an incipient revolt.[134] A decade later in Burma a rural uprising, the Saya San rebellion, which was embraced by members of Burma's proto-nationalist movement during 1930–31, was suppressed with the same ruthless, exemplary violence as used against the Yen Bay mutineers in northern Vietnam.[135] Elsewhere, sources of British colonial dissent were rather different. Palestine stood out in this regard. Its disputes were written in Britain's conflicting wartime promises to Arab and Jewish leaders. Never during the mandate's sorry twenty-eight year history did Palestine's British rulers reconcile their contradictory commitments to a Jewish national home and protection of Palestinians' rights as charges of the League of Nations. By 1937, sub-dividing Palestine between Arabs and Jews, something dismissed by British politicians of all stripes in the 1920s as an admission of imperial failure, had acquired the

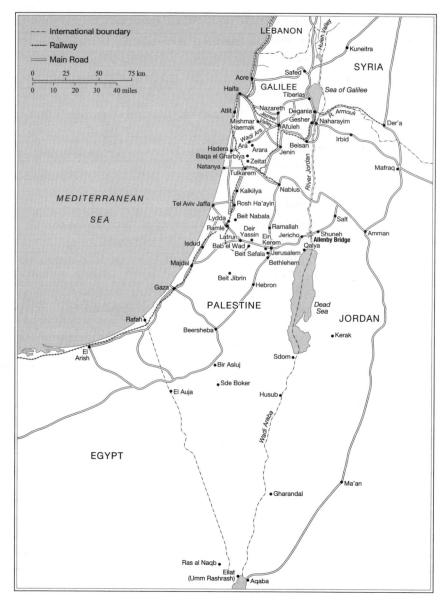

Map 4. The British Mandate in Palestine.

dismal respectability of the last resort solution. Partition became policy, its planned outlines evident in Map 4. Perhaps because Britain's Palestine problems were self-inflicted, its administrators excelled other British colonial bureaucrats in expressing their frustration.[136] Jerusalem High Commissioner

Sir Ronald Storrs was among those exasperated by the challenges of communal impartiality: 'Two hours of Arab grievances drive me into the synagogue, while after an intensive course of Zionist propaganda, I am prepared to embrace Islam.'[137]

Storrs' cynicism is easily explained. Neither he nor his successors could dampen Palestine's inter-communal friction. Indeed, the combination of early 1930s depression conditions, rising Jewish immigration from Europe, and intensified competition over land, property, and religious observance made it worse. Sickening outbursts of internecine violence proliferated.[138] From the early 1920s to the late 1930s riots along communal frontlines in Jaffa, Hebron, Nablus, and, above all, Jerusalem, culminated in orgies of killing.[139] Fearful about accusations of partiality and betrayal of trust, successive British Cabinets turned to the final expedient for a cornered government: a decorous Royal Commission to conduct a judicial investigation and offer advice on lessons learnt.[140] One such commission of inquiry into the worst of these clashes, the Wailing Wall riots of August 1929, recorded 133 Jews and 116 Arabs killed with a further 572 seriously injured.[141] The Mandate's security forces, reliant on local paramilitaries and targeted by rebel groups from both communities, became caught up in the cycle of killings and counter-killings. Increasingly brutal, Palestine's police and the British army garrison were a hated occupation force by the time full-scale Arab revolt erupted in early 1936.[142]

Even a temporary ceasefire in October 1936 only highlighted the limits to British influence. Negotiated in part to facilitate Palestine's all-important citrus harvest, in part to offset demands for martial law, the ceasefire underscored the ability of the Palestinian Arab leadership to orchestrate the violence. As General Sir John Dill, recently dispatched to suppress the revolt, commented, 'I regard the most disturbing side of the situation as being the demonstration of power which the Arab Higher Committee has given in calling off the rebellion so completely and so quickly—by a word.'[143] The cycle of killings and retribution would resume in 1937. British security forces began manipulating the law to justify a savage policy of counter-terror against Palestinian civilians.[144] This time it was the British public that did not seem to care.

Liberal leftists throughout Europe were drawn to the against-the-odds bravery of the anti-fascist international brigades in the Spanish Civil War. Left-leaning anti-colonial nationalists like Algeria's People's Party (*Parti du Peuple Algérien*) or the Indian National Congress also

Figure 3. Minimum force? The Palestine Police, actually a paramilitary force, take to the streets during January 1936 riots in Jaffa.

professed their opposition to fascism while stressing the double standards of European Socialists who did little about colonial oppression. In February 1938 Jawaharlal Nehru, for one, criticized the 'curious and comforting delusion' among Labour leaders who presumed that resisting fascism could be accomplished without freeing India.[145] According to this logic, the Labour leadership brushed the moral equivalence between anti-fascism and anti-colonialism under the carpet. Certainly, no British politicians looked favourably on the Palestinian peasant insurgents who resisted Mandate rule in precisely the same three-year period of 1936 to 1939 that witnessed the death of Republican Spain.[146] This elision of memory is typified by the figure of Shaykh 'Izz al-Dîn al-Qassâm, a Syrian-born Haifa imam and insurgent organizer who became the hero of the Palestinian Revolt after he was shot dead by police in November 1935. His tomb in the village grave-yard of Balad al-Shaykh has since been repeatedly vandalized, a reminder that the village's 5,000 Palestinian inhabitants fled their homes in the first wave of Jewish Haganah attacks during the 1948 Arab-Israeli war in April 1948. Balad al-Shaykh is now subsumed within an Israeli township, its name, like its original residents, long since replaced.[147]

As for the rebellion that Qassâm helped inspire, its failure is usually ascribed to factionalism among rebel bands faced with superior British and Jewish paramilitary firepower and intelligence-gathering capability.[148] There is some truth in this depiction. During the opening months of the rebellion in 1936–37 insurgent bands typically coalesced at village level, without wider 'national' coordination or command.[149] There was a logic to this, however. Rooted in their local community, insurgents were better placed to recruit supporters, to maintain their supplies, to hide when necessary and, most important, to establish alternate structures of local administration. Far from being the 'criminals' or 'outlaws' depicted in British propaganda or subsequent Zionist accounts, Palestinian rebel groups adhered to a strict moral economy in which careful target selection, the protection of loyalist villagers, and the redistribution of land to those who served the rebel cause was integral to their capacity to operate at all. Ultimately, however, rebel efforts to sustain the rhythm of revolt were undone by brutal British military tactics of aerial bombing, collective punishments, destruction of Palestinian property, and systematic torture of detainees. Destroying a farmstead, cutting down citrus and olive orchards, or pouring oil over a family's winter store of cereals and pulses were acts of violence as ruthlessly effective as beating prisoners to extract information.[150]

The Palestine Revolt drove Neville Chamberlain's government to adopt that most bastardized of flight strategies: partition as the prelude to withdrawal. Improvised and unpopular, especially within the Jewish community, the 1939 partition plan bore the seeds of renewed post-war conflict.[151] In the event, the Government's May 1939 White Paper subdividing the Mandate into Jewish and Arab mini-states was overtaken by the war. But the essence of British thinking was clear enough. Palestine was a net liability.[152]

Co-option and control

Sustaining British political influence elsewhere in the inter-war Middle East proved only marginally less troublesome. Collusion with monarchical elites, cajoling of their nationalist opponents, and outwardly generous concessions—mock independence for Egypt in 1922, a similar arrangement with Iraq in 1932, and a Suez defence treaty in 1936—were expedient but fundamentally duplicitous. In one of its first acts in office, Ramsay

MacDonald's second Labour government confirmed in September 1929 that Iraq should pass from Colonial Office to Foreign Office control. The signal would go out home and abroad that Britain recognized Iraqi statehood, while imperial interests could be upheld through partnership.[153] These political tactics amounted to what we might usefully think of as 'pre-flight': the backstairs dealing that, for the most part, conserved British strategic and economic interest through negotiation backed by the threat of force, rather than its actual use. Take, for example, the royal succession crisis of 1936, not in Britain, but in Egypt. There, the death of King Fuad in April cleared a path for Wafdist leader Mustafa al-Nahas to advance nationalist interests at the expense of the monarchy's conservative supporters and their British backers. In the event, High Commissioner Sir Miles Lampson's badgering of Wafdist politicians and his choosing to support Fuad's sixteen-year-old successor, King Farouk, kept negotiations for the Anglo-Egyptian treaty (signed in August) on track. The fiction of peaceful co-existence with Wafdist nationalism survived.[154]

Lampson pursued the same tactics as his predecessor, Sir Percy Loraine. Both preserved the appearance of cooperation with Britain's long-standing allies among Egypt's royalist elite while bargaining with their natural opponents in the Wafd. The resultant treaty was a compromise, subject to later renegotiation at what probably seemed a distant and not particularly significant date: 1956. One thing that the 1930s negotiators on both sides did realize was that each would try to strengthen their position at the other's expense in the intervening twenty years. This was implicit in the 1936 treaty bargain that the two High Commissioners helped to strike. Britain might have secured a more advantageous deal with previous Egyptian governments, but, in signing a treaty with Wafdist support, it co-opted the group otherwise bound to oppose it.[155] This was British imperial diplomacy inter-war style. In place of the gunboats of old, more subtle pressure was applied. As if to make the point, the young Farouk, who had been studying at the Woolwich Military Academy, travelled home to Egypt aboard an ordinary passenger liner, P&O's *Viceroy of India*—but with the cruiser HMS *Ajax* providing a Mediterranean escort.[156]

The image of benign, restrained intervention was equally cultivated in other British territories where client rulers remained in place. A March 1931 letter written by a deputy of Sir Cecil Clementi, Governor of Malaya, while his boss was back in London conveyed the unflappable calm so beloved by British colonial officials. It began dismissively by telling Clementi that there was no news 'of sufficient interest to bother you with' while on leave. Of Malaya's component states, Johore had been 'jogging along quietly except for a little Communist trouble in the Muar District', while Trengganu was 'financially on the rocks'. Yet, these were mere asides. The sole newsworthy item was that in Brunei 'the Sultan's mother has been making rather a nuisance of herself'.[157]

Before the Japanese invasion in 1941 colonial Malaya had some claim to be genuinely multicultural. The growth of English educational curricula and elite, but ethnically-mixed schools informed their Malay, Chinese, and Indian pupils with a shared sense of Britishness. Beyond the school gate, increasing consumerism also made for fluid identities yet to crystallize into the sharper communal divides associated with Malaya during the post-war Emergency. By 1931 Singapore's population had risen to over half a million, making it Southeast Asia's largest and most cosmopolitan city. There, as on the neighbouring Malayan Peninsula, nationalist sentiment was weak; overseas ties of ethnicity, commerce, and culture commensurately strong.[158]

The picture in another multi-ethnic British colony—Kenya—could hardly have been more different. In October 1936, the Conservative colonial secretary William Ormsby-Gore wrote to Air Chief Marshal Sir Robert Brooke-Popham to offer him the Kenya governorship. With Italy's bloody takeover of Ethiopia still unfolding, it seemed vital to have a dependable appointee in Nairobi's Government House. The job was a tough one. At least four of Kenya's previous governors had departed prematurely, usually after clashing with the colony's implacable settlers. Ever since the Colonial Office 'Devonshire Declaration' of 1923 (pejoratively labelled the 'Devonshire fudge') affirmed that Kenya was 'primarily' African and unsuited for white 'self-rule', the colony's settlers viewed Westminster edicts with poisonous disdain.[159] There was more to this than the resentment of the pioneer for the interfering bureaucrat. The Great War destabilized minds as well as empires, communities and families. As Patricia Lorcin, a sharp analyst of women settlers' writing, notes, the '14–'18 War undermined the rock-solid belief in the excellence of European civilization and the advantages of social modernity. And it broke many of the ties between settler societies and their home governments. Elspeth Huxley, writing in 1935, almost a generation after the armistice, captured the point in her otherwise laudatory biography of Lord Delamere, the champion of white settlement in Kenya: 'Behind the almost fanatical manner in which many African questions are approached today lurks the feeling that we who so obviously and tragically fail to manage our own affairs in Europe should not meddle in Africa.'[160]

Ormsby-Gore admitted that Kenya was acutely divided between 'the very vocal British settlers, mostly of the ex-officer and public school class, a large Indian middle class of traders, artisans and some lawyers, and three million African natives of the most heterogeneous types in any colony in Africa'. Yet it remained, 'a country people fall in love with and acquire an emotional rather than a strictly rational attitude toward—a paradise of big game with superb scenery, but bristling with "problems" and controversies, many of them arising from the fact that at 6,000 feet above sea level on the Equator everyone wants to run before they can walk in an atmosphere which doesn't permit of quite such strenuous exercise.' The colony, he thought, 'wants somebody who is a good mixer, has plenty of self-reliance, and a sense of humour quite as much as an energetic administrator...I know it well enough to know that it is a "man's" job.'[161] Suitably flattered, Brooke-Popham was in Nairobi six months later. His 'self-reliance' was soon tested, neither by the Kikuyu nor by his unwelcome Italian neighbours, but by settler opposition to any whisper of reform.[162] The irony was that land policy, taxation, and social spending served settler requirements. Official reluctance—or inability—to tackle these structural problems before the war stored up African resentments that would emerge with more strength and political coherence after it.

Conclusion

The notion of an 'inter-war period' makes sense for the two imperial powers. In France and Britain the war just ended and the next to come combined proud accomplishments with dreadful memories, proximate threats with reluctance to countenance another conflagration. Europe's conflicts weighed less heavily than other factors in the lives of colonial peoples. Economics was perhaps paramount. Structural poverty in some places, in others, the alternation between boom and bust as raw material prices rose and fell affected levels of political engagement and dissent to a greater extent than the cultural resentments precipitated by specific colonial policies. To sustain political control in their inter-war empires France and Britain followed similar colonial paths of low-level coercion, occasional, ruthless repression, and concessions to local elites identified as empire loyalists. Yet their differing trajectories of fight or flight, admittedly more apparent after the Second World War than before it, were nonetheless evident in their contrasting ideas about the purposes served by empire and the ways in which these ideas informed their colonial actions.[163] How would the impending war change things for rulers and ruled?

2

Empires and the Challenge
of Total War

In the spring of 1939 four young army officers set off from the Paris Military Academy along the Champs de Mars to begin an arduous motor-
cycle journey to Dakar, French West Africa's federal capital.[1] Stories of their
progress, a precursor to the latter-day Paris-Dakar rally, were celebrated as
part of a fortnight-long 'imperial market fair' in April. The sights and smells
of colonial products helped take Parisian minds off the Nazi menace.
Department stores vied with five kilometres of roadside stalls in the city
centre that offered exotic commodities for all tastes and pockets. Eager
shoppers could buy everything from exquisite African carvings and Malagasy vanilla pods to musky Vietnamese perfumes and leopard-skin coats.[2]
'Buy empire', a message more familiar to consumers across the English
Channel, resounded louder than ever in 1939 as politicians and public in
France drew comfort from the reassuring vastness of their colonial assets on
the eve of war.[3] How far were these hopes realized over the next six years?

For an 'imperial nation-state' the challenge of total war was to mould its
empire into a strategic asset—a global 'power system' as opposed to a disparate agglomeration of territories, peoples, and interests.[4] Raw materials and
foodstuffs, colonial revenues, strategic bases and, above all else, additional
manpower were the hard currency of imperial power in war. Just as important from a social perspective were the greater confidence and common
purpose that a united empire might confer. But there was an altogether different construction of empire in a global conflict, one that was overwhelmingly negative. Far-flung colonies, remote naval bases, and other useful prizes
were vulnerable and hard to defend. Policy-makers on both sides of the
Channel thus came to regard some colonies as hostages to fortune. Imperial
resources and attachments might be precious, but the financial and strategic

implications of keeping global empires intact against at least two, perhaps three, enemies among the great powers were nightmarish. At the heart of that nightmare were excruciating choices. In the British case, deathly Flanders fields beckoned once more for home and empire forces because only commitment to a continental fight alongside France could protect Britain from Nazi invasion. On the other hand, only by conserving limited military capacity could exposed colonial territories be protected at the same time. The simplest solution—spending more on rearmament in order to meet both European and imperial obligations—was precluded for the sound reason that unrestrained defence expenditure would undermine the one incontestable advantage that Britain retained next to Nazi Germany: sane finances.[5]

While British strategic planners wrestled with this dilemma, France's Minister of Colonies Georges Mandel reassured his nation's anxious radio listeners in the winter of 1939 that their empire's reserves of people, money, and supplies would save them. The son of a Jewish tailor from Alsace, a territory only re-assimilated into France after 1918, Mandel was a virulent critic of fascism. His faith and his republican patriotism would later cost him his life.[6] But in the autumn of 1939 his imperial rhetoric purred reassurance. Unfortunately, it left French service chiefs unconvinced. They worried that the colonies, which Mandel identified as saviours of France, might, in fact, drain vital reserves needed for the looming *Wehrmacht* onslaught.[7] For both imperial powers the actual position after war broke out in Europe lay somewhere between these two positions. Some colonies became warehouses, their food and other raw material exports indispensable. But numerous dependent territories faced new foreign occupations. More serious in the long term, the coercive means employed to mesh local populations into serving imperial war efforts fed antagonism to foreign rule.[8] The contradictory messages of wartime imperial propaganda were also unsettling for home audiences. Was Britain a global power or a 'plucky little island'? Was the fight for freedom a European or a global one? Conscious that their Home Service and forces programming could reach an estimated thirty-three million adults in Britain alone, in September BBC controllers identified the essential challenge of broadcasting propaganda about the colonies: demonstrating 'that our democratic professions are not a hypocritical pretence'.[9]

The ways in which Britain and France mobilized their empires to fight World War—and the representation of these efforts at home and overseas—would shape post-war decisions about resisting or accommodating local pressures to decolonize. This chapter reviews these events. It illustrates that in those locations where anti-colonial sentiment was most keenly felt—India, Burma, and Palestine among British territories, Algeria and Vietnam among French ones—the end of the Second World War would be immediately followed by the outbreak of anti-colonial uprisings that heralded decolonization's first wave.

Britain and France entered the war as allies in the struggle against Nazi Germany; but what about imperially? Franco-British staff talks had been held in London, Beirut, Singapore, and Aden over the summer of 1939 to work out joint regional strategies for the protection of neighbouring imperial territories. These meetings were high on grand schemes: a 'Balkan front' alongside Turkey, naval cooperation in the South China Sea, a common defence plan for the Indian Ocean.[10] But they were short on tangible results. Turkey, despite signing up to a tripartite alliance with Britain and France on 19 October, stayed out of the war, alarmed by the implications of the August 1939 Nazi–Soviet Pact for its northern frontiers.[11] In the Far East French negotiators could offer nothing to tempt British naval planners to venture east of the so-called 'Malay barrier' into the waters off Indochina. The discussions held in Singapore during late June had a particularly Never-Never Land quality. French navy representatives confirmed that their government would construct battleship base facilities at Camranh Bay and Saigon but had no battleships to spare. Admiral Sir Percy Noble explained where a British Far Eastern fleet might eventually operate but, as yet, commanded no fleet to speak of.[12] Here was 'imperial overstretch' writ large in the obvious lack of warships to block hostile incursion.[13] It proved easier to pool resources in the Indian Ocean because the British and French naval resources in Aden, Kenya, Djibouti, and Madagascar were relatively small and the threat from Japan more remote.[14]

This combination of closer Franco-British partnership with limited outcomes was equally apparent in economic affairs. Certain categories of French products were exempted from the import restrictions announced by Neville Chamberlain's government on the outbreak of war. September 1939 also saw talks begin over fuller commercial integration between the two partners. The French Premier Édouard Daladier declared his support for a system of 'federal trade' between the two empires in a high-profile speech to the French Senate on 30 December 1939. Yet, while further discussions on broader inter-imperial economic cooperation got under way in London in January 1940, free trade between British and French territories was never agreed.[15] The arrangement which pertained instead for most of the war saw Britain bankroll those French colonies that 'rallied' to General de Gaulle's Free French movement in return for which these territories were subsumed into Britain's war effort, supplying primary products, mainly foods and minerals, in return for the sterling needed to finance Charles de Gaulle's nascent government-in-waiting.[16]

British backing for de Gaulle's Free French movement reflected the way that France and its Empire splintered after defeat by Germany in June 1940. Part military force, part quasi-government-in-exile, Free France was certainly committed to fighting the Axis Powers, but it operated outside France for most of the war.[17] Until mid 1943 its principal strategic assets were in sub-Saharan Africa, President Franklin Roosevelt's administration blocking de Gaulle's move northwards to 'liberated' Algiers following the American landings in North Africa the previous November.[18] The Free French should not to be confused with the diverse civilian resistance networks that sprang up within metropolitan France. Indeed, these homeland resisters vied with Free France for power and influence once the Vichy regime established under Marshal Pétain became more venal and collaborationist from 1941 onwards. Meanwhile, because their movement coalesced around General de Gaulle in London and among his supporters in the colonies, followers of Free France—a politically diverse group of armed forces personnel, politicians, diplomats, bureaucrats, and African colonial troops—were often misleadingly described by the catch-all term 'Gaullists'.[19]

For some, support for the General and his unique vision of French greatness—or *grandeur*—verged on the fanatical. For others, de Gaulle's attractions were incidental to the more urgent priorities of fighting fascist occupation, ousting Vichy, and restoring republican democracy to France. As for Free France's colonial troops, who campaigned arduously in North Africa, Italy, and southern France, serving de Gaulle was, initially at least, as much circumstantial as deliberate. For what one historian dubs these 'soldiers of misfortune', it usually reflected the location of a particular garrison or the loyalties of its senior officers, not the political leanings of the rank-and-file.[20] The estimated 16,500 Free French military losses during campaigning in North Africa and Italy were primarily colonial. Villages in Morocco, Mali, and Algeria, not Brittany, the Ardèche, or the Pas-de-Calais, mourned the largest numbers of soldiers killed in French uniform after June 1940.[21]

The ambivalence within the Free French movement towards its symbolic figurehead points to other aspects of wartime France that bear emphasis.

First, French people and society—at home and overseas—were as much politically as physically divided by the 1940 collapse. The circumstances of the defeat, the massive population exodus that preceded it, the removal of at least 1.65 million French prisoners of war (POWs) to Germany, and the carving of mainland France into occupied and unoccupied 'zones' turned people's worlds upside down.[22] The French population experienced warfare fitfully, first in May–June 1940, then following the Allied landings in northern and southern France in June and August 1944. In between-times their experiences of violence and loss derived from the consequences of occupation and population displacement. The absence of so many POWs, later compounded by German recruitment of 840,000 forced labourers, plus the forced enlistment of young men from Alsace into the *Wehrmacht*, weighed heavily. Worst of all, French Jews were systematically wiped out in the manner of their co-religionists and other persecuted groups in Eastern Europe.[23] Another cruel irony was that allied bombing killed so many French civilians, the 600,000 tons of British and American bombs dropped on France resulting in an estimated 60,000 civilian deaths, a figure broadly comparable to the number of Britons killed in German raids on the United Kingdom.[24]

The Vichy state took shape amidst the chaos. Its authority was confirmed by National Assembly parliamentarians who obligingly voted themselves out of office—and the Third Republic out of existence—by an overwhelming majority of 569 to 80 on 10 July 1940. Granted full powers by this act of political hari-kiri, the innate authoritarianism of Marshal Pétain's regime was set free at home and in the colonies.[25]

Vichy signified what American historian Stanley Hoffman memorably dubbed 'the revenge of the minorities'. Right-wing anti-republicans, Catholic traditionalists, and proto-fascists, the outsiders of the pre-war political system, moved to centre-stage.[26] In a sweetly ironic twist, the regime's improvised Ministry of Colonies took up residence in Vichy's Hotel Britannique.[27] It is doubtful whether many French citizens or colonial subjects immediately grasped the implications of France's ideological lurch to the extreme right. Their lives thrown into confusion, the dominant emotion among the domestic population was bewilderment. Missing relatives, shortages, and black market iniquities generated greater anxiety than high politics.[28]

Those prepared to express firm convictions or adopt life-changing positions for or against Vichy were a small minority. Some were ideologically motivated, welcoming the opportunity to build a disciplined and

Figure 4. Marshal Pétain appears as Napoleonic saviour in this Vichy propaganda poster produced for dissemination in French North Africa.

hierarchical society shorn of what they considered the decadent excesses of republican liberality.[29] Others felt compelled to keep fighting by the very opposite political and ethical values. Pre-eminent among them were Communists. Their party outlawed back in September 1939, a month after Stalin's signature of the Nazi–Soviet Pact, Communist supporters were driven underground well before the 1940 defeat.[30] If resistance organization came naturally to Communist activists, still others were animated by patriotic resolve, by personal loss, or, as in the case of numerous Jewish families, by an ethno-religious background that placed them in mortal danger.[31] Settler communities in the empire, most with family or military connections 'back home', were also shattered by the defeat. But they had greater scope to express opinions than their kith and kin in France. Although their attachments were commensurately diverse, a high proportion welcomed Vichy's authoritarian machismo, which came with a pronounced racist tinge that celebrated settler virility and identified authentic French identity with whiteness.[32]

Another point, then, is that colonial communities, marginal to pre-war French politics, were more intimately involved in the wartime struggle over France's long-term destiny. The consequences were acutely divisive. For much of the Second World War, combat within colonial territory was Franco-French, part of an undeclared civil war between Vichy and its domestic enemies. Measured by the objectives of its principal combatants, this colonial civil war was about the future of France and was not colonial at all. Yet this internecine struggle was fought in the midst of colonial subjects and frequently exploited them to do the actual fighting. The line between voluntary military contribution and coercive recruitment of colonial soldiers was sometimes impossible to trace. Even so, the Franco–French struggle remained curiously removed from the daily lives of colonial communities for whom more fundamental questions of food supply, employment, and basic rights figured larger.[33] Not so for the French Empire's white populations. Even when the wider war impinged on them, as, for instance, when Japanese forces occupied southern Indochina in 1941, or when US and British (including imperial and other Allied) forces fought to expel Erwin Rommel's army from French North Africa in 1942–3, the quarrels between Vichy supporters and their resistance opponents predominated in French minds and actions. This raises a final point. For the uncomfortable fact confronting all sides in this French civil war was their de facto reliance on stronger external backers. Vichy existed only as long as it was expedient for Nazi Germany to leave Pétain's regime in place, not just in unoccupied southern France, but in much of French Africa as well. And the Free French movement, as well as the internal resistance groups fighting Vichy and its German and Italian overseers, were themselves dependent on some type of Allied support: Anglo-American facilities, money, and war materiel for some; Soviet ideological inspiration for others. The upshot was that France's wartime faction fights, although substantially played out in colonial theatres, were peculiarly skewed towards a domestic struggle for power. Phrased differently, empire provided the terrain but not the agenda for the French leadership contest fought out between 1940 and 1945.

The British Empire, of course, was also fighting for its existence, a fact that left no room for sentiment about the fate of former allies. British naval bombardment of the largest component of the French Mediterranean fleet at anchor in the Algerian port of Mers el-Kébir in July 1940 drove the point home. Intended to nullify the risk of the French vessels falling into Axis hands, Royal Navy shelling killed 1,297 French sailors. Their commanders had rejected British entreaties to come over for two reasons above all. One was that remaining in North Africa seemed essential to keep the French Empire intact after the armistice. The other was that, alongside the Empire, an operational fleet was the only strategic card remaining to a France in defeat. These reasons seemed justification enough to ignore the ultimatum to surrender the ships into British hands or face bombardment, a fatal mistake.

The inevitable cries of Perfidious Albion went up loudest among senior French naval commanders, already seething over Britain's ingratitude for the French maritime cover provided for British troops evacuating from Dunkirk. What Churchill portrayed as a remarkable combination of British improvisation and courage was viewed rather differently from a French perspective: as an indecently premature retreat only accomplished thanks to the French Navy. Furthermore, France's naval leaders had pledged after the Franco-German armistice to scupper their ships rather than cede them to Germany. And they later proved their word by sinking their remaining warships in Toulon harbour after German forces overran unoccupied Vichy France in November 1942. The loss of so many lives at Mers el-Kébir added injury to insult.[34] Most galling of all to Vichy's new politico-naval elite was that Britain, which had so recently relied on French military strength to protect its home islands from German attack, rounded on France in its most agonizing hour of need.[35] Their anger had longer-term implications. Several French Admirals—Jean-Marie Abrail, Jean Decoux, Jean-Pierre Esteva, Charles Platon and, of course, Darlan—rose to prominence as ministers and colonial governors under Vichy. This made the task of persuading French colonial administrations from North Africa to Indochina to join the allied cause all but impossible.[36]

As the Mers el-Kébir attack indicates, after the fall of France British military engagements took a more desperate turn. The British Empire's war thereafter was one of paradoxes, revealing the best and the worst of imperial connections. Dominion engagement was for the most part willingly offered. Only Éire chose neutrality, although Afrikaner opinion in South Africa favoured it as well.[37] Once committed, every Dominion provided invaluable support. Even neutral Ireland contributed 43,000 volunteer servicemen and women. Army divisions from Australia, New Zealand, South Africa, and Southern Rhodesia helped expel Italian forces from East Africa in 1940–1 before joining the North African campaign against Rommel's *Afrika Korps* during 1940–3. Dominion accents could also be heard throughout the wider

Mediterranean theatre from the defence of British Egypt and the ill-fated landings in Crete in May 1941 to the attack on Vichy French Syria two months later and the invasion of Italy over the summer of 1943. Australians and New Zealanders also fought in the Pacific War, where, inexorably, they came under the wing of an American war effort that eclipsed the remaining British presence in the region.[38]

Some young Australians also followed the fortunes of France with particular interest. A Melbourne High School pupil recalled that the war was brought to life in French lessons when *Le Courier australien*, a fervently pro-de Gaulle weekly published by the country's tiny French community, recounted the latest acts of derring-do by the General's followers.[39] Schoolboys enthralled by de Gaulle were one thing, but most Australians were more animated by decisions taken in their name in London. Three factors sapped Australians' and New Zealanders' belief in British capacity to sustain a global, fighting role. First were the crushing imperial defeats experienced in the opening weeks of war against Japan. The collapse of the Far Eastern garrisons of Hong Kong and Singapore between December 1941 and mid-February 1942 were seared into popular memory by press reportage of the killings, rapes, and internments that accompanied them.[40] These calamities underscored the failure of Britain's limited attempt to enforce a naval perimeter around its East Asian possessions. As we have seen, inter-war plans to send a 'main fleet' to Singapore withered by 1939 as the German and Italian threats loomed larger.[41] The improvised naval force eventually dispatched met a tragic end. *Repulse* and the *Prince of Wales*, the only two British battleships sent to patrol the South China Sea, were sunk by nine Japanese bombers off the Malayan coast on 10 December 1941. There was a macabre echo of Mers el-Kébir here: the lethal bomber squadron took off from a Japanese-occupied airbase in French Vietnam.

These disastrous British defeats on land and sea left the Australasian Dominions without effective protection. Churchill, 'stupefied' by the news according to his doctor, Lord Moran, made no attempt to portray the garrison's surrender as anything less than an imperial disaster. Even in New Zealand, always characterized as the most loyal, unflappable Dominion, there were understandable signs of public anxiety born of a dawning recognition of powerlessness.[42] Australia's Labour Prime Minister John Curtin recalled his country's two army divisions home, rejecting their assignment to active theatres, particularly in the Middle East and Mediterranean, remote from the more present dangers in Australia's Near North. The sense that

Britain disposed of Australasian men and materiel without providing tangible insurance in return became a second source of disillusionment. Incontrovertible evidence of British dependence on American support in Asia added the third dimension to this crisis of confidence, contributing to what one historian describes as Australia's 'dedominionization'.[43]

It was Canada, however, that made the most decisive Dominion contribution to the British Empire's struggle for survival.[44] Although the Ottawa Parliament convened to discuss it, Canada's entry to war alongside Britain was, in John Darwin's words, 'the merest formality'.[45] Shaky French Canadian support had been bolstered some months earlier, principally by Prime Minister Mackenzie King's pledge that conscription would be avoided. This was a promise he could not keep. Pushed by popular demand in English-speaking Canada, Mackenzie King's government eventually conceded a referendum on conscription in April 1942. The result revealed a nation still sharply divided along linguistic lines with 83 per cent of English Canadian voters supporting the measure and 72.9 per cent of French Canadians opposing it.[46] In late 1939, however, these ethno-regional cracks were papered over well enough and by December Canadian troops were stationed in Britain. Indeed, Canada should be acknowledged for what it was: not just one of many cogs in an imperial wheel but a major ally in its own right. Justifiable Canadian sensibilities about equal treatment in dealings with Britain were appeased, mostly by Chief of Imperial General Staff Sir Alan Brooke. It fell to him to placate two highly political Canadian Army commanders: Generals Andy McNaughton and Harry Crerar. Brooke enjoyed several advantages in doing so. Among them were common patterns of Anglo-Canadian training and military doctrine, plus a shared commitment to fight together, even in integrated formations.[47]

Over 85 per cent of the 1,086,771 male and female service personnel from Britain's oldest Dominion were volunteers. So many passed through Britain that the BBC Forces Programme began airing ice hockey highlights on Sunday evenings.[48] Many were lost in dreadful circumstances—as members of the isolated Hong Kong garrison that surrendered to a rapacious Japanese assault on Christmas Day 1941; as the hapless assault brigade cut down during the August 1942 Dieppe Raid.[49] It was Canada that dominated the Commonwealth Air Training Scheme, providing vital replenishment to the service arm that suffered the largest proportionate share of frontline losses. And, owing to the circumstances of their deployment, relatively large numbers of Canadian service personnel became POWs.

One of those captured was Captain Lionel Massey, son of Vincent Massey, Canada's High Commissioner in London, who helped devise Britain's POW policies.[50] The Royal Canadian Navy was also integral to the North Atlantic convoy system, which was fundamental to Britain's capacity to fight on. Finally, Canada manufactured more and lent more than its smaller Dominion cousins, facts which confirmed that the old asymmetries of Anglo-Canadian—and Anglo-Dominion—relations were changing.[51]

India's contribution to Britain's war effort was larger still in human terms but its involvement in the war—demanded, rather than requested by Viceroy Lord Linlithgow in September 1939—exposed the fallacy of British claims to fair and equal treatment of its subjects overseas.[52] The All-India National Congress, although internally divided over its attitude to the war, was uniformly outraged at Britain's short-term rejection of constitutional reform. Congress representatives promptly resigned from seven of India's eleven provincial governments.[53] As Yasmin Khan has suggested, India occupied a liminal space, an uncomfortable, median position between loyal imperial home front and restive, quasi-war zone. It was certainly a place where decolonization beckoned.[54] Little wonder that signs of disaffection proliferated among Indian army divisions stationed in Singapore and Hong Kong before Japan attacked Pearl Harbor. Soldiers' sense of being taken for granted was sharpened by the limited results of long-promised 'Indianization' of officer and NCO positions in Indian Army units. Not surprisingly expatriate Indian nationalists and the Japanese military found enthusiastic recruits for the anti-British Indian National Army among the thousands of *Sepoys* taken prisoner during Japan's unstoppable progress through Malaya to Singapore in January–February 1942.[55]

Almost as damaging as the 32,000 or so Indian troops who agreed to take up arms against the British Empire were the million-plus Indian migrants who lived in Burma where they formed the majority ethnic group in the capital, Rangoon. By May 1942 over 300,000 Indian refugees had arrived in Calcutta (Kolkata), the teeming cultural hub of Bengal. Most arrived destitute from the Burmese port of Chittagong. With every disembarkation, the refugees' harrowing stories of Japanese cruelty and British disarray sent rumour and panic pulsing throughout north-eastern India. The plight of these migrants confirmed that the early stages of the Pacific War caught the British looking the wrong way, too preoccupied with the Mediterranean theatre and colonial India's north-west frontier and not enough with the encroaching menace from the East.[56] Matters quickly went from bad to catastrophic. On 8 August 1942 Congress told Britain to 'Quit India', inspiring a nationwide movement in support of the call. War Cabinet approval for the arrest of Gandhi and other Congress leaders a month later heralded a vicious police crackdown.[57] Perhaps because assignments to India were liable to involve such repressive policing, military postings there were considered unglamorous and insalubrious. Although the regulation of intimate contacts between British and Allied troops became an increasing official obsession, the sexual exploitation of local women remained prevalent.[58] Venereal disease among British imperial troops garrisoned in Indian cantonments reached almost fifty per thousand by 1945—the highest rate in any British military theatre.[59]

Other colonial peoples made proportionately large sacrifices in defence of the Empire, whether eagerly or not. In their cases the discomfiting juxtaposition between imperial patriotism and the empire's structural racism was even harder to ignore. Black African troops fought Italians in Ethiopia and Japanese in Burma, but still in white-officered colonial units. The colour bar that prevented non-white service personnel from becoming officers was formally relinquished in October 1939. But its spirit lived on. To avoid 'cross-contamination', even military blood banks kept separate stocks for whites and non-whites. Young men from the British Caribbean, West Africa, and the Indian subcontinent eager to take to the skies had to wait until bomber command became truly desperate for replacement air-crew before they could do so.[60] Discriminatory treatment was just as stark beyond the armed forces. Forced labour, which had been nominally abolished in the British, if not the French, Empire at the behest of the International Labour Organization in 1930, reappeared in several sub-Saharan colonies. Coercing labour from wider swathes of the African civilian population was impelled by the war's insatiable demand for strategic war materiel and foodstuffs like Nigerian tin or Tanganyika's agricultural produce. And thousands of colonial sailors from Africa, Asia, and the Caribbean flocked to Britain's merchant navy in which an estimated 5,000 died (about a sixth of total merchant navy losses). Many worked below decks as boiler-room stokers, the location notorious among seamen as the most lethal in any submarine attack.[61]

Ashore in Britain's ports, some of these seamen faced other humiliations. So did the colonial war workers serving Britain's armaments industry. Where Merseyside was once remarkable for its relatively low incidence of overtly anti-black sentiment, racist attacks on West Indian munitions workers in Liverpool mounted once large numbers of American GIs began transiting through the city from 1942 onwards. The city's hotels, dancehalls, and pubs began closing their doors to Jamaicans and others, probably aware of the injustice involved, but reluctant to risk losing GI trade. Responding to the rising incidence of racial violence in British port cities, in September 1942 the Colonial Office even toyed with the idea of requiring black colonial war workers in Britain to wear a badge 'so they can be easily differentiated'. Thankfully, the proposal was soon abandoned.[62]

Widening cracks in the French Empire

Disintegration of the French Empire continued inexorably over three war-time stages. From the Phoney War, through Vichy dominance in 1940–2, to the Free French ascendency cemented by de Gaulle's triumphal return to Paris on 25 August 1944, life remained very hard for colonial subjects. The three stages thus shared one point in common despite the fact that French political leadership differed in each one. Throughout the war years, economic hardship, typified by foodstuff shortages and chronic price inflation, matched social exclusion and political repression in bearing more heavily on colonial lives than the progress of allied campaigns or changes at the top of the colonial tree.

French North Africa is a case in point. Typically discussed in relation to the aftermath of French defeat in 1940 as well as in terms of the outcome of Operation Torch, the French-ruled Maghreb was convulsed by other pressures entirely. From the economic impact of conscription in autumn 1939 through the foodstuff crises and urban public health scares that sapped French capacity to overcome the material consequences of metropolitan defeat, French North Africa's war looked very different to the local administrators and wider populations that lived through it. Viewed in this way, the war years were most notable for the irreversible damage they wrought to economic stability and the hierarchies of colonial rule in North Africa. By the time General Maxime Weygand took over as Algeria's Governor-General on 17 July 1941 French North Africa's economic fortunes had declined precipitately. Fuel and foodstuffs were in short supply, the agricultural economy was profoundly disrupted, and average wages languished at subsistence level.[63]

For all that, economic crises and limited sovereignty proved no barrier to the embrace of Vichy's 'National Revolution' by colonial regimes enthused by the Pétainist cults of xenophobic ultra-nationalism, stricter social hierarchies, and a rural nostalgia flavoured with Catholic pro-natalism.[64] Peasant values, large families, and veneration of conservative, often anti-republican institutions—the Catholic Church and the military foremost among them—came naturally to settlers and authoritarian administrators. Thus we find Jean Decoux, another Admiral catapulted to political promi-nence as Vichy's Governor of Indochina, promoting Pétainist youth move-ments in French Vietnam, celebrating the cult of Joan of Arc (Vichy's preferred symbol of patriotic self-sacrifice), and lauding the 'magnificent' fecundity of a settler couple from Tonkin whose twelve children holidayed near the Governor's Palace in the Vietnamese hill station of Dalat.[65] The air of detachment from reality was hardly surprising when the realities in ques-tion were so alarming: the dual menace of a Japanese takeover and an incipi-ent Vietnamese revolution impelled by French inability to satisfy the most basic needs of Indochina's peoples—for security and food.[66]

Across the French political divide, it is easier to see why the senior Gaullists in London were determined to exploit the colonies when one remembers how few cards they had to play with their British patrons. And the British mission to the Free French National Committee was more than an intermediary. Not only did it relay Gaullist economic requests for funds, supplies, shipping, and other transport to the War Cabinet, it also filtered out such demands when they conflicted with the overarching priorities of the Anglo-American supply boards that controlled the circulation of goods between allied and imperial territories.[67]

Furthermore, British officialdom's enduring scepticism about de Gaulle and Free France as rulers of a revitalized French Empire was writ much larger across the Atlantic.[68] In February 1942 Maurice Dejean, foreign affairs commissioner in the French National Committee, articulated a widely-held view among Gaullist staff about the underlying reason behind the Roosevelt administration's enduring coolness towards Free France. The answer, Dejean insisted, lay in a secret US-Vichy deal whereby Marshal Pétain's regime agreed to minimize strategic concessions to Germany provided that the United States left Vichy's empire alone. US recognition of de Gaulle was allegedly withheld as part of the bargain.[69] The simpler reason for Washing-ton's derision of Free France was that Roosevelt loathed de Gaulle, a man he considered pompous, autocratic, and selfish.[70] But Dejean's conspiracy theory was less outlandish than it seemed. Roosevelt's special envoy, Robert Murphy, agreed with Admiral Darlan in March 1941 to trade US foodstuff convoys to Vichy for the promise (quickly broken) to limit collaboration with Germany, particularly in North Africa.[71] Murphy's talks marked the beginning of a longer-term association that climaxed in the so-called 'Darlan deal'. It left Vichy's former premier at the head of government in Algiers in return for the regime's acquiescence in Operation Torch, the US takeover in Morocco and Algeria after only seventy-two hours of fighting in November 1942.[72]

De Gaulle's supporters were incandescent, although far from surprised. Adrien Tixier and Pierre Mendès France, later ministers in the post-war Fourth Republic, spent their war years in Washington trying to win support for the General. By mid 1942 both men were at the end of their tether. The Americans did not understand what Free France stood for, they were hopelessly naive about the Vichy regime, and Roosevelt simply followed his instincts most of the time.[73] In late August, after the US State Department once again refused to recognize the Free French movement as the legitimate voice of France, Dejean let rip again:

> American policy continues to be the result of several diverse factors: wild romanticism, brutal materialism, economic imperialism, anti-colonialism, anti-British and anti-Russian tendencies, Machiavellianism and puerility, the whole lot combining into something Messianic and unconsciously sure of itself.[74]

Excluded from Torch planning, de Gaulle was even more incensed by American support of his new rival for leadership of the Free French, General Henri Giraud, in the limited handover of power that followed Darlan's assassination in Algiers on 24 December 1942.[75] The mutual incomprehension that characterized the Roosevelt–de Gaulle relationship only deepened when they met for the first time at the inter-allied conference in Casablanca in January 1943. Side-lined during the summit, de Gaulle's attitude went from frosty to glacial as he watched the Americans fete the rather wooden and politically obtuse Giraud.[76] When de Gaulle eventually came face to face with Roosevelt, members of the President's secret service detail hid behind the meeting-room curtains, their tommy guns poised.[77] Hardly the beginning of a thaw.

Operation Torch also cast a spotlight on the changing economic balance of power in the Maghreb as the US invasion force moved rapidly eastwards. Its supply needs took precedence over all else and the Americans' dollar purchasing power placed the French North African franc under strain. After Torch, the Algiers authorities quickly negotiated a provisional franc–dollar exchange rate with the US Treasury Department. This was, in turn, supplanted at the Casablanca conference by a stabilization accord that pegged the value of the franc throughout French Africa at fifty to the dollar.[78] Although the greater price stability that resulted was welcome to North Africans, the Casablanca economic agreements did not curb the overweening power of a local black market in which dollars reigned supreme to the detriment of rural consumers least able to obtain them.[79]

It was no coincidence that, during the 1943–4 hiatus of transfers of executive power between Vichy and Free French administrations, the founding statutes of leading nationalist groups, including Algeria's *Amis du Manifeste et de la Liberté* and Morocco's *Istiqlal* (*Independence*) movement cited poverty and economic exploitation as justifications for their anti-colonial platforms.[80] Likewise, Messali Hadj's *Parti du Peuple Algérien*, still the major force in Algerian domestic politics despite being banned outright since 1939, insisted that any ideological differences between Vichy and Gaullist leaders were eclipsed by their shared colonialism, a phenomenon epitomized by ruthless wartime economic extraction. Whether Algeria's foodstuffs, minerals, and other primary products were shipped to Marseilles and thence to Germany or to Allied ports, the essential fact was that Algerians, denied any democratic choice over participation in the war, went hungry. Messali received a fifteen-year sentence of forced labour from a Vichy military tribunal on 28 March 1941. So he might have been expected to welcome the advent of a Gaullist provisional government in Algiers, the French Committee of National Liberation (FCNL).[81] The nomenclature was telling. As Messali asked FCNL members on 11 October 1943, why should Algerians support French liberation when their own national freedom was denied?[82]

Meanwhile, to the east, US forces moved into Tunisia over the winter of 1942–3. Local sections of the country's dominant nationalist group, *Néo-Destour* (the 'new constitution' party) had been denuded by police harassment and long prison terms. Hoping that the party leader Habib Bourguiba and his followers would repudiate their erstwhile French persecutors the German authorities freed the *Néo-Destour* executive in January 1943. They were disappointed. Bourguiba denounced the Nazi occupation of Tunisia, thinking that his bravery might be rewarded by de Gaulle's followers. This, too, proved a vain hope. Repression of nationalist activity resumed once Rommel's forces were evicted. During 1944 the Free French re-imposed the ban on Bourguiba's party and ignored Tunisia's status as a protectorate with its own monarchical administration by enacting legislation that centralized political power under French authority. This signalled the beginning of Bourguiba's turn away from France towards the cultivation of Arab and US opinion, a strategy pursued until Tunisia achieved its independence in March 1956.[83]

North Africa's political violence in 1944 was gravest in Morocco. The ill-advised FCNL decision to arrest the four leaders of the *Hizb el-Istiqlal*, Morocco's foremost nationalist voice, on 29 January provoked rioting in Rabat, Salé, and Fez, the death of at least forty protesters, and the arrest of over 1,800 more.[84] As urban disorder became endemic in Morocco even the Algiers authorities admitted that supply problems, iniquitous rationing, and consequent shortages had become inseparable from nationalist dissent.[85] Perhaps inevitably, the nature and scale of Maghribi recruitment to the First French Army, which was meanwhile fighting northwards through Italy, Corsica, and southern France, deepened the animosity between the Gaullist imperial establishment and their nationalist opponents. To the former, these units confirmed the unity of purpose between France and its North African subjects, although the army's cadres were progressively 'whitened' the closer they got to the French capital. To the latter, the large numbers of North African army volunteers merely indicated how desperate they were for a steady income.[86] And it was a different story for Algerian conscripts among whom desertion rates climbed towards twenty per cent by July 1943 with some 11,119 out of 56,455 avoiding the call-up over the preceding six months.[87]

The Free French were hard-pressed to conceal the signs of unrest in their newly-consolidated African empire. But the breakdown of colonial authority went furthest in the Indochina federation. Admiral Decoux's faltering pro-Vichy government was isolated and broke.[88] It was also threatened from three sides. For General Tsuchihashi's Japanese military administration the bureaucratic convenience of leaving a bankrupt colonial regime in place became questionable.[89] For the regime's internal opponents, many of them loosely connected in a Communist-dominated coalition called the Vietminh, the implosion of French colonial authority enhanced the prospects for a rapid seizure of power. Finally, for the Americans it made sense to work with Vietminh guerrillas, the sole group capable of mounting any serious local challenge to the Japanese.[90]

None of these three alternatives appealed to de Gaulle's supporters, of course. Without the resources to intervene independently in Indochina and unable to 'turn' Decoux's government their way, de Gaulle's provisional government newly installed in liberated Paris could do little.[91] Observing the situation in Vietnam, the Gaullist military attaché in Nationalist China conceded that the Indochina Federation had become 'a no man's land' for the major allied powers. None dared intervene decisively lest they antagonize one another or, far worse, trigger the Japanese takeover they all feared.[92] It was the Vietnamese who seized the initiative. By December 1944 Ho Chi Minh and Vo Nguyen Giap, the Vietminh's leading strategic thinkers, had established the National Liberation Army of Vietnam, which operated from 'free zones' in the far north.[93] Choosing to overlook the Vietminh's ideological leanings, the US and British special services—the OSS and SOE—offered training and equipment for sabotage attacks on the Japanese.

Three months later the Japanese struck back. The American re-conquest of the Philippines in early 1945 had alerted Japan's Supreme War Council to the possibility of similar US amphibious landings in Indochina. These might be supported, not just by the Vietminh but by Decoux's government as well. Tokyo therefore presented the Governor with an ultimatum: place his administration and the French colonial garrison under Japanese command or face the consequences. Decoux's '*non*' spelt the end of French rule—albeit temporarily. Japanese units swept through Hanoi on the night of 9 March, killing scores of French bureaucrats and troops, and interning those unable to make a fighting retreat northwards to China.[94] A puppet regime under Emperor Bao Dai was set up in Hue, Vietnam's imperial capital. Parallel monarchical regimes were re-established in Laos and Cambodia, which reverted to its pre-colonial title of Kampuchea. All three promptly declared 'independence' from France under the approving gaze of General Tsuchihashi's occupation forces. From taxation systems to school curricula, symbols of French colonial power were hastily removed. Kampuchea's Prince Norodom Sihanouk even restored the Buddhist calendar and urged his subjects to abandon the use of Romanized script.[95]

The limits to this independence soon became tragically apparent in northern Vietnam where the new authorities under Premier Tran Trong Kim could not prevent heightened Japanese requisitioning, which destabilized the local rice market. Chronic price inflation made food of any kind unaffordable for the poorest labourers and their families. Famine took hold. It was especially devastating in the Red River Delta and two densely-populated provinces of northern Annam.[96] Village populations collapsed. Some locked their doors, resolved to die together as a family. Others became famine refugees begging on the streets of local towns and cities. One Hanoi resident described the scene: 'Sounds of crying as at a funeral. Elderly twisted women, naked kids huddled against the wall or lying inside a mat, fathers and children prostrate along the road, corpses hunched up like foetuses, an arm thrust out as if to threaten'.[97]

Starvation dominated North Vietnamese politics by early 1945. The faction fighting among the French colonial rulers was at best an irrelevance, at worst an act of shocking insensitivity. Not surprisingly, the combination of Japan's military coup and the tragic shortcomings of its new surrogate authorities in Indochina enhanced the Vietminh's legitimacy as a popular resistance movement. For the Western Allies, impatient to secure victory over Japan, as for Vietnamese, Cambodians, and Laotians facing Japanese exactions and resultant food shortages, the Vietminh counted for more than the French as spring turned to summer 1945.

Looking to the Future of the British Empire

By 1943 Britain had its own colonial insurgents to worry about from the Indian National Army to the Communist-influenced anti–Japanese resistance groups in Burma and Malaya. Nevertheless, growing confidence in eventual allied victory fed renewed bureaucratic interest in the mechanics of colonial administration and the empire's economic potential. The BBC mirrored the trend, increasing its empire-related output and encouraging wireless listeners to 'Brush Up your Empire'.[98] Politicians' involvement in post-war planning for empire was, by contrast, minimal. Knocking Italy out of the war, preparations for D-Day, and the uncomfortable fact of Japan's continued occupation of Southeast Asia confined colonial forward-thinking to the back-burner for Cabinet Ministers.[99] Not so for the large numbers of Colonial Office civil servants frustrated by the fact that the War had placed legal reforms, industrialization projects, and constitutional redesign in cold storage.[100] Closely attuned to the war's insatiable appetite for manpower, food, and raw materials, managing empire became more centralized and technocratic even so.[101]

Colonies' sterling balances (in other words, British war debts to colonial creditors such as India) were managed from London.[102] Government Marketing Boards brought unprecedented regulation to colonial economies in their quest to increase export production. Whitehall departments previously tangential to imperial policy—the Board of Trade and Ministry of Supply, for instance—were now at its heart.[103] Grandly-named 'Resident-Ministers' (Harold Macmillan among them) were appointed to help manage strategic priorities across vast regions—the Middle East, North, and West Africa. Scientific research was enlisted to help solve problems of development.[104] Even missionaries were depicted as adjuncts to government—educators and institution-builders rather than quixotic pioneers.[105] Despite this more complex bureaucracy, indeed, perhaps because of it, running the wartime empire was superficially depoliticized. Numerous confrontations of the immediate pre-war years, such as violent clashes between colonial business and organized labour in the British Caribbean or contested partition in Palestine, were treated as if in suspended animation.

This impression of stasis was profoundly misleading. Past imperial problems were, at best, deferred; at worst, they were complicated by unforeseen wartime pressures. Take British East Africa, where unprecedented British governmental interest in the region's agricultural output brought mixed consequences for local populations. In Kenya, African farmers had already been encouraged to produce more during the depression years. The war brought a host of new restrictions for Kenya's producers and consumers, even famine conditions for the poorest. At the same time, rising food costs nourished a burgeoning black market. For Africans living as squatters on settler farms in the Kenyan highlands—later, an epicentre of the Mau Mau rebellion—the war brought a reprieve from threatened eviction under the 1937 Resident Native Labour Ordinance. Wartime demand for farm labour and the food grown on squatters' smallholdings allowed them to consolidate their presence on the margins of settler farmland. Now a more permanent fixture, antagonism between the squatters and their settler employers emerged stronger after the war.[106]

In the Far East, from Malaya and Singapore to Shanghai, Hong Kong, and Burma, colonial politics were partly conditioned by seismic economic changes, partly by local responses to the Japanese occupier. Meanwhile, in London, members of the 'Malaya Planning Unit', what Tim Harper wryly describes as 'a kind of court in exile', took the war as an opportunity for a fundamental redefinition of the purpose and scope of colonial governance. Central to this was 'a general belief that the fall of Malaya, and reports of local "collaboration" with the Japanese, represented the failure of colonial government to secure the allegiance of the subject populations'.[107] The pre-war system of 'government by advice', it was suggested, was too narrowly focused on cultivating relations with Malay elites.[108] Malaya's Chinese and

Indian immigrant populations, many of whom laboured in mines, on rubber plantations, and in agriculture, lacked any representation or investment in British colonial rule. As Harper suggests, the wartime schemes for Malaya's post-war renovation signified 'an attempt to replace the confused loyalties of the pre-war period with a sense of allegiance to the colonial state'.[109] In March 1942, weeks after the fall of Singapore, the sociological organization Mass Observation, well known for its public opinion surveys, found echoes of this Whitehall reformism in a widespread 'guilt feeling about the way Empire has been acquired, and the way the colonies have been administered'. Few people levelled specific criticisms against particular policies, but many felt 'bad' about the old ways of British imperialism.[110]

Was it too late to make amends? In British India, British attempts to defuse anti-colonial sentiment by invoking wartime imperial unity were not very successful. The impetus for reform generated by Congress in the late 1930s was too powerful to ignore. Several Ministers in Churchill's coalition were keen to respond, dismissing their prime minister's unbending defence of the Raj as ethically indefensible.[111] One such was Stafford Cripps. Credited with helping to bring Soviet Russia into the war as Churchill's Ambassador to Moscow, Cripps joined the War Cabinet as Lord Privy Seal in early 1942. Once in government, he rode a surging wave of public support for greater concessions to India in recognition of the country's sacrifices in the fight against Japan. George Orwell got it right in describing the resultant 'Cripps Mission' to restart negotiations with Indian leaders as 'a bubble blown by popular discontent'.[112]

Cripps and his close-knit advisory team—dubbed 'the Crippery'—spent three energetic weeks roaming India in March and April 1942 trying to coax Congress and the All-India Muslim League into government as members of the Viceroy's Executive Council. The Cripps Mission stopped short of any formal offer of independence, postponing detailed consideration of British withdrawal until after the war. Gandhi's famous repudiation of Cripps' proposals as a 'post-dated cheque' from a failing bank was harsh even so. Through sheer persistence, Cripps almost secured an agreement despite the manifest reluctance of Gandhi, Churchill, and Lord Linlithgow to contemplate one. Defence cooperation was one stumbling block, the future status of India's Princely States another. As historian Nicholas Owen observes, 'Weakened by the feeble support of Labour for Congress and of Congress for the war, the Cripps Offer could never have taken the weight that each side wished to put on it. Although they did more, Churchill and

Linlithgow had merely to point this out.' Moreover, at the heart of that offer was the pledge that individual Indian provinces could opt out of an Indian Union if they disliked the constitution to be drawn up by a constituent assembly. Gandhi was horrified, considering this tantamount to inviting the Muslim League to press its March 1940 demand for an independent Pakistan.[113]

The Cripps Mission may have failed, but it was hugely significant, conceding the principle of Indian-run Cabinet government several years before the final talks on British withdrawal began.[114] The propensity to flight was clear, albeit temporarily thwarted. The negotiation process was further stalled by India's worsening political violence and appalling British mismanagement of the country's internal foodstuff market, which brought famine and massive loss of life to Bengal after 1943.[115] By the end of the war, up to three million Bengalis had died of malnourishment and related diseases, a direct result of the ruthless extraction of Indian resources to serve Britain's war effort.[116] Failure to guarantee enough food, perhaps the ultimate symbol of state failure in the Indian sub-continent, delegitimized British rule as surely as the collapse of social solidarity among Bengal's starving population redoubled Gandhi and other Congress leaders' determination to build greater national cohesion among India's poor.[117]

The Bengal famine stands as a dreadful reminder of the horrors that unremitting prioritization of an imperial mother-country's needs could cause.[118] Yet it was the technocratic, economic turn in wartime colonial administration that underpinned the re-conceptualization of relations between Britain and its colonies immediately after the war.[119] After years spent devising elaborate schemes for the empire's post-war constitutional and social renovation, financial imperatives dominated imperial policy-making by 1945. Consistent with Labour's thumping electoral victory in the July 1945 general election, the imperialist luminaries, many of aristocratic descent, who once set the agenda for parliamentary, City, and press discussion about Britain's imperial future, were eclipsed by a younger generation of administrators. Less colourful, if better qualified, what excited them were infrastructure projects and heightened agricultural productivity, not appeals to Britain's imperial destiny. Lord Hailey's espousal of pragmatic colonial development was back in vogue.[120] This shift in British imperial governance mirrored the new age of austerity. Amidst harsh post-war rationing, statistics on dollar purchases of Malayan rubber and Colonial Office estimates of the potential for expanded peanut production in Tanganyika figured large in Cabinet discussion.[121] John Maynard Keynes captured the reason for this triumph of the accountants over the romantics: 'We cannot police half the world at our own expense when we have already gone in pawn to the other half.'[122] Predominant among that other half was the United States. Its financial leverage over Britain would be exerted to devastating effect in the Suez crisis of 1956. Yet, in the decades either side of that pivotal imperial collapse, the US imposed remarkably little pressure on the British, preferring the strategic certainties of colonial anti-Communism to the political uncertainties of a post-colonial world.[123]

Nowhere was Washington's more benevolent view of European imperial restoration more apparent than in Southeast Asia. British strategic planners, who had been finalizing plans laid in September 1944 to 'liberate' Singapore and Malaya, were overtaken by Japan's surrender after the atomic bombings of August 1945. With US approval, a decorous British amphibious assault went ahead in Malaya on 12 September, its purpose symbolic rather than military. An intelligence officer remembered their bizarre quality: 'A full-dress landing was made through the surf', and he spoke feelingly of the experience 'of wading ashore with rifle in hand before an admiring audience of Malays dressed in their holiday best and applauding eagerly.'[124] One reason for this demonstration of British military prowess was to conceal the fact that the Communist guerrillas of the Malayan Peoples Anti-Japanese Army (MPAJA) had actually fought the Japanese during the war's closing stages. Whether in British Malaya, French Indochina, or Dutch Indonesia, the spectre of Communists seizing control before colonial administration could be restored was too much for President Truman's new administration to swallow. Superficially at least, Malaya posed fewest problems. Speedy establishment of a transitional British Military Administration enabled Admiral Mountbatten's South East Asia Command to marginalize the MPAJA. Disbarred from mainstream colonial politics, the Malayan Communist Party instead consolidated its grip over two discrete constituencies: Malaya's industrial trade unions and its rural Chinese workforce; their appeals to both enhanced by severe post-war rice shortages.[125] This was to have devastating consequences. In the short-term, though, Indochina's social breakdown loomed larger. In southern Vietnam British imperial forces took over as transitional occupiers pending the arrival of a French 'expeditionary force' in Saigon in September 1945. But the Vietminh was not about to be cast aside.

Fighting for a New French Empire?

With an empire wracked by internal division and violence, the ebullience of French imperialism in 1945 seems puzzling.[126] Whereas, over the ensuing decades, Britain would adjust, albeit painfully, to America's new global dominance, successive French governments reacted in contrary fashion, equating retention of empire with resurgent international power. It was, after all, the colonies that made Free France credible, not just as a political force but as a territorial entity. Even though, in terms of volume and value, French colonial trade improved sharply over the course of 1944, in purely monetary terms France's empire was not generating foreign exchange revenues comparable to the sums derived from British territories.[127] So it was perhaps unsurprising that de Gaulle's senior advisers viewed imperial affairs in instrumental terms. In the months preceding the D-Day landings, this boiled down to a simple calculation: colonial reforms should enhance French power, not diminish it.[128]

In January 1944 the Governors of the Free French Empire assembled in Brazzaville, the sleepy Congolese capital of French Equatorial Africa, to consider the empire's post-war consolidation. The tenor of their discussions was deeply conservative. North Africa and Indochina—the regions where wartime disruption was greatest—were scratched from the conference agenda.[129] And plans for administrative restructuring, economic diversification, and greater electoral representation in territories south of the Sahara were profoundly cautious. They were framed, not in terms of preparation for independence, but the acquisition of a more francophone *personnalité politique* in individual colonies.[130] Put differently, wider citizenship rights, political responsibilities, and improved living standards, however enacted once the war was over, were intended to make colonial peoples more French, not less.

The 'colonial myth' that keeping empire intact was somehow pivotal to French grandeur was not confined to the Gaullist right, despite its self-proclaimed role as arch defender of France's historical greatness. The imperialist reflex was prevalent throughout the political community in liberated France. Even the Communist leadership, rhetorically anti-colonial to be sure, was not immune. Why? The unique circumstances of France's wartime defeat, liberation, and reconstruction offer some explanation. France's acute weakness compared with its major allies in 1945 nurtured the presumption that empire was fundamental to French recovery.[131] This view spanned the restyled French party-political spectrum. It was readily accepted by former resisters, erstwhile Vichyites and, it appears, newly-enfranchised women voters. The acrimonious circumstances of France's eventual pull-out from Syria and Lebanon in 1944–6 helped turn presumption into dogma by the time the Indochina War broke out in December 1946.

Having negotiated (but not implemented) treaties of independence with the two Levant states in 1936, French governments exploited communal unrest and the outbreak of war in Europe to postpone consideration of a transfer of power. This pattern of obfuscation, justified by reference to internal disorder and France's primordial strategic requirements, continued during the war years, unaffected by the sequence of Vichy and Free French rule. France's imperial authority drained away regardless. In November 1943 Lebanese and Syrian parliamentarians took decisive steps towards unilateral declarations of independence that made French rule untenable. In Beirut and Damascus populations enthused by long-delayed fulfilment of their claims to sovereignty understandably refused to knuckle under when the French authorities tried to re-impose their mastery. Local opposition to it proved unrelenting. And British determination to rebuild its Arab connections precluded support for a hated French administration.[132] The stern resistance of Syria's pro-Vichy garrison to a British-led imperial invasion force in June–July 1941 nourished British contempt for French sensibilities. So incensed were the Vichy authorities of the time that they lobbied Hitler's government to authorize *Luftwaffe* raids against British Palestine's oil installations and urban centres.[133]

Beneficiaries of Syria's regime change over the summer of 1941, the Free French were no less suspicious of ulterior British motives. By 1944 the French Levant was critical of emerging British plans to redraw the boundaries of a 'Greater Syria' as part of a definitive Palestine partition.[134] De Gaulle raged against this scheming. It was, he said, tantamount to covert imperial warfare against an ally.[135] From its inception in July 1944 de Gaulle's provisional government railed against what were regarded as British diktats imposing withdrawal. Far from admitting the inevitability of a pull-out, throughout 1945 the Paris authorities interpreted British pressure for evacuation as a conspiracy to buy Arab friendship at French expense.[136] Meanwhile, in the fast-developing secret intelligence war between the two imperial powers, French security services began supplying arms and information to the Zionist terrorist groups *Irgun Tzva'i Le'umi* (National Military Organization) and the Stern Gang.[137]

Syria provoked the severest breakdown in Anglo-French imperial relations of the decolonization era. Last-ditch French efforts to stave off Syrian and Lebanese independence were matched by countervailing British pressure to accelerate the process (an ironic counter-point to subsequent British anger over US actions over Palestine). Faced with uncompromising nationalist opposition and Britain's decisive military presence, French evacuation was unavoidable. That it occurred only after bloodshed and amidst bitter acrimony between France and the nationalist governments in Damascus and Beirut was not. The venomous divisions between French and British authorities in the Middle East were partly to blame. So, too, was the reconstructed imperialism of the early Fourth Republic, which fed the mistaken presumption that France might yet salvage its position. This hard-line stance was doubly ironic in Syria, where the French had twice abandoned territory at the Mandate's northern margins in order to placate Kemalist Turkey—first in Cilicia in 1921 and, second, in the sanjak of Alexandretta in 1938. Such pragmatism—and readiness to choose flight over fight—was forgotten amidst the fury of France's final withdrawal.[138]

For all sides involved, the material aspects to the Levant dispute—control over local security forces, provision for base rights, and the recognition of French educational privileges—held particular symbolic value. To the Syrian and Lebanese authorities the right to raise sovereign security forces was the yardstick of true independence.[139] For French negotiators, continued control over a handful of schools and military bases retained a cultural significance disproportionate to their material value. Meanwhile, for the British government, and Ernest Bevin's Foreign Office above all, the Levant settlement was subsumed within the central preoccupation of their Middle East policy—to conserve Britain's regional influence after the end of the Palestine Mandate.[140]

Neither France nor Britain emerged with much credit from this contest. The unpopularity of the local French administration, the *délégation générale*, made a mockery of the high price placed by French negotiators on their cultural legacy in the Levant states, something that American, Arab League, and United Nations observers found incomprehensible. But it was the violence that attended the Syrian endgame that utterly discredited French imperialism in the Middle East. Over two days on 29–30 May 1945 French artillery pounded the Damascus Parliament building and its environs. The bombardment marked the culmination of three weeks of smaller-scale clashes in the capital as French army reinforcements battled with Syrian security forces for control of the streets. The French commander General Fernand Oliva-Roget lost patience with this skirmishing and let loose his forces to teach the Syrians 'a good lesson'.[141] Hundreds died. North and West African colonial troops were quickly put to work burying Syrian gendarmes and other protestors in mass graves, making it impossible to calculate the numbers killed.[142] This bloody show of imperial defiance tipped the balance. Britain's Middle East Army Command, technically the ultimate military authority in the region, assumed full control in Syria, imposing martial law and confining the French garrison to its barracks. Negotiations over the terms of the French pull-out resumed, but their Mandate was already dead.[143]

The French coalition government, smarting from this humiliation, became doubly resolved to hang on elsewhere. As we shall see, the Syrian experience compounded French intransigence in talks with Ho Chi Minh's Vietnamese Republic in early 1946. Covert French support for Zionist terrorism in Palestine was stepped up, as much a means of exacting revenge against British betrayal as a shrewd strategic gamble on the future power of Israel.[144] The British, preoccupied by the problems of Palestine partition, a Hashemite Greater Syria, and the renegotiation of Anglo-Arab treaties, had exploited the opportunity to capitalize upon French weakness to curry Arab favour. Viewed from this perspective, withdrawal from the Levant revealed as much about the complexities of Britain's effort to safeguard its Middle Eastern power as it did about France's reluctance to decolonize.[145]

Conclusion

Britain's efforts to spread limited military resources widely enough to safeguard its empire against all potential threats were doomed once Japan resolved on its own bid for imperial supremacy in eastern Asia. What John Darwin has called Britain's 'strategy of shuffle' was quickly revealed for what it was: a sleight of hand with only half the cards necessary for success.[146] Although phrasing things rather differently, Keith Jeffery, another shrewd analyst of Britain's wartime imperial problems, reaches a similar conclusion: 'Paradoxically, the ultimate cost of defending the British Empire during the Second World War was the Empire itself.'[147] Both writers agree that this, the biggest fight undertaken by Britain in defence of its empire, undermined the entire construct. The door was thereby opened to new strategies of accommodation with those demanding colonial change after the war. Britain's post-war turn towards flight, soon to reach fulfilment in South Asia, was rendered possible, imperative even, by the preceding commitment to keep the empire intact under the stresses of World War. This connection between victory and empire dissolution was, at once, paradoxical and remarkably simple. The imperial cost of Britain's triumph of arms was decolonization.

What about France? The country moved, in rapid succession from a nation defeated and occupied to one liberated and resurgent. A longer wartime constant was the state of undeclared civil war in its colonies. From June 1940 until Japan's final overthrow of the Vichyite regime in Hanoi on 9 March 1945, the French empire was torn apart by an internecine war between the civil–military elites who ran it. Its endless factionalism antagonized the local elites essential to empire governance, presenting a golden opportunity for radical anti-colonial groups like Algeria's PPA and the Vietminh resistance. The result was a crisis of colonial legitimacy that the French Empire never quite shook off. The Vichy–Free French antagonism was also sharpened by the weaknesses of each protagonist. Leaders on both sides of this Franco-French divide were acutely conscious of their relative powerlessness next to stronger European, American, or Asian clients. It was these outsiders—British, American, German, or Japanese, who, time and again, demonstrated that they controlled the wartime disposition of French colonial territory.

Nazi Germany, perhaps unrealistically, treated French North Africa as a strategic pawn until America took over following the Torch landings of November 1942. And where Gaullist administrations refused to bend to American wishes, as in Pacific New Caledonia or the tiny islands of St Pierre and Miquelon off the Newfoundland coast, the political consequences of deeper US antagonism were greater than the *amour-propre* satisfied by petty displays of French independence. Britain, meanwhile, pulled the key imperial levers in Syria and Lebanon after July 1941. British and Dominion forces also precipitated changes of administration, although not of underlying colonial conditions, in French Somaliland and Madagascar in 1942. Ultimately, though, it was Japan that did most to knock over France's house of colonial cards. Its occupation of Indochina, partial at first, total and brutal at last, catalysed the first of France's major fights against decolonization—an eight-year war against the Vietminh that reverberated throughout Southeast Asia and the colonial world.[148]

3

Brave New World?
Rebuilding Empire after the
Second World War

On a June evening in 1947 Seretse Khama, a young trainee barrister at
London's Inner Temple, attended an evening 'social' for colonial students at Nutford House, a London University hall of residence. There he met
Ruth Williams, clerk in a London underwriters' firm. The two got on famously
and began dating. They married at Kensington Register Office fifteen months
later on 29 September 1948. Inter-racial relationships, and particularly one
involving a white British woman, were unusual at the time, although less
scarce than they had been before the arrival of African-American GIs in wartime Britain. Seretse, though, was African royalty, heir to the Ngwato kingdom in the Bechuanaland Protectorate (now Botswana).[1] His Christian
Mission education, and the strong ties between the Congregationalist London
Missionary Society (LMS) and Ngwato's people, the Bangwato, added a strong
religious dimension to what would soon develop into the most notorious
case of British official racism in the immediate post-war years.

The marriage of an African prince to an English commoner was controversial. It was some time before the Bangwato's foremost political council,
the *kgotla*, endorsed the union and, with it, Seretse's succession. The couple
had become popular, especially among Bangwato women. LMS leaders in
London and Bechuanaland also accepted the arrangement—reluctantly.
Privately they deplored the match, alarmed by the hostility it provoked
locally among the Ngwato elite and, more broadly, within British southern
Africa.

The outcry against Ruth Williams' choice of partner was loudest among
Southern Rhodesia's white settlers and Raymond Malan's recently-installed

apartheid regime in South Africa. The governments in Salisbury and Pretoria, the empire's most implacable white troublemakers, were fierce opponents of partnerships that crossed the colour line. Indeed, South Africa was stiffening its legal penalties against 'mixed marriages' and inter-racial sex. In their eyes Seretse was unfit to rule. Sadly, this reaction was only to be expected. Sadder still was that the Commonwealth Relations Office under Labour Minister Patrick Gordon Walker gave way. On 6 March 1950 Gordon Walker told the House of Commons that Seretse would be banished from the Bangwato reserve. The decision was more geo-politically than racially motivated, although in its attempt to keep South Africa sweet—and within the Commonwealth—the two motivations were obviously interlinked.[2] The resultant outcry in Britain also entwined two hitherto discrete strands of anti-colonial opinion—on the one hand, radical and liberal-minded Church leaders such as Michael Scott and Father Trevor Huddlestone; on the other hand, the anti-imperialist left, personified by Fenner Brockway and Barbara Castle. Official reaffirmation of Seretse's banishment by Winston Churchill's Conservative government in May 1952 catalysed the formation of influential lobby groups, including the Council for the Defence of Seretse Khama and the more wide-ranging Africa Bureau. Each developed links to the radical left.[3] Refracted through the dignified stoicism of Seretse and his wife (by now a young mother), the controversy exposed the hypocrisy of official pronouncements about post-war inter-racial partnership between Britain and its colonial dependencies. The Labour government's decision to mollify South Africa and Southern Rhodesian whites while ignoring the manifest injustice involved deserves criticism.[4] But it is most relevant to us here because it illustrates the seamier side of a flight strategy: of the human costs of the triumph of pragmatism over principle. The British Empire's brave new world of post-war modernity and inter-ethnic harmony was a pipe-dream.

We saw in Chapter 1 how the disappointment felt by colonial leaders whose demands for additional rights went unanswered after the First World War spurred the growth of anti-colonial protest. British and French imperial rule survived nonetheless.[5] The Second World War, by contrast, undermined the territorial, economic, and intellectual certainties of European imperialism itself.[6] The United Nations Charter of 1946 fell short of demanding an end to colonial rule. Indeed, its key authors showed little enthusiasm for explicit reference to any presumptive right to 'self-determination'.[7] The Charter did, however, commit its signatories to develop 'self-government', a

term for which French colonial officials developed an acute loathing.[8] And
it soon became apparent, not just that colonial nationalist leaders expected
the Allies to uphold their wartime pledges of support for self-determination
but that countless people around the world did too. Galvanized by transnational networks of shared interest that, for instance, linked African Americans seeking an end to discrimination at home with Africans and Indians
who wanted freedom from colonialism, the perceived right for people of
shared ethnicity to govern themselves became more closely bound up with
demands for an end to racial discrimination.[9]

With this in mind, perhaps the most surprising facet of the imperial policies emanating from London and Paris in 1945 was the ready assumption
that colonial ties undone by wartime occupations, uprisings, or deprivation
could be renewed. The human and material costs of maintaining empire fell
on two European countries devastated by war: the one, Britain, bankrupted
by it; the other, France, torn apart and traumatized by its 'dark years' of collaboration.[10] Domestic crises, whether economic, political, or cultural, were
matched by their colonial equivalents. Imperial promises of new constitutional arrangements, development funding, inclusive governance, and new
eras of partnership were remarkably similar, whether articulated in English
or French. And they hit the same rocks when colonial voices turned this
rhetoric of reform against colonial administrations, demanding that governments live up to pledges they were reluctant to keep. Colonial disturbances
of one kind or another became a constant feature in the post-war landscape,
sometimes confined to the shadows of metropolitan politics, but occasionally jostling domestic or European issues out of the frame.

For the French Empire the post-war decade was one of exceptional violence, brutality, and dissent even by the standards of European colonialism.
It was bookended by two horrors. First was the famine that ravaged Northern Vietnam in the winter of 1944–5, leaving hundreds of thousands dead.
A lethal combination of ruthless Japanese requisitioning and French
maladministration, in the worst-affected regions of Tonkin and northern
Annam at least ten per cent of the population died of starvation.[11] Last
was the outbreak of rebellion in Algeria on 1 November 1954, the beginning of an eight-year 'dirty war'. Events such as these make it difficult to
view the ten years after the Liberation as anything other than a history of
organized violence, whether that violence stemmed from ruthless economic extraction or military intervention. Yet was French colonialism so
exceptional? For famine in Vietnam, read British Bengal in 1944; for

repression in Algeria, read Dutch 'police action' in Java in 1948 or British suppression of Mau Mau from 1952. Another discomfiting truth is that the archival record, French and colonial, speaks only fitfully, and often dismissively, of violence. French concerns lay elsewhere. More ambitious plans for the redesign of France's overseas Empire were tabled in the years 1944 to 1954 than throughout the preceding century. The UN Charter's challenge 'to develop self-government' would be read, not as a injunction to lay the groundwork for colonial independence, but as a call to transmit France's models of administration, citizenship, and ever closer cultural union to its overseas dependencies.[12] If it required force to do so, so be it. This juxtaposition between domestic and imperial reconstruction on the one hand and a colonial fight strategy on the other is the central tension in the history of the Fourth Republic. To focus upon it is also to move away from the preoccupation with Cold War, with the first steps towards European integration, and with the French culture wars over 'Coca-Colonization' and dependence on US dollar assistance that still dominate histories of la Quatrième.[13]

Superficially at least, the French and British political figures so determined to revitalize their Empires immediately after the Second World War made unlikely imperialists. In Britain, as in France, most were ideologically left-of-centre. Several leading French Socialists, like the fiery Corsican Paul Giacobbi, Minister of Colonies in the critical 1944–5 transition, had been imprisoned for resistance activities. Giacobbi's Labour Party counterpart, Arthur Creech-Jones, also had a singular prison record, having been jailed in September 1916 for conscientious objection.[14] Premiers Clement Attlee and Léon Blum, both exceptional intellects, cultivated an image of pragmatism, the product of long political careers. Still others, like Adrien Tixier in France or Ernest Bevin in Britain, were no-nonsense trade unionists, proud of their working-class origins. Other discrete groups—Jean Monnet's dirigiste planners and Stafford Cripps' Treasury team—were technocratic modernizers. Their fondness for scrutinizing output statistics and economic forecasts also convinced them that colonial assets were more vital than ever. For them, left-wing sympathies often translated into a commitment to mobilize state resources to develop colonial economies, improve welfare provision, and raise living standards.[15]

In Britain and France marriage and birth-rates increased sharply after 1945 and post-war social policies venerated the 'normal' nuclear family as an ideal state of being.[16] Socialistic reformism did not, though, necessitate the recognition that colonial subjects should be treated as politically mature like

the idealized British families at home. Labour Chancellor of the Exchequer
Hugh Dalton's diary records his hostile reaction to a February 1950 suggestion that he consider the Gold Coast governorship: 'I had a horrid vision of
pullulating, poverty-stricken, diseased nigger communities, for whom one
can do nothing in the short run, and now, the more one tries to help them,
are querulous and ungrateful.' Dalton could be exceptionally blunt but this
combination of racial arrogance and frustrated reformism was not untypical.[17] In British Africa at least, Labour Ministers and colonial officials talked
of self-government but locked up those who asked for it too soon. Left-
wing politicians in liberated France, their reputations built on careers in the
resistance, ordered mass arrests and the internment of colonial opponents in
squalid re-education camps.

Even so, unlike their forebears in 1919, these were not politicians deaf to
colonial complaint. For the 1945 generation, the impetus was not to ignore
the political fissures opened by the War but to remodel imperial structures
more fundamentally. Huge wartime debts and worsening East–West tensions transformed the economic and strategic context in which imperial
rebuilding was supposed to occur, making it easier for British and French
officials to spurn 'flight', or negotiated reform, because of the overweening
requirements of austerity and Cold War. Attlee's government, for instance,
ring-fenced colonial economic assets to assist the recovery of sterling and
redeployed British national servicemen to replace the vast manpower reserve
lost after Indian independence.[18]

This observation brings us to another of the War's most critical effects:
the changing connection between money and empire. Sterling's precarious
position as both a reserve and a transactions currency in an emergent global
trading system dominated by US dollars bore heavily on official thinking
about fight or flight. India was Britain's largest colonial creditor. With over
1.3 billion of sterling assets in July 1946, it was pivotal to British liquidity.
Other colonies cumulatively held another 550 million, Egypt and Sudan a
further 400 million, and the Australasian Dominions some 190 million. Each
could destabilize Britain's monetary system by demanding their money
back. There was little prospect of any write-off of what were, in effect, British war debts to its overseas dependencies, despite occasional Treasury musings about how wonderful this might be. It took hard negotiation during
1946 and 1947 with prominent empire creditors, notably India and Australia,
to produce the interim agreements that kept the sterling balances problem
under control.[19] Self-interest trumped fellow feeling here. It made no sense

for Commonwealth governments or soon-to-be-independent India to undermine sterling's value in international markets. Indeed, the former Dominions, their trade and financial interests bound up with the City of London, became strong supporters of the sterling area even though Canada, the most economically powerful, remained outside it.[20]

As for the Cold War, it was the imperial powers' misfortune to set about post-war imperial reconstruction along the conflict's fault-lines in South-east Asia, the Middle East, and Africa. John Darwin captures the resultant fragility: 'A forward move by a rival great power (hostile or friendly), a show of resistance by local nationalist leaders, an open quarrel with an indispensable ally, a spasm of weakness in an overstrained economy: each was enough to produce symptoms of crisis.'[21] Crisis after crisis there would be, tumbling over one another within the British and French empires over the next quarter-century. As in 1919, so after 1945, the United States was critical. It weakened the grip of colonial powers: the Dutch in Indonesia; the British in Palestine; initially at least, the French in Indochina. At the same time Washington disappointed those colonial subjects who anticipated a brave new world of democratic freedom.[22] Just as 1919 witnessed a fleeting Wilsonian moment, so the years 1944 to 1947 might be identified as a second 'moment' in which America might have played its diplomatic and strategic cards in the anti-colonialists' favour.[23]

Events turned out otherwise. Ailing President Roosevelt's grand ideas for a system of international 'trusteeship' in which formerly colonial territories would be guided to independence under UN supervision were swiftly curtailed.[24] Indeed, post-war US administrations, supposedly anti-colonial by emotional reflex, did more to prop up colonial systems than to destroy them.[25] In the hands of Harry Truman's White House team, talk of resurrecting 'trusteeship' became a diplomatic lever to extract strategic advantage and commercial concessions from reluctant European governments.[26] American politicians, diplomats, and business figures still invoked an anti-colonialist vocabulary of rights and nation-building in their dealings with subject peoples to differentiate themselves from Europe's inveterate imperialists. But US race relations were hardly exemplary. Southern segregation marked the extreme expression of widespread racial discrimination at home. Aspects of so-called 'Jim Crow colonialism' also persisted in America's dealings with Caribbean and Latin American neighbours.[27] Meanwhile, American strategic influence, military capacity, and economic power entrenched new forms of dependency in the colonial world, often in *de facto* collaboration with the European imperial states being vilified as political dinosaurs.[28]

Once overwhelmingly explained in terms of Cold War zero-sum thinking—the imperatives of western strategic interest trumping the empty rhetoric of US anti-colonialism—historians have, more recently, been drawn to other explanations for this shift in American approach. The most subtle posit that the United States worked with its British and French partners to ease their withdrawal from empire, clearing a path for US dominance while, for the most part, avoiding open confrontation. President Truman's 'layered conception of sovereignty' cast self-determination, not as a basic right, but as an ideal condition contingent on the abilities and willingness of the people involved to adhere to western standards and political loyalties.[29] Cruder arguments, more prevalent since America's Middle Eastern wars of the recent past, indict American political leaders for conspiring to replace one empire with another.[30] Common to these differing interpretations is the recognition of what Michael Hunt terms the 'promise–performance gap'.[31] Having pledged to transform power relations in the colonial world at the end of the Second World War, the United States first bolstered European colonial rule in some quarters, and then, from Vietnam through to Iraq and Afghanistan, fought its own quasi-imperial wars in others.

Back in 1945 it was in the Far East that the European imperialists were feeblest and American military might most decisive. In their Southeast Asian colonies, Britain, like France, had suffered crushing defeat at the hands of the Japanese. The endurance of General Slim's 'forgotten army' in the Burma campaign notwithstanding, Britain's humiliation was compounded by dependence on the United States to bring Tokyo to surrender. India was increasingly ungovernable; Bengal devastated by the famine whose estimated three million victims bore stark witness to the bankruptcy of imperial rule.[32]

In Malaya, too, the British Military Administration that assumed power in autumn 1945 confronted a profound social crisis, the most visible signs of which were food shortages, malnutrition, and epidemics. Regional outbreaks of typhoid, cholera, and smallpox joined malaria as major killers. Displaced persons and refugees, many of them migrant workers misleadingly characterized as vagrants, flooded into Singapore and other urban centres. Health scares, rising criminality, workplace disorders, and the radicalization of Malaya's trade unions formed the backdrop to the restoration of civil administration in 1945–6.[33] These were hardly propitious circumstances in which to pursue the ill-fated Malayan Union, a scheme launched in April 1946 in a bid to couple the restoration of British civil government with a more equitable redistribution of power between Malaya's three principal ethnic groups— Malays, Chinese, and Indians. Ambitious but poorly sold, the Malayan Union was deeply unpopular among the dominant Malay community. Its abandonment in January 1948 was also hastened by the growing militancy of the Malayan Communist Party, which drew most of its support from the ethnic Chinese community. Post-war dislocation, the ill-advised Malayan Union, new strains of ethnic nationalism, and the threat of leftist subversion: Malaya was in ferment. Whitehall plans for inter-communal cooperation and eventual self-government, for flight on British terms, unravelled.[34]

Few drew parallels with Indochina's situation at the time. But there, too, the Second World War's impact was visible in internal rebellion, heightened nationalist legitimacy and a northern famine that claimed hundreds of thousands of lives. Elsewhere, the contrast in British and French fortunes was sharper. The fall of France in June 1940 did not open the floodgates to nationalist overthrows of colonial government in North and West Africa, Madagascar or the Caribbean. Rather, as we saw in the preceding chapter, defeat at home gave rise to an undeclared Franco-French imperial civil war as Vichy and Free French political elites vied for local control. British Africa seemed tranquil by comparison. Fratricidal violence and competition for influence in the French colonies mirrored the wartime struggle for power in mainland France. This was as much a contest to determine the long-term direction of France's political destiny—as ultra-conservative and autocratic or as republican democracy restored—as it was about the immediate issue of opposition or accommodation to defeat and occupation.

The outcome, of course, was the triumph of those forces representing the internal resistance, broadly speaking, the parties of the left, plus a Christian Democrat centre-right, and those representing the external, overseas-based resistance, in other words, pro-de Gaulle Free France: politically right-wing but also republican in temperament.[35] French liberation did not heal the wartime divides, but it did change the terms of the arguments involved. Enfranchised at last, women gained a stronger voice in national affairs. With the wartime past still too raw to confront, there was little appetite for a thorough autopsy on the Vichy period. The popular *épuration,* or purge, of alleged collaborators, while in many respects arbitrary, strongly biased against women, and fundamentally unjust, was, by wider continental standards, relatively mild and mercifully short-lived.[36] With peace restored, social questions—shortages, rationing, and the black market; family policy, job prospects, and 'getting back to normal'—predominated over broader political concerns.[37] That being said, a 'good' war record was vital for the aspiring post-war French politician.

Party political conflict in the Fourth Republic was embittered by a simple underlying problem. Four parties, each of them closely tied to the internal resistance—the Socialists, the Christian Democrat MRP, the social democratic UDSR, and the Communist PCF—supported the new Republic's constitutional settlement.[38] Some of the key politicians involved were comparatively new faces—the erstwhile resister Guy Mollet, who became Socialist Party Secretary-General in 1946; the heavy-drinking history teacher Georges Bidault, a former prisoner of war whose role as an MRP founder was prefigured by his leadership of a unified National Resistance Council. Others were brasher: the former Dachau inmate and Christian Democrat-turned-Gaullist cheerleader Edmond Michelet; the fearsome Charles Tillon, a Communist naval mutineer in 1919, International Brigader in civil war Spain, and leader of the *Francs-Tireurs et Partisans* resistance group, who made an unlikely Armaments Minister in November 1945.

Most of this younger generation—all born in the ten years after 1895—cut their teeth as decision-makers within resistance networks. Others returned to politics after their pre-war careers were interrupted by war, Vichy, and, in several cases, imprisonment. The veteran Socialists Léon Blum, Vincent Auriol, Marius Moutet, and Félix Gouin fell into this category. So, too, did the Christian Democrat and European Community founder Robert Schuman, and the Radical Party's rural affairs specialist Henri Queuille, surely the ultimate '*ministrable*' who had already served in nineteen cabinets between 1920 and 1940. For different reasons, all of these senior figures favoured a basic constitutional design in which coalition governments were accountable to parliament, a viewpoint that brought them into conflict with de Gaulle's followers. The Gaullist movement saw only a repetition of the ministerial merry-go-round politics of the old Third Republic in this new arrangement. Perhaps unsurprisingly, Gaullists favoured a strong executive presidency, a job description tailor-made for their beloved General.[39] The party that represented de Gaulle—the RPF, established in 1946–7—soon transferred its distaste for the post-war constitutional settlement into outright opposition to 'the system' of the Fourth Republic itself.[40] Meanwhile, much of the established, mainstream French right, tainted by accusations of collaboration or, at minimum, Vichy sympathies, took time to recover reputation and influence. As a result, the Fourth Republic suffered from its association with a narrowly sectarian vision of how post-war French democracy should work.[41]

Fundamental differences among politicians and the wider public about the shape of democracy in post-war France inevitably reverberated through French foreign and colonial affairs. But the various alignments involved were not always predictable. It was, for instance, de Gaulle as premier who signed up to a post-war alliance with the USSR. A treaty of mutual assistance with Soviet Russia against German attack, something that made sense when unsuccessfully sought in 1939, was less of a strategic prize when it was finally concluded in December 1944. Gaullist enthusiasm for the Soviet connection soon cooled, leaving the French Communists as the alliance's only unequivocal supporters as Cold War tensions mounted. The more that de Gaulle's RPF moved rightwards on imperial and foreign policy questions, the more it stood to benefit from the loss of electoral support for the older right-wing parties discredited by actual or presumed Vichy connections.

Wary of the RPF's ability to secure right-wing ground, France's governing coalitions could be remarkably imperialistic when circumstances demanded. Even so, a shared loathing for the Gaullist alternative was not enough to prevent the fragile unity between Socialists, Christian Democrats, and Communists from cracking. The Communist Party increasingly laid exclusive claim to the resistance heritage, a rhetorical strategy that concealed the ambivalence within Maurice Thorez's Party executive about the Cold War's implications for French international alignments and colonial connections. The Socialists, anxious about the Communists' surging popularity, were in the process of reinvention with a changing of the generational guard at national and local leadership level. And the Christian Democrats of the MRP, despite being welfare reformers at home and prescient advocates of Franco-German reconciliation, were more hawkish than their left-wing coalition partners about empire questions.

Women's suffrage also tended to drive the governing parties apart. The Socialists, like their fellow anti-clericals in the reconstituted Radical Party, were fearful that newly-enfranchised women voters would either follow the advice of their priest or the call of their heart, meaning, in practice, that most would vote either for the Catholic right or the heroic figure of de Gaulle. The abiding sexism among the main anti-clerical parties had been a massive obstacle to universal suffrage in pre-war France.[42] And its presumptions were belied in the October 1945 French general election when the majority of women voters opted in fairly equal measure for the Communists and the MRP. But the crude Machiavellianism of the supposedly egalitarian left pointed to the endless calculations of electoral advantage that dogged coalition politics during the Fourth Republic's twelve-year history between October 1946 and May 1958.

The colonial implications of this labyrinthine inter-party competition are well illustrated by certain political careers. As leader of the UDSR, René Pleven tried to navigate a path between de Gaulle's RPF, the MRP, and the Socialists within a new coalition configuration, known by the short-hand appellation the 'Third Force', between late 1947 and 1951. It was a difficult task. Clearly left-of-centre, the UDSR nonetheless defined itself by what it opposed: first the Communists' domination of the internal French resistance in 1945, then Gaullist opposition to the Fourth Republic 'system' after 1946.[43] These were hardly messages likely to electrify voters. The UDSR's two leading figures, Pleven and François Mitterrand each made a name for themselves in colonial affairs even so. Mitterrand's role as Interior Minister in the opening phase of the Algerian War is described in Chapter 10. But it was Pleven who rose first. A Free French resister 'from the first hour', he joined two military men, Claude Hettier de Boilambert and Pierre Leclerc, aboard a four-engined seaplane, *The Clyde*, which flew shakily out of Poole harbour on 6 August 1940. After crash-landing in Lisbon, the plane limped on to Bathurst, British Gambia, thence to Freetown in Sierra Leone, and finally to Lagos, Nigeria. It was there, in the company of Governor Sir Bernard Bourdillon that the French trio organized a Free French takeover of French Equatorial Africa. Its success assured Pleven's political rise, first as secretary-general in the federation's government, then as Commissioner for Colonies in the Free French Committee of National Liberation in Algiers.[44] Born in Rennes and a former US telephone company executive, Pleven had few empire connections before 1940. But his wartime career was overwhelmingly colonial, a fund of experience he drew upon in ministerial and prime-ministerial posts well into the 1950s.[45]

Already complicated enough, the Fourth Republic's politics became increasingly acrimonious from 1948. The two most dynamic political movements in France—the Communist PCF and the Gaullist RPF—attacked the coalition centrism and perennial deal-making that characterized Third Force supremacy. The people's will, they insisted, was being ignored by a political elite obsessed with keeping office. Even with experienced coalition builders like Henri Queuille, Robert Schuman, and Pleven himself at the helm of government, Third Force administrations could be fractious. Radical Party ministers argued with the Christian Democrats of the MRP. Independents who provided vital backbench support demanded local rewards, introducing pork-barrel concerns to coalition politics.[46]

French political in-fighting also irritated Attlee's ministers who longed for greater political stability across the Channel.[47] For all that, seen from London's perspective, the singular virtue of Third Force ministers next to their predecessors in the left-of-centre tripartite governments of Socialists, Communists, and the Christian Democrat MRP was that they divided over social and economic questions, not over foreign or colonial policy.[48] But the threat of outright political paralysis was never far away. On 2 November 1948 an editorial in *The Observer* suggested that France was 'not an ally on whom we could rely'. Although French industrial unrest had receded, neither the Communists nor the Gaullists showed any sign of making peace with the new regime.[49] The Stalinists of the PCF decried France's 'Coca Cola-nization' by American consumerism. They depicted US loan assistance through the Marshall Plan of 1948–52 as evidence of Washington's (and Wall Street's) economic imperialism.[50] For the RPF, the fundamental problem was simpler. The post-war Republic lacked strong, purposeful government because it lacked a unifying, presidential figure. And that figure should, of course, be de Gaulle. The fact that the General had voluntarily, and rather petulantly, walked out of government in January 1946 was conveniently forgotten.

These observations about France's post-war political system may be summarized with two comments. One is that the acrimony, instability, and factionalism in parliamentary politics in the years 1946 to 1958 stemmed from a lack of consensus about how France should be governed and on whose behalf.[51] The other is that the wonder of the Fourth Republic was not that it collapsed, but that it survived for so long. Indeed, in some areas—economic growth and the first steps to European integration for example—this supposedly dysfunctional system performed spectacularly well.[52]

France underwent twenty-three changes of government over these years. Some of these administrations were fleeting—de Gaulle's first ministry formed on 21 November 1945, which lasted only two fraught months before the General resigned; Georges Bidault's second government, in existence for barely forty-eight hours in October 1948. Yet these episodes could be interpreted differently, less as changes of government than as ministerial reshuffles. It is thus in the endurance of particular coalition groupings that one discerns the underlying continuity in France's post-war politics: the centre-left tri-partite alignment of 1944 to 1947, the centrist and avowedly 'anti-extremist' Third Force of 1948 to 1951, and the resurgence of centre-right parties between the general elections of June 1951 and January 1956.[53] Seen this way, essential changes of political direction in the Fourth Republic years are reduced to four: May 1947, July 1948, and the two elections in 1951 and 1956. Coalition governments survived reasonably well in-between times and are deservedly remembered for major achievements: the social reforms, ambitious economic planning, and constitutional renovation of the tripar-tite coalition; the first, decisive steps towards Franco-German partnership at the heart of a Western European Community pursued by Third Force ministries; and the promise of fundamental change in international policy partially delivered by the Radical Party reformer Pierre Mendès France in late 1954.[54]

Party politics only explains so much anyway. The unbroken commitment to state intervention and industrial modernization that underpinned the 'thirty glorious years' of post-war economic growth is more significant than the comings and goings in the National Assembly.[55] So, too, the consumerist turn in French society in the 1950s represents a stronger cultural shift than the decision to elect this or that party to office. Cementing France's place at the heart of Europe by laying the foundations of the European Commu-nity counted for more than individual foreign policy spats.[56] All of this may be true. But, in colonial affairs, the Fourth Republic's changing party polit-ical complexion mattered. Particular coalitions promoted reform; more often, others precluded it. A handful of deservedly influential politicians from Algeria, West Africa, and the French Caribbean found their niche within coalition politics in Paris, but they were hardly representative. Far more colonial leaders were exasperated by the limitations imposed by French party interests. Alienation from France's post-war political system ran deeper still among the professional soldiery commanded to fight its colonial wars. Army officers, not colonial firebrands, brought down the Fourth Republic, the ultimate proof that party politics was central to France's end of empire.

For all the hiatus characteristic of French domestic politics after 1945, the irony was that the political cultures of colonial governance—by which I mean the way that decisions were implemented, in consultation with which people, and for what purpose—changed more dramatically in the British case than in the French. With so much wartime division among the rulers of French empire, one might expect more fundamental changes in the out-look, practices, and personnel of colonial administration to have occurred in French territories rather than in British colonies where, in comparative terms at least, disruption was less dramatic. Yet the reverse applied. The French Empire after 1945 was notable for the prevalence of old faces at all tiers of government, not for the emergence of new ones.

The point seems odder still when one considers that the French Empire's administrative system was redesigned between 1944 and 1946 in tandem with the launch of the post-war constitutional settlement at home. The French Union, in other words, took shape alongside the Fourth Republic and was meant to complement it, not only politically and economically, but culturally as well. The empire's new inclusiveness was intended to signify the renunciation of discredited colonial habits in the same way that the Fourth Republic spurned Vichy's authoritarian discrimination against women, racial minorities, and supporters of republican values. France also shared with the United States a strong intellectual interest in federalist schemes that, by transcending the old boundaries and competition between nation states, would make conflict less likely in future.[57] At first glance, then, the immediate post-war period in France and its empire heralded a radical departure from what had existed before. Yet British colonial rule underwent the more profound post-war turn, albeit with less fanfare. Why? Answering this question requires us to consider its two constituent parts: the gap between image and reality in the case of the French Union and the reasons for the greater changes in British colonial administration. Both issues would have lasting implications for the pursuit of fight or flight strategies in the late 1940s and beyond.

The politicians and colonial functionaries of the so-called 'tripartite period' from the Liberation of Paris in August 1944 until the collapse of centre-left coalition government in May 1947 drew their legitimacy from years of resistance to Nazism, to Vichy, and, more broadly, to the 'mistakes' that brought France to its knees in 1940.[58] Alongside their rise to power, an entire political system—the Vichy state, its national leadership, its local government apparatus, and associated civil society groups—was vilified and purged from French society and, in the short term at least, from national memory.[59] This replacement of one governing elite by another was messier and less thorough in French imperial territory. Vichy sympathies were more widespread in the corridors of colonial administration, making a clear-out of personnel unfeasible. Herein lies the clue to a very different perspective.

Unusually in the country's parliamentary history, many parliamentarians in post-war France had direct experience of life in the colonies, if only because *faut de mieux* so many had congregated in Algiers, home from mid 1943 of what would become the first proto-parliament of the Fourth Republic, the Constituent Assembly. Few came away with a love of the place. Most itched to get out of the empire and back to France, away from the grubby realities of colonial hardship to begin the process of putting France back together again after four years of occupation, division, and war. Established colonial interests were thus familiar and yet, somehow, disregarded; even, in some quarters, disliked. No wonder. Governors' palaces, planters' clubs, officers' messes, and the boardrooms of the Bank of Indochina figured among the most staunchly anti-republican and overtly reactionary centres of influence anywhere in the francophone world. For the *arriviste* politicians of the Fourth Republic, the colonies were essential but secondary; important but not *that* important.

Even from the perspective of its chief architects, the reconstruction of empire had only a bit part in the grander scheme of post-war French recovery.[60] Some scored notable victories even so. African and Antillean deputies such as the Senegalese Lamine Guèye and Léopold Senghor and the Guyanese Gaston Monnerville used their positions as deputies in the newly-elected French Constituent Assembly to call time on some of the worst injustices of the pre-war empire. Forced labour and arbitrary imprisonment were outlawed, although worker recruitment in many places remained highly coercive. Racially-configured voting systems were overhauled, if not quite abandoned.[61] Worryingly, those politicians and social commentators with the greatest investment in it were side-lined the closer that imperial reform came to the statute book. As a result, the project to recast the French Empire as the French Union was always likely to disappoint. The Ministry of Colonies was rebranded as a Ministry for Overseas France, the dread word 'colony' being scrupulously avoided. Its backroom functions were reorganized to accommodate more specialist divisions, including a discrete development arm.[62] In conformity with this technocratic redesign, ambitious proposals emanated from Ministry planners. Most sought to square the circle between deeper cultural integration between France and its overseas territories (the former 'colonies'), the need for partnership agreements with its associated states (formerly 'protectorates'), and promises of longer-term state-driven investment to modernize colonial health, housing, and industry.

Obvious questions remained unanswered. How would this be funded at a time of national insolvency? What sort of security relationships did France expect with these re-categorized dependencies? Would individual territories be required to pool money and men into a 'French Union' army?[63] More critical, to adapt Zara Steiner's comment about the peacemaking of 1919, none of the usual foundations for state identity—language, religion, ethnicity, geography, ideology—commanded universal assent as a basis either for individual colonial statehood or for common identity across the French Empire as a whole.[64] With little money and no unifying principle to guide them, where were the advocates of a French Union to begin? The dilemma was never resolved. Instead, it was fudged.

Few historians have a good word for the French Union.[65] Those who view the project sympathetically stress its transformative aspirations, rather than its practical effects.[66] These aspirations were articulated in the federalist terms of a new colonial equality that would render local separatism or national independence irrelevant. Autonomy within a federal system certainly appealed to numerous colonial politicians later identified with violent struggles for independence. Ferhat Abbas' UDMA in Algeria, even the Vietminh in Indochina, talked the language of federal autonomy, drawing comfort from the fact that Soviet Russia was, outwardly at least, a federal union of diverse republics.[67] René Capitant, Gaullist Minister of Education during the early debates over the French Union's political complexion, insisted that the new scheme would be federal or nothing. France and its overseas dependencies would be united as never before because egalitarian ideals would be made flesh in binding constitutional arrangements and shared imperial citizenship. The veteran Socialist Vincent Auriol shared these dreams. As the Fourth Republic's head of state, Auriol became President of the French Union as well. He saw himself as arbiter, persuading colonial politicians that their interests were served in partnership with France, not in opposition to it. The French Union Assembly—an empire-wide parliament that sat alongside the French National Assembly—would thus become the centre for a vibrant imperial politics.[68] Both Capitant and Auriol were proved wrong.

In place of the early hopes of structures that might replicate the 'separate but equal' ethos of the British Commonwealth, the French Union, as its title implied, promised closer assimilation between France and its empire. Admittedly, Henri Laurentie, senior policy adviser at the Ministry for Overseas France, devised a federal system of elected territorial parliaments as well

as extended colonial representation in the French National Assembly.[69] Dispassionate and scrupulously logical, Laurentie was also politically naive. He
and his Ministry officials also lacked reliable information from some of the
territories whose political futures they were beginning to redefine. Indochina, economically devastated and internally divided in late 1945, stood out
in this regard.[70]

Ordered to re-write the empire's basic administrative rules at break-neck
speed, Laurentie carried on as if grand imperial schemes could progress
from planning to implementation with the same facility as plans for a town
bypass.[71] His provision for differing levels of attachment to the Union
promised substantial autonomy to 'associated states' like the Vietnamese territories identified as more advanced in their socio-political 'evolution'.
France would retain a tighter grip over less developed regions, including the
black African federations. French authorities across West Africa, for instance,
sponsored increasing numbers of local Muslims to perform the *hajj* to
Mecca, but as a measure to deepen identification with France as a sympathetic 'Muslim power'.[72] Elsewhere, local elites in the North African protectorates and the Indochina federation were, understandably, preoccupied by
the precise implications of autonomy. Who would control budgetary purse-
strings, defence policy, and policing for instance? Would there be a multinational French Union high command or would separate French and local
security forces co-exist alongside each other?[73] Black Africans fixed on the
hypocrisy of egalitarian promises that came hedged with colonialist presumptions about their limited capacity to run things themselves.

Laurentie's other French Union proposals paid too little heed to the disparities of power within and between colonies. Settler lobbies could frus-
trate plans for a single, colour-blind franchise by focusing on necessary
criteria for citizenship such as literacy, property ownership or public service.
In the 'overseas territories' of black Africa, as well as in Algeria, voting systems based on dual electoral colleges—the lesser one elected by African
'subjects', the stronger one representing 'citizens', principally settlers—gave
the lie to universal political participation. And, in French West Africa especially, well-organized trade unions, students' associations, and political parties that operated trans-nationally could mobilize opposition across borders.[74]
Laurentie's formulation, as well as the variants that followed it, also ignored
the fact that the most influential voices in places as diverse as Morocco
and Vietnam were implacably opposed to subsuming their claims to
nationhood.[75]

Further problems arose from the efforts made to accommodate various local claims to special status within the new system. In consequence, the French Union's original unitary vision became clouded by a complex array of arrangements for individual territories and regional federations. Voting rights, the powers of elected colonial assemblies, and the extent of local autonomy were all diminished relative to the arrangements within the so-called 'Senghor constitution'—the previous French Union draft that was rejected in a French referendum vote on 5 May 1946.[76] That first French Union draft was highly ambitious. Everyone in overseas France was to gain citizen rights, which, for the first time, were decoupled from an individual's 'civil status'. A person's religion, gender, wealth, and educational attainment, let alone their ethnic origin, would no longer determine imperial citizenship. Individual territories might retain their own civil status regimes, but all adults in the French Union would become citizens of it. The implications of Senghor's ideas—equal civil rights and universal suffrage—united the governing parties against him. As veteran Radical Party leader Edouard Herriot famously put it, France risked becoming the colony of its former colonies. It would be swamped by colonial people's demands for the same legal rights, the same welfare benefits, the same living standards as their French counterparts. These were claims it was manifestly impossible to concede.[77]

The die was cast as soon as the second, more conservative version of the French Union was approved in October 1946. A political instrument of the French centre-right, the convoluted associational, electoral, and legal arrangements of the French Union became a means to shut down reformist alternatives that threatened a real democratization of colonial politics and consequent popular votes for independence.[78] A settler interest group, the 'States-general of French colonization', set up in September 1945 by members of various colonial Chambers of Commerce to defend the interests of whites in francophone black Africa, lent vocal support to ministers temperamentally inclined to recoil from deeper reform.[79] In its second-draft incarnation, the French Union, originally promoted as the means to end colonial discrimination, institutionalized it afresh in the smarter colours of a definitive constitutional settlement.[80] The peoples of French black Africa became citizens of the French Union but remained subjects of France. Under the separate Statute for Algeria, voted in 1947, Algerian Muslims, paradoxically, *were* acknowledged as citizens of France because Algeria was constitutionally an extension of metropolitan France overseas. Yet within Algeria itself these same Algerians remained second-class citizens, or citizens of 'Muslim civil status', unlike the European settlers, who retained an iron grip over the levers of political power and economic influence.[81] Even more confusing, their neighbours in Morocco and Tunisia, territories whose subordination to France was regulated by protectorate treaties, remained outside the French Union altogether. These countries, although still directed by France, were theoretically sovereign, so their peoples retained national citizenship rights as 'Moroccans' and 'Tunisians'.[82]

A brutal verdict on the French Union would be that it merely replicated the undeclared racial hierarchies—from white, through North African and Asiatic, to black African—of the pre-war empire. A kindlier judgement would be that the original French Union scheme was over-ambitious while its second, timorous incarnation was hamstrung by the vicissitudes of post-war coalition politics. What is certain is that hardly anyone in the empire liked it. Even Henri Laurentie was, by late 1946, profoundly dissatisfied with the French Union's final, adulterated form.[83] Most of the Empire's anti-colonialists responded in one of two divergent ways. In much of franco-phone black Africa, political parties, student groups, and above all industrial workers turned the French Union's rhetoric of shared rights and entitlements against their political masters.[84] Demands for equivalent freedoms, economic opportunities, and workplace entitlements to their French counterparts spurred the development of West African trade unionism and more hotly-contested local politics.[85]

If West Africa's political leaders and trade union organizers chose the path of constructive engagement with France after 1946, their counterparts in Algeria, Madagascar, and Vietnam saw no alternative to violent rebellion. In each case, the most influential—the Algerian People's Party, Madagascar's MRDM, and the Communist-led Vietminh coalition—had all been outlawed long before the French Union was launched. But French efforts to marginalize these groups were less significant than the party political manoeuvrings of post-war France itself.[86] From the start of the Indochina War in 1946 until the final collapse of French Christian Democracy in 1958, the movement's representatives, the MRP, refused to give an inch in matters colonial.[87] The explanation generally advanced is that Christian Democrats feared being outflanked by the Gaullists, their chief rival for votes.[88] That may be part of the equation, but it underplays the MRP's commitment to wage Cold War in the empire and to crush those that threatened Christian Democracy's most lasting creation: the constitutional architecture of the Fourth Republic and the French Union.

British post-war colonial planning had a much lower profile. Colonial development schemes for black Africa and elsewhere intersected with war-time welfare reforms and the extension of state control over utilities, health-care, and other public services that followed Labour's landslide victory in July 1945. It is doubtful that many Labour voters, whether in the Party's established Northern and Scottish strongholds or among its newer converts of the suburban South linked their choice at the polls to empire questions.[89] But, for many Fabian-type imperial reformers, improving basic standards of life in the colonies was a logical corollary to the New Jerusalem being fash-ioned in metropolitan Britain.[90] Development was not imagined as the means to recast colonial societies in a British image by replicating metro-politan economic conditions. If anything, its advocates sought the opposite outcome. Their aim was to mitigate what were perceived to be the damag-ing social consequences of economic modernization, such as unbridled urban growth and mass unemployment, by making better use of farmland and other rural resources.[91] Alongside renewed investment in infrastructure and agronomy, colonial social policy, a catch-all term for initiatives in health-care, welfare, and educational provision, was the stuff of development plan-ning. Self-consciously 'modern' in approach, its practical benefits were meant to foster community spirit and improved economic performance.[92] Anti-colonialism might lose its appeal as the health and skills of colonial workforces increased.[93]

Newly 'hyperactive' colonial administrations in the tropics were packed with technical specialists to provide the impetus to this imperial renovation. A BSc in civil engineering or forestry management now offered a surer route into Britain's colonial bureaucracy than a BA in Classics as the number of scientific 'experts' increased.[94] For all the pragmatism inherent in this 'second colonial occupation' by well-intentioned 'doers' rather than old-school 'thinkers', the post-war accent on development retained its school-masterly ethics and Fabian undertones.[95] It was paternalism with a progressive edge.[96]

At a macro-economic level, colonial development was also of a piece with Keynesian ideas about post-war reconstruction and global trade recov-ery. Each was supposed to rest on state investment and international clearing arrangements designed to facilitate capital flows between creditor and debtor nations. It was not to be. Keynes' 'visionary hope' was frustrated, in part, by the conservative turn in US financial policy.[97] And Britain lacked the monetary wherewithal to transform its colonial economies alone. Far

from investing huge sums of British money in the empire, the grandly-
named 1945 Colonial Development and Welfare Act drew on budgetary
surpluses built up by the colonies themselves.[98] The supreme irony of post-
war British imperial development was that colonial peoples were, for the
most part, expected to pay for it. Over and above this contribution, thanks
to rapidly rising commodity prices during the primary products boom
ignited by the Korean War in 1950, some territories, notably Malaya and the
colonies of West Africa, remained net contributors to Britain's sterling
balances.[99]

The point, though, should not be taken too far. Development was never
devised as a panacea for Britain's financial woes; quite the reverse. In East
Africa especially, vaunted schemes such as an irrigation programme to assist
Sudanese cotton cultivation and investment in brick- and tile-making facto-
ries in Kenya only antagonized the farmers and workers they were supposed
to help. A vast project to make Tanganyika a leading peanut producer—and
an exporter of the nut oil required to manufacture margarine for ration-hit
British families—typified the absurdity of poorly coordinated development
planning. Despite planting over a huge area, a dismal crop of only 9,000 tons
translated into a cost of over £700 per pound of peanuts produced.[100] Perhaps the muted public reaction to the exorbitance of the grandly-named
'East African groundnut scheme' was explained by the fact that, according to
a 1948 Colonial Office survey, fewer than half of the 2,000 adults surveyed
could name a single Crown Colony, and only sixteen per cent knew that the
scheme was in some way connected to East Africa.[101]

It may not have resonated with the public, but there were strategic
dimensions to this developmental agenda as well. Between 1946 and 1949
Foreign and Colonial Office staff forged closer Anglo-French imperial connections in sub-Saharan Africa.[102] Foreign Secretary Ernest Bevin envisaged
a 'Eurafrican' bloc led by Europe's two premier imperial nations as an economic and strategic counterweight to the Cold War super-powers. The
British, the French, and their African subjects stood to benefit from freer
trade and stronger colonial partnerships between them. Western Europe,
fortified by its two African empires combined, might stake its claim as the
'third force' in international politics, capable of resisting America's dollar
supremacy and creeping Soviet influence in the colonial world. In the event,
Bevin's geo-political hopes came to nothing.

One reason was that the logic of Franco-British partnership below the
Sahara was nullified by the bitterness that characterized relations between

the two imperial powers in the Arab world.[103] French grievances over their unceremonious eviction from Syria were slow to heal. Indeed, Gallic animus for Britain's Middle East primacy was reflected in France's outspoken backing for an Israeli state in place of the Palestine Mandate.[104] The fact that the Cairo-based Arab League preferred to work with Britain, and often against French interests in North Africa, also caused annoyance among French officials. The nationalist leadership of Morocco's Istiqlal Party reportedly saw the Arab League and the newly-established United Nations as levers to compel France into conceding early independence, a measure they hoped Britain and the United States would endorse.[105] On 1 February 1946 the French administration in Tunis complained that 'British agents' were involved in Arab League efforts to secure weapons, money, and vital UN backing for Tunisia's principal nationalist group, Habib Bourguiba's Néo-Destour Party.[106] In July 1947 the Maghreb nationalist groups opened a New York 'publicity bureau'—in reality, a filing cabinet in the Fifth Avenue apartment of a Moroccan activist, Sidi Mahdi Bennouna—to make their case in the American media. BBC Arabic broadcasts were cited to lend objectivity to the bureau's claims of French repression.[107]

Little wonder that Bevin's ideas about an Anglo-French marriage south of the Sahara struck some as strange. Despite the conclusion of a Franco-British security alliance, the Treaty of Dunkirk, in March 1947, Franco-British enthusiasm for the Foreign Secretary's 'neo-colonial entente' soon waned. It was eclipsed by other, more realistic prizes: US Marshall Aid funds, a NATO pact, and, for France especially, the prospect of lasting peace with Germany through European integration.[108] A flash in the diplomatic pan, Bevin's Eurafrica scheme was also the last sustained attempt at colonial partnership before Britain and France combined disastrously over Suez in 1956.[109]

Much as closer Anglo-French colonial cooperation proved elusive, so Britain's hoped-for imperial consolidation turned into an 'initial phase of disengagement' in which withdrawals from the Indian subcontinent and Palestine transformed the geographic and imagined reaches of empire. None of Attlee's ministers regarded these pull-outs as the prelude to complete imperial collapse. They were right. What William Roger Louis calls the 'era of liquidation' began only after 1957. Even then, 'the goal was not that Britain should sustain the Empire but that the Empire, in a new form, should continue to sustain Britain'.[110] For the most part, Attlee's Labour governments and their Conservative successors favoured negotiating decolonization, not fighting it. In doing so, British post-war governments combined bullish Cold War rhetoric with subtler arguments about Britain's peculiar genius for gradualism, local democracy, and practical welfare reforms. As Anne Deighton notes, 'the ending of empire was conceptualised and presented as a necessary modernisation'. Adaptation to the new concept of commonwealth was conceived as nothing less than a 'world-wide experiment in nation-building'. It was an attempt to create a set of global partnerships with new Commonwealth countries that would shore up the West, and that would be part of a 'global resistance to the "onrush" of communist influence'.[111]

It is doubtful that the British public bought into this vision of continuing world leadership. Perhaps more typical were the views expressed by constituents in Hammersmith and Shrewsbury during a 1946 Mass Observation survey into attitudes towards the United Nations and the prospects for peace.[112] The survey's authors found people less concerned about British power or the preservation of British imperial primacy than anxious to see peace consolidated by whatever means:

> the vast majority of "the common people" are deeply conscious of the dangers of international anarchy and would be only too ready to give up a portion of their so-called sovereign rights for the sake of achieving a new order in world affairs based on justice, security and common sense. The tragedy is that so often they feel that their own wishes in such a matter are of little consequence, and that the continuance of the old hopeless state of affairs is inevitable because of the designs of that mysterious section of the community who are always referred to with cynical resignation as "They". We know that, generally speaking, "they" do their duty according to their lights, regarding themselves as trustees for the welfare and happiness of the people. But... the people, for all their lack of specific knowledge, are far more advanced in "thinking internationally" than is generally supposed and are more than ready for sweeping reforms in the relationship of nations.[113]

Maybe the great British people cared less about fighting for empire than Bevin and his colleagues imagined.

Conclusion

Historian Todd Shepard identifies a fundamental contradiction at the heart of struggles over empire after 1945. The contradiction turns on the centrality of the nation-state in decolonization. And its starting-point is the trauma of the Second World War itself. The ultra-nationalism of fascism and the war it provoked did much to discredit the nation-state as the 'logical' political form it was presumed to be after 1918. Governments, NGOs, academics, economic interest groups, and public health bodies looked instead to supra-national organizations, many of them tied to a United Nations superstructure, to create a more peaceable and effective post-war international order. British and French politicians and public intellectuals were caught up in this turn towards the supra-national.[114]

For Britain, the post-war future of dependent territories seemed to lie in regional combinations—territorial federations or larger economic units that would be better placed to modernize under British guidance. In this view, 'self-determination' or sovereign independence for potentially small states with few financial or resource assets made little sense and could be ruled out in good conscience for the foreseeable future.[115] Meanwhile, the foundations of the 'French Union' laid between the Brazzaville Conference of colonial governors in early 1944 and the establishment of France's Fourth Republic in October 1946 posited ideals of integration, cooperation, and transnational partnership that, in theory at least, also rejected a binary opposition between the imperial 'mother country' and its individual colonies.[116] These need not be 'nations in the making', whose freedom could only be achieved by rejecting France. Rather, they were members of a new-style community in which the promise of liberty could be fulfilled with France's assistance.[117]

Similar claims, albeit couched in less lofty terms, might be advanced for Britain's oft-professed transition from Empire to Commonwealth. Furthermore, several of the most radical anti-colonialists of the next twenty years would propose their own versions of supra-nationalism: Kwame Nkrumah's pan-Africanist union, Léopold Sédar Senghor's dream of a francophone West African federation, or Gamal Abdul Nasser's United Arab Republic to cite three of the most far-reaching. For all that, the contradiction remained: supra-national alternatives to the nation-state model failed. Ultimately, as Shepard puts it, 'It was instead the establishment of formally independent nation-states that became the marker of decolonization's success'.[118] Such was the unwritten rule of fight and flight politics for the next thirty years.

4

Fiery Sunsets:
Fighting Withdrawals
in Asia, 1945–8

Contemplating their colonial options in Asia, the governments elected in
Britain and France in late 1945 confronted stark alternatives of fight or
flight. The British Empire risked being engulfed by an unstoppable wave of
colonial withdrawals spreading across the vast South Asian agglomeration of
British-ruled India, Ceylon, and Burma. A similar deluge threatened in the
Palestine Mandate, departure from which lacked 'even the pretence of fore-
thought'.[1] Historical treatments of these events are divided between those
that consider enforced British pull-outs the prelude to disastrous political
violence and those that take a more sympathetic view of British readiness to
leave. This chapter takes a different line. It examines the arguments among
Clement Attlee's ministers and Asian leaders, and between Whitehall officials
and their counterparts in New Delhi, Jerusalem, and elsewhere. It suggests
that the unworkable combination of fight and flight strategies, most notably
in British India and Palestine, contributed to worsening inter-communal
clashes and the descent into partition and war soon afterwards.

Colonial violence was endemic to the French Empire by 1945. Colonial
troops turned their guns on domestic populations to suppress uprisings in
Algeria and Syria as the Second World War drew to a close. As we shall see
later, Algeria's Sétif uprising marked a critical step towards colonial breakdown in France's pre-eminent colony. By contrast, army shelling of nationalist strongholds in Damascus during the conflict over withdrawal from Syria
in 1945 barely registered in France even though the bloodbath occasioned
the first appeal for consideration of colonial abuses to the newly-established
United Nations. The main French governmental preoccupation at the time

was not Syria but the Indochina federation. There, the likelihood of armed conflict against the Vietminh ebbed and flowed with the fortunes of negotiations over the form and extent of France's post-war return to Vietnam. Another ruthless bombardment of France's opponents—this time in the northern Vietnamese port of Haiphong—triggered the outbreak of the Indochina War at the end of November 1946. It would be another eight years before warfare gave way to 'fighting withdrawal'. The original French decision to fight was approved by left-leaning Paris governments packed with former resisters against Nazi occupation, men and women who struggled to come to terms with the disastrous escalation of the conflict in Vietnam.

The Franco-Vietnamese war was the first of Indochina's three major international conflicts of the twentieth century (the second was unleashed by America in 1964, the third by China in 1979). And, more than most other armed confrontations in the colonial world, it pitted East against West as well as imperial North against anti-colonial South.[2] Not surprisingly, Vietnam became a focal point for Third Worldism—the idea, popularized by 'new left' thinkers from the late 1950s onwards, that anti-colonial struggles were the vanguard of the major ideological clashes transforming global politics. Next to the icy stasis of the European Cold War, there was some substance to this claim that the collapse of European empire in Asia and Africa represented the more fundamental reorientation of the international system.[3] Vietnam's tragedy was central to the process.[4] From the 1940s to the 1980s the country remained a cockpit for international strategic rivalry and competing visions of how post-colonial societies should be organized.[5] Decolonization from the Indian subcontinent also occasioned human tragedy on a calamitous scale. And India and Pakistan's subsequent, mutually-hostile international alignments flowed directly from their roads to independence and the acrimonious partition that followed.

The Indian subcontinent

Impending partition was announced to India's peoples by wireless broadcast on 3 June 1947. Attlee's matter-of-fact statement to the House of Commons was followed by equally downbeat speeches recited into giant microphones at Delhi's All-India Radio Station by Viceroy Admiral Louis Mountbatten, Congress leader Jawaharlal Nehru, the Muslim League's Mohammed Ali Jinnah and Baldev Singh, who spoke for India's Sikhs. Their subdued tone was easily explained: no one knew what partition implied. Where and to whom would it be applied? How would it be implemented—or enforced? Bengal's Legislative Assembly, for instance, was required to subdivide itself into two parts, the one representing Hindu-majority districts, the other Muslim-majority ones. The members of each were then to vote for or against partition and attachment to India or an East Pakistan. Little wonder that the process here, as elsewhere, while rational in theory, was messy in practice, stoking local battles for political influence in the new successor states.[6]

British ministers and officials meanwhile devoted greater effort to maintaining the façade of Indian responsibility for the impending division than to refining its detail.[7] The final partition lines were only made public on 17 August 1947, two days *after* formal independence, not before. Sketched on the basis of wartime census figures indicating the location of Muslim, Hindu or Sikh majority populations, the frontiers demarcating West and East Pakistan from independent India paid little heed to topography, land ownership, natural resources, or the existence of mixed communities. The British judge, Sir Cyril Radcliffe, given responsibility for delimiting borders, was 'a rank outsider' to India. Clever, secretive, and rarely seen without his characteristic thick-lensed spectacles, he never visited the areas to be partitioned and remained in India for only six weeks.[8] The judges assigned to Radcliffe's Boundary Commission faced insistent political lobbying as they pored over the maps. But they never developed an observer's 'feel' for the communities they were about to destroy. Far from being amputated cleanly with a surgeon's dispassionate skill, the regions Radcliffe's pen divided were left torn and bleeding without the administrative support necessary to staunch the flow. At the micro-level, cultivators were separated from their lands, earners from their employments, families from their relatives.[9] As is evident from the population displacements recorded in Map 5, at the macro level, partition frontiers fuelled communal hatreds, inter-state disputes, and future wars.

One such conflict zone, the princely state of Jammu and Kashmir, claimed by both India and Pakistan, offers a notorious example of imperial—and imperious—partition. Three-quarters of its four million people were Muslim. But their autocratic Maharajah, Hari Singh, a pampered ruler out of touch with the strength of communal affiliation, was given the option by Mountbatten of deciding which dominion his state should join.[10] First he dithered. Then he fled, taking his royal jeweller with him as his state descended into civil war.[11] British administrators put a different gloss on things. Lord Mountbatten, faced with the unenviable task as last Viceroy of winning

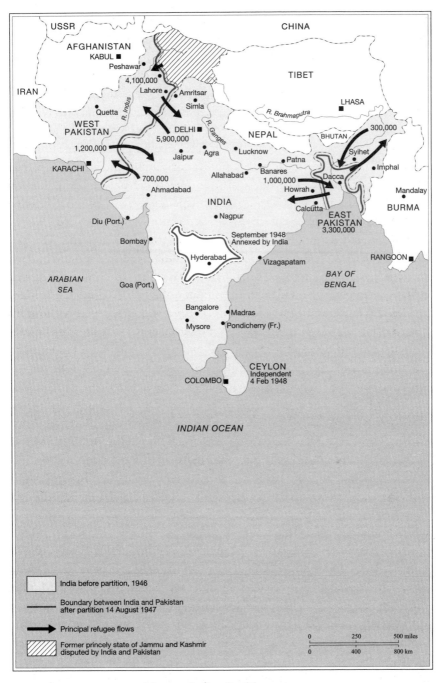

Map 5. Indian Partition, 1947.

acceptance for Radcliffe's partition, described Kashmir's partition to former India Office minister Arthur Henderson thus:

> He had advised the Maharajah in July 1947 to ascertain the will of the people by any accepted means and accede as quickly as possible to one Dominion or the other; and when nothing had happened by the end of August, Lord Ismay had tried again to induce the Maharajah to make up his mind on this point. But the Maharajah was apparently constitutionally incapable of coming to any decision and was, in fact, almost entirely to blame for the present disaster in Kashmir.[12]

Here was the politics of partition in a nutshell. By ceding responsibility for implementation to local rulers, the British authorities put safe distance between their improvised decolonization and the problems it induced.

For Yasmin Khan, one of partition's most eloquent historians, the high politics of Britain's decision to divide from a distance cannot—should not—be divorced from its ensuing human disasters.[13] The point is well taken. For Britons, in particular, the path to Indian independence is more familiar as a courtly play, the colourful relationships between a handful of leading actors—Lord and Lady Mountbatten, Nehru, Gandhi, and Jinnah—occupying centre-stage. Spoiling the narrative of early decolonization generously bequeathed, partition's horrors are confined to the wings.[14] Yet, even before the British departed, dividing India was a blood-soaked affair. It created a massive refugee problem for both newly-independent states, crystallizing the enduring animosity between them. India's partition was also a double division into West and East Pakistan—later Bangladesh—for the subcontinent's Muslims. Its cultural fallout dominated the popular politics of the subcontinent and seared itself into collective memory far more than the constitutional niceties of formal independence.[15] To be fair, the Labour Government and Mountbatten's departing colonial administration were horrified, albeit not surprised, by the clashes attending these splits. But they saw no alternative to them. So cataclysmic was the violence that accompanied Indian independence that neither British officials at the time, nor subsequent nationalist accounts of anti-colonial struggle cared to dwell on it.[16] Politically expedient and financially imperative it may have been, but Britain's flight from India came at exorbitant human cost.

It was as spring turned to summer 1946 that pre-partition killings began in earnest. In mid-March a trio of Labour Ministers flew to India to pursue talks with leading politicians. Cripps, the real leader of this Cabinet 'mission', was hoping to reheat his wartime recipe of concessions. His two ministe-rial colleagues, the bumbling Secretary of State for India Freddie Pethick-Lawrence and the unlikely First Lord of the Admiralty A.V. Alexander, a man better informed about his beloved Chelsea F.C. than about India, were largely superfluous. Despite Cripps' best efforts, the mission merely stimulated the opposing Indian parties to adopt more uncompromising positions.[17]

The British by this point regarded their two principal negotiating part-ners, the Muslim League and the Indian National Congress, very differ-ently. The League's impressive performance in March 1946 provincial elections confirmed the movement's success in exploiting the economic distress in the Punjab's rural heartlands to mobilize traditional client net-works among Muslim landlords, kinship groups, and sufi religious orders.[18] Jinnah could now claim to be a genuine national leader rather than a Raj insider indulged by the British since the 1930s. Much the same could be said of the Muslim League. The election results confirmed that it repre-sented more than the Punjab's Muslim urban elite. Invigorated by his party's unprecedented rural support, Jinnah reiterated his central demand for Muslim 'self-determination' within a separate state. This was the log-ical consequence of the longstanding British tendency to link Indians' identity and legal status to their religious affiliation, Muslims having been designated a separate Indian electorate since 1909.[19]

Mountbatten's vice-regal team, no friends of Jinnah, at least knew the likely Muslim League response when negotiating the terms of partition. By contrast, the Congress leadership framed their demands in terms that left Attlee's government exasperated.[20] Part of Gandhi's brilliance lay in the connections he made between Hindu and Indic traditions of asceti-cism and rejection of alien, colonial values. The result was what Mithi Mukharjee terms the adoption of 'renunciative freedom' based on the Hindu ideal of the *samnyasin*, or renouncer, who rejects earthly corrup-tions in pursuit of true personal liberty, or *moksha*. Gandhi's role as India's foremost *samnyasin* was a potent one. It provided the philosophical ground-ing for the strategy of passive resistance and undermined long-standing British claims that India was a hopelessly divided society, which required the firm hand of colonial guidance to keep it from anarchy.[21] Even so, the idea that Congress might be a better guarantor of India's domestic peace was not something that British negotiators found easy to swallow. Nicholas Owen puts it well:

The Congress high command seemed to Labour leaders in Britain to demonstrate all the worst faults of the irresponsible politician: unwilling to give ground in negotiations, but unreliable once settlements had been reached; reluctant to shoulder the burden of administration, but happy to wield unaccountable power from the sidelines; prepared to raise popular emotions through demagoguery and agitation, but capable only of floundering blindly in the wake of those they had inspired when public order collapsed as a result.[22]

Greater Congress ambivalence towards negotiation when compared with the Muslim League was unfortunate. It enhanced Jinnah's standing as 'sole spokesman' for Muslim claims and fuelled local confrontations between supporters of the rival movements.[23] Imperial bureaucracy was meanwhile adjusting to the unprecedented hubbub of provincial politics after March 1946 elections brought into office Congress or Muslim League-dominated governments throughout India's directly-administered states. With so many provincial administrations rigidly divided, Congress politicians struggled to hold the political centre. Prospects for a working relationship within India's Constituent Assembly between rancorous Congress politicians and the Muslim League receded as the clock ticked towards British withdrawal.[24]

Sir Francis Mudie, a senior figure in the New Delhi administration soon to take up the Governorship of Sind, had summarized the essential dilemma at the end of the war:

> August 1942 [Quit India] made it clear that we have in this country two very different communities, or to use Jinnah's words, nations, struggling for power, not two parties competing for office. From this point of view the real offence of the British in Congress eyes is that they stand in the way of the Hindus, led by the Congress, in imposing their rule over the whole of India. Muslims at present advance Pakistan as their only adequate safeguard: we must either accept this or bypass it and produce an alternative: this alternative must involve the removal of Hindu domination at the centre, which is the essence of the Pakistan demand. It would seem to be impossible to negotiate on Pakistan: the answer must be "yes" or "no": it would have to be imposed, a very dangerous course: we should therefore try to bypass it by agreement.[25]

Forewarnings that no such agreement could be struck came thick and fast. Food riots and sporadic religious disputes in towns from Gujarat to Madras; the noisy acclamation for former Indian National Army rebels; a mutiny among naval ratings in Bombay who trained their ships' guns on venerable shoreline establishments including the city yacht club and the Taj Hotel.[26]

All pointed to a powerful surge of leftist radicalism that added complexity to the challenges of communal coexistence.[27] Still the scale and ferocity of the clashes in Calcutta during three days of Hindu–Muslim rioting between 16 and 19 August was profoundly shocking. At least 4,000 people died following Jinnah's call for a day of direct action to demonstrate Muslim support for an independent Pakistan. Touring Calcutta's most devastated districts, one British official mixed modern and pre-modern metaphors. The city, he said, looked as if it were simultaneously blitzed and hit by bubonic plague.[28]

Violence—actual or potential, physical or psychological—haunted the remaining months of British rule. The threat of it crept into family homes and political meeting rooms. Inter-communal killings and population displacement multiplied, with the most sustained clashes in the Punjab, the north-western epicentre of partition.[29] Communal massacres, mass rapes, lootings and abductions, often systematically planned with the complicity of openly sectarian administrators and police, certainly point to state failure.[30] Reprisals against exposed minority communities were to some degree predictable. So were attacks on obvious targets like refugee columns and

Figure 5. Inter-communal violence on the other side of partition's divide: Indian police use tear gas against Calcutta rioters, January 1949.

trains. Each pointed to a chronic absence of effective security force protection, a source of tremendous guilt for dedicated imperial bureaucrats.[31] But
which state was failing? An incumbent colonial regime on the point of leaving that could neither impose its authority nor 'police the police'? Or the
political actors in Congress and the Muslim League, plus the panoply of
provincial governments and local administrative agencies set to fill the vacuum after British withdrawal?

In the Punjab especially, the cycle of violence between March and August
1947 implicated both the colonial authorities and their local counterparts. It
began with massacres in Rawalpindi and then escalated into even larger
pogroms in Lahore, Amritsar, and outlying districts nearby.[32] In those locali-
ties where politicians, administrators, and police acted swiftly and impar-
tially to quell violence, they were often successful. But where rioters went
unprosecuted and the civil authorities stood by as vigilantes roamed, levels
of sectarian attacks and ethnic cleansing were commensurately higher. Sir
Francis Mudie, by now relocated to West Punjab as Governor, instructed
provincial police on 20 September 1947 to allow all columns of departing
Hindu and Sikh families to pass through without any searches or other
interference. His order was partially heeded in Lahore. But it was generally
ignored the further the columns headed eastwards from the provincial capital.[33] Muslim refugees heading in the opposite direction from East to West
Punjab faced similar perils. A spate of attacks in the Jullundur and Amritsar
districts between 21 and 23 September 1947 culminated in the killing of
every person aboard a packed refugee train making for the border.[34] Whatever the official instructions to the contrary, security force connivance in all
of these cases was undeniable. Because so many administrators and police
put communal loyalty before public service or, more often, conflated the
two, the tendency to construct India and Pakistan as 'communalized' states
became harder to reverse.[35]

Even in the socially conservative princely states where party politics were
less entrenched than in India's directly-ruled provinces, inter-communal
violence broke the surface repeatedly in the last years of colonial rule.[36]
After independence the strains of refugee resettlement, often conducted
with government assistance, sharpened these divides.[37] The eastern frontier
demarcating East Pakistan ran for 4,000 kilometres. It bisected villages, isolating some communities, arbitrarily re-assigning others. Refugee movements—
some voluntary migrations, others the result of riots, dispossession, or land
exchanges—poisoned cross-border relations for years to come, cementing

the iconographic image of the Bengali refugee as victim of both colonialism and communalism.[38] There were similar legacies in the north-west. Certainly, the ethno-religious composition of the Punjab after partition was unrecognizable next to what it had been before. The Indian Punjab, fifty-three per cent Muslim according to 1941 census figures, was overwhelmingly Hindu- and Sikh-dominated a decade later.[39] At least twelve million people were displaced in the Punjab alone; close to twenty million across the entire subcontinent. The shock of partition and its lingering effects were physically constituted in the two capitals of India and Pakistan. Muslim refugees in their tens of thousands fled Delhi, once the hub of the Muslim-ruled Mughal Empire.[40] Many of them settled in Karachi, the new capital of Pakistan, whose Hindu population collapsed as refugees travelled in the opposite direction. Inexorably, communal loyalty was mapped onto national identity in the two states, feeding mutual antagonisms typified by the struggle for control of Kashmir.[41]

Assessing partition and the early withdrawals

Some imperial historians have suggested that partition, the last resort for British governments confronted by irreconcilable communities, represented settlement of a sort. The chaos and killing, as well as the lasting animosities that attended British pull-outs from India and Palestine make this argument untenable. Yet the rationale for partition in each of these cases remains hard to challenge. Short-term calamity was, in British governmental eyes, a price worth paying to avoid still greater bloodshed were imperial attachments not relinquished. Like all counter-factual arguments, this one is impossible to disprove. But the underlying point is straightforward: the logic of partition was to choose the lesser evil.[42] There is, of course, a less indulgent interpretation of Britain's withdrawal from India, one in which enforced partition was the inevitable, awful consequence of mismanagement and scuttle. Perhaps the truth lies somewhere between these two positions.

It is equally difficult to represent the road to Arab–Jewish war in Palestine, the forcible expansion of the new Israeli state, and the resultant eviction of thousands of Palestinians from their homes as any kind of solution.[43] But the contrasting levels of partition planning also bear emphasis. British governments, as the map below indicates, had toyed with various Palestine partition schemes since 1937.[44]

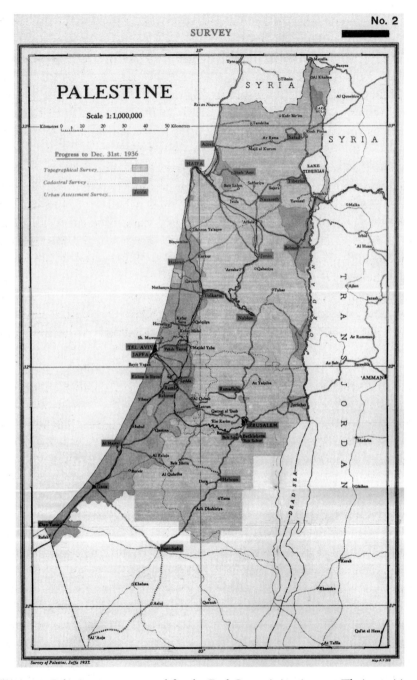

Figure 6. Palestine map prepared for the Peel Commission in 1937. Their partition scheme was rejected.

Yet, a decade later, the Labour government handed responsibility for the Mandate to the United Nations, thereby distancing Britain from the resultant UN partition plan. In India, Sir Cyril Radcliffe was only appointed to head a Boundary Commission in the spring of 1947. As the date for British withdrawal was brought forward in response to India's worsening violence and mounting pressure on Britain's sterling balances, so, too, partition lines were hastily redrawn. Indian partition or, in the Palestinian case, its disavowal were driven by British political requirements.[45]

The British preference for flight from India was distinguished by five core elements from the French decision to fight in Indochina. First was the consistent leadership provided by Clement Attlee when compared with the procession of politicians who took France into war in Vietnam. Well apprised of Indian questions, Attlee recognized that the principal Indian political movements—Congress and the Muslim League—held the moral high ground after the war. He was disinclined to moan about the ramifications of British departure for Britain's global power, its trade prospects, or the 'empire families' whose lifestyles were gone. He also directed negotiations, albeit usually from behind the scenes. Significantly, the British Prime Minister was also eager to cut British commitments in the Arab world. He would have endorsed withdrawal from the Middle East but for the fierce opposition of Ernest Bevin's Foreign Office and the British service chiefs.[46] Contrary to Attlee's preference for the concentration of a British strategic reserve in Kenya, it became axiomatic among British defence planners that defence of the African continent against Soviet incursion required a British military presence along a 'northern tier' running from Turkey to Pakistan. Looking ahead, this strategic vision of a vast defensive perimeter arcing across northwest Asia became the basic precept of the Baghdad Pact, signed in May 1955.[47] Over India, however, Whitehall divisions were less severe.

Here was the second cornerstone of British flight from India: civil–military agreement about its wisdom. Where the heads of the armed forces located a Middle East presence at the centre of British global strategy, they doubted that India could be internally policed any longer.[48] Indeed, for Attlee personally, the acrimonious end of imperial rule in Burma cut deeper than Britain's withdrawal from India five months earlier. Independent Burma turned its back on the Commonwealth. Far more serious, the Burmese political elite clustered around nationalist leader General U Aung San (father of Aung San Suu Kyi) and his Anti-Fascist People's Freedom League (AFPFL), leaders willing to work with the British in a post-independence partnership, were either pushed aside or, like Aung San himself, fell victim to assassination. Their elimination destroyed British presumptions about underlying Burmese goodwill.[49]

The idea that the Burmese were well disposed to Britain derived from wartime experience. During the Burma campaign retreating British troops sometimes left their wounded behind to be cared for in secret by local families who faced harsh Japanese retribution if their charges were discovered. Yet so assured were the sympathies of Burmese villagers that British officers even carried vernacular language letters instructing their potential hosts on basic remedial care.[50] The war not only devastated Burma's rural economy, but the capital Rangoon (Yangon) was more severely 'blitzed' than London. Around sixty per cent of its commercial quarter and twenty-five per cent of its residential housing were flattened.[51]

Whitehall recognition of Britain's responsibility for Burma's reconstruction costs helped the notion of shared suffering take hold.[52] But only to a point: with peace restored, the returning colonial government pushed aside Aung San's AFPFL, determined to curb the movement's influence within a Burma Executive Council established in October 1945 to assist the Governor in drawing up plans for self-government.[53] Divided over whether or not to participate in the Executive Council, the AFPFL split. In one sense the movement was akin to the Vietminh, a coalition bringing together Communist and non-Communist nationalists.[54] But the AFPFL's fault-lines were as much generational as ideological. Its younger activists were more hard-line. They saw the Executive Council scheme as a ruse to undermine an AFPFL provisional government set up on liberation much like its equivalent in North Vietnam.[55] Aung San was caught in the middle. Burma's Communists and other AFPFL militants accused him of being too conciliatory. But he knew that Governor Sir Reginald Dorman-Smith would crack down if the nationalists pushed for too much, too soon.[56]

By the time it dawned on Dorman-Smith's successor, Sir Hubert Rance, that Aung San offered the best hope of a negotiated settlement, Burma was teetering on the brink of civil war.[57] During late 1946 various strands of nationalist opinion, not to mention a well-armed Communist opposition, traded accusations about the opportunities lost to evict the British.[58] Government House negotiators had overplayed their hand, fatally undermining constructive nationalist partners in the process.[59] From September onwards police and civil service strikes in Rangoon brought the nightmare of unreliable security forces so dreaded by officials in India to life.[60] Police unionists loyal to the AFPFL ignored government pleas to put aside their politics in the interests of public security. As a result, the preservation of law and order became contingent on the AFPFL's internal divisions.[61]

By December, the Communists, fortified by Mao's advances in China, were urging millions of Burmese peasant cultivators not to pay taxes in anticipation of eventual land redistribution. It was at this low point that Attlee stepped in, inviting Aung San and his fellow Executive Council members to London for a fortnight's discussions beginning on 13 January 1947. The outcome was a Government White Paper endorsed by an AFPFL majority. It promised early elections and a quicker hand-over of responsibility for internal security.[62] Burma's independence was confirmed twelve months later. By this point Aung San and several of his Cabinet colleagues were dead. Their assassination pointed to the internecine warfare within AFPFL ranks and between the movement and its non-governmental rivals.[63] Army and police mutinies in August 1948 heralded outright civil war.[64] Yet, in Burma, as in India, British withdrawal preceded the escalation of political violence. What remained of British commercial and financial interests were relatively insignificant. No one in Whitehall suggested that Britain's exit from Burma had gone to plan, but most agreed that flight was accomplished just in time.[65]

Returning to the distinctions between British and French approaches to fight or flight, a third advantage enjoyed by the Labour government was its greater freedom of domestic political manoeuvre next to its counterparts in Paris. Labour's convincing election victory in July 1945 and the fact that imperial concerns counted for less among its rank-and-file than among Conservative voters were helpful in this regard. Paradoxically, the failure of earlier initiatives constituted a fourth advantage. Flawed experiments with provincial self-government in the late 1930s and Cripps' later attempts at negotiation only reinforced the case for leaving India quickly. Fifth and finally, hard-nosed British calculations of cost, whether expressed in terms of military commitment, commercial consequences, or Britain's overall deficit position weighed more heavily in the scales of decision-making than in equivalent French evaluations of Indochina's importance as an imperial asset. Rather than focusing on the critical fine details of the Radcliffe Commission's partition plan, Attlee's ministers and senior Treasury officials were more concerned that the independent governments of India and Pakistan would draw down their sterling balances. In the event, the two dilemmas proved inseparable. The appalling violence of partition sapped British capacity to challenge the right of either nation to gain access to their monetary reserves.[66]

For all the political mistakes and devastating social consequences of Britain's chaotic withdrawals from India and Burma, the end of the Raj made evacuation from other, smaller territories easier to contemplate. The largely peaceful decolonization from Ceylon (renamed Sri Lanka in 1972) stood out in this respect.[67] Aware that Ceylon's socially conservative Sinhalese elite were unlikely to press violently for independence, the Labour government devised stringent pre-conditions and a longer timetable for a transfer of power. The aim was to make plain that, despite the spate of withdrawals from South Asia, British capacity to secure favourable terms endured. D.S. Senanayake, elected prime minister three months before Ceylonese independence on 4 February 1948, proved an ideal partner, willing to maintain the base facilities and trade connections British negotiators craved.[68]

Predictably perhaps, after the horrors of Indian partition, Ceylon's more placid route to independence prompted effusive commentary in the British media. Tom Reid, Labour MP (Member of Parliament) for Swindon and a bitter opponent of Palestine partition, used an article in *The Listener* to suggest that Ceylon highlighted alternate possibilities:

> A few days ago Ceylon was a Crown Colony; today it is a British Dominion. A miracle has happened. Without the loss of a single life, without one act of violence, without a frown or secret reservation, the transfer of power from British to Ceylonese hands has taken place ... Perhaps as a Briton and one who has served Ceylon and eaten its salt, I am prejudiced, but I doubt if this miracle could have happened anywhere outside the British Empire. We had the power to retain our hold over the little island and its peoples, but gladly we told them to be free like ourselves. They know that we genuinely desire their prosperity and happiness, and that when and if necessary we will prove our goodwill by our acts. And the outside world, often bemused by propaganda about British imperialism, looks on in surprise and asks, "Can such things be?"[69]

Gushing prose, but it seems doubtful that the Ceylonese precedent reverberated much among nationalist groups in other dependent territories. A solitary instance of managed decolonization was immediately contradicted by Britain's utter failure to impose a Palestine settlement.

Flight or rout? Palestine

Several factors conspired to thwart British hopes of a compromise solution. The Second World War turned the gap between Arab and Jewish territorial demands into a chasm. Holocaust suffering underpinned new strains of militant Zionism and assured international sympathy for the plight of Jewish refugees in Europe, many of them languishing in resettlement camps in post-war Germany. Palestinian and Arab League representatives, still clinging to Britain's pre-war partition scheme as the basis for agreement, struggled to evoke similar concern for dispossessed Palestinians.[70] Nor had Palestinian political leadership recovered from British repression during the Arab uprising of 1936–9.[71] Recriminations over the Revolt's failure and divisions among its leading sponsors, the Husaynis and their Nashashibi clan rivals resurfaced once the Mufti of Jerusalem Haj Amin Al-Husayni and his cousin Jamal took charge of a reconstituted Arab Higher Committee (AHC—the putative Palestinian authority in the earlier rebellion) in the spring of 1946.[72] This raises a second issue.

In 1939 Neville Chamberlain's government planned to divide Palestine in conformity with British Middle East interests. Insofar as the League of Nations constituted a court of international opinion, it was, by then, moribund.[73] By 1945 that court was in session at the newly-established United Nations.[74] And a US administration favourable to the Zionist cause was its presiding judge. Thus the third consideration: Britain's imperative need for American financial and strategic backing to sustain domestic and imperial reconstruction. If this inclined some British decision-makers to give way over Palestine, the countervailing need for Arab acquiescence in Britain's Middle Eastern presence pointed in the opposite direction. Friction with Egypt over base rights in the Suez Canal Zone and the ambitions of Transjordan's King Abdullah for annexation of Palestinian land on the River Jordan's West Bank added extra layers of complication. As if to prove the point, Transjordan's increasing strategic importance to Britain as Palestine slipped away was confirmed by the conclusion of a partnership treaty in 1946.[75] Finally, and most importantly, the monetary and human costs of holding on in Palestine were rising fast to the dismay of the Treasury and the disgust of a British public fed up with the entire problem.

What was to be done? The solution favoured by Bevin's Foreign Office was a bi-national state whose autonomous cantons would preserve a broad two-to-one ratio between Arabs and Jews in a single independent country. The design was rational, possibly even fair, but hopelessly unrealistic. Other alternatives proved equally unpalatable. An enlarged Jewish state would antagonize the Arab partners whose cooperation was pivotal to Britain's regional strategy. The Arabs' continued endorsement of partition was, in turn, dismissed by Zionist groups, President Truman's administration, and, to British surprise, by the Soviet government as well.[76] Turning the problem over to the UN—Palestine was, after all, a Mandate territory formally established by the UN's forebear, the League of Nations—was also risky. On the one hand, Arab states in the General Assembly might steer the organization away from accepting a Jewish-dominated state. On the other hand, the dominant American presence in the United Nations Special Committee on Palestine (UNSCOP), the organization's key advisory group, suggested the opposite outcome. The pervasive anti-colonialism among UN members also militated against British intercession in favour of either solution.[77]

Bevin's personal unpopularity on America's East Coast also nullified Britain's influence. The Foreign Secretary's indiscreet suggestion that Truman called in August 1945 for 100,000 Jewish refugees to be admitted to Palestine because Americans did not want any more Jews arriving in New York was the first of many insensitive public relations 'gaffes' that punctuated British ministerial responses to decolonization. In fact, Truman's consistently pro-Zionist position, although later influenced by electoral considerations, was, in 1945, driven by pervasive sympathy in Washington for the plight of Jewish Displaced Persons in Germany.[78] That sympathy was amplified by sophisticated Zionist lobbying directed by the shadowy 'American League for a Free Palestine'. Its propaganda connected Zionist efforts to throw off the shackles of British rule with America's fight for independence in the 1770s. Backed by celebrity endorsements that included Eleanor Roosevelt, Bob Hope, and Frank Sinatra, the organization raised hundreds of thousands of dollars, some of which funded the Zionist military organization *Irgun Tzva'i Le'umi*.[79]

Behind the scenes, other Labour ministers were neither insensitive nor despairing. But they were arguing. The Cabinet's leading Zionist supporters, Hugh Dalton, Aneurin Bevan and Emanuel Shinwell, were outflanked by Bevin's Foreign Office and Britain's service chiefs for whom broader imperial strategy counted most. Attlee, unconvinced that Britain could hold the ring in the Middle East and sceptical of a workable Palestine compromise, gave Bevin his head nonetheless. The Prime Minister's stance encouraged the more timorous Colonial Secretary, Arthur Creech-Jones, responsible for the Mandate's collapsing internal administration, to follow in the Foreign Secretary's slipstream. Inside Parliament Richard Crossman, the young Labour Member for Coventry East ranked alongside Churchill as the most stinging back-bench critic of the government's Palestine policy. As a journalist, Crossman was among the first British personnel to enter Dachau after its liberation in April 1945. This emotional scarring that set him apart from numerous British politicians in accepting the moral imperative of a Jewish state refuge after the slaughter of the Holocaust. Crossman also served on an Anglo-American Committee of Inquiry appointed to make recommendations on Palestine over the winter of 1945–6. The committee's April 1946 endorsement of Truman's 100,000 proposal confirmed that British policy was unravelling under the weight of hostile external pressure.[80]

Continuing impasse over the next two years was signified by two decisions above all: the referral of the Palestine issue to the UN in February 1947 and the Cabinet's rejection of the resultant UNSCOP partition plan in September. Turning down the UNSCOP recommendations marked the decisive step towards withdrawal.[81] Their bi-national state option killed off in New York and calls for compromise drowned out within a Palestine sliding towards civil war, Attlee's government was set on the road to a unilateral pull-out in May 1948. Bevin consoled himself by recalling that Palestine's calamity was written in the contradictions of the Balfour Declaration and Britain's assumption of mandate obligations a generation earlier. Still, the government's decision to quit Palestine was not quite an admission of defeat. The hope was that, once the problem was placed in UN hands, the carving up of Palestine between a putative Israeli state and neighbouring Arab territories might yet be ruled out on the grounds that it would spark an Arab–Jewish war.[82] In this fatal misapprehension lay ultimate British humiliation and tragedy for the Palestinians.

As the drift to war in Palestine indicated, high policy wasn't everything. Worsening inter-communal friction, Britain's administrative and financial exhaustion, and public exasperation with Zionist terrorism counted for more. Jewish insurgent attacks and Arab counter-violence increased sharply over the winter of 1945–6.[83] Ignoring these clashes, trade unionists and other left-wingers within both the Palestinian community and the Yishuv (the Jewish community in Palestine) tried to maintain unity among low-paid public-sector workers. Their efforts to do so culminated in a general strike in April 1946. Unfortunately, this defiant show of cooperation across the ethno-religious divide was never repeated as violence took hold.[84] Jewish insurgent groups clashed over tactics and targets. But their disputes paled next to the internecine divisions among Palestinians. In some areas of the West Bank the Husaynis' grip over the AHC was bitterly contested, feeding support for King Abdullah's irredentist designs on Palestinian territory.[85] Hardening Jewish resolve and persistent British loathing for the AHC leadership destroyed any prospect of dialogue.[86]

British administrators, seeing only worsening anarchy around them, longed to leave. Their morale never recovered from the shock when, just after midday, on 22 July 1946 Menachem Begin's Zionist military organization, *Irgun Tzva'i Le'umi*, blew up an entire wing of Jerusalem's King David Hotel, home to the Mandate secretariat. Over ninety men and women were killed, many of them locally-hired Jewish office staff. The bombing prompted the removal of British personnel to fortified bunkers, so-called 'Bevingrads' that accentuated their isolation from surrounding communities.[87] Senior administrators and military personnel lost friends in the attack and their sense of outrage was palpable. High Commissioner Sir Alan Cunningham and Army commander Lieutenant-General Sir Evelyn Barker petitioned the Colonial Office to approve the imposition of a collective fine on Palestine's Jewish population. Rebuffed by Whitehall, Barker then took it upon himself to advise all British personnel to boycott Jewish businesses:

> No British soldier will have contact with any Jew, and duty contacts will be made as short as possible and will be limited to the duty concerned. I understand that these measures will create difficulties for the troops, but I am certain that if my reasons are explained to them they will understand their duty and will punish the Jews in the manner this race dislikes most; by hitting them in the pocket, which will demonstrate our disgust for them.[88]

Barker's incendiary comments, leaked to the US media by various Zionist groups, were echoed by Lieutenant-Colonel Richard Webb, commander of the 1st Battalion, Argyle and Sutherland Highlanders. His troops were at the sharpest end of Palestine counter-insurgency. Visibly inebriated, Webb lashed out before the international press corps after two of his men died in another bomb attack: 'These bloody Jews, we saved their skins in Alamein and other places and then they do this to us.'[89] Politically naive, these senior officers' words exposed the latent anti-Semitism among some British personnel as their thankless task got ever harder. Others, though, were determined to remain neutral. In private correspondence, many British personnel expressed sympathy for the ship-borne refugees that arrived in often appalling conditions in Haifa only to be sent packing to Cyprus or to internment elsewhere.[90] If most security-force personnel managed to contain their emotions, brutality there certainly was, encouraged by the hyper-masculine, heavy-

drinking culture of the Palestine Police. Violence was also a mark of alienation: few considered the Palestine mission worth pursuing.[91]

In the spring of 1947 another Zionist underground movement, *Lehi
b'Herut b'Yisrael* (Fighters for the Freedom of Israel), better known as the
Stern Gang, took the battle to London. An ex-servicemen's club near Tra-
falgar Square was bombed.[92] Not far away, a striking young woman with a
discernable French accent smuggled another device into the Colonial
Office, slipping past an indulgent security guard on the pretext that she
needed to visit the lavatory to mend a laddered stocking. She left behind a
large parcel bomb containing twenty-four sticks of French-manufactured

Figure 7. British recruitment poster for the Palestine Police aimed at National
Servicemen. The final phrase speaks volumes.

gelignite. Only a failed detonator saved the British Empire's bureaucratic heart from destruction on a scale comparable with the King David Hotel.[93]

Worse was to come. Two kidnapped British army sergeants, Cliff Martin and Mervyn Paice, were hanged on 30 July 1947 in retaliation for the capital sentences handed down to three *Irgun* members after a breakout from Acre jail. The ground beneath their feet was mined, preventing their comrades from cutting down the bodies. Unusually, press photographers were allowed to capture the scene, and images of the dead men appeared on British breakfast tables the next day. *Irgun's* execution of the soldiers, found guilty of 'illegal entry into the Hebrew Homeland', unleashed a wave of anti-Semitic attacks in British cities from Liverpool to London.[94] Mutual incomprehension deepened between aggrieved Britons to whom Jewish terrorism seemed inexcusable and wider international opinion for which the plight of Jewish refugees loomed larger.

As 1947 wore on, more mundane considerations deepened Britain's mood of impotent anger about the Palestine problem. Austere rationing, an incipient sterling crisis, an exceptionally cold winter, and, of course, impending withdrawal from India all dampened enthusiasm for another expensive commitment that conferred only insults and brickbats. Rationing was at its most stringent in 1947, and bore down heaviest on poor urban households and housewives who frequently gave part of their ration to other family members.[95] The sense of lingering post-war hardship was mirrored by disgruntlement in the services. Army and police frustrations with trying to hold the line between warring communities inside Palestine were matched by the Navy's grumbling about the miserable task of policing refugee traffic in the eastern Mediterranean.[96] Matters were not helped by indications that the French authorities not only revelled in Britain's Palestine embarrassments but were deliberately slack in monitoring Jewish refugee traffic through French ports.[97] A sign of growing British desperation as much as of its security service's derring-do, during 1947 MI6 began sabotaging freighters to impede the flow of Jewish refugees from French and Italian Mediterranean harbours.[98] Evidence also mounted of something even more serious: French weapons supply to Jewish fighters. In January 1948 Foreign Minister Bidault signed off a twenty-six-million-dollar arms deal with the *Haganah*, the prelude to larger and more sustained arms deliveries that resumed in May 1948.[99]

Meanwhile, it fell to insurgents across Palestine's sectarian divides to rein in the terrorist activities of their more radical splinter groups. A secret instruction issued by the *Irgun* executive on 10 February 1947 identified all

Britons in Palestine as legitimate targets. Aside from *Irgun* and *Lehi* shootings and car bombings aimed at British officials, fighters on both sides mounted larger attacks on Jewish settlements or Arab villages. By the start of 1948 the death toll was fast approaching 2,000.[100] If the British faced terrorist violence, the losers among Palestine's permanent residents faced ethnic cleansing.[101] This was not how the wider world saw things, however. In the weeks preceding the murder of the two sergeants, international press attention focused on the enforced return from Haifa to Marseilles of 4,493 refugees. Their evocatively-renamed ship *Exodus 1947* was boarded by a Royal Navy forces off Gaza on 18 July. Scuffles broke out, but the ship's crew were eventually overpowered and escorted into Haifa. Within hours the refugees were forcibly transferred to three British vessels for return to France.[102]

In private, British officials vented their fury at the French customs service for permitting so many people with obviously forged visa documents to set sail.[103] In public, hostile reaction in the United States and France multiplied when, in a move redolent of the death camps, some of the returning refugees were herded aboard trains and back to holding camps in Germany.[104] Leading French Socialists were especially critical. Interior Minister Edouard Depreux, former premier and concentration camp survivor Léon Blum, and Minister of Transport Jules Moch, whose Midi constituency included the port of Sète at which the refugees first boarded the *Exodus*, accused the British of 'closing, one after the other, all the avenues of hope to the Jews of Palestine and the Zionists across the world'.[105] The refugee crisis was now doing grave damage to Britain's international standing—and for what? The Cabinet's decision to cut Britain's losses in September 1947, an abnegation of imperial and ethical responsibility for the Palestinian imbroglio, certainly chimed with domestic opinion. By this point the prevailing sentiment at home was 'Why bother?'

Similar traces of British fatalism and self-righteousness resurfaced as Palestine descended into civil war following the final pull-out of Britain's forces in March 1948. Again, the immediate human consequences were staggering. Over 600,000 Palestinians left their homes, many of them forcibly expelled. Massacres accelerated the process.[106] Within a matter of months the ethnic composition of once predominantly Arab towns like Haifa and Jaffa was unrecognizable, a transformation even more complete than those in Punjabi cities like Lahore or Amritsar. Over 400 Palestinian villages were emptied, the Arab signifiers in their cultural landscape systematically effaced.[107] Controversy continues over the form and extent of this cleansing and the resultant plight of Palestinian refugees.[108] But the point to stress here is the speed with which Britain turned its back on partition's aftermath. Nor was it alone in doing so. In April 1946 the Anglo-American inquiry commission's estimate that 226,000 Jewish refugees remained in Europe, the majority in camps in Austria, Germany, and Italy, unleashed a storm of protest in the United States. By 1949 the fact that numbers of legally-certified Palestinian Arab refugees were climbing towards one million passed virtually unremarked.[109] Having struggled to find a way out of the Palestine morass, the Attlee government, not to mention the Truman administration, proved more dexterous in avoiding blame for what followed.

Diverse and hard to compare, the first cluster of British decolonization in the late 1940s drove home important lessons. First was that combating armed insurgency contained escalatory dynamics that were innately difficult to control. Military repression tended to increase in severity, in financial cost, and in its divisive consequences at home and abroad. Linked to this was a second conclusion. Insurgents capable of mobilizing international support—particularly American, Soviet or Arab—could cause diplomatic defeats to an extent unseen in pre-Cold War imperial politics.[110] This, in turn, drove home the third lesson: at the United Nations, in the international media and elsewhere, evolving ideas of self-determination, citizenship and individual human rights were sure to expose colonial rule to hostile scrutiny.[111] The fourth and final point was equally inescapable: schemes to relinquish colonial authority, no matter how sensible on paper, were liable to fail if inter-communal frictions boiled over into political violence. While it might be feasible to dress things up in terms of 'transfers of power', the longer decolonization was allowed to drag on, the deadlier and more ignominious it was likely to be.

More by accident than design, British bureaucracies, civil and military, colonial and metropolitan, absorbed these lessons, acquiring a working knowledge of accelerated withdrawals and the mechanics of evacuation and handover even in chaotic situations.[112] Equally significant, the limited economic, political, and strategic consequences for the home country, even of Indian decolonization, made crossing the Rubicon of colonial flight elsewhere immeasurably easier to contemplate.[113] Remarkable as it may seem in hindsight, the devastation left behind—partition violence in India, civil war then a wider Arab-Israeli conflict in the Middle East—had limited material consequences for Britain, helping the idea of low-cost 'escape' from empire take root in the public imagination and the British official mind. Besides all of this, much of Britain's imperial power remained intact. Reviewing Churchill's accusation that Attlee's government was liquidating the British Empire, in May 1947 René Massigli, the French Ambassador to London, reminded Georges Bidault, his ministerial boss, that other British imperial connections were being strengthened. Jordan and Libya were likely to fill the strategic gap left by Palestine. Malaya's dollar-earning exports compensated for losses in India. And the new language of Commonwealth partnership made British imperialism seem less domineering.[114] France had faced nothing comparable—as yet.[115]

The fight alternative: France returns to Indochina

The French fight for control of their Southeast Asian empire did not begin as armed resistance to decolonization but as a military re-conquest of territories already substantially decolonized.[116] At the end of the Second World War, France, although still a factor in Vietnamese politics, exerted less influence over events than other outsiders—Chinese, American, and British.[117] Japanese defeat and a terrible famine allowed the Vietminh to ride a wave of social discontent to power on 19 August 1945, a surge that was never entirely controlled by the Communists at the heart of the Vietminh coalition.[118] Faced with this groundswell of popular support for the Vietminh, the monarchical regimes previously installed in Vietnam, Laos, and Cambodia after Japan's March 1945 coup against Admiral Decoux's administration soon faltered. Emperor Bao Daï's Vietnamese regime was the first to go. Its internal security forces proved unwilling or unable to defend the incumbent regime against armed Vietminh organizers, noisy youth groups, and other inchoate rural protest movements determined to rid themselves of hated local officials. Bao Daï chose to ride the wave, not fight it. First he abdicated. Then he made the astonishing decision to join the Vietminh as an adviser to Ho Chi Minh. The end of Vietnam's centuries-long history of dynastic politics was revolutionary, but it was not an end in itself. The speed with which an array of local parties, religious sects, and village-level revolutionary 'committees of national salvation' (*hoi cuu quoc*) filled the resultant power vacuum revealed the weight of popular expectation that fundamental social transformation was imminent.[119]

Vietnam's revolution, capped by the establishment of a Democratic Republic Vietnam (DRV) in Hanoi on 2 September 1945, was also a race against time.[120] It was vital for the Vietminh's constituent groups to seize power before the occupation arrangements made by the Allied Powers at the Potsdam conference were implemented and before any French re-conquest began. These two imperatives precluded leisurely debate over the revolution's ideological direction or the distribution of power within the DRV's provisional government. Vietminh troops entered Hanoi on 26 August, five days after Ho Chi Minh had slipped into the city from his village HQ at Tan Trao, seventy miles distant. To the delight of a crowd several hundred-thousand strong, early in the afternoon of the 2nd Ho ascended a wooden stage decorated with Vietminh flags outside the Governor-General's palace. With flights of rhetorical fancy he announced the DRV's creation. The location became part of the celebration too. Hanoi's Ba Dinh Square was renamed to honour a heroic 'last stand' against French occupation forces in the 1880s. Ho's associate, Vo Nguyen Giap, the Vietminh's leading military thinker, described the scene in jubilant terms: 'Red brightens Hanoi. Flags, lights, flowers fill the sky as far as one can see. Red banners float above houses; the stores and small shops are closed... The population of the capital—the old, the young, men, and women—is in the streets. All have understood that they must participate in this first great gathering of their homeland.'[121] Ho's speech, though, avoided triumphal posturing. He borrowed instead from two definitive eighteenth-century pledges: the 1776 American Declaration of Independence and revolutionary France's 1791 Declaration of the Rights of Man and the Citizen.[122] Vietnam's people, he said, deserved freedom.

The ceremonial goodwill in Hanoi contrasted with the disorderliness elsewhere. ICP activists planned to relay Ho's independence speech to tens of thousands of their supporters gathered in the steamy heat of Saigon's Norodom Square. Wires were strung up between buildings and loudspeakers positioned above the crowd in anticipation of Ho's declaration. But the radio transmission failed. Exuberant, but disappointed, the crowd fastened instead on the French onlookers around the Central Post Office and the city's Catholic Cathedral. In a fatal misjudgement, these French spectators made their contempt for the Vietnamese celebrations clear. Shots were exchanged. By late afternoon scores of French settlers and interned military personnel had been intimidated, beaten, or stabbed. Saigon's French- and Chinese-owned commercial premises were looted in a settling of scores across Vietnam's racial divide.[123] Sectarian inter-Vietnamese violence exploded meanwhile. Communists battled it out with the pro-Chinese nationalists of the VNQDD and the Vietnam Revolutionary League (Dong

Minh Hoi). Religious sects fearful of marginalization in the new revolutionary
state joined the melee. The most murderous struggle occurred within Communist ranks in the Saigon hinterland where the ICP's Stalinist hard-liners
moved to eliminate their Trotskyite rivals.[124] This bloodletting pitched the
South into civil war.

Vietnam's quickening tempo of political violence also followed the
rhythm of inter-allied bargaining as Chinese and British imperial occupation forces prepared to take up positions north and south of the 16th
parallel, ostensibly to disarm and repatriate the Japanese garrison still in
Indochina.[125] Agreed at Potsdam, this neat north–south split ran rough-
shod over Vietnamese and French sensibilities.[126] But at least the French
found General Douglas Gracey's 20th Indian Army division—the occupation force dispatched to Saigon by Lord Mountbatten's South East Asia
Command—more or less convivial peace enforcers.[127] France's centrality
to the future of the Indochinese territories was always more evident in
southern Vietnam. Bustling Saigon counted more settlers, more banks, and
more commercial investments than elegant, but distant, Hanoi. Saigon was
also the launching pad for the French military re-conquest begun by
General Philippe Leclerc's expeditionary force in September 1945. For the
British, the April 1946 handover to the returning French administration in
Indochina could not come soon enough. Predicting that skirmishing
between French troops and militia units loyal to the DRV could easily
erupt into full-blown war, and aware that the French planned to seize
control in Hanoi and the nearby port city of Haiphong, Mountbatten was
unequivocal: it was imperative to put distance between French and British
policies in Southeast Asia.[128]

Above the 16th parallel, the impact of foreign occupation was even
harsher. Northern Vietnamese provinces still in the grip of acute foodstuff shortages and inflation could not cope with the presence of more
than 150,000 Chinese troops, many of whom arrived exhausted and hungry from months of fighting the Japanese. The Chinese contingents that
moved southwards from Yunnan under Generals Lu Han and Zhang
Fakui soon acquired a reputation for looting and ill-discipline. But it
was another large contingent from Kwangsi headed by General Hsiao
Wen that provoked the greatest alarm in ICP ranks. Their backing for the
VNQDD and the Dong Minh Hoi against Ho's Communists injected
extra venom into the rivalry between Vietnam's nationalist and Communist groups.[129]

By the time the Chinese forces departed in June 1946 much of northern Vietnam had been pillaged. Demonstrating remarkable forbearance, the Hanoi provisional government mollified the Chinese Nationalist occupiers whenever possible, anxious to conserve Vietminh militia units for the impending struggle against the French military contingents moving north-wards. Ho Chi Minh side-stepped discussion of contentious issues with Chinese headquarters staff in Hanoi, ensuring that they had plentiful sup-plies of opium each evening. Efforts to placate Chinese Nationalist suspi-cions culminated on 11 November 1945 when the ICP formally dissolved. Having failed to draw recruits among more nationalist-minded elites, ICP cadres resumed an underground existence in the guise of 'Marxist Study Groups'.[130]

As this manoeuvre implies, ending the Chinese occupation was the utmost priority for Ho's Communists; settlement with France was second-ary. That being said, their shared longing for the Chinese to leave was one of the few points of agreement between French and DRV negotiators over the winter of 1945.[131] The point requires qualification. The Chinese occupiers did not, after all, evict the DRV from power. And it was they who com-pelled the Hanoi regime to reach an interim agreement with their French adversaries in March 1946. Both sides kept the peace until the last Chinese troops were gone. The dangerous implication of this external pressure became apparent as soon as it was no longer applied. Desperate to consolidate his grip over the Hanoi coalition government and anxious to extend Vietminh influence further south, Ho clearly hoped that the March accords would endure, allowing the Communists to tighten their grip on northern Viet-nam without Chinese or French interference. He was soon disappointed.[132] Once Chinese forces began pulling out in June, French authorities in Sai-gon refused to honour the terms of the March agreements, an accord they dismissed as a mere expedient to get Nationalist China's soldiers out.

Anticipating that French military forces would return to Hanoi, over the summer of 1946 Vietminh officials mobilized thousands of their supporters to remove as many useful resources as possible from the city to the DRV's new improvised capital in the hills of Thai Nguyen to the north. Commu-nications equipment from the French broadcasting station; telephones, typewriters, paper, and pens from schools and government offices; vaccines and other medicines from the Hanoi Pasteur Institute: some 40,000 tons of goods and equipment were transported out of the city by an army of civil-ian couriers in anticipation of a violent French takeover. Within months over half of Hanoi's resident population would follow them, evacuating the city before the back-streets of its old quarter became the first battleground of the coming war.[133]

Franco–Vietminh talks limped on meanwhile, their focal point shifting to Fontainebleau near Paris. Ho Chi Minh endeared himself to the French public during this further round of negotiations in June–July 1946.A shrewd, if unlikely, self-publicist, Ho was gregarious and likeable. Finding himself with time to kill, he renewed acquaintances with old left-wing comrades in the French capital. Ho's empathetic qualities also shone through during ceremonial visits to convalescing French soldiers and newly-minted resistance memorials up and down the country. To the delight of onlooking cameramen, he chatted with fishermen on the Biarritz waterfront, comparing their work clothes with his own. Hard as it was to believe that the charming, stick-thin Vietnamese would soon become public enemy number 1, there were clues. Back in Hanoi the DRV's Defence Ministry was working frantically to recruit, organize and equip the new Vietnamese 'national armed forces' whose expansion Ho had approved in May.[134] Meanwhile, in Paris the contrast between Ho's Gandhi-like unpretentiousness and Prime Minister Georges Bidault's snobbish, sometimes drunken, awkwardness came into sharp relief when the two men were seated together during the capital's 1946 Bastille Day festivities. The incongruity of Ho's polite applause for the French army march-past was overshadowed by Bidault's petulant insistence that Ho's chair be set back a few inches from his own.[135] This spat, not the easy informality of Ho's day-to-day encounters with the French public, indicated how negotiations were going.

Behind the scenes, there was growing anxiety in Ho's negotiating team. The Vietminh emerged triumphant from January 1946 elections to the DRV National Assembly. But the Kwangsi Generals' endorsement of pro-Chinese nationalist groups, combined with bitter arguments over how to handle the French, precipitated a ministerial shake-up in Hanoi. Only when the Communists took a firmer grip within a multi-party 'Government of Resistance and National Reconstruction' on 2 March, did Ho feel secure enough to renew talks with French envoy Jean Sainteny in Vietnam or with French Ministers in Paris.[136]

Even though Communists now controlled the key DRV portfolios, Ho worried about challenges from Party rivals and was justifiably suspicious of his nationalist coalition partners.[137] Still, on the central question of freedom for Vietnam he left no room for doubt. In a February 1946 conversation with General Raoul Salan, who would eventually assume command of French military operations in Indochina and, later, Algeria, Ho warned of the dreadful consequences of a French takeover: 'blood will flow and it will be terrible. I do not want it to happen, but French men and women will be killed. I will not be able to hold back the masses...It is simply the reaction of people who do not want to be enslaved.'[138]

A dire prediction indeed, and yet relations between the Vietminh leadership and French negotiators in Paris and Saigon might have been sustained even in the midst of worsening local conflict, much as they were in the case of India. Vietnam's Communists, after all, went further than did India's Congress movement in offering to keep their country inside an imperial formation as an 'associated state'. And Indochina was already a federation in which the requirements of its other constituent polities—Cambodia, Laos, and, above all, the southern Vietnamese colony of Cochin-China (Nam Bo) could be used as counter-weights to any extreme demands emanating from Hanoi.

So the dialogue intermittently pursued in France and Vietnam over long months in 1946 was never futile. Nor was it reducible to a circle that could never be squared, which pitted French claims for imperial suzerainty against Vietnamese demands for independence. The discussions were more flexible, more prone to external influence than such a characterization allows. Leading actors on both sides might have entered the discussions with seemingly irreconcilable 'bottom lines', but they also shied away from armed conflict. Not quite inevitable, war was always probable unless two pre-conditions were met. First was that the advocates of peace in Paris and Hanoi should retain the upper hand, not only in general but in the minutiae of day-to-day decision-making. Second was that both sides be genuinely prepared to give ground over the timing, nature, and extent of eventual Vietnamese self-rule within some sort of wider French imperial framework. To some, this might appear ridiculous: hopelessly unrealistic, at odds with the irresistible tide of decolonization, and at variance with the Marxist determinism of the ICP, the real power within the DRV regime. The bitter irony is that it was the first and not the second pre-condition that triggered the outbreak of hostilities.

It was not the rivalry between Vietnamese nationalist groups but persistent disunity among the French negotiators that set Vietnam on the path to war. By June 1946 French disagreements over the wisdom of compromise escalated into something more: first the arrogation, then the abuse of power by the Saigon high commission where the advocates of military confrontation reigned supreme. None more so than the High Commissioner himself: Georges Thierry d'Argenlieu. A former Carmelite monk who rose to the rank of Free French Admiral, d'Argenlieu spent most of the war governing the nickel-rich former penal colony of New Caledonia. There, his sanctimonious obduracy infuriated virtually everyone, US officials above all.[139] Saigon's embattled settlers found their champion in d'Argenlieu, but it was his Cabinet team headed by federal commissioner of political affairs Léon Pignon and Jean-Étienne Valluy, Leclerc's successor as expeditionary force commander, that turned d'Argenlieu's mulish stubbornness into a strategy of dissent.[140] Consistently pursued with the connivance of sympathetic Paris bureaucrats and politicians (notably, the Christian Democrats in government and de Gaulle's parliamentary supporters outside it), this diplomatic sabotage was criminally insubordinate, ranking among the most egregious of the Vietnam conflict's many 'tragedies'.[141]

On 1 June 1946 d'Argenlieu's team engineered the creation of the 'Autonomous Republic of Cochin-China', pushing the limits of the tacit support the High Commission enjoyed among MRP ministers and Gaullists. Only four days later did the government's inner cabinet, the awkwardly-named Inter-Ministerial Committee on Indochina, or COMININDO, accord its seal of approval to the initiative. Intended as a reliable client regime, the truncated South Vietnamese Republic was led by the fervently anti-Communist Dr Nguyen Van Thinh. His first objective was to supplant the pre-existing, and Vietminh-dominated, Saigon Committee of the South.[142] D'Argenlieu, meanwhile, intended to use the new Republic of Cochin-China as the wedge to drive through a wider reorganization of the Indochina Federation. His plan was to sap the Hanoi government's overweening influence over Vietnam as a whole. Having got away with it so far, d'Argenlieu and Pignon soon took their audacity further, moving to seize control of the entire negotiation process. On 25 July the high commissioner announced a conference at the hill station resort of Dalat with hand-picked representatives from areas of Vietnam under French administrative control to determine Indochina's future structure.[143] This Dalat conference, ostensibly the follow-up to an earlier meeting in April, was transparently designed to torpedo the parallel Franco-Vietnamese negotiations taking place at Fontainebleau.

The manoeuvre worked. Chief Vietminh negotiator Pham Van Dong stormed out of the Fontainebleau talks in protest.[144] Ho Chi Minh almost followed him. Invited to the Paris apartment of the socialist Minister for

Overseas France Marius Moutet for dinner on 14 September, the Vietminh leader eventually agreed to resume the Fontainebleau exchanges: but not until 1947. It was stalemate. The cardinal Vietminh goal of Vietnamese unification was undermined by the Bidault government's endorsement of the openly separatist regime in Cochin China. Another prescient warning from Ho: that taking this step was akin to Germany's amputation of Alsace-Lorraine from France in 1871, went unheeded. On 19 December 1946 the DRV military supremo Vo Nguyen Giap issued the decisive order for Vietminh cadres in Hanoi to begin shooting. Formally at least, the Vietminh thus began the first Indochina War.[145] But by this point the High Commission had shut down any alternatives.

How seriously should we take these other 'might-have-been' outcomes? Some of the barriers to a flight solution were institutional, and political. Critical here were the changing complexion of French government coalitions in 1946 and the resultant configuration of the all-important Inter-Ministerial Committee on Indochina, a decision-making forum swayed by MRP hardliners. Strategic presumptions also played their part. French policy-makers' insistence that speed was of the essence in overthrowing the Hanoi regime militarily was matched by Vietminh anxiety to strike before the French expeditionary force consolidated its presence in northern Vietnam. But the irresponsibility of d'Argenlieu and his backers in the COMININDO did most damage. The outbreak of the Franco-Vietnamese war in December 1946 was less a clash of ideologies than the product of missed opportunities, miscommunications, and misapprehensions. It was not that negotiations failed to go to plan; after all, few do. It was more that well-crafted solutions were unpicked as the war's advocates took control.

On 4 January 1947 Léon Pignon, still d'Argenlieu's fixer as federal commissioner in Saigon, insisted to his superiors in Paris that the fighting in Hanoi confirmed that Ho Chi Minh headed a government bent on conflict. Any resumption of talks with the current Vietminh leadership should be ruled out. Pignon was flatly contradicted two days later by Claude de Boisanger, head of the Foreign Ministry's Asia division. He read the start of the war quite differently: as evidence of the depth of popular Vietnamese nationalism and as a wake-up call to invest renewed effort in a negotiated solution before it was too late. Unfortunately, these divergent policy options were presented just as Léon Blum's caretaker administration was about to be replaced by Paul Ramadier's new socialist-led coalition.[146] With the diplomatic sand draining away, news of further skirmishes between French and Vietminh forces solidified backing for the war in Paris and Hanoi.

Epitaph: Britain, France, and the early tests of fight or flight

In 1946 the British government appointed former Egyptian High Commissioner Sir Miles Lampson, by then Lord Killearn, to a new, impressively-named post: Special Commissioner for South East Asia. With Britain soon to leave the Indian subcontinent, its remaining, more easterly territories acquired greater economic, strategic, and symbolic importance; hence, Killearn's new job.[147] Killearn's remit was to ensure that diplomatic initiatives, colonial reforms, and economic priorities were not pursued piecemeal throughout the region. His task was to weld diffuse policies into more than the sum of their parts—a coherent package of viable imperial policy East of Suez.[148] A grand ambition for a grand old imperialist; almost, but not quite: Killearn was replaced after two years in the job by a younger, more dynamic figure, Malcolm MacDonald, son of Labour's first Prime Minister. He combined the Commissioner role with that of Malayan Governor. The energetic MacDonald seemed to be everywhere, roving between negotiations, ceremonial functions, and informal get-togethers between officials and loyalist headmen in his trademark short sleeves and bowtie.[149] Here were the alleged benefits of talking not fighting personified, the affable MacDonald pointing the way to an era of partnership between Britain and its remaining Asian dependencies.

The Special Commissioner's office, a Singapore-based imperial bureaucracy in miniature, was the closest approximation to the far larger federal administration of French Indochina in Saigon, still the colonial capital of Cochin-China. The parallel, on closer inspection, does not withstand scrutiny. The Special Commissioner's office lacked executive powers. Whatever regional influence it enjoyed derived from the persuasive skills of its titular head. His staff, although capable were few. Indochina's federal administration, housed in a Governor-general's palace of classic late nineteenth-century French design, was very different, always the hub of France's imperial power in its Southeast Asian territories. Indeed, as France fought to re-establish colonial control from the south to the north of Vietnam in 1945–6, Saigon's senior officials emerged as more than a colonial bureaucracy. They became a clique planning for war. Little wonder that after France and Britain signed their first peacetime alliance of the twentieth century—the Treaty of Dunkirk—on 4 March 1947, French officials in Saigon tried to enlist

Britain's support for their efforts to defeat the Vietminh. The British response was, understandably, cautious. The Foreign Office offered only informal exchanges between the authorities in Malaya and Indochina, some swapping of intelligence, and the occasional *tour d'horizon* between Killearn and d'Argenlieu.[150]

Having just extricated British Indian occupation forces from southern Vietnam, there was no appetite for any kind of strategic partnership to fight anti-colonial insurgencies throughout the region. Earlier, on 26 January 1947, barely a month into their military operations against Ho Chi Minh's forces, French liaison officers in Singapore petitioned Killearn for large quantities of British arms and ammunition. He was reluctant to comply, telling his Foreign Office masters that overt material support for the French war in Vietnam 'will land us in extremely deep waters'. British war materiel previously sent to assist ill-fated Dutch military actions in their vast colony of Indonesia as well as French military over-flights of India and Burma were painful sources of political embarrassment. Why risk more Asiatic opprobrium when, as one Foreign Office specialist commented, 'the future is with the native peoples throughout the Far East'? The Admiralty and the War Office agreed; it was unwise to waste British equipment on dubious colonial military ventures that only complicated matters in Britain's turbulent Asian empire. Only Foreign Secretary Bevin demurred. What about the imminent Treaty? What about needs of a friend, an ally, and a fellow colonial power facing 'attacks organized by a native leader (Ho) who is a Moscow-trained Communist'? Not for the first time, Attlee stepped in with a compromise solution: Britain could supply military aid to mainland France. Where it went thereafter need not be advertised. Cynical perhaps, but Attlee viewed indirect assistance for the war in Indochina as a cheap way to mend imperial fences battered by an earlier clash over fight or flight: Britain's enforcement of French withdrawal from Syria. Furthermore, the French were sure to get their hardware somehow.[151]

1947 was a watershed year insofar as France turned definitively towards the pursuit of fight strategies to retain its grip over dissentient colonial territory. Centre-left tripartism finally collapsed in the spring. Nine months of bitter confrontation between Communists and their opponents—in parliament, in industrial relations, and on the streets—dominated French politics from March to December. Worsening ideological polarization poisoned French political culture, making reasoned discussion of colonial abuses impossible.[152] Communist Party refusal to vote military credits for the Indochina War in early

March catalysed the Ramadier government's decision to break with them on 5 May. A combination of factors made the Indochina conflict an acutely divisive issue in French politics. One was the increasing militancy of the PCF rank-and-file, epitomized by Communist dockworkers' refusal to load war supplies destined for Vietnam. Another was the closer identification of the centre-right 'Third Force' parties (especially the MRP and the Radicals) with support for outright military victory.

But 'Third Force' politicians acted in the knowledge that the general public, still quiescent about the deepening crisis in Indochina, would only tolerate so much. This ruled out the dispatch of young national servicemen to a colonial war, but it also left room for an escalation of the expeditionary force's campaign. There were other reasons for French public acquiescence in the war. For one thing, within eighteen months of the start of hostilities, France claimed to be fighting for something more laudable than the re-imposition of colonial authority. For another, there was at least a plan to install a new Vietnamese leadership, albeit one that lacked significant popular backing. By December 1947 Robert Schuman's government, dominated like most 'Third Force' administrations by the MRP and the Radical Party, seemed wedded to the idea of restoring Bao Daï, former Emperor of Annam, as ruler of a unified Vietnam. In Southeast Asia the new French republic vested its hopes of colonial salvation in a dissolute monarch.

Did this mark a new beginning, in tune with the French Union aspirations that the Vietnamese territories should become an autonomous 'associated state' of France? Tempting as it is to scream 'No', the investment in Bao Daï allowed successive Third Force governments to claim that their war effort was endorsed by a Vietnamese national government supportive of the French Union. Above all, the success of French policy was now harnessed to Bao Daï's ability to garner Vietnamese support. To do this, his supporters had to prove their effectiveness as a bulwark against Communism by building a coalition from diverse nationalist parties and religious sects. They also had to ensure that economic conditions outside Vietminh-controlled areas compared favourably with those inside. The Bao Daï solution failed on both counts. In microcosm it pointed up the inherent inadequacies of French Union reformism as a whole: externally imposed, locally unpopular, and an untenable halfway house between colonial control and national—in this case, Vietnamese—independence.

In fact, from the beginning of the first Indochina war to its dramatic end, French governments never wholeheartedly pursued any of the objectives

for which France was supposedly fighting. The initial war of colonial re-
conquest, presumed at first to be integral to the reassertion of French international power, was all but abandoned by the end of 1947. There was an
inherent contradiction thereafter between a French military campaign to
guarantee the survival of a loyal Vietnamese state and the fact that the war
itself sapped residual Vietnamese loyalty to any non-Vietminh alternative.
Putting aside Bao Daï's shortcomings as playboy turned national leader and
the instability of Franco-Vietnamese government in Saigon, no southern
Vietnamese regime could compete with the Vietminh for popular legitimacy. And, as we shall see in the next chapter, after Mao's victory in China
in October 1949 and the massive increase in Vietminh military potential
that followed, the French strategic position sped downhill.

One of the few consolations for the French as the Indochina War went
from bad to worse was that they acquired a stronger partner in resisting
decolonization from the Far East. By the time the Dutch finally relinquished
Indonesia in 1949, the British were militarily committed in nearby Malaya.
Asked by Attlee's Cabinet the previous September to consider transferring
army battalions from the Malayan Peninsula to help evacuate British nation-
als from worsening civil disorder in Rangoon, the British service chiefs
scotched the idea. Newly-independent Burma was no longer a British strategic priority whereas Malaya most emphatically was.[153] There, too, fighting
had broken out between Communists and their opponents. But conserving
Britain's interests was handled very differently in Southeast Asia. Following
the spate of withdrawals from the Indian subcontinent, fight replaced flight
as the guiding principle of decision-making.

5

Troubled Roads: War and Revolution in Southeast Asia, 1948–57

On May Day 1948 British authorities banned two protest marches on opposite sides of the globe. Oswald Mosley's Union Movement, successor to his pre-war British Union of Fascists, wanted to parade through the East End of London, aiming to capitalize on the anti-Semitic feelings stirred by recent events in Palestine. Fearing a 1930s-style 'battle of Cable Street', the Labour Home Secretary James Chuter Ede said no.[1] Seven thousand miles away the government of Malaya prohibited a march by striking Singapore dockworkers, many of them Chinese Communist sympathizers.[2] Empire problems, it seemed, were everywhere.

Two months later Palestine again came to mind when the Colonial Office cast around for a robust and experienced imperial official to handle the rebellion that had just erupted in Malaya. Sir Henry Gurney, the man chosen to take over as Malaya's High Commissioner, had served as Chief Secretary in Jerusalem, where he had tried to conserve the administrative fabric of British rule as the Mandate fell apart. This was dangerous work, but it proved less perilous than Gurney's new post. On 6 October 1951, three years to the day after beginning his job in Malaya, Gurney's motorcade approached Fraser's Hill, an idyllic hill station sixty-five miles north of Kuala Lumpur. Gunmen of the pro-Communist Malayan Races' Liberation Army (MLRA) raked the High Commissioner's car with machine-gun fire. His chauffeur was hit and, as Gurney clambered out, he was immediately shot dead.[3]

Gurney's assassination has been viewed as a tipping point in the Malayan 'Emergency'. This was an undeclared war between the British colonial authorities, their Malay allies, and a small army of Communist guerrillas largely composed of ethnic-Chinese immigrants. It began with a spate of

twenty-six murders in the last fortnight of June 1948 in which British managers of isolated rubber plantations were primary targets.[4] Communist
rebels, so the conventional story goes, wrought havoc in the Emergency's
first three years, their reign of terror capped by the High Commissioner's
murder. Yet, soon afterwards, fundamental changes in British counter-
insurgency and new faces at the top of Malaya's colonial administration
transformed the conflict, heralding eventual British victory and a remarkably smooth transition to independence on 31 August 1957. Few Malaya
specialists accept this version of events, with its neat chronological watershed and unabashedly rosy outcome.[5] The underlying narrative of fight
successfully supplanted by flight is not so straightforward.

The breakdown of order in Malaya was not some spontaneous calamity,
but was closely related to the acrimonious collapse of the Malayan Union
in late January 1948. Diluting the *de facto* supremacy of ethnic Malays by
opening up political space and economic opportunity for Chinese and
Indian immigrants, the Malayan Union promised a more equitable future
for a multi-racial society that Britain would steer towards self-government.[6]
In practice, stripping sovereign powers from local Sultans and promoting
the rights of non-Malay residents galvanized a more self-consciously Malay
nationalism. Its tangible expression was a powerful new political grouping,
the United Malays National Organization (UMNO). Avowedly reformist,
the Malayan Union was profoundly imperialist in its presumption that
Malaya remained a blank slate whose cultural identity and socio-ethnic
composition could be redrawn at will.[7] And yet, pause for a moment at Map
6. As the multiple internal frontiers of peninsular Malaya's component states
confirm, colonial Malaya was superimposed onto more long-standing structures of Malayan regional and political attachment.

For the ethnic Malays, the affront to their communal authenticity as
'true' Malayans was exacerbated by the imperious manner in which British
officials, especially 'Special Representative' Sir Harold MacMichael, imposed
the new constitution over the heads of the Sultanates and other local representatives.[8] The post-war influx of technocratic administrators, no matter
how well intentioned, compounded the sense of old ways trampled down.[9]
Historian Tony Stockwell gets to the heart of it: 'By the Malayan Union the
British not only were assured of full power, but also—and here lies the new
factor in Anglo-Malay relations—were seen to wield this power; the new
constitution was a gross misunderstanding of the importance for the Malays
of the illusion of authority.'[10] With the Malayan Union project in ruins,

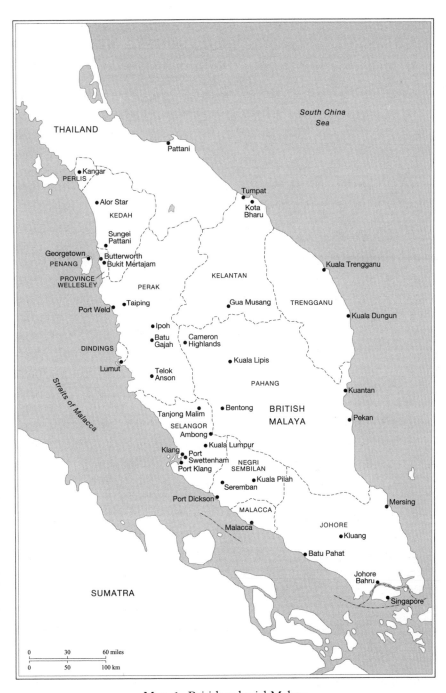

Map 6. British colonial Malaya.

High Commission staff, Malaya's political parties and civil society groups, as well as British business interests were still adjusting to the reversion to a federal system of government as the Emergency began.[11]

It was also far from clear to British officials in Malaya or London when violence broke out that the Malayan Communist Party (MCP) was directing it.[12] Before the Emergency developed as a full-blown armed rebellion, strikes and other workplace protests were the favoured battleground between Malaya's Communists, the colony's large industrial workforce, and the colonial authorities.[13] Between 1945 and early 1947, the Malayan Security Service basked in the knowledge that the MCP's Secretary-General Lai Tek could be relied upon to tell them what Malaya's Communists were planning; he was, after all, a British double-agent in their pay. But verifiable intelligence about MCP intentions dried up when Lai Tek was replaced by a more orthodox Stalinist, Chin Peng, in March 1947.[14] Beyond the reach of police and civil affairs officers in Malaya's jungle interior, Chin Peng reactivated the *Min Yuen*, the networks of rural support, predominantly among the ethnic Chinese labourers who had sustained the Communist resistance to wartime Japanese occupation.[15] Gurney's predecessor, High Commissioner Sir Edward Gent, was slow to react. Identified with the failed Malayan Union experiment, his job was on the line. Having lost the confidence of Colonial Secretary Creech-Jones and Malcolm MacDonald, still the Commissioner-General for Southeast Asia, Gent was more anxious to mend fences with the UMNO than to pay heed to Communist machinations.[16] This mistake ended his career. Acrimony over Malaya's constitutional structure (primarily a dispute over the ethnic hierarchies within it) overshadowed mounting evidence of Communist influence spreading throughout Southeast Asia.[17] In this increasingly toxic environment no one showed much willingness to compromise before the shooting started; still less so afterwards.[18]

Even so, the first Communist attacks on British targets in Malaya in June 1948, whether systematically planned or not, shocked colonial reformers in Britain just as the earlier outbreak of fighting in Hanoi had done in Paris. Although Malaya's Communists never achieved the levels of mass mobilization of their ideological brethren in Vietnam, the political effects of their rebellion were, for a while at least, the same.[19] Escalating violence silenced those who favoured dialogue over force, flight over fight. Assaults on rural police stations, grenade attacks on commercial premises, assassinations of Chinese businessmen, sabotage of railway lines, and systematic destruction of thousands of rubber trees on large, British-owned estates disrupted the colonial economy. Demands for a decisive response increased. Indeed, the security forces, heavily criticized at the time for knowing so little about Malaya's Chinese communities, operated with minimal restraint in the Emergency's opening stages.[20] This was part of a deliberate policy of counter-terror, devised by the Malayan Security Service (MSS), implemented by Army and police units, and designed to nip the rebellion in the bud. In the absence of reliable intelligence from members of rural Chinese communities who were terrified of Communist retribution if they were seen to be co-operating with the British, the security forces turned to collective punishment

Figure 8. Counter-insurgency in action in this July 1948 interrogation during the early days of the Malayan Emergency. Note the Gurkha soldier with characteristic *kukri* conducting the search of the labourers' dwelling.

instead.[21] The closest comparison was with British suppression of the Arab Revolt in Palestine before 1939. There, as in Malaya ten years later, mass arrests, deportations, the destruction of suspects' property, and arbitrary killing defied ethical or legal restriction.[22]

The grim consequences of fighting terrorism with terror were illustrated when soldiers of the Scots Guards shot dead twenty-four alleged suspects in December 1948. The massacre occurred in Batang Kali, a tiny settlement in Selangor inhabited by Chinese rubber tappers. Initially celebrated as a successful fire-fight against Communist bandits, but later the subject of a government investigation, Batang Kali was the largest single killing of unarmed detainees.[23] The numbers involved in other incidents may have been smaller, but the shooting of individuals and groups of alleged escapers became sufficiently commonplace to suggest deliberate tactics of summary execution.[24] There was fierce repression in other sectors, too. During the three years between the Emergency's outbreak in June 1948 and Gurney's death in October 1951, British suppression of the Communist-controlled Pan-Malayan Federation of Trade Unions (PMFTU), the execution of the Federation's former president S. A. Ganapathy, and official sponsorship of a neutered and non-political Malayan Trade Union Congress revealed that even a Labour government would swing an iron fist against Communist sedition.[25]

Bevin's Foreign Office, not surprisingly, was keen to show that there was more to British policy in Southeast Asia than brute force. But, by the time the Foreign Secretary had floated a scheme for closer economic cooperation and increased foodstuff production among Southeast Asia's non-Communist states in January 1950, the Malayan situation was spiralling out of control.[26] What became known as the Colombo Plan, a scheme backed by Anglo-American investment and technical expertise, pointed to a post-colonial future of regional partnership in which former colonial masters became mentors.[27] In the short term, however, dreams of harmonious times ahead collided with a harsher reality: the forcible relocation of rural communities to cordoned encampments administered under martial law, a practice defended by reference to a growing Communist threat.

Was this justified? Throughout the Malayan Emergency the Foreign Office Information Research Department, which directed the production of British overseas propaganda under the auspices of MI6, advised British Ministers and local officials about how to depict their Communist opponents.[28] The aim was to delegitimize them. In the conflict's early stages, insurgents were labelled 'bandits', a pejorative term replete with criminal associations but pleasingly devoid of serious political intent.[29] But killing bandits might not persuade Washington that Britain was 'doing its bit' in fighting the Asian Cold War. So the adjective 'Communist' was added and the word 'terrorist' substituted for bandit: hence the epithet 'CTs'.[30] Alarm over impending Communist victory in China and heightened pressure on the British colony of Hong Kong strengthened this Cold War inflexion in British official thinking.[31] Perhaps most important was rigid adherence to the concept of colonial 'Emergency', not anti-colonial war. Familiar in numerous decolonization conflicts, careful avoidance of any mention of war was more than a rhetorical gambit. It was also good politics. It underplayed the significance of the conflict to home and imperial audiences; it discouraged international scrutiny of what remained an ostensibly 'internal' affair; it denied opponents the rights under international law attaching to 'enemy combatants' or 'prisoners of war'; and it ensured that businesses which suffered commercial losses because of the violence could file ordinary insurance claims, something that most insurers precluded once 'war' was declared.[32]

    This brings us to the question of Gurney's successor and the ensuing change in the British approach. A civil–military supremo, who combined the responsibilities of Governor and Director of Military Operations, from his arrival in February 1952 General Sir Gerald Templer injected greater urgency into Malayan policy.[33] Endorsed by the new Conservative government's Colonial Secretary Oliver Lyttelton, Templer's role was not so much to redraw counter-insurgency plans as to reinvigorate them.[34] This meant convincing the security forces, the Malayan Civil Service, and, above all, the rural populations worst affected by the violence that Communist attacks would be stopped. Constantly touring administrative districts, resettlement camps, and contested villages, Templer strove to inspire confidence in the certainty of British victory and a rapid transition to Malayan self-rule. Intolerant of any 'under-performance' by his subordinates, Templer inspired trust, but not affection. Trust in government pledges to cut the links between the MRLA and their rural suppliers; trust that living conditions within resettlement camps would improve; trust that there could only be one outcome to the Emergency. None of this pointed to particularly original thinking or any fundamental change in a long-term strategy predicated on isolating Communist guerrillas from their often reluctant *Min Yuen* backers among the Chinese immigrant workforces, on plantations, in tin mines, and in agriculture.[35] In this respect Templer's impact as a strategist has been overblown. But, as energizing figures determined to get quick results, Templer and his tireless deputy Sir David MacGillivray changed the psychological climate of administrative action from sullen desperation to almost arrogant self-confidence.

Could single individuals make such a difference? The question divides 'Emergency' specialists.[36] Some suggest that the conflict's tide was already turning in Britain's favour, thanks to the population resettlement programme begun by General Sir Harold Briggs, the man appointed 'director of anti-bandit operations' in March 1950.[37] A model for subsequent counter-insurgency operations from Algeria in the late 1950s to Vietnam in the mid 1960s, the Briggs Plan's objective was to cut the umbilical cord between the *Min Yuen* and MRLA fighters in the Malayan jungle by forcibly relocating Chinese squatters and estate labourers to designated camps. Later rebranded as 'New Villages', these camps were closely monitored by the security forces. Thousands of additional police and Malay Home Guard were recruited, providing extra security, albeit at the cost of freedom of movement for the civilian population in the 'resettlement areas'.[38] By the end of 1951 over 600,000 were forcibly confined within these zones.[39] Intelligence officers working with Chinese-language translators checked the identities, intentions, and movements of people, money, and goods. Suspects were interrogated, imprisoned, or repatriated to China. Anyone found passing information, food, or other supplies to 'CTs' was liable to the death penalty, an indication both of the Draconian emergency restrictions that under-pinned security force actions and of the ruthlessness with which the New Villages programme was enforced.[40] It was colonial population control on a grand, coercive scale. Relocating communities and screening camp residents had slow, cumulative effects, appealing not to hearts but to minds.[41]

Briggs was always candid in this regard, noting that 'in a campaign such as this, where pitched battles between organised armies do not occur . . . success depends on the morale of and the help given by the population and the breaking of Communist morale and organisation'. Commenting on the progress achieved by June 1951, he continued, 'While it cannot yet be said that the Chinese are no longer "sitting on the fence", our policy of committing them to our side by getting them to join our Home Guard organisation, which they are doing in very great numbers, is bearing good fruit.'[42] The statistics tended to confirm Briggs' assessment. The MRLA could muster perhaps 8,000 fighters. Yet, by the end of 1952, the 40,000 or so military personnel in Malaya were outnumbered by 67,000 Malayan Police and some 300,000 Home Guard members. With a population of barely six million, Malaya had become the most highly-militarized colony in the British Empire.[43]

The Briggs Plan's thoroughness, while bitterly resented, persuaded many Chinese that the MRLA could not win. Formulated before Templer's arrival, he reaped its political harvest.[44] The combination of his authoritarian powers, his close attention to sources of intelligence, and the groundwork done by his predecessors under the Briggs Plan achieved success by extending the scope of government intervention in Chinese rural affairs. In line with Templer's vigorous activism, information-gathering was stepped up; anti-insurgent propaganda intensified.[45] The tempo of security force operations increased and, with it, the numbers of insurgents killed. A greater emphasis on rewarding 'Surrendered Enemy Personnel' with amnesty and financial recompense for disgorging weapons or information also achieved results. Former MCP members were enlisted to write imploring articles, replete with Marxist dogma, for the government's *Freedom News*, a propagandist newspaper ingeniously produced on a captured MCP printing press.[46] For all that, Templer was not the key to the subsequent transition from fight to flight. The safer interpretational ground lies in longer-term trends and other impersonal factors that helped decolonization succeed. Among these, four stand out.

First is the MCP's inability to build a mass following across Malaya's communitarian and socio-economic divides. Historian Karl Hack summarizes the position: 'Locally, Malaya's communal patterns ensured neutrality or support for the government from Malays. Within the "Chinese community", many of the commercially orientated and pro-KMT [Chinese Nationalist] elements were hostile to communism, even if a significant number paid communist "subscriptions" when the MRLA was strong in their area.' A silent majority gravitated towards the moderate Malayan Chinese Association to defend their communal identity, a development that the colonial authorities encouraged.[47] Unable to surmount these obstacles, the Party, its MRLA armed wing, and its civilian networks of support remained overwhelmingly poor Chinese in composition.[48] The stringent population control at the heart of Harold Briggs' resettlement plan, so critical to Templer's counter-insurgency drive, delivered a painful blow to the MRLA. But it was not quite the killer punch that protagonists of British counter-insurgency in Malaya have claimed it to be. Guerrilla units were already struggling to provision themselves or to draw new recruits. They could never boast the urban support networks that the Vietminh enjoyed. Nor did the MCP follow their Vietnamese counterparts in developing fraternal links and logistical supply chains with Communist China. Lacking a city presence or external sources of support, the

MRLA fell back on the squatters. These poor labourers were literally caught in the middle, denied the opportunity to avoid taking sides by the counter-vailing pressures of Communist exactions, the risk of denunciation, and the security forces' expectation of compliance. All this at the very moment when the outbreak of war in Korea over the summer of 1950 sparked a boom in commodity prices that left the Malayan authorities flush with the cash nec-essary to finance the resettlement programme.[49]

The second consideration—the economics of the Chinese labour market in Malaya—comes into play here. It cannot be stressed enough that the rural Chinese were always the primary target of the colonial government's emer-gency measures. These could be staggeringly harsh, ranging from detention and deportation to communal fines and curfews. By February 1951, a full year before Templer's arrival, almost 3,000 ethnic Chinese had been deported to China. By the start of 1952, 22,667 Chinese figured in the total of 25,641 Malayans held for more than twenty-eight days under the Emergency Regu-lations. Templer was by no means alone in recognizing that such levels of repression were not only unsustainable but politically counter-productive.[50] This returns us to the economic impact of the Korean War boom, which, in driving up wages, diminished the appeal of the Communist alternative for the Chinese labour force in the rubber and tin industries. Meanwhile, improving security in the Malayan interior, notably along the northern frontier with Thailand, assured continuing imports of Thai rice, the key staple in the Malayan diet.[51] Herein lies the significance of the Communists' abandonment of unrestricted warfare in October 1951, a decision substan-tially taken in response to the exasperation and internal division among Malaya's Chinese community as the Emergency dragged on.

Talk of communities brings us to the third factor: those who the British claimed to be protecting. Paradoxically, although British forces fought the MCP, in part, to defend the settler community, the Emergency also signalled the end of their social supremacy. Relations between the colonial authori-ties and Malaya 'old-hands' were generally testy. Malcolm MacDonald per-sonified the shift. As South East Asia Commissioner-General he cultivated cross-communal ties with an easy informality that, as Tim Harper notes, spurned 'the oppression of the necktie'. The influx of bureaucrats, national servicemen, and police reinforcements diluted settler influence further, dissolving former links between whiteness and wealth. In 1955 Singapore was scandalized by claims that up to fifty service wives struggling to make ends meet had organized a prostitution racket that worked the city's

hotels.[52] Whatever else it was, the Malayan Emergency was never a reactionary defence of white minority privilege. In this respect it was quite different
to decolonization conflicts in Africa because the cultural dynamics of
Malaya's politics were conceived in terms of the triangular relationship
between the Federation's three principal ethnic groups: Malays, Chinese, and
Indians. Britons were, in this sense, incidental to the conflict. The consolidation of new inter-communal partnerships predicated on Malay dominance
was what counted.

And so we come to the fourth and final long-term factor. This was the
steady accretion of local and federal government reforms that the High Commission pursued, often in cooperation with the UMNO and other moderate
groups representing Malaya's Chinese and Indian communities. Municipal
elections were organized between 1951 and 1953, a resurrection of what Templer described as politics at the 'parish-pump level', which occurred beyond
MCP reach.[53] The restoration of local government was later followed by the
establishment of a Federal Council, elections to which in July 1955 cemented
a working Malayan Alliance that brought together the UMNO, the Malayan
Chinese Association and the Malayan Indian Congress. With the political
building blocks for Malayan self-government in place by the summer of 1955,
the British could accelerate the rundown of their security commitment.[54] On
9 September Alliance leader and newly-appointed Malayan Chief Minister
Tunku Abdul Rahman offered a renewed amnesty to any insurgents who surrendered, the prelude to formal talks with the MCP leadership in December.[55] Far from laying the foundations for British neo-colonial influence, these
measures to bring an end to the Emergency were increasingly organized and
implemented on Malayan terms.[56]

Escalating war in Indochina

If Britain's decision to fight in Malaya was forced upon it by the combination of insurgent violence and the colony's enduring value to the Exchequer, the dynamics of conflict escalation in Indochina were almost the exact
reverse. The Saigon High Commission and its COMININDO supporters
had pitched France into a premeditated war, while, over time, the mounting
costs of military commitment drained the French Treasury of precious
funds.[57] Vietminh forces grew stronger meanwhile. Conditions for the poorest in Communist-held rural areas were ameliorated by improving peasants'

access to communal land and sources of credit. Upper limits were imposed on landlords' rents. A mass literacy drive to widen usage of the Romanized Vietnamese script *quoc ngu* proved popular.[58] Knowing that French troops planned to re-occupy Hanoi, the DRV authorities withdrew Vietminh forces northwards over the summer of 1946, consolidating their grip over the highlands of Tonkin (North Vietnam) and the uncontested regions of Annam (central Vietnam). As Map 7 indicates, the reality was that France simply never reconquered a good deal of central and northern Vietnam. This large region, home to ten million people by the early 1950s, was what constituted the DRV state, its administrative system, regional trade networks, and interior policies regulated from Hanoi. Its insurgent origins and internal coalition rivalries declining in importance, the Hanoi regime was, by 1950, harder to equate with the 'Vietminh' of old. Determined to deploy all its human and material resources to defeat the French, the lands controlled by the DRV formed a highly-militarized command economy mobilized for combat. France, in other words, was at war with a sovereign Vietnamese state in all but name.[59]

Meanwhile, far to the south, fighters, intelligence agents, and couriers continued to infiltrate Saigon, sabotaging military and administrative services, extracting valuable information, and spiriting away essential supplies from medicines to rubber-soled sandals for the militia. Dockers and arsenal workers, housemaids and drivers, students and coolies, all became critical to Saigon's Vietminh network, moving supplies, exchanging information and, on occasion, taking up arms.[60] According to Saigon colonial police records, in August 1948 alone nine million units of penicillin and 60,000 malarial prophylactics 'disappeared' from the city's pharmacies. A more potent symbol of urban insecurity was the number of daylight killings of French soldiers, officials, and settlers. These became so frequent that café-owners erected protective wire 'cages' around their premises to prevent Vietminh supporters from lobbing grenades among customers' tables. Others, including the Chinese owners of Saigon's premier casino, *Le Monde*, whose trade was hit by an earlier grenade attack, paid Vietminh 'taxes' as protection. Many of these assaults were carried out by young women, and children who were orphaned during the war or the preceding famine. They used their intimate knowledge of the city's back-streets to evade the increasing numbers of troops—15,000 by 1950—brought in to restore calm.[61]

Saigon's urban disorder pointed to the uncertainty characteristic of the war's early years. This uncertainty was everywhere to be found: in the shifting

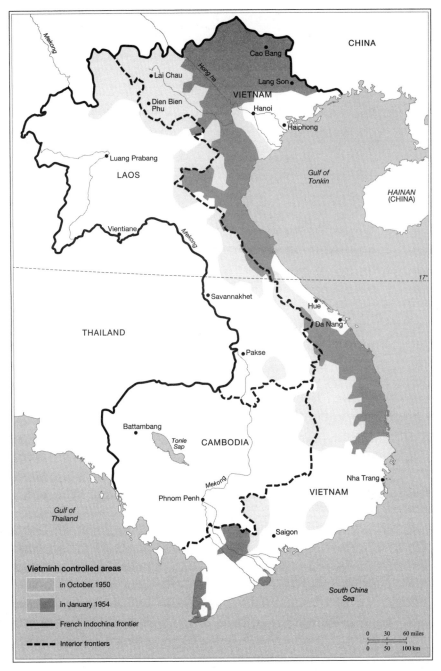

Map 7. Territorial control in the Indochina War, 1950–4.

configurations of the multi-party coalitions that governed France between
1947 and 1949, which managed to accommodate individual ministers, more
briefly, even an entire party (the PCF) that opposed the war; in the military
strategy adopted by French commander-in-chief Jean Valluy, who divided
his limited forces between consolidating their hold in Cochin-China and
evicting the DRV from critical economic regions further north—Tonkin's
coal-producing region and the densely-populated industrial centres of
Annam; and in the half-hearted French efforts to keep the door ajar to the
Hanoi regime through surreptitious dialogue. Unsurprisingly, neither General
Leclerc's regional adviser Paul Mus nor the young Socialist Deputy Alain
Savary made much headway. Their attempts to find common ground with
Ho were stymied by hard-liners in Paris and the Saigon High Commission
still insistent that the Hanoi regime should capitulate by surrendering
sovereign control over north-central Vietnam.[62] In the event, this early
period of drift was brought to an end by the convergence of two events, one
internal, the other external.

On the internal plane, the French decision to press ahead with the launch
of a Vietnamese 'associated state' built around an anti-Communist government in Saigon signified a burning of diplomatic bridges. By investing in
the creation of an alternative, southern locus of Vietnamese national power,
the so-called 'Bao Daï solution' redoubled France's commitment to oust
Ho's northern republic. French officials persuaded policy hawks within the
US government to back their two-pronged strategy of war against the Vietminh and consolidation of a pro-western Saigon regime.[63] In mid March
1949 the State Department reiterated Washington's support for the Bao Daï
solution. French negotiators, meanwhile, traded on the ex-emperor's animus against the Vietminh to persuade him to head a national authority in a
unified Vietnam.[64] By cajoling the former Emperor into accepting Vietnam's
autonomy as an associated state of the French Union, Henri Queuille's
Third Force government denied him the means to build an independent
following in opposition to the Vietminh. This paradox was never confronted.
France insisted that Bao Daï was the authentic representative of the Vietnamese
nation, yet withheld national independence, the only concession likely to
secure popular endorsement. By early 1950, the Saigon regime relied on
more sectarian elements: the commercial classes, fervent anti-Communists,
and Catholic and sect leaders hostile to Marxist atheism.[65]

These domestic realignments were vitally important, but they were overshadowed by a more dramatic change on the external plane: the creation of

the People's Republic of China on 1 October 1949. Ho moved quickly to conclude a military alliance with Mao's Chinese regime after dispatching his envoy Hoang Van Hoan to prepare the ground for an approach.[66] Spurred by China's recognition of the DRV in mid-January 1950, Ho resolved to conduct the negotiations personally.[67] Leaving in secret, he walked for seventeen days from northern Tonkin to conduct talks with Mao's deputy Liu Shaoqi and Zhu De, senior commander of China's People's Liberation Army (PLA). From there he travelled by more modern means to Moscow for discussions with Stalin and, more importantly, another Chinese duo: Foreign Minister Zhou Enlai and Mao himself, both of whom were visiting the Russian capital at the time. Stalin was non-committal. But Mao, consistent with the Chinese Communist policy of 'leaning to one side' by promoting revolution throughout East Asia, promised 'every military assistance needed by Vietnam in its struggle against France'.[68] The war in Indochina was about to get much bigger, confronting France with decolonization's first 'total war'.[69]

By late July 1950 a Chinese Military Advisory Group (CMAG) was established over the frontier at Nanning, Guangxi Province. Preliminary training of DRV cadres began, much of it by Chinese military advisers installed with Vietminh regiments and battalions. Although the Chinese introduced some Maoist innovations, including much greater mobilization of Vietnamese women, this was less a case of revolutionary insurgency—or people's war—than the systematic construction of a large field army capable of matching the French in open encounter.[70] In line with this rapid expansion of the DRV's military capability, General Chen Geng, commander of the PLA's 20th Army Corps and an old associate of Ho, took charge of plans to launch a major offensive along the Vietnam–China frontier. Expelling French forces from the border region was the prerequisite to the free passage of Chinese weapons and equipment into the DRV's national territory.[71]

The irony was that the French were thinking in similar terms. At precisely the same time that the Chinese aid plans were finalized, General Marcel Alessandri, the Expeditionary Force's northern commander, was pushing French units towards the Chinese frontier. Colonial troops fanned out along the heavily-populated Red River Delta while others seized Dong Khe, a strategic border outpost. These advances, critical if the Chinese lifeline was to be cut, were reversed within months. By September the CMAG had sent over 14,000 guns, medicines, uniforms, and 2,800 tons of grain southwards, part of a regular supply-line that continued virtually uninterrupted for the next four years.[72] On 16 September DRV soldiers, now better equipped, better fed, and better organized into larger regimental formations, moved onto the attack. A Vietnamese force of 10,000 recaptured Dong Khe after two days of intense fighting.[73] By now, the DRV's field army, fortified by Chinese supplies, bore scant resemblance to Malaya's isolated and unsupported Communist insurgents.

For the Expeditionary Force, losing Dong Khe was the prelude to catastrophe. Pounded by Chinese-supplied shells and outnumbered by DRV troops, three French battalions at Cao Bang, the principal French garrison in north-eastern Tonkin, were ordered by Commander-in-Chief General Georges Carpentier to evacuate. Aware that their retreat might leave them exposed, Carpentier ordered another four battalions under Lieutenant-General Marcel Lepage into the area to provide cover as the columns snaked along *Route Coloniale 4*. Neither the evacuees nor the reinforcements got far. Lepage's force was severely mauled in an ambush on 8 October. Two days later the units leaving Cao Bang were hemmed in on the roadside and wiped out. Almost 5,000 soldiers were lost, some missing, most killed. French humiliation was sealed by the capture of Lepage and Lieutenant-Colonel Pierre Charton, his opposite number in Cao Bang.[74] Other remaining northerly garrisons at Lao Kay, Lang-Son, and Hoa Binh were immediately instructed to withdraw. They did so with such haste that 11,000 tons of ammunition was left behind for the DRV units closing in.[75]

General Chen's strategy was working. So much so that the war's strategic balance shifted. Ho was delighted, telegramming Stalin with news of what he called a victory for 'proletarian internationalism'. DRV regiments in Tonkin could now link up with fighters further south, thereby controlling a single 'liberated zone' spanning rural Tonkin and northern Annam. Over the winter of 1950–51 Chinese-supported DRV forces split into three, systematically retaking the ground along the Red River Delta occupied by Alessandri's colonial troops the year before. By June gunfire could be heard within twenty kilometres of Hanoi.[76]

René Pleven was four months into the job of Prime Minister when details reached Paris of what the newspapers immediately dubbed the Cao Bang 'disaster'. On 19 October 1950, during the National Assembly's ill-tempered autopsy on the events, he dismissed suggestions from Pierre Cot, a left-wing renegade and veteran of the Popular Front, that the time had come to open talks with Hanoi. Instead, Pleven began customarily enough by paying homage to the dead soldiers' bravery. His detractors would have none of it. Interruptions from the floor forced him to concede that the government was planning troop reductions in 1951. No matter, Pleven insisted. Tonkin would be defended 'as it had been on numerous occasions over the past ninety years'. It was an unconvincing performance. The Minister left the Chamber to jibes from Communist Deputies that France was a handmaiden to America's Asian imperialism.[77]

Within days of the fractious National Assembly debate, the security service analysts of Britain's Joint Intelligence Committee saw only bad things ahead for France in Vietnam. The expeditionary force, they said, lacked 'the will to win'. The Communists' grip on northern Vietnam would tighten as Chinese military instruction, bigger and better weapons, and assured food supplies transformed the DRV army into a professional and dangerous strike force.[78] More significant than these military developments was the political context, the most striking feature of which was the 'almost universal unpopularity' of the French among the Vietnamese. Promises of autonomy remained unfulfilled. Only unequivocal French endorsement of national independence and democratic institutions might persuade Vietnam's people to question their faith in a Communist/DRV alternative.[79] French opinion poll evidence compounded British doubts about France's 'endless battle' in Indochina, indicating worrying shifts in metropolitan attitudes to the war. French voters, it seemed, were 'turning off' media coverage of Vietnamese events that were too dismal and too remote to absorb.[80]

Those inclined to apathy or anxiety may have closed their eyes to French problems in the Far East, but the bleak events of 1950 did spark French religious opposition and louder intellectual criticism of the conflict, albeit outside the mainstream of domestic political opinion.[81] Human rights organizations, Church groups, and prominent literary figures questioned the wisdom, the methods, and the ethics of a war costing more and more lives.[82] Relatively few establishment figures were willing as yet to air their pangs of conscience. Leclerc's former adviser, Paul Mus, who had returned to France to assume the headship of the colonial service training academy, the *École nationale de la France d'outre-mer*, was a notable exception. In 1949 he published a sequence of articles in the magazine *Témoignage Chrétien* ('Christian witness') that exposed the folly of French policy. They cost him his job. Mus's former boss in Saigon, Léon Pignon, demanded his removal, aware that Mus's knowledge of Vietnam was unrivalled within government.[83] Meanwhile, among the major parties in France, only the PCF maintained an anti-war line. But the Communists' hectoring tone only antagonized wider French opinion.

Indeed, Communist opposition to empire struck their domestic opponents as nakedly self-serving. They droned on about the evils of imperialism in coldly ideological terms but said next to nothing about the war's human suffering. And they chose not to advertise Ho Chi Minh's unwavering Stalinism. One could even argue that Communist anti-colonialism was counter-productive, precluding other peace-inclined moderates from speaking out for fear of being smeared as fellow-travellers.[84]

The Socialists squirmed on the horn of this particular dilemma. The Party had never devised a workable Indochina policy. Its parliamentarians paid lip service to the need for a negotiated solution but ran scared of its obvious implication: talks with the DRV.[85] They disliked mounting defence spending but voted credits for the war even so. Jules Moch, former resister, industrial policy specialist, and arch anti-Communist, personified the Socialists' agony. As Minister of Defence in 1950–51 he knew the war was slipping from France's grasp, not least because of chronic troop shortages in the expeditionary force. But as the government's leading Cold War strategist, he maintained that the requirements of European defence had to come first.[86]

The MRP was, as ever, more hard-line. The Fourth Republic's perennial party of government, its ministers—Jean Letourneau, Maurice Schumann, and Georges Bidault prominent among them—were closest to the day-to-day running of the war. The MRP's collective leadership stuck to the mantra of no talks without military victory. But, behind the scenes, other senior Party figures, including Robert Schuman and Pierre Pflimlin, grew increasingly pessimistic.[87] As Foreign Minister in early 1949 Schuman avowed that Ho was 'a creature of the Communists'. But this conviction nourished Schuman's desperation to find a viable Vietnamese negotiating partner before China fell under the complete control of Mao's forces.[88] Once the Chinese–DRV alliance was in place, Schuman began to lose hope. Much the same could be said of the Radical Party's leading lights, a fact which helps explain Party leader Pierre Mendès France's outspoken attacks on the war's pointlessness after the calamity at Cao Bang.[89] Basking in the warm sunlight of political opposition, de Gaulle's RPF relished the discomfort of party rivals without offering any clear alternative to fighting on.[90] Not a propitious political climate for a renewed effort by Pleven's government to resuscitate French policy in Indochina.

In the picturesque setting of Pau in the Pyrenean foothills on 29 November 1950 a French delegation led by Albert Sarraut, a former governor of Indochina, concluded a series of 'inter-state conventions' with the governments of Cambodia, Laos, and [South] Vietnam. The Pau agreements were the latest in a sequence of accords with Indochina's 'Associated States'. Intended to place the individual Indochinese territories on an independent economic footing, they covered everything from postal services and customs tariffs to the creation of separate national treasuries with autonomous budgets. To read them, one could almost imagine there was no war going on at all, let alone a vicious campaign in northern Vietnam recently expanded thanks to fresh injections of Chinese advice and support to the DRV army. In fact, the Pau accords, just like the Along Bay agreements that preceded them, were as much about what they symbolized as what they said. These conventions were integral to the struggle for Indochina's soul, the diplomatic contribution to a propaganda war in which France refuted the accusation of imperialism. The Pau accords were meant to demonstrate that France had no intention of preserving colonial control. Quite the reverse: France was fighting to secure its non-communist partners in Saigon, Phnom Penh, and Luang Prabang; fighting to sustain authentic national traditions and customary forms of government against an illegitimate DRV challenger.[91]

The fine details suggested otherwise. Admittedly, the conventions ended the long financial reign of the hugely influential Bank of Indochina, largest of France's colonial investment houses. The old Bank was to be replaced from late 1951 with a more sober budgetary 'Institute' that would manage currency levels, trade, and loan funding. But the 'standing inter-governmental conference' established to oversee implementation of the Pau conventions was soon bogged down. French negotiators insisted that their country's preferential commercial rights in Indochina be retained. Colonial bureaucrats also clung on to key advisory posts in the Associated States governments. Not until 1952 did the Associated States take greater control of their national finances—at just the wrong moment. Rampant inflation threatened to destabilize the Indochinese currencies, sending living standards crashing. The core problem was war costs—to which the Cambodian and Laotian administrations contributed alongside their Saigon counterpart. None had a taxable base large enough to meet their fiscal obligations. Each still depended on colonial backers old and new: on French monetary support for domestic spending; on US financial aid for military spending. This combination of limited autonomy, financial dependency, and grinding poverty did not bode well for their longer-term political future. Indeed, so unpopular were the Saigon government's 1952 budgetary provisions that in August Bao Daï chose to approve them without first consulting the

Vietnamese National Assembly. To complicate matters further, the Americans insisted on disbursing aid without French interference, eager to see the southern Vietnamese push ahead with the 'Vietnamization' of the expeditionary force. This bilateralism offended the French preference for statist planning. And it fed suspicions in Paris about Washington's growing financial and strategic hold over the Saigon regime.[92]

Rather than ameliorating French–US relations, the drip-feed of American funds and military supplies that underpinned the final three years of the French war effort in Indochina drove another wedge through France's bitterly divided politics between 1951 and 1954. Money, more than lives, explained this acrimony. US financial support grated as tangible proof of French incapacity. Damning statistical calculations in the Paris press reinforced the point. In every year from 1946 France had ploughed a yearly average of between six to ten per cent of annual government expenditure into fighting the Indochina War. Unsustainable in the long term, this cost burden was holding back the rate of domestic reconstruction in the short term. By 1950 some 150,000 of France's 659,000 members of the armed forces were serving in Indochina. To the embarrassment of Pleven's government, an eighty-billion-franc supplementary budget issue was required to equip these troops properly.[93] What, people asked, was the point in expending so much blood and treasure, especially as businesses and investors, anticipating the DRV's triumph of arms, began moving specialist staffs, factory plant and, above all, funds out of Vietnam from late 1952.[94] The war's dwindling number of party political backers had no convincing answer.

These recriminations highlighted something else. The brief winter 1950 respite for those still eager to prosecute the fight against the Hanoi regime was over. With the Parisian political establishment floundering in the wake of Cao Bang, with the Pau agreements ridiculed by the DRV, and with US guns and dollars yet to register their impact in Vietnam, most expected 1951 to be another year of French reverses. Remarkably, it was anything but. Far more so than in Malaya this transformation in colonial fortunes during 1951 could be attributed to changes at the top. If Templer capitalized on the preparatory work done by Briggs and others in Malaya, his French counterpart, General Jean de Lattre de Tassigny, enjoyed no such head-start. Dispatched to pick up the pieces of civil and military command after Cao Bang, de Lattre had little foreknowledge of Vietnam. An infantry officer from the same Vendée village as Georges Clemenceau, de Lattre cemented his reputation by rebuilding the French Army into an esteemed fighting force during the final months of World War Two. He proved his political acuity by helping cleanse the military of its Vichy connections.[95] Now de Lattre brought his skills to bear in restoring expeditionary force morale and quietening the hubbub of divided counsels in Saigon.

Reliving his achievements of 1944–5, de Lattre made best use of American equipment to roll back the DRV's advance on Hanoi. In a move more redolent of Templer, he integrated military intelligence with policing the better to pre-empt DRV attacks and begin restoring French control in the Vietnamese interior.[96] Finally, he drew on his wartime experience in constructing a viable Vietnamese National Army loyal to Bao Daï. The General was always a good speaker—frank, uncomplicated, and honest. His speech to potential National Army recruits gathered at Saigon's Lycée Chasseloup-Laubat in June 1951 was typical in this regard: 'Stand up like men,' he implored them. 'If you are Communists, join the Vietminh; there are certain individuals among them who fight very well for a very bad cause. But if you are patriots, fight for your country, because this is your war.' Over the conflict's three remaining years, tens of thousands did so.[97]

De Lattre's achievements roused the Foreign Minister Robert Schuman from his gloom, persuading him to take the war to the DRV regime. This was a Damascene conversion. Justifiably venerated as an architect of European integration, it was Schuman's misfortune during successive spells as French premier and minister from 1947 onwards to be in the thick of the war from its inception.[98] His room to challenge French actions was further limited by his party's identification with the war's prosecution.[99] De Lattre promised salvation at last. The result was a dual-track fight strategy. Schuman capitalized on his reputation in Washington as a European visionary to persuade Dean Acheson's State Department that France could turn the political tide in Vietnam.[100] General de Lattre exploited his formidable reputation with the US Joint Chiefs and other Pentagon insiders to secure larger, speedier deliveries of military aid.[101] Feted in the American press as an inspirational leader, de Lattre drew on his reputational credit during hard bargaining with American officials over additional weaponry.[102] Together, the elderly politician from Lorraine and the ailing General from the Vendée convinced the Americans to up the ante in Indochina. It was a staggering turn-about, coming less than three months after Schuman's predecessor, Edgar Faure, confessed to Dean Acheson that France could never meet its NATO commitments in Europe and fight the Hanoi regime at the same time.[103]

Inspired by de Lattre, might the American hand of intervention outreach the Chinese? The question is moot on two counts. One is that US military involvement in Vietnam outlived the French stake in Indochina and was never entirely bound up with it. The other is that de Lattre, the individual acclaimed for reviving French fortunes, was beset by personal tragedy. On 30 May 1951, the General's twenty-three-year-old son Bernard, another serving officer, was killed during a battle with DRV forces at Nam Dinh in northern Vietnam. Grief accelerated the progress of his father's cancer, which exacted its price in January 1952. The General was posthumously awarded a Marshal's baton and accorded a state funeral at which his erstwhile colleagues Bernard Montgomery and Dwight Eisenhower were pallbearers. France responded to his passing as if to the death of a cherished illusion that defeat in Vietnam could be averted.

De Lattre's successors could hardly have been more different either from their predecessor or from each other. General Raoul Salan could boast more extensive experience of the Indochina peninsula than virtually anyone in the French High Command. But boasting was never part of Salan's armoury. Years spent working for the French military intelligence service in Laos and Vietnam fostered the quiet inscrutability for which Salan was renowned. Sometimes compared to a Chinese mandarin and known for his fondness for opium, Salan felt more at home in Saigon than the city of Nîmes in the Midi from which he came. Henri Navarre, a relative newcomer to the Far East, shared Salan's background in colonial intelligence-gathering, but in Arab territories, not Far Eastern ones. A suave Parisian with impeccable Saint Cyr credentials, his reputation was enhanced by serving the reconstructed French Army that helped liberate his home town in 1944.[104] Neither commander had enough men or equipment to turn the Indochina campaign their way.[105] Salan came closest. In mid-October 1952 DRV forces drove the French units strung across Tonkin retreating towards the Black River after the spectacular capture of garrison outposts in and around Nghia Lo. Almost a thousand members of the Expeditionary Force were lost. Salan improvised a quick response, consolidating all his available forces to mount Operation *Lorraine*, the largest French counter-offensive of the war's final years. Meant to split DRV forces, to rupture their communications and bolster the French defensive position north-west of Hanoi, *Lorraine* was still too small a venture to turn the tide of the war. By the time that Navarre replaced Salan in May 1953 the Expeditionary Force was chronically short of experienced officers and NCOs. So much so that it was impossible to sustain the rhythm of offensive operations. Navarre's task, as a result, was retrenchment, not victory—holding the line in the hope that the politicians might extract French irons from the Vietnamese fire.[106]

Local British observers got things more or less right. H. A. Graves, Consul in Saigon, summarized the position thus:

> When the Vietminh launched their autumn offensive in October [1952] they rapidly dispelled any immediate hope of a French military initiative…The fault is not only on the side of the French High Command in Indochina. Inhibited in their military freedom of action by political caveats from Paris, directed to plan for the withdrawal of French forces when their crying present need is reinforcements, they have been reduced to waiting to be hit. When they are hit, French opinion at home takes another plunge into despondency and pessimism and so the vicious circle continues.[107]

On the military side, British estimates varied about whether France could sustain its current defensive positions or accomplish a fighting withdrawal.[108] On the political side, Churchill's government was openly disdainful about the shifting party coalitions of the Fourth Republic. Reviewing the intelligence on Indochina presented to him, the British Prime Minister was typically blunt:

> The French are naturally afraid of being "Dutched out" of Indochina by the same sloppy United Nations methods as lost Indonesia. On the other hand they will not take the only step which could restore their position, namely two years' military service and sending conscripts to the Front. France cannot be a great nation, still less an overseas empire, without a good French Army. A strong French Chamber [of Deputies] breeding Prime Ministers by the score and the Deputies having splendid fun in politics is no substitute for the hard simple decisions which they have to make to remain a great power.[109]

The result, most British estimates agreed, was policy paralysis, which translated into a sullen resolve to fight on for little tangible reward.

While the Expeditionary Force edged towards eclipse, the DRV's star was rising. As the October 1952 capture of Nghia Lo had confirmed, during the campaigning of winter 1952–3 the DRV could field over seven divisions capable of set-piece battle encounters. These forces not only controlled most of northern and central Vietnam but exerted an economic stranglehold over much of eastern Laos as well.[110] Their commercial networks extended overland and by sea from China to Thailand, trading everything from narcotics to artillery.[111] French special forces units were reduced to using secret service funds to buy up locally-produced opium in the hope that this might win the loyalty of Laotian farmers and the Vietnamese traffickers who traded in the 'golden triangle' between Laos, Vietnam, and Thailand.[112] Reporting on a tour of Indochina in May 1953, Chief of Air Staff General Charles Léchères made no effort to conceal his pessimism. DRV forces made war 'totally' by coordinating all aspects of their political and military initiatives. Their presence was deeply felt throughout the Federation, 'even in the zones that we outwardly control'.[113]

It seemed unlikely that creeping DRV influence could be countered. De Lattre's earlier efforts to develop a self-reliant Vietnamese army had not been crowned with success. Indeed, French military evaluations of their local allies became bluntly dismissive over the course of 1953. There was a chronic shortage of reliable senior commanders. Officer training was behind schedule. Most serious of all, no Vietnamese army battalions were capable of acting alone, leaving Bao Daï's regime more exposed than ever.[114] A prerequisite for American aid, 'Vietnamization' of the war continued, but next to its DRV opponents, the National Army of Vietnam was a weak reed. Staunchly anti-communist, highly combative but poorly trained, its battalions exemplified French unwillingness to cede real control to the local authorities.[115] Matters were made worse by continued French string-pulling of the Associated States' governments, which made plain that their professed autonomy was a sham. These problems came to a head in May 1953 when French premier René Mayer made a snap decision to devalue the Indochinese piastre. The three Associated State governments were left with reduced treasury holdings and declining purchasing power. Infuriated by such high-handed French action, Prince Sihanouk seized the initiative. He demanded and, in November 1953, secured full independence for Cambodia.

Back in Paris, war weariness was exacting a heavier toll. All of the governing parties identified with starting, expanding, or sustaining the war—the MRP, the Socialists, the Radicals, and the UDSR—were now internally divided over it. Public opposition to the conflict was also harder to ignore. Journalists took the lead. Some wrote for a reinvigorated Catholic press, tending to focus on the conflict's ethical dimensions. Others criticized the war's shadowy politics in the Fourth Republic's flagship newspaper Le Monde, founded in 1946. And longer, in-depth critiques appeared in another newly-established title, the weekly, L'Express. Throughout the national press a steady stream of press editorials decried past administrative failures and questioned the wisdom of continued military engagement.[116] Watching France's fight strategy unravel, in late 1953 Eisenhower's Republican administration worked behind the scenes to ensure that a new coalition government under Joseph Laniel conceded independence to the governments in Phnom Penh, Luang Prabang, and Saigon.[117] The Associated States idea, a cornerstone of the original French Union scheme, was dead.

Vo Nguyen Giap and other senior DRV army commanders were taken aback by de Lattre's earlier advances and the extensive US aid and equipment, including aircraft and napalm, that made them possible. In tune with CMAG advice, the DRV responded accordingly. Guerrilla raiding resumed while DRV forces continued building their capacity to wage major encounter battles. Indeed, the Vietnamese Communists were, if anything, more committed than ever to securing outright military victory. Their movement re-launched in February 1951 as the Vietnamese Workers Party (VWP or *Dang Lao Dong Viet Nam*), Ho, Giap, and Party General Secretary Truong Chinh stressed that Vietnam's revolutionary transformation was attendant on first evicting the French.[118] To do so, the VWP Politburo concerted plans with Mao's government to consolidate their grip over Vietnam's north-western provinces and neighbouring territory in Laos. After Giap's regular units opened the Xam Neua offensive in Upper Laos in late March 1953, DRV forces began infiltrating southwards from their Viet Bac stronghold. This time around it was harder to envisage them being dislodged.[119] The revolution proceeded meanwhile. The pace of communal land redistribution within liberated zones quickened. Party propagandists warned that peasant families who remained loyal to Bao Daï would be denied a share of the spoils. This was a direct riposte to the Emperor's last-ditch efforts to sway the rural population with the promise of land reforms, a programme derailed by furious opposition from Vietnamese landlords along the fertile banks of the Red River and the Mekong Delta.[120]

As French Commissioner-General for Southeast Asia, the former Free French diplomat Maurice Dejean served as intermediary between France and its client regimes in Vietnam, Cambodia, and Laos as the Indochina War neared its conclusion. During 1953 it fell to him to issue official denials that any diplomatic back-channel to Ho Chi Minh existed. Dejean also upheld the fiction that the Cambodian and Laotian governments were willing and equal partners in the fight against the Hanoi regime. By this late stage in the war the Laotians were the keener of the two. From August 1953 onwards intensive French-Laotian frontier patrolling disrupted DRV supply lines and base areas in Laos.[121] But these minor successes in the north were overshadowed by a worsening crisis of authority in Saigon. Bao Daï was caught in a cleft stick, too compromised by his long-standing association with the French to make a credible national leader. Although the southward flood of refugees pointed to popular longing for a decent, non-Communist alternative in Vietnam, Bao Daï did not fit the bill.[122] Instead, the list of his diverse internal opponents kept getting longer, among them the separatist Popular Front for South Vietnam, the socialist Vietnam National Party, and the Hoa Hao Buddhist sect, which fielded its own paramilitary force.[123]

Declining French capacity to control events in Saigon was matched by an inability to regulate international involvement in the war. Communist China's immersion in the conflict was, of course, an accomplished fact. But the cessation of the Korean War in July 1953 released Chinese strategic energies to focus on securing victory in Indochina. With a Korean armistice finally concluded, as autumn 1953 turned to winter it became clearer that the Cold War giants were positioning themselves for Indochina's future without France. On 19 September 1953 Georgy Malenkov, appointed Soviet premier following Stalin's death six months earlier, proposed a negotiated settlement, reasoning that the USSR's Chinese ally should figure large in any peace talks. Six weeks later US Vice-President Richard Nixon met the heads of government in Saigon, Phnom Penh, and Luang Prabang. The Indochinese Peninsula, he insisted, had overtaken Korea as America's foremost strategic priority in eastern Asia. The Vice-President pledged that Eisenhower's administration would redouble its efforts to defeat Hanoi, the implication being that France might have to do America's bidding if it failed to make military progress soon.[124] The fight in Indochina was slipping out of French hands into the grasp of stronger outsiders.

By 1954 the sense of a conflict no longer in France's power to decide became overwhelming. This loss of control converged in two decisive events. One was the five-month siege that befell the French garrison at a northern fortress complex called Dien Bien Phu. The other was the convocation of an international conference at Geneva to negotiate an armistice to end the fighting.[125] In a move redolent of French efforts to prove Germany's 'war guilt' after the Great War, in the weeks before the conference opened the Saigon High Commission compiled a dossier of alleged Chinese misdemeanours in northern Vietnam. Combining diplomatic traffic with intelligence material, the dossier confirmed that the Chinese Nationalist regime had impeded the return of French administrators north of the 16th parallel in 1945–6. Similar evidence from 1950 onwards was adduced to suggest that Ho's government was the puppet of its larger Communist cousin. The DRV

Figure 9. A fight already lost? The jubilation is clear in this image of a 1954 Vietnamese youth rally in Hanoi.

war effort was portrayed, not as popular mobilization in support of a 'people's war', but as the vanguard of Mao's 'military-industrial complex' in Southeast Asia.[126]

Diplomatic skirmishing was one thing, but the French nation, only fitfully engaged by the preceding eight years of the Indochina War, was in early 1954 gripped by the unfolding tragedy of Dien Bien Phu. Night after night from January through to May, Pathé, and Gaumont newsreels relayed the garrison's depletion to cinema audiences. Between 20 March and 15 May *Paris Match* published 144 battlefield photographs, including five front covers variously depicting stretcher-bound casualties and stoical defenders hopelessly outnumbered. Staring out from newsstands, these graphic, sorrowful images registered a huge impact, making a national heroine of one aristocratic French air-force nurse, Lieutenant Geneviève de Galard, nicknamed 'the angel of Dien Bien Phu'.[127]

The DRV's gargantuan logistical task in relaying troops, munitions, and food to the hills surrounding Dien Bien Phu was only tangentially apparent in the images of artillery bombardments and wave after wave of infantry assaults.[128] But photographs and film footage of bodies strewn across Dien Bien Phu's valley floor were real enough. Stark warnings from French military intelligence officers in Saigon about the vast scale of Chinese aid to a DRV army estimated by March 1954 at over 300,000 strong no longer seemed outlandish.[129] The siege was colonial war on a Second World War scale. Both sides were pushed to breaking point by the battle, a killing field whose intimate horrors were brought home to the French public like no other empire confrontation hitherto.[130]

By the time the Geneva conference opened on 26 April the French garrison and the DRV's assault brigades were beyond exhaustion.[131] A day later, French premier Joseph Laniel begged his British counterpart to join President Eisenhower in a statement of support for the French position in Indochina. Politely, Churchill declined. He added, rather unhelpfully, that he 'thought it a great mistake to have left this large and important force in so isolated a position'.[132] Churchill's remark was merely a statement of what was by then obvious. On 7 May Dien Bien Phu's battered inmates surrendered. Laniel's six months in office ended five weeks after that.

Keeping a new French Cabinet together through the lingering humiliation of Dien Bien Phu and the trials of the Geneva Conference was not the only political miracle performed by Laniel's successor, Pierre Mendès France. The Radical Party leader also reconciled French parliamentarians to the final collapse of long-held plans for greater integration of Western security forces within a European Defence Community (EDC). This was a scheme originally devised in 1950 to ensure French control over future West German rearmament. But, by 1954, seemingly endless negotiations over the EDC had soured relations between French ministerial colleagues, as well as with Washington and London.[133] Foreign Office head Sir Ivone Kirkpatrick captured the mood in a note penned for Churchill during the project's dying days in August 1954: 'Monsieur Mendès France reported the members of his Government whom he had consulted on EDC as being united on one point, namely that they disagreed with everyone else.'[134] That Mendès France not only came through this but through the final admission of defeat in Vietnam confirmed what appeared to be a sea-change in French public attitudes about the acceptable price of overseas commitments.

Having lost the fight in Indochina, France fared better in agreeing terms for its flight from the territory. These stopped short of acknowledging the extent of defeat. French negotiators entered the Geneva Conference with minimal bargaining power. Three factors worked in their favour, nonetheless. First among them was the eagerness of the VWP leadership to limit international involvement in Vietnam's longer-term future, particularly in regard to the elections expected to determine whether Communist North and non-Communist South should unite into a single independent state. Linked to this was the second of the Hanoi government's prerequisites: the withdrawal of remaining French forces as soon as possible. To speed this process along, VWP negotiator Pham Van Dong chose not to press demands for political control over all territory held by DRV forces, which included large areas of southern Vietnam.[135] Finally, Hanoi government fears of dealmaking by the Chinese, British, and other representatives at Geneva increased their amenability to direct talks with their former French enemies.[136] And here they met a positive response. Mendès France moved quickly to prevent French involvement in any future Vietnamese conflict. Working closely with Jean Sainteny, who had come closest to negotiating an agreement with Ho before the war began in 1946, Mendès France's government encouraged neutralism among the Indochinese peninsula's newly-independent states.[137] China's principal negotiator, Foreign Minister Zhou Enlai was delighted. Mendès was, in effect, refusing to back US plans to undermine the North Vietnamese regime by investing more heavily in the regime of South Vietnam's prime minister-designate, Ngô Dình Diêm.[138]

A silent majority of the French public respected Mendès France for taking decisions that were long overdue. But, for a certain brand of French politician, for serving professional soldiers, and for France's North African settlers, Dien Bien Phu was Suez *avant la lettre*: a country's imperial prestige sacrificed on the altar of domestic political miscalculation; a valiant Cold War contribution against an anti-western regime under-appreciated at home and misinterpreted abroad; France confounded by its mistaken presumptions about American goodwill. Admittedly, no one could argue, as they would in relation to the enforced withdrawal from Egypt in November 1956, that defeat was snatched from the jaws of victory. But the manner of that defeat resonated especially strongly with the Gaullist right and the army officer corps. It became axiomatic to both that the French 'system' of parliamentary democracy, coalition ministries, and political compromises betrayed its bravest sons in time of direst need. For May 1954, read June 1940. The parallel was explicitly drawn by Henri Navarre, the Indochina expeditionary force commander. His 1957 memoirs cast Dien Bien Phu as the inevitable outcome of weak-kneed political leadership, public neglect, and sluggish American intervention. Little wonder that the young army parachutist Jean-Marie Le Pen dated his decision to enter French politics to May 1954.[139]

In meetings between 17 and 19 August 1954 Britain's senior security officials in the Joint Intelligence Committee reflected on Southeast Asia's future after the Geneva Conference settlement. Their only confident prediction was that, aside from a French pull-out, nothing else was settled. Laos, Cambodia, Vietnam, Burma, and Siam (Thailand) looked acutely vulnerable to internal destabilization. None was well placed to resist China's overweening influence.[140] As for Vietnam, its renewed partition into North and South looked no more viable in 1954 than it did in 1945. Vietnamese refugees were pouring southward, a sorry human tide accompanying the French military evacuation. Unification under Hanoi's control seemed unavoidable, but its timing was likely to be determined 'in Moscow or Peking, rather than in Nam Dinh'.[141] Neighbouring Laos and Cambodia were hostages to Vietnam's fortunes, their future as independent countries contingent on the ideological complexion of Vietnamese government.

Beyond Southeast Asia the fallout from Dien Bien Phu was quickly felt. Algeria's young nationalist guerrillas, still to emerge as a fighting force, drew succour from Vietnamese success. They studied the revolutionary war doctrine at its heart absorbing the lesson that victory in colonial fights was contingent on mobilizing international support and material aid. Their French army opponents were equally determined that hard-won military gains should not be undone by crass political decisions or public indifference.[142] Dien Bien Phu thus exposed the most dangerous fissure in the political landscape of the late Fourth Republic: collapsing civil–military relations. Indochina spelt death for the two most lionized Generals of France's post-war army—Philippe Leclerc and Jean de Lattre de Tassigny— each of them political moderates whose sons also died during the fighting in Vietnam. With them perished the army officer corps' respect for civilian authority. Dien Bien Phu, its tragic drama inexorably unfolding over weeks and months, incubated a stab in the back legend stronger even than the mourning over the loss of two inspirational generals.[143] The collusion between Gaullists, Algiers settlers, and senior army officers that brought de Gaulle back into office in May 1958 was built on the memories of a heroic garrison unjustly abandoned in the northern Vietnamese highlands four years earlier.[144]

Conclusion

The Malayan Union experiment indicated that British colonial administrators could devise constitutional arrangements almost as elaborate as the French Union. The difference lay in the speed with which Britain's imperial rulers dropped such schemes once they became unworkable. Greater British readiness to steer colonial government into an abrupt U-turn when compared with French determination to drive on regardless helps explain why the insurgencies in Malaya and Indochina developed so differently from 1948 onwards. When examined comparatively, they are typically explained as opposites: Communist-nationalist victory and French defeat in Vietnam; Communist defeat and British success in Malaya.[145] An unspoken assumption here is that the revolutionary challenges facing the colonial powers in Southeast Asia were broadly equivalent: Communist rebellions rooted among rural labour forces radicalized by Japan's wartime military occupation and the hardships that came with it. It is also contended that, once the old colonial powers resumed control, the British and, especially, the French authorities rejected dialogue with their opponents. Each opted to fight because of the economic and strategic resources and the questions of 'prestige' at stake. But it was the political choices made that mattered more. Britain regained control thanks to its accommodation of Malay elites. France lost control because it backed a corrupt and unpopular South Vietnamese regime. Fighting dominated; flight was considered too little and too late.

   This chapter has cast a sceptical eye over these presumptions. Each conflict had distinct phases and the two were, in some ways, interrelated. One indicator of this was the Attlee government's decision to provide arms for the Indochina expeditionary force. Although never an arms supplier on anything like the American scale, the British kept selling military equipment to the French and their South Vietnamese proxies. But even the weaponry supplied conveyed a sense of British pessimism about French prospects. Top of the Franco-Vietnamese shopping list were helicopters, particularly Westland's S.51 or 'Dragonfly', an aircraft modified for casualty evacuation.[146] By 1952 the rate and quantity of arms sales had mushroomed. By this point the Canadians and New Zealanders had joined the British in offloading surplus military equipment for use in Vietnam. Churchill's government agreed to double the scale of its provisions to the expeditionary force in 1953 to a value of two billion francs, but only if the French paid cash on delivery.[147]

Much as under the preceding Labour administration, Conservative ministers chose not to advertise this lucrative supply-line. Selling guns did not indicate any new-found optimism about the likely outcome of the conflict. In June 1953, by which time General Templer's administration was riding high, the Colonial Office warned that 'major Vietminh successes in Indochina' could have disastrous knock-on effects. Southeast Asia's rice economy and, with it, Malaya's food supplies would be disrupted; MCP violence might be rekindled.[148] Churchill's War Office advisers issued equally dire, domino-theory warnings, predicting that not just Vietnam, but Cambodia, Thailand, and Burma might fall to Communism, leaving Malaya fatally exposed.[149] For all that, interrelatedness is not equivalence. The Indochina War started as a Vietnamese anti-colonial rebellion that was both nationalist and national. And it was organized around a functioning state in North Vietnam with extensive links to neighbouring states, Communist China first among them. Between 1950 and 1952 the conflict therefore mushroomed into a massive proxy war that pitted Chinese and US strategies, resources, and ideologies against one another.

The point here is that French alternatives, including the 'Bao Daï solution', became increasingly irrelevant to the outcome. Months before the Indochina War began Ho told an American journalist, David Schoenbrun, that the conflict would be:

> ...a war between an elephant and a tiger. If the tiger ever stands still, the elephant will crush him with his mighty tusks. But the tiger will not stand still... He will leap upon the back of the elephant, tearing huge chunks from his side, and then he will leap back into the jungle. And slowly the elephant will bleed to death.[150]

A graphic image and one that, as DRV resources expanded from 1950 onwards, grew outdated. France never regained the military initiative in the Indochina War during the four years separating the Sino-Vietnamese military alliance in February 1950 from capitulation at Dien Bien Phu in May 1954. 1951 may have been the exception that proved the rule, but the so-called *année de Lattre* was just that; a single year of achievement named after an exceptional commander-in-chief after which French fortunes declined once more. Both France's initial decision to fight and, more tragically still, its subsequent readiness to consider 'flight' were eclipsed by the internationalization of the Vietnamese conflict. By contrast, the Malayan Emergency, which the British authorities took several years to contain, was never internationalized. From 1951 onwards it was gradually de-escalated thanks to a relentless lockdown of the Malayan interior.

The dominant historical interpretation of British 'success' in Malayan counter-insurgency has it that only after the killing of high commissioner Gurney in October 1951—an event almost coincidental with the end of General de Lattre de Tassigny's short-lived revitalization of French military fortunes in Tonkin—did a disjuncture appear between British advances in Malaya and French setbacks in Vietnam. This view cries out to be challenged for three reasons. One is that it underplays the extent of British problems that still lay ahead while, paradoxically, ignoring the distinct British strategy of counter-terror pursued in the first eighteen months of the Malayan Emergency.[151] Linked to this is the second point. What would come to be known as 'the Malayan model' of targeted counter-insurgency was less cogent and far more violent than its supporters, to this day influential in British military thinking, acknowledged.[152] Finally, the British success—French failure dialectic is not just inaccurate, it is distasteful, close to the erroneous 'league tables' of colonial misdeeds that David Anderson has, quite rightly, dismissed as banal.[153] The fight in Indochina was of a different magnitude altogether—a major war with an estimated half a million Vietnamese victims. For France, which lost 59,745 military personnel killed or missing, the conflict was an enormous strategic reverse; a critical factor in the Fourth Republic's deepening political and cultural divisions, and a lasting source of friction between civilian governments and a professional military that felt unsupported and unappreciated.[154] The soldiers' alienation was profoundly dangerous, both for France and for the societies in which colonial security forces would go on to act with less and less restraint.

6

Fighting Together, Drifting Apart: The Suez Crisis

The Suez Canal Zone, 31 October 1956: the one event in the calendar of decolonization when British and French resolve to fight against imperial withdrawal spectacularly and calamitously converged. 'I cannot imagine a worse act of aggression,' wrote India's Premier Jawaharlal Nehru on hearing news that Egypt had been invaded by Israeli, British, and French forces: 'the whole future of the relations between Europe and Asia hangs in the balance'.[1] The invasion to which he referred was the outcome of a secret Franco-British deal with Israel, the Sèvres protocol of 24 October. One of the most infamous arrangements in the entire history of modern European empire, it concocted false pretexts to attack Egypt. The aim was to depose the country's troublesome ruler, General Gamal Abdel Nasser, quickly, before either his armed forces or his foreign friends could do much about it.[2]

The protocol was agreed over three days of discussion. At its centre was a high-level Israeli negotiating team consisting of Prime Minister David Ben-Gurion, Chief of Staff Moshe Dayan, and Defence Ministry director Shimon Peres who met with their counterparts in Guy Mollet's French government. The talks were held in the quiet suburban home of the Bonnier de la Chapelle family. The family's devotion to the Resistance was exemplary, like that of the French premier, who had endured repeated arrests and Gestapo interrogation. Indeed, their eighteen-year-old son was executed for involvement in the assassination of Admiral Darlan, Vichy's imperial plenipotentiary, in Algiers on Christmas Eve 1942. All of this endeared the Israeli visitors to their French hosts. Foreign Secretary Selwyn Lloyd, who represented British interests at Sèvres with two Foreign Office advisers, arrived later by which time the *bonhomie* between the French and Israelis was in full flow. A rather stiff character at the best of times, Lloyd was ill at ease in the matey, gung-ho atmosphere that pervaded the Franco-Israeli exchanges. Lloyd's starchiness was, on this occasion, hardly surprising. All of the French and Israeli participants, even Lloyd's opposite number, the softly-spoken Christian Pineau, a noted writer of children's books, had at one time or another served in resistance groups, whether fighting against Nazi occupation or the British Mandate in Palestine.[3] These were experiences that served them well at Sèvres where another overthrow was being plotted. It was all a far cry from Lloyd's war service as a senior officer in the British Second Army that had pushed through north-west Europe after D-Day.[4]

Whatever Lloyd's discomfort, the British government's commitment to the deal eventually done was never in doubt. It was just that neither the Foreign Office nor the Cabinet wished to advertise the fact. Israeli forces would advance into the Sinai Desert paving the way for an Anglo-French expeditionary force to occupy the Canal Zone and 'separate' the warring Israeli and Egyptian armies. Ruthlessly Machiavellian, Operation *Musketeer* was worthy of Stalin, whose political heirs were, at the time, busy crushing a popular uprising in Budapest.[5] Western democracies and NATO partners, even those with mounting imperial worries, supposedly upheld higher standards.[6] Or did they? Nehru had a point. Invasion turned into fiasco in barely a week.

'Suez' is commonly described with favoured historians' terms like 'turning point' or 'watershed' to describe its impact on decolonization. Anthony Eden, Britain's ailing Prime Minister, chronically ill with liver disease after a botched operation, attracts more negative epithets. 'Misguided' is perhaps the kindest.[7] 'Deceitful', 'delusional', or 'criminal' figure more often.[8] Eden stepped down in January 1957, a broken man after the Eisenhower administration condemned the Suez venture and pulled the financial rug from under it.[9] His career in ruins, the former premier remained unrepentant, if anything even more convinced in the aftermath of the crisis than before it that overthrowing the Cairo regime made sense.[10] Such blinkered intransigence left him exposed to ridicule. Eden's opposite number was the bespectacled, football-loving Anglophile, French Socialist leader Guy Mollet. The Frenchman was blessed with neither Eden's suaveness nor his good looks: Eden, the old Etonian, had been dubbed 'Lord Eyelashes' by Italian journalists in the 1930s; Mollet, a former schoolteacher from Arras in Normandy, bore a striking resemblance to comedian Arthur Askey. But Mollet did escape the opprobrium that felled his British counterpart. The French Socialists, by then a highly-disciplined party, held together despite vigorous complaint from the

Young Socialist wing led by Michel Rocard.[11] Yet Mollet's centre-left 'Republican Front' also collapsed a few months later, not over Suez, but over the issue that inspired the visceral French hatred of Nasser: the Algerian War.

   The stronger language used to describe Eden's mistakes add to the impression that the Suez crisis brought down a dark and heavy curtain on the British Empire, its strings pulled by the impatient hands of irresistible American power. Contemporary accounts lend colour to this image of a long-running, but hackneyed imperial show forced to close early.

   Emerging from Downing Street on 28 June 1956 Harold Macmillan, still Chancellor at the time, recorded the sense of imperial problems clamouring for Cabinet attention in the weeks before Nasser's announcement of the Suez Canal nationalization: 'terrible agenda—Cyprus, Malta, Libya,

Figure 10. President Nasser announces the nationalization of the Suez Canal in Cairo, July 1956.

Egypt—all trouble and mostly blackmail'.[12] After nationalization on 26 July, 'Suez' became the all-consuming issue for an inner circle of favoured ministers in an 'Egypt committee'. Its deliberations were often closed to wider Cabinet or Whitehall advice.[13] For three months from mid July to mid October Eden and fellow committee members including the Foreign Secretary (Lloyd), Macmillan, and Lord Salisbury (Robert Cecil, formerly Viscount Cranborne) talked of using force only as a last resort.[14] But, in a way, their past imperial rhetoric had already boxed them into a corner. Previous right-wing criticism of Labour's 'scuttle' from Palestine and its handling of Persia's nationalization of the Anglo-Iranian Oil Company in the Abadan crisis of May 1951 constrained Conservative choices in late 1956, suggesting that a firm hand in the Middle East was overdue.[15]

Sections of Fleet Street agreed. The three right-wing *Dailys*: the *Express, Mail*, and *Telegraph*, blustered about firmness in adversity. All three remained unrepentant when it backfired. Their imperialism, at least, was openly displayed.[16] Most of Eden's fellow ministers were less forthright—in public. The majority either shared their leader's apocalyptic vision of Nasser as an Arab Mussolini bestriding the Arab world, or they acquiesced in it. Only two junior ministers resigned in protest. A third, more senior figure, the Minister of Defence Walter Monckton, quit his job for the lesser stresses of Postmaster General.[17] More typical was Macmillan. 'The leader of the bolters', in other words, those ministers quickest to disavow their earlier backing for Eden, he was pre-eminent among the Cabinet members anxious to draw a veil over their earlier enthusiasm for military intervention.[18] The British service chiefs were more honest. Chief of Imperial General Staff Sir Gerald Templer endorsed the tripartite invasion or 'Operation *Musketeer*'; First Sea Lord Mountbatten opposed it; and Air Chief Marshal Sir Denis Smallwood dismissed Eden's excuses for action as 'utterly phoney'. (The complexity of the invasion—and the consequent scope for plans to go awry—is evident from Map 8 below.) In Parliament and the country, political parties, no less than radio listeners, pub drinkers, families, and long-time friendships, split over the issue. Labour boasted several strongly pro-Zionist figures who were willing to back Israel. The Conservative back-benches, rather like the Whitehall civil service, were never monolithically imperialist but expressed a wide spectrum of opinion from moral disgust to the die-hard empire loyalism of 'Suez Group' rowdies, Lord Salisbury, Julian Amery, and Neil 'Billy' McLean.[19] One of the most high-profile ruptures was between the government and the BBC.

The Corporation was uncomfortable with the role of semi-official government cheerleader both in its domestic programming and in its Arabic-language broadcasting.[20] That Suez was immensely divisive is beyond doubt. But was it *the* definitive post-war turning point for the British Empire (or, indeed, the French)?

Again, the interpretational tide has flowed strongly in one direction for many years. As Scott Lucas puts it, the fates of the two principal imperial actors in this version of events are easily summarized: 'France colludes, invades, but then leaves for the morass of Algeria and the demise of the Fourth Republic. Britain colludes, invades, and fails with an epilogue of imperial decline...'[21] For all that, as he, Anthony Stockwell and others have shown, Suez was not the 'beginning of the end' for British colonial rule. Nor, as we are all now painfully aware, was it the last ill-judged western intervention in the Middle East. By 1956 British decolonization from the Indian subcontinent was an accomplished fact and its progress was far-advanced in Southeast Asia and sub-Saharan Africa. After 1956 Britain's Middle Eastern presence no longer hinged on Egypt, but it did not disappear. Instead, it shifted steadily eastwards towards the Persian Gulf and southern Arabia.[22] Deposing Nasser was never an end in itself for France but, as we shall see, was adjunct to a strategy of conflict escalation in Algeria that continued regardless of the failure in Egypt.

Further complexity emerges when one recalls that Eden's Middle Eastern record as Churchill's Foreign Secretary after 1951 boasted some successes. He helped negotiate an Anglo-Egyptian treaty settlement in 1954 to evacuate British forces from the Suez Canal Zone and mend fences with the Colonels' regime that seized power in the Young Officers' revolution of 23 July 1952.[23] The scale of Eden's personal achievement in securing what was a hugely symbolic transfer of power emerges when one remembers three things. First, that an almost identical agreement on British military evacuation and redeployment had eluded the Attlee government.[24] Second, that Eden persuaded Churchill to accept the case for withdrawal.[25] And third, that in late January 1952 British forces from the vast Suez Canal base had been involved in bloody clashes with Egyptian police that left scores of policemen dead. This 'battle of Ismailia' helped ignite the revolution that brought the Egyptian military to power.[26] Conclusion of the Canal base agreement two years later suggested—wrongly, as it turned out—that the British could do business with the Egyptian Colonels.[27]

Elements of the new French leadership also made unlikely warmongers at the start of 1956. Mollet's Socialists and Pierre Mendès France's Radicals, mainstays of the 'Republican Front' formed a month after a general election on 2 January, went to the polls promising a political breakthrough in Algeria to match independence accords in neighbouring Morocco and Tunisia. The voters who put them in office—younger, more bourgeois, and more female than those who preferred their right-wing opponents—hardly constituted a 'war party'. As a 'young Turk' secretary general of the Socialist Party in 1946–7 Mollet had lambasted the older generation of socialist politicians that had engaged France more deeply in the Indochina War.[28] Ten years later, under Pierre Commin, Mollet's successor as party secretary, the Socialists directed secret contacts with Algerian nationalist leaders based in Cairo for much of 1956 hoping to negotiate a ceasefire.[29] But Mollet had, by this point, dropped his earlier objections to engaging in colonial conflict. Within weeks of becoming premier, Mollet defied those among his socialist colleagues in France and abroad who considered immediate independence the only just outcome for Algerians. Nonsense, he argued. Algerian majority-rule would not be democratic or equitable; it would be dystopian and violent. Algeria's settlers would be marginalized, evicted, or maybe even worse in a country likely to become either a one-party state, a theocratic Muslim regime, or a perverse mixture of both.[30]

Mendès France, too, was no imperial sentimentalist. But his recent experience of negotiating France's pull-out from Morocco and Tunisia kept him from prophesying doom for an independent Algeria. Mendès was guided instead by his humanitarian convictions and his economist's eye for the 'cost-benefits' of colonial commitments. He was also more accustomed to vitriolic right-wing criticism than Mollet. Applauded by some, he was loathed by others for making France face up to the imperatives of withdrawal from Vietnam and the two North African protectorates.[31] Mendès France might have steered the Republican Front towards a flight solution constructed around early talks with the FLN had he remained in government. Instead, he resigned his ministerial post in May, unimpressed by the coalition's financial management and disconcerted by its adventurism in Algeria.[32] Mollet was, by then, heeding other, more belligerent voices: the Minister of Defence, Maurice Bourgès-Maunoury, the Army Minister Max Lejeune, and Pierre Boursicot, head of the French overseas intelligence service (the *Service de*

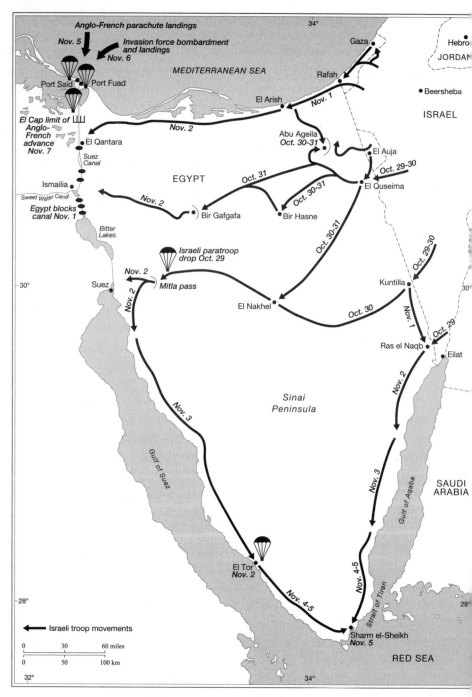

Map 8. The Suez Operation, 1956.

Documentation Extérieure et de Contre-Espionnage, SDECE).[33] The Social-ist leader was now in the camp of the die-hards.

What turned these once shrewd British and French proponents of 'flight' into implacable advocates of 'fight' in 1956? Or, to avoid reducing Suez to the wrong-headed adoption of a harder line by individual leaders, what drove Britain into such a disastrous confrontation in defiance of interna-tional law, UN opinion, and its Washington ally? And why did Mollet's administration follow suit? Avowedly committed to talks with Algeria's National Liberation Front (*Front de Libération Nationale*—FLN), the Repub-lican Front reversed course, making regime change in Cairo a central plank of its scheme to keep Algeria French. Answers lie in two things. First, the pervasive political atmosphere in which key decisions were made within the governing 'inner circles' in London and Paris, Second, the underlying con-viction amongst the decision-makers that decisive action was essential to arrest their declining imperial position. The mistakes of Suez, in other words, derived, in part, from the flawed assumptions within tight-knit governing groups that were increasingly unreceptive to contrary advice. A classic case of 'group think', or the mutual reinforcement of shared presumptions among crisis decision-makers, this also amounted to a breakdown of Cabi-net government in both countries.[34] It became more difficult in conse-quence to respond constructively to deeper, impersonal forces—the inexorable disaggregation of the British and French empires, the height-ened importance of the Middle East within the global Cold War, and the rising militancy among various strains of Arab nationalism.[35] None of these dilemmas was new. But each was fatally misinterpreted as policy planning became more restricted, secretive, and uncompromising. The task now is to trace this drift towards 'fight' solutions in Britain and France.

To do so, it is first worth glancing below the Egyptian horizon to the country's southern neighbour, Sudan. Here was another imperial interest that, in British eyes, faced a Nasserite threat. The key dynamics in this vast territory, technically a condominium—or joint protectorate of Britain and Egypt—were the permissible extent of Egyptian influence and the coun-tervailing wisdom of 'Sudanization', by which was meant the progressive indigenization of administrative services. Over the preceding decades the British, as Heather Sharkey puts it, 'unwittingly gave nationalism an insti-tutional framework' because of their operating principle that a colony should pay its way. The frugality that this imposed made reliance on locally-educated and trained Sudanese government servants inevitable. Most of these Sudanese officials were northerners and graduates of Khartoum's Gordon College secondary school. This all-male administrative elite became the local officials, known as *mamurs* and *sub-mamurs*, who were charged with policing and tax collection tasks in tandem with the assistant district commissioners of Britain's Sudan Political Service. Sudanization accelerated further in the decade 1945–55, making an orderly flight seem predictable, logical, and only a matter of time. This was a view expressed by the Sudanese Graduate Congress, educated future officials who, in 1942, demanded self-government after the war.[36]

Increasing talk of self-rule did not imply an end to British intervention-ism, however. The controversial practice of clitoridectomy was a case in point. Spurred by criticism from British women's groups, colonial opposi-tion to clitoridectomy, or female genital cutting, culminated in a February 1946 law banning the practice. Was this 'progress' or an attack on customary tradition? Surely it was both. But this late colonial campaign against female circumcision was, if anything, driven by economic concerns. Officials and medical staff concurred that 'infibulation led to poor maternity outcomes'. Eliminating the practice was intended to spur population growth and foster women's mothering skills.[37] Sudan's British rulers, it seems, were still con-vinced they knew best.

The foundational justifications for British imperial supremacy in the Sudan—to protect the Sudanese from otherwise certain domination by their northern neighbour—collapsed once the leaders of Egypt's new mili-tary government declared their support for Sudanese self-determination. From 1953 onwards, the Egyptians and the Sudanese set the agenda and the pace for Sudanese independence.[38] Conservative Ministers and Foreign Office diplomats meanwhile hoped that their accommodating attitude to Sudan would be reciprocated by Egypt's new leadership in the more impor-tant discussions over the long-term future of the Suez Canal zone. Redolent of the 'high imperialism' of the Victorian era, trade and military prerogatives triumphed over concern for Sudanese internal stability.[39]

The growing alarmism about anti-imperial trends in the Middle East becomes easier to read when placed in this light. In late November 1955 General 'Pasha' Glubb, head of Jordan's Arab Legion security forces warned Eden that not just Egypt, but Saudi Arabia, Yemen, and Syria were all 'irrevocably in the Soviet bag'. Glubb's hyperbole was a transparent attempt to secure additional funding for his beloved Legion.[40] But it pointed to the greater prevalence of Cold War rhetoric in high-level discussions of Britain's

Middle East prospects in the year ahead. Typical in this regard was a Foreign Office paper, 'Communism and Africa', circulated to ministers in mid April 1956. The Soviets, the Foreign Secretary Selwyn Lloyd averred, were fast acquiring a deeper knowledge of African affairs. And they used arms sales, 'cultural' exchanges, and front organizations such as the World Federation of Trade Unions to enhance their influence over nationalist groups. Pointing to a raft of new African studies academies in Moscow, Lloyd was unequivocal, 'When suddenly the history, economics, languages, and social relations of Africa are stepped up by political directive to the point where the work now being done on Africa compares with that done in South-East Asia, it is clear that this is for operational reasons rather than an academic love of science.'[41] Months before the nationalization of the Canal, the Egyptian regime's anti-colonial pan-Arabism was recast as quasi-Communistic.

Admittedly, the Cairo government courted international backing for the causes of Arab independence and the right of return of Palestinian refugees expelled from their homeland in the Arab-Israeli War of 1948. Integral to this process were procuring arms from the Eastern bloc and cultivating ties with socialist regimes in the Non-Aligned Movement, Tito's Yugoslavia especially.[42] The one thing that Britain, France, and the US agreed upon in early 1956 was that the Egyptian leadership was becoming more vigorously anti-imperialist as it grew militarily stronger. Anglo-American efforts to broker an Egyptian–Israeli settlement sweetened by the offer of financial assistance for construction of Egypt's Aswan Dam proved fruitless. The scheme, known as Project *Alpha*, also looked increasingly naive.[43] By contrast, French investment in military cooperation with Israel, previously vilified as avaricious realpolitik, began to look shrewder.[44] When Jordan's King Hussein, previously considered reliably Anglophile, dismissed Glubb on 1 March 1956, Downing Street and the Foreign office mistakenly attributed the sacking to Nasser's malign influence. The ousted General became an oracle for hard-liners in Westminster and Whitehall.[45] Eden rehearsed Glubb's dire predictions in correspondence with Eisenhower in the months ahead. In late July he told the American president that Nasser was 'active wherever Muslims can be found'. He was no Hitler, but the parallel with Mussolini, another Mediterranean empire-builder, was 'close'.[46] On the night of 27 July, after news reached London of the Suez nationalization, the Prime Minister summoned the French Ambassador Jean Chauvel, telling him that France, like Britain, faced an acid test of western solidarity.[47]

In early September Eden took his doom-laden analogies a step further. Egyptian seizure of the Canal was 'the opening gambit in a planned campaign...to expel all Western influence and interests from Arab countries'. If successful, Nasser's pan-Arabist ideology would foment revolution throughout North Africa and western Asia. Once Operation *Musketeer* began, Eden distilled his earlier musings into three self-justificatory sentences: 'if we had allowed things to drift, everything would have gone from bad to worse. Nasser would have become a kind of Moslem Mussolini and our friends in Iraq, Jordan, Saudi Arabia and even Iran would gradually have been brought down. His efforts would have spread westwards, and Libya and all North Africa would have been brought under his control.'[48]

With the benefit of hindsight, Eden's nightmarish vision of Egyptian-backed military regimes from Iraq to Libya was less outlandish than it seemed to his opponents at the time. Even the Labour opposition accepted that Nasser's actions were blatantly provocative. With more than a tinge of racism, Aneurin Bevan commented, 'if the sending of one's police and soldiers into the darkness of the night to seize somebody else's property is nationalisation, Ali Baba used the wrong terminology'.[49] No one on the government or opposition frontbenches recalled that Nasser-inspired interventionism was a recent phenomenon, the Egyptian state not having been at the forefront of the Arab nationalist movement before the revolution that brought the Colonel to power in July 1952.[50]

The idea of Arab dominos falling because of Egyptian prodding certainly resonated in Paris where official preoccupation with the Algerian FLN's external sources of support was becoming an obsession. French politicians and press were even more outspoken in their condemnation of Nasser's regime. Again war memories cast a long shadow. For Mollet, the Colonel was a 'Hitler', his writings comparable to *Mein Kampf*. The Minister of Justice François Mitterrand, proponent of an expanded war effort in Algeria, spoke of 'liquidating' the troublesome Pharaoh. For newspapers of right and left, overthrow of the Egyptian regime presented an opportunity to prevent another Munich. If the rhetoric was familiar, its articulation in the language of 'resistance' was not. Mollet's closest ministerial colleagues, including Bourgès-Maunoury, the principal architect of French intervention, had resistance backgrounds. So did many of their senior advisers, military figures, colonial appointees, and security service operatives. Like their Israeli allies, they adapted more easily than their British counterparts to the practices of covert planning, sabotage, and audacious 'behind the lines' actions that characterized the Suez invasion.[51] Former intelligence officers and Suez group members Julian Amery and Billy McLean were, in this respect, exceptions and not the rule.[52] Behind everything the Frenchmen did lay the Algerian fixation.[53]

The French Army had over 320,000 soldiers deployed in Morocco, Algeria, and Tunisia on 1 January 1956. 180,451 were in Algeria alone.[54] Yet remarkably few politicians thought these huge numbers were large enough. New Year bombings in two Algerian provincial towns—Bône (Anneba) in the east and Tizi Ouzou, capital of Berber Kabylia—announced an intensification of attacks by the FLN's military wing, the National Liberation Army (in French: ALN). French settlers, powerfully represented by Algeria's mayoral federation, insisted that the first responsibility of the new French government was to ensure security, not rush ahead with reform.[55] As is explained more fully in Chapter 11, this sequential mantra of 'order before reform' would be repeatedly cited to postpone major policy initiatives from the reorganization of local government to land redistribution and tax reform.[56] If any government were to buck this trend, it was Mollet's. This was not because the Socialists received a strong mandate from the electorate in the January elections (indeed, the Communist PCF fared much better with 5.5 million votes), but because the two political parties most critical of generous concessions to the FLN saw their vote collapse. The Christian Democrat MRP, the moving force behind the escalation of war in Indochina, lost out to the Radicals. And electors punished persistent squabbling within the Gaullist RPF, which mustered fewer than 850,000 votes, down from four million plus at the last national election in July 1951.[57] (It is worth remembering this in light of de Gaulle's conspicuous silence as the Suez crisis developed.)

Conclusive only for its losers, the 1956 election result was not a mandate for peace in Algeria. It took a month before the new coalition was invested in office. Yet over the eight weeks of February–March 1956 the Republican Front government wrought more fundamental change in the Algerian War than that which would follow de Gaulle's spectacular return to power in the 'May crisis' of 1958 (discussed in Chapter 10). The transformation in the Algerian scene in early 1956 did not mark the fulfilment of pre-election promises for a wider Algerian franchise, local government reform, and an end to conflict. It signalled their abandonment. Algerian settlers, a constituency that the *New York Times* identified as a 'dictatorship of the populace', were the reason why.[58]

Mollet visited Algiers on 6 February hoping to galvanize support for a package of reforms. Twenty years to the day after bloody rioting between ultra-rightists and their opponents in Paris, he was greeted by settler protests coordinated by a new generation of die-hards—post-war inheritors of the anti-republican, ultra-rightist mantle.[59] Three were colonial establishment insiders: Jean-Baptiste Biaggi, right-hand man of the former governor Jacques Soustelle; Amédée Froger, mayor of Boufarik, a *colon* farming town south of Algiers; and André Achiary, the infamous sub-prefect who directed vigilante killings in Guelma in 1945. Two others were rabble-rousers: Joseph Ortiz, thuggish leader of Algeria's Poujadists, a reactionary petit-bourgeois movement that had just broken through at the polls; and Pierre Lagaillarde, student activist at Algiers University and, later, a founder of the terroristic *Organisation de l'Année Secrète* (OAS). As Mollet struggled to be heard behind a cordon of paramilitary CRS at the Algiers cenotaph, demonstrators pelted him with tomatoes, their 'ammunition' supplied by a wholesaler's truck concealed from police view.[60]

The settlers were furious that their man, the former governor Soustelle, was to be replaced with a 'Resident-Minister', Georges Catroux. Both men shared wartime associations with de Gaulle's Free French movement. But their colonial paths had since diverged. Catroux, a retired Army General, wartime Governor in Syria, and key negotiator of Moroccan independence, was an imperial pro-consul with over forty years' experience, patriarchal in the tradition of his original mentor, Marshal Lyautey.[61] Soustelle was a professional anthropologist turned Gaullist apparatchik, fervent in his commitment to Algerian 'integration' with France and, by 1956, a darling of the settlers.[62] Catroux suffered by comparison. He was derided as the government's placeman, the unpopular receiver sent in to wind up the company as the inevitable prelude to withdrawal. For all their playground antics, the settlers, many of them ex-servicemen from the capital's poorer districts, were deadly serious. Mollet, herded by police into the government buildings of the *Palais d'été*, was visibly shaken by his first brush with settler politics. Told about the incident over the telephone later that afternoon, Catroux resigned immediately. 6 February 1956, the *jour des tomates*, looked like the settlers' first successful coup d'état of the Algerian War.

It is, indeed, tempting to ascribe the French government's subsequent decision to request parliamentary 'special powers' to place Algeria under emergency rule as an abject capitulation to reactionary settler demands. FLN activists saw it that way. They were contemptuous of the Socialists' sham liberalism; still more so of the French Communists' willingness to support war in contravention of their so-called internationalism. An understandable reaction, it neglects three considerations. First was Mollet's interpretation of the Algiers protests as the authentic reaction of Algeria's 'poor white' working class to the threat of abandonment by a political elite ignorant of the realities of FLN terrorism. Government approval of extended military powers was justified in the language of republican defence, of safeguarding loyal citizens and making Algeria safe for eventual reform.

Second was the implicit acknowledgement among the Fourth Republic's centrist parties, the Socialist Party included, that the professional army, having been inadequately supported in Indochina, deserved wholehearted backing. The strategic rationale for this was always secondary to the tense politics of French civil–military relations. French public opinion, wavering but generally unsympathetic to the settler cause, was also more inclined to back the armed forces. This explains why the Communists, still angling for a place in the ruling coalition, backed the parliamentary vote on 'special powers' on 12 March.[63] The PCF decision was all the more remarkable because their client Communist party in Algeria was facing a renewed government ban.[64]

The third point was that Robert Lacoste, the man selected to replace Catroux, was assigned the task of combining extended repressive powers with the resumption of welfare reforms, educational provision, and other improvements to Algerian living standards. A veteran trade unionist and another left-wing politician with immaculate resistance credentials (his father was shot by German occupation forces in March 1944), Lacoste was republican patriot personified.

Each of these factors points to the emotional and cultural perceptions of the Algerian conflict among politicians of the Fourth Republic, many of them, like Mollet (born 1905), Bourgès-Maunoury (born 1914), and Lacoste (born 1898), for whom wartime resistance and the restoration of republican democracy in France was the defining event of their adult lives. It was no coincidence that the Army Minister Max Lejeune named the decision to begin sending young conscripts (*Appelés*) and twenty-something reservists (*Rappelés*) to serve in Algeria from April onwards Operation *Valmy* in evocation of French citizens' defence of an imperilled First French Republic in 1792. Operation *Valmy*'s call to arms failed to resonate with those affected by it—national servicemen not previously called upon to fight nasty colonial wars; older reservists, often their family's sole bread-winner; and the loved ones thrown into confusion by their unanticipated departure. A grass-roots

protest movement mushroomed, but failed to win party political endorsement. In Rouen, Paris, Limoges, and Lyons police herded reluctant soldiers
onto trains bound for the Mediterranean embarkation ports. Mothers, wives,
and girlfriends blocked the tracks. Barrack-room indiscipline was widespread.[65] Hatred of officialdom, the military, and the Algerian War melded
into a kind of generational alienation from the former *résistantes* in government whose good fortune had been to fight for something worthwhile.[66]

The stakes involved changed dramatically soon after dawn on 18 May
1956 when ALN fighters ambushed a French infantry patrol picking its way
through the massifs of the Palestro gorge, eighty kilometres south-east of
Algiers. Seventeen soldiers were killed, four more captured. The corpses
were stripped then mutilated, some beyond recognition. With the exception
of their junior officer, sub-Lieutenant Hervé Artur, an eager recruit from
Casablanca, the dead men were all *Rappelés* from the Paris region. Among
them, as the tabloid *France Dimanche*'s banner headline phrased it, were
'seven husbands, four fathers, seven fiancés'. Larger massacres than this one,
often involving French troops as killers not victims, were not uncommon in
Algeria. And local civilians in dirt-poor areas like the Palestro region were
their principal victims. But 'Palestro' shocked France precisely because the
annihilation of these suburban family men, reluctant warriors coerced into
uniform, encapsulated so much: the cruel arbitrariness of Plan *Valmy*, the
anguish of families ignored by government; the FLN's terrifying ruthlessness; the dystopian cycle of worsening Algerian violence.[67]

One month later, prison warders dragged Ahmed Zabana and Ferradj
Abdelkader Ben Moussa into the courtyard of the Algiers *Barberousse* jail.
The unfortunate duo was bound hand and foot, their heads locked into position
inside the contraption that dominated the yard. When the blade came down
they became the first FLN prisoners guillotined for terrorism. More would
follow, to the delight of the settler press. But the majority of political killings
in the Algerian capital occurred on its streets. Assassinations, disappearances,
and indiscriminate bombings at traffic intersections, in cafés, and in the city's
Casbah continued into the autumn. Bombings in Muslim *quartiers* were
orchestrated by settler extremists led by André Achiary, a confidant of the
SDECE's shadowy counter-espionage unit. Saadi Yacef and a team of young
women bombers, including Zohra Drif and Djamila Bouhired, planned the
explosions in the capital's European districts.[68] After the notorious 'Milk Bar'
bombings on 30 September, immortalized in Gillo Pontecorvo's 1966 film
The Battle of Algiers, the overwhelming impression was of a city and a conflict

spiralling out of control. Special powers, Lacoste's reforms, Plan *Valmy* were plainly not working. Might an Egyptian solution exist?

This was certainly the message given to a British parliamentary delegation that toured Algeria between 15 and 22 October. Led by Walter Elliott, a former Secretary of State for Scotland whose time at the Ministry of Agriculture deepened his attachment to France, the nine British MPs received red carpet treatment. After visiting new housing projects in Algiers, they were entertained by Resident Minister Lacoste and the city's mayor Jacques Chevalier. Each insisted that France had to win the war—for the sake of moderates on all sides, for the sake of western influence in Africa. Nasser, they went on was behind everything but was himself probably just an unwitting Moscow stooge. This was music to the ears of Elliot and Julian Amery, the two most active members of the British delegation. So, too, was the message they received during their next formal engagement, a meal with the 'super-prefect' (or IGAME) for Eastern Algeria, Maurice Papon. Better known to history for his 1990s trial for war crimes against French Jews, Papon spent much longer serving the Algerian colonial state than Pétain's Second World War regime. A notorious hardliner who played a crucial role in constructing the institutional apparatus of the Algerian police state, Papon was at the time much respected by French governmental and Gaullist oppositional opinion in France. Talking to his British guests with customary frankness, he convinced them that France would crush its FLN opponents. A final, well-orchestrated army visit saw the MPs' delegation deposited at the Oran arsenal where weapons captured from Algerian fighters were stored. Over half, including 1956-model Bren guns, were of British manufacture, definitive proof, it was stated, that the weapons came, not from British but from Egyptian military sources.[69]

Not all shades of British parliamentary opinion were so willing to be convinced. Speaking a month before the delegation visit, John Strachey, a former Labour War Office minister, told an audience in Dundee that of all the stupidities to which Eden's government might fall prey, the worst would be to embark on a joint military venture with France against Nasser's Egypt. Labour leader Hugh Gaitskell said much the same in private correspondence with Eden and Selwyn Lloyd in the weeks after nationalization, adding that firm US backing was an absolute prerequisite should intervention take place.[70] Instead, by mid-October Britain risked becoming involved in an unjustifiable fight to undermine Arab support for Algerian independence. The results would be disastrous.[71] With the exception of the Communists, few French parliamentarians had any such reservations. To understand why, we need to wind the clock back a little.

'France considers it more important to defeat Colonel Nasser's enterprise than to win ten battles in Algeria.' Thus did Foreign Minister Christian Pineau justify French calls for a riposte to nationalization of the Suez Canal in discussion with his British and US counterparts in London on 30 July 1956.[72] At this stage, it was not weapons but bugging and the theft of documents from Egypt's Paris Embassy by the French internal security service, the *Direction de la Surveillance du Territoire* (DST) that registered greater impact. Conducted as part of an intelligence war against FLN fundraising inside and outside France, the 'active surveillance' of the Egyptian Embassy allegedly confirmed Nasser's pivotal role as the Algerians' chief foreign backer.[73] The British security services also did their part, passing on information to Paris about illicit Egyptian arms supplies via Tunisia to the FLN for eighteen months before the Suez Operation.[74] Little wonder that on 23 June 1956 SDECE head Boursicot, and Defence Ministry representatives Abel Thomas and Louis Mangin agreed a major arms contract with Shimon Peres and Israeli Chief of Staff Moshe Dayan. Its centrepiece was seventy-two state-of-the-art Mystère IV jets, enough to transform the balance of air power in the Middle East. Israel's lugubrious premier David Ben-Gurion, not a natural Francophile, enthused that, 'with an ally like France, Israel is willing to go all the way'.[75] Israel's decisive aerial advantage might not last long, however. Aware that Egypt's closest Arab partner, Syria, was awaiting delivery of two squadrons of Soviet MiG 15 fighters, the French general staff was sure that speed was of the essence.[76] The stresses of Algeria had set France on the path to collusion.

After the special powers vote, Plan *Valmy*, and public revulsion at Palestro, conspiring with Israel to overthrow Nasser was less of a departure for the French government than for the British. Put simply, the more remarkable fight decision—to escalate in Algeria—was taken in March. (The importance of this decision is discussed in Chapter 11.) Its significance becomes clearer in light of France's financial position in early 1956. The preceding government achieved a modest balance of payments surplus in 1955, the first since the end of the Second World War. So the Republican Front came into office with the budgetary books in relatively good order. Algerian War costs changed this. 300 billion francs were spent in 1956 alone, adding to a budget deficit, which was careening towards the one trillion franc mark as the Suez venture crumbled. In desperation, the government drew heavily on its foreign currency reserves to maintain franc values. External trade plummeted meanwhile, increasing the risk of recession at home.[77] There was, though, a crucial difference between the French and British financial positions. The Bank of France had secured necessary US loan funding prior to the invasion decision at Sèvres. The French could afford to be brazen, if only in the short term, whereas the British, as we shall see, could not.

That brazenness, and the absence of political accountability to which it pointed, was hidden from public view in the Sèvres discussions.[78] Instead, French voters were still left with the image of cool responsibility conjured up by the Foreign Minister, Pineau, when he took to the French airwaves four weeks earlier, on the evening of 14 September. Pineau's aim, he said, was to prove that the proponents of talks with Nasser were misguided. It was not that Mollet's government was determined to use force no matter what. Quite the reverse: the French government wanted peace. It was working hard to lessen Cold War tension and was committed to improving living standards for the world's poorest communities. But advances in these and other fields of overseas policy demanded respect for the rules of international law and existing treaties.[79] Nasser was the outlaw, not France. Events later indicated that Pineau was being somewhat economical with the truth.

By the time the Sèvres talks began, the French authorities were facing bitter criticism from Arab and African governments over another breach of international law—a mid-air hijack of the FLN's external leadership. The background to this event lay in the earlier secret exchanges between Socialist politicians and the FLN executive, central to which were Habib Bourguiba's Tunisian government and Morocco's monarchical regime. The lynch-pin between them was Alain Savary, Minister for Moroccan and Tunisian Affairs and the Socialists' veteran negotiator with the Vietminh.[80] After Mendès France's resignation in May, Savary personified the liberal wing of Mollet's government, which was rapidly losing ground to the hard-liners grouped around the Defence Minister Bourgès-Maunoury. Both men achieved political prominence young. Savary, an outstanding student at Sciences-Po, helped organize the Free French takeover of the tiny island colony of St Pierre et Miquelon off the Newfoundland coast. He became the territory's Governor at the tender age of twenty-three. A more doctrinaire socialist than Mollet, Savary instinctively grasped the confluence between popular nationalism and leftist egalitarianism represented by anti-colonial groups like the Vietminh and Bourguiba's Neo-Destour as well as by senior FLN figures like Mohamed Boudiaf and Hocine Aït Ahmed.[81] A *Polytechnicien* and, later, an accomplished resistance organizer, Bourgès-Maunoury also cemented his reputation as a young man. He was, though, a more strident nationalist than the cosmopolitan Savary. Bourgès-Maunoury invested his energies in consolidating the Radical Party's regional, south-western power-base in and around Toulouse. Hawkish in colonial affairs, he stood at the heart of the French security establishment of senior military personnel, intelligence officers, and police prefects. A firm supporter of Papon's repressive methods, Bourgès-Maunoury had no time for the ideological pretensions of their Algerian opponents, whose contacts with Savary he was impatient to end.

It was Sultan Mohammed V who, in mid April, organized preliminary talks with FLN envoys on neutral ground: the Spanish cities of Madrid and Seville. Anxious lest its own pending independence be jeopardized by the violence in neighbouring Algeria, Morocco's governing elite, like their Tunisian brethren, were understandably eager to mediate a settlement. The French government, and especially the Defence Ministry, responded coolly, nervous that cherished base rights in Morocco might form part of any bargain.[82] Savary was, however, allowed to keep the door ajar. With his encouragement, the Moroccans and Tunisians organized a round-table conference in Tunis scheduled to begin in late October to give a fillip to negotiations. Four members of the FLN executive—Boudiaf, Aït Ahmed, Mohammed Khider and Ahmed Ben Bella— therefore accepted the Sultan's offer of a DC 3 aircraft to fly them from Rabat to the Tunisian capital on the 22nd.[83] Alerted by the DST to the plane's VIP cargo, once it entered Algerian air space the bait proved irresistible to the French air force and army commanders Air Marshal Frandon and General Lorillot. Frandon ordered the pilot to land in Algiers, disgorging his passengers for immediate arrest.[84] Neither Governor Lacoste in Algiers nor Mollet in Paris were alerted beforehand. Coming only six days after the French navy had intercepted the steamship *Athos*, seizing a substantial cargo of Egyptian-supplied weaponry destined for the ALN, detention of the four FLN executive members, although unauthorized, proved wildly popular among Algerian settlers and commentators in France.[85] Security service officers were quick to publicize details of twelve kilograms of FLN documents found aboard the aircraft, which indicated that the Algerian rebellion was sustained financially and militarily with Egyptian aid.[86]

Whatever the expediency of arresting the FLN leaders, the Algiers hijack exposed breaks in the chain of government decision-making between Paris and Algiers. Although Eisenhower's administration chose to keep quiet—for now—the hijack, a flagrant violation of commercial air-space, convinced the White House that the French government was out of control.[87] Mollet had even offered the plane safe passage so that Savary's negotiation effort could be sustained. The two intransigents—Bourgès-Maunoury at Defence and the Army Minister Max Lejeune—approved the action before their prime minister even knew about it. Mollet's subsequent acquiescence, partly in response to the favourable French public reaction, partly because he anticipated that the FLN would be significantly weakened by the 'decapitation', was also misplaced.[88] Incarcerated in the Paris La Santé prison, the four Algerian nationalists could do nothing to prevent the emergence of a more combative ALN strategy to which Ben Bella and Boudiaf in particular were strongly opposed. The temporary eclipse of the FLN's external directorate consolidated the power of the movement's internal leadership as a result. Organized into a five-member committee (*Comité de Coordination et d'Exécution*—CCE) at a critical secret FLN meeting—the Soummam Congress—five months earlier in August, the CCE approved the extension of FLN terrorism to Algeria's urban centres, Algiers especially. According to the capital's mayor Jacques Chevalier, a reformer with an unofficial back-channel to the FLN, the movement was now firmly in the hands of hard-line regional (*wilaya*) commanders: Belkacem Krim, Ramdane Abbane, and Omar Ouamrane.[89] The Republican Front's Algerian strategy was going disastrously wrong even before the attack on Egypt began.

In a sense, the same was true for Britain, albeit for monetary, more than political, reasons. The supreme irony of Suez was that a key motive for British action against Nasser was to defend the sterling exchange rate and the sterling area. Yet Britain's currency, its foreign exchange reserve, and its vital oil supplies were all undermined by the confrontational path chosen. Eisenhower was unconvinced by Eden's arguments about the extent of the Egyptian danger and the best way to handle it.[90]

'Anthony, are you out of your mind?' was the President's first reaction.[91] Opposed to military intervention and infuriated at being deceived with the apparent fait accompli of invasion, the US government made expert use of its 'economic artillery' to sink British plans.[92] Eisenhower's Republican administration, preparing for presidential elections on 6 November 1956, included several former bankers and corporate lawyers. They included Secretary of State John Foster Dulles and his brother Allen, head of the CIA, as well as the industrialist George Humphrey, US Treasury Secretary. All agreed that the time had come to flex American financial muscle.[93] Withholding loan funding precipitated a disastrous 'run' on sterling in the first week of

November that spelt the end for the Suez operation.[94] The Bank of England's dollar reserves collapsed as the Treasury struggled to defend the pound and avoid a last-ditch appeal to the IMF for monetary aid. It was a hopeless task. Only when the British backed down did Washington reverse its position, making IMF credits worth 1.3 billion dollars available on 10 December.[95]

Reduced to its essence, Suez marked a definitive rebuff to what Martin Lynn terms, 'imperial unilateralism': the mistaken belief that Britain could still pursue imperial policies at variance with US interests.[96] British imperial 'prestige', for so long critical to maintaining colonial control, was revealed as an elaborate fraud, less substance than hot air.[97] This was precisely what Secretary of State Dulles told Eisenhower's National Security Council on 1 November as *Musketeer* reverberated through Washington: US alliance commitments to Britain and France should not imply any indulgence towards their colonial policies.[98]

In fact, the crisis was less definitive than Dulles' remarks suggest. Once American displeasure was made plain, 'normal service' quickly resumed. The Treasury got the financial bailout. Extensive military spending on imperial defence was barely affected, particularly in Malaysia and Singapore, where the end of the Malayan Emergency would be followed by the emergence of a more substantial threat—an expansionist Indonesian state. Suez Group die-hards blustered in the Commons and in the press about American interference and the threat it posed to the Atlantic alliance. But, as the French Ambassador Jean Chauvel commented, by the end of November their complaints carried little weight.[99] Relations with Washington were bruised but not seriously wounded by the Eden government's flawed pursuit of an imperial fight. And it cannot be reasonably claimed that any Anglo-American 'special relationship' suddenly became unequal. The commanding strength of America's financial lever had been apparent since at least 1945 when John Maynard Keynes took the Treasury's begging bowl to Washington in search of a loan. Frequent UN General Assembly attacks on Britain and, more especially, France would confirm that the case for empire was 'morally disarmed' by the dishonesty and stupidity of Suez. Like so many capable civil servants who might have warned against it, the British delegation to the UN, including a young Douglas Hurd, was not even informed about the impending invasion.[100] Yet, with the important exception of nearby Cyprus, Britain's imperial connections were only marginally contaminated by the crisis and its international fallout.[101]

Perhaps, then, Julian Amery's rueful identification of Suez as Britain's imperial Waterloo was overdrawn. It is harder still to make the case that the

1956 crisis marked an equally decisive defeat for France.[102] Admittedly, some leading figures in French political life were outraged by their government's Machiavellian behaviour. On the afternoon of 31 October, the first day of the Franco-British invasion, Pierre Cot, a former Popular Front minister and alleged Communist fellow-traveller who we encountered during the acrimonious parliamentary inquest into the Cao Bang 'disaster', took the floor in the Chamber of Deputies to condemn this latest French colonial misadventure. 'What right did France have to intervene?' he asked. Surely his fellow deputies could see that the pretexts for attacking Egypt were a sham? Cot's speech was impressively forthright, but the National Assembly was engaged in a dialogue of the deaf. There was no appetite on the Left to take Mollet to task when the Soviet Union was acting in equally flagrant disregard of sovereignty and human rights in Hungary. Indeed, Cot was repeatedly interrupted by furious right-wingers insistent that France at least had a case for sending in the troops unlike the Soviet Union.[103] Members of the French diplomatic community were less sanguine about France's disregard for international law, although the Foreign Ministry issued a ludicrous circular to all of France's overseas embassies on 31 October stating that France was invading Egypt to restore peace to the Middle East.[104]

Behind such bravado, senior French diplomats took steps to prevent details of the Sèvres collusion from leaking out. Embassy staff in Washington and in European and Asian capitals reassured their host governments that, whatever the rumours, France was acting in the interests of regional stability.[105] But this brief panic soon passed. Unlike Eden, Mollet did not fall from grace. Indeed, the country united behind him, accepting the government's argument that Nasser's overthrow was a moral imperative because it would shorten the Algerian War.[106] On 20 December he won a parliamentary vote of confidence resoundingly 325 to 210. Opinion polls confirmed that more French people approved of the invasion *after* it than before.[107] For France, by contrast, Suez was less a short-term humiliation than a long-term reverse. Although Mollet's Republican Front survived, and was even commended for its resolve, the fact remained that the Fourth Republic 'system' they represented had suffered another crushing blow. The regime's Gaullist opponents savaged the fallacy of strategic alignment with either one of the 'Anglo-Saxon' powers. Efforts to thwart the internationalization of the Algerian conflict were in vain. French standing in the Arab world and its prickly relations with Washington were sorely tested for years afterward. In these circumstances, the case for accelerated development of French nuclear weaponry seemed to make itself. So did the argument for a continental European Community, enthusi-astically underlined by the West German Chancellor Konrad Adenauer and soon underwritten by the Treaty of Rome in March 1957.[108]

Just as significant as the international ramifications were the consequences for Algeria and the fraught relationship between French officialdom and its armed forces. The keenest proponents of the French fight strategy against Nasser were its executors—the professional army elite in Algiers. The exten-sive French military commitment to *Musketeer* came with a strongly North African flavour. French assault forces comprised two elite divisions—the 10th parachutists and the 7th rapid mechanized—each based in Algeria. These units, along with the aircraft carrier *Georges Leygues* (which shelled Rafah on 1 November in support of Israeli ground forces) and French air-craft operating from Israel and Cyprus, were placed under British com-mand.[109] British commanders were acutely embarrassed by the Rafah shelling and the fact that French aircraft sported joint forces markings.[110] Both actions brought the extent of Franco-British collusion with Israel into plain sight, prompting Eden to telegram a personal plea to Mollet for greater discre-tion.[111] Labour MPs, led by Richard Crossman, were looking for evidence of double-dealing both to make the case for a full parliamentary inquiry and to prove the moral argument against Eden's government.[112] Little wonder that ministers and military commanders urged French discretion.

British calls for restraint seemed nonsensical to senior officers of the 10th Division, another empire fighting force. It included one Foreign Legion regiment and another designated solely for colonial operations. They were assigned the toughest element in the *Musketeer* plan—capturing Port Said and Port Fuad. Their success in doing so nourished the conviction among the French assault troops that it was British wavering that snatched defeat from the jaws of victory.[113] Here, again, the British seemed peevish, not to say racist, in asking the French Chief of Staff General Paul Ely to ensure that Senegalese troops were not included among the Port Said occupation force.[114] Rumour had it that disgruntled French parachutists, returning to Algeria via Cyprus after the 6 November ceasefire, 'lost' some of their equipment—small arms that fell into the hands of Cypriot EOKA guerril-las. Like his men, their commander, Jacques Massu, soon to achieve notori-ety for directing the battle of Algiers in 1957, had spent years on active service in Indochina and North Africa, including Second World War service with the Free French in the Libyan Fezzan. Fiercely independent, with a distinctive moustache and prominent, hooked nose, Massu exemplified a strain of thought among professional officers in the colonial army, suspicious of Parisian politicking and certain that decisive military leadership was the empire's only salvation. The illicit supply of weapons nearly changed matters for him too. He had narrowly escaped assassination a month earlier when his staff car was peppered with bullets—probably fired by an Egyptian-supplied machine gun.[115]

The Defence Ministry autopsy on the Suez operations submitted to defence chiefs by the overall French commander Admiral Pierre Barjot, on 31 December pleased Massu more than it did Mollet. Unrepentant, it reached three telling conclusions. First, the collapse in British political resolve denied France the opportunity to secure decisive advantage in Algeria. Second, it was therefore vital that France acquire the means—amphibious vessels and long-range strike aircraft—to conduct comparable ventures alone, possibly outside NATO's restrictive command structure. Third, there was no reason to be apologetic. Fighting for France and its empire might require further operations of this type in future.[116] Decidedly Gaullist in his conclusions, Barjot's unashamedly bullish analysis pointed to the further expansion of French military involvement—and military control—in Algeria where, by the year's end, force numbers had risen to almost 400,000. It was a bleak, combative vision, the full horrors of which would become apparent in the months ahead.

Conclusion

The Suez crisis presents the clearest instance in which Britain and France chose to 'fight' together to defend imperial interests in the face of hostile international opinion. For all the rivalries, jealousies, and confrontations supposedly characteristic of British and French imperial co-existence, the two countries, on occasion, worked as close allies when the demands of colonial inter-dependence became obvious to both sides. The consequences could be devastating, and not just for the objects of their joint military ventures. As we saw in Chapter 4, British military occupation of southern Vietnam, initially presented as a facet of the disarmament of Japanese occupation forces in Southeast Asia, was actually driven by support for the restoration of French colonial authority in Indochina. So critical was this intervention that Britain has been depicted by some analysts as undermining the Vietnamese revolution of August 1945 and thus catalysing the outbreak of the Indochina

War.[117] But the Suez War of November–December 1956 was the most infamous case of joint imperial interventionism in the era of decolonization.

In the short term, Suez weighed heavier on Britain as both a political disaster and a symbolic eclipse. It cost Anthony Eden the premiership and sent Britain's stock of international prestige plummeting. Yet its longer-term consequences were less explosive. The gradual realignment of Britain's Middle East interests, moving inexorably away from the eastern Mediterranean and towards the Persian Gulf, was not much affected. In this sense, the changing focus in the regional operations of British Petroleum's antecedent, the Anglo-Iranian Oil Company, in the Middle East—broadly speaking, away from Iran and Egypt and towards Kuwait and the Persian Gulf—mirrored the strategic shifts in British policy as the dust settled after the 1956 crisis.[118] Most important, the country's cherished relationship with the United States was soon rebuilt.

Remembered in Britain for the political earthquake it triggered at home, 'Suez' is rarely acknowledged for what it was. Suez was a covertly planned Franco-British war of aggression against a sovereign state. Its protagonists (particularly in the security services and imperial armed forces of both countries) tried to justify it as an expedient means to safeguard imperial and trade interests—Britain's in the Middle East; France's in North Africa. The crisis has not been short of its historical analysts. Yet the colonial interdependence and imperialist cultures that underpinned this Franco-British alliance still merit closer scrutiny, not least because the intervention went so disastrously wrong, ending in bitter recriminations on all sides. Here, then, was an instance—perhaps *the* instance—in which the limits to effective bilateral collaboration in an international system grown more intolerant of old-style colonial interventionism were finally laid bare.

France decided to attack Egypt to help win a colonial war. Britain did so to consolidate the neo-colonial relationships with client Arab regimes that seemed pivotal to its imperial power. Both pretexts for fight over flight were empire derived, the former narrowly so, the latter an element in grand imperial strategy. Neither withstands close scrutiny. The Algerian conflict was internally generated and, while its international dimensions were crucial, its ultimate solution lay inside Algeria not outside it.[119] The impending battle of Algiers could no more be avoided than it could be won on the shores of the Suez Canal. British intervention, meanwhile, significantly weakened its favoured Middle East partners, Iraq and Jordan above all. It undermined the region's one pro-Western multilateral alliance—the Baghdad Pact.[120] It made

Britain 'public enemy number one' among the non-aligned states of Asia, Africa, and Latin America, increasingly ranged alongside one another in the UN General Assembly.[121] And it opened the door for America to assume the primordial role among Western powers throughout the Arab world.

There were warning signs hidden amid the welter of diplomatic paperwork occasioned by the crisis that the operation might backfire. French diplomats in Cairo were never in any doubt that Nasser enjoyed overwhelming support from what we now term 'the Arab street'.[122] And the French military attaché in Washington also picked up the significance of a State Department conference with twenty Latin American state representatives on 7 August 1956. Talking informally and without Washington lobby correspondents present, Secretary of State Dulles blasted the British and French for provoking the crisis. It was folly to think that they could act with impunity.[123] This was consistent with the 'overriding lesson' that General Sir Charles Keightley, commander of the Anglo-French task force, drew from the operation's collapse: 'world opinion is now an absolute principle of war and must be treated as such'.[124]

7

The Return of the Red Shawls?
Fighting Insurrection
in Madagascar

In October 1938 the French steamer *Ville de Reims* loaded an unusual cargo on the Algiers dockside. It was a casket containing the mortal remains of Queen Ranavalona III, the last monarch of Madagascar's Merina dynasty.[1] Ranavalona spent twenty years in Algerian exile before her death on 23 May 1917. She was evicted from her homeland by Madagascar's first colonial pro-consul General Joseph Gallieni, a rarity among France's senior soldiers in his fervent republicanism. Of relatively modest background himself, Gallieni was hostile to monarchical privilege in principle and hostile to Ranavalona's dynasty in particular. He reserved his deepest loathing for certain members of the Merina elite who refused to submit to a French colonial conquest, which on 30 September 1895 culminated in the occupation of the capital Tananarive (now Antananarivo), centre of the pre-colonial monarchy of Imerina. Concentrated around the highland plateaux of central Madagascar, the Merina had long been the Island's dominant ethnic group. Many, including the Queen's family, were Protestants, converted by British missionaries in the nineteenth century.[2] Indeed, popular hostility to Merina notables, and the missionary state-church they supported was integral to the Menalamba or Red Shawls revolt of 1896–7.[3] The uprising was substantially traceable to local causes. Among these, worsening famine conditions, forced labour requisitions, and a domineering ecclesiastical system left in place by the conquest figured largest. But the Menalamba revolt was also a last-ditch resistance to creeping French imperial control, and it was for this that it was popularly remembered—and celebrated. The revolt of the Red Shawls remained a cultural reference point for Malagasy nationalists for decades.[4]

Gallieni's plans to implant French imperial administration required the displacement of Merina influence and the subjugation of the inhabitants of Madagascar's rural interior. Subsequent colonial administrations, first military, then civilian, although avowedly committed to a policy of cooperative 'association', followed the General's lead in exploiting the economic divisions between Malagasy social groups and the acute provincial suspicion of the old Merina elite.[5] For those Malagasy, including former East African slaves once subordinated to the Merina, collectively assigned the colonial appellation *côtiers*, or coastal peoples, the French takeover was not quite the disaster that it was for the old royal elite.[6] For one thing, the French colonizers formally abolished Malagasy slavery in 1896. For another, the entire colonial project rested on the construction of a new export economy at variance with the slave-based economic system of Imerina.[7]

Not surprisingly, in subsequent years and decades, Merina notables figured within secret societies and, later, political parties, whose central objectives were to cast off the colonial yoke and restore Merina primacy.[8] As time wore on, other more modern ideas, socialism and nationalism prominent among them, exerted a stronger grip over Malagasy politics. Long before the people of Madagascar rebelled against French rule, the issues of independence and the role of the state had become entangled with historic ethnic divisions between Malagasy communities of Malay and Bantu origin. Thus, by the time that Ranavalona was shipped home in 1938, it was hard to distinguish the older accents of Merina communal loyalty from the newer inflexions of Malagasy popular nationalism.

Why, then, was the *Ville de Reims* steaming southward with the Queen's remains in late 1938? The answer, at one level, is that the colonial administration, still affected by the Popular Front's reforming humanism, wished to give tangible expression to its message of inter-ethnic reconciliation under benevolent French control. The pomp of a state-conferred funeral for a once-revered monarch conveyed a simple message: the violence and injustice of conquest were things of the past. Certainly, the returning Queen was treated with greater dignity in death than in life. She was re-interred alongside her royal forebears in an elaborate ceremony presided over by the French head of Madagascar's Protestant mission.[9] At another, deeper level Ranavalona's burial was sheer expediency. It helped disarm persistent Merina criticism of cultural insensitivity. And it offered a memorable public display to obscure the crackdown against Malagasy political parties then under way.

Madagascar's promised reconciliation with its colonial overseers was not to be. The coming of war in 1939 accentuated the divisions in island politics, both French and Malagasy. At the centre of colonial power, the sequence of Vichy administration followed by a British-backed Gaullist takeover in 1942–3 brought with it the familiar strains of increasingly authoritarian rule and extractive economics as Madagascar was coerced into serving a distant war effort.[10] For the wider population, mounting forced labour exactions provoked especially deep resentments that would resurface after the war.[11]

For a brief post-war moment during 1945 and 1946 the political skies brightened, even so. Renowned for consolidating a labour inspection service in French West Africa, a new colonial governor, Marcel de Coppet, promised a clean break with the wartime past.[12] Government was overhauled and new provincial assemblies elected over the autumn of 1946.[13] In practice, these measures backfired, opening up enough political space to reveal the depth of Malagasy antagonism to French domination. In short, the underlying tensions revealed by Ranavalona's return were still evident when Madagascar exploded into rebellion ten years later. Administrative practices and the disbursement of money and favour still exploited Malagasy ethnic divides. Suspicion of surreptitious Merina disloyalty endured, especially within the colony's security services. And the government's 'native affairs service' refused to accept the advent of political modernity signified by a vibrant, left-leaning Malagasy nationalism.[14] Most important of all, rural antagonism to externally-imposed systems of cultural belief, land use, and labour recruitment was, if anything, stronger than ever. The grievances of the Red Shawls resonated still.[15]

The 1947 rebellion

Rebellion broke out on the island of Madagascar on the night of 29 March 1947. Coordinated attacks were launched against widely-separated targets, including a military base at Moramanga in the centre of the island. Here and elsewhere the rebels were unsuccessful in their key objective: to secure modern weapons.[16] Planned urban uprisings in Tananarive and Fianarantsoa fell through, largely because additional troops and police were deployed, although the colonial infantry garrison in the northern port of Diego-Suarez did go over to the rebels.[17] After these initial reverses, the uprising never engulfed the entire island. But, in large swathes of eastern farmland and forest, disorder was sufficiently widespread to prompt a large-scale military intervention led by Foreign Legion and other specialist empire infantry trained for the dirty business of imperial policing. During April and May 1947, before these reinforcements arrived, the insurrection escalated steadily. The insurgents took advantage of dry-season conditions to move relatively freely through the countryside. For the authorities, the island's rail system was judged particularly unsafe. Locomotives sat in station sidings daubed with nationalist graffiti; bridges and sections of track were destroyed. In the first days after the outbreak the Governor was even compelled to requisition two Air France civil aircraft to allow him to visit victims of rebel attacks.[18]

The rebels meanwhile edged closer towards the capital, Tananarive, in Madagascar's central highlands. Road and rail links were cut, although the city itself never suffered sustained attack.[19] The strategic balance shifted once the colonial troops, spearheaded by two further battalions of West African *tirailleurs sénégalais*, disembarked in May and June.[20] Some estimates point to a French suppression so severe that, by the time the island's rebellion was declared over in 1949, over 100,000 Malagasy people among a population less than four million-strong had been killed. Certainly, the revolt marked the worst violence in a French African territory since the Rif War in Morocco twenty years earlier. Among those who lost their lives, the elimination of an entire political class of Malagasy opposition illustrates both the devastating legacy of a colonial power's decision to fight rather than negotiate and the narrowing of political choices it produced.

Leading Malagasy politicians were among over 600 arrested for sedition within the first days of the disorders.[21] Among them were Joseph Raseta, Joseph Ravoahangy, and Jacques Rabemananjara, the island's three deputies, the elected parliamentary representatives to the National Assembly in Paris. Ravoahangy and Rabemananjara were taken into custody by the island's police chief Marcel Baron on 12 April 1947. Raseta, already a marked man, remained free a little longer as he was in Paris at the time.[22] On 6 May he took to the floor of the National Assembly to refute the allegations against him. Few remembered his speech because of the spectacle of what followed. Jules Castellani, one of Madagascar's settler deputies, outraged by Raseta's temerity, slapped him in the face.[23] Why such fury? Raseta and Rovoahangy were founding members of the *Mouvement Démocratique de la Rénovation Malgache* (MDRM), the nationalist party established in February 1946 that

Figure 11. Post-war French recruitment for the Troupes Coloniales. Madagascar is included, alongside Indochina, Morocco, and the black African federations, as likely destinations for service.

was accused of directing the uprising.[24] Rabemananjara put his elite Merina lineage and outstanding literary skills to good use as MDRM secretary-general and chief orator for Malagasy nationalism.[25] They would soon achieve greater international notoriety as the Fourth Union's pre-eminent political prisoners. Two French-trained medical doctors and a noted writer, the trio made unlikely revolutionaries.[26] So much so that the details of the MDRM's rapid rise and the trial of its leaders are worth dwelling on because of the unscrupulous colonial officialdom they reveal.

The MDRM's cellular structure and executive 'bureau' mimicked the working practices of the Madagascan Communist Party, which had itself emerged in the freer political atmosphere created by Popular Front reforms in 1936–7. MDRM leaders, including Ravoahangy and Raseta, honed their organizational skills as Communist activists, a path that earned them the enduring hatred of Madagascar's colonial police.[27] Sûreté suspicions deepened when both men rubbed shoulders with their old colonial comrade Ho Chi Minh during the Vietnamese leader's stay in Paris during 1946.[28] By January 1947 MDRM organizers were being tailed, informants monitored party meetings, and government clerks thought to sympathize with the movement were brought in for questioning.[29] For all that, the MDRM was becoming a broader ideological church. It enjoyed the support of both the *Parti nationaliste malgache* (PA.NA.MA.), a group particularly strong in the south of the Island, as well as the 'JINA', pre-eminent among the secret societies that were a constant fixture of Madagascar's colonial politics. With a membership estimated at 300,000, on 21 March 1946 the MDRM leadership demanded French recognition of Madagascar as a free state within the French Union with its own government, legislature, and armed forces.[30] But not all the Malagasy were enthused by the prospect of MDRM control.

The socio-ethnic divisions between the peoples of the western and north-western coastal provinces and the Merina of the high plateaux around Tananarive, closely identified with the pre-colonial monarchy, still resonated. In several provinces, victory for the MDRM was widely seen as the precursor to Merina domination. Bitterness towards Merina elitism was perhaps sharpest amongst the Hova Mainty, formerly a slave caste under the Merina dynasty in the nineteenth century. These two anti-Merina constituencies, one regional, the other caste-based, united in the *Parti des déshérités de Madagascar* (Party of the Disinherited of Madagascar—PADESM), a political party whose nomenclature revealed its animus against the MDRM and Merina hegemony more broadly.[31] Within weeks of its foundation in June 1946, the PADESM was co-opted by Governor de Coppet's administration to thwart the MDRM's advance. Plans were agreed, but, as yet, unimplemented, with the Ministry of Overseas France to outlaw the Movement. And at local level, the settler community willingly bankrolled PADESM candidates in provincial elections in January 1947.[32]

Back in Paris, meanwhile, colonial problems had driven a wedge into Paul Ramadier's government, the last of the post-war centre-leftist coalitions in office between 1944 and 1947. It is worth revisiting these before we return to Madagascar. To begin with, modernization schemes to partner the launch of the French Union were still to be finalized. Like its domestic equivalent, Jean Monnet's grand plan for French industrial renovation, colonial development divided *dirigiste* planners from economic liberals.[33] Whichever proposals were approved seemed likely to hit the rocks of France's chronic dollar shortage.[34] Algeria raised other problems. The coalition partners and their local party sections within Algeria concurred that independence was out of the question, but agreed on little else.[35] These differences crystallized around Algeria's post-war 'Statute', meant to define the status of France's premier overseas possession in relation to the new Fourth Republic and the French Union. With minimal underlying agreement, the necessary legislation was slow in coming. The governing parties divided over Algerian voting rights and the extent of the territory's assimilation to France.[36] And recriminations continued about the disastrous Sétif uprising in Eastern Algeria, whose suppression over the summer of 1945 had cost at least 7,000 Algerian lives, probably more.[37]

The most immediate colonial problem, though, remained Indochina. Ramadier's Socialists were becoming uncomfortable at their identification with an expanding war in Vietnam, whose prosecution their Christian Democrat coalition partners the MRP increasingly controlled.[38] The dynamics of coalition-making and the recurrence of votes—over the new constitution, as well as national, provincial, and municipal elections—in a country rebuilding itself after war and occupation was especially damaging in this regard. A sideways glance at the MRP explains this point. Hitherto the strongest of the Fourth Republic's new political parties, the MRP's grassroots support had three distinct traits: it was provincial, female, and Catholic. Christian Democracy put down its deepest roots in Brittany and the strongly Catholic eastern provinces of Alsace and Lorraine.[39] Unfortunately for the Party's electoral planners, this profile of support corresponded closely with that of the Gaullist movement, the RPF. True to their leader, the Gaullists remained unremittingly hostile to a constitutional settlement that precluded strong presidential politics in favour of multi-party consensus.[40] If things went badly for the incumbent government, disenchanted MRP voters were liable to be seduced by the RPF's blend of social conservatism and uncompromising patriotism. De Gaulle's supporters at this stage had little truck with anything that smacked of imperial retreat.[41] Looking warily over their right shoulder at the strengthening Gaullist challenge, MRP ministers like Robert Schuman, Georges Bidault, and Paul Coste-Floret gravitated naturally towards a colonial hard-line.[42]

The other major partner in the tripartite coalition, the Communist Party, was, by contrast, fast approaching outright opposition to the fight against the Vietminh.[43] This was problematic not least because a Communist Defence Minister, the Marseille deputy François Billoux, technically oversaw the military strategy pursued. In a March 1947 National Assembly debate that descended into a brawl, Billoux, an International Brigade volunteer of the Spanish Civil War, pointedly withheld his support for expeditionary force intervention in Vietnam.[44] The French left's longstanding inter-party rivalries, never dormant in spite of the coalition partnership between Socialists and Communists, intervened here. The PCF registered major gains in the November 1946 general election, during which the Socialist vote, in particular, fell back. To complicate matters further, the UDSR, centre-left cousins of the Socialists, had fought the November election in partnership with the Radical Party as a combined block, the *Rassemblement des Gauches Républicaines* (RGR, the Left-Republican Group). Neither much of a group nor especially left-wing, the one thing RGR members agreed on was their opposition to the Communists.[45] Outflanked by the Communists on one side and by the RGR on the other, it became harder still for Ramadier's Socialist Party colleagues to swallow their objections while PCF ministers and the Communist daily *L'Humanité* vilified official policy.[46] Coalition government, they insisted, required responsible—and collective—decision-making, not electoral grand-standing and a narrowly ideological approach to difficult policy options.[47]

With a long hot summer of French labour unrest looming, the Communists, their Stalinist credentials no longer hidden up their sleeve, looked increasingly out of place inside a Cabinet that aligned itself against workers' demands at home, with imperial interests in the empire, and alongside Washington in the emerging Cold War. 1947, in other words, was a year of fateful choices for those in power in France.[48] Within a matter of months these testing policy choices caused centre-left tripartism to unravel only for a new coalition combination to take shape around the MRP and the Radical Party—the so-called Third Force. By the end of the year France had moved firmly rightwards.

Framed within this shifting political, imperial, and strategic landscape, Madagascar represented an unwelcome problem at an unpropitious time. Ramadier's senior ministers wanted it quickly contained. This helps explain why the government acceded to an 11 April request from Marcel de Coppet to revoke the three Malagasy deputies' parliamentary privileges.[49] The Governor insisted that the MDRM executive was solidly united behind the uprising. Police seizures of party documents, as well as interrogation of the first detainees, revealed that the key decisions were taken on the night of 17 March. It was then that plans were finalized for coordinated attacks in the capital and regional party cells were given instructions on targets to attack.[50] Armed with such damning evidence, National Assembly members, who did not even debate the rebellion until a full month after its outbreak, wasted little time questioning their fellow parliamentarians' guilt. The MDRM trio's immunity from prosecution was lifted by a vote of 324 to 195 on 6 June.[51] Raseta was taken into custody as he left the Assembly building. With all three MDRM deputies now behind bars and gruesome revelations of the murders of settlers hitting the headlines, the trio were condemned as 'murderers' in the French press before their cases went to trial, a blatant violation of basic judicial standards that outraged the writer Albert Camus.[52] But this was as nothing compared to events in Tananarive.

The charges of 'conspiracy against the state and endangering national security' levelled against the three parliamentarians rested on three main sources of evidence.[53] First was an MDRM Political Bureau telegram sent on 27 March 1947, two days before the rebellion began. With an eye to impending elections, the leadership advised local party sections to avoid involvement in political violence. Although Raseta and Ravoahangy were elected in November 1946 on a pro-independence ticket, the MDRM's senior leaders recognized that nationalist militancy simply invited a ban on the Party's activities.[54] So their instructions reminded their local supporters that the movement stood for Malagasy autonomy within the French Union. In an extraordinary act of evidential reinterpretation, prosecutors read the telegram's contents as a coded message to MDRM organizers to unleash the revolt.[55] The second source of 'evidence' against the deputies was a series of confessions extracted from several local MDRM activists. Some confessed under police torture; others did so in response to death threats. Insistent that these admissions were reliable nonetheless, Sûreté chief Baron advised prosecutors that they confirmed the coded telegram accusation. The third piece of evidence was the testimony expected from the defence team's star witness Samuel Rakotondrabé, a Tananarive tobacco factory manager who was also a leading activist in the JINA. The problem for the authorities here was less the reliability of what Rakotondrabé might say, but the prospect of him saying anything at all. The deputies' defence team were relying on Rakotondrabé's testimony to confirm from a participant's perspective that the rebellion was locally organized. The case built up by the police and the colonial authorities would explode. Not surprisingly, the prosecution preferred the account of Rakotondrabé's associate Edmond Ravelonahina. He suggested that the parliamentarians masterminded the original uprising in the critical nights preceding 29 March. It was only after the deputies' trial that Ravelonahina's evidence was proved inconsistent and false; in short, a police concoction.[56]

A great deal was hanging on Rakotondrabé's willingness to contradict the emerging official story. Unlike Ravelonahina, whose trial before a military court was still pending, Rakotondrabé had nothing to lose by telling the truth. He was among seventeen former rebels already sentenced to death for involvement in the rebellion's first killings. But his march to the guillotine awaited the outcome of clemency appeals to the Minister for Overseas France. The minister in question, the socialist veteran Marius Moutet, might have been expected to look kindly on the condemned men. He had ordered the release of thousands of Vietnamese and Malagasy political prisoners in 1936–7 as part of the Popular Front's brief experiment with colonial reform. A decade later, in the midst of the Indochina War and with memories of a horrendous 1945 uprising in eastern Algeria seared into French memory, Moutet reacted very differently. With the Malagasy politicians' trial looming, on 5 July Madagascar's colonial government formally asked the Minister to make his mind up, warning that further delay in carrying out the executions diminished their power of 'intimidation'. To the delight of the colonial authorities, the police, and the prosecutors in Madagascar's capital, Tananarive, Rakotondrabé was executed on 18 July 1948.[57] This was three days before the trial of the deputies and twenty-nine other alleged rebel organizers opened in Tananarive's criminal court.[58]

Madagascar's Bar Association prohibited any of its members from acting as defence counsel for the MDRM detainees. It was a Paris lawyer, Pierre Stibbe, who agreed to take on the case. He faced relentless harassment after his arrival on the island and narrowly escaped a grenade thrown from a police car. Stibbe's associate Henri Douzon was even less fortunate. He was kidnapped, almost certainly with police connivance, and badly beaten. The abuse of the trial lawyers and the obvious flaws in the evidence, which the judge admitted but discounted, portended the inevitable outcome. Few were surprised when, in one of the French Empire's most infamous show trials, Raseta and Ravoahangy were handed down death sentences on 4 October 1948.[59] Rabemananjara got forced labour for life. The manner of their conviction illustrated the dismissive intolerance of Malagasy dissent that characterized French actions throughout the rebellion years.

Ultimately, the deputies escaped the guillotine, but not lengthy prison terms. On 15 July 1949 President Vincent Auriol commuted their death sentences to life terms in a high-security prison, the prelude to their transfer to a Corsican jail in September 1950.[60] The three deputies' imprisonment made them an early focal point for French intellectual and confessional opposition to colonialism just as the conviction of Captain Alfred Dreyfus had galvanized opinion against racial injustice half a century earlier. In the first months of the rebellion, the League for the Rights of Man, the leading human rights group in France established in response to the Dreyfus case, joined student groups, French and colonial lawyers' associations, church leaders, and anti-colonial activists in condemning the abuse of Malagasy political prisoners.[61] Its volume steadily increasing, this clamour of opposition was slow to register with France's rulers. Despite the glaring flaws in the case against them, like Dreyfus, it was years before the three politicians were finally amnestied—in March 1956.[62] Their fate became emblematic of a fight strategy that, by crushing dissent, halted Madagascar's path to decolonization for over a decade.

At its most severe along Madagascar's eastern coastal belt, particularly in what is now Toamasina province, where estate farming and labour requisitioning went furthest, the Malagasy uprising destabilized Madagascar's principal export industries. Eastern settlements from Moramanga, southward to the port of Tamatave (Toamasina) and on towards Mahanoro and Manajary all saw local commerce collapse within weeks of the start of the fighting in late March 1947.[63] The island's coffee growers were especially hard-hit. Some settler-owned plantations were targeted, their properties and crops burned. Others were looted, their stores of dried coffee sold on to fund rebel arms purchases. Even those who escaped such violence complained that continuing insecurity prevented them from recruiting estate labour and continuing to cultivate. Most planters in the eastern regions badly affected by the rebellion were unable either to harvest their coffee crop or to distribute it for sale. And with so much stolen coffee flooding Madagascar's domestic market, prices collapsed. Much the same occurred within rice-growing areas around Fianarantsoa further to the south, where crop production ground to a halt during late 1947. This was what peasant rebellion meant for those caught up in it.

Episodic violence on estates and smallholdings stifled agricultural production, choked off sources of labour, and, in remarkably quick time, brought small- and large-scale cultivators face to face with economic ruin. Seen from a colonial perspective, the underlying issue was security. Without an assured military and police presence, the rhythm of local economic activity could not quicken. Reviewing the rebellion's opening months between April and August 1947, the Ministry of Overseas France conceded that locally available troops and police had no hope of guaranteeing such security across broad stretches of northern and eastern Madagascar.[64]

Pending the arrival of army reinforcements, mainly professional colonial army units en route to the war in Indochina, security operations were largely confined to the protection of urban centres, railways, and other strategic nodal points. Thereafter, the colonial authorities applied a simple measurement for the restoration of security: could Europeans travel safely without a military escort? Judged by that criterion, the colonial government acknowledged that they controlled less than five per cent of the terrain and only two per cent of the population in heavily-settled areas along Madagascar's east coast. Numerous rural settlements and isolated estates were totally cut off. Food was parachuted in because travel by road was deemed too dangerous. In all, some 150 Europeans lost their lives during the rebellion, a figure far in excess of the numbers of *colons* murdered in Algeria's Sétif uprising two years earlier.[65] Admittedly, the numbers of planters and local villagers killed by rebels were relatively small when compared with levels of violence in Indochina and, later, Algeria. But the manner of their deaths— hacked with farm implements, sometimes tortured—and the sense of exposure to sudden attack without hope of rescue was profoundly unsettling.[66]

This pattern of isolated European farmers exposed to outpourings of collective violence would recur in a British colonial context with the coming of Mau Mau to Kenya. But it was French Madagascar that experienced it first. And, as in the Kenyan case discussed below, it was this utter collapse in colonial order that led to the massive security force violence that followed.[67] The outcome was never in much doubt. Although they adopted an army's nomenclature and ranks, the insurgents lacked the advantages of military communications or transport. Coordination, even basic connection, became harder to sustain as French forces imposed security perimeters around areas of rebel activity.[68]

Aside from suppressing the Mandritsara uprising, a separate rebellion in the island's far north, the army set about 'caging' the entire rebel-controlled zone to the east. This amounted to over 100,000 square kilometres of territory of which about forty per cent was heavily forested.[69] Forest fighting was slow and dangerous. Targeting the rebels' supporters and, it was presumed, their suppliers in farming settlements was quicker and easier. Punitive columns swept through villages dispensing instant retribution because, in security force parlance, the entire area was hostile ground. Villages were burned to a cinder, sometimes with the occupants trapped inside their homes. Levels of destruction were such that entire rural communities were erased from the map. The impact of state coercion was as much ethnic as party political. French repression had particularly devastating effects on the Betsimisaraka people in eastern Madagascar. Their villages gone, their livestock slaughtered, unable even to conduct customary burial and mourning rites, families hiding in the forests were now denied access to food. Yet, even as starvation took hold, few rebel fighters surrendered. Some had taken oaths to protect their ancestral land to the death.[70] And many were surely aware that summary execution or lengthy punishments of forced labour awaited them.[71]

By April 1948 the official list of political prisoners reached 5,750.[72] Making prisoners perform hard labour was also highly symbolic. Before the revolt erupted, Madagascar's settler farmers expressed outrage at the impending abolition of forced labour throughout the empire. This long overdue reform was finally secured in March 1946, twelve months before Madagascar's insurrection. Its passage into law followed intensive lobbying by several African deputies including the Malian Fily Dabo Sissoko, the Senegalese Lamine Guèye and Léopold Senghor, and, above all, Ivory Coast's Félix Houphouët-Boigny.[73] The success of their efforts in Paris suggested to Madagascar's estate-owners that the colonial world was being turned upside down. They complained of estate operations rendered unviable overnight. For its part, MDRM propaganda identified the harsh exploitation of Madagascar's agricultural labourers as the clearest evidence of colonial iniquity.[74] Yet still the official rhetoric insisted that military saturation and severe punishment were the essential preludes to the restoration of normality, the resumption of traditional patron–client relationships in the countryside, and eventual inter-communal reconciliation.

The Governor, de Coppet, and his successor Pierre de Chevigné, reclassified as a High Commissioner as part of the French Union's elision of direct colonial references, were firm supporters of the clampdown. In October 1947 the administration imposed stringent limits on party political activity, backed by strict press censorship. Suspected MDRM sympathizers were purged from administrative posts. De Chevigné took charge of the repression from February 1948, insisting that most of the Malagasy had remained 'non-political' and, through it all, loyal. Government statements conflated the MDRM with Merina exclusivity and rebel violence, not an authentic popular nationalism.[75]

Even Marius Moutet at the Ministry for Overseas France maintained that
it was the MDRM who were guilty of racial killings, not the French.[76] Their
rationale for these statements drew on a familiar strand of imperialist thought,
popular among liberal republicans. Its self-serving logic was transparently
obvious: a subject population, unschooled in the ways of politics, had been
misled by extremist outsiders, in this case, supporters of a Messianic and racist
nationalist group. The silent majority, whose horizons were bounded by the
village, the crop cycle and their customary beliefs, responded best to unequivocal lessons and exemplary discipline.[77] Even the small minority of rebel troublemakers probably had little idea of what they really wanted and were
themselves victims of the even smaller nationalist intellectual elite. Most
within this latter category were members of the Merina ethnic group that
once ruled independent Madagascar. Many were educated town-dwellers or
landowners with little appreciation for the lives of the rural poor. Thus, to the
ethnic stereotyping that underpinned colonial disciplinary violence a layer of
class war was added. The Merina, usurped by a benevolent and modernizing
French colonial regime, were accused of cynical manipulation. They hid their
efforts to reclaim lost pre-eminence by dressing in the garb of anti-colonial
nationalism.[78]

In line with this thinking, MDRM activists faced the harshest punishments of all. By late December 1947 the area under rebel control had contracted by over two-thirds. At least 200,000 Malagasy nationalists submitted
to government authority, and the MDRM was utterly broken, with some
2,500 of its members imprisoned on sedition charges. Some were summar-
ily executed, others tortured first.[79] Still more were beaten unconscious and
dropped from aircraft into the Indian Ocean. In one notorious case in May
1947, 165 rebel suspects were executed aboard a train in Moramanga. None
of this appeared to influence Madagascar's governors. De Coppet's attitude
was clear from the start. When first told of the rebellion, he promised to
meet war with war.[80]

As for de Chevigné, in his mind statehood for Madagascar made no sense:
remove the rotten apples, get economic activity and welfare reforms going
again, and all would be well.[81] Even the Communist Party, more critical of
army repression after leaving the coalition in May 1947, soon afterwards
issued a formal statement at their annual congress inviting the Malagasy to
work alongside the French working class within the fold of the French
Union.[82] The ban on the MDRM, and the execution or detention of its
senior cadres, changed the terms of political engagement in post-rebellion

Madagascar. With so many MDRM organizers in detention, the movement relied on local activists, many of them Merina women with familial as well as political ties to the party, to sustain the movement's grass-roots organization and journalistic output.[83] Understandably, their activism focused less on party issues, more on campaigning for the release of Malagasy political prisoners from the harsh confines of places like Nosy Lava, infamous as Madagascar's *bagne* (penal colony).[84] The fight to re-impose French rule had purchased another decade of colonial control, but at enormous human cost and for scant political or economic benefit.

Towards independence

Madagascar's colonial politics may have been thrown into stasis but elsewhere the fate of empires moved on. By mid 1954 French withdrawal from Morocco and Tunisia was a realistic expectation. Indochina was lost. And a more peaceful path to decolonization in francophone West Africa was being carved by electoral reforms, inward investment, and gradual loosening of administrative control. The Non-Aligned Movement was making its presence felt on the international stage at the United Nations, in socialist internationalist gatherings, new development projects, and health initiatives. Aid agencies and other NGOs, civil rights groups in the United States, and the gradual shift of anti-colonialist thinking from the margins of European politics towards the mainstream, all these transnational factors also worked slowly but surely to help inject new vigour into Malagasy domestic politics. There were other, more tangible, changes as well. Madagascar fell within the ambit of the Gaston Defferre law, an enabling act eponymously named after the Minister for Overseas France (and discussed at greater length in Chapter 9). The law's fundamental purpose was to kick-start democratization in francophone black Africa, albeit at a rate still determined by France. Introduction of universal suffrage underpinned other, practical, measures designed to make vibrant local democracy a reality. Piece by piece, colonial administration, once highly centralized and autocratic, was dismantled and supplanted by regional assemblies and communal councils.

    The principal beneficiary of this gradual political thaw was likely to be the PADESM, the pro-administration party long favoured as an antidote to the MDRM. With the prospect of exercising real sovereign power tantalizingly close, the PADESM grew more factionalized. The party's more progressive wing, led by Philibert Tsiranana, a French-educated *côtier*, broke away to form a new coalition with the *Front national malgache*, the party that had filled the void left by the MDRM in the Merina heartland. In December 1956 the two groups fused into the *Parti social démocrate* (PSD), a broad-church grouping with genuine inter-ethnic appeal. The PSD romped home in December 1956 municipal elections, the first held after introduction of Gaston Defferre's electoral reforms. From the outset Tsiranana made endorsed amicable long-term relations with France, thus assuring the PSD the unswerving support of the outgoing French administration. Few were surprised at the strongly PSD complexion of Madagascar's first national government established in late 1958.[85]

Soon afterwards 83 per cent of Malagasy voters approved Madagascar's inclusion within the new constitutional arrangements of the French Community, the looser imperial organization launched alongside the French Fifth Republic as replacement to the French Union. But certain indicators gave the lie to the image of normality restored. A more telling result was registered in the province of Tananarive, where a narrow majority of 50.5 per cent voted 'non'. The capital and the surrounding central highlands retained at least some of their nationalist militancy, and were contemptuous of Tsiranana's honeyed promises of harmonious Franco-Malagasy partnership.[86] Clearly, memories of revolt lingered. Over the summer what remained of the colonial garrison and the island's gendarmerie were surreptitiously reinforced in anticipation of renewed disorder.[87] In the event, public disaffection in and around Tananarive never exploded into violence. The Republic of Madagascar was proclaimed on 14 October 1958 in the Place d'Andohalo, the forum in which the Merina dynasty's royal decrees were announced to Tananarive's nineteenth-century inhabitants.

Conclusion

Madagascar's 1947 revolt was the largest rebellion in French-ruled Africa for a generation. Soon eclipsed in French popular memory by the even more cataclysmic Algerian War, this island uprising has been remarkably overlooked by historians of French imperialism and of European decolonization more generally. Yet, as we have seen, there is a strong case to be made that the rebellion set the Fourth Republic on the road to increasingly violent post-war fight strategies that tore apart not only Malagasy society but those of Vietnam and Algeria as well. The French ethnographer Octave Mannoni, a long-serving official in Madagascar's colonial administration who developed a keen interest in 'native psychology', characterized the brutal French suppression of the revolt as a type of 'theatrical violence'. Mass killings of villagers and novel forms of murder such as dropping victims from aircraft were equally demonstrative. These were acts intended to restore order to the minds of an indigenous population whom Mannoni considered psychologically dependent on the stern hand of external authority.[88]

Mannoni's diagnosis seems crass in retrospect. But nor can popular motives for revolt be reduced to 'national independence', a term whose bland homogeneity flattens out the multiplicity of grievances felt by Malagasy of different ethnicity, socio-economic status, and occupation. In the rebellion's eastern heartlands, dissent was impelled by labour requisition, loss of ancestral land, and perennial rural poverty. To these material grievances, long experience of cultural denigration and ethnic discrimination were added. And then there was the pressure of MDRM activism in towns and village settlements across the island, its messengers sometimes genuinely appealing, occasionally locally coercive.[89] For some MDRM activists, particularly those in the major towns who were indoctrinated into Communism in the 1930s, independence was the stepping stone to socialist transformation. For others, including the senior leadership, autonomy with the concomitant end to French manipulation of Malagasy civil society and cultural practices was the more viable goal. For still others, the death or incarceration of family members catalysed political engagement.

Extraneous factors and transnational pressures also came into play. The post-war return of thousands of Malagasy ex-servicemen, many of them highly politicized, was one such. An awareness of international public and media interest in manifest colonial abuses was another. The Madagascar revolt and the manner of its suppression were, in this sense, intimately linked with contemporaneous decolonization on the other side of the Indian Ocean and, further on, to Vietnam.[90] Finally, the apparent efficaciousness of severe French repression, not so much targeted counter-insurgency as mass punishment, fostered more permissive official attitudes towards the containment of colonial disorder.

Ethical opposition in France and elsewhere to the crackdown was insufficient to counter this, a fact confirmed by the detention of thousands of Malagasy political prisoners. Even the macabre theatricality of the revolt's violence would soon be repeated. Ten years after the uprising began, when

the urban warfare between French security forces and their nationalist opponents in Algiers was at its peak in February 1957, the secretary-general at the
city's police prefecture let slip that some 3,024 people had been 'disappeared',
the majority of them thrown from helicopters into the sea.[91] Madagascar's
revolt and the fight it elicited would prove less the exception than the rule.

8

Emergency!
Paths to Confrontation
in Black Africa

The paths to confrontation of the chapter title refer to the two main regions of British Africa—East and South—to which fight strategies were applied after 1945. Communal tensions and political impasse fuelled violent dissent in both places during the 1950s. First, the chapter considers the differing ways in which black majority rule was blocked in the Central African Federation (CAF) of Northern and Southern Rhodesia (now Zambia and Zimbabwe) and Nyasaland (now Malawi). The Federation's acrimonious ten-year existence was punctuated by sporadic internal disorder that prompted declarations of state of emergency in its component territories in early 1959. The introduction of martial law did not, on this occasion, signify a British decision to fight for continued colonial control. It pointed instead to the worsening conflict between the imperial authorities and the local white settler elite in the Rhodesian territories, a confrontation set to escalate even further in the 1960s. Finally, the chapter turns northwards to British East Africa to explore Kenya's Mau Mau rebellion. In some ways similar to the Madagascar uprising, Mau Mau had quintessentially colonial origins—settler privilege, contested access to land, and racially-framed structures of law and entitlement. Yet the rebellion was misrepresented as something else entirely: a fanatical tribalism that laid bare the underlying primitivism of Kenya's majority people, the Kikuyu.[1] Here, too, extreme repression ensued. Again redolent of Madagascar, the co-option of Kenyans into the ensuing state violence represented a low point in British 'fight' strategy.

Fights in British Africa: The Central African Emergency

There is a case, so far as the halting strides of British decolonization are concerned, for thinking of 'a short 1950s' bookended by the election victory of Winston Churchill's Conservatives in October 1951 and the appointment of the reformer Iain MacLeod as Harold Macmillan's Colonial Secretary in October 1959. Over the intervening eight years three successive Conservative governments courted their favoured nationalist collaborators and picked fights with others they deemed too radical. British military force and covert interventions were used with seeming abandon, not as a last resort, but as a first—to restore the Shah of Iran in 1953, to prevent left-wing victory in the Latin American colony of British Guiana that same year, and, more generally, to ramp up counter-insurgency efforts in Malaya, Kenya, and Cyprus.[2] In this sense, the attempt to overthrow Egypt's Colonel Nasser in November 1956 fitted a broader trend. Certain Conservative ministers were also willing to defend white settler privilege in southern Africa in a way that their Labour opponents found increasingly repugnant.[3]

In the case of the Central African Federation (CAF) of Southern Rhodesia and the protectorates of Northern Rhodesia and Nyasaland, it is particularly difficult to untangle 'fight' from 'flight'. The three territories were federated in January 1953 in a state-building exercise the objective of which was never wholly agreed between the participant governments. Ironically, one of its main designers was Andrew Cohen, the far-sighted Colonial Office mandarin often credited with formulating schemes for the peaceful dismantling of Britain's African empire.[4] Welded together against the wishes of its African majority populations and against the advice of the colonial governors in Lusaka and Zomba, the federation would last a decade before crashing to destruction leaving a tangled wreck of constitutional debris to pick through as the component territories went their separate ways.[5] Bitterness about the Federation's demise was strongest among Southern Rhodesia's whites, by 1963, well on the road to rebellion. Yet it was their politics that made the Federation so toxic.

During the CAF's ten-year existence meaningful reforms were withheld from black Africans while, at the same time, the white settler minority, and especially those in Southern Rhodesia—consistently the most intransigent 'nationalist' constituency in Central Africa—was shamelessly placated.

(Southern Rhodesia contained by far the largest settler population of the three federated territories—close on 200,000, next to Nyasaland's 9,000 and Northern Rhodesia's 70,000.) The majority of Southern Rhodesia's whites were neither wealthy farmers nor civil servants but skilled workers. Their employment prospects and economic status were threatened by the Africanization of local industry. In Northern Rhodesia, whose all-important copper-belt was dominated by three part-British-owned mining conglomerates, company interest in promoting opportunities for their African labour force clashed with the preferential status once accorded to white mineworkers through an industry colour bar.[6] To be sure, post-war British governments had diminishing means to restrain settler demands, whether in the labour market or in matters of politics and cultural privilege. Colonial Governors wielded executive power in Northern Rhodesia and Nyasaland, but Southern Rhodesia had been internally self-governing since 1923. Its model of white rule based on a narrow franchise and a firm grip on the levers of local economic power was always liable to spread to its two neighbours once the Federation took shape. Confusion persisted over the division of responsibilities between Britain, the three territorial administrations, and the new federal authorities even so. 'Defence', for example, was a federal matter, policing remained in the hands of individual territorial governments, and the British government maintained direct interests in both. These overlapping jurisdictions would cause intense friction between all sides from 1958 onwards as the choice between oppression or conciliation of the African majority in all three federated territories became urgent. Much clearer was that the apparatus of federal government would be settler built and settler led. Once established, the Federation enjoyed law-making powers, British Ministers and Whitehall officials scrutinizing legislation but not initiating it.[7]

The underlying tensions between government in London and Salisbury over the wisdom and purpose of a territorial amalgamation were of long standing. A Central African Council set up in wartime to contain pressure for the amalgamation of the two Rhodesias was sidelined when hostilities ended. But the white-dominated governments in Salisbury and Lusaka acquired a stronger financial hold over mining-company profits, internal trade, and the crucial rail network linking the three Central African territories with one another and with South Africa.[8] Meanwhile, the 'danger' presented by the post-war immigration of thousands of Afrikaner South Africans—perceived as even more reactionary than their Anglophone cousins north of the Zambezi—mounted steadily.[9] This allowed Rhodesian settler politicians like Sir Godfrey Huggins and Roy Welensky, successive leaders of the United Federal Party (UFP), to make the case for federation as a 'better than' solution next to the creeping influence of apartheid. Some British ministers, backed by officials of the Commonwealth Relations Office (CRO), which handled the Federation's administrative business, were happy to go along with this.[10] Negotiators on both sides colluded in making a white-dominated federation between Southern and Northern Rhodesia, with Nyasaland thrown in, appear a reasonable compromise rather than the institutionalization of settler domination that it actually was.

Why, then, did successive Conservative governments, various Whitehall departments and a broad spectrum of British political and press opinion consider the federation scheme a good idea? The answer was that, in the eyes of its British sponsors, far from making inter-racial conflict more likely, the federation seemed to offer 'a middle way' between racial authoritarianism in the South African style and the surrender of Britain's Central African interests to black nationalist regimes. The CAF supposedly offered a different, gradualist route to racial harmony. The Federation's settlers were supposed, eventually, to share power with 'moderate' African representatives.[11] Such multi-racialism, integral to the Conservative Party's approach, not only to the CAF but to Kenyan politics as well, turned out to be a pipedream.[12] From the outset Southern Rhodesian settler leaders exploited the apparatus of federal rule to weaken countervailing British authority and thereby ensure continuing white supremacy. For them, the Federation was both the prelude and the means to transform its component territories into a white-governed Dominion, a greater Rhodesia whose racial politics would approximate South African standards, not British.

But the CAF's chequered history was never reducible to a two-way fight between settler reactionaries and British liberal reformers; far from it. On the one hand, African nationalist groups, including Southern Rhodesia's African National Congress, Joshua Nkomo's breakaway Zimbabwe African Peoples Union, and their northern cousin, the Zambia African National Congress led by Harry Nkumbala and Kenneth Kaunda, rejected cooption on principle. Each proved their fitness to govern through quite extraordinary forbearance in the face of mounting repression.[13] On the other hand, Westminster politicians, mainly on the Conservative right, sympathized with settler fears of reverse discrimination under black majority rule. White farmers were unlikely to thrive under such a regime. Many produced tobacco and foodstuffs on well-run estates employing large numbers of African labourers. Agricultural revenues were fundamental to Southern Rhodesia's prosperity. What would happen if the land made productive by the white pioneer was no longer farmed efficiently? The countryside might be destabilized, the cities flooded with unemployed. The security services and some Foreign Office personnel fretted about Communist infiltration facilitated by African nationalist fellow-travellers.[14] Most of all, for Cabinet ministers, the CRO and the Colonial Office, the Federation, once established, acquired a status akin to an inconvenient stretch of green belt: worth protecting to a point, but an obstacle to the pressures of modernization. When push came to shove, it was not worth fighting over.

Avoiding conflict in Central Africa proved impossible, however. The British did little initially to block the Federal government in Salisbury from reconfiguring the CAF constitution to block democratic reform. Indeed, it fell to the protectorate governors, particularly Sir Arthur Benson in Northern Rhodesia, to warn against devolving too much authority to the federal authorities, especially in relation to policing, internal security, and the detention of political opponents.[15] 'States of emergency' designed to stifle African protests such as pithead strikes and a boycott of beer halls in Northern Rhodesia's copper-belt in 1956 and 1957 were periodically enacted even so.[16] In response, between 1957 and 1959 African nationalist parties in all three Federation territories coalesced around three central concerns: the institutional basis of discrimination, the threat of Federation independence under settler control, and the barriers to reform within the CAF next to the gathering pace of decolonization elsewhere. In their eyes, federal rule, its agenda always set by Southern Rhodesia's settlers, was the enemy.[17]

By the start of 1959 the fundamental choices in Federation politics had narrowed as a result. In place of a middle way, only two markedly different routes to independence seemed open, one leading to South African-type reaction, the other to Ghana-style black majority rule.[18] With the nationalist parties moving towards open confrontation of federal rule, the threat of African political violence was exploited, and certainly exaggerated, by the Southern Rhodesian and Nyasaland governments to justify a clampdown. With strong encouragement from Welenky's federal administration, longing to make martial law the pretext to take unilateral control over internal security matters, states of emergency were declared in all three territories between 25 February and 11 March. Opposition parties were banned, hundreds of activists locked up. Pre-eminent among them was Dr Hastings

Banda, the Edinburgh-trained GP and Church of Scotland elder, who had returned home to the territory where disturbances went furthest to resume direction of the Nyasaland African Congress (NAC).

'On-the-spot' colonial officials watched the people of Nyasaland mobilize against British and white Rhodesian domination with a mixture of shock and surprise. Historian Megan Vaughan highlights the persistence among colonial health professionals, psychologists, magistrates, and police of crudely racist stereotypes about Africans, their mental acuity, and supposed lack of initiative. Commenting on the incidence of suicide, or rather, its presumed absence, in Nyasaland, Vaughan notes that '"Africans" were generally held to be a happy-go-lucky "race" of people with few cares in the world.' They were alleged to attribute any worries they did have to the malign influence of others, 'via the medium of witchcraft or the intervention of spirits'. 'African people', so the argument went, 'did not suffer from introspection and guilt, and so one rarely encountered depressive illness among them.'[19] These layers of prejudice and lazy thinking about Africans lacking political conviction were gradually stripped away by well-organized popular protest and a resilient NAC leadership.

Nyasaland's Emergency made plain what critics—African, British, and American—had known for some time: the Central African Federation was unworkable.[20] Divisions between the individual territorial administrations and Welensky's federal government had been allowed to fester in the absence of clear direction from London. For the defenders of the Macmillan government's approach this was commendable light-touch restraint; for his opponents it was woeful indecisiveness. Macmillan's anxiety to avoid having to say or do anything definitive was understandable. For one thing, there was a general election coming in October 1959. For another, Welensky's supporters believed that the British government would concede independence to the Federation within the next year or so; a dangerous hostage to fortune because internal African opposition was proving stronger than anticipated. Banda's noisy, but largely non-violent return to Nyasaland politics as chief opponent of the Federation may have precipitated the Emergency.[21] But his two core arguments had been incontrovertible for years. Firstly, Nyasaland, an overwhelmingly black country lacking the mineral wealth of Northern Rhodesia, was a poor fit within the Federation. Secondly, it was manifestly unjust for Nyasaland's three million blacks to be governed in the interests of a settler community numbering under 10,000. Unfortunately, releasing Nyasaland and allowing it to chart its own course to independence, logical and ethically defensible though it was, remained politically inexpedient for politicians in London and Salisbury. The plain fact was that if Nyasaland went the entire Federation would collapse. Northern Rhodesia's nationalists would demand the same freedoms. Their Southern Rhodesian counterparts would be emboldened to challenge settler authority once and for all. Even more likely was that Welensky's federal government would take pre-emptive action, proclaiming Dominion status in defiance of Britain's failure to stand up for its kith and kin in southern Africa.[22]

In the histories of British and French decolonization, few nightmare scenarios came to fruition much as their doomsayers predicted. But Central Africa came close. Ultimately, the rulers of Southern Rhodesia, rather than the Federation as a whole, rebelled against British authority, declaring unilateral independence in November 1965, a subject examined in Chapter 10. The Central African Federation had imploded over two years earlier, a victim of its internal contradictions. Its dissolution was rendered inevitable earlier still: by the disastrous manner in which the Nyasaland crisis unfolded in 1959. Sir Robert Armitage was the protectorate's governor at the time. An administrator with previous experience of emergencies in the Gold Coast and Cyprus, he was wary of ceding responsibility for the maintenance of internal order to Welensky's federal government and the white Rhodesian-led security forces at his disposal. But his hand was forced by worsening clashes between police and Banda's supporters, as well as purported evidence of an NAC plot to attack key installations and assassinate leading Europeans. The territorial governors and the federation executive met in Salisbury, first on 20 February 1959, then a week later on the 27th to discuss emergency powers. In between times, police reinforcements from Northern Rhodesia and Tanganyika, in addition to regular troops from Southern Rhodesia, began moving into Nyasaland. Most were in place by 26 February.[23]

By this point Welensky's party colleague Sir Edgar Whitehead, the Prime Minister of Southern Rhodesia, had resolved to move against his territory's ANC organizers. Hundreds were detained in nationwide police sweeps authorized under Southern Rhodesia's new emergency provisions. Sir Arthur Benson, still Governor of Northern Rhodesia, refused to act in similar fashion against the Zambia nationalists in his territory. He insisted that local police could handle the nationalists' occasional acts of intimidation and Northern Rhodesia's ANC could be outlawed without recourse to martial law.[24] It was intimidation from another quarter that Benson feared rather more. On 4 March he complained to London of a 'most spectacular and coordinated campaign' by the federal government to force him into declaring an emergency in Northern Rhodesia. Its object was to seize control over all aspects of internal security.[25]

According to Benson, Welensky and other members of the Federal government were 'flushed' with a pride 'that swelled them up like frogs' after Armitage, the Crown representative, conceded that only the federal authorities could protect a British domain.[26] Colonial Secretary Alan Lennox-Boyd seconded Benson's determination 'to avoid if humanly possible' any comparable resort to emergency rule in Northern Rhodesia. But Lennox-Boyd's principal objective was to prevent the backstairs wrangling over the crackdowns from leaking out. He cabled Benson with the following advice on the 5th:

> It is, as I know you realise, of vital importance at this moment that no whisper of Federal pressure to declare a State of Emergency should get out. So I hope you will be able to avoid press conferences where all (repeat all) of us can say things which give rise to conjecture. I have often been caught out this way![27]

The tragedy was that Governor Armitage opted to follow Whitehead's example, not Benson's.[28] He authorized a crackdown against Banda's NAC, similar to that conducted against the Southern Rhodesia ANC. In the first act of Nyasaland's state of emergency on 3 March 166 NAC members were arrested. They included a dishevelled Hastings Banda, bundled into a police vehicle still in his pyjamas. Far from silencing dissent, Operation Sunrise unleashed a wave of protests. In the worst single incident, on the morning of the 3rd a contingent of King's African Rifles, part of the newly-arrived reinforcements, shot dead twenty demonstrators at Nkata Bay on the shores of Lake Nyasa. News of the killings reached London at much the same time as reports arrived from Kenya indicating that eleven Kenyan detainees had been beaten to death at a Mau Mau detention camp in Hola.[29] Two massacres in a single day; Operation Sunrise gave way to imperial sunset within a matter of hours.

Downing Street was left reeling by the damning press coverage and international outcry over this bloody turn in colonial policy. Barbara Castle and Jim Callaghan led stinging Labour Party attacks, which accused ministers of turning a blind eye to murder.[30] On the night of 5 March, in what was his preferred method of letting off steam—privately—Macmillan took up his

pen to write his latest diary entry. He railed against 'extremist native leaders', British Socialists and their acolytes in the *Manchester Guardian* and
The Observer. They were all out to embarrass him by highlighting the
'most regrettable division of responsibility' in the Central African Federation. The Prime Minister closed with a classic 'note to self': 'I must try to
get the facts and take a hand in this affair, or it may prove really difficult
as well as politically damaging at home.'[31] Macmillan's government duly
sought refuge in the bureaucratic devices customarily used to defuse
criticism—an inquiry commission and a consultation exercise. Neither
went to plan.

The undeclared purpose of both investigations was, as Macmillan put it,
'to keep Parliament and public steady'. To further the cause, secret political
intelligence about NAC subversion was hastily compiled into a White Paper
to prove that the Nyasaland clampdown was justified.[32] The Prime Minister
meanwhile returned to his other, larger preoccupations: the emerging Cold
War crisis over Berlin, a partial French withdrawal from NATO, heightened
tension in the Middle East, and a Cyprus settlement.[33] Central Africa, for all
its devilish complexity, was still small beer. Macmillan, though, was shrewd
enough to recognize that this could change. In early June he set up a Cabinet Africa committee to review colonial affairs week by week; its aim: 'to
give us a grip on the situation'.[34]

The Nyasaland inquiry commission led by Lord Justice Sir Patrick Devlin
began its work in early April 1959. The Cabinet meanwhile closed ranks
over continuing press and parliamentary criticism of its lapses in Kenya and
Central Africa although, behind the scenes, Lennox-Boyd offered to resign
from the Colonial Office.[35] All of this changed in mid July when Devlin
published his findings. They were brief—and devastatingly blunt. The Governor's pretexts for invoking emergency powers were inadequate and, by
implication, bogus; the repression they unleashed excessive. The NAC, the
legitimate voice of majority opinion, had been strangled in what had
become, albeit temporarily, 'a police state'. Macmillan vented his spleen at
the Devlin Report in his diary. This time he focused his ire on Devlin personally. He lambasted the judge's naïve streak. He damned Devlin's disloyalty, allegedly traceable to Catholic Irish roots and a Jesuit priest brother.
And he accused Devlin of vindictiveness. This he ascribed to Devlin's resentment at having missed out on the post of Lord Chief Justice. No wonder the
Prime Minister concluded that Devlin's report was 'dynamite', which 'may
well blow this Government out of office'.[36] Any remaining hopes that Hugh

Gaitskell's Labour Party might agree a bipartisan approach to African problems evaporated.[37] After winning the October 1959 general election, Macmillan did hold further meetings with Gaitskell, Aneurin Bevan, and Jim Callaghan in November in a last-ditch effort to win Labour's backing for the government's Central Africa policy, but to no avail.[38]

Explosive they certainly were, but there was no way to argue with Devlin's conclusions without seeming ridiculously out of touch. Luckily for the government, their other defensive move—the consultation exercise—offered some respite. Macmillan and the Secretary of State for Commonwealth Relations Lord Home had selected former Conservative minister Sir Walter Monkton to lead an investigative commission into the Federation's troubles and future prospects. This at least gave a breathing space. It would be over a year before the Monkton Commission report confirmed what most impartial observers already knew. The clunking constitutional machinery of the Central African Federation had turned into a blundering instrument of repression blocking the road to black majority rule.[39]

Only the shock of the Nyasaland Emergency in 1959 compelled a fundamental reconsideration of Britain's 'strategy' for departure from Central Africa. Its limitations, so candidly described by Devlin were amplified by South Africa's harsh racial divides and shocking political violence. The shooting of scores of unarmed pro-ANC protesters outside Sharpeville police station on 21 March 1960 finally exploded the myth of austere but well-intentioned white paternalism in southern Africa. During the early 1960s, after twenty years of pandering to settler demands—tellingly described by one historian as 'government by blackmail'—it became clearer still that white diehards demanding fight not flight were the more serious obstacle to ending empire on British terms.[40]

Time and money spent on gathering intelligence about nugatory African nationalist links with the Communist bloc would have been better devoted to monitoring what the settlers might do to block franchise reform and democratic elections.[41] Fuller information about the underlying sources of settler fears would also have been useful. British policymakers were perhaps too dismissive of the visceral panic that gripped southern Africa's settler communities as the bloodletting of decolonization elsewhere edged ever closer. As novelist Doris Lessing remembers, for white Rhodesians Mau Mau was like 'a burglar alarm in a rich house'. Growing concern with personal security reached fever pitch in response to news of renewed racial violence during the Congo Crisis in 1960. Iron bars were added to farmstead window-frames. Volunteer home guards began patrolling white neighbourhoods after dark.[42] Back in Britain, Kenyan and Rhodesian settlers, once viewed as representing all that was best about their home country, were becoming an embarrassment, out of touch with the home country to which they claimed attachment.[43] Historian Will Jackson sees three areas in which distinctly colonial facets of Kenyan settler experience emerge clearly. In the physical and emotional hardships of colonial life and family separation; in the prevalence of hostile, anxious feelings towards African neighbours, servants, and workers; and in the growing awareness that white domination hung by a thread. It was this final quality that imposed exacting standards to behave as 'Europeans' should in front of 'the natives'.[44] These were people never entirely 'settled' in their colony of choice. To adapt Lessing's insight about Southern Rhodesia's whites, settlers were in exile, not from Britain, but from Africa.[45] For all that, a striking feature of Mau Mau violence was the intra-African focus. Settlers were certainly integral to this Kenyan conflict, but most escaped the worst of it. We need to consider why.

Mau Mau

The Mau Mau rebellion was a revolt centred among Kenya's largest ethnic group, the Kikuyu. It was also the dirtiest of Britain's colonial fights, 'the great horror story of Britain's empire in the 1950s' as historian David Anderson describes it. Sir Evelyn Baring's Nairobi government introduced sweeping emergency powers on 20 October 1952. This followed numerous killings of pro-administration figures, including Kenya's paramount chief Waruhiu wa Kungu.[46] An experienced colonial administrator, Baring was the son of Lord Cromer, a famed Victorian pro-consul in Egypt. Following in his father's footsteps, Baring had the gravitas to play patrician governor in Kenya.[47] But the transformation in the colony's security apparatus that he oversaw soon acquired a momentum of its own.[48] The regular Kenya Police, a white-dominated Kenya Police Reserve, and, subsequently, a 'Home Guard' of Kikuyu loyalists led the fight against Mau Mau. Emergency powers allowed them to detain suspects without trial, to prohibit access to operational zones, and to impose curfews.[49] As in Malaya, a revitalized Police Special Branch led the intelligence war against Mau Mau, relying on local informants for leads. Within three months of the declaration of the Emer-

gency an additional twenty-seven police stations were built in the Kikuyu
'reserves'. By late 1953 the combined police forces had trebled in size from
approximately 7,000 to almost 21,000.[50] British troop reinforcements were
also brought in.

The expansion of local security forces was merely the thin, cleaner end of
the wedge. Kenya's Emergency Regulations, their scope steadily extended,
underpinned wholesale human rights abuses. These included over a thousand hangings after peremptory trial, mass population removal, lethal beatings, sexual torture, and a network of detention camps, the principal examples
of which are shown on Map 9. It was the most ruthless repression in any British colonial dependency after the Second World War.[51] The rebellion itself
was largely spent by 1956. And Dedan Kimathi, the titular leader of the Mau
Mau fighters based in the forests of the Aberdare Mountains, went to the
gallows in February 1957. Yet it was only three years later, on 12 January 1960,
that the Emergency was declared over. By this point hundreds of thousands
of Kenyans had passed through the camp system. Once released, many found
their families gone, their homes broken, their access to land denied. Any
appreciation of why the British authorities, metropolitan and colonial,
approved all of this must, therefore, engage with the origins of Kikuyu grievances, the nature of the revolt itself, and the methods of repression adopted.

Logically enough, the account begins with the first President of independent Kenya, Johnstone (Jomo) Kenyatta. As general secretary of the
Kikuyu Central Association (KCA), an early voice of moderate Kenyan
nationalism, a young Kenyatta sailed for Britain in February 1929.[52] His
aim? To make the case that the Kikuyu formed a coherent society dispossessed and fragmented by colonial government and the white settlement it
upheld. His trip, an early example of direct African anti-colonial lobbying
in London, went unrewarded. Leftist anti-colonialists had little time for the
minutiae of African sociology, which seemed to stress ethnic particularity
over class solidarity. Conservative parliamentarians simply denied him
appointments. Colonial Office specialists, better informed about what the
Kikuyu were suffering, still rejected Kenyatta's arguments about a fairer
distribution of agricultural land and labour. Deeply frustrated, he departed
for Moscow where he began a brief flirtation with the Comintern. This,
too, ended in disillusionment.[53]

Returning to London in 1933, Kenyatta turned to academic study. Two
years later he enrolled with the Polish exile Bronislaw Malinowski for a
postgraduate diploma in social anthropology at the London School of

Map 9. Kenyan 'White Highlands' and main detention camps.

Economics. Much like the Trinidadian intellectual George Padmore, with
whom he shared interests in Marxism and anthropology, Kenyatta was convinced that the European powers still regarded Africa as a continent to be
divided and exploited at will.[54] The work he produced under Malinowski's
supervision was ultimately published as *Facing Mount Kenya: The Tribal Life of*

the Gikuyu in 1938. Perhaps read by only a few hundred fellow specialists at the time, Kenyatta's thesis revealed the singularity of his vision. He explained the complexity of Kikuyu land-holding, its distinct individual and collective forms, its regulation by *mbari* or sub-clan elders, and the rules governing its transfer between families. The core argument was devastatingly simple: the British were wrong to presume that 'tribal land' could be alienated without undermining the very foundations of Kikuyu society.[55] It was a theme to which Kenyatta and other, later supporters of Mau Mau would revert time and again in the years ahead. Colonial capitalism, with white settlers its willing foot-soldiers, was denying Kenyans the capacity to acquire and bequeath their key source of wealth and social independence. Colonial rule meanwhile robbed Kenyans of decision-making responsibilities, as much in the domestic and familial sphere as in the realm of national politics. For Kikuyu this social autonomy was a measure of adult status. Mau Mau was about individual self-respect and a household's 'capacity to produce and eat'.[56]

Following established colonial precedent, the Conservative governments in office throughout the eleven years separating Mau Mau's outbreak from Kenya's independence in December 1963 insisted that the rebellion was a purely internal issue, a matter for Kenyans and Britons alone; an 'Emergency', not a war. But as the Dutch had discovered to their cost in Indonesia and as the French would soon realize in North Africa, the convenient fiction that decolonization struggles could be handled without outside involvement or hostile international reaction was unsustainable. The reconfiguration of the post-war international system into mutually antagonistic Cold War blocs militated against it. So did US concern about the long-term strategic alignment of independent African and Asian states. The United Nations, its membership expanding to include newly-independent, often non-aligned countries, including former colonial giants India and Indonesia, as well as black African states led by Kwame Nkrumah's Ghana, took an interest. The UN's affiliate health and aid agencies were another influential African presence. Other Non-Governmental Agencies, the Red Cross and Oxfam prominent among them, were working in Kenya already. Indeed, as the conflict escalated they were probably better informed about life inside detention camps and embattled Kikuyu villages than many Colonial Office advisers.[57] Finally, both sympathetic allied powers and generally unsympathetic colonial nationalist movements elsewhere in British Africa were watching to see how Mau Mau would affect Britain's capacity to maintain imperial control elsewhere.

Partly because British characterizations of Mau Mau were so emotive and partly because this is a book comparing British and French colonial experience, the reader may find it useful to see what French observers thought of Britain's repression of Mau Mau. On 13 January 1953 French Consul Beaudouin reported from Nairobi that Kenya's settler community in the so-called 'white highlands' (largely former Maasai land heavily populated by Kikuyu whose ancestral lands had been alienated to whites) was close to revolt. Settler landowners felt unprotected. Night-time attacks on isolated farmhouses, often organized in collusion with servants and house-boys, were a more or less weekly occurrence. The sense of being cornered was all pervasive. The rhetorical analogies with hunting were no accident. As Patricia Lorcin observes in her study of women settlers in colonial Algeria and Kenya, 'women lived and imagined their lives in ways that reflected both the values and customs of their homelands and the opportunities and experiences of their "adopted" land … In Kenya it was the British traditions of the landed gentry with their class convictions and their love of the hunt. Wild animals were … essential to the creation of Kenya's nostalgic space.'[58] Now it seemed that it was the settlers themselves who were at bay. The killing of the Ruck family—husband Roger, wife Esme, and six-year-old son Michael—at their farm in Kinangop on the night of 24 January 1953 raised settler outrage to fever pitch.

The much larger population of Britons living in the Kenyan capital also felt increasingly insecure and joined the chorus demanding instant retribution.[59] Those concentrated in classier Nairobi suburbs, described by one historian as resembling 'the better part of Woking', complained of the colonial government's ineffectiveness in halting both Mau Mau attacks and the more general breakdown of strict inter-racial deference for which Kenya was renowned.[60] There were other, less privileged settler voices as well. Kenya's 'poor whites' were equally anxious about black dissent, albeit for different reasons. After 1945 Kenya's settler community not only grew in number, but became poorer and more urbanized. 'Poor whites', for decades the classic outsiders of colonial settler society, became starkly visible. Usually described in terms of transgression—of racial boundaries, of social norms, of economic minima—the lowest strata of white settler society was highly problematic. Their poorer circumstances subverted the official rhetoric of modernization and unravelled finely woven settler myths of respectability and moral superiority. As Jackson puts it, in the figure of the 'poor white' degeneracy and deviancy converge.[61]

The influx of new settlers in the late 1940s produced greater social diversification in the settler population, a diversity typified by the unprecedented numbers of single, white working-class men and women drawn to Nairobi and Mombasa. Working in low-paid occupations, the women as typists, hairdressers, receptionists, and shop-assistants, the men as garage mechanics, building-site labourers or store-men, these new settlers were closer to modern-day economic migrants than the hardy pioneers who stride through settler literature. They had little in common socially or culturally with Kenya's 'old hands'. But they were generally apprehensive of rapid socio-economic change, fearful of being displaced by cheaper African labour. Alongside them was another discrete band of new settler immigrants. These were civil service and commercial retirees from India, who moved to Kenya in large numbers after Indian independence to retain their colonial lifestyles. They tended to be even more reactionary. Few had much recent experience of life in Britain or of changing British attitudes to empire. In Will Jackson's words, 'As aristocrats and socialites were replaced by demobilised soldiers, economic migrants, and retirees from the Raj, what had always been (and remained) the *sine qua non* of settler Kenya—the maintenance of distance between colonisers and colonised—began to dissolve. At the same time, Africans—urbanised, and politicised as never before—impinged on those spaces previously demarcated white.'[62] Little wonder, then, that both the well-to-do settler and their poorer cousins were unimpressed by the post-war stewardship of Governor Sir Philip Mitchell. He was a conservative administrator to be sure, but one who spoke an unwelcome language of development and multi-racial partnership.[63] Far from preserving the racial difference in which all strata of Kenya's settler society placed such value, Mitchell began dismantling it.[64]

This more permissive environment allowed Jomo Kenyatta's fledgling Kenya African Union (KAU—the post-war reincarnation of the KCA) to grow in the late 1940s. It also opened up political space for the KAU's radical offshoot, the Mau Mau (literally translatable as the 'greedy eaters' of chiefly elders' authority). Mau Mau's emergence was problematic for KAU leaders. They struggled to bridge the cultural and generational divides between their rural supporters in Kikuyuland and the more confrontational trade union activism and youth politics of post-war Nairobi.[65] Even so, what startled the colonial administration most about the character of the non-violent KAU was its apparently 'pan-tribal'—for which we might read 'national'—basis of support.[66] What alarmed them about Mau Mau was precisely the reverse: its sectarian violence and it secretiveness.[67]

These two features coalesced in British official minds thanks to highly
sensationalist reports of Mau Mau oathing ceremonies in which tens of
thousands in central Kenya pledged support, often in small groups and frequently under duress.[68] Equally effective as instruments of political mobilization and social discipline, oathing ceremonies drew on Kikuyu religious
practice. Earlier dramatic increases in the numbers making oaths of allegiance to the KAU were instrumental to the efforts of younger, Nairobi-
based militants to usurp the party's established leadership of rural elders
typified by Kenyatta and another senior Kikuyu chief, Koinange wa Mbiyu.
By 1951 the party was profoundly radicalized and moving rapidly towards
anti-British and internecine violence.[69]

Where declarations of support for the KAU were conventionally political and limited in number, Mau Mau oathing was ritualized and conducted
on an enormous scale. Exaggerated, vulgarized accounts of these newer
oathing ceremonies became staples of settler conversation and British press
accounts. Their garishness sought to demonize Mau Mau by proving the
movement's backwardness, deviancy, and cruelty. Numerous reports from
district administrators, officially-sponsored ethnographers and government-
appointed psychologists interpreted oathing through the cosmologies as
early modern witchcraft. Ceremonies, which often involved animal sacrifice
and the eating of raw goat meat, were interpreted in highly sexualized terms
as frenzied acts of satanic depravity.[70] New initiates, estimated to number
around ninety per cent of the population in parts of Kenya's Central Highlands, were thereby represented as having been duped. Either they were
coerced into compliance or they fell into a trance-like state in which all
reason and inhibition was lost.

Not surprisingly, a propaganda war soon developed over the meaning
and validity of Mau Mau oaths, and of the movement they endorsed. If, as
British official statements insisted, followers of Mau Mau had succumbed to
a form of collective psychosis, corrective treatment rather than colonial
reform was what was required. So-called 'counter-oathing' ceremonies
became a central plank of counter-insurgency strategy. Theatrical public
recantations were organized in which Mau Mau detainees ceremonially
repudiated their earlier vows—sometimes kissing a male goat's foot, spitting
and then spurning Mau Mau allegiance. Such performances, instrumental
to British 'rehabilitation' of their Kenyan captives, perpetuated the idea that
the Mau Mau was closer to a cult than a political quest for 'land and freedom', the movement's core slogan.[71]

Despite the obsession with its covert practices, Mau Mau had other, more pragmatic origins. It was rooted among Kikuyu agricultural labourers living as squatters on settler estates. They identified colonial authority, white landowners, and chiefly elders as obstacles to their acquisition of land, personal status, and wealth—components of what Kenya scholars term 'self-mastery'.[72] Household wealth, individual opportunity, marriage, procreation, and peer recognition of one's status as an autonomous adult: these were the prerequisites to successful transition through the life stages of Kikuyu culture. All were bound up with the availability of land and livestock resources that were harder than ever to come by. Population growth added to overcrowding in the districts colonially designated as Kikuyu 'reserves'. In response some thirty per cent of Kikuyu left these areas to become squatters contracted to work for white landowners in the White Highlands of west-central Kenya. The injustice inherent to their legally marginalized and landless status became starkly apparent immediately after the Second World War as white farmers, anxious to take advantage of higher prices for agricultural produce, began evicting squatters to expand their holdings.[73] At a time when development initiatives elsewhere in the British Empire sought to break down racial barriers to wealth creation, the White Highlands remained a colonial throwback—the exclusive preserve of a settler over-class.

As Kenyatta had warned, the structural iniquity of Kenya's colonial farming economy provoked cultural degradation by undermining customary Kikuyu practices of capital accumulation and household consolidation. Long-established patterns of rural life, gender relations, and generational deference were ruptured, pushing Kikuyu society into crisis.[74] To borrow Caroline Elkins' well-chosen words, in 'Kikuyu notions of being: landlessness was anathema to indigenous civic virtue'.[75] Mau Mau, then, was closer to a conventional peasant revolt against unsustainable agricultural economics and unjust rural politics than the ritualistic cult of irrational bloodlust depicted in sections of the British press from late 1952 onwards. *The Daily Mail* was particularly sensationalist in its coverage of the conflict.[76] But animal-loving British readers were also sickened by images of European-owned cattle slashed with traditional *panga* knives and left crippled and bleeding to death.

Images of dead children killed in the same way were deemed too extreme for UK publication but were used in Swahili pamphlets distributed by government officers in Kenya.[77]

By March 1953 it was clear that reasoned discussion in Nairobi or in Whitehall about Kikuyu grievances was out of the question. Settler anger was inflamed by delays in Kenyatta's criminal trial. As KAU president, he was falsely accused of masterminding the rise of Mau Mau.[78] Some of the rowdiest settlers even threatened to lynch Kenyatta's defence lawyer Dennis Pritt, accusing him of collusion with a murderous fanatic.[79] Ridiculous accusations, but indicative of the pervasive sense of terror caused by isolated Mau Mau killings. These attacks were, in turn, becoming more audacious, particularly in the areas surrounding the Aberdare Mountains where policing operations were concentrated. It was there in the village of Lari that the worst massacres of the entire war occurred on the night of 26 March.

Lari's local chief Makimei, an authoritarian figure, had organized a loyalist Home Guard before the Emergency was declared. Local support for Mau Mau was strong, particularly among ex-squatters who had returned to the Rift Valley region landless and poor. On the night in question Home Guard members were lured away from the village, leaving their families unprotected. Several Mau Mau gangs converged on Lari burning the huts of loyalist families and killing anyone trying to escape. 120 were murdered. Most were women and children who either died in the flames or were hacked down as they fled. This first massacre was immediately followed by another as the returning Home Guard wrought vengeance on suspected Mau Mau supporters. Again no family members were spared. In all, some 400 people died in and around Lari in a night of bloodletting that exposed the fault-lines between residents and returnees, haves and have-nots that were tearing Kikuyu society apart.[80] Revenge attacks continued over subsequent days and weeks. Mass trials of Mau Mau allegedly involved in the original massacre also made a mockery of basic evidential standards, confirming that the colony's judicial system was becoming a key instrument of repression.[81]

Watching events unfold, the French Foreign Ministry noted that the quickening rhythm of killings and retribution indicated that the revolt had turned a dreadful corner before Kenyatta and five co-accused KAU leaders were finally convicted in early April. The five sentenced alongside Kenyatta were Fred Kubai, a Kikuyu trade unionist; Richard Onieko, a former Nairobi city councillor; Bildad Kaggia, Secretary of the KAU's Nairobi section; Paul Ngei, another KAU activist; and Kunga Karumba, a member of KAU executive committee.[82] Their imprisonment made little difference. Far from Mau Mau activity decreasing, attacks grew more sophisticated and deadly.

Ironically, because of the security crackdown, fighters of Mau Mau's Land Freedom Army (LFA) had greater access to automatic weapons, most of them stolen during ambushes on isolated Home Guard posts manned by loyalist Kenyan auxiliaries. LFA bands like those in the Mount Kenya forests expanded during 1953.[83] The largest was estimated at 300 strong, capable of shooting it out with the army patrols sent to track them. But the fighters of Mount Kenya had other priorities. Led by Waruhiu Itote, the infamous 'General China', a former King's African Rifleman who had served in the Burma campaign, they targeted loyalist villages, Home Guard encampments and mission schools.[84]

Itote's past military training was not unusual. Increasing numbers of ex-servicemen joined Mau Mau bands, including Askaris with recent experience of the Malayan Emergency. The forest war gradually turned the British way even so. Fighters moved further into the forests during late 1953 to escape detection. Their support networks in the villages of the Kikuyu reserves were tightly locked down by loyalist paramilitaries, making it harder for Mau Mau to procure food, weapons, and new recruits. And when fire-fights did take place the security forces usually prevailed, sometimes capturing young men exhausted, half-starved, and with harrowing personal testimonies of enforced recruitment.[85] General China himself was shot and captured on 15 January 1954. Sentenced to hang, he was reprieved in exchange for cooperating with Special Branch officers in tentative negotiations intended to coax remaining rebel units into surrender. His change of fortunes personified the conflict's shifting balance.[86]

Within the confines of Nairobi assassinations of policemen and local officials persisted throughout 1953. The slum quarters of Pumwani and Bahati became virtual no-go areas for whites. Once again the French diplomatic advice was sobering. Removing Kenyatta from the equation was no solution because his work was already done. The KAU's political education programme and Mau Mau indoctrination reached further into Kikuyu society than the colonial authorities had realized. Even if it were possible, reversing this process would take years.[87]

British security operations certainly intensified following General Erskine's arrival as commander.[88] By August 1953 Nairobi commanded his attention. The problems the British confronted—and the way they depicted them—anticipated the challenge of urban insurgency in Algiers, which climaxed four years later in 1957.[89] Much as in the later Algerian case, the success of military operations in rural areas, in this case, in Kenya's Fort Hall district, displaced insurgent activity to the capital city. Home

Guard auxiliaries were better armed and were given leeway to conduct additional rural sweeps, notably south of Nyari. Meanwhile, Nairobi police, assisted by regular army units, began what French observers described as a series of 'gargantuan round-ups' to clear Nairobi's three principal shantytowns of Mau Mau sympathizers. 'Operation Ratcatcher' relied on hooded informants, the so-called *gikunia*, to identify suspects. It was a process open to abuse. Few British officials could converse with Kikuyu detainees. Their reliance on translators, intermediaries, and informants left ample room for mistakes and score-settling while opportunities were missed to gather intelligence about impending attacks.[90] Colonial Information Service propaganda pointing to Mau Mau killings of fellow Kenyans and the risk of falling living standards proved equally ineffective. Mau Mau boycotts of European goods and services proliferated. And drive-by shootings in hijacked taxis eliminated several of Nairobi's higher-profile loyalists.[91]

Security force killings outside the capital quickened in late 1953.[92] Official statistics listed a death toll averaging 50 to 120 Kenyans per week. Actual figures were probably higher. In Nairobi, meanwhile, Mau Mau organizers imposed a bus boycott that severely disrupted the city's economy. The French diplomatic observers saw only one solution: military saturation to filter out rebel suspects.[93] In fact, Erskine went further. Additional police were joined by an extra battalion of troops, the prelude to a grim shift in the conflict's dynamics. As a first step, economic migrants and slum dwellers, many of them recent Kikuyu, Embu, and Meru arrivals, faced security 'screening', a combination of searches and identity checks, interrogation, and the use of informants to pinpoint alleged Mau Mau supporters. Screening offered the pretext for a massive programme of population removal and mass detention.

Formally proposed on 22 February 1954, Operation Anvil was depicted as a logical response to the uncontrolled growth in Nairobi's population and the heightened criminality that resulted. Mau Mau attacks were presented, not as political violence, but as the delinquency of an indolent under-class.[94] Only the drastic solution of mass population transfer, Erskine claimed, would break Mau Mau's grip over the Kikuyu. In detention camps remote from the corruptive effects of the city the process of re-indoctrination and social re-integration could begin. The obvious contradiction here between the denial that Mau Mau had rational political objectives and the recognition of the need for long-term political re-education was not something that Erskine's commanders acknowledged. Anvil, they insisted, was a matter of law and order, not political struggle.[95]

Whatever the case, its results were dramatic. Mau Mau's urban support networks were broken; security force intelligence gathering transformed. But the hunt for Mau Mau fighters was now tied to a population control programme whose pillars were mass detention and ruthless counter-terror.[96] By the time Erskine was replaced in early 1955 the insurgency was set to change again.[97] With violence once more concentrated in the countryside, the rebellion's internecine character emerged more strongly. The mass detentions integral to Anvil also heralded British repression of unprecedented intensity. Numbers of convicted Mau Mau hanged or awaiting execution climbed rapidly through the hundreds, reaching a figure of 1,090 by 1960.[98] It was this harsh legal regime alongside the internal dynamics of the detention camp system that increasingly consumed British—and French—government and media reportage of the emergency from 1955 onwards.[99]

Figure 12. Mau Mau detainees packed off to detention camps in specially-modified army lorries during Operation Anvil in February 1954.

The disjuncture between the moral universe of Mau Mau adherents and the operating assumptions of their British and Kenyan loyalist opponents lies at the heart of the changing nature of repressive violence in the four discrete environments in which it was practised between 1953 and 1960. First among these were the forested areas of Kenya's Central Highlands, seen at the time as the war's military 'front-line' but increasingly marginal to its outcome. Second was the capital, Nairobi. Kenyan refugees and economic migrants flooded into the city's fast-expanding shantytowns from outlying provinces in the grip of the security force clampdown. Their arrival connected the networks of rural insurgency to the politics of urban deprivation and criminality in Eastlands, home to the capital's sprawling African estates.[100] This urban dimension to Kenya's insurgency peaked in early 1954 when, as we have seen, it was robustly challenged by Operation Anvil, the gargantuan military operation to isolate and evict the city's newcomers.

Anvil accelerated Mau Mau's transformation from limited emergency to outright civil war, a shift that was exemplified by two quite different locales, each of them critical in shaping Kenya's longer-term future. One of these—the third in my list of four—was the detention camps. Their size and number increased after Anvil to such an extent that a vast system of incarceration, what Caroline Elkins has memorably labelled Britan's 'colonial gulag', became a key arena in the contest between Mau Mau followers and the Kenyan authorities.[101] The largest of them, at Mackinnon Road and Manyani, were situated on the railway line connecting Nairobi and Mombasa. Designed to serve as reception centres in which Mau Mau suspects could be filtered out, both were soon filled to bursting. Sanitation was minimal. Epidemics struck. By the end of October 1954 Manyani, which only opened months earlier, contained 760 prisoners suffering from typhoid. An additional 63 had died already. Camp medical reports were also highly politicized documents, the probability being that the camp authorities concealed those inmates who died from beatings among the statistics for typhoid fatalities.[102] Manyani and the other detention camps were predominantly, although not exclusively, male in composition.[103] Official figures suggested that up to 80,000 people passed through them, a conservative figure that perhaps underestimates the total number of inmates by as much as a quarter of a million.[104] It is, though, worth recording that the Prime Minister, Macmillan, believed the lower figure, comforting himself that the 'original' 80,000 detainees had fallen to under 1,000 by the time of the Hola killings in 1959.[105]

With so many men detained, their original rural settlements were left largely populated by women, children, and the elderly. These denuded communities, struggling to survive became the fourth site of conflict as the colonial administration embarked upon a massive exercise in social engineering. This time people were herded into 'Emergency villages' guarded by loyalist, pro-administration auxiliaries. It was a brutal process. The scope of Kenya's emergency regulations, which, in practical terms, it fell to local Home Guard units to enforce, had opened an enormous grey area in which collective punishment and local settling of scores became permissible. 'Suspect' settlements were burned, land and livestock seized, and families, on occasion, separated. It was here in the rural heartland of Kikuyu society that the equation between violence and the reordering of power went furthest. Within the new villages, beatings, rape, and requisition, predominantly conducted by loyalist Home Guard, became sufficiently commonplace to qualify as systematic. Less visible but also devastating, denying access to food was another favoured weapon against recalcitrant families.

The changing environs of Kenya's counter-insurgency go some way to explaining how a fight, supposedly mounted against terrorism, degenerated into a systematic assault on the colony's majority ethnic group. But to pin down the British rationale for such extreme measures one needs to consider the political arguments between the proponents of heightened repression and the advocates of other, lesser, alternatives. These disputes were never reducible to a clear divide between hard-liners, many of them members of Kenya's 29,000-strong settler community, including most of their eleven representatives on the colony's Legislative Council, versus the proponents of Malayan-style 'hearts and minds' or 'rehabilitation' (the synonym generally preferred by officials in Kenya at the time). The reason why the hard-liner vs moderate equation makes little sense is that remarkably few civilian or military personnel conceded the validity of Kikuyu grievances. Instead, the main fault-line within British and settler politics was over the permissible extent of repression under the legislative restrictions of Kenya's 'Emergency Regulations'.

Even the supporters of rehabilitation posited that Mau Mau suspects had to be broken down psychologically before they could be built back up into responsible colonial subjects.[106] After 1954's mass sweeps and detentions, rehabilitation was championed by Thomas Askwith, head of Nairobi's native affairs office. A committed Quaker and former district officer, he was appointed Commissioner of Community Development on the strength of his writings about Kenyan social welfare and family cohesion.[107] Askwith sat alongside the psychiatrist J. C. Carothers and social anthropologist Louis Leakey among others on a 'Sociological Committee' that strove to identify Mau Mau's deeper causes and, by extension, its remedies. Carothers, formerly the superintendant at Kenya's one psychiatric hospital, was especially virulent in his diagnosis of Mau Mau as a form of collective mental breakdown in Kikuyu society, which, he insisted, was suffering the ill-effects of colonial modernization too rapidly imposed.[108] Convinced that the movement was sustained by the psychological traumas inculcated through oath-taking, collective intimidation, and fear of denunciation, Carothers, Askwith, and their colleagues helped devise the screening, counter-oathing ceremonies, and community development projects that were supposed to mend Kikuyu society.[109] The inquisitorial foundations of this strategy were most apparent in the detention camps. Suspects were identified—and often literally daubed—as either 'white' (innocent and eligible for immediate release), 'grey' (having confessed their involvement), or 'black' (unrepentant intransigents). Those categorized as 'grey' thus began their journey along the so-called 'pipeline' of political re-education, hard labour, and strict camp discipline identified as prerequisites to eventual rehabilitation.[110]

A system with the dubious moral underpinnings of the Victorian prison system, 'rehabilitation' was always less than the sum of its parts. For one thing, the detention camps lacked trained personnel to make the pipeline system work. For another thing, the detainees themselves developed their own educational programmes and other strategies of passive resistance in defiance of the camp authorities.[111] By late 1956 repeated camp riots, the settlers' clamour for stronger punishments, and the burgeoning detainee population combined to discredit 'rehabilitation'. Blunter instruments of enforced compliance took its place. The transition was symbolized by the 'dilution technique', a euphemism for harsher camp regimens, the nub of which was the brutalization and systematic humiliation of prisoners culminating in confessions beaten out of detainees by their guards.[112]

Just as the camp system and the new villages programme drove a wedge into Kikuyu society, so the overwhelming majority of Mau Mau war victims came from that same community. Village elders and other prominent community members that refused to take Mau Mau oaths figured among the earliest casualties. Deaths among villagers on either side of the Mau Mau-loyalist divide later overtook the numbers killed in army and Kenya police operations in the conflict's first eighteen months. In total, thirty-two white settlers were murdered. Most died in a spate of attacks on farmsteads spanning eight months between November 1952 and July 1953. Fewer than 200 members of the regular security forces—army and police—lost their lives. An additional 1,920 African 'loyalists' were also recorded as killed. The number of rebels killed remains unknown and estimates move upwards from the official figure of 11,503 'terrorist' deaths, certainly a tremendous underestimate.[113]

The shocking disproportionateness of these figures should remind us of at least four singularities in British responses to Mau Mau. First is the correlation between the concentration on Mau Mau's European victims among settlers, colonial officials, and the judiciary and the resultant extension of Emergency Regulations that laid the foundations for killings, torture, and other abuses by the security forces and their loyalist auxiliaries. Second is the fact that, although members of Churchill's government, including the Colonial Secretaries Oliver Lyttelton and Alan Lennox-Boyd, and the Prime Minister himself questioned the usefulness of heightened repression, they never overruled the Nairobi government's endorsement of it.[114] Equally, while some settlers, notably the owners of larger, more profitable estates, were willing to countenance multi-racialism and Kenyan independence, their 'new Kenya group' was overshadowed by others who saw compromise as treachery.[115]

A third factor arises here: the changing nature of the war itself. From 1954 onwards direct military involvement in Kenya's counter-insurgency gave way to increased Home Guard involvement. This Africanization of the conflict signalled the transition to internecine warfare between loyalists and their opponents. Sir Arthur Young, a veteran of the Malayan counter-insurgency, appointed as Kenya's new Commissioner of Police in 1954, found this reliance on loyalist paramilitaries intolerable. He resigned in January 1955 complaining that police powers were unlawfully arrogated to Home Guard units that habitually committed dreadful crimes. Most shocking of all, some provincial and district administrators connived in the process, certain that Home Guard violence—including rape and murder—was destroying the Mau Mau presence in rural communities.[116] When set alongside the abuses committed within the camps' 'pipeline' system, this civil war aspect to villagization points to the fourth important factor: Mau Mau does not really fit the conventional chronology of British decolonization ascribed to it. Interpreting its course through the lens of Emergency powers enforced and eventually lifted ignores the uncomfortable truth that the war was increasingly waged between Kenyans, on Kenyan terms. Its aftermath lingers in Kenya's distribution of power, wealth, and influence to this day.[117]

Conclusion

Permit me to bring the last couple of chapters together in this brief conclusion. Madagascar, Mau Mau, the Central African Emergencies; at one level, these instances of colonial fight reveal similar patterns of conflict escalation, government manipulation and shocking disregard for human life. Party political leaders victimized and jailed after sham trials; draconian punishments for insurgents; destruction of rural communities: between Madagascar and Kenya, in particular, the similarities seem strong. Dig deeper, however, and any idea of a generic model of fight responses in post-war black Africa collapses. The Madagascar rebellion remains the most obscure of the Emergencies examined here. Partly nationalist in inspiration, substantially orchestrated by members of the dispossessed Merina elite, the insurrection's regional concentration in the island's eastern farming corridor suggests that it was as much a rural revolt against the harshness of the colonial labour regime as anything else. It was the islanders' dual misfortune to rebel at a time when the Fourth Republic's rulers were gearing up to fight a major colonial war in Indochina and, second, to be situated at the midway point taken by expeditionary force units heading to Vietnam. France, in other words, had both the will and the means to crush the uprising over the summer of 1947.

Mau Mau emerges, at one level, as a multi-stage counter-insurgency drive pursued with quite staggering intensity under ruthless Emergency Regulations. Directed at first by the army, the police, and their African auxiliaries operating in Central Kenya and, during 1954 especially, within greater Nairobi, the fight over Kenya changed its terms after Operation Anvil. From 1955 the military took a back seat while the civil administration, local security forces, and Kikuyu loyalist Home Guard played a greater role in the screening process, the camp system, and the enforced villagization programme until the Emergency's official end in 1960. Explaining who held responsibility for what takes us only so far, however. The horrors of the Mau Mau conflict stemmed from the wide margin left for abuses by the powerful against the powerless in each of its phases. The breadth of the Emergency Regulations encouraged first the regular security forces, then the loyalist auxiliaries and camp administrators to go beyond a strictly demarcated counter-insurgency campaign. The result was a sustained onslaught against Kikuyu society, which uprooted hundreds of thousands, incarcerated tens of thousands, and executed, tortured, or otherwise abused thousands more.

The sheer brutality of state-sponsored violence sets Mau Mau apart in British, if not in wider European, colonial decolonization. Yet the war involved cannot be wholly understood as one conducted on British terms to defend either white settlers or Britain's colonial and commercial interests. For Mau Mau was also a Kenyan civil war. It was an intra-Kikuyu struggle between loyalists and their Mau Mau opponents over which British officials and security forces exercised only partial influence. Throughout the Central Kenya provinces worst affected by the bloodletting, killings, rape and intimidation, land seizures and local networks of power were all privatized, in the sense of being either conducted or refashioned without formal state sanction. This is emphatically not to suggest that the British authorities did not know what was taking place. The shocking fact is that British governments and their colonial administrations chose to condone this violence and the disfigurement of Kikuyu society even though they could not control it.[118]

As for Central Africa, John Darwin's damning verdict on the procession of failures during emergency rule in Nyasaland is telling: 'perpetrating a mini-Amritsar [massacre] on day one; being forced into an imperial (not even a local) inquiry within days; selecting as chief inquisitor the judge who was least likely to take a relaxed view of boisterous colonial methods; suffering the inquiry's public dismissal of the official reason for declaring the emergency; and finding the political views of the "extremists" against whom the emergency had been declared vindicated by the inquiry as an accurate expression of local opinion'.[119] Little wonder that the 1959 crackdown in the Central African Federation, although expiated to a degree by the resumption of negotiation with the nationalist leaderships in Nyasaland and Northern Rhodesia, would slide into the crisis of white settler rebellion further south in Salisbury. The days when imperial government could be assured by the alternation of repression and limited dialogue with favoured clients had long gone. Fight and flight were becoming stark alternatives, not reciprocal elements that could be combined.

9

Keeping the Peace?
'Constructive Nationalism'
in West Africa

Reflecting on his illustrious career, Hubert Deschamps, a former governor of the Côte d'Ivoire (Ivory Coast), told an audience at London's International African Institute in 1963 that apparently profound doctrinal differences between French and British imperialism in West Africa were nothing of the sort. In fact, they were irrelevant. Few successful colonial officials were great theoreticians. Once 'on the spot', at all levels of colonial administration everyone soon worked out that compromise and co-option worked better than rigid adherence to programmatic change. Assimilation versus association in the French case, indirect versus direct rule in the British; these theoretical opposites became homogenized in practice thanks to the inescapable force of expediency. A tired, rather cynical judgement perhaps, but Deschamps, once a committed 'assimilationist' himself, pointed to an underlying truth. The stylistic differences between French and British colonialism in West Africa were less important than their common motivations. Each traced a path from conquest, through political consolidation to economic extraction and eventual departure.[1] And neither wanted expensive fights along the way. Deschamps' comments, perhaps tailored to flatter his British audience by extolling the virtues of pragmatism over principle, could be put differently. Ruling empire was all about muddling along, a matter of getting away with it for as long and as cheaply as possible.

Was it really this simple? To be sure, the less confrontational paths to colonial withdrawal in this region, unusual in its melange of French and British-ruled colonies, are sometimes depicted as an exemplar of constructive nationalist engagement with reforms more or less willingly conceded—a counterpoint to the violence in East and southern Africa described in the preceding chapters. But the idea of 'managed' decolonization that this implies does not hold up. The manoeuvrings among rival African political groups as well as various forms of 'pressure from below' suggest that colonial withdrawal was less serene.[2]

A telling example of such pressure—and an indication that it began early—was the mass walkout by leprosy patients at the central leprosarium in Djikoroni, French Sudan (now Mali), on 24 August 1945. Angry about reduced rations and heavy labour obligations, the patients gathered outside the director's office to demand improvements. Gendarmes were called in and ten of the demonstrators were expelled from the leprosarium. A defeat for the patients, their protest revealed something deeper nonetheless; a strengthening community will to press claims for better treatment from colonial institutions. A full government investigation of the patients' complaints ensued.[3] In its way, the 'revolt' at Djikoroni's *Institut Central de la Lepré* exemplifies the pattern of negotiations resumed after spells of repression, pointing to the dominance of 'flight' solutions in West Africa.[4] But, as we shall see, the general absence of long-term political violence is not enough to confirm Deschamps' judgement that colonial policies throughout West Africa were inter changeable. For one thing, political violence there certainly was, particularly in the sphere of labour disputes. For another thing, the differences between British and French decolonization in West Africa remained profound. These differences are reducible to two things: first, their contrasting attitudes towards independence and its desirability, and second, the presence of a federal system in the French case, its absence in the British. To untangle these points we need to look at the institutional apparatus and economic characteristics of West African colonial rule.

Colonial structures in West Africa

Two vast colonial federations dominated France's sub-Saharan empire. French West Africa (*Afrique Occidentale Française*, AOF, shown in Map 10) comprised seven territories: Senegal, French Sudan (now Mali), Guinea, Ivory Coast, Mauritania, Niger and Dahomey (now Benin). An eighth was added in 1948 with the re-designation of Upper Volta (now Burkina-Faso), an inland territory formerly incorporated into its neighbouring

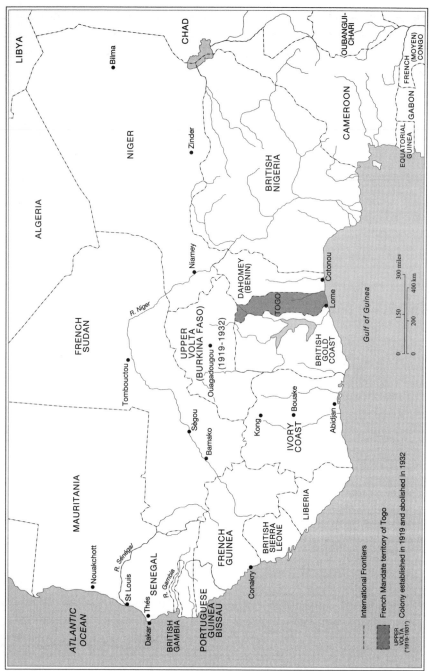

Map 10. French West Africa.

territories. French Togo, previously a League of Nations Mandate, became a UN trusteeship territory in 1945. It, too, gravitated economically and politically towards AOF. The outward appearance of federation, so appealing to metropolitan governments, belied AOF's economic and cultural disparities. Three of its colonies were landlocked, making it hard for them to prosper alone.[5] Contrasts were stark between widespread poverty in the *Sahel*—the semi-arid pre-Saharan north—and extensive plantation agriculture, forestry, and commerce in more southerly communities.[6]

Acute regional variation in population density, economic opportunity, and wealth made economic migration crucial to AOF's socio-economic structure. Peasant labourers headed south and westwards to work in the cash crop and forestry sectors in Senegal, Guinea, Côte d'Ivoire, and Dahomey.[7] Senegal and Ivory Coast stood out as the federation's 'pearls'. Yet, much as these two colonies were, respectively, political and economic showcases of French rule, both were centres of the earliest and most significant African political mobilization against colonial abuses. An added political complication was that remnants of imperial reforms from the mid nineteenth century survived in the original French slaving settlements in West Africa: the 'Four Communes' of Senegal (the towns of Dakar, St Louis, and Rufisque, and Gorée Island). After 1848 the Communes' administration was modelled on the French system of local government. From October 1916 their inhabitants enjoyed 'citizen' status as opposed to that of mere colonial 'subjects'.[8] By 1936 there were some 100,000 black African and mixed race (*métis*) citizens in the Four Communes, but under 2,500 throughout the rest of AOF.[9] No surprise, then, that the Four Communes' uniquely assimilated status made them, at once, a model, a magnet for political activism, and a monument to the inequity of colonialism elsewhere in AOF.

The colonial economies of AOF remained beholden to export crop production, rubber extraction, and forestry; industries still dominated by old-style colonial trading companies at the end of the Second World War.[10] Two stood out. The *Société Commerciale de l'Ouest Africain* (SCOA), founded in 1887, and the *Compagnie Française d'Afrique Occidentale* (CFAO), established in 1906, towered over French West Africa's export trade.[11] But their dominance was beginning to fade. On the one hand, growing industrial unrest among African wage earners was matched by recognition in France that the old exploitative ways of colonial business were an embarrassment. The introduction in 1945 of a distinct colonial currency, the franc CFA, pointed to a renewed French commitment to develop a more integrated French African economy. But the new currency regime did not silence African cash-crop farmers clamouring for an end to price controls and labour restrictions.[12] Among them was Félix Houphouët-Boigny, a Baule cantonal chief and future national leader of Ivory Coast. It was his coffee-cultivation interests that led Houphouët-Boigny to organize an African planters' association, the *Syndicat Agricole Africain* (SAA) in 1944. His call for substitution of forced labour with a competitive wage market in Ivory Coast's plantations won him the backing of African farmers and labourers alike.[13] Their demands were soon answered, albeit not as they envisaged. The surge in metropolitan demand for African commodities as France's reconstruction proceeded in the late 1940s was immediately followed by sharper increases in raw material prices triggered by the Korean War rearmament boom of 1950–53. Black African colonies, for the first time, acquired economic importance as dollar earners, and were soon integrated into the US-directed bureaucracy of the Marshall Plan.[14]

In late 1945 the Dakar government established a planning directorate to vet development projects put to the federal authorities. The first criterion for approval was that such programmes improve the welfare of the African population.[15] Investment capital was made available as never before. State funding for infrastructure modernization through the Economic and Social Development Fund (*Fonds d'Investissment pour le Développment Economique et Social*, FIDES), created on 30 April 1946, was quickly followed by some 10 billion francs of Marshall Aid spending in AOF between 1948 and 1952.[16] The annual GNP of the AOF territories grew by an average 13.8 per cent between 1947 and 1951.[17] Although little of the increased wealth in French West Africa trickled down to the wider population, but the post-war trade boom still had momentous social effects. It stimulated urbanization and added to the numbers of politically active African wage earners. The new commercial prospects presented to adventurous capitalists also increased the opportunities for African workers to press claims for a decent wage, better working conditions, and employment protection. So much so that the greatest shift in the post-war balance sheets of the large trading companies was not the surge in capital investment and annual profit, but the rising proportion of turnover allocated to wage payments.

Towards flight solutions in French West Africa?

These structural factors go a long way to explaining differing local reactions to what the imperial rulers proposed and did. The French African leaders who sat in the French Constituent Assembly at the end of the war were models of Francophile refinement. Most were French educated, products of Dakar's William Ponty Lycée, a training school for administrators, lawyers, and mid-level managers. Through its corridors passed most of the first generation of French West Africa's politicians, including eleven of the African deputies elected to Paris in 1945. William Ponty graduates were modernizers, educated to view a republican state as the key agent of social change. They endorsed the closer partnership between France and West Africa to which the French Union aspired. Several of them helped define it in the first place.[18]

French West Africa's new political elites were also quick to recognize something else: that the political architecture of AOF, combining a federal administration with national constitutions, partnership agreements, and electoral arrangements in individual francophone West African states, while complex, maximized the opportunities for constructive engagement. The experience in neighbouring British-ruled territories was very different. Few British policy-makers thought nationalism an existential threat to their strategic and commercial interests in Nigeria, the Gold Coast (now Ghana), or Sierra Leone. The fact that key British industrial concerns, some of which counted senior Conservatives among their board members, were equally sanguine was valuable, but not decisive.[19] 'Fighting' the consolidation of West African anti-colonialism with the full force of military intervention was no more seriously contemplated in the City of London's square mile than it was in nearby Whitehall. In part, this was because hostility to European rule in anglophone West Africa, although heartfelt, left room for compromise. Even the more radical politicians—Kwame Nkrumah in the Gold Coast or I.T.A. Wallace-Johnson in Sierra Leone for instance—ultimately recognized the benefits of dialogue. In part, it was because the rapid acceleration in plans for self-government, local and national elections, economic reorganization, and eventual withdrawal left British officials preoccupied with more pressing concerns.

Indeed, the term 'nationalist' is too simplistic to explain the ways in which West African politicians such as the future presidents, prime ministers, party and union leaders, Nkrumah in Ghana, Nnamdi Azikwe in Nigeria, and Wallace-Johnson in Sierra Leone, articulated their vision of independence and pan-African cooperation. Several of British Africa's leading anti-colonial radicals had attended the Fifth Pan-African Congress, which opened in the unlikely setting of Chorlton-on-Medlock Town Hall in All Saints, Manchester, in mid October 1945. Perhaps the location was less unusual than might appear. Many of the delegates had backgrounds in trade union activism and left-wing journalism that chimed with Manchester's radical tradition. Eschewing the label of 'nationalist', the delegates stressed a more fundamental objective: they were, they said, 'determined to be free'.[20]

Their French African counterparts, the Senegalese Léopold Sedar Senghor, his colleague Mamadou Dia, even the Guinean trade unionist Sékou Touré (ultimately, the most militant among West Africa's 'big men'), approached the challenges of African identity, self-rule, and economic development with a similar clarity of vision. They, too, recognized the fundamental importance of questions of liberty and sovereignty. But they were less consumed than the English-speaking pan-Africanists by the idea that racial division and the need to overcome it were the fundamental goals of anti-colonialism.[21] What is so striking is that so many francophone African politicians embraced the possibilities offered by French claims of greater inclusivity, welfare entitlements, and citizenship rights for west Africans within the framework, first of the French Union and, after 1958, of the French Community. Even Touré, who eventually spurned such a partnership, did so in reaction to the overweening influence that France exercised nearby. Touré was the exception, not the rule. Numerous political leaders from Senegal's cosmopolitan administrative hub of Dakar in the west to dusty Niger in the east sought additional rights and improved social welfare for their compatriots, not within wholly independent states but as autonomous members of a West African confederation still tied to France.[22]

Their logic in doing so rested on four elements. Two were negative, the product of anxieties about the terms on which independence might be secured, and two were positive, reflecting hopes for a better future for West Africans. The negatives first. One was that French West Africa's colonial boundaries, some barely fifty years old, were ethnically artificial, commercially nonsensical, and socially limiting. Underlying this view was a second anxiety: the fear that independence would precipitate what Senghor dubbed 'balkanization' or sub-division into territories that were neither economically nor politically viable. Viewed this way, 'nationalism' in the narrowly instrumental sense of support for individual nation states roughly equivalent in size and structure to the erstwhile colonies was deeply unattractive.[23] For Senghor and other federalists who thought like him, national independence of this sort promised only lasting poverty, under-development and political marginalization. As for the positives, first was the belief that cultural, economic, and strategic partnership with France offered greater possibilities for Africans as workers and citizens to attain improved living standards and guaranteed individual rights. Linked to this was a second, regionally-focused ambition—to transform the old federal structures of colonial West Africa into a free association of autonomous territories. Each would be sovereign in domestic affairs, and thus effectively independent. But all would be connected to something greater: a confederation with shared economic interests, a single global voice, and free internal movement for all its peoples; in short, a West African Union to match the institutions and cultural ambitions of the European Community.[24]

The peoples of French West Africa would thereby transcend the limitations of 'national' independence based on a replication of former colonial frontiers, bureaucracies, and economies. They would, instead, attain something better: a powerful regional grouping that overcame the national particularity imposed by colonial rule.[25]

As these ideas indicate, both the complexion of politics and the substance of political debate in French West Africa were quite unlike their equivalents in adjacent British-ruled territories. For one thing, francophone African politicians, trade union leaders, student organizers, and other civil society activists had an entire imperial constitution, the French Union, from which to draw their claims for everything from higher wages and employment protections to educational entitlements and legal rights as citizens of an imperial super-state. Admittedly, as we saw in Chapter 3, the French Union in its final form was vague about the rights conferred by imperial citizenship. It was ambiguous about the scope for African political participation in decision-making. And it was conspicuously silent about the extent to which metropolitan welfare benefits would be extended to overseas territories.

Yet, for all its ambiguities, indeed, perhaps because of them, the French Union presented West Africa's new political parties with numerous opportunities to make political and economic claims to which French governments had to respond. The French African politicians pitching these demands worked assiduously to pin down the rights conferred by citizenship and the entitlements due to colonial workers performing tasks comparable to their French equivalents.[26] The governments of the Fourth Republic and their subordinate colonial administrations were thus presented with a basic dilemma. How to reconcile the persistence of a French-directed imperial system with the republican rhetoric of equality, inclusivity, and democratic participation that France and the French Union purported to represent?[27] The written articles of the Union, the presence of elected African deputies in Paris as well as in individual colonial capitals, and the institutional structures set up under the FIDES and its associated economic programmes were tangible and arguable in a way that the Commonwealth's more decorous but largely vacuous conventions were not.

Differences were equally apparent in the realm of party politics. There was no equivalent in British West Africa of Houphouët-Boigny's *Rassemblement Démocratique Africain* (RDA). This was an inter-territorial alliance that functioned as an umbrella organization for several of the leading nationalist groups in individual territories. Although its reach extended throughout French West Africa, the RDA pivoted around the Parti Démocratique de la Côte d'Ivoire, its largest component party and the core of Houphouët-Boigny's regional power. More importantly from the French domestic perspective, between 1946 and 1950 the RDA maintained a working relationship with the Communist Party in France. Several RDA activists underwent their political apprenticeship as members of the Communist Study Groups that proliferated in French West Africa's major towns at the end of the War. Orchestrated by Raymond Barbé, head of the French Communist Party's colonial section, the Study Groups were meant to align young African radicals with the French Party's opposition to colonial capitalism.[28] They also provided valuable organizational training, which helped RDA sections survive renewed repression that gathered momentum following the Communists' eviction from the French government in May 1947. In Guinea, for instance, Sékou Touré, Madéïra Kéïta, and Léon Maka, joint founders of the colony's RDA branch, all passed through the Communist Study Group in the capital, Conakry.[29] The RDA, formally launched at the Bamako Congress in October 1946 (itself part funded by the PCF), thus drew more from Communist political culture—the Party's way of seeing and doing things—than from Marxist ideology.[30]

Other French African parties, Senghor's Senegalese Socialists for instance, cultivated similar filial ties with their metropolitan party political counterparts.[31] And still others remained close to the French West African labour movement. Industrial trade unions were a rich source of leadership cadres for national parties in Guinea, Côte d'Ivoire and Niger, individuals who proved equally adept at mobilizing public support for political demands as for workers' rights.[32] There were no British echoes of the formal ties between French and colonial political parties, although the Labour Party fostered looser transnational connections with socialist parties in Asia and Africa through the framework of the Second International. Nor was there any British equivalent to the complexities of imperial citizenship facing franco-phone populations whose rights and economic opportunities would be materially affected by the alternatives of post-colonial federation, looser confederation, or unitary 'national' independence.[33]

Conflict and negotiation in Nigeria

Nigeria perhaps came closest to the institutional complexities of French West Africa. It also acquired unprecedented importance within British colonial policy in the late 1940s. Immediately after Indian independence, Nigeria's population of thirty-one million constituted one in four of Britain's remaining colonial subjects. Bewilderingly diverse and territorially extensive, the Nigerian state was ethnically, religiously, economically, and politically divided between north and south, east and west. Its main urban centres and regional divisions are shown in Map 11 below. Flying in the face of its substantial material and cultural disparities, Nigeria's colonial exist-ence represented a loose federation from which the north in particular might secede as the reality of a southern-dominated post-colonial state loomed larger. As in French West Africa industrial unrest destabilized the major port cities of Nigeria's south immediately after World War II. A highly politicized general strike in May 1945 brought Lagos, the colony's commer-cial capital, to a standstill.[34] The political effervescence in the south only accentuated the social and cultural divide with the generally more placid Nigerian North. Efforts to prevent secession through the cultivation of conservative Muslim chiefs in Northern Nigeria were, therefore, as pivotal to British policy as the end of the colonial period as they had been at its beginning.[35]

On 4 December 1929, a time when imperialist propaganda helped allevi-ate the looming reality of economic depression, a future Conservative Colonial Secretary, William Ormsby-Gore, explained Nigeria's importance

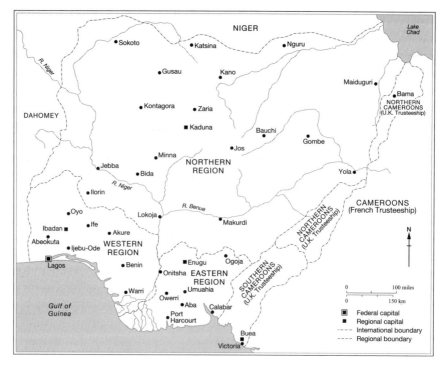

Map 11. Nigeria before independence.

in simple terms in a BBC radio broadcast for British schoolchildren: 'our largest African dependency is nearly seven times the size of England, with about twenty million inhabitants, that is, as many human beings as Canada, South Africa, and Australia put together.' He went on to describe a tour around the magnificent northern city of Kano whose 'great walls are fourteen miles round'. 'Towards evening', he continued, 'the market places are absolutely thronged with people, and you can buy and sell almost anything—cotton goods from Manchester, hardware from Birmingham, mixed up with native medicines made of bits of birds' legs, lucky stones, dried fish; and, of course, animals galore being driven in and out of the thronging crowd.' Relatively tame as colonial propaganda, Ormsby-Gore's effusive broadcast still encouraged his listeners to swallow the colonial construction of Northern Nigeria's distinctiveness under British rule. 'All this trade has brought tremendously increased prosperity to all sections of the community. Education is advancing. New hospitals are going up, but nowhere else does society seem to be so little affected. Hausa and Fulani [northern Nigeria's largest ethnic groups] alike are dominated by a sense of courtly dignity. Good manners are expected from everyone. The casual visitor must, I think, be impressed by the fact that of all the Mohammedan countries Northern Nigeria comes closest to living up to the ideal of fraternity which is the best element of the Mohammedan code.'[36]

In the late 1940s Nigeria fell short of the exuberant, harmonious co-existence that Ormsby-Gore conjured up twenty years before. Racial segregation excluded black Nigerians from hotels, bars, even town districts, firing an animosity to British racism that cut across the colony's internal ethnic divides. The prevalence of Nigeria's 'colour bar' was brought to light in February 1947 when the owner of the Bristol Hotel in Lagos made plain that he would have refused admission to a senior British colonial official of mixed race parentage had he known he was 'black'.[37] Nigeria's colonial authorities eschewed such overt discrimination but there was a pronounced racial flavour in their intolerance of labour unrest, which occasionally exploded into lethal police violence in the decade after the war ended.[38]

The worst such incident occurred on 18 November 1949 when police fired into a crowd of striking miners at Enugu colliery in Nigeria's south-eastern coalfield. Twenty-two died and a further fifty were injured, provoking rioting throughout the region.[39] Dedicated officials and Nigerian progressives did, on occasion, bridge these racial and workplace divides, a point proven by the rise of the Gaskiya Corporation, an Anglo-Nigerian publishing house that disseminated Hausa literature in the immediate post-war years.[40] But 'spatial apartheid' between whites and blacks was more common, the gradual 'Nigerianization' of the colony's civil service rarely being matched by any commitment among foreign-owned corporations to employ local personnel in Nigeria.[41] Royal Dutch/Shell, which, in 1946, resumed oil exploration operations in and around Owerri in south-eastern Nigeria's Delta region, could boast only three Nigerians among its staff of over 2,000 in 1954.[42]

Three communally-based parties were contesting power at regional and national levels meanwhile. Strongest among them was Nnamdi Azikiwe's National Council of Nigeria and the Cameroons (NCNC). It was founded in 1944 and was strongest among the Igbo peoples of the south-east. The NCNC also made inroads into Lagos, where Igbo economic migration was increasingly visible.[43] For all that, Obefami Awolowo's Action Group (AG) remained the dominant force in the Yoruba territories of the south-west with Lagos at their heart. The two southern movements favoured rapid independence with a powerful central government, knowing that it was likely to come under their control. For the same reason, their Muslim Hausa-Fulani rivals in the Northern People's Congress (NPC) dreaded 'southernization', a phenomenon the NPC equated with Igbo and Yoruba dominance.[44]

Between 1948 and 1953 Governor Sir John Macpherson, his chief secretary Hugh Foot, and Sir Bryan Sharwood-Smith, Governor of the Northern Region, worked assiduously to placate northern anxieties that Britain's relatively light colonial touch in the North risked replacement by an all-controlling central government after independence. Macpherson promised a harmonious future in which regional particularities would be respected. His hopes rested on a new constitution designed to counter-balance the power of a national parliament with three strong regional governments.[45] Much of this was devised to safeguard northern interests, the Governor's inner circle of advisers finding the cautious NPC leaders more congenial than their southern counterparts.[46] Colonial Secretary Oliver Lyttelton felt the same way, praising the 'courtly manners' and 'high bearing' of NPC representatives in London, whose conservatism 'democracy and the *Daily Mirror* have not yet debased'.[47]

For all this admiration, British negotiators did not ignore southern concerns entirely. The key issue here was the inter-relationship between the ethnic and regional power-bases of Nigeria's three major parties and their standing in a national parliament or House of Representatives. Simply put, the dangers were that each would remain sectarian and that the two southern groups—the NCNC and AG—might, in combination, negate the collective voice of Nigeria's seventeen million northerners. Other factors came into play. The Gold Coast's march to independence and the quickening pace of reform throughout much of French West Africa after the RDA broke with their Communist mentors in 1950–1 (both discussed below) increased the pressure for an accelerated devolution of ministerial authority in Nigeria.[48] Chief among the local issues was to guarantee the status of minority communities by fostering cooperation among the regional party groups.[49]

Macpherson and his colleagues soon found their elaborately-laid constitutional plans for Nigeria's future unravelling around them. Under the new political arrangements put in place in 1951, Nigerians elected to the impressively-named Council of Ministers were denied real authority. The colonial government could still act independently of them. In June 1952 the AG

leadership began insisting that, without genuine Nigerian ministerial responsibility and additional local government powers, Macpherson's new constitution was an elaborate sham. By the end of the year the AG had joined
the NCNC in demanding full self-government within four years.[50] On
31 March 1953 Anthony Enahoro, a leading AG organizer and editor of
the Lagos *Morning Star* newspaper, reiterated the demand during a House
of Representatives debate. With this, Macpherson's flawed attempt to play
Nigeria's political puppeteer collapsed.[51]

Voted down amid chaotic scenes in the chamber, Enahoro's historic
demand accomplished several things regardless. For one thing, it stole
NCNC thunder, compelling Azikwe to work more closely with the AG in
its Lagos heartland. But this jockeying for influence between the two southern parties was as nothing when compared with the hostility each directed
towards their NPC rivals from the north. Seen from an NPC perspective,
Enahoro's call for full self-government raised the prospect of northern subordination within a Nigerian state permanently ruled in southern interests.
Vicious caricatures in Enahoro's *Morning Star* and other Lagos newspapers
depicted northerners as parochial, reactionary stooges of British colonialism. NPC representatives ran a gauntlet of southern railway-workers' jibes
as they returned northwards by train.[52]

This accusatory tone was matched by escalating inter-communal friction on the streets. On 17 May 1953 a provocative AG rally in Kano, the
city so beloved by Ormsby-Gore and still the largest in the north, ignited
a week of ethnic violence. At least 36 died and hundreds more were
injured.[53] A train rumoured to be ferrying NCNC politicians was attacked
in Kaduna to the south. Government and police were losing control and
the break-up of Nigeria, once a remote spectre, was becoming a real possibility. In the event, the principal political victim was Governor Macpherson.
Recalled to London before the Kano riots, he was overruled by Colonial
Secretary Lyttelton. There would be an immediate cession of power to
regional governments to take the heat out of northern secessionism.[54]
Nigerian party delegates were instead invited to London in late July 1953
to discuss constitutional revision.[55] No one in the Colonial Office anticipated how far this meeting would go. But, when faced with Azikwe's
renewed insistence on self-government by 1956 and the threat of an inter-
party boycott unless a firm date for independence were agreed then and
there, British negotiators gave way. In July 1954 a new 'Lyttelton constitution', which ought, more accurately, to have born Azikwe's name, confirmed

the London conference deal.[56] Nigeria's internal ferment had catalysed independence.

The irony was that once Macpherson's schemes for Nigeria's long-term future went up in smoke, the political air cleared. The policy reverses precipitated by the 1953 self-government crisis made it easier for Macpherson's administration to resuscitate its other main objective—inter-ethnic 'national' cooperation. Central to this was an NPC–NCNC alliance. Colonial officials nurtured this tender flower assiduously, helping to assure victory for NPC leader Tafawa Balewa during national elections in 1959. Strongly Anglophile, Balewa became independent Nigeria's first prime minister in the following year.[57] British championing of compromise between Nigeria's 'big three' political groups marked the logical end-point of indirect rule. Insofar as Nigeria's decolonization was 'managed' at all, this was its essence. The point was that such collaboration was feasible only after the colonial authorities had retreated on the more fundamental question of Nigerian self-rule. Flight, in this case, was a two-stage process in which Macpherson's initial efforts to impose constitutional devolution on British terms disintegrated amidst the violence of the Kano disorders. A Nigeria taken to the brink of uncontrollable inter-communal violence was the dismal, but essential prelude to renewed negotiation. Only then could the self-government scheme embodied in the Lyttelton constitution, its outlines freely negotiated with Nigeria's political leaders at the London conference, take flight.

A Ghanaian model of constructive nationalism?

Gradual, orderly transition to 'responsible' self-government (translatable as hopefully democratic, but definitely pro-British) was also the aspiration for the Gold Coast (Ghana), Britain's other main wealth-generating colony in West Africa. By 1947 the hope was that a new African elite, British-educated and commensurately respectful of Britain's advice, would take up the reins, first of local government, then of national affairs, abandoning the old ways of 'chieftaincy politics' and ignoring the temptations of pan-African or leftist ideologies.[58] The 'romantic cultural conservatism' of indirect rule, in which the British singled out the African institutions that could be accommodated before prodding them to follow their bidding, would be supplanted by the mechanisms of English local government.[59] Direct taxes would at last be introduced to provide money for domestic spending. 'Customary' law-making, poorly understood by the Colonial Office reformers who despised it, would be rationalized into a network of magistrates' courts.[60] Framed in this light, Gold Coast self-government was less the prelude to decolonization than the institutionalization of British practice.[61] Government of the shires was coming to Accra.

The problem was that such imperial managerialism, so much in vogue at the Colonial Office, was overtaken by events before the Second World War even ended. During three years from February 1944 Gold Coast politics was held in thrall by a well-publicized murder case. Seven high-born southern Ghanaians were convicted of the gruesome killing of a local Akan-speaking chief. The prosecution persuaded a largely African jury and a Turkish Cypriot colonial judge that the accused used the blood of the dead man, Akyea Mensah, in an elaborate royal funeral ritual. At a time when colonial administrations were proclaiming the impending triumph of development and reform, the case came as a jolt; at best, a discomfiting throwback to customary practices out of step with social modernization; at worst, a glimpse into a Conradian heart of darkness.

Gold Coast Governor Sir Alan Burns was at the time putting the final touches to a more inclusive colonial constitution designed to engage not only young Ghanaian government officers but also chiefly elders akin to those on trial. Politically, the case had concluded at just the wrong moment. Burns acted quickly, confirming the jury's verdict and the judge's choice of the death penalty. All seven were condemned to hang. But the Governor's authority was eroded by a tortuous appeals process, much of it conducted via increasingly acrimonious correspondence between Whitehall and Accra. In March 1947 Burns threatened resignation, a move sufficient to send three of the defendants to the gallows. There was uproar, not just in the colony, but in Westminster too. Barristers-turned-MPs on both sides of the House of Commons, including the Conservatives R.A. Butler and Quentin Hogg and Labour members Sidney Silverman and Leslie Hale figured among eighty-five MPs who petitioned the Colonial Secretary, Creech-Jones, to commute the remaining death sentences. Ostensibly, it was the Minister's flip-flopping on the matter that so infuriated Governor Burns. His anger was intensified by the fact that the condemned men's all-Ghanaian defence team was led by an eloquent lawyer, Dr J.B. Danquah, a former Gold Coast youth–movement leader. Within months of the executions, Danquah went on to establish the United Gold Coast Convention (UGCC), the colony's first nationalist party.[62]

What should we make of this? Three points bear emphasis. Firstly, although the actual circumstances of Chief Mensah's murder remained obscure, its legal outcome was openly adjudicated by local people and freely discussed by a local press, albeit operating within the confines of a colonial legal system. A second, countervailing observation is that, while the conduct of the case was fair by the standards of the day, it became highly politicized. So much so that it destroyed the relationship between a previously success-ful colonial governor and his Whitehall superiors. Burns' increasing obses-sion with the case fed his hostility to Danquah and the relatively moderate political organization he founded—the UGCC. This rendered the Accra administration better disposed to another party political grouping that emerged from a subsequent rift within the UGCC: Kwame Nkrumah's Convention People's Party (CPP). Ironically, this latter organization was the more militant. Casting further doubt on the idea that decolonization could ever be 'managed', the third point is simply to highlight the importance of historical contingency, of the unforeseen. Although Burns is recalled in his-tories of decolonization for the new Gold Coast constitution that bore his name, a dramatic, in some ways atavistic murder case did more to shape official reactions to the emergence of an organized nationalist challenge in the colony.[63]

Wider social pressures also came into play. Most important was a severe crisis in the agricultural economy caused by swollen-shoot disease, a virus afflicting the Gold Coast's staple export: cocoa. The virus devastated cocoa farms in the colony's Eastern Province and was prevalent throughout the Gold Coast rainforest. Government agronomists prescribed aggressive con-trol measures, dubbed 'cutting out', to halt its advance. In December 1946 the Accra administration duly enacted 'Swollen Shoot of Cocoa Disease Order Number 148', a compulsory tree-felling programme. Government-recruited labour gangs brandished the requisite administrative order on the estates selected for cutting out. Fury among growers and labourers whose livelihoods were literally destroyed before their eyes was compounded by uncertainty about compensation arrangements. Amid the felled timber a political firestorm was about to ignite.[64]

It took seven years from planting before a cocoa tree yielded its distinctive pods for harvest. What would happen meanwhile? Farmers' credit lines were broken. Their workers were laid off. The entire agricultural economy might disintegrate. Large commercial trading companies dominated the cocoa market, selling to the British chocolate giants Cadbury and Fry's. Long-standing complaints that the cocoa market, always geared to British export requirements, operated to cultivators' disadvantage grew louder. Expatriate banks offered little in the way of start-up loans to put agriculturalists back on their feet. Urban moneylenders and pawnbrokers, many of them Syrian and Lebanese, filled the gap to some degree but were often decried as sharks. In this tense atmosphere, rising goods prices turned seething resentment, first into a consumers' boycott, then into street protest. Uniting rural chiefs (many of them cocoa district landowners) with unemployed city youths, a farmers' movement with UGCC lawyers, this was popular opposition to manifest unfairness rather than anti-colonial mobilization.[65]

And it snowballed. Former members of the Royal West African Frontier Force pressed their case for the fulfilment of government pledges of support for demobilized Ghanaian soldiers. On 28 February 1948 a contingent of the ex-servicemen's union sporting old uniforms, their campaign medals glinting in the sunshine, marched on Accra's Christiansborg Castle, seat of the colonial government. They aimed to present a petition detailing economic grievances about pensions and unfulfilled promises of resettlement.[66] Accra's police chief, Commissioner B. E. A. Tamakloe, did not anticipate problems from men who had served King and Empire loyally in the past. He not only authorized the demonstration but limited police numbers on the day.[67] Gradually, however, the orderly veterans' procession was hijacked by the city's young unemployed. By the time the demonstrators encountered the police cordon at the Christiansborg crossroads their numbers had swollen to several thousand. Visibly intimidated, the policemen's fright turned to violence. Shots were fired, killing three protesters and wounding many more.[68] News of the incident triggered rioting in Accra and several of the Eastern Province towns worst affected by the cocoa crisis.[69] Briefly, it looked as if colonial politics in the Gold Coast would trace a path depressingly familiar from recent experience in Kenya or even Palestine. The inevitable commission of inquiry into the 1948 disorders hunted obsessively for reds under beds before acknowledging the colony's post-war economic problems as the real driver of dissent.[70] Colonial government meanwhile resumed its preparations for what turned out to be an abortive new constitutional settlement, something that the CPP, from its inception in 1949, pledged to oppose.[71]

For the authorities at least, these apparently dark clouds revealed unexpected silver linings. First, escalating disorder in 1948–9 led to expanded police intelligence-gathering. The colony's Special Branch dedicated itself to collecting information about internal political threats in general and Communist infiltration of the CPP in particular. Thanks to informants within the CPP executive, the resultant political intelligence suggested that Nkrumah's party was not a Marxist Trojan horse but a viable political client.[72] Better information about their political adversaries illuminated another change taking place. Far from driving the CPP towards extremism as was initially feared, the Party's espousal of non-violent protest, or 'positive action' in support of self-government, provided the platform for the CPP's rise as a nationalist party with practical ideas about how Gold Coast/Ghana should be run. As several British MPs pointed out, recognizing that the CPP's alternative proposals were negotiable made it imperative to release Nkrumah, who had been imprisoned for directing the CPP's civil disobedience campaign.[73] A third change, then, lay in the colonial authorities' reversal of past policy. The previous indulgence of chieftaincy politics was dropped in favour of dialogue with Nkrumah's new party as the more viable alternative.[74] The turn towards cooperation with the CPP signalled that the colonial authorities favoured negotiation and concession over force and inflexibility. Having flirted with a fight strategy at the height of the swollen-shoot crisis, by late 1951 flight was preferred.

Nkrumah's CPP, a self-consciously modern party with a young, literate, largely urban membership, won elections in 1951, 1954, and 1956. But its voter support was never rock solid. Northern Muslim groups grew disillusioned with Nkrumah's hostility to chieftaincy politics and Islamic tradition.[75] The challenge presented by an emergent Asante nationalist alternative was stronger still.[76] In all, the CPP's rapid rise was more vigorously contested than Nkrumah's lieutenants cared to admit. Still, it heralded the decisive transition of power in the Gold Coast.[77] This shift occurred on two levels. The first, the gradual relaxation of British colonial control, is well known—a short-lived turn to Indian-style diarchy or 'joint rule' with the CPP before the de facto admission of self-government that preceded 'formal' independence in 1957. It is the second, the rise of CPP predominance and the commensurate demise of customary chiefly authority in the countryside that held greater significance for most Ghanaians. Once Nkrumah was appointed 'leader of government business' after the 1951 elections, then prime minister in 1952, the CPP's determination to dismantle the political and juridical apparatus of 'chieftaincy politics' became apparent. This signified a revolutionary transformation in the social relations at the heart of

Ghana's civil society. And it prefigured the establishment of a one-party state. Few could have been surprised by the CPP's impatience to assimilate the Ewe-speaking regions of British-administered Togoland, Ghana's eastern neighbour and a former UN trust territory. In its quest to absorb this territory, the party steamrollered over the demands of villagers and townspeople in the region for a separate Ewe state.[78] More unusually, these developments took place, not just under the noses of British colonial officials, but with their blessing.[79]

West African commonalities: pressure from below

Largely because of its agricultural crisis, the Gold Coast missed out on the spectacular post-war economic growth taking place in nearby French West African territories like Ivory Coast and Guinea. But there, too, popular dissent intensified in the late 1940s. Aggrieved that the export boom conferred few local benefits, French African salaried workers provided the impetus for social reform. Many were organized into local trade unions, several of which were tied to France's Communist-affiliated *Confédération Générale du Travail* (CGT). French organizers played little part in the resultant worker protests that swept through West Africa's cities after the war, however Vestigial paternalism, entrenched racism, plus a limited understanding of the region's industrial sector impeded the growth of working partnerships between French trade unionists and their West African counterparts.[80] A cautionary note here: under five per cent of French West Africa's working population were wage labourers, perhaps no more than 70,000 by 1948. This was fewer than the number of African ex-servicemen who drew army pensions from the French state after 1945.[81] But force of numbers was not everything. If former colonial soldiers inclined towards conservatism, unionized workers did not. Their capacity to shape events reflected their urban concentration in strategic industries. Unionization registered its biggest impact in French West Africa's dockyards and the federation's largest industrial conglomerate, its railway company, the *Régie des Chemins de Fer de l'AOF* or 'RAN'.[82]

Spurred by a reform-minded Governor, René Barthes, the federal government's Labour Inspection Service tried to steer African trade unionism towards moderation. Success hinged on an implicit recognition by both sides that industrial disputes were facets of capitalist modernization, not the seedbed for anti-colonialism. The administration enjoyed a critical advantage here. Thanks, in part, to their CGT connections, African trade unionists typically sought parity in wages and conditions with their French counterparts rather than a clean break with France.[83] Even so, industrial unrest persisted throughout the late 1940s, notably in Senegal and the Guinean capital, Conakry, where rank-and-file militancy was strongest.[84] Wildcat strikes that began on Dakar's dockside in December 1946 mushroomed into an eleven-day general strike in mid January 1947. Government clerks, market women, skilled and manual labourers joined the dockworkers in claiming equal pay for equal work irrespective of race. Additional demands for a guaranteed minimum wage and family allowances confirmed that the strikers were well aware of similar concessions being extracted by their French counterparts. Just as significantly, rather than colonial-style repression, the strikes were arbitrated by the Labour Inspection Service.[85] The principles of colonial assimilation were being turned upside down. Union action secured equivalent rights for black public-sector workers without any prior requirement to adopt the cultural trappings of 'Frenchness'.[86]

For all these successes, leading African political figures in AOF remained ambivalent about trade union power. Suspicion of African organized labour ran deep among the ten West African deputies elected to the Constituent Assembly in October 1945. Anxiety about workers' demands came naturally to the five deputies elected by citizens; in other words, principally by Europeans, other than in the one seat reserved for the Four Communes of Senegal. But the other five deputies elected by AOF's 118,000 enfranchised African subjects—Léopold Senghor (Senegal), Félix Houphouët-Boigny (Ivory Coast), Sourou Migan Apithy (Dahomey), Yacine Diallo (Guinea), and Fily Dabo Sissoko (Soudan-Niger)—also distanced themselves from the post-war strike-wave.[87] This was an ominous portent. African national leaders, some of them former union officials, proved less sympathetic towards industrial dissent once they held the levers of power. Trade unionism in French West Africa, impelled by a grass-roots activism that blazed a trail in consolidating workers' rights, was eventually felled by the insecurities of post-colonial regimes.[88]

Repression and its abandonment

In the late 1940s West African trade unionism filled the void left by the government's clampdown against RDA organizers. During the three years of centre-right 'Third Force' coalitions in France between 1948 and the general elections of June 1951, government hostility to the RDA was personified by several newly-appointed hard-line governors. Foremost among them was the Ivory Coast's Laurent Péchoux.[89] Mass arrests, party bans, and press censorship appeared increasingly irrational even so. Was the RDA menacing because of its inter-territorial organization? Or did the threat lie in its Communist connections? Neither viewpoint withstood scrutiny. For all its federal connections, the RDA rested on individual territory-based parties. Several of these were already haemorrhaging. And only two of them, Sékou Touré's Guinean RDA branch and Djibo Bakary's Parti Progressiste Nigérien, faced pressure from their grass-roots supporters for any kind of socialist transformation.[90] As for the RDA's alignment with the Communists in France, this, too, was fraught with the tensions of a loveless, unequal marriage. Surely negotiation with the RDA made more sense than driving local activists, trade unionists, and student protesters in West Africa's port cities underground? Numerous Third Force politicians realized this. But they had a pre-condition: the RDA leadership had to break with the Communists. Only this would rupture the links made in French official minds between the RDA's radical populism and Communist subversion.

Three senior politicians in France performed the necessary U-turn. Unsurprisingly, the first was RDA leader Félix Houphouët-Boigny. Second was the Martinique-born Senator for Guinea, Raphael Saller. Third was François Mitterrand, appointed Minister for Overseas France by Prime Minister René Pleven on 12 July 1950. Houphouët-Boigny pushed through the RDA's disaffiliation from the PCF, splitting the party in the process as a minority of Communist diehards rallied to RDA secretary-general Gabriel d'Arboussier.[91] Raphael Saller was Pleven's closest adviser on colonial affairs. His achievement was to persuade his boss to seize the chance to drive a wedge between RDA moderates and the radical party branches in Guinea and elsewhere.[92] With Pleven on board, Mitterrand began advocating the RDA's rehabilitation. The colonial administrators identified with the previous crackdown, including Governor-General Béchard and his deputy, the Ivory Coast Governor Péchoux were replaced. The deal was sealed by Houphouët-Boigny's January 1952 decision to affiliate his movement with the *Union Démocratique et Sociale de la Résistance* (UDSR)—which just happened to be Pleven and Mitterrand's party.[93] The RDA's rightwards shift was more than a political bargain to end years of persecution; it also played into the power-struggle between the movement's Paris leaders and their militant

party sections, trade union followers, women's groups and student supporters at the bottom.[94] This battle was far from over.

Towards independence in French West Africa

The RDA was not alone in spurning its former mentor on the French left.[95]
West African Socialists also turned away from their metropolitan counterparts in the early 1950s. The actions of the RDA and of Senghor's Senegalese
Socialists in particular reflected their exasperation with the French left's
hypocrisy in colonial affairs. Communist anti-imperialism was less unequivocal than it seemed. Its guiding precept was hostility to capitalism, not to
colonialism itself. Neither the PCF executive nor their rank-and-file members were as racially colour-blind as their internationalist rhetoric suggested.
Time and again the Communists used the language of Marxist structuralism
to stifle colonial demands for equality or national autonomy. Ever since Party
leader Maurice Thorez disappointed Algerian hopes in 1939 by defining the
colony as a 'nation in the making', the argument went that French-led
modernization would be the catalyst to class formation or 'proletarianization'
in Marxist terminology. This was identified as the prerequisite to genuine
working-class liberation rather than the 'false freedom' advocated by colonial
nationalists. It was a clever argument but impossible to sell to the very political leaders that the Communist Party disparaged. These limitations were
amplified within the Socialist Party. It had struggled for years to reconcile
its republican egalitarianism with enthusiastic support for empire. Socialist
claims that colonial rule was justifiable as a modernizing, humanist project
only seemed credible for a post-war instant: when the first, reformist French
Union scheme was in preparation in 1945 and before the Party sanctioned
war against the Vietminh in 1946.[96]

    Despite the French left's dismal colonial record, the French African poli-
ticians who served in the National Assembly after 1945 regarded French
republicanism as a worthy political ideal. Steeped in French values, at home
in the politicking and literary ferment of Paris, Senghor and Houphouët-
Boigny especially were Fourth Republic 'insiders'.[97] Houphouët, as we have
seen, became alienated from the RDA's grass-roots as a result.[98] African trade
unions were increasingly unsympathetic; West African student groups still
more so. Each suspected that the RDA executive had sold out: to UDSR
politicians, to conniving colonial officials, to the comforts of Paris.[99] Certainly,

the UDSR recognized the need to burnish Houphouët's credentials as a man of influence.[100] Young educated city-dwellers were a key target and 1,320 bursaries were awarded to black African students to study in French universities by 1954. Up to four times that number studied in France with the financial backing of their families. But hopes that graduates would return home, their faith in France restored, proved misguided. Student journalists of the Federation of black African students in France spearheaded criticism of politicians seduced by 'the system'.[101]

What about other parts of West Africa's civil society? It is hard to fit either religious or literary dissent into a pattern of mounting friction between people and colonial regime. Yet each was highly significant. Rarely directly confrontational, the pull of Islamic devotional practice with its implicit rejection of French values and integrationist ideas highlighted how limited colonial influence over African cultural expression really was.[102] This autonomous 'Islamic sphere' remained a marker of the superficiality of French control.[103] Nor is it easy to see French churches or missionary societies as championing an alternative model of social integration. French missionary groups in Senegal and elsewhere, theoretically committed to racial equivalence in the eyes of God, proved less accommodating to black advancement within the ranks of West Africa's Catholic churches. During and after the Second World War it was the Vatican that pushed for greater 'Africanization' of Senegal's Catholic Church in defiance of the colony's French apostolic elite whose positions of authority were threatened by it.[104] The cultural assertiveness of black African writers and artists also shaped the form that decolonization took. The West African poets and essayists who discerned a uniquely African cultural resilience—or négritude (literally, 'blackness')—challenged colonialism's capacity to remould the ideas and practices of colonized peoples. Indeed, the very eloquence of négritude writers disarmed imperialist presumptions of Africa's backwardness.[105]

Real enough, the contesting visions of French Africa's future between federalists and nationalists, between parties, across generations, and between secular republicans and the devout never spiralled out of administrative control as occurred in North Africa. But Maghreb disorder and the pullout from Indochina did have consequences south of the Sahara, encouraging Pierre Mendès France's government to press ahead with plans for West African self-government over the winter of 1954.[106] The outcome was the Gaston Defferre enabling law, passed by the newly-elected National Assembly in February 1956. The legislation marked a decisive turn away from assimilation.

The ideal of cultural and political convergence between France and West Africa was replaced by recognition that independent states should chart distinct paths to autonomy, devising legislation in accordance with their local circumstances.[107] Defferre was a good choice as the law's advocate. A well-respected Marseilles mayor, the Socialist Defferre enjoyed his Prime Minister Guy Mollet's confidence. He was given free rein to ensure that his eponymous legislation got through. The Gaston Defferre law was duly voted on 23 June 1956. It heralded the introduction of universal suffrage and the election of national governments throughout French West Africa, marking the culmination of the constitutional reforms toyed with since the launch of the French Union a decade earlier.[108] And it helped convince French ministers and officials that they, and not the peoples of French West Africa, retained control over the pace and extent of decolonization.[109] Even though French army commands throughout the region quietly activated plans to impose military control in case of major unrest, power, it seemed, was being devolved territory by territory without a fight.[110]

The politics of African claims to greater rights and entitlements, pursued incessantly since 1946, had reached a crossroads. Unwilling to meet each and every African demand, Mollet's government deflected back to the individual colonies the tasks of defining the limits to welfare, rights, and benefits—and of finding the means to finance them. Alongside the election of national governments came the devolution of budgetary powers. For the first time, African electors would choose, not just their governing authority but the scope of its spending as well. Often interpreted as the beginning of the end of French political oversight and an accelerated transition towards national independence, this 'territorialization' of French West African politics marked a huge reverse for the advocates of confederation and inclusive imperial citizenship.[111] With each territory shortly to match greater political autonomy with control of its own financial resources, the likelihood receded of pooled sovereignty or any redistribution of 'national' wealth from French West Africa's richer coastal territories, Côte d'Ivoire first among them, to its poorer, land-locked ones.[112]

Conclusion

When explaining the absence of sustained political violence in the history of French West African decolonization one factor stands out. It is that the redesign of French imperial rule, one that embraced both its constitutional form and its basic purpose, enabled West African political leaders, trade unionists, and civil society groups to press demands for additional civil rights, improved working lives, and more inclusive politics. Challenging the political elites of post-war France to live up to their claims that colonialism would give way to authentic partnership, these West African voices grasped the opportunities offered by the rhetoric of reform, development, and shared imperial citizenship. In simple terms, West Africa's political elites saw greater potential in exploiting the new rules of empire than in defying them.[113] Equipped with the legislative instruments and institutional tools to press demands without recourse to violence, it became possible to navigate a peaceful route to decolonization. The dream of *Eurafrique*, the economic and cultural integration of France and French black Africa, meanwhile helped French politicians and investors stomach negotiations over withdrawal.

For all that, the idea of dialogue sustained by a combination of rights conceded and pledges irrevocably made should not be taken too far. The very different French approach to Sékou Touré's Guinean RDA, the leading French West African political group to reject French tutelage in any form, reveals a different side to French colonial politics. First wooed, then cajoled, Touré's independent Guinean state was ostracized from the club of francophone West African states that retained close political, financial, and cultural ties to France. Among these countries, the battle between Senegal's future president Léopold Sedar Senghor and his Ivoirian rival, Félix Houphouët-Boigny, over the relationship between French West Africa and France also reminds us that it took some spectacular policy reversals to reinvent former political opponents, notably the 'quasi-Communist' RDA, as favoured partners once flight became policy.

The British administrations in Nigeria and the Gold Coast also struggled to keep one step ahead of popular protests triggered by economic problems, ethnic tensions, or unfulfilled government pledges. Anything but planned, one might even argue that decolonization in these two British colonial cases boiled down to the attempt to wrest the initiative for reform from local politicians increasingly able to press demands without serious threat of repression. This explanation may account for the pattern of flight solutions in British West Africa's elite politics, but it remains limited all the same. For most Nigerians the balance of ethnic forces in an independent Nigeria was always more significant than the fine detail of British concessions (although the two were never mutually exclusive). For most Ghanaians, the condition

of the agricultural economy, its cocoa sector especially, as well as the reaction upon it of Nkrumah's piece-by-piece dismantling of chieftaincy politics were every bit as crucial as their famed status as British Africa's first
post-colonial nation state. The conclusion implicit in this is deceptively simple. The key to the success of Britain's flight solutions in West Africa was less
a matter of engagement with 'constructive nationalism' and more a reflection of the irrelevance of British preferences. It was to the credit of most
senior officials and ministers that this was a trend they eventually chose not
to buck. Keeping the peace in British and French West Africa was a triumph
of adaptation, not planning. It also pointed the way to something deeper,
the dawning recognition that decolonization need not represent the total
breach so much feared by its long-term opponents. Perhaps empire could
be ended with a whisper and not a scream after all.

10

From a Whisper to a Scream: The Politics of Letting Go

On the evening of 10 November 1959 Harold Macmillan went for dinner at the Savoy. The famous hotel in London's West End offered a convivial meeting point for dignitaries and heads of state. It was especially favoured by those whose embassies had no sumptuous accommodation to offer. One such was Sékou Touré, the union organizer-turned-president of independent Guinea with whom the British prime minister chewed the fat that November night. The two men enjoyed an easy informality. They had previously spent two days shooting grouse together. But blowing little birds out of Scottish skies did less to cement their friendship than their shared exasperation with General de Gaulle.[1] Macmillan, fresh from election victory, but mired in the problems of a collapsing Central African Federation, had Africa on his mind. The Moroccan and Ghanaian governments were leading a chorus of UN disapproval over the first French atomic tests at Reggane in southern Algeria. The blasts were the prelude to de Gaulle's proud announcement of France's *force de frappe*. Confirmation that France not only had 'the bomb', but reserved the right to use it unilaterally infuriated Eisenhower's administration and made it harder still for the British government to keep in step with de Gaulle's Algerian policy.[2]

Other, more fundamental challenges lay ahead. It was less than two months before a more anxious Macmillan, his face drained of colour, would rise to the podium in the South African parliament building in Cape Town to deliver perhaps the best-known affirmation of British governmental intention to close the book on colonialism in Africa.[3] When he sat down to dine with Touré, however, 'SuperMac's' 'wind of change' speech was yet to be written.[4] In the event, the Prime Minister shared the task with Sir John Maud, British High Commissioner in South Africa.[5] Macmillan's words

before a shocked audience of South African MPs, most of them apartheid
supporters, have been cited ever since as evidence that Britain was, by then,
committed to peaceful flight from empire.[6] That withdrawal is often favourably contrasted with the upheaval that attended African decolonization elsewhere. Did the British Empire end with merely a whisper a few short years
after Eden's Suez misadventure? This chapter tests the proposition that it
did. To do so, let's first return to the Savoy dinner companions.

    Like Macmillan, Sékou Touré blamed de Gaulle for many of his troubles.
The Frenchman insisted that Touré's Guinean regime be ostracized because
it chose immediate, full independence during French West African referenda held in September 1958. Appearances, though, were deceptive. Touré's

Figure 13. Macmillan's Wind of Change speech as depicted by the *Daily Herald*
on 4 February 1960.

isolation was less total than it seemed. For one thing, Guinean diplomats had tried to alter the terms of the 1958 referendum to make the choice, not a total break with France, but a more equitable 'Community' whose African members need not be in thrall to their former imperial master.[7] For another thing, French diplomats became less hostile once it became apparent that discarding Guinea was tantamount to casting the country into a British and Ghanaian orbit. Touré, for his part, was happy to play all sides off each other. By the summer of 1959 there was a palpable sense that fundamental strategic realignments were taking place throughout the region.[8]

Decolonization's second wave

In April 1959 British, French, and US governmental representatives convened in Washington to discuss their long-term strategic plans for Africa.[9] These exchanges were a dialogue of the deaf. American delegates mocked French insistence that 'the spread of Islam' was dangerous. The British were equally dismissive of French alarmism about Soviet incursion into sub-Saharan Africa via Sudan or Ethiopia. More importantly, the notion that the three powers could determine the scope and pace of political change in Africa, or elsewhere for that matter, was increasingly ludicrous. Much of the European colonial presence in Southeast Asia was gone, replaced either by combative post-colonial regimes, as in Indonesia and North Vietnam, or by western clients in soon-to-be-independent Malaysia and Singapore. In the Caribbean, some of the oldest colonial settlements of all were edging towards independence via the detour of a short-lived British West Indies Federation for Jamaica, Barbados, Trinidad, the Leeward and Windward Islands. The geo-political complexion of empire, always predominantly African for France, was becoming more so for Britain as well. As we have seen already, both fight and flight approaches were adopted south of the Sahara. But the insurgencies that rocked French and British territories from Madagascar to Kenya were, by the end of the decade, in eclipse. There was less cause for optimism in the white-ruled regimes of Algeria and Southern Africa. But in the African expanses intermediate between them, adjustment to a post-imperial future was under way.

   The re-design of African colonial relationships went furthest in French black Africa. Discussed in the next chapter, the Algerian political crisis of May 1958 that propelled de Gaulle's return to office triggered constitutional reorganization not just in France and Algeria, but south of the Sahara too. Referenda were held in the member territories of the French Union to determine whether or not they wished to become members of a replacement confederation—the French Community, its name suggested by Madagascar's premier, Philibert Tsiranana.[10] De Gaulle insisted on a single, blunt alternative for any that did not: complete secession with the loss of French revenues that this implied. Hence, the position in which Touré's regime found itself after selecting the latter option. Promulgated on 4 October 1958, Article 78 of the Fifth Republic constitution defined the local prerogatives that Community territories could expect. Matters of foreign policy, currency and finance, strategic exports, justice, higher education, transport, and telecommunications, were reserved for decision by the Community as a whole. Reading between the lines of this stipulation implied something else entirely: that France, still the Community's sole independent state, would reserve ultimate control in key areas.[11]

In theory, the way remained open for some sort of federation of francophone African states within the larger Community. This was something to which the Senegalese leaders Léopold Senghor and Mamadou Dia remained attached.[12] In practice, the entire Community project was hostage to the referenda decisions of its designated African members in September 1958. Only Guinea unequivocally rejected Community membership, and by a thumping ninety-seven per cent.[13] Niger, another territory with a strong tradition of RDA-tinged radicalism, might have followed suit but for the lobbying, vote-rigging, and police intimidation organized by its colonial authorities.[14] Such crude manipulation was the exception, not the rule. Most of the governments in French West Africa recognized what could be gained by negotiating concessions from Paris. Fewer were drawn to the Senegalese-led federation idea. The majority endorsed the Community in return for pledges from Paris of preferential economic treatment and a rapid transition to self-rule.[15] Dialogue over the rights and benefits attendant on imperial connections was a logical progression from the claims-making culture of Francophone black African politics defined during the French Union's early years. By 1960, during which year fourteen Francophone African territories became formally independent, the Community's decision-making structures were reworked again, into the apparatus for a Franco-African clientelism that lasted for decades.[16]

British plans for Africa risked getting left behind by the French Community's metamorphosis into a club of insider elites.[17] The Suez expedition triggered an earthquake in British politics but it did not change relationships with African colonies to the extent that the May crisis did for the French Empire in late 1958. There were cross-Channel similarities even so. One was that from 1957 onwards Macmillan's first government set about the most comprehensive stock-taking of empire since the Second World War. Cabinet committees with impressively grand titles—for Defence, for Africa, for Southeast Asia, reviewed the strategic, political, and economic worth of imperial territories. Overseas commitments, defence spending, and, of course, colonial policy looked set to be scaled back. All of this implied a magisterial redesign where none existed. There would be no empire-wide transformation. But the hubbub of backroom discussion did change the terms of Cabinet and Whitehall thinking, making colonial withdrawal seem more proximate and less earth-shattering.[18] Another similarity was that British ministers and colonial administrators shared their French cousins' concern with Africa's pro-western orientation. Nasser, by now the leader of an Arab Federation incorporating Egypt and Syria, remained a worry; for the British at least, the racist militancy of apartheid South Africa even more so.[19]

Though usually at pains to deny it, government ministers in London and Paris were also increasingly sensitive to external criticism of colonialism, particularly if such attacks were framed in the language of human rights. A signatory to the 1953 European Convention on Human Rights, Britain was taken to task at Strasbourg over the hanging of nine Cypriot fighters.[20] A Greek Cypriot lawyer, Glafkos Clerides, provided the Athens government with the evidence necessary to make a case before the Strasbourg judges. He went on to expose cases of detainee torture that led to the court-martial of two army interrogators in April 1956.[21] Unfortunately, this did not herald any marked shift in counter-insurgency practices. The execution of two Greek Cypriot gunmen a month later provoked outrage in Greece. The hanging of another three in September was held to prove that the British were becoming more Draconian towards the Greek Cypriot community, not less.[22] With the worst of the Algerian War and revelations about the killing of Mau Mau detainees still to come, external condemnation of colonial dirty war methods was set to intensify.[23]

America, as ever Britain's leading diplomatic partner, could also be a severe critic, Eisenhower's administration exploiting obvious opportunities to burnish its anti-colonial credentials.[24] From 1954 onwards the annual round of UN General Assembly debates witnessed stinging denunciations of colonial abuses that united otherwise antagonistic states across the Cold War divide.[25] Newer General Assembly members, generally supportive of the Non-Aligned Movement, rejected any distinction between British and other colonialism, tarring all imperial powers with the same brush.

In the colonies whose futures were being debated, first demonstrations and civil disorders, then sophisticated media campaigns and backstairs lobbying were organized to stir sympathetic UN delegates into action. Women and children were especially potent propaganda weapons. School strikes in Cyprus achieved greater prominence after urban marches were banned. Images of blood-spattered schoolchildren beaten to the ground by police in Limassol did more to discredit British actions than any number of Greek diplomatic protests.[26] Newsreel footage of Algiers women crushed against a CRS-cordon in defiant support of the FLN was equally poignant. An incontrovertible shift was occurring. Beyond the confines of inter-state politics, public criticism of empire was becoming globalized, registering in diffuse cultural milieu from anti-colonial writings and civil rights activism to hostile coverage on film and its bumptious sibling, television.

These transnational forces of civic activism also had their equivalents closer to home. Strongest among these in Britain was the Movement for Colonial Freedom (MCF), founded in 1954 on the remnants of older, less strident anti-imperialist groups whose political impact had been limited. The MCF was confrontational. Fiery press articles, hostile parliamentary questions, and a nose for unearthing embarrassing episodes of colonial violence combined into a strategy calculated to win public support. The MCF's leading lights, Fenner Brockway, former general secretary of the Independent Labour Party, and two of the newer stars in Labour's firmament, Anthony Wedgwood Benn and Barbara Castle, ran rings around the stodgy arguments put forward by Hugh Gaitskell's Labour Party leadership to justify gradual reform. But we should not take the argument too far. Few of the MCF's three million rank-and-file members, most of them trade unionists automatically 'affiliated' to the Movement, shared the radicalism of the group's activist core.[27] And the MCF's leftist rhetoric facilitated official efforts to discredit it, making it harder to mobilize public opposition to colonialism in general rather than against egregious human rights abuses in particular.[28]

South Africa was the one territory to provoke broader-based popular opposition to colonial-style abuses. Opposition to racist rule, formerly confined to a loose coalition of anti-colonial groups, trade unionists, and anti-nuclear protestors, entered the British political mainstream as the 1950s drew to a close. While Macmillan headed towards Cape Town in early 1960, Britons were being urged to boycott South African products including Outspan oranges and *Craven A* cigarettes. In January Liverpool City Council became the first metropolitan local authority in Britain to ban South African goods. The Council's decision only affected some £2,000-worth of canned fruit, but the worthiness of the principle involved became sickeningly clear after the police shootings of South African protestors in Sharpeville three months later. Public revulsion at the killings transformed the cause of anti-apartheid into something approaching a mass protest movement.[29] By now the strongest common thread linking French and British trajectories of decolonization was the persistence of colonial conflicts that sullied international reputations and divided domestic opinion. For France, Algeria was, by 1960, more or less everything. For Britain, less blood-soaked conflicts—in Cyprus and in Southern Rhodesia above all—proved even more intractable.

The Cyprus Emergency

Despite the prosecution of 'successful' counter-insurgency strategies in Malaya and Kenya, the Cyprus Emergency indicated that anti-British violence was not subsiding everywhere. Between 1954 and 1959 increasing numbers of British troops were used to lock down the island through curfews, searches, collective punishments, and targeted operations.[30] As a result, the garrison island of Cyprus, under British colonial rule since 1878, became the unlikely setting for some of the severest restrictions anywhere in the British Empire. Unlikely because the island's Turkish minority remained substantially pro-British. Unlikely, too, because the Cypriot Greek majority, uniquely among anti-colonial movements of the day, wanted, not independence but unification with another state. It was this *Enosis*, or union with Greece, that the British denied. Greek Cypriot representatives dismissed new constitutional arrangements in 1948 that conceded limited home rule.[31] The British authorities responded in kind by ignoring a January 1950 plebiscite organized by the pro-*Enosis* Ethnarchy Bureau, which registered overwhelming Greek Cypriot backing for union.[32] Countervailing demands from Turkey, NATO's eastern linchpin, were harder to overlook. Prospects for a flight solution looked grim.

The repressive turn in Britain's Cyprus policy also had a longer history. Press censorship, broader prerogatives to lock up protesters and prosecute sedition, and, most controversially, the authority to deport 'troublemakers' were added to the Governor's legislative armoury after Government House was razed to the ground during previous *Enosis* demonstrations in Nicosia in October 1931. The colonial government in Nicosia bolstered its arsenal of arbitrary powers after the UN rejected Greek demands for Cypriot self-determination in December 1954.[33] So the island was already subject to stringent regulation before a state of emergency was declared following the latest assassination of a British serviceman on 26 November 1955.[34] Colonial policy, it seemed, began from the proposition that Cypriot political expression should be discouraged. To borrow the phrase of Labour MP Richard Crossman, the policy's most trenchant British critic, Cyprus resembled 'an amiable police state'. Hard-line parliamentary statements by Conservative ministers flatly ruling out Cypriot self-determination confirmed Crossman's impression that the British were spoiling for a showdown with the pro-*Enosis* insurgents of Colonel George Grivas' National Organization of [Greek] Cypriot Fighters, the *Ethniki Organosis Kyrion Agoniston* (EOKA).[35]

The array of legislative instruments available to the authorities in Nicosia goes some way to explaining this combativeness. The peremptory replacement of the Governor Sir Robert Armitage following the September 1955 riots in Nicosia, with Britain's most senior soldier, Field Marshal Sir John Harding, underlined the government's willingness to wield these powers to the full.[36] Also critical was the mounting official exasperation with Archbishop Makarios, the political voice of *Enosis* and, in British eyes, an exceptionally slippery customer.[37] The accretion of various emergency powers and the visceral dislike of Makarios do not tell us much about the solution preferred in London. Anthony Eden dispatched Harding with only vague instructions 'to get moving on the road to self-government if possible', and, more pessimistically, 'to have a look around first' before resorting to emergency rule.[38]

The Field Marshal never claimed to have a particular political solution in mind, but he held stronger views about the heightened security measures necessary to avert another Palestine-type humiliation. The gloves were about to come off in the war against Cypriot 'terrorism'. Within weeks of Harding's arrival the island was sealed off to prevent arms supplies coming in. Police and army ranks swelled. An intelligence war was launched in a bid to flush out EOKA cells. In December the Communist Progressive Party of Workers (AKEL) was banned.[39] To cap it all, on the afternoon of Friday 9 March 1956, Makarios was herded onto an RAF transport plane at Nicosia airport. To the dismay of Greek Cypriots, their leader was deported first to Mombasa, then onwards by sea to the Seychelles where, in an unfortunate coincidence, the house reserved for his arrest bore the name *La Bastille*.[40]

Unfortunately for Harding, the flaws in Britain's response to the Cyprus revolt were laid bare by each of these measures. The depth of national sentiment shared by Greek Cypriots and their mainland brethren was mistakenly read as illicit complicity, not fellow feeling. The island's police, reliant on Turkish Cypriot recruits, was badly placed to play arbiter and poorly equipped to penetrate Greek Cypriot society in the hunt for EOKA. Policemen living in fear of EOKA assassination and army units frustrated by the walls of community silence they encountered became increasingly thuggish. The Communists, far from being seditionist, offered the one secular, interethnic alternative to Church-influenced *enosis* nationalism. With AKEL proscribed and Makarios removed, there were no viable interlocutors left to discuss a compromise solution. Perhaps worst of all from the perspective of global media coverage, the image of stone-throwing youths in school uniform running from heavily-armed riot squads through the back-streets of Nicosia made a mockery of Harding's clampdown. Harding's emergency rule as a fight solution was no solution at all.[41]

The conventional explanation for this clash is that it was the Cypriots' misfortune to inhabit an island strategically pivotal to Britain's Mediterranean and Middle Eastern presence. In this reading of events, Tory 'Suez groupers', service chiefs, Foreign Office staff, and others with vested Middle East interests redoubled Britain's hold over Cyprus after the pull-out from Egypt in December 1956. The island's bases and listening stations, in other words, rose in importance in inverse proportion to the declining viability of Britain's grip on the Suez Canal zone.[42] The neatness of this explanation is its weakness. British service chiefs discerned no such linear progression. They complained that Downing Street improvised Cyprus policy, lurching from one expedient to another because the politicians had neither the stomach for confrontation nor the wherewithal to negotiate withdrawal. Bitterly opposed to Cyprus partition, which they feared would make British military bases unworkable, in July 1957 the heads of Britain's armed forces pleaded for clarity: either an unequivocal commitment to fight EOKA or the admission that flight was the sole option.[43]

In fact, efforts to break the political logjam were being pursued. The problem was that the political atmosphere in Cyprus was slow to improve. Makarios was allowed back to Athens in the spring of 1957 and a new, liberal
Governor, Sir Hugh Foot (brother of Labour MP Michael Foot), took office
that December. On Christmas Eve the new Governor eased curfew restrictions and ordered the release of 100 detainees, plus all women being held
without trial. But Foot's longer-term scheme to concede Cyprus independence foundered on the rocks of Turkish governmental opposition in early
1958.[44] In the absence of a workable plan for British withdrawal, inter-ethnic
violence spiralled out of control. EOKA killings not only targeted security-
force personnel but Turkish Cypriots and Greek Cypriot 'traitors' as well.
A shadowy Turkish Cypriot self-defence organization, *Turk Mukavemet Teski-
lati*, appeared on the scene. Its leader, Rauf Denktash, a future president of the
Turkish Cypriot Republic, shared Grivas' fondness for bombings and other
terror tactics.[45] Determined to protect themselves and distrustful of the army
and police, rural communities turned to vigilantism, generating bloodier
inter-communal clashes. By 1958 Cyprus was close to civil war.[46]

The uncomfortable parallels between the internal dynamics of the
Cyprus conflict and the final, chaotic months of the British presence in
Palestine caused alarm in Nicosia and London.[47] Turning from fight to flight
at local level was not yielding results. Two points bear emphasis here. First is
that surreptitious exchanges with Makarios and even Grivas about settlements and ceasefires had gone on, albeit fitfully, for years. Second is that the
Labour Party effectively endorsed Cyprus independence at its October 1957
party conference. As a result, Harding and his influential chief secretary,
John Reddaway, both men identified as Tory placemen, found it impossible
to negotiate for anything less with Greek and Greek Cypriot representatives.[48] Reluctant to contemplate partition, the last resort of the cornered
imperial politician and, in this case, a choice identifiable with Turkish preferences, Macmillan turned instead to international diplomacy.

As in Palestine a decade earlier, the chosen 'solution' amounted to recognition that the problem defied clear-cut answers. Macmillan confessed as
much in his diary on 7 July 1957. Cyprus, he said, 'is one of the most baffling
problems which I can remember. There are objections to about every possible course.' The lull in terrorist activity was merely temporary; the military forces needed to quell it were unaffordable. In any event, Labour, if
re-elected, was sure to give Cyprus away. Meanwhile, 'if we give in to Greece
there will be a war between Greece and Turkey. If we "partition", it is a

confession of failure' and the prelude to civil war. And yet all Britain really wanted was the military bases.[49]

Sensibly enough, the Prime Minister concealed his gloominess, putting on a brave face in Cyprus diplomacy. During May he proposed an 'adventure in partnership' with the Greek and Turkish governments. Lennox-Boyd followed up, proclaiming a 'new course' when the Commons debated Cyprus policy on 26 June.[50] Both men were referring to what came to be known as the 'tri-dominium' scheme. This was a plan sketched out during lengthy sessions of an inner-Cabinet of Macmillan, Lennox-Boyd, Selwyn Lloyd, Duncan Sandys, R.A. Butler, plus senior Foreign Office and military personnel. Cabinet Secretary Norman Brook worked out the fine details in early July.[51] The plan rested on power-sharing between Greek and Turkish Cypriot representatives to be jointly overseen by the Greek, Turkish, and British governments. Agreed ratios of Greek and Turkish personnel at all levels of island government were backed by strict guarantees of minority rights. Britain would retain its precious bases.

What did this actually mean? Not full independence certainly; not quite partition either, although the explicit commitment to protect minority—in other words, Turkish Cypriot—rights could be read as opening the door to the island's division along communal lines. And while Britain was not washing its hands of Cyprus as it did Palestine, the 'adventure in partnership' carried an implicit threat that it might yet do so.[52]

In discussions over defence spending in December 1958 the chiefs of staff redoubled the pressure for a decisive political break, using the Cyprus problem to illustrate the military complications created by inadequate investment in the internal security services of individual colonies. The Army's strategic reserve, much of it located in Kenya, was persistently depleted by calls from colonial governors for reinforcements to work alongside local police 'in aid of the civil power'.[53] Nicosia led the field in making such requests—and to what purpose? The service chiefs noted that 'EOKA is as strong and effective as it ever has been, both in personnel and arms, and support for EOKA among the general Greek Cypriot public is stronger than ever'. Policing and intelligence gathering were so hapless that five army battalions were needed to cope with the resulting insecurity. Again, the senior soldiers identified the policy-makers as culprits: 'the Cyprus Emergency has always been treated as one of short duration, with success always "just around the corner".' Investment in the island's local security forces was therefore neglected with predictably bad consequences.[54]

Days later, on the night of 17 December 1958, Costas Constantinados and Yiannakis Athanassiou, the last two EOKA fighters condemned to hang, were being comforted by an Orthodox priest before facing the gallows in Nicosia's Central Prison. Governor Foot was temperamentally inclined to clemency. But he withheld a reprieve fearing that more hard-line Cabinet ministers and army commanders would see red. Unbeknown to him, the Greek and Turkish Foreign Ministers Evangelos Averoff and Fatin Zorlu, then attending a NATO Council meeting in Paris, had just issued a joint appeal for mercy. A sign of things to come, Greece and Turkey were setting the agenda in Cyprus. That two historic antagonists should be willing to compromise made British insistence on hanging the two EOKA men seem vindictive and out of touch. A U-turn was agreed. Frantic Colonial Office efforts were made to contact Foot before the executions went ahead. The result: a Governor's pardon with barely half an hour to spare. Traumatized, the young EOKA fighters survived. Two RAF servicemen, identified by Grivas as targets for a tit-for-tat reprisal, were less fortunate. Early on the morning of 20 December their van was bombed in EOKA's final lethal attack on Britain's armed forces.[55]

Seen from the military standpoint, implementation of the tri-dominium scheme through a new Cyprus constitution could not come fast enough. This was not, however, an outcome that Britain's politicians could arrange. Months of complex negotiation lay ahead, much of it conducted under the aegis of the three outside players with most vested interests in the outcome: NATO, the UN, and the United States. All three welcomed the settlement agreed, not by the British, but by the Greek and Turkish governments after a week-long conference in Zurich between 6 and 11 February 1959.[56] A breach between two NATO partners was averted, the communal power-sharing and rights guarantees provided benchmarks for UN monitors, and Cypriot Communism was marginalized. Even so, an agreement derived from the original tri-dominium plan contained a fatal flaw; it frustrated Greek Cypriot hopes and lent heavily towards Turkish preferences. This iniquity rendered the Cyprus Republic established on 16 August 1960 dangerously unstable. But when renewed inter-communal clashes broke out in December 1963 it was the UN that stepped in at Britain's invitation. The spectre of Palestine partition that had hung over British official thinking was ultimately made real, first by UN peacekeepers, then by Turkish military intervention following a Greek Cypriot coup a decade later.

British politics and ending Empire

The Cyprus emergency was clearly a special case that, for all its frustrations, exerted little influence over British colonial policies elsewhere. In
the years before Macmillan discerned the force of African nationalist
wind-power, neither the revision of plans for Nigerian self-government at
the London Conference in July 1954 nor even full independence for
Ghana in March 1957 convinced Ministers and colonial officials that a
conveyer belt of British African decolonization was about to start moving.
Indeed, Nigeria could be held up to prove exact opposites: the merits of
proceeding cautiously or accelerating final withdrawal. British negotiators
tried to combine the two. Broadly amicable talks continued between 1957
and 1959, first consolidating regional self-government, then agreeing
terms and dates for full independence in October 1960. Underlying this
negotiated flight were two factors beyond British control. One was imminent independence in neighbouring French West African states. The other
was the arrangements made between Nigeria's ethnically-based parties for
the division of power. Not intrinsically unwelcome, these arrangements
presumed the British were already gone.[57]

   The combination of outward calm and ceremonial politeness on the one
hand, hasty reappraisals of declining British options on the other, was equally
apparent in the next wave of independence settlements agreed with eastern
and southern African territories. In Julius Nyerere, leader of the Tanganyika
African National Union, the British were blessed with a far-sighted inter-
locutor determined to follow his party's programme of socialist development.[58] Hastings Banda of Nyasaland and Kenneth Kaunda of Northern
Rhodesia also tolerated Britain's schizoid alternation between imperial jailor
and glad-handing negotiator with extraordinary forbearance. In each case,
the dynamic was the same. Fearing protests or civil unrest that could not be
stifled without incurring international condemnation, Macmillan's government ultimately acknowledged that the substance of imperial power was
draining away.[59] In this sense, preoccupation with the minutiae of electoral
arrangements and the precise timing of final independence accords—
December 1961 for Tanzania, July 1964 for Malawi (formerly Nyasaland),
and October 1964 for Zambia (formerly Northern Rhodesia)—obscures the
essential point. Attitudinally speaking, by late 1960 the key decision-makers
in Macmillan's second government had crossed the Rubicon from imperial

to post-imperial mind-sets. Conserving international reputation and post-colonial influence meant letting go sooner, not later.

Economic factors

Does such high politics really matter or were changing British and French calculations about decolonization undergirded by economic factors? Put differently, how important were their empires to the wealth of post-war Britain and France by the late 1950s? This basic question divides the scholars who have addressed it. There are two reasons why. The first relates to measurement, the second to interpretation of the parts played by private industry and the state in colonial economies. Focusing, first, on the indicators of colonial economic importance, some statistics look unequivocal. Received wisdom suggested that the 'sterling area' was a cornerstone of Britain's post-war financial position. And during the 1950s the value of sterling assets held by remaining British colonies, mainly the producers of high-value primary goods, more than doubled. In 1958 the sum touched £1.45 billion. Colonial holdings, in other words, comprised almost half of Britain's overseas sterling reserves.[60]

The sterling area's member countries not only valued their own currencies against sterling but deposited their dollar earnings in a British-managed currency pool to the immense advantage of Britain's balance of payments. The London market remained their primary source of borrowing. Colonial Office specialists were, not surprisingly, reluctant to see Britain's control over the issue of currency and the dominance of British banks in issuing commercial loans to colonial borrowers replaced by national banks in independent African territories.[61] But whether the sterling area or the predominance of Britain's banking sector within it could last was a moot point. The 'convertibility problem' dominated proceedings at a Commonwealth heads of government conference in London that stretched over a month in September–October 1952.[62] Efforts to resolve it were stymied by the attendees' greater interest in accumulating dollar reserves. It was a salutary lesson for the few British Treasury officials who claimed the London Conference was the most important imperial economic gathering since the Ottawa Conference twenty years earlier.[63] The dollar was clearly the stronger benchmark currency for international trade. And the Bretton Woods agreements of July 1944, which saw the establishment of the International Monetary Fund and the World Bank, were predicated on a global liberalization of free trade in which the dollar was king.[64] Gold-producing South Africa led the way, eliminating its sterling reserves by 1957. Less dramatically, India, Pakistan, and Australia, once pre-eminent holders of sterling reserves, diversified their currency holdings, gradually reducing the proportion of sterling they held.[65] The founding members of the European Economic Community (EEC), with France in the vanguard, meanwhile laid the foundations for a continental trade system that, it turned out, proved more accommodating to French black African territories than to Britain.[66]

Early EEC reservations about British admittance to their market system were hardly surprising. The British Empire–Commonwealth still accounted for fifty-one per cent of British exports and forty-five per cent of imports in the last five financial years of the 1950s. In 1960 fully sixty per cent of British capital invested overseas was tied up in Commonwealth or colonial territories. Indeed, colonies accounted for the majority of public issues on the London stock-market during the 1950s with loans typically raised to cover major infrastructure projects. The London imperial investor, a type usually identified with heady Victorian capitalism, was alive and kicking in the 1950s. Furthermore, the empire's major raw materials producers, as well as newer client states in the oil-rich Middle East, were major holders of sterling assets by the end of the decade, replacing the money withdrawn by former Dominions. Kuwait alone, for instance, accumulated some £260 million in sterling reserves by late 1958, a sum almost equivalent to the holdings of Australia, the country that was still Britain's biggest export market.[67]

Unquestionably high, these figures mask two other developing trends— one away from exporting heavy industrial products and importing primary goods, the other towards more remunerative trade with continental Europe. To the consternation of its backbenchers and much of the right-wing press, the Conservative government embraced this change. Macmillan had little time for 'anti-marketeers' who imagined that British national identity was bound up with empire and who insisted that Britain's industrial and farming interests were protected by historic ties to the Commonwealth.[68] It was not only pointless to set a British world 'us' against an encroaching European 'them', a tactic perfected by Lord Beaverbrook's *Daily Express*, it was irresponsible, too.[69] At the conclusion of a Commonwealth Prime Ministers' conference in September 1962 Macmillan made an evening broadcast to the nation on the BBC Home Service. In his warmest avuncular tone he rejected the notion that Britain had reached an economic crossroads

between the Commonwealth and Europe. Then he changed tack, telling
listeners that European economic connections held greater material significance to their daily lives than the old Commonwealth ties.[70] That significance would only increase as the 1960s unfolded.

Turning to the second source of historical argument—the relative importance of the government and private business in colonial economies—the
issues are these. Was development state led? Or were government and business co-dependent? And did political decolonization necessarily herald economic decolonization as well? As we will see, these questions merge into
one another.

Colonial budgets were usually small, the income from taxing dependent
peoples limited by extensive poverty. Without investment, loans, or other
stimulus packages from Britain or France, colonial states were poorly placed
to lead 'development'. Acknowledging that local governments lacked the
financial wherewithal to undertake major internal spending, in November
1951 the Conservative Colonial Secretary Oliver Lyttelton confirmed that
Britain's new Colonial Development Corporation would provide start-up
capital for favoured projects. These, it was hoped, would then be adopted by
private industry.[71] In fact, much as before the Second World War, the British
Treasury would never authorize large-scale expenditure on the colonies.
Currency boards also prevented colonies from spending their sterling
reserves to fund development, forcing them to drive up dollar-earning
export production in the service of Britain's balance of payments.[72]

Lack of state capital and restrictions on the use of colonial reserves tell
only part of the story, however. The Treasury could still use strategic investment, customs tariffs, and tax breaks to foster a climate favourable to home
industries and, by extension, less favourable to outsiders. Government relationships with key multinational conglomerates and banks, though frequently acrimonious, were sustained by mutual recognition of a shared
interest in retaining access to former colonial markets. In this sense, government, finance, and commerce remained mutually reliant. Lending in Africa
and the British Caribbean by the Barclays Overseas Development Corporation, a Barclays Bank subsidiary founded in 1946, quickly supplanted government investment in development projects. And it was industry more
than government that drove efforts to diversify colonial economies. British
industrialists worked alongside state-run marketing boards to encourage
Britain's imperial subjects to buy additional UK manufactures from cars to
domestic appliances.[73]

If this suggests that the private sector predominated in post-war empire economics, it does not quite convey the mounting pessimism among British and French business communities about their long-term prospects as colonial insecurity increased in the 1950s. Such anxiety registered in the phenomenon of 'flight capital' as investors, sometimes industries too, withdrew from one colonial territory only to reappear more strongly in another. Gloomy corporate predictions about their prospects in post-colonial societies also refracted persistent disagreements over certain 'red rag' issues between politicians and businessmen (white collar colonial business was still overwhelmingly male). The legalization of trade unions and collective bargaining, exclusive licences to prospect for minerals or sell particular goods, and differential rates of corporation tax in various dependent territories were guaranteed to raise the blood pressure of stockholders and company boards. More basically, company personnel increasingly found themselves in the firing-line of violent decolonization. Plantation managers and mining engineers in Malaya and Indochina, oil-workers in the Middle East and North Africa, even bank managers in Cyprus and Algeria became targets for anti-colonial violence or extortion. Little wonder that, behind the closed doors of company boardrooms, there was rarely much enthusiasm for accelerated pull-outs and military draw-downs. Yet the ultimate irony lay elsewhere. Having worried for years about seditious trade unions, nationalist firebrands, and the menace of nationalization thought to be lurking behind most independence settlements, British corporations lost most ground, not to nationalizing regimes but to US commercial rivals. In the business of decolonization, as in its politics, the trend towards Americanization was irresistible.[74]

Arms sales

In one area British business acclimatized quickly to impending decolonization. Overseas arms sales to Commonwealth partners and client states rose steadily in the late 1950s. This was particularly so in the Middle East where the provision of tanks and aircraft supplanted boots on the ground as evidence of British influence. In this context, preceding withdrawals not only reduced Britain's over-extended strategic commitments but presented a feast of commercial opportunity. In October 1954 the Minister of Defence Earl Alexander accepted Whitehall recommendations that 'older'—for which, read 'white'—Commonwealth countries should retain the privilege to purchase British military equipment through government-to-government transactions, rather than paying private manufacturers' market prices. Other branches of government seized on this recommendation and, over the next two years, sought to extend it. The Foreign Office and Air Ministry wanted to include Iraq and Jordan among the favoured clients allowed to buy arms direct from Her Majesty's Government. The Commonwealth Relations Office petitioned for the Central African Federation to do so. Against these Departments' political and strategic arguments, the Treasury and Ministry of Supply raised financial objections. The resulting compromise, agreed on 8 June 1956, extended the range of favoured imperial clients for British arms, but expected those included to pay 'fair commercial prices'.[75] Its linkage with government policy clarified, in certain regions Britain's empire arms-dealing took off.

Still reeling from its Egyptian humiliation, in mid November 1956 the Conservative government authorized arms exports licences to its favoured Middle East clients: Iraq, Jordan, Libya, the Persian Gulf Emirates, and newly independent Sudan.[76] Britain also played on American caution about selling weaponry to Israel's Arab neighbours and the concomitant desire in Washington to ensure that Arab states did not follow Egypt and Syria in seeking Soviet supplies instead.[77] Hard on the heels of a Board of Trade mission to five Middle Eastern countries in April 1959, the year's largest single British arms deal, for instance, saw sixty *Centurion* tanks sold to Israel and another forty-two to neighbouring Jordan. Highly lucrative, the anti-Egyptian thrust of these deliveries was also obvious.[78]

The Middle East was not Britain's sole arms export market of course, but it was the most strategically sensitive. While orders would keep rolling in, after the July 1958 overthrow of the pro-British monarchical regime in Iraq, White-hall defence planners recognized that British influence in the Middle East's eastern Mediterranean arc was diminished. Again, the criticisms of past imperial policy voiced by the military men were remarkably forthright. Government, they suggested, had been duped by supposedly 'moderate' nationalists. Ministers were too willing to believe that supporting development and keeping fast friends supplied with weapons would nurture democratic, pro-Western regimes. Their options shrank inexorably meanwhile. Thanks to Suez, high-risk military intervention was political suicide. And the pro-Soviet turn in Arab strategic thinking from Algeria to Yemen suggested that western influence might only be conserved in black Africa.[79] The chiefs of staff's advisers on a specially-appointed 'Africa committee' conceded, in other words, that Attlee had been right when he argued back in 1947 that Britain was better advised to draw its strategic line south of the Saharan sand, not to its north.[80]

This portrayal of receding strategic reach proved overly pessimistic. Otherwise disunited Baghdad Pact powers still conserved their anti-Communism. And as the Chiefs of Staff commented wryly, concern over oil supplies was bound to sustain British preoccupation with the Arab world's strategic alignments.[81] Their point was borne out by the earlier decision, taken in December 1957, to keep British garrison forces in Libya indefinitely rather than to withdraw them in 1959 as previously envisaged.[82] Britain was also in the throes of expanding—not contracting—its influence in the Persian Gulf, and in Kuwait and Aden especially. Each became hubs for its regional power in the 1960s.[83] While British military intervention in Kuwait in 1961 was somewhat reticent, its actions in South Arabia were anything but. In a bid to secure some payback for the humiliations of Suez, the Conservative hardliners—the Minister for Aviation Julian Amery, the Colonial Secretary Duncan Sandys, the Minister of Defence Peter Thorneycroft, and their backbench confidant Colonel Neil McLean—exploited the involvement of Nasser's Egypt in Yemen's developing civil war by secretly backing his Yemeni opponents.[84] None of this erased the legacies of Britain's earlier Suez misadventure. The army planners were surely right that, after 1956, Britain was 'unable to accept the odium of military domination' and denied 'the initiative of political action'.[85] Whatever the compensatory work elsewhere, Suez put paid to Britain's Middle Eastern 'moment'.[86]

Fights ahead?

So was Britain still an imperial colossus as it entered the 1960s? Few colonies remained in which withdrawal was neither an accomplished fact nor an imminent possibility, least of all in Africa. Social attitudes were changing irrevocably, popular culture becoming more irreverent about supposed imperial greatness.[87] Occasionally, this combination of apathy and mockery left politicians reeling but more frequently, if imperceptibly, these cultural markers encouraged government to accelerate flight schemes that were already in prospect. The politics of letting go was, in this sense, an intellectual journey towards an acceptance of irreversible change that the British public seemed refreshingly willing to take.

On 21 June 1960 Mountbatten, then Chief of Defence Staff, and his deputy Sir Francis Festing, still bearing the title Chief of *Imperial* General Staff, submitted their findings from a wide-ranging strategic review. It focused on the most likely conventional (i.e. non-nuclear) conflicts to confront British forces in the decade ahead. Their assessment was, at best, post-colonial, at worst, neo-colonial in its conclusions. Britain's priorities in the Middle East should be 'economic co-operation, non-interference with inter-Arab affairs and, as far as possible, disengagement from the Palestine problem'. Working with the United States was essential.[88] Mountbatten and his colleagues counselled 'benevolence towards Arab ideals', just as they recommended 'inter-dependence' with Far Eastern allies like Malaysia in their continuing struggle against communism. As for Africa, the adverse consequences at the United Nations of any use of force in British colonial territory should be at the forefront of decision-making. No stranger to the requirements of hasty, even chaotic decolonization, Mountbatten's imprint was clearly visible in the service chiefs' Africa recommendations. Retaining the goodwill of newly-independent states was everything. Flexibility, the essence of any successful flight strategy, demanded that long-cherished privileges and slower timetables for reform be sacrificed.[89]

Six months later, in January 1961, Macmillan's private secretary Philip de Zulueta advised him that Britain's major problem in Africa was how to guarantee the rights of European minorities once former colonies achieved independence. The underlying issue here was not race, but wealth: despite their loss of privileged status, settlers and company staffs would still be the dominant economic force in numerous territories. The Foreign Secretary Lord Home agreed. Referring explicitly to Ghana under Nkrumah, he noted that safeguards agreed at independence for British-owned businesses, bank deposits, and property rights were easily circumvented.[90] There was talk in Macmillan's Private Office about a combined Anglo-French approach to protecting African settler rights. But the idea was rejected because of France's deepening unpopularity throughout Africa.[91]

Conclusion

It is tempting to represent the quickening pace of late 1950s decolonization as a steepening curve, but its contingencies defy reduction to a linear model. As Frederick Cooper, a leading historian of African decolonization has it,

'What gets lost in narrating history as the triumph of freedom followed by failure to use that freedom is a sense of process. If we can, from our present-day vantage point, put ourselves in the position of different historical actors, in 1958—or 1945, 1966 or 1994—we see moments of divergent possibilities, or different configurations of power, that open up and shut down.'[92] For many contemporaries, decolonization in its many regional variants was less something inevitable than a question of difficult choices: either a transient opportunity to be seized and negotiated, or a looming threat to be contested and fought.

At its best, British colonial policy in the last days of African empire was both principled and pragmatic. Even in some places where ministers, officials, generals, and others initially resisted decolonization, determination to cling on eventually crumbled under the weight of hostile external scrutiny, the greater economic pull of European trade, and lack of public enthusiasm for costly colonial fights. Few among the new cohort of Conservative MPs elected to Westminster in the October 1959 election displayed the imperialist reflexes of their predecessors. Most backed Iain MacLeod's reformism, aware that diehard colonialism was no vote winner.[93] It was not all political calculation. *Africa, New Year 1960*, a pamphlet produced on the eve of Macmillan's 'Wind of Change' tour by the young Conservative progressives of the Bow Group, concluded starkly that Britain's primary African obligation was 'to govern justly or to get out'.[94] The heat once intrinsic to cross-party exchanges on empire questions would also diminish over coming years.

On the other side of Britain's party political divide, Barbara Castle, a tireless critic of Britain's colonial abuses, respected the view that, when accomplished peacefully and without rancour, formal transfers of power were curative procedures, exuberant and dignified at the same time. Invited to attend Kenya's independence ceremony on 11 December 1963 in recognition of her work on behalf of Mau Mau detainees, she found herself affirming her own ideas of British decency:

> Just before 6pm an African military band beautifully turned out marched with perfect precision up the central lawn to the steps of the terrace of State House to which the Duke [of Edinburgh], Jomo [Kenyatta], the Governor-General [Malcolm MacDonald] and Duncan Sandys had returned from their tour among the crowd. After some spirited playing and marching about the band came to rest in front of the terrace, played "Abide with Me" and then the British national anthem as the Union Jack was hauled down above State

House for the last time. Frankly I felt my eyes pricking with tears at the symbolism of this moment: the peaceful abdication of rule by an imperialist power. Then, to crown the emotion of the moment, the band marched off to the tune of Auld Lang Syne and we all broke up.[95]

The festivities continued into the evening when Kenyan dances gave way to a 'magnificent' King's African Rifles parade that culminated in handing over their battalion colours to the units now rebranded as the Kenya Army. Then, just before midnight, Jomo and Malcolm MacDonald walked into the centre of the huge parade ground facing two flag-poles on the far sides, one flying the Union Jack (Rumour had it that the Duke turned to Jomo at this point and said: 'Want to reconsider? There's still time.') Dead on midnight the National Anthem was played and slowly the Union Jack was hauled down. The Kenyans tactfully extinguished the floodlight so that the act of capitulation took place undetected in the darkness. Then the lights were triumphantly switched on again to reveal the ascent of the independent Kenya's flag.[96]

So frequent did ceremonies of this type become in the first half of the 1960s that it is at least questionable whether the British public took much notice. Empire-mindedness survived, not just on the hard right or among those with family or career attachments to former dependencies, but in a dogged belief—still remarkably resistant to countervailing historical proofs—that British colonialism, whatever its mistakes, was rooted in fairness and 'play the game' spirit. The staunchest advocates of Britain's imperial connections struggled to square the circle between the post-war reinvention of empire as something inclusive, progressive, and developmental and the proliferation of anti-colonial protests and rebellions requiring military intervention. Andrew Thompson captures the dilemma: 'even for those politicians and officials steeped in notions of racial superiority, the human cost of suppressing dissent could easily give rise to a feeling of distaste . . . Stripped of much of its romance, invincibility, and moral validity, the imperial relationship during the 1950s, 1960s, and 1970s offered significantly more scope for disappointment.'[97] The stories of colonial fight or flight from the late 1950s to the early 1960s confirm that letting go made more sense than clinging on.[98]

I I

Open Wounds:
Fighting the Algerian War

On 25 January 1955 Jacques Soustelle, a renowned social anthropologist-turned-Gaullist politician, was appointed Algeria's Governor-General.[1] The rebellion launched by the Algerian National Liberation Front (*Front de Libération Nationale*—FLN) was, by then, well into its third month. The organization behind it remained obscure nevertheless. Local administrators struggled to brief the novice governor about what or who the FLN was.[2] The movement's nine 'historic leaders' were relatively young, aged in their twenties and thirties. They emerged from the fringes of an older nationalist group, the Movement for the Triumph of Democratic Liberties (whose French acronym was MTLD). Most senior FLN figures had humble origins in the east of the country. Some hailed from Berber families, others from Arab. Several took part in the abortive Sétif uprising of May 1945.[3] Their earliest pronouncements were issued under the banner of a 'Revolutionary Committee of Unity and Action'. To those inside the Algiers Governor's Palace, the Committee's statements seemed naïve and inflated. The call for Algerians to rise up against their colonial oppressors was even a little clichéd.[4] But underestimating the FLN was a mistake.

The fight begins

The National Liberation Front may have been new but, although the police and security services were slow to make the connection, its organizers were 'known to the authorities', men like Amar Mostefa Benaouda, Lakhdar Ben Tobbal, and Abbane Ramdane.[5] Their radicalization underlined the counter-productiveness of colonial repression in the decade after 1945. Some, like

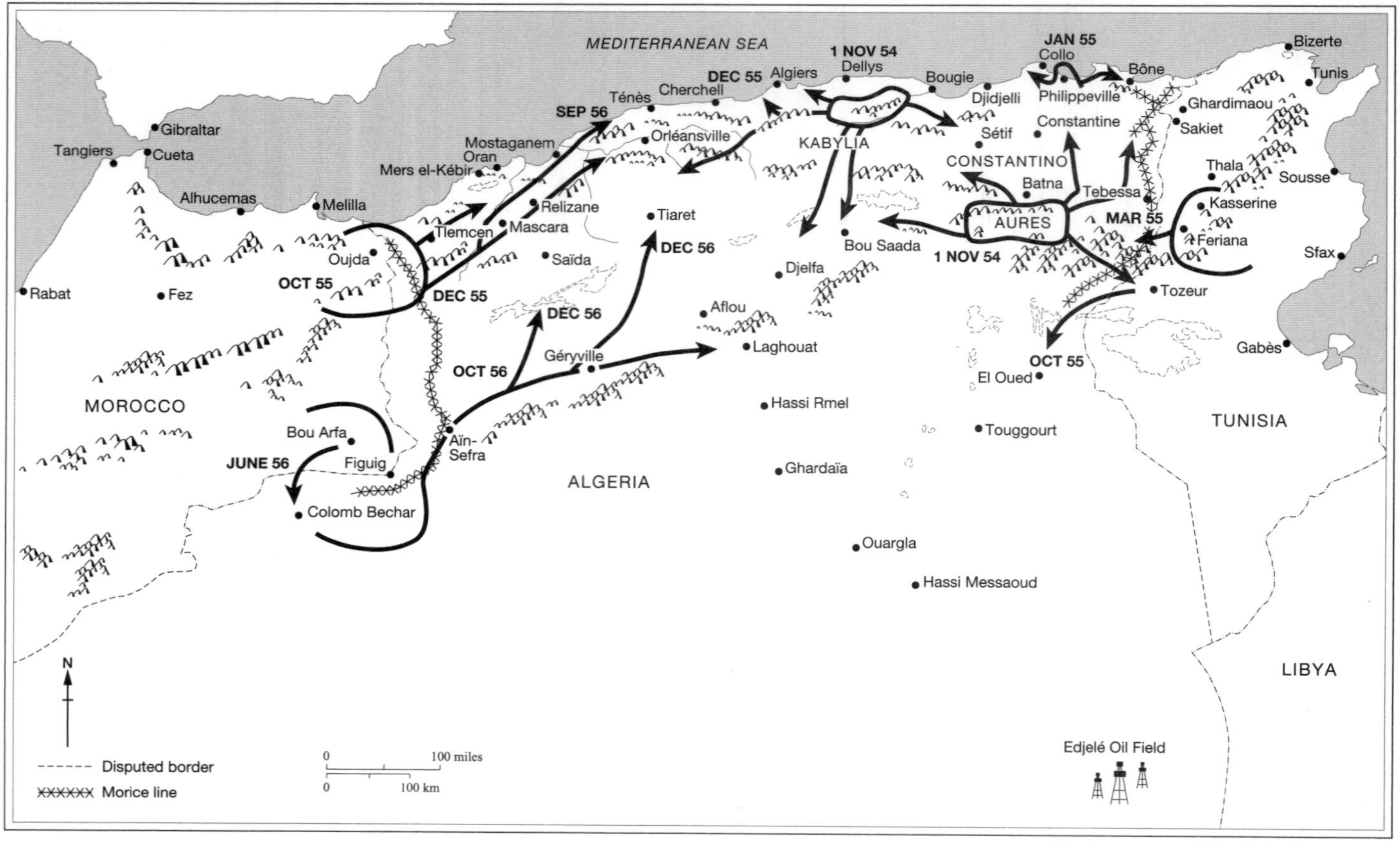

Map 12. The spread of rebel violence in Algeria, 1954–6.

Abbane, had seen French retribution at first hand following the Sétif uprising. Thereafter, he, like others, became acclimatized to clandestine political
activity as MTLD activists.[6] Lengthy spells in prison were the norm. Indeed,
shared experiences of incarceration linked the police crack-down against
the MTLD's paramilitary wing, the 'Special Organization', in early 1950,
with the consolidation of the FLN's inner core of regional (wilaya) commanders four years later.[7] Still, for weeks after the initial rebel attacks on
1 November 1954, the authorities in Algiers attributed the disorder—
wrongly—to one or more of Algeria's established nationalist groups, even
to a spill-over from neighbouring Tunisia where, for much of 1954, anti-
colonial violence was more virulent.[8]

What was incontrovertible was that attacks against government buildings,
administrative personnel, and settlers were spreading far and wide, a trend
clearly evident in Map 12. But precisely who was responsible? Struggling to
piece together its intelligence about the small number of FLN activists,
Soustelle's administration pressed for more firepower.[9] Rebel attacks were
proliferating, particularly along Algeria's rebellious eastern flank from the
vertiginous slopes of the Aurès massif through the market centres of Sétif
and Guèlma to the port of Philippeville, all of them centres of the last major
challenge to French rule in May 1945.[10] Furthermore, the case for additional troops would have been made anyway, regardless of the changes at the
top in Algiers. Three days before Soustelle replaced him, Algeria's outgoing
Governor Roger Léonard discussed the worsening insecurity with his military commanders and regional prefects at the funeral for seven parachutists
killed near the eastern city of Batna. Operation Véronique, a two-day sweep
by 5,000 troops through the Aurès highlands, had yielded only twelve rebel
'kills'. At least 3,500 villagers suspected of concealing or assisting local fighters were to be forcibly evicted.[11] Viewed in hindsight, Véronique might have
given pause for thought. A handful of 'rebels' eliminated; an entire local
community antagonized: the grim escalatory dynamics of France's fight for
Algeria were falling into place.

Soustelle did not see things this way. For him there could be only one
outcome to the developing Algerian War of Independence. Faith in his
capacity to turn the situation around came naturally. A Protestant south-
erner with the twang of a Montpellier accent, the forty-two-year-old
Soustelle had led a busy life. A distinguished résistant and erstwhile deputy
for Lyon, he was also an expert on the Mayan and Aztec civilizations
of Central America. True to his ethnographical training, Soustelle was

convinced that complex societies could be understood through observational fieldwork.[12] At first glance, the erudite Soustelle looked out of step with settler opinion.[13] Events would prove otherwise. Soon after touching down in Algiers he sought to reassure the city's European population. Whatever the drift towards decolonization in the neighbouring protectorate territories of Morocco and Tunisia, the French presence in Algeria was permanent: 'France is at home here, or rather, Algeria and her inhabitants form an integral part of France, one and indivisible. All must know, here and elsewhere, that France will not leave Algeria any more than she will leave Provence and Brittany. Whatever happens, the destiny of Algeria is French.'[14]

Soustelle pledged to cement Franco-Algerian ties with welfare reforms, investment in infrastructure, housing projects, plus enhanced citizenship rights for the Muslim majority. This was merely to repeat the stock 'official line'.[15] It was Pierre Mendès France who, as prime minister when the Algerian rebellion began on 1 November 1954, selected Soustelle for the Governor's position. Two months earlier, Muslim members of the regional council in Constantine, Algeria's eastern-most *département* and an epicentre of nationalist militancy, congratulated the French premier for advocating a pull-out from neighbouring Tunisia. Mendès France, it appeared, knew that colonial flight—negotiations and orderly withdrawal—made sense.[16] But on 12 November the prime minister disappointed them, reassuring his French parliamentary colleagues in the same terms that Soustelle would employ in Algiers: 'We do not negotiate when it comes to defending the *internal security* of the nation and the integrity of the Republic. Between Algeria and the metropole, secession is unthinkable.'[17] Adherence to the idea of Franco-Algerian indivisibility, its achievement encapsulated in policies collectively termed 'integration', precluded official talk of decolonization before the Fourth Republic collapsed amidst the Algerian protests of the May crisis in 1958.[18]

In France's one substantial settler colony, a peculiarly republican form of colonial intransigence had descended into war. The Franco-Algerian conflict, perhaps the most vicious and scarring of any decolonization, illustrates the appalling consequences when fight and flight were eventually combined in an effort to protect a white settler minority. Acutely divisive in North Africa and France, Algeria's dirtiest colonial war stands out as the most egregious example of a fight strategy running out of control.

Violence

This, inevitably, brings us to the war's violence. Casualty numbers remain unconfirmed, but a conservative estimate suggests that at least 300,000 Algerians died in the eight years of conflict between 1954 and 1962 among a population of less than ten million.[19] The great majority of these fatalities fell on Algeria's Muslim population. We get a better sense of this within the official statistics for wartime 'disappeared', among which 13,296 of the 13,671 total were registered as 'French Algerian Muslims'.[20] More shocking still, a large proportion of these were killed by fellow Algerians, victims of the 'compliance terror' that characterized the FLN's quest for dominance.[21] Losses among the settler population were fewer, although still far greater than those suffered in any British colonial emergency of the period. Over the war's first three years 1,315 European civilians were killed. A further 740 police personnel—technically, civilians—might be added to this total. Using the lower figure, exclusive of police losses, we arrive at one European civilian casualty for every three military deaths between 1954 and 1957.[22] Telescoping forward to the conflict's final months in 1961–2, the diehard French terrorists of the *Organization de l'Armée Secrète* (OAS) murdered in excess of 3,000 people, among them pro-government officials, schoolteachers, and other alleged 'traitors' to French Algeria. Many OAS victims were slain after the 1962 ceasefire.[23]

These shocking figures were mirrored in the behaviour of the French security forces, who also killed with minimal restraint. In what we now recognize as a common pattern in wars of decolonization, local insurgents were variously treated as criminal, terrorist, rebel, or traitor; never as recognized combatants with commensurate rights under international law. In Algeria especially, the familiar colonial axiom that disorder was an internal affair was elevated to official dogma. Codes of military conduct—in particular, Article 3 of the 1949 Geneva Convention, devised to uphold human rights protections in 'non-international armed conflict'—were consistently ignored and blatantly violated. The intimacy of the killing conducted by both sides made the circle of violence exceptionally vicious. The knife, the razor, and the homemade bomb, classic 'weapons of the weak' but capable of inflicting horrible injury, became trademarks of FLN violence, a violence meant to be publicized. Security force auxiliaries, informers, and other 'traitors' were dumped in market squares or on hamlet roadsides, their disfigured corpses arranged into grotesque poses that parodied their alleged crime. Gaping wounds from slit throats or multiple stabbings were a blunt display of FLN power. Often the victims were hacked down by new recruits to the FLN's guerrilla force, a sanguinary initiation that tested the commitment of any waverers and ensured their complicity in the cycle of killings. Settler landowners, often entire farming families, were butchered by their farmhands; long-serving employees sometimes acting under duress, sometimes not. On rare but notorious occasions entire village populations were massacred for allegedly crossing the line—undiscernible to some, crystal-clear to FLN militants— that separated authentic nationalist loyalty from support for a party rival or co-existence with the colonial occupiers.

On the French side, security forces combined the impersonal killing of occasional military encounters with organized 'national liberation army' bands (rendered as 'ALN' in French) with the face-to-face violence of raids on homes, detainee executions, and the abuse of suspects. This culture of killing with impunity was not invisible to the French public; far from it. The popularity of 'photo-journalism' typified by *Life* magazine and *Paris Match* brought shocking montages of colonial violence to news-stands, waiting rooms, and lounge coffee tables as never before. French readers were invested with the power of judge and jury, invited to pass judgement on the 'faceless FLN killers' who slayed civilian innocents or on the 'terrorists' hunted down by the security forces. Only rarely were the polarities of such judgements reversed.

In December 1955 the magazine *L'Express* printed a sequence of photographs that clearly showed a gendarme in the village of Aïn Abid shooting an unarmed Algerian civilian in the back. The gendarme then calmly reloaded his rifle while his victim lay dying before him. The stills in question were from newsreel footage that captured the event from start to finish; a murder played out before the camera. This was no isolated act of rogue criminality. It was one of the thousands of reprisal killings that took place in eastern Algeria after the FLN's first sustained massacre of European settlers earlier that year. Rock-solid evidence; or so one would have thought. Predictably enough, the editors at *L'Express* took the moral high ground. But they had an agenda: to embarrass Edgar Faure's right-of-centre coalition before the impending general election. It didn't work. A brief, pre-ballot media storm, then nothing.[24] For French society, the reality of unjustifiable violence in Algeria was, as yet, no reality at all.

Gradually, painfully slowly, eye-witness accounts did make their mark back home. Raw recruits in some army units were shocked and traumatized by what they saw, let alone by what they were ordered to do. Some refused to be compromised. From mid 1956 onwards, a small but not insignificant minority, many of them Communist supporters, resisted the draft, disobeyed orders to use their weapons, or in other, lesser ways, subverted military discipline.[25] But, for others, particular styles of killing, notably without leaving tell-tale marks of abuse, became a speciality. Professional torturers came to know their victims, probing their minds for information, probing their bodies to maximize pain.[26] Often, the experience was highly sexualized. The army's use of torture was predicated on a perverted intimacy in which a concentration on sexual acts, sexual organs and the domination of torturer over victim magnified the inequalities of power evident in colonial society and the ultra-masculine military culture of frontline units.[27] Put in a torturer's hands, mundane items—pliers, a beer bottle, the battery connections from a field telephone—became instruments of horror. Always illegal, torture became routine, so integral to army operations that, at the end of the conflict, the French state granted former army torturers immunity from prosecution.[28]

The laws of the Republic, when applied colonially, were never colour-blind. Nor was the law gender neutral, if anything offering fewer protections to women than to men.[29] Algeria's women faced multiple degradations within legal parameters and outside them. Their freedom of movement was curtailed. Their homes were invaded during army searches. Soldiers tampered with their clothing during roadside checks for hidden weapons or supplies.[30] Captured women fighters, the ALN's rural *moudjahida* and the FLN's urban couriers, or *fidayate*, whose numbers grew rapidly from 1957, were more likely than their male counterparts to be spared summary execution. But army and police torturers were less scrupulous about sexual boundaries.[31] Here, too, the humiliation of being forced to strip, a practice applied to detainees of both sexes, could be the prelude to far worse.[32] Rape of women and men became commonplace inside police stations, army torture chambers, and isolated settlements along the war's rural frontlines. Partly because fewer died in custody, women were liable to suffer multiple assaults.[33] Nor did women escape FLN retribution. As symbols of national purity, guardians of the family, and educators of children, they faced punishment if they or their loved ones showed less than exemplary loyalty to the cause.[34] Village women were expected to provide the shelter, to ferry the food and water that ALN guerrillas needed to survive.[35] And this while

successive waves of health workers, army medical teams, and other 'women's
affairs' specialists drew Algeria's women under a government umbrella, making *de facto* collaboration harder to avoid.[36] Arguments over the rights and
duties of 'French Muslim women' (*Françaises musulmanes*—the colonial
juridical designation for Algerian women) in everything from language
usage and suitable dress to marriage and inheritance politicized all aspects
of women's existence.[37] The fear or actuality of violence wove itself into the
very fabric of Algerian domestic life as the war dragged on.

Intellectuals, immigrants, and the war in France

Was all of this unknown to the French public? Reports of security force
torture surfaced within weeks of the rebellion's outbreak. In January 1955
Claude Bourdet, editor of *France Observateur*, printed an article provocatively
titled 'Your Gestapo in Algeria'. The liberal Christian magazines *L'Esprit* and
Témoignage Chrétien also exposed instances of the abuse and murder of
detainees. Sympathetic human-rights lawyers and academics in France and
Algiers took up individual detainees' cases and began investigating the sys-
tematization of torture, rape, and summary execution as weapons of colonial war. Criticism also emanated from within the security forces, notably
after conscripts went sent to Algeria from 1956. Harrowing accounts of
deaths in custody, of repeated sexual violence, of soldiers coerced, corrupted,
or brutalized into shooting FLN prisoners after capture, confronted the
French public with the exact inversion of their recent experiences under
Nazi occupation. For some, these reports induced a kind of intellectual tor-
por, a refusal to countenance the facts; for others, torture in Algeria became
the decisive issue confronting French democracy in the 1950s. Earlier struggles of principle were invoked. For a tiny minority of French people active
support for the FLN became a moral imperative akin to joining the resistance.[38] For many others who cherished French republicanism as a humanitarian ideal the Dreyfus case came to mind. The unjust, racist treatment of
Captain Alfred Dreyfus, wrongly accused of divulging military secrets to
Germany in the 1890s, had mobilized a wide spectrum of republican opinion in opposition to military abuses conducted for reasons of state. Sixty
years later the maltreatment of Algerians called French values into question
once more.[39] Still others, among whom de Gaulle was one, were never wedded to the republican conception of France as a nation built on shared

values rather than common ethnicity. They were affronted by something else: the damage done to valued institutions and traditions; the army as repository of patriotic grandeur, the state as guarantor of basic rights.[40]

The tension between republican principles, 'reasons of state', and the cultural validity of 'French Algeria' also divided leading French intellectuals over a twenty-year period book-ended by the expulsion of the French Communists from government in 1947 and the cultural upheaval of May '68. Best known were the venomous clashes between prize-winning novelist Albert Camus, the settlers' son raised in the working-class Algiers district of Belcourt, and Jean-Paul Sartre, existentialist writer, epitome of Parisian sophistication, and voice of the anti-war hard left.[41] Sartre and his philosopher-partner Simone de Beauvoir's repudiation of colonialism as an outgrowth of market capitalism meshed with their attacks on France's postwar republican establishment. Sartre and de Beauvoir reserved their strongest contempt for those like Camus: liberals who professed a commitment to assimilation between France and Algeria that, according to French literature's golden couple, negated the structural causes of colonial racism. Sartre and de Beauvoir each spoke out passionately about the Algerian War, often in *Les Temps Modernes*, the journal they had co-founded in 1945.[42] The café-bar intellectualism of the Paris left bank was an ocean away from Camus' visceral attachment to the Algiers back-streets, and his genuine, if misguided, belief that the social divisions of Algeria's colonial past could be transcended through inter-communal reconciliation. The crisis of conscience that Camus suffered over French repression in Algeria turned on the issue of violence—when and if it could be justified by either side.[43]

While Camus, himself a former resister, applauded the spirit of self-sacrifice of those driven to rebel by injustice, he condemned the FLN's escalating terrorism just as he did the military's use of torture. It was the immoral equivalence he drew between the two that angered other intellectual opponents of the war. For them, rebel attacks were a justifiable last resort whereas security-force killings were not.[44] Strongest among these was Frantz Fanon, a psychiatrist from Martinique, who practised in French Algeria from 1952. Within a year he had written *Peau Noir, Masques Blancs* (*Black Skin, White Masks*), a searing indictment of the ways in which colonial iniquity sapped the cultural integrity of the colonized. Where Camus viewed Algeria's communal blood-letting as a downward spiral of atrocity, Fanon defended killings by the FLN as the reclamation of Algerian identity through violence.[45]

French sociologist Pierre Bourdieu joined the criticism of Sartre, Fanon, and others who romanticized the Algerian rebellion as a popular revolution.[46] Bourdieu's theories about the cultural factors that enable groups and individuals to dominate one another built on fieldwork he conducted at the war's height among Berber peasant communities in Kabylia, a mountainous northern region profoundly disrupted by the conflict. Bourdieu's ethnographic vantage point left him pessimistic about the war's emancipatory potential.[47] Algeria's peasantry was 'uprooted' from its moral economy, traditional cultural practices, including forms of land tenure, inheritance, and extended family solidarity undermined by dispossession and poverty.[48] He had a point. Although France was investing heavily in Algeria, development funding failed to curb the ethnic inequalities typified by soaring Algerian unemployment and the growth of shanty towns.[49] 145,000 Algerian Muslims did enter industrial employment between 1948 and 1956, but this number was dwarfed by Algeria's rising population, which climbed from 8,811,100 in 1955 to 9.875,000 in 1960.[50] Bourdieu's subsequent fieldwork inside the massive army resettlement camps to which destitute Algerians from rural conflict zones were forcibly relocated in the war's latter stages left him even more convinced that Algerian society was already despoiled.[51]

Bourdieu's scholarly pessimism did not reflect how Algeria's European population viewed the society around them. In the words of settler poet Gabriel Audisio, Algeria was the sole colony in which 'the creation of "France" really succeeded'. It was made French, not by some privileged 'plantocracy', typical of an older, discredited imperialism, but by workaday folk from France and other Mediterranean countries. There were almost one million white European residents in Algeria when the war began; seventy-nine per cent were Algerian born. Many had family connections with Spain, Malta, or Italy, but not in mainland France. The majority were urbanites—industrial workers, low-ranking civil servants, shopkeepers, and artisans; poor to middling by French standards.[52] Stories of grand settler estates and Algerian rural misery were almost as remote to them as they were to Parisians. It was easy to depict these *pieds noirs* (literally, 'black feet') as obstinate in their racism, emotive in their reading of the war's deeper causes. Racist bigotry there was, yet instances of casual discrimination were matched by enduring friendships across communal divides in the languid heat of Algiers.[53]

Tragically, the logic of civil conflict made such inter-ethnic mixing harder to sustain.[54] Algeria's cycle of urban killings, in particular, transformed cul-

tural interchange.[55] Police arrested Rosa Serrano, a settler of Spanish origin, because she supported the outlawed Algerian Communist Party.
Released pending her trial, she recalled that French neighbours and child-
hood friends in the Bab el-Oued district of Algiers neither spoke to her,
nor made eye contact, whereas local Algerians embraced her, wishing her
well. Later, these same settler neighbours began a campaign of intimidation against her.[56] Part of the war's disturbing geometry was that while
Algerian Muslims faced worsening bloodletting as the FLN imposed its
dominance, so, too, the settler community and their military protectors
turned on one another as victory slipped from their grasp.[57] Patricia
Lorcin frames it nicely: 'The socio-political violence of the colonial era
was vertical being restricted largely to conflict between the dominant
French and the subordinated Algerians. During the war, however, it was
vertical *and* horizontal. In addition to fighting each other, the French and
the Algerians had to contend with internecine struggles that bordered on
civil war.'[58]

There were settlers of a different sort. And they added another layer of
complication to the fight or flight choice. These were migrants who moved
in the opposite direction from North Africa to France. They, too, found
themselves in the grip of a civil war, one waged on the poor margins of
France's industrial cities. Thousands of Algerian immigrants, the majority,
single working men, had lived in Paris, Marseilles, Lille, and elsewhere since
the First World War. Some made the northward crossing of the Mediterranean for good. Others were temporary workers whose remittances to families helped sustain rural communities with strong traditions of economic
migration in regions like Kabylia, Algeria's Berber heartland. Several factors
contributed to the spatial segregation of these immigrant communities from
surrounding French society. The most obvious was the relative poverty of
most North African workers. Others included tight official screening and
persistent discrimination in the allocation of social housing.[59] Perhaps most
compelling was the understandable tendency among the immigrants themselves to cluster together. The *bidonvilles* [so-called because of the large gas
bottles or '*bidons*' favoured by residents to provide affordable fuel for cook-
ing] which mushroomed on the margins of Paris and Marseilles typified
these processes in action. 'Huts,' notes the historian Neil MacMaster, 'were
constructed of wood, corrugated iron, tarred felt, and breezeblocks, and had
no basic services like running water, electricity or sewerage.' Aside from poor
sanitation, 'the greatest risk to the inhabitants, a source of continuous anxiety,

was from fire and asphyxiation due to primitive stoves.' By 1955 at least 4,300 Algerians, around half of the total in the Paris commune of Nanterre, lived in such conditions. By the time the war ended in 1962 Nanterre's *bidonville* housed close on 7,000.[60]

Ghettoized, confined to low-paid employment and stringently policed, by the early 1950s the Algerians of the northern Paris *banlieues* seethed with resentment. Many were 'Messalists', followers of Messali Hadj's Movement for the Triumph of Democratic Liberties (the MTLD in French), a party boasting a thirty-year history of opposition to French rule in Algeria. But by 1953 the MTLD was splitting. Its internal fault-lines exposed ideological and generational shifts in Algerian nationalism that pitched the Messalists into self-destructive conflict with their offshoot, the FLN.[61] On 14 July 1953, the horrors of this intra-Algerian civil war—one in which an estimated 8,000 Algerian immigrants died in internecine fighting in mainland French cities between 1955 and 1962—lay in the future.[62] Messalist organizers were determined to use the 1953 Bastille Day commemoration to protest at their leader's imprisonment and the colonial subjugation that his incarceration signified.

The marchers first assembled into neat columns, then set out for the Place de la Bastille. Few got there. Scuffles broke out with parachutists on leave from the war in Indochina drinking in a roadside café. The police called for back-up from nearby city stations at Charonne and Bel Air. In what would be a recurrent feature of Paris policing during the Algerian conflict, the line between corralling demonstrators, aggressive riot control, and the targeted killing of protesters evaporated. Some Algerians struck out with placards and broken street furniture once the police moved in to shut down the march. Several policemen drew their side-arms. Multiple shots were fired. By the early evening of an unusually rainy 14 July seven demonstrators lay dead amidst the puddles between the Place de la Nation and the Bastille monument. At least forty more had gunshot wounds. Some of the injured avoided hospital treatment for fear of arrest, making it harder to verify casualty numbers. The subsequent growth of discrete police units to monitor Maghreb immigrants brought repressive practices refined in colonial Algeria to the epicentre of the Republic.[63]

The fact that Algeria's colonial war spilled over into mainland France has helped convince historians of its singularity. Was the Algerian case really so different? Several long-term processes entrenched the privileges of European settler communities within African colonial societies. On the economic side, the extractive nature of colonial economies and the introduction of monetary taxes helped turn Africans into wage workers, often dependent on European-owned concerns to provide employment. Typically associated with industries like mining where company control of African labour was especially rigorous, this trend was equally evident in the countryside where land seizures and the introduction of large-scale, estate-type farming consolidated the racial hierarchies of settler power. On the juridical side, colonial civil law became an instrument to legitimize settler property-holding and European commercial primacy, while criminal law imposed differential scales of punishment for whites and non-whites. Racially-codified restrictions on freedom of movement and access to public space underpinned systems of segregation that, to be sure, were more vigorously enforced in some places than others, but which were never entirely absent from Africa's settler colonies.[64] Government legislation meanwhile restricted access to citizenship, ostensibly by non-racial criteria such as education, religious attachment, or property ownership. The effect, deliberate but fervently denied, was to align political rights and economic opportunity with those of white skin.[65]

Little wonder that, during the 1950s and 1960s, the most intransigent ultra-nationalism in French and British Africa emanated from settler communities determined to resist majority rule.[66] These were the societies where the implications of moving from the rights attached to an ethnically-based national identity towards an inclusive and racially-neutral civic nationalism provoked the bitterest argument. Often, these disputes culminated in heightened inter-ethnic violence as the prelude to imperial withdrawal.[67] Yet, as we have seen, viewing Algeria's European residents as politically united, culturally homogeneous, or singularly affluent does them a disservice. The large proportion of what in British colonial parlance were known as 'poor whites' among Algeria's *pieds noirs* should unsettle our understanding of settler lives, which come loaded with preconceptions about privileged communities at one remove from the local populations surrounding them. A brief digression to colonial Kenya proves the point. The experiences of its poor whites as revealed in Kenya colony's legal and medical records expose the thinnest of lines separating successful farming or business ventures from foreclosure, the idealized settler family from dysfunctional relationships marred by domestic violence and alcoholism.[68] Comparable encounters with poverty, drink, and unhappiness figured as prominently in Algerian settler lives.

Extending the fight

Returning now to the politics of the Algerian conflict, the situation changed fundamentally a year after Governor Soustelle's arrival in Algiers. Critical to that change was the question of who should replace him. A darling of the settlers, Soustelle was out of step with the Socialist Party that won France's general elections in January 1956. Determined to reward a domestic elector-ate impatient for a decisive Algerian breakthrough, the new prime minister, Guy Mollet, called on the former Free French General Georges Catroux to take Soustelle's place. To ensure that Catroux could push ahead with consti-tutional reforms and economic redistribution without being derailed by the settler-dominated Algiers Assembly or the equally intransigent Federation of Algerian Mayors, Mollet assigned him enhanced powers as 'Resident Minister'. This welcome reorientation in policy was not to last.

On 6 February 1956, a day after announcing his government's legislative plans in the National Assembly, Mollet flew to Algiers to prepare the ground for Catroux. Hours later he was barricaded inside the Governor's Palace, his suit smeared with rotten tomatoes and clods of earth after a bruising encoun-ter with Soustelle's disgruntled supporters. As we saw in Chapter 6, the demonstrators were a loose coalition that included leading settler polit-icians, mayors, and media figures, Pierre Lagaillarde's Student Action Com-mittee, and ultra-rightist followers of Pierre Poujade's small traders' movement.[69] Afraid that the new government was on the point of selling out to the FLN, they shut down the capital before venting their anger on Mollet himself. The prime minister's first full day in office culminated in a riot, decisive evidence of settler power in Algiers. Catroux tendered his res-ignation without ever taking up his post, leaving Mollet to fly home with little prospect of imposing a liberal alternative in defiance of settler wishes.[70]

The left-leaning Republican Front coalition had begun its eighteen months in office with a crushing about-turn in Algeria. Without entirely abandoning its reform proposals or even exploratory talks with FLN inter-mediaries, Mollet's government embarked upon a massive escalation in the war.[71] What linked these seeming opposites was French parliamentary approval of extended Algerian 'special powers'. Voted on 12 March 1956, the special powers combined rule by decree with extended martial law. Algeria's resi-dent minister could implement constitutional changes, reorganize Algerian local government, and assign development funding by fiat.[72] The army acquired full police powers. These were backed up by the promise of huge reinforcements as national servicemen lost their previous exemption from serving in colonial conflicts.[73] Algeria was careening towards dirty war.

For a brief moment, it all seemed quite sensible. Catroux's newly-designated replacement, Robert Lacoste, was a straight-talking former industrial arbitrator willing to surrender his position as Finance Minister to push ahead with the reform plans. Operation *Valmy*, its title invoking the French revolutionary army's defeat of the Prussians in September 1792, heralded the largest French army deployment overseas since the age of Napoleon. Troop numbers nudged half a million by December.[74]

Three fatal flaws lurked within this strategy of top-down reform and military saturation, however. First was the admission, implicit in the Special Powers vote, that governmental restructuring of Algerian society could not be achieved through consent. Second was that sending teenage conscripts to Algeria invested workmates, classmates, girlfriends, and, above all, parents with a stake in events across the Mediterranean.[75] Third, the failure to disconnect dialogue from violence; indeed, the pursuit of an alternate logic that imposing military order was a prerequisite to reform, made matters far worse for Algerians.[76] Bizarre as it may seem, in the four years that separated Mollet's 1956 election from the start of formal negotiations with the FLN's 'provisional government of the Algerian Republic', successive French administrations justified heightened restrictions, collective punishments, and forced population removal as prerequisites to talks and eventual peace. Algeria, then, was another instance in which efforts to combine fight with flight went disastrously wrong for the country's colonial rulers.

To understand why Mollet's government chose to do what an equally ill-fated American President, Lyndon Johnson, would do nine years later in Vietnam: namely, to authorize a massive expansion in an anti-insurgent war, to commit conscripts to the fight, and to blur the line between population control and human rights abuses, we need to consider three factors.[77] One is the political setting in which strategic decisions were made in Paris and Algiers. Another is the wider international context in which the Algerian War was fought. Finally are the changing understandings of the war's nature and purpose among the French and Algerian populations, Muslim and European alike. These three factors folded together as the war expanded in the months before the Socialists came to power.

1955 had witnessed a steady growth in Algerian disorder. Even though the largest ALN guerrilla bands numbered perhaps 500, their principal locales were in Algeria's mountainous interior, regions where cultural resistance to colonial demands was strongest and French authority commensurately weak. The ALN's strict internal discipline drew on longer traditions of communal solidarity against French exaction.[78] The result was an enemy that remained invisible most of the time. Soustelle's administration responded by imposing state of emergency restrictions on 6 April. Curfews and other restrictions on freedom of movement were, at first, confined to so-called *zones d'urgence*, those areas worst affected by FLN violence: much of upland Kabylia, the Aurès–Nementchas highlands, and the eastern *Constantinois* region more generally.[79] Months later a broader swathe of Algeria's northern coastal belt stretching southwards towards the colony's military-administered Saharan territory was similarly locked down. Algerian local government, civilian prefects at its apex, village *djemaa* assemblies at its base, was co-opted to the army's divisional commands, a process consolidated when Algeria's three *départements* were sub-divided into twelve, smaller units in June 1956. Martial law had collapsed the boundaries between civil administration and army rule, crushing basic safeguards of individual rights along the way.[80]

Algerian political meetings were prohibited. In some places, Chambers of Commerce and Agriculture, even religious services, Muslim, Christian, and Jewish, were suspended. The FLN responded in kind. Algerians known to be working for the administration in any capacity became prime targets for FLN retribution. Army checkpoints, curfews and police round-ups, night-time disappearances and FLN bombings and killings of alleged 'collaborators', all disrupted economic activity, fractured community loyalties, and sent fear creeping into family homes, Algerian and European alike. Ten years after the 1945 Sétif uprising, in the market towns of eastern Algeria inter-communal distrust bubbled back to the surface. Once again, funerals for murdered settlers became flashpoints for violence. Fearful that anyone in Muslim dress might be lynched, police advised Algerian bystanders to keep off the streets as cortèges passed by. There was talk of defunct ultra-rightist groups, the Action Française, and the Parti Populaire Français, being resurrected. Vigilante death squads also reappeared. As much in desperation as in hope, a group of Algerian councilmen lined up with Constantine Prefect Pierre Dupuch on 9 July to plead for calm, inter-faith dialogue, and respect for the emergency laws.[81] It was to no avail.

The Constantine massacres and after

During seventy-two hours beginning at midday on Saturday 20 August 1955 FLN supporters in the towns and villages decimated by French repression of the Sétif uprising took their revenge. From the port of Philippeville to the market town of Guèlma, settler families, members of the security forces, and alleged Algerian collaborators were hacked to death. 171 Europeans were killed. They included ten children who were among the thirty-seven victims hunted down in the worst single episode of violence at the El-Halia mining compound outside Philippeville.[82] Although the weapons used—farm implements, knives, clubs—were primitive, this was neither a simple pay-back nor a spontaneous peasant *jacquerie*. Coordinated by Lakhdar Ben Tobbal and Zighoud Youcef, ALN leaders in northern Constantine, this was terrorism as provocation. Intended, in part, to divert army resources, in part, to demonstrate the FLN's capacity to mobilize popular support, the Constantine massacres mocked official insistence that a silent Algerian majority wanted the French to remain.[83] In this sense, the massacres not only replayed the events of 1945 but formed part of a cycle of violence the motor for which was the earlier imposition of martial law. With numerous forms of public dissent already liable to capital punishment, the military authorities made no pretence of restraint as order was re-imposed. As was the case with the 1945 uprising after which Algerian deaths ran into several thousands, security-force killing was industrial in scale. Algerians in the neighbourhood of El-Halia were shot without trial; suspects in Philippeville were executed *en masse* on the town's football pitch. Settler vigilantism, so much a feature of the reprisal killings in 1945, resumed.[84] Uneasy Franco-Algerian co-habitation in north-eastern Algeria unravelled in a matter of weeks.

In 1955, as in 1945, the shared bias of colonial bureaucracy, military tribunals, and prosecuting magistrates contributed mightily to this breakdown. The official record of the 1945 Sétif uprising, largely derived from police reports and the colonial gendarmerie, painted a lurid picture of attacks on settlers. Missing from archival accounts or later trial documents are any comparable official records revealing how Algerians viewed the more widespread violence done to them.[85] The imbalance reflected long-practised colonial skills in hiding the details of state repression. Euphemistic language, clerical imprecision or, quite literally, burying evidence by hurriedly interring victims in mass graves, set terrible precedents for the many forms of rhetorical elision and archival concealment , and the 'disappearing' of victims used to mask the murder or torture of detainees during the Algerian War.[86]

Unsurprisingly, French security analysts had no truck with the view that the original Algerian violence stemmed from maltreatment and material hardship. To have done so would have conferred a measure of rationality, even defensibility, on these uprisings ten years apart.[87] The colonial authorities instead wanted things both ways: the Sétif rebellion and the Constantine massacres *were* political violence, but of a sort that only immature and innately dangerous individuals could perpetrate. In plain terms, it was the work of criminally-misguided colonial subjects, not fully-formed citizens.[88] But how should we, in turn, understand the scale of French repressive violence that began in May 1945, was resumed in August 1955, and continued with varying intensity until 1962? Can it, or should it, be rationalized? Was it simply a case of meeting fire with firestorm? As historian James McDougall suggests, 'any assessment of collective colonial violence should begin with the social and political conditions in which such practices arose'.[89] It was exactly this connection—between the violence produced by an exclusionary colonial system that set an ethnic minority over an indigenous majority— which the French authorities refused to make.[90]

Others were less reticent. Arab states, with Egypt leading the charge, condemned the ferocity of the French clampdown in August 1955. The pro-Western Iraqi and Yemeni governments appealed to Britain and the US to help end the killings.[91] Even Konrad Adenauer's West German administration described the army's retribution as a 'blood bath'.[92] France was losing friends over a colonial war that was rapidly acquiring global dimensions. Britain's Conservative government, by contrast, remained conspicuously silent. Stuck inside their own colonial glass-houses, British observers were reluctant to throw accusatory stones. Brigadier A.C.F. Jackson, military attaché in Paris, played down press reports of army atrocities in Algeria. For him, the tragedy was that it took the 20 August massacres before ministers in Paris woke up to the FLN threat and began 'supporting' their troops as they should have from the beginning.[93] Among soldiers 'tried beyond the reasonable restraints of military discipline' by a combination of political neglect at home and horrific terrorist violence in the field, army atrocities were remarkably scarce.[94] Jackson's case was soon disproved. Better informed US consuls in North Africa indicated a death

toll of between six to eight thousand Algerian civilians during the punitive operations mounted in and around Philippeville during August and
September 1955.[95]

At the local level, the Constantine massacres turned the constant hiss of
settler complaint about inadequate security force protection into a cacophonous drone. Its clamour reached Paris thanks to outraged settler parliamentarians in the National Assembly.[96] Pierre Dupuch, the beleaguered
Prefect in Constantine, struggled vainly to keep cross-community relations
alive amidst the poisonous atmosphere of recrimination and vigilantism.
Having failed to prevent the massacres, he was too discredited to make any
impact.[97] His long-term replacement would be Maurice Papon, the former
Vichy official convicted for crimes against humanity in the 1990s for his
role in sending thousands of French Jews to Auschwitz. Granted extended
powers by Mollet's government as one of Algeria's new 'super-prefects' or
'IGAME' (*Inspecteur-général de l'administration en mission extraordinaire*) Papon
was no stranger to Constantine. He had reorganized the region's police and
gendarmerie forces in the aftermath of Sétif, work that secured his selection
as the region's prefect between 1949 and 1951.[98] Less than five years later, he
was back coordinating another 'pacification' of Algeria's rebellious east.

Determined to sever the links between ALN fighters and the surrounding population, Papon acted with little constraint. Torture centres became
busier; forced population removal more extensive.[99] Speaking the language
of revolutionary warfare in vogue within the army's Fifth Bureau psychological warfare division, Papon insisted that the Algerian conflict was a battle of wills. People's compliance would be secured by convincing them that
the security forces would go further than the FLN to achieve their objectives. Papon repeated his dictum time and again: through force came protection; from protection flowed confidence.[100] This was the 'order before
reform' rationale of colonial government in Mollet-era Algeria.

Papon's appointment indicated something else as well. The Constantine
attacks created the permissive environment necessary for the expansion of
the emergency powers imposed by Edgar Faure's governing coalition during 1955. In the months that followed the French general election in January
1956, parliamentary criticism of Mollet's escalation strategy was nugatory. To
the shock of its grass-roots activists, even the French Communist Party
leadership endorsed the Special Powers vote, earning itself lasting FLN
derision.[101] In July 1956 a group of opposition deputies led by former
Finance Minister Pierre Pflimlin toured Algeria's army districts. They were

shocked to discover their local supporters so terrified of FLN retribution that they barricaded themselves in their homes at night. What did the deputies conclude? That total military pacification was the essential prelude to national elections and the resumption of socio-economic reform.[102] As if reading from the script of the government's Algerian policy, Pflimlin's colleagues repeated the unconvincing official mantra that ordinary Algerians, once freed to vote in secure conditions, would desert the FLN for moderate, pro-French alternatives.[103] This was a pipe-dream.

Algeria's discriminatory voting system and years of government vote rigging—known among colonial bureaucrats as *élections à l'algérienne*—ensured derisory participation long before the FLN announced a boycott of local and national elections in 1955.[104] Algeria's electoral practices were fairly typical of white minority-ruled colonies in which Europeans selected representatives to one (usually more influential) assembly, while the local majority population voted for a second, largely decorous assembly packed with compliant yes men—*Beni Oui Ouis* in the parlance of French Algeria. Once FLN enforcers began slicing off the lips and noses of those Algerians who defied its boycotts of French wine and tobacco, even fewer people were willing to venture into polling stations.[105]

Although it was the Algerian rebellion that propelled Mollet's government into the Suez collusion, few French politicians were prepared to question the wisdom of this ever-widening war. As we saw in Chapter 6, on 18 May 1956 an ALN unit ambushed a patrol of newly-arrived reservists near the Palestro gorge, a beauty-spot south-east of Algiers. Twenty soldiers were killed. The loss of family men and youngsters just starting out in life sent to their deaths by the requirements of national service intensified public debate about what was at stake in Algeria and about military obligation more generally.[106] Leading intellectuals, including Sartre, the pioneer surrealist André Breton, and acclaimed writer François Mauriac, signed up to a 'Committee opposed to the sending of conscripts to North Africa'.[107] Others, including a Catholic Cardinal, several Sorbonne professors, and Paul Rivet, France's premier ethnographer, came out in support of Mollet's policies.[108] Inside the National Assembly, there were some dissenting Socialists—former minister André Philip, Algiers-born colonial specialist Alain Savary, and Young Socialist leader Michel Rocard. But most mainstream politicians toed the official line.[109] At street level, public anger over the Palestro ambush added impulse to the protests at railway stations, ports of embarkation, and other conscript assembly points that began in the wake of the special powers vote. Seventy-seven such demonstrations were recorded in thirty-six of France's ninety *départements* between April and the end of June 1956. Communist Party militants, the rail and dockworkers' unions, and other anti-war activists talked of mobilizing the public against Mollet's government and the Fourth Republic. This was to misunderstand what was taking place. The protesters' ranks were not comprised of ideological fellow-travellers but of family members and friends appalled that their loved ones were being sent to fight such a wretched cause.[110]

Cinema newsreels, early television reports, and radio coverage of the war were still relatively upbeat, but the press much less so. *Le Monde*, the magazines *France Observateur* and *L'Express*, as well as the progressive journals *Esprit* and *Les Temps Modernes*, became sharply critical of the war and especially the way it was being fought.[111] Here, the newspapers were reacting to something else. Personal accounts of village massacres and of army torture turned from a trickle into a flood during the two years that separated the Palestro ambush from the Fourth Republic's demise in the May crisis of 1958. Particularly damaging was *La question*, the account by Henri Alleg, Communist editor of the left-wing daily *Alger Républicain*, of his experiences under torture by army parachutists during the battle of Algiers in 1957. It caused a media storm in France and overseas that lasted long after its February 1958 publication.[112]

Central to the disconnection between French politicians and public was the underlying popular belief that the governing parties that had dominated the Fourth Republic's imperial policy-making since 1946 had no idea how to arrest France's slide deeper into the Algerian morass. Leading figures in the ruling Socialist and Radical parties, as well as participants in previous coalition administrations from the MRP and the UDSR, were increasingly tarred with the same brush. From the Communist left to the Gaullist right flowed accusations that ministers, wedded to the rhetoric of order before reform, of fight before flight, were playing fast and loose with French lives, money, and international reputation. Still, Mollet's government refused to change course.

Algeria had become a war of political attrition, a slow, grinding conflict punctuated by shocks and scandal.[113] But, as we shall see in the next chapter, there were those willing to risk negotiations. To understand this impending change of political direction, we need briefly to turn our attention to the extraneous influences on the Franco-Algerian conflict.

International and transnational pressures

The skies over the Mediterranean witnessed some revealing airborne encounters during the autumn of 1956. We saw in Chapter 6 how a Paris governmental clique, working in conjunction with military commanders in North Africa, engineered the hijacking of the aircraft carrying senior members of the FLN executive on 22 October. A month earlier an older Algerian nationalist figure, Ferhat Abbas, for years held up in France as a 'moderate' negotiating partner, had met an unnamed British contact aboard a flight between Geneva and Milan. Abbas told the Briton that only the FLN could deliver Algeria's freedom. His decision to endorse his former rivals was old news by then. More interesting was his description of the ALN's numerous overseas backers. Nasser's Egypt was not even first among them.[114] Franco's Spain, hostile to French policy in Morocco, was providing essential small arms.[115] And Eastern bloc regimes were expected to send far more. There was, it seemed, more than a kernel of truth in the French army's insistence that Algeria was a Cold War frontline. It was a viewpoint graphically illustrated in posters, such as the one reproduced below, depicting the FLN as mere puppets of the Soviet Union and the Arab League.

Three weeks after Abbas' revelations a French aircraft ferried nine British MPs on an Algerian observation tour. Their visit was organized by the Algiers authorities to convince international observers of the progress being made by civil and military administrators on the ground. Taken to see urban housing projects, rural health centres, and a team of the army's elite 'special administrative section' (or 'SAS') local government workers, the MPs finished their inspection with a 'frank, impressive' discussion with the IGAME, Maurice Papon. He reassured them that, thanks to this nuts-and-bolts approach to development, peace was returning to the eastern regions worst affected by the August 1955 massacres.[116]

These episodes pointed to a discernible trend. The Algerian War of Independence was being internationalized, coming to symbolize the rights and wrongs of colonialism in the eyes of the world. Algerian nationalists found ideological inspiration in numerous foreign sources, including Nasser's call for pan-Arab solidarity, Kwame Nkrumah's vision of pan-African unity, and the socialist non-alignment perfected by the Yugoslav premier, Tito.[117] Young Algerian fighters inspired by Vietnam's against-the-odds struggle also drew

Ne soyons pas aveugles!

"Le terrorisme ne suffit pas. Il faut partout une lutte armée du typ... AURÈS . Ce sera une questio... rapport de forces, et la... devra céder"...

"le Comité de Libération de l'...

Lybie

Radio Le Caire

Figure 14. 'Ne soyons pas aveugles!' ('Don't be blind!'), 18 April 1956. The quotation from the ALN executive committee reads: 'Terror isn't enough. We need armed struggle akin to that in the Aurès everywhere. It a matter of the relative strength of forces and France will have to give way.'

Source: SHD-DAT, 1H2595/D2, DSTT, 5ème Bureau poster.

succour from the successes of their brethren in Morocco and Tunisia to the consternation of police personnel who fretted about the traffic of people, weapons, and ideas across Algeria's land frontiers.[118] Algeria's ulama clerics, as well as the devout within FLN ranks, looked to fellow Islamists, notably Egypt's Muslim Brotherhood and Qur'anic scholars at Cairo's Al-Azhar University.[119]

Internationalization involved more than learning lessons from foreign example, however. As early as December 1948 Hocine Aït Ahmed, one of the FLN's original nine leaders who became the FLN's principal spokesperson in the USA and elsewhere, had urged the MTLD's central committee to greater diplomatic efforts to win friends, sympathy, and influence overseas. Citing examples from Ireland's Easter Rising to Mao's imminent victory in China, he defined 'people's war' as inherently transnational—part of a universal struggle against injustice that transcended international politics. Aït Ahmed's rhetorical flourishes registered with his fellow revolutionaries.[120]

In August 1954 Messali Hadj, elder statesman of militant Algerian nationalism and still MTLD leader, instructed his party executive to devise a strategy
for the internationalization of the Algerian conflict through the United
Nations. And internationalization of the Algerian crisis was the primary
objectif extérieur outlined in the FLN's first proclamation, issued at the rebellion's outbreak. Two months later the Saudi delegation raised the Algerian
situation with the Security Council, the first of numerous attempts to place
France in the dock at the UN.[121]

  After a hesitant start that reflected the divisions between the FLN's internal and external leadership, the movement became an adept practitioner of
this transnational battle for foreign hearts, minds, money, and guns. Aside
from petitioning the UN, relief agencies like the Red Cross were assiduously
cultivated, further isolating the colonial authorities at home and abroad.[122]
The FLN's external leadership, a de facto government-in-waiting that operated principally from Cairo and Tunis, coordinated press, radio, and other
publicity campaigns. Their propagandist output chimed with the cycle of
UN General Assembly sessions and other multilateral gatherings as diverse as
the Socialist International, the World Council of Churches, and the NATO
command. Little by little, the war sucked in other states, foreign sympathizers, charities, and social commentators whose interest in colonial problems
was not evident hitherto.[123] By 1957 high-profile figures from the Indian
premier Nehru to the ANC leader Nelson Mandela, and a young Massachu-
setts Senator, John F. Kennedy, had condemned French actions in Algeria.[124]
Nor did FLN propaganda neglect its home audience. Transistor radios, omni-
present in Algerian rural homes, spread the word of revolution. Calls to arms,
stirring accounts of ALN victories, and reminders about boycotts were inter-
spersed with news from across the Arab world and the latest tunes from
popular Maghreb singers.[125]

  Sensitivity to foreign opinion also shaped the war's violence. From
the Constantine massacres onwards, the timing of ALN offensives, bombings, and urban demonstrations were calculated to maximize international impact.[126] The French army found itself disarmed by this kind of
propaganda war. Indeed, the greater its military success against ALN
bands and the FLN's urban networks, the more oppressive it appeared to
outsiders. Faced with this dilemma, the authorities in French Algeria
(and British Kenya) resorted instead to what historian Fabian Klose
terms the 'humanitarian double standard'. Critical of rights abuses in
the Communist world, they insisted that purely 'domestic' colonial

problems escaped the supposedly global protections of international human rights law.[127]

Such defiance of international opinion became harder to sustain as dissentient Algerian voices reached a global audience. Assured of the support of Eastern bloc countries and non-aligned states from Asia and Latin America, FLN lobbyists registered additional successes with the UN General Assembly as newly-independent African countries gained admission from 1957 onwards. French diplomatic efforts to confine UN scrutiny of the Algerian situation to backroom committees peaked between 1955 and 1957.[128] UN delegations in New York, the State Department in Washington, prominent US media commentators, and the 'opinion-forming' newspapers of America's major cities were all sent Algiers government publications highlighting levels of French investment, improving welfare, and educational provision. Gruesome booklets with pictures of the FLN's civilian victims prominently displayed were also dispatched as evidence of the true complexion of Algerian nationalism (see figure below).

For all that, it was French, not FLN, misdeeds that resonated strongest. Worsening army abuses made French denials that a war was going on seem laughable. The guillotining of FLN prisoners in Algiers tarnished France's image as a cradle of democracy. The French legal system became tainted. With sometimes minimal consideration, prosecutors sanctioned some 1,500 capital sentences. Almost 200 were carried out, a fraction of the number of extra-judicial killings by the army.[129] Most devastating were the testimonies of torture victims and their lawyers. There was no more powerful ammunition to mobilize public sympathy overseas. The abuses suffered by two *fidayate* detainees, each condemned to be guillotined for their role in the FLN's urban bombing campaign, drew unprecedented international attention. Djamila Bouhired's trial was conducted in July 1957 at the height of the 'battle for Algiers' between the city's FLN cells and General Jacques Massu's 10th Parachute Division. Her unstinting defence of her actions stimulated the production of a booklet, *Pour Djamila Bouhired*, a hit Egyptian film, *Djamila l'Algérienne*, and a string of popular songs broadcast across North Africa.[130] Sixty-five British Labour Party MPs signed a petition describing her trial as a travesty of 'western standards' of justice.[131] With international pressure mounting, Bouhired's death sentence was commuted.

The torture and rape of Djamila Boupacha, another female detainee arrested alongside Bouhired, attracted even greater hostile international attention.[132] Accused of planting a bomb at Algiers University, Boupacha's

Figure 15. One of the least gruesome images from a 1957 Algiers government booklet, *Mélouza et Wagram accusent*, showing Berber women grieving over children's corpses after a village massacre carried out in reprisal for villagers' support of the FLN's rival, the MNA.

Note: The propaganda uses to which the French authorities put the Mélouza massacre are discussed in Le Sueur, *Uncivil War*, 165–79.

fortitude in the face of her torturers inspired a portrait by Picasso. The image featured in a book written by her lawyer, Gisèle Halimi, to which Simone de Beauvoir, Boupacha's pre-eminent French defender, contributed.[133] Petitions demanding her reprieve were organized from Latin America to India, although only after the war ended was she amnestied.[134] The quest for global sympathy did not mean that the FLN was about to become less ruthless.

Senior leaders led by Abbane Ramdane sensed that Mollet's government, reeling from humiliation in Egypt and losing domestic support for its 'order before reform' approach, could be pushed beyond the brink, either into defeat or international isolation. At the start of 1957 the campaign of city bombings and targeted assassinations was intensified. The shift towards urban terrorism transformed the war's image irrevocably.

Terror and counter-terror: fighting the battle of Algiers

Algeria's FLN was one of three national liberation movements whose resort to terrorism achieved devastating results. Along with the Jewish *Irgun Zwai Le'umi* (Irgun), which targeted British security forces in the last years of the Palestine Mandate, and the National Organization of Cypriot Fighters (EOKA), the FLN applied merciless violence to achieve four objectives. First was to enforce popular compliance, to eliminate party rivals, and to sap the will of administrators, settlers, and the French public to resist them. These eliminations advanced the second objective: building a disciplined party apparatus to take on the mantle of local government. The FLN, by forming a state within a state inside its 'liberated zones', made the transition to independence commensurate with its assumption of power.

Linked to the construction of the institutional fabric of a functioning state was the third strategy—destabilization of the hubs of French colonial rule: Algeria's coastal cities. The FLN learnt from Vietminh tactics of urban bombings, extortive taxation from businesses, boycotts, civilian intelligence-gathering, and courier work. But the impact of colonial warfare on the urban demography of Vietnam and Algeria was markedly different. After 1946 the Vietnamese urban population shrank, especially in Hanoi. Residents fled the cities to find shelter with families in the countryside or to join the Vietminh. In Algeria, by contrast, the urban population mushroomed, the fastest expansion occurring within the *bidonvilles* on city fringes. In neither case could France win. Whether the cities emptied or overflowed, the net result was the same: growing popular conviction that the security forces were losing control of the situation.[135]

Fourth and finally was the FLN's readiness to defend its right to resist colonialism by all means necessary. For all its brutality at home, the FLN enjoyed conspicuous success in persuading foreign audiences that France had shut off all non-violent routes to Algerian self-determination. Part of their success lay in exposing the hollowness of French assimilationist rhetoric; part in establishing Algeria's emblematic status as symbol of a burgeoning 'Third World'. For Algerians, so the message went, read black Africans, Vietnamese, or Latin American Amerindians, peoples long silenced by colonialism, whose demands for equitable treatment were at last being heard.[136] Paradoxically, the force of this message was enhanced by a crushing defeat.

Over a ten-month period from January to October 1957 the French army dismantled Saadi Yacef's network of FLN cells in Algiers. In late February, Larbi Ben M'Hidi, one of the FLN's original founders, was captured and later murdered in army custody. Other locally-based members of the movement's executive 'Coordination Committee' fled the city. Several departed for foreign exile. Yacef, too, was ultimately caught, his deputies, including Ali Ammar (alias Ali La Pointe) cornered and killed.

Several aspects of this asymmetric 'battle' between urban guerrillas and professional soldiers gripped international attention. As anyone who has seen Gillo Pontecorvo's 1966 film dramatizing the battle's signal events will know, women couriers—Djamila Bouhired, Zohra Drif, Samia Lakhdari, and others— took the war into the heart of European Algiers. They planted bombs in government offices, cafés, dancehalls, and sports venues. Scores of settlers, young and old, were killed. Entire sections of the capital were locked down. The knotty backstreets of its *casbah* became the battle's lynchpin. The heart of Yacef's secretive political fiefdom, the *casbah* was the concrete embodiment of a people hemmed in by colonial oppression. Barriers, checkpoints, and curfews fostered the image of a dual, segregated city, its poorest inhabitants in its most authentically Arab quarter besieged by foreign occupiers. The apogee of this urban warfare came on 8 October 1957 after the army surrounded the hideout of the *casbah's* most notorious bombers, a team of four led by Ali La Pointe, the bomb-maker Mahmoud Bouhamidi, their female assistant, the teenaged Hassiba Ben Bouali, and a twelve-year-old boy, 'petit' Yacef Omar. After they refused to surrender, their flat was dynamited. So many charges were laid that not only were the quartet blown to bits, but seventeen of their neighbours died as the entire tenement came down. The bombing was a final, unforgettable illustration of the army's loss of tactical focus and ethical constraint. The revolution had four more martyrs to celebrate; the *casbah's* residents yet more reason to detest the troops.[137] Their moral compass spinning wildly out of control, the actions of these military occupiers, spearheaded by General Massu's parachutists, made the battle of Algiers infamous.

As in other colonial counter-insurgencies, the fight against local opponents concealed among a civilian population was intelligence led.[138] The
strategy adopted and the troops assigned to lead it transferred direct from
a predominantly rural rebellion where extreme measures—free-fire zones,
collective punishments, summary executions—were endemic, although,
as yet, little publicized. Nairobi's Operation Anvil was an obvious precedent. But the means used to extract the information necessary to discover the connections between FLN leaders, bomb-makers, couriers, and
their supporters was what set the Algiers experience apart. To be sure,
beatings, torture, and rape had been used—indeed, were being used—in
other wars of decolonization, but Massu's lieutenants set about it with
cold, systematic efficiency. Torture was part of a well-organized process,
not a departure from the norm, but the very norm itself. Its ostensible
objective was to extract usable information quickly, but its grotesque
ingredients, dehumanizing and highly sexualized, defied such matter-of-
fact, 'for the greater good' logic. Torture centres sprang up, their fearsome
reputations evoked by the merest reference to the quaint-sounding villas—
Rose, Susini, Tourelles—that housed them. The quantity of Algiers residents taken into custody at some point during the 'battle' ran into the
thousands. In an information-gathering system otherwise known for its
card indexes and mathematical precision, the numbers killed were never
precisely tallied. In addition to those who turned up dead on street cor-
ners or floating in the Bay of Algiers, over 3,000 Algiers residents were
permanently 'disappeared'.[139]

For publics and media commentators worldwide it was the chilling parallel with France's own tragic past under Nazi occupation that distinguished
the battle of Algiers. Individuals, including leading politicians, writers, and
academics tortured for resistance activity, as well as French associations representing victims of Nazi deportation began to speak out, insisting that such
practices should never be used in their name. On 27 July 1957 *Le Monde*
published the findings of an 'International Commission against the regime
of concentration camps', which shone a spotlight on the thousands of Algerians who were arbitrarily arrested and forcibly removed to detention centres or resettlement camps. Justified by the Algiers authorities as a means to
cut off the ALN's civilian sources of supply and as a way to protect isolated
rural communities from the guerrillas' predations, the camps in fact represented the largest forcible internment of a civilian population conducted
anywhere in the colonial world.[140] A day earlier the newspaper printed

harrowing accounts by five members of the International Voluntary Service for Peace, picked up and tortured by a parachutist patrol.[141]

Where *Le Monde* led, others followed. While the paper's editor, Hubert Beuve-Méry, focused on human rights abuses, contributors to *Le Monde's* right-wing broadsheet rival *Le Figaro* highlighted the war's financial drain on the French economy, implicitly connecting unsustainable expenditure with indefensible military tactics.[142] By the end of 1957 the FLN's Algiers apparatus was, for a time at least, broken. The FLN's *casbah* cells were destroyed, but the movement's international reputation as self-sacrificing and legitimate was cemented. For most observers the world over, the French presence in Algeria became something repellent: dictatorial, sadistically cruel, and morally bankrupt. Until South African troops mowed down ANC protestors at Sharpeville three years later, the battle of Algiers did more to delegitimize white minority rule in Africa than any other security force action of the decolonization era.

The link between order and reform, between the restoration of security and the promotion of constructive social change, was now impossible to sustain.

Algeria's uniqueness

British imperial authorities and right-wing media outlets matched their French counterparts in their preference for euphemism and prosaic vocabulary to describe sustained colonial violence. There were obvious advantages in deploying the language of the ordinary, of law, order, and 'the restoration of calm' to describe extraordinary violence and social breakdown. Prosaic terminology was meant to depoliticize anti-colonial rebellion and make the resultant European repression seem limited and excusable. It was also critical to avoid the vocabulary of war, which conferred combatants' rights and brought both international law and foreign scrutiny into play.[143] For French professional soldiers in Algeria, describing napalm bombs as 'special delivery tins', torture with electric shocks as 'rock 'n' roll', or escorting a detainee outside for execution as 'firewood duty', trivialized the killing involved while erecting the psychological barriers needed to cope with it.[144] Described by Roland Barthes in relation to French depictions of the crackdown in Algeria, this 'African grammar' was spoken equally fluently in British colonial conflict zones where the extraordinarily large numbers of 'prisoners shot while trying to escape' speak for themselves.[145]

In a sense, then, the issue at hand is quantitative, not qualitative. The Algerian War was longer, bigger, and nastier than anything in the British experience. A simple tally of the overall French military commitment underlines the difference: never less than 400,000 French military personnel deployed in Algeria between 1956 and 1961; more than two million armed forces personnel who served in the war, of which 1,179,523 were conscripts performing national service.[146] These numbers were redolent of world war, not the 'internal affair' of a colonial emergency. And, as we shall see, in the next chapter concluding the examination of fight and flight in Algeria, by the start of 1958 the war was not just tearing the colony apart; it was destroying the fabric of republican democracy in France.

12

Endgames in Algeria
and Rhodesia

The Algerian conflict expanded massively in 1956 and became dirtier over the course of 1957. It changed fundamentally once more in 1958. It was obvious by that point that the Algerian War was the most pressing unresolved colonial dilemma of the late 1950s. Algeria's endgame was bound to affect choices between fight or flight more generally because it encapsulated the most basic of all the questions thrown up by decolonization: could white Europeans and Africans live together after empire was gone? The British, too, faced problems with intransigent, white-minority regimes in apartheid South Africa and, more directly, the Central African Federation, the cluster of three territories under the sway of the Southern Rhodesia government. But the fact that France was already sinking in its North African quagmire lent influence to those British observers who knew most about it.

Outsiders looking in: British reactions to Algeria's unfolding war

In mid January 1957, during the week that General Jacques Massu's elite forces began their merciless 'clean-up' of the Algiers *casbah*, Lieutenant-Colonel A.J. Wilson, Britain's military attaché in the Algerian capital, reported on the contrasting morale of French regular and conscript troops. His comments were prophetic. Professional soldiers were remarkably up-beat, reluctant conscripts less so. But the 'real danger' was the senior officers; the Colonels and Generals, many of whom had been on uninterrupted colonial service since 1947.[1] These empire centurions, enthusiasts for revolutionary warfare, were the architects of dirty war. They even dubbed their opponents '*les Viets*' in reference to the bitter lessons they claimed to have learned from the Vietminh.[2] Their embrace of ultra-nationalism and ultra-violence, and, for some, their psychotic alienation from civilian life, made them difficult for less troubled minds to comprehend. Sitting opposite the inquiring British attaché, Commander-in-Chief Raoul Salan was so inscrutable that the Englishman was reduced to complimenting the General's famed blue rinse. Massu was more forthcoming, even jocular; but his messianic views on population control left the attaché baffled. Lieutenant-Colonel Feaugas, a moving force in the Algiers psychological warfare bureau and an early defender of the expediency of torture, 'had something of the spell of Laurence [*sic*] of Arabia about him'.[3] One thing was clear about this trio. Their fondness for 'spectacular' military operations blinded them to the consequences of their own actions. More than anything else, it was hard to take seriously the army's additional roles as protector, pacifier, and administrator while its frontline hard-core espoused such radical violence. To be sure, the army had a softer side. Its 600-strong *Sections Administratives Spécialisées* of countryside administrators were central to the government's rural development programmes. But for most Algerians the appearance of French soldiers inspired fear and loathing, not relief and reform.[4]

Eight months later, in August 1957, Wilson's superior, Paris military attaché Brigadier Jackson, revisited French army prospects at the height of the battle for Algiers. Writing as Massu's parachutist snatch squads and back-room torturers tore open the FLN's urban cell structure, Jackson recognized that the war's two strategic epicentres lay elsewhere: in the struggle over the ALN's principal overland supply-line along the Algeria–Tunisia frontier and in the contest between French army and FLN for control over Algeria's rural masses.[5]

At the level of strategic assessment, British military observers persisted in evaluating French success in terms of the losses inflicted on the ALN rather than in relation to other intangible factors more critical in counter-insurgency. Next to the bald facts about army killings and skirmishes with ALN units, little was said either about the corrosive effects of insurgent violence on Algeria's economy and society, or about the war's moral economy as registered in the shifting loyalties of the civilian population.[6] Typical in this regard was Brigadier Jackson's April 1958 assessment of the success of the Morice Line. 200 miles of barbed wire, minefields, blockhouses, and electrified fence, largely constructed during 1957, the Line promised several advantages. ALN bands could no longer traverse the Algeria–Tunisia frontier easily.[7] Crossing into Algeria to conduct operations in the eastern province of Constantine or returning the other way to seek sanctuary and supplies in Tunisia became perilous. In the event, the Morice Line slowed, but did not stop ALN incursions. As total interdiction proved impossible, interception became more critical. The objective was to eliminate the ALN as an effective fighting force. Jackson did not mince words:

> The French have also now appreciated the need for high quality troops for the final kill. At the start, a number of rebel bands were able to slip away or avoid total destruction because the attacking units were not really prepared to come to close quarters. When the majority of the 25th Parachute Division and some units of the Foreign Legion were moved in to act as shock troops, the final part of the operation ceased to be in doubt. The French have suffered casualties which were quite heavy for peacetime, but they are killing rebels at the rate of somewhere between 5 to 10 to 1, depending on the toughness of the bands.[8]

In July 1958, Lieutenant-Colonel Breil, acting head of French military intelligence in Algiers, briefed Wilson about the FLN–ALN structure of administrative regions, or *wilaya*. Their increasingly sophisticated local sub-divisions are shown in Map 13. The Frenchman focused on rebel numbers (an estimated 21,000 'regulars' and 30,000 auxiliary *supplétifs*), their weaponry (including an estimated 800 machine-guns), and their regional deployment (densest in Eastern Algeria).[9] Again, Wilson was impressed by news from the Morice Line. Breil told him of an intense encounter, which occurred over four days in May at Souk Ahras. By the time the shooting stopped, over 800 ALN fighters were dead.[10] The Military Attaché came away convinced that the ALN was close to destruction. But he still knew precious little about the decisive relationships between the FLN and the civilian population.[11]

Indeed, the striking omission from these British observers' assessments was the Algerian people. Appreciations of public sentiment, of shifting allegiances, of changing opinion there certainly were, but most derived from elite sources, whether ministers, colonial officials, army commanders, or nationalist party representatives. Reports based on unmediated dialogue with Algerians of no particular political influence were non-existent. The void was partially filled by Roderick Sarell, British consul in Algiers. A deeply compassionate man, he was shocked by the daily discriminations and psychological violence inherent to inter-communal relations in the Algerian capital. Only Muslims were stopped at road blocks. Their freedom of movement between locales was restricted by a network of block wardens;

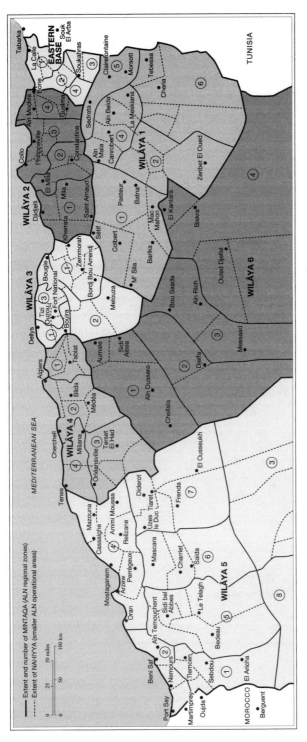

Map 13. FLN and ALN administrative districts, 1959 (adapted from SHD–DAT, 1H1600).

only they were under strict curfew at night. Police beatings were reserved for them.[12] Inevitably, Algerian civil society mutated, becoming more impenetrable under the pressures of war. French official pronouncements conveyed no sense of this—of ordinary people's *attentisme*: their daily struggle to avoid taking sides by steering clear of the violence.[13] It was this effort *not* to commit, at least not in public, despite the unrelenting pressure from both sides to do otherwise, that consumed 'ordinary' Algerians.[14] The stark alternatives of fight or flight were mirrored in personal lives as much as in national politics. Might Charles de Gaulle make a difference?

De Gaulle returns

Early indications suggested so. In May 1958 de Gaulle returned to power riding a wave of Algiers protests against a French political elite accused of having lost its way. For all the settler euphoria attending the General's intervention, the war had four more years to run. And de Gaulle made an unlikely colonists' darling. He held no strong attachment to Algeria. His northern-French family contained few emigrants. He had forged his military career in the metropolitan army, not its colonial equivalent. Admittedly, he knew Algiers well, but he held no fondness for it. His wartime memories of settlers backing his Vichy opponents hardly endeared him to the cause of French Algeria. For all that, de Gaulle was a republican, albeit an imperious, rather autocratic one. And Algeria was part of the French Republic. Surely no one knew better what consequences a French military defeat in its colonial backyard might have. Despite the fog surrounding his intentions for Algeria, the conflict had reached a tipping point.

The manner of de Gaulle's return to office underlined the point. In April the Minister of National Defence Jacques Chaban-Delmas made plans for Léon Delbeque, a Gaullist fixer from northern France, to visit Algiers. Jacques Soustelle's Union for the Salvation and Renewal of French Algeria (USRAF in French) ensured that Delbeque reeled in a prize catch on his political fishing trip. Half party, half protest movement, the USRAF brought together renegade Gaullists like Soustelle and André Morice with former colonial governors and pro-settler interest groups. They encouraged Delbeque not merely to evaluate, but also to nurture support for de Gaulle among *colon* leaders and the army command.[15] Another Gaullist networker, Jacques Foccart, a secretive deal-maker with close links to the French overseas intelligence service, the SDECE, consolidated these contacts with the Algiers Generals.[16] De Gaulle was thus made aware that influential settlers and senior officers favoured more than a change of government. They wanted a change in regime.

International pressures also came into play. The tide of decolonization had engulfed Morocco and Tunisia two years earlier, making for troublesome neighbours on Algeria's flanks. Indeed, it was Tunisian outrage at a French air force search-and-destroy mission against the Tunisian border town of Sakiet Sidi-Youssef that helped precipitate the May crisis itself. French bombs aimed at an ALN re-supply centre destroyed a Sakiet primary school killing scores of children.[17] The press images were shocking. The UN became involved. Washington joined the chorus insisting on a French admission of guilt.[18]

Decolonization's floodwaters were also rising below the Sahara. A series of French West African elections over the spring of 1957 produced governments-in-waiting and the possibility of new partnership arrangements both with France and with one another.[19] Closer to home, the settlers' sympathetic governor Robert Lacoste faced replacement. Worst of all for the imperialist diehards in Algiers, French Prime Minister Pierre Pflimlin seemed keen to emulate Mendès France's decisive 1954 break with the colonial past by entering negotiations with a hated nationalist enemy—the FLN. Rabble-rousers like student leader Pierre Lagaillarde and the Poujadist Joseph Ortiz took to the streets; indeed, these and other local USRAF organizers threatened to unleash 'ungovernable settler anger' if Paris politicians went soft on the war.[20] Colonels Roger Trinquier, Yves Godard, and Michel Goussault, zealots of the influential psychological warfare 'Fifth Bureau', were perfectly willing to manipulate local opinion as required, utilizing the army's urban social work teams (the *Section administrative urbaine*—SAU) to do so.[21] Massu, their divisional commander, also harboured Gaullist sympathies.

In the aftermath of the battle of Algiers, Fifth Bureau officers and SAU personnel assigned to the city's *bidonvilles* knew how to coerce the capital's population into doing their bidding. Outwardly at least, colourful demonstrations in which settlers and professional soldiers linked arms with *harki* auxiliaries and Muslim ex-servicemen evoked inter-communal solidarity against FLN violence. In fact, apparently spontaneous expressions of such 'fraternization' were no such thing, the participants having been tutored by Fifth Bureau officers beforehand.[22]

Figure 16. Ever loyal? Algerian veterans of the First World War parade through Algiers during Armistice Day commemorations on 11 November 1957.

Mass unveilings of Muslim women in the Algiers forum, officially cele-brated as symbolizing Franco-Algerian 'sisterhood', marked the next step in the sinister social engineering of the May crisis. A group of young women who ceremoniously removed their *haïks* on the 17th were selected for their 'modern', 'attractive', and 'European' appearance from a group of secretaries in a nearby typing pool. And the poorer women who followed them a day later were recruited from the Cité Mahiéddine, a dockworkers' *bidonville*, where the SAU was especially active.[23] SAU officers had ordered repre-sentatives of local residents' blocks to produce suitably compliant candidates for unveiling.[24] Orchestrated with Machiavellian precision, these powerful demonstrations of integration in action were a propaganda triumph—photographed, filmed, and broadcast worldwide. The stage was set for a populist alliance between settlers, military professionals, and ostensibly loyalist Algerians united under the banner of *Algérie française*. By the time the fraternization ceremonies occurred, that banner was already raised. A week of settler demonstrations between 9 and 15 May called repeatedly for a change in French government. The protests, at first organized by a shadowy 'Committee of Vigilance' led by Lagaillarde, Ortiz, and like-minded diehards, were taken over by a successor 'Committee of Public Safety'. Their rabble-rousing tone suggested that a *coup* was imminent. But Massu had a more limited objective in mind. He imposed himself on the new Committee to focus its efforts on securing de Gaulle's ascendancy. The allusions to the French Revolution in the committee's title were deliberate. Popular will, it implied, must be obeyed. The point was underlined by the threat of hard-bitten units from Algiers descending on Paris to overthrow a rotten regime. De Gaulle, not surprisingly, concealed any foreknowledge of the plotting or any clear stance on the war. As Macmillan noted drily in his diary on the night of 16 May, 'De Gaulle has made an equivocal statement, but one which has terrified the French politicians. It is cast in his usual scornful, but enigmatic language.'[25] Did the General favour fight or flight? Neither before, during, nor after the May crisis did he intend to say. In the event, despite a parachutists' 'takeover' in Corsica on 24–25 May, there was no bloody revolution.[26] The menace was enough. Pflimlin at the head of a crisis-bound coalition, and Guy Mollet, the leader of the National Assembly's largest voting bloc, bowed to the protestors and approved de Gaulle's investiture as prime minister on 29 May.[27]

Some of their long-time political partners were less quiescent. On 1 June 1958, in the first Chamber of Deputies debate since the Algiers protests, François Mitterrand condemned the abuse of legal process intrinsic to the General's resumption of power. He was followed by Pierre Cot. The veteran left-winger simply asked de Gaulle, 'Who made you King?' The obvious answer was that de Gaulle and the unelected head of his Private Office, Georges Pompidou, owed their positions to the conniving between their political fixers, the army officers behind the 'Committee of Public Safety', and the settler crowds determined to conserve white minority rule. De Gaulle was catapulted back into power by an ugly combination of surreptitious pre-planning, a local military takeover, and plebiscitary mob rule that subverted French democracy. 'So what?' parliamentarians and public in

France appeared to say. The subsequent vote granting the new government emergency powers and the right to reform the constitution went decisively in the General's favour. 329 deputies supported de Gaulle's investiture against 224 (141 of them Communists) who opposed it.[28]

With this, the certainties of Fourth Republic party politics collapsed. The relative ease with which de Gaulle swept away, not only the incumbent government but the institutional apparatus of France's post-war regime confirmed what had been apparent for some months. France's coalition politics had become unworkable. Most important, the French public's clear preference for decisive leadership over parliamentary horse-trading and turnstile coalitions condemned the Fourth Republic's governing elite to the wilderness. The political centre fell way. Parties once integral to post-war government—the Socialists and their UDSR cousins, the Radicals and, above all, the Christian Democrat MRP—were never likely to become a 'loyal opposition'. Both the Socialists and the MRP fractured; the latter irredeemably so. For the once mighty MRP, proud creation of former premiers Georges Bidault and Robert Schuman among others, internal factionalism would dominate internal party affairs for the remainder of the Algerian War.[29] For some, including the MRP's affiliate Christian Trade Union Confederation, the rough-shod manner of de Gaulle's restoration was too much to swallow.[30] For others, including Bidault and the Party's Algerian federations, the problem was less how de Gaulle got the keys to the Elysée Palace than what he planned to do with Algeria once inside. Utterly intransigent in their faith in Franco-Algerian integration, some MRP hardliners, Bidault foremost among them, would end up condoning the terrorism of the Secret Army Organization (OAS) if it helped keep Algeria French.[31] The Algiers shockwave had travelled northwards across the Mediterranean with devastating political results.

As we shall see, the dramatic turn of events in Algiers bore some comparison with settler rebellion in Souther Rhodesia, which, by the 1960s, was Britain's sole remaining white-ruled dependency. Rhodesia's unilateral declaration of independence (UDI) in 1965 confirmed the failure of British efforts to steer the territory towards black majority rule. Or, to phrase it differently, it exposed the limitations of a flight strategy lacking the muscle to persuade Rhodesia's settler leaders to change political course. Prior to that, the question facing France and Algeria in the summer of 1958 was whether de Gaulle's government would follow or defy the combination of settlers and army officers that had been so instrumental in creating it.

Winning but losing

It was not long before de Gaulle disabused the Algiers radicals who had mistaken him for their saviour. On 3 October the new French government raised the possibility of political amnesties for ALN fighters who laid down their arms. Three weeks later came the first official offer of a full ceasefire since the war began. De Gaulle's so-called 'peace of the brave' responded to the FLN's establishment of a 'Provisional Government of the Algerian Republic' (GPRA in French) on 19 September.[32] French ministers and officials privately disparaged the GPRA. The dismissive description by the London ambassador Jean Chauvel of a 'so-called Algerian government' without any territorial basis and 'no means of influence other than assassination and terror' was fairly typical.[33] But, as de Gaulle knew, the new FLN executive was not going away. Formally recognized by most Arab governments and feted by fellow non-aligned states, the GPRA also received highly publicized 'best wishes' from Nikita Khrushchev in Moscow.[34] Its public face, represented by Algeria's elder statesman Ferhat Abbas and Information Minister Mohammed Yazid, a familiar presence in the UN's New York headquarters, concealed the fact that the GPRA's real powerbrokers were a more hard-line trio of original FLN founders, Belkacem Krim, Vice-President with responsibility for armed forces, Lakhdar Ben Tobbal (at Interior), and the secret services boss Abdelhafid Boussouf. These three were immune to de Gaulle's coaxing. They heaped scorn on the General's 24 October promise that the French army would protect Algeria's Muslims as well as its Europeans.[35] This was rash. His peace offer rejected, de Gaulle reverted to other, more conventional means of persuasion.

During the first six months of 1959 unrelenting French army offensives pushed the ALN to the brink of military defeat. Their architect was Maurice Challe, a diminutive, pipe-smoking air force general, appointed on 12 December 1958 to replace the inscrutable Raoul Salan as commander in Algeria.[36] As mentioned earlier, between July 1957 and November 1959 army engineers erected over 1,300 kilometres of electric fencing along Algeria's eastern frontier with Tunisia. Blockhouses, over a million anti-personnel mines, and almost 80,000 French assault troops completed the so-called Morice Line, shutting off the ALN from its principal refuge and primary source of overland resupply.[37] An equivalent barrier was also established along Algeria's western border with Morocco. These frontier defences were the prerequisite to Challe's transformative year of command. Militarily, it was every bit as significant—and, as it turned out, as transient—as de Lattre's impact on Indochina had been seven years before.[38] Like de Lattre, Challe was an enthusiast for bold, some would say risky, initiatives. It was he who devised the key elements of the Suez Operation in October 1956.[39] His Algerian schema was reducible to two elements. Helicopters to chase down guerrilla bands, plus *harkis*, the Algerian paramilitaries recruited to assist frontline operations: these were the keys to victory in 1959.[40]

Challe's 60,000-plus *harkis* and his airborne troops' ever-expanding search-and-destroy missions cut ALN cadres by well over fifty per cent.[41] Yet over the course of the same year de Gaulle's administration edged closer towards negotiations with the FLN, opening the door to French withdrawal from Algeria. How do we reconcile these apparent opposites? Answering this question is important. For one thing, the evidence that tens of thousands of volunteer militiamen were willing to side with France, placing their families at risk of FLN retribution, suggests either that the army was winning the battle for Algerian loyalties or that the FLN was losing it through its terroristic methods and the naked self-interest of some of its *wilaya* commanders.[42] For another thing, the events of 1959 made plain that de Gaulle could square the circle between short-term military advance and longer-term decolonization whereas the army's senior officers in Algeria could not. The result was the worst crisis in French civil–military relations since the creation of the Vichy state in July 1940. The opposing logics of fight and flight were now institutionally personified in confrontation between a purposeful civilian government and the heads of a disaffected colonial army.

Matters first came to a head with the 'Barricades week' in Algiers in late January 1960. Before that, the widening gulf between the army leadership in Algiers and de Gaulle's supporters in Paris had provoked angry exchanges over political and economic planning for Algeria's long-term future. While Challe propelled his offensives forward during 1959, schemes to modify Algerian citizenship status, to improve access to welfare services, and to modernize the Algerian economy through massive housing and infrastructure projects were all undone by the underlying stresses of the war. Was such investment affordable at a time when the army was swallowing so much money? And who would risk moving into government-sponsored homes in defiance of the FLN? The advocates of such schemes were undeterred. As these ideas evinced, the Paris government and its civilian representative in Algiers, Paul Delouvrier, abandoned the old 'order before reform' logic of fight before flight that had condemned the reformist planning of the Mollet era to irrelevance. A man of sharp suits but cautious pronouncements, Delouvrier was the embodiment of his technocratic training inside the Franco-German Coal and Steel Community. The antithesis of the populist Soustelle and the impassioned Lacoste, Delouvrier assumed the unambiguously subordinate position of 'delegate-general' rather than governor.[43] But Delouvrier's title also conferred one clear advantage: a hot-line to his presidential boss. Fastidiously bureaucratic, he soon alerted the Elysée Palace to the twin problems of funding shortfalls and local obstructionism that would thwart any rapid achievement of Algerian development. On the one hand, military expertise was essential to provide the security and specialist personnel necessary to put rural welfare into practice. On the other hand, the cash to finance the government's transformative development scheme, the Constantine Plan, was never likely to be forthcoming from a French exchequer faced with mounting war costs and costly expansion of France's nuclear programme.

Ironically, the Constantine Plan, named after the city where de Gaulle first announced its outlines on 3 October 1958, was supposed to complement the ramping up of military operations.[44] But finding the money for a million new homes or the investment to create 400,000 new jobs—the taglines of de Gaulle's Constantine speech—was impossible while bankrolling a major ground war as well.[45] On 10 February 1959, with the Challe offensive rolling on, premier Michel Debré assigned implementation schedules to specialist planning commissions in Paris, the 'super-prefects', or IGAMEs in Algeria, and the departmental authorities beneath them. Serious in intent, the Constantine Plan was a sham even so. Some basic economic facts help explain why. At least 6.5 million Algerians still depended on an agricultural sector in which approximately 22,000 settler-owned farms produced a volume of saleable produce equivalent to that of an estimated 600,000 Algerian-owned smallholdings. The Constantine Plan skirted this, the fundamental injustice of Algerian rural life. Instead, the central problem of economic survival in the Algerian countryside—chronic land shortage—went unanswered.[46] The obvious colonial roots of this agricultural iniquity were replicated within Algeria's public sector as well. Here, the Constantine Plan had more to say. Clerical jobs in the administration, once reserved for full French citizens, were opened up to 'French Algerian Muslims'. But decades of under-education and fear of FLN retribution left three out of every four bureaucratic vacancies unfilled after the Plan finally secured government approval on 13 June 1960.[47] By that point, the prospect of flight through negotiation rather than fight-plus-development made sounder financial sense.[48] Indeed, it was policy.

On 16 September 1959 de Gaulle made a decisive speech, simultaneously transmitted on French TV and radio, announcing his government's support for an Algerian ceasefire, amnesty, elections, and eventual self-determination. The FLN, increasingly factionalized and reeling from Challe's military onslaught, was slow to respond.[49] It did not matter. The French authorities had made the decisive shift towards negotiated withdrawal, to decolonization by flight.

The USRAF diehards, now organized into an ultra-rightist 'French National Front' (FNF), channelled their outrage into plotting. The revelation in January 1960 that their military hero Jacques Massu was being recalled to France, spurred them to action. Decked in Castro-like military fatigues and dark sunglasses, Pierre Lagaillarde and another, younger student leader, Jean-Jacques Susini, took their defiance over the brink from May '58-style protests to violent direct action. Algiers University was occupied by scores of youthful paramilitaries. Street barricades were thrown up in downtown Algiers.[50] Numerous army officers as well as Massu's parachutists, disgusted by the cold ingratitude of their home government, clearly sympathized with this resumption of *Algérie française* disorder.[51]

The 'barricades week' in late January 1960 did not signify a return to the exuberance of the May crisis, but something darker: a desperate bid to keep Algeria French that prefigured the counter-terrorist killings conducted by the disaffected soldiers and FNF militants who joined forces in the OAS. Whereas the May 1958 demonstrations had been scrupulously planned, the scenes in Algiers during the final days of January 1960 were riotous, anarchic, and reactionary. This time around, the revolutionary symbolism implicit in the romanticized moniker 'barricades week' was wholly inappropriate. On the evening of Monday 25 January the Algiers gendarmerie in full riot gear moved in to clear the barricades and reopen the university. Settler vigilantes fired down on the unfortunate riot squad from apartment balconies, killing fourteen. Others set upon the gendarmes in the street, seriously injuring many more.[52] The stresses of colonial conflict were culminating in a dystopian mirror image of the Algerian-vs-Algerian civil war between the FLN and Messali Hadj's MNA. The cycle of internecine bloodletting amongst Algeria's European population had begun.

To this tragic irony was added another. Before barricades week, disdain for *pieds noirs* extremism was one of the few things on which professional

soldiers and conscripts could agree. Meanwhile, among rural settlers in particular, there was growing realization that heavy-handed military interventions, supposedly mounted on their behalf, only compounded their exposure
to danger in the longer term. Operations against ALN bands were mobile
and fleeting, at odds with the seasonal routines of country life in which
farming families were often left alone to face increasingly hostile Algerian
villagers and farmhands.[53] After barricades week it was harder to disparage
settler politics or inappropriate military tactics without risking ostracism or
OAS retribution.

Clearly, the war's grim political logic was changing. In the three months
between October and December 1960 the French army listed 1,214 'kills' of
ALN fighters, a figure that pointed to the continuing intensity of military
operations. Yet perhaps more significant was the FLN's response. Rather
than fighting harder against French forces, the ALN increasingly focused its
own efforts on the elimination of Algerian rivals and other 'collaborators'
such as elected officials and local government employees. The movement's
short-term priority, in other words, was to clear the path for its seizure of
power.[54]

Warning signs for Britain

The string of unbroken French military successes, beginning with the
Morice Line's construction and climaxing with the Challe offensives in
1959, convinced British military observers in the months preceding Macmillan's 'wind of change' speech in February 1960 that the FLN might yet
accede to de Gaulle's call for negotiations.[55] Barricades week made British
ministers think again. After a year of humiliating revelations of British colonial violence in Kenya, the Central African Federation and Cyprus, the sight
of rebellious troops and *colon* ultras manning the Algiers barricades in
January 1960 conjured up frightening images of something similar happening in anglophone southern Africa.[56] The first open revolt since May 1958
against de Gaulle's dual-track strategy of heightened operations and offers
of dialogue helped persuade Macmillan that settler extremism in Africa
must be checked.[57]

Almost as troubling, de Gaulle seemed to have other strategic concerns
entirely. Hostile to NATO's multilateral command structure, the General's
inner circle of military advisers were fixated on France's imminent acquisition

of a working nuclear bomb.[58] The prospect of Gaullist obstreperousness enhanced by a nuclear trigger was something that, to put it mildly, Whitehall, Number 10, and the White House disliked.[59] But it was Algeria's widening conventional war that provoked greatest alarm. Those, such as Iain MacLeod's Colonial Office advisers, Britain's UN delegation in New York, and the mandarins of the Foreign Office, who viewed colonial violence through the prisms of African regional politics, international diplomacy, and changing transnational norms of acceptable state action, were coming to realize through bitter experience that further killing, no matter how effective in narrowly military terms, was deeply counter-productive.[60] In part, this perspective signified belated recognition of Britain's diminishing scope for repressive violence after its string of African humiliations in 1959 and the tightening of budgetary strings expected in the new decade ahead.[61] In part, it was a game of catch-up with the Americans as the handover to John F. Kennedy's new presidential administration became imminent.[62] And, in part, it stemmed from shock at the lengths to which settler and army reactionaries would go to salvage white minority rule.[63]

Meanwhile, inside Algeria and France, a strange inversion of political positions occurred between the supporters and opponents of negotiations and French withdrawal. Proponents of de Gaulle's flight strategy ridiculed what were once self-evident republican 'truths', namely, that Algeria was genuinely French and that its population, European and non-European alike, could be fully-fledged citizens as well. For the first time a French executive conceded that integration could never succeed. Inherent in this was the admission that legal, political, and economic equality between French and Algerians was unachievable. This drift in official rhetoric was most apparent after independence became a reality in 1962. In historian Todd Shepard's neat summation, 'French public officials and many French people would assert that Algeria and Algerians had never really been French with the same certainty that had previously accompanied their insistence that Algeria was French.'[64] The supreme paradox was that it fell to the last defenders of *Algérie française*, the OAS, an ultra-right terrorist group that allied long-serving army officers with settler extremists, to defend the French presence in Algeria in republican terms. With uncompromising, if twisted, logic, OAS supporters justified their killings as part of the struggle for assimilation between two peoples united in the single trans-Mediterranean nation that was 'French Algeria'. Ludicrous as it may seem, a quasi-fascist movement adopted the language of cultural integration and shared Franco-Algerian citizenship that de Gaulle discarded.[65]

The gulf between the official and OAS versions of French Algerian history was linked to changes in de Gaulle's government, which increasingly
resembled a presidential 'regime' as the General augmented his decision-
making powers. He did so by appealing directly to French voters through
successive referenda, particularly in relation to France's future in Algeria.
Parliamentary debate and party political opposition to de Gaulle's Algerian
policies was side-lined, leaving the field open to the OAS to attack the government line. Perhaps none of this mattered. The government's abandonment of Franco-Algerian integration mirrored the prevailing conviction
among France's people that Algerian independence and a complete pull-out
were inevitable. In this sense, de Gaulle did not transform public opinion, he
followed it. What was only in hindsight identified as 'decolonization' was
viewed at the time as something else—*le courant de l'Histoire*, the 'tide of
History'.[66]

De Gaulle's war or de Gaulle's peace?

In the two-year interval between barricades week in January 1960 and the
final round of high-level talks between French and FLN representatives at
the spa town of Evian, several factors increased de Gaulle's freedom to
pursue what he tellingly described as an 'Algerian agenda'. Within the
colony, the steady advance of French military control proved less significant than the FLN's elimination of its internal rivals. As 1960 unfolded it
became clear that Algeria's dominant nationalist movement had weath-
ered the storms of 1957–9. Incursions across the frontier barrier with
Tunisia redoubled. Weapons supplied by Eastern bloc countries and Mao's
China transformed the ALN's fighting capacity. And the GPRA's announcement in May 1960 that several hundred foreign fighters, including Jorda-
nians, Libyans, and Syrians, had joined the struggle underlined the Algerian
War's capacity to galvanize Arab opinion and destabilize pivotal Middle
Eastern regimes.[67] No matter that French military forces could still eliminate ALN bands whenever they tracked them down; their movement
remained the only nationalist show in town. Seeking alternative negotiating partners was pointless.

   Refusing to acknowledge this fact of Algerian political life, in early 1961
four senior French military commanders passed from exasperation to outright mutiny. Mounted in April, the so-called 'Generals' coup' quickly

descended into farce. But it might have been otherwise. With a powerful whiff of double standards, de Gaulle, the chief beneficiary of a similar act of officers' indiscipline three years earlier, this time insisted on total military loyalty to the constitution, to the law, and to the presidential office. He took to the air-waves to broadcast repeatedly to rank-and-file soldiers, settlers, and Algerians alike. Stiff and awkward at diplomatic gatherings, de Gaulle was a masterful radio and TV performer. His sonorous voice, sometimes booming, other times reassuring, inspired confidence in radio listeners. On television he was, by turns, magisterial and avuncular, speaking passionately but calmly, occasionally waving his thick spectacles for dramatic effect. His April 1961 broadcasts portrayed the rebellious Generals as reactionaries, out of touch with Algerian realities and the French public's appetite for peace.

Their treachery aside, the last-ditch defenders of *Algérie française* were made to look foolish. Adding insult to injury, de Gaulle ordered the release of 6,000 FLN detainees as a curtain-raiser to the first round of Evian negotiations on 20 May.[68] Some never forgave him. In a 29 April letter to the MRP executive, one of the plotters' supporters in Algiers complained that the city's 'prisons, still warm from the presence of recently-freed rebels, all known killers, have opened their doors to admit the true patriots of French Algeria...veterans of Second World War campaigns to liberate Italy and France from fascist oppression'.[69]

Within France, the issue was less about the need to fight on and more about the need to get on with getting out. The start of the Evian talks was broadly welcomed; their breakdown in mid June lamented. The disappointment was compounded by the apparent failure of further discussions in late July, which stalled over guarantees for settlers and the long-term status of Algeria's strategically- and economically-critical Saharan region. Public disaffection was matched by bitter press criticism. Reflecting the mood, demonstrations against the war by Algerian immigrants, French trade unionists, church groups, and intellectuals peaked in late 1961.[70] On the eve of the Bastille Day festivities de Gaulle had confided to the British Ambassador Sir Pierson Dixon that he planned to recall more troops from Algeria. It was absurd, the General said, to have 400,000 men stuck over there when the war was all but over.[71] Two months later, 121 leading public intellectuals, including writers, academics, and 'New Wave' film directors, took the logic of de Gaulle's comment one step further, putting their names to a 'manifesto', which affirmed that conscripts were morally entitled to refuse to serve their country in Algeria. Orchestrated by long-time FLN sympathizer

Francis Jeanson, this 'Manifesto of the 121' gripped the public imagination. Its message was devastatingly simple: no one should be compelled to support an unjust cause.[72]

It would be wrong to imply that the French public shifted *en bloc* to an anti-war stance. There was fundamental difference between war fatigue and active anti-colonialism, between support for de Gaulle's Algerian flight solution and positive recognition of past French misdeeds in North Africa or elsewhere. While the majority of French voters wanted out of Algeria, most refused to go as far as the 121 petitioners had done in acknowledging the legitimacy of Algeria's fight for independence.[73] The limits to French public sympathy for Algerian nationalism, and Algerians more generally, were starkly illustrated by the muted reaction to a night of state terror, not in Algiers or Constantine, but in the heart of Paris.[74]

In some ways reminiscent of the MTLD's fateful Bastille Day march in 1953, on 17 October 1961 well-disciplined columns of Algerian demonstrators, representing the 180,000 immigrants domiciled in the Greater Paris region, set out for the capital's downtown boulevards. They wanted to protest against a night-time curfew imposed twelve days earlier.[75] The curfew, restricted to North African immigrant *quartiers* and *banlieue* shanty-towns, was the harshest of several restrictions devised by the Prefecture of Police. The capital's police chief Maurice Papon we have encountered before. His colonial methods of surveillance, repression, and extra-judicial killing, refined during his service in eastern Algeria after 1945, were now transposed to Paris.

Papon saw no reason for restraint. Beginning in August 1961, French police officers and informants had been targeted for assassination by FLN militants within the immigrant community. The curfew was his central riposte. But what followed on the night of 17 October went much further. Demonstrators' anger at the curfew condensed their resentment at poor-quality housing, social marginalization, and, of course, discriminatory policing. Amongst them were members of FLN commando gangs, veterans of the internecine war against MNA supporters. Some came armed with revolvers. But it was the police, reinforced by *Compagnie Républicaine de Sécurité* (CRS) and *Gendarmes mobiles* riot squads, who were spoiling for revenge. Scuffles broke out at the margins of the demonstration as snatch squads extracted those identified as ringleaders. In the resultant confusion police began using their wooden nightsticks, or *matraques*, raining blows on those too slow to disperse. Shots were exchanged, although the facts of who fired first and why were disputed. Those demonstrators dragged off by the police were bundled off to nearby police stations or hauled into darker backstreets. Within a matter of hours well over a hundred Algerians had been fatally shot, strangled, or beaten to death by members of the Paris police force. Several were murdered by death squads comprised of hard-bitten personnel shipped in from Algeria, their activities organized in secrecy by Papon as part of his war against the FLN's immigrant supporters.[76]

In a practice perfected over preceding months during which surreptitious killings of FLN suspects had intensified in response to the movement's targeting of police personnel, officers covered their tracks by stripping the bodies, which were then thrown from city centre bridges into the Seine.[77] The river's downstream lock-gates were conveniently opened to help sluice away the evidence of a colonial war now being fought in the French capital. Papon's official press release, issued in the early hours of 18 October, described the events curtly. The police, called in to disperse a demonstration, returned fire after being shot at by FLN militants among the crowd. Only two deaths were acknowledged. In fact, taking into account the victims murdered by police in the weeks running up to the demonstration, the number of Algerians killed ran into the hundreds. Paris, 17 October 1961 was the worst peacetime massacre of civilian protestors in Western Europe since the end of the Second World War.[78]

Demands for a public inquiry into the killings were led by the Socialists' veteran colonial reformer Gaston Defferre and the former Resistance organizer Eugène Claudius-Petit. Summarizing evidence from doctors who had treated 210 wounded demonstrators, his was the first voice in the National Assembly to connect police brutality with colonial racism. For all that, neither the judiciary nor the French public seemed particularly animated by what had taken place. The press, too, moved on to news of other street violence—the death of seventy-four Algiers demonstrators commemorating the 1 November anniversary of the war's outbreak in 1954, the threat of heightened OAS counter-terror. Nor did de Gaulle's government or the GPRA make an issue of 17 October, reluctant to block the path to a negotiated Algerian settlement. Its outlines had become clearer after de Gaulle's negotiators abandoned plans for an Algerian partition intended to reserve designated urban areas for Europeans and huge tracts of the Sahara for French commercial and military exploitation. In the short term, at least, a shocking low-point of the fight over French Algeria was confined to the shadows by the emerging prospects of flight.[79]

It took single-minded optimism to see Algerian peace on the horizon as the war's violence plumbed new depths in early 1962. Factionalized and desperate, the OAS expanded its bombing campaigns in Algiers, Paris, and elsewhere. Government offices, even the homes of Jean-Paul Sartre and another writer, the Minister of Culture André Malraux, were targeted. The cycle of bombings was even worse in Algiers. Daily attacks were launched from the downtown settler neighbourhood of Bab El-Oued. These became increasingly indiscriminate once it became clear that government talks with the FLN, resumed in early February, were likely to culminate in a peace deal.[80]

French public revulsion at OAS tactics far outstripped the muted response to 17 October. Malraux was absent when his Boulogne-sur-Seine home was bombed on 7 February 1962, but Delphine Renard, the four-year-old daughter of a neighbour, was not. Her bloodied, disfigured face dominated the next day's press coverage, sparking trade union and left-wing calls for a mass protest against OAS violence. The resultant 'anti-fascist' demonstration on the evening of Thursday 8 February was rowdy. There were running battles with police in and around the Place de la Bastille. *Matraques* were much in evidence once more. Terrified protesters ran for cover down the stairs of the nearby Charonne metro station. Its entrance locked, the station became a crush of humanity in which eight people died. The victims included three women and a sixteen-year-old boy. The funerals for the victims, interred on 13 February in the section of the famous Père Lachaise cemetery reserved for Communist Party supporters, were accompanied by a general strike and the largest public march in Paris since Liberation in July 1944.[81] 'Charonne' became a by-word for the sheer futility of the Algerian War and the tensions—between ideologies, ethnicities, and generations—which gnawed deeper into French society as the 1960s rolled on. A once silent majority of French people found their voice: military defence of the sham creation *Algérie française* was an indefensible human expense.

The role reversal implicit in the government's admission that the French republican project in Algeria was a mirage became manifest in the National Assembly debate that followed de Gaulle's broadcast on 18 March 1962 announcing an Algerian cease-fire. Algiers Deputy Pierre Portalano denounced de Gaulle's repudiation of past pledges as a violation of the cardinal principle of a democratic republic: 'For the first time in the history of the Free World', he thundered, 'a Western government has freely abandoned guarantees of domestic liberty and the rights of man.'[82] Clearly, it was settlers' liberty that most concerned him, but still Portalano's argument had force. All that successive Algerian governors and Paris governments had pledged over decades about the progressive eradication of difference between France and Algeria as the two peoples were forged into a single nation had been dropped like a hot coal, rejected as irrelevant frippery next to decolonization's irresistible advance. Portalano, then, had a point. But he was also profoundly wrong. Juridical arguments and appeals to republican idealism ignored the central facts that de Gaulle, his ministers and officials, and the overwhelming majority of the French public recognized. To the bitter end Algeria had been ruled as a colony in all but name. And the great majority of its own people wanted the French to leave. Even de Gaulle's rhetorical flourishes in an evening broadcast on 18 March, in which he emphasized that the final Evian agreement ensured orderly self-determination, guarantees for settlers, plus economic and strategic privileges for France, could not disguise the underlying truth. The FLN had won.[83]

From his 'hiding place' in Algeria, twelve days before the war's 19 March 1962 ceasefire OAS leader General Salan sent letters to Kennedy, Macmillan, and Adenauer. Salan implored the three Western leaders to understand his movement's loyalist motives and humanitarian purpose. The OAS, he insisted, was neither fascist nor out to seize power. Its sole aim was to protect Europeans' rights to fair treatment. The suggestion that colonial whites were victims of a new discrimination inherent in the rush to bring empire to a close was a familiar refrain among those on the losing side of decolonization's bloodiest confrontations. Stripped of its overblown claims about loyal sons of the soil cruelly abandoned by uncaring home governments, the argument was always the same: those who fought to sustain imperial ties were betrayed by political elites and domestic populations who failed to grasp the realities of colonial life.[84]

In fact few OAS leaders were ever optimistic that Algeria could be kept French. Their shockingly indiscriminate terrorism during 1961–2 was closer to despairing nihilism than the violent expression of a coherent strategy to seize power. Those OAS militants that evaded capture inhabited a looking-glass world of inverse logic, one in which Oran, always the most European of Algeria's cities, might yet be preserved as a white enclave in an independent but truncated Algeria deprived of its Saharan south. By late 1961 all talk of settler enclaves and autonomous Saharan regions had been

Figure 17. Victory! Residents celebrate the re-opening of the Algiers *casbah* on 22 March 1962.

officially dropped.[85] Not surprisingly, OAS diehards would make common cause against such betrayals of 'western civilisation' in Africa with Katanga separatists in the Congo, with Francisco Franco's fascist regime, and, most pertinent to us here, with Ian Smith's Rhodesian Front.[86]

Britain's fight over Southern Rhodesia

As we have seen, the Algerian spectre of kith-and-kin conflict between settlers and metropolitan armed forces haunted British Ministers and service chiefs from the late 1950s onwards.[87] A Cyprus settlement in 1959 ended Britain's colonial oversight and saw its military presence reduced just as General Challe was launching his Algerian offensive. This juxtaposition between a negotiated settlement and an escalating conflict seemed to suggest that, unlike France, Britain was turning away from protracted colonial fights.[88]

Whatever the contrasting 'lessons' of Cyprus and Algeria, they produced less clear-cut rejection of British military intervention against recalcitrant settlers in southern Africa than might be imagined. There was a strong civil–military divide here. By March 1961 senior military figures, including the service chiefs Sir Francis Festing and Lord Louis Mountbatten, as well as the intelligence analysts of the Cabinet's Joint Intelligence Committee, ruled out deploying British aircraft and soldiers against the white minority regime in the Central African Federation. It is not hard to see why.

There were sound strategic reasons for rejecting the use of overwhelming British military force to overthrow white minority rule and clear the path to African self-government in Nyasaland and Northern and Southern Rhodesia. For a start, British troops would have to be ferried in from some distance, probably from Kenya, making a surprise operation unfeasible. The airfields of the Central African Federation would have to be secured in the opening phase of any attack. But this could not be done without risking large-scale civilian casualties because the C.A.F.'s airbases also served as commercial airstrips. Parachute drops and the use of poor-quality roads to transport supplies presented innumerable difficulties. Reliable intelligence about Federation military units and their likely reaction was sparse.[89] It was clear, however, that Federal security forces were quite capable of acting unilaterally—and contrary to British wishes. This point was brought home by their support for Moise Tshombe's secessionist government in the Congo's mineral-producing eastern province of Katanga after the Congo Crisis erupted in 1960.[90] Roy Welensky's federal government in Salisbury also took steps in February 1961 to secure additional weaponry and munitions from apartheid South Africa, whose imminent departure from the Commonwealth only increased the probability that the Pretoria regime would relish the opportunity to help give Britain a bloody nose.[91]

What, then, if white Rhodesian forces resisted invasion? The Federation's greatest strategic asset was the Royal Rhodesian Air Force. Aside from its potential to attack incoming British forces, it afforded the local defenders greater mobility than their potential British opponents. Destroying RRAF aircraft, whether by commando raids against airbases or by aerial bombardment might have been possible.[92] But at what cost? Rather than pre-empting a wider conflict, knocking out the RRAF might escalate military confrontation into all-out war between Britain and Rhodesia's whites. Behind all these calculations lay the unspoken assumption that British soldiers and airmen might be unwilling to fire on fellow white servicemen, including former comrades in earlier conflicts.[93]

What about the politics of it all? The greatest oddity is that, first Macmillan's government and, later, Harold Wilson's successive Labour administrations between 1964 and 1970 kept returning to the idea of military intervention. And this in spite of the convincing objections to it. Fight was not entirely abandoned despite the overwhelming arguments for flight. The point should not be over-stressed, though. Faced in early 1961 with the prospect of a constitutional breakdown in Central Africa in which the white-controlled Rhodesian regimes used force to block African self-rule, it was incumbent on Macmillan's Cabinet to explore the possibilities of applying countervailing pressure of their own. The same held true three years later as Southern Rhodesia's settler militants edged towards a Unilateral Declaration of Independence (UDI) in defiance of Wilson's government. For all that, in each case military and intelligence advice was unequivocal: 'limited' military action was unfeasible, so intervention meant war. This was a bridge that neither Conservative nor Labour ministers were willing to cross. Wilson ultimately said so, telling the Rhodesian Front regime on the eve of UDI that Britain would not intervene militarily to stop it. The Prime Minister was lambasted in the press and by Cabinet colleagues, including, the Minister of Defence Denis Healey, for throwing away Britain's bargaining chips. But Wilson was merely stating the obvious. By doing so he also made clear to African nationalist leaders in the region that it was pointless to hope for a British takeover as the prelude to any transfer of power.[94]

Wilson's renunciation of force on 30 October 1965 was not quite the end of the story. Senior Labour Party figures including Barbara Castle and Jim Callaghan, not to mention other influential opinion-makers, the Archbishop of Canterbury Michael Ramsey for one, insisted that violence might yet be required; this time to impose a form of decolonization rather than to prevent it.[95] However genuinely meant, these sentiments persuaded few inside Rhodesia that Britain's armed forces might risk all for the cause of black freedom. The Wilson government had, for instance, played tougher than its

Conservative predecessor with South Africa over arms sales and sports boy-cotts while stopping short of cutting economic or military ties.[96] Ultimately, none of Britain's 1960s administrations enjoyed much success in bolstering their diplomacy of decolonization with the threat of military action. The fact was that neither side in Rhodesia's bitter racial struggle believed that British forces would ever be deployed. Few were surprised, then, when Smith's government raised the stakes.

Rhodesia and UDI

At 11 a.m. British time on Armistice Day, 11 November 1965, a phalanx of journalists and press photographers gathered in Rhodesia's Government House to witness the ultra-loyalist imperialists of Smith's Rhodesian Front (RF) government sign their Unilateral Declaration of Independence. A shambling, rather bizarre ceremony concluded with the opening verses of 'God Save the Queen'. Smith later told Rhodesian Broadcasting Company listeners that he and they shared the same spirit of 'kith-and-kin' solidarity with ordinary Britons that had seen them through two World Wars. It was Labour's 'doctrinaire philosophy of appeasement and surrender' to Soviet-inspired African nationalism that was beyond the pale.[97] With this blast of faux-Churchillian rhetoric a settler regime determined to resist black majority rule ostracized itself from the mother country whose values it claimed to cherish. The anglophone settlers of Southern Rhodesia had done what the francophone *colons* of Algeria never quite did. They rebelled. In Donal Lowry's words, 'thus the white Rhodesians became, however reluc-tantly, the first people of largely British origin to throw off the Crown since the American Revolution'.[98]

The Crown representative, the Governor Sir Humphrey Gibbs, duly 'sacked' the offending RF Cabinet, a pointless exercise insofar as UDI signi-fied the repudiation of Britain's authority over Southern Rhodesia. Similar confusion reigned elsewhere. There were no British soldiers in Rhodesia, and few civil servants. So Wilson's government had no means to contest Smith's decision by enforcing special Orders in Council that, on paper any-way, provided the constitutional basis for upholding British sovereignty.[99] Nor was the rupture complete. Rhodesia did not declare itself a republic until 2 March 1970, part of a white supremacist constitutional settlement uncompromisingly hostile to black majority rule. Over the preceding five years, the central plank of the Labour government's effort to reverse UDI—economic warfare waged by the imposition of wide-ranging sanctions—was also more equivocal than it appeared. For one thing, sanctions imposed in November 1965 in the hope of catalysing Smith's overthrow, were, from April 1966 onwards, harnessed to British efforts to cajole the RF regime into talks. For another thing, the Southern Rhodesian government retained crucial economic and strategic advantages. Friendly regimes to south, west and east: apartheid South Africa, plus Portuguese Angola and Mozambique, minimized the impact of sanctions. As for Zambia under Kenneth Kaunda, the one black-led Commonwealth state on Southern Rhodesia's borders, whose copper exports were vital to British industry, Smith's ministers could easily retaliate by shutting down its power supplies.[100]

Furthermore, there were plenty in Britain who either opposed Labour's sanctions policy outright or retained some sympathy for the 230,000 or so white Rhodesians, many of whom, like Smith himself, boasted impeccable war records.[101] Men like Smith, after all, had not only fought alongside British 'mates' against Hitler and Mussolini, but against other, darker-skinned foes in Malaya and Aden who were determined to bring down the British Empire. For their apologists 'back home' it was sixties Britain that was changing for the worst, not Rhodesia. Here were the British echoes of the same political and inter-generational conflicts apparent in France at the close of the Algerian War. Edward Heath, the Conservative Party's new leader, installed only five months earlier in July 1965, therefore faced a dilemma. He was amenable to a bipartisan approach to otherwise divisive issues of decolonization, but many of his backbenchers thought otherwise. When it came to a parliamentary vote over oil sanctions on 21 December, Tory MPs split three ways. Some endorsed sanctions on principle; others rejected them as ineffectual; and a vocal minority backed the Smith regime.[102] What would become an annual ritual of acrimonious Conservative opposition to any renewal of sanctions had begun.

As Christmas 1965 approached goodwill messages to Rhodesia's prime minister began appearing in *The Times* classifieds. Smith's noisiest British parliamentary backers were the Monday Club members led by Lord Salisbury. They defied the Conservative Party Whip and opposed any imposition of sanctions. Salisbury had told the Conservative Party conference a month before UDI that white Rhodesians deserved credit for bringing health, hygiene, and 'British ideas of peace and justice' to a backward land. Labour's support for majority rule was unethical and politically self-defeating, the abandonment of a British ethnic community that had built a thriving African economy. This was a view echoed in the editorial columns of the *Daily Express*.[103] The gift selected by another group of Smith's British supporters to show solidarity with the rebellious premier was a painting of two Spitfires taking off at dawn. Playing on 'Good Old Smithy's' reputation as a heroic patriot, the evocation of wartime glories carried a powerful subliminal message: 'that the betrayal of white Rhodesia provided yet another distressing example of how a powerful nation, triumphant in war, had become abject, compromised and defeated in peace'.[104]

Until its closure in 1969, Rhodesia House, the former home of the British Medical Association at 429 The Strand, symbolized the limbo in which Smith's UDI regime existed and the reluctance of Wilson's government to act decisively against it. Denied the status of a high commission, Rhodesia House remained open despite virulent media criticism and periodic 'sit-in' occupations by student protestors from the nearby London School of Economics. Time and again Whitehall officials carpeted Sydney Brice, the senior figure at Rhodesia House, for breaches of diplomatic protocol. These ranged from flying the illegal UDI regime flag to collusion in espionage. Still Rhodesia House survived; an embarrassing bricks and mortar reminder of sanctions' failure to bring down the Smith regime.[105]

Back in Rhodesia attitudes hardened as sanctions pushed the RF government closer to its regional allies, Pretoria's apartheid defenders and Portuguese-ruled Angola and Mozambique. Significantly, in the years after UDI the 103,000 settlers who emigrated were outnumbered by 127,000 new arrivals, mostly from South Africa. White support for the RF increased as a result, despite the turnover in the settler population. Among Smith's most fervent backers were Rhodesian housewives for whom the colony's Britishness was axiomatic. Although the security of white land tenure, guaranteed by legislation passed in the early 1930s and reaffirmed by the Land Tenure Act in 1969, was central to settler politics, by the start of the 1970s only seven per cent of whites worked in agriculture, giving the lie to the Algeria-style myth of the pioneer farmer. Far more were in white-collar employment or directly employed by the security forces. White Rhodesia may have fought a bush war, but most of its fighters came from the suburbs of Salisbury and Bulawayo.[106]

The sense that these settlers were closer to conservative 'middle England' than to Kenya's privileged Happy Valley set or the unapologetic racists of South Africa was even reflected in the pages of *The Guardian*, which, despite its progressive reputation, reported with only the faintest trace of irony about the defining features of Rhodesia's white suburbanites: 'there are no beatniks, and people dress up to go to the cinema (where they will certainly not see a French film)'.[107] Perhaps the irony lay elsewhere. Parisian movies may not have been to Rhodesian taste, but numerous French firms, notably in the petro-chemical sector, made hay, busting Britain's sanctions regime by diverting banned exports via a dependable, shockingly corrupt French client-state, Omar Bongo's Gabon.[108]

Unwilling to use force to get Smith out and aware that a sanctions regime would take time to bite, Wilson's government had little choice but to negotiate even after the UDI breakdown. Having aligned fellow Commonwealth members behind them, in late September 1966 Labour ministers resumed their approaches to the Smith regime through gritted teeth. The new Commonwealth Secretary Bert Bowden, like Smith a wartime airman, twice visited the Rhodesian capital in an effort to kick-start dialogue. During Bowden's first trip, in late September, the Salisbury government denied him access to opposition politicians, including the leader of the Zimbabwe African People's Union (ZAPU) Joshua Nkomo and Ndabaningi Sithole, founder of the Zimbabwe African National Union (ZANU), the party led, after independence, by Robert Mugabe. According to Wilson, 'At the end of the visit Bert Bowden and Mr Smith managed to agree on one thing: a statement listing the areas of disagreement. It was almost total.'[109] Bowden's follow-up visit in November looked to be going worse. He and Smith 'glowered' at one another during two fractious—and fruitless—encounters on 25 November. Only when the Governor Sir Humphrey Gibbs brokered another meeting between them did Smith concede that he might be willing to resume 'constitutional rule'—meaning, in practice, the renunciation of UDI. The way was suddenly open for face-to-face talks—or, as Wilson later put it, 'a direct confrontation'—between the opposing heads of government.[110]

Wilson and Defence Secretary Healey resolved to hold this meeting aboard a Royal Naval vessel. They considered three alternative island venues: Cyprus, Malta, or Gibraltar. The cruiser HMS *Tiger*, docked in Casablanca on a goodwill visit, swung the decision Gibraltar's way. Seeing the opportunity for a once-only deal, Wilson insisted that Smith should come equipped with plenipotentiary powers. With the agreement of the Cabinet's Rhodesia Committee, and reassured by Labour's Chief Whip that any backbench rebellion against a settlement could be contained, Wilson, Bowden, and

Attorney-General Sir Elwin Jones flew down to Gibraltar to be met by a winter gale. Negotiations with Smith's team began early on the morning of 1 December 1966. Threatening more stringent UN sanctions, Wilson pressed Smith to abandon UDI and hold an early general election. A Royal Commission would, meanwhile, submit recommendations on a new Rhodesian constitution. Its proposals would require acceptance by 'the Rhodesian people as a whole'. Nudging Smith towards elections, an agreed transfer of power, and eventual majority rule, the British prime minister further proposed that, in the short term, the Rhodesian leader reshuffle his Cabinet. The British team produced a list of suitable 'moderates' whose presence in government might dilute RF influence, thereby affording Smith greater room for manoeuvre. At first, the Rhodesian premier seemed overwhelmed. Wilson's proposals, coming thick, fast, and fully formulated, were hard to challenge and, for a while, Smith looked close to caving in. In the end, however, he insisted that his hard-line government colleagues in Salisbury must be consulted. This was tantamount to rejection. 'The rats', as Wilson put it, would get at their man.[111]

He was right. 1967 was remarkable for the absence of any significant movement in the Rhodesian problem. Perhaps inevitably, a problem without much prospect of resolution moved down the list of the Wilson government's priorities. Rhodesia was neither Britain's principal economic difficulty nor its major strategic concern. Financial affairs were dominated by 1967's devaluation crisis. International affairs were consumed by more pressing issues, among them the resumption of efforts to join the EEC, the fallout from the Arab-Israeli Six Day War, civil war in Nigeria, and the advancement of plans to pull back British forces from east of the Suez Canal.[112] Rhodesia's defiance only hardened in the years that followed. In early March 1968 Smith spurned global appeals for clemency, authorizing the hanging of three black Rhodesians convicted of murder, James Dhlamini, Victor Mlambo, and Duly Shadrack.[113] The executions prompted the UN to introduce mandatory sanctions against Rhodesia on 29 May.

Few now expected that British negotiators or British bullets could secure a favourable outcome for Rhodesia's black majority. Wilson, though, made a final bid to break the deadlock, ignoring his Cabinet colleagues' scepticism. Over five days in mid October 1968 he renewed his face-to-face talks with Smith aboard another Gibraltar-docked warship, HMS *Fearless*. Prepared to leave the UDI regime in place during a lengthy 'transitional period' before the eventual introduction of democracy to Rhodesia, Wilson came perilously close to abandoning the moral high ground that was the principal asset left to a British government confounded by the intransigence of Rhodesia's settlers. Albeit otherwise than in Algeria, the problems caused by the privileged position of a white European minority within another African dependency defied peaceful solution.

Conclusion

This chapter began by reflecting on how British observers interpreted Algeria's violent colonial meltdown. An obvious contradiction dogged the resultant British assessments of the conflict's dynamics. All conceded that the Algerian War, the most traumatic of empire's endgames, was no longer being played by French rules. Yet most looked to France, its constitutional system, its governments, its military, its cultural values, and its changing societal concerns for explanations of what was happening. Few evaluated Algerian socio-economic conditions, nationalist demands, and the progress of the ALN's rural insurgency on their own terms. Tellingly, this metropolitan bias in British evaluation of France's fight or flight alternatives still tilted towards acknowledgement that the FLN was the future. The transition was encapsulated by the September 1961 decision to invite FLN representative Mohamed Kellou to address an unlikely audience: the Conservative Party Conference in Brighton. Furious French protests provoked a last-minute withdrawal of the invitation, but the point had been made.[114]

Decolonization was a cataclysm for Algerians, European and Muslim alike; far less so for a French public fatigued by the conflict's slow progress towards negotiated withdrawal. President de Gaulle not only read this public mood, he shared it. The supreme irony of the May crisis was that the presumed emotional connections between de Gaulle, the settler *ultras*, and their army heroes never existed. Sceptical about republican ideas of ever-closer cultural union, the General was dismissive of the integrationism to which his political predecessors were attached. Crudely put, de Gaulle was never persuaded that Algerians could or should be made French. As he told his Minister of Information Alain Peyrefitte in October 1959, weeks after his call for Algerian self-determination,

> We have premised our colonization, since the beginning, on the principle of assimilation. We pretended to turn negroes [*nègres*] into good Frenchmen. We had them recite 'The Gauls were our ancestors' [*Nos ancestres les Gaulois*] ... [That]

was not very bright. That is why our decolonization is so much more difficult
than that of the English. They always admitted that there were differences
between races and cultures.[115]

De Gaulle's willingness to confront the decolonization dilemma also pointed
to deeper shifts in French military and scientific culture. As historian Dominique Pestre suggests, long-term involvement in colonial wars where conventional equipment predominated caused France to fall behind the United
States in developing new military technology. Culturally, too, matters scientific caught the public imagination less than social and philosophical questions, not least the ethical issues surrounding the Algerian conflict. De
Gaulle broke the mould. His abandonment of colonial war was tied to his
embrace of nuclear technology and the promotion of scientific innovation
in France's private and university sectors.[116]

Asked in the early 1990s to reflect on their hasty departures from Algeria
some thirty years earlier, numerous elderly *pieds noirs* still saw themselves as
'exiled' in a France that had little time for their stories of colonial dispossession. The exodus from Algeria of approximately 600,000 settlers between
January and August 1962 was largely unplanned and commensurately chaotic. The French authorities were reluctant to accept so many returnees and
even reduced ferry services during the spring months in a bid to stem the
inflow. Little wonder that so many of Algeria's *pieds noirs* struggled to comprehend what had befallen them. To the shock of Algerian dispossession was
added a profound sense of cultural alienation from a mother country that
few recognized and in which most felt unwelcome. These were sentiments
amplified among the families of Muslim *harkis*, thousands of whom were
forced out of their homeland at independence. Trapped on the wrong side of
history, these Algerian loyalists faced social invisibility and economic ghet-
toization in mainland France. Viewing these experiences at a fifty-year distance one can see that the end of French Algeria triggered the most
destabilizing and traumatic of the many population 'refluxes' or return migrations of 'colonials'—whether settlers and officials or policemen and paramilitary auxiliaries—that accompanied European decolonization.

But the Algerian exodus was untypical. For the most part, European
return migration was relatively peaceful. Ironically, the very absence of
comparable mass evictions from British colonial dependencies has perhaps
helped conceal the scale of departures, the great majority of which were
more or less voluntary. One researcher has identified 328,080 'whites' in
Britain listed under the 1991 census as having been born in former colonial

territories.[117] The root causes of the eviction of white Rhodesian farmers from independent Zimbabwe at the behest of Robert Mugabe's regime might lie in the UDI era, but the fact remains that there was nothing in the British experience of 1960s decolonization that matched France's tumultuous endgames in Algeria.

13

New Dawn:
After Fight or Flight

In February 1991 Georges Boudarel, a Paris University professor, became the unwilling catalyst for a vitriolic media debate in France. At issue was the rectitude, ethical or otherwise, of fight or flight strategies. To say that Boudarel was an unusual case is an understatement. A one-time seminary student from the southern French city of St-Étienne, he lost his faith as a young man. Boudarel, like many of his wartime generation, turned instead to Communism. A teaching post in post-war Saigon reinforced his ideological conviction. Soon his commitment became so strong that he decided to work for the Vietminh. His devotion to Marxist anti-colonialism carried him northward where, in 1950, he took charge of propaganda at one of the Vietminh's notorious POW camps. It was in the prosaically-named 'Camp 113' that Boudarel allegedly combined Communist indoctrination with the maltreatment of disease-ridden French military prisoners. Forty years later, it was a handful of these former inmates who denounced him.[1] Their accusations were serious enough for Boudarel to be charged with 'crimes against humanity'.[2] In the event, the case never made it to court. But the 'Boudarel affair' did precipitate the professor's early retirement from his university post ten months after the claims against him were made.

Coming almost a century after the infamous trial of Captain Alfred Dreyfus, this new 'affair' provoked almost 300 articles in the French press. Some were predictable. Right-wing newspapers, including the broadsheet *Le Figaro*, vilified Boudarel. They traced a moral equivalence between his actions and those of René Bousquet, Paul Touvier, and Maurice Papon, former servants of the Vichy regime whose dark wartime pasts finally caught up with them in another series of trial proceedings for crimes against humanity belatedly launched in the 1990s.[3] But others on the French right, including the blunt-speaking Minister François Léotard, denounced the 'lynch-mob' mentality that prevailed among Boudarel's accusers. Léotard was clearly fascinated by the ethical choices that Boudarel had faced forty years earlier. How could a once patriotic Frenchman be transformed into a fanatical prison overseer for an anti-colonial movement? Did this place Boudarel on the right side or the wrong side of history? Most on the French liberal left concurred that, while Boudarel's support for the Vietminh's fight against France was, in hindsight, defensible, his participation in the abuse of French captives was not. Boudarel, then, was not a traitor, but his actions at Camp 113 were unjustifiably cruel. France, it seemed, was still unsure when or if fight or flight made sense and for whom.

Several decades having elapsed since the culmination of British and French fights and flights from Africa, the Boudarel affair, itself more than twenty years past, suggests that the legitimacy of decolonization could still be bitterly contested. Is this still the case? To conclude the book, this last chapter tries to answer this basic question. It does so in several ways. One is by connecting the circumstances in which empire was ended with the evolution of post-colonial relationships between newly-independent nations and their former imperial masters. Another is by asking what impact the increasingly multi-cultural composition of the populations of Britain and France has had on attitudes to empire. Finally, the chapter revisits the book's central propositions: that ending empire is better understood comparatively and that ideas of 'fight or flight' provide a useful basis for comparison. The end of empire, in other words, was inherently transnational insofar as it collapsed the boundaries between the imperial mother country and its colonies just as it did between rulers and ruled, between citizens and subjects. Furthermore, the basic similarity in the colonial choices confronting Britain and France also tied imperial policy-makers and publics on both sides of the English Channel together, their successes or failures reverberating through one another's empires time and again.

In recent years three interpretational strands have been prominent in historians' assessments of British and French imperial pasts and the conflicts that ended colonial rule. The first concentrates on the politics and economics of the imperial mother-country as well as the changing attitudes towards empire among its people. In this way of thinking, especially popular among social and cultural historians, Britain's nineteenth and twentieth centuries (as, indeed, France's) occupy the same analytical field as that of their empires. British, French, and colonial histories, it is argued, are part of a single whole, interdependent and mutually constituted.[4] A second, quite contrary strand sticks doggedly to the opposite view. Broadly, it suggests either that colonial peoples liberated themselves or that changing colonial conditions made it impossible for the imperial power to cling on. Implicit here is the notion that, while metropolitan and colonial histories overlapped, the story of decolonization must be approached and understood within colonial territory first and foremost. Metropolitan and colonial histories may be intertwined but they were dominated by struggle, not shared experience. Simply put, the history of decolonization is African or Asian first, European second.[5] A third strand of interpretation steers a different course entirely. It relegates tired European imperial nations and their restive colonial subjects almost to the role of observers of their own fate, and focuses instead on the wider global setting in which decolonization took place. This line of reasoning identifies Cold War pressures, capital flows, and the inexorable spread of 'proxy wars' pitting East against West throughout much of Southeast Asia and Africa to explain why the British and French empires collapsed at much the same time. Here, the end of empire becomes a sub-plot in a bigger story of international competition, the disintegrative effects of world war, and the inexorable rise of mutually hostile superpowers.[6]

Each of these viewpoints has something to commend it. It is surely impossible to write a meaningful history of the British or French empires without acknowledging the interdependence of change at the metropolitan centre and the colonial frontier. Could British or French 'declinism' be understood without some sense of the fate of their empires? It seems equally apparent that imperial episodes which might have seemed marginal to the inhabitants of Birmingham or Bordeaux could be critical to those of Bombay or Bamako. People's ideas of political geography inevitably reflected their own sense of place. What for some were distant or peripheral concerns were imminently local to others. Yet all took place within the frameworks of empire, of trade links or family ties, of transnational and international connections, which bound European and colonial lives together for most of the twentieth century. Finally, there can be no denying that, in comparative terms, Britain and France were lesser players on the global stage of Cold War than they had been during the preceding forty years of European bloodletting that began in the early 1900s.

The myths of 'managed decolonization' or orderly 'transfers of power' that once predominated in imperial history—and, even more so in the first official accounts of the process—are also untenable. A single example illustrates the point. In December 1958 General de Gaulle's new presidential administration distributed thousands of brochures about France's colonial achievements to American government offices, universities, and media outlets. 'A Decade of Progress' combined glossy photographs of hydro-electric plants, housing projects and educational facilities with a text packed with figures and charts that drew unflattering comparisons between meagre British colonial spending and the larger share of French national income invested in empire. The brochures caused little complaint in London, aside from some mild Colonial Office huffing about unreliable French statistics.[7] In hindsight, the real significance of the 'Decade of Progress' material was its American target audience. This pointed to a simple but profound transformation: by the late 1950s opinion-makers inside the Washington, DC beltway, the UN building in New York, and within nearby press offices in Manhattan were all vital actors in the unfolding drama of decolonization. Alongside the bullets and bombings of colonial wars, subtler weapons were deployed: words and images, propaganda and diplomatic persuasion, claim and counter-claim in the world's press. This was a war of rhetoric, of pithy comments, and searing imagery. Its mounting significance highlighted the fact that colonial conflicts were less about controlling territory than about controlling populations and swaying international opinion.

The quickening pace of imperial collapse was transforming the grand strategies of the Cold War protagonists.[8] New ideas of individualized human rights and growing transnational revulsion at the 'claimed ethnic superiority' integral to colonialism made hierarchical systems of imperial domination harder to defend physically, intellectually, and morally.[9] Some of the decade's most famous pronouncements on decolonization emanated from unexpected sources—not just Washington, Moscow, or Peking, but Tehran, Guatemala City, Pyongyang, and Havana. Anti-colonialist luminaries such as Kwame Nkrumah and Frantz Fanon rode this wave of mounting global interest, their views and writings avidly studied by African American civil rights activists and other supporters of protest movements determined to rid the world of racial inequality.[10] The emergence of a firmly anti-colonial Non-Aligned Movement and the prominence of colonial disputes within the UN General Assembly add lustre to this picture of a multi-polar international system in which rights politics played a critical role.[11] But this 'internationalization of decolonization' also demonstrated two trends sometimes overlooked in studies of empire after 1945. One is that non-governmental actors—charity workers and human rights groups, churchmen and women, artists and intellectuals, among others—did just as much to convince international opinion of the bankruptcy of colonial rule. The other is that direct foreign interventions, whether diplomatic, military or economic, in British or French colonial affairs could be counter-productive. Heightened foreign involvement in colonial crises sometimes encouraged imperial powers to resist more tenaciously when negotiated withdrawal—flight—was otherwise unavoidable.

This observation has its limits. International criticism contributed to British exasperation with the Palestine Mandate for example. And direct foreign involvement escalated the Indochina War. Yet it seems equally obvi-ous that a Cyprus settlement would have been impossible without the active participation of the Greek and Turkish governments. Perhaps, then, a safer 'general rule' is that the tendency among colonial authorities and settler communities to dig their heels in deeper when faced with unwanted for-eign involvement only intensified nationalist efforts to internationalize their struggles for freedom. In much of Africa and Southeast Asia the result was countervailing pressure, louder calls from the international community for negotiated solutions on the one hand and stronger imperialist resolve to resist decolonization on the other.

Sometimes it was local demands for change that registered most: think of the Vietnamese revolution in 1945 or the Gold Coast protests of 1948 for instance. At other times, disenchantment within Britain or France with seemingly unending imperial conflicts had greater impact; perhaps Palestine and Algeria provide the most striking cases here. The story of British and French decolonization therefore emerges as being more complex than a straightforward narrative of decline and resentful withdrawal in which once powerful imperial nations succumbed to resilient colonial opponents and insistent international pressure.[12] Indeed, the harder task is not to explain why the British and French empires disintegrated but, rather, to account for the enduring belief among their supporters that imperial possessions could—and should—be retained. It is this central dilemma that, I think, justifies the focus on alternate strategies of fight or flight.[13] To make the case more clearly, let's remind ourselves about the politics of post-war France.

In the immediate post-war years, French society, struggling to come to terms with the traumas of defeat and occupation, turned sharply to the left. This was a nation that would define its political identity afresh in terms of the republican troika of *liberté, égalité*, and *fraternité*, creating a participatory democracy to match. Yet between 1945 and 1954 France also launched the two bloodiest colonial wars of the twentieth century, first in Vietnam, then in Algeria. A spirit of metropolitan reform, a commitment to European renewal, and a thirst for economic modernization co-existed alongside a profound intransigence in colonial affairs.[14] So much so that post-war French governments took their determination to keep the overseas empire intact to the point of self-destruction. The stresses induced by colonial fights precipitated the Fourth Republic's collapse in 1958. More liberal at home than either its predecessors or its successors, the immediate post-war French regime was also shockingly illiberal overseas. Its political elites, capable of far-sighted decision-making and selfless gestures in European affairs— witness the French hand guiding the process of European integration and the settlement of Franco-German rivalries—proved incapable of similar benevolence in colonial matters.

This was not crude racism, inveterate Eurocentrism, or misplaced optimism about the durability of empire. It was, instead, the product of the very paradox that was the Fourth Republic: a political system in which governments were direct emanations of parliament and completely dependent on it. This, then, was a regime trapped by its elaborate constitutional architecture and the promises made by its leading political groups to preserve France's imperial power. For historians of French political history, the point becomes more poignant still when we recall that 1958 would also see the parties of left and centre cast into the political wilderness for the next quarter-century. In this sense, only François Mitterrand's presidential election victory in May 1981 marked the Left's belated return from the long, cold winter of decolonization.

Algeria, the French empire's core territory, was always the place where fight or flight alternatives would be most sorely tested. So much so that some British observers concluded that France's colonial problems were incomparable with Britain's lesser imperial difficulties. An 'inter-departmental study group', established after the Constantine massacres of August 1955 and coordinated by the Foreign Office to review French actions in North Africa, certainly thought so. The experts identified rapid population growth, the strengthening appeal of political Islam, settler intransigence, and, above all, French governmental indecision as barriers to progress in Algeria. But the study group's deliberations do not seem to have figured in Cabinet-level discussion.[15] Ministers and their secretarial advisers focused on other observed realities entirely. First among these was the belief that the constitutional malfunctions and political immobility thought to be endemic in post-war French—and French colonial—politics were uniquely francophone phenomena. The comforting conclusion, from a

British imperial perspective, was that 'it can't happen here'. Further solace
came from the calculation that, while the British public's interest in empire
might be waning—indeed, perhaps because of it—the country was less divided
over issues of colonial repression. If 1950s cinema newsreels and media coverage are any guide to domestic opinion, there was something of a British 'siege
mentality' about an empire still holding but under threat, the dangers facing
it translated into human terms by rare but sensational killings of Britons
overseas.[16]

Decolonization, then, had not divided British society to the extent that
it had the French. But empire still had its defenders, and some colonial
misdeeds were, as yet, only dimly understood. Certain long-term trends
were plain. British public, press, and parliamentary attitudes to the costs of
white minority rule were changing, settler privilege becoming a source of
embarrassment for many. At the high political level, the Suez crisis taught
the Conservative Party leadership the dangers of taking public opinion for
granted in imperial affairs. Other instances of colonial wrongdoing, from
Malaya's Batang Kali massacre to the thousand-plus hangings of Mau Mau
detainees, often after sham trials, registered less, failing to dent popular
perceptions of British fairness and minimum force solutions pursued from
the late 1940s onwards.

Britain's most reactionary colonial settlers were also more remote and
less embattled than their European cousins in Algeria. The troublesome
colons, after all, were a mere hop across the Mediterranean from mainland
France. That is not to minimize either the iniquities of white rule in eastern
or southern Africa or the conflicts it generated. It is, rather, to point out that
only a minority on the outer fringes of British politics were willing to go
to the wall to conserve settler society in the way that their French counterparts did in defence of *Algérie française*. Nor did Kenya's white highlands or
Rhodesia's prim settler suburbs exercise the emotional hold over the British
military that drove some French officers into their fatal alliance with the
colons to defend the farmlands of the Mitidja plain and the sun-kissed apartments of Algiers.[17] There was no need to go to such extremes. After independence, Kenya's settlers did not flee *en masse*. Those who did leave were
soon replaced by new white immigrants.[18] White Rhodesians, meanwhile,
remained all too firmly in the political driving seat.

Lest we conclude too easily that Britain was unlikely by the late 1950s to
take the French route to colonial war and Algeria-style repression, two final
points should give us pause for thought. One is that by the time these 1950s

perspectives crystallized, inter-communal blood-letting and population transfers far in excess of French imperial proportions had occurred in Britain's very recent colonial past. The end of the Palestine mandate and, above all, the partition of India were pull-outs in which the requirements of British political expediency registered above the needs of local civilian populations. The grim fate of displaced Palestinians and millions of Punjabi and Bengali refugees could, of course, be viewed as the result of simmering communal conflicts boiling over, as products of the absence of imperial authority not its presence. But British colonialism with its imposition of particular territorial boundaries, ethnic hierarchies, and differential political and social rights, had generally made matters worse, not better.

The ensuing disorder had been predicted by many inside and outside British and colonial government circles in London, Jerusalem, and Delhi. In each case, partition unleashed mass killings, forced removal of particular ethno-religious groups, and attendant social upheaval that outstripped even the egregious violence of the Madagascar rebellion or the early stages of the Indochina War. The fact that these dreadful events were temporally compressed into the immediate post-war period diminishes neither the horrors involved nor their enduring legacies. What is remarkable is the bold-as-brass manner in which British government pronouncements subsumed this first wave of chaotic withdrawals within a narrative of negotiated decolonization—of orderly flight—that skated over its calamities.[19] The second point to note is that the Conservative and Labour governments of the 1950s and 1960s looked on Algerian colonial violence, its settler dimension especially, not merely as a road not taken, but as a path best avoided, no matter what. The prospect of British Crown forces sucked into a conflict that pitched majority rule against settler rights was not outlandish. Uppermost among the conclusions drawn from Algeria was the redoubled conviction that nothing comparable should be allowed to develop in anglophone southern Africa.

Whether due to violent social breakdown or not, colonial withdrawals also triggered huge population movements and altered long-established economic and cultural relationships within and between countries and communities. By 1949 the extent of the refugee crises within former British territories in the Middle East and the Indian subcontinent rivalled those left in the aftermath of the Second World War in Europe in terms of sheer numerical scale.[20] Thousands of Britons also left their erstwhile Indian homes, albeit in less obviously traumatic circumstances. Once the public face of imperial rule, many of these Raj returnees faced uncertain futures and social invisibility in post-war Britain.[21] From communal displacement and expanding proxy wars to post-colonial returns and voluntary migration, the end of empire changed the points of contact between first world and third.

Does it make sense to explain these shifts in terms of globalization? Did decolonization, which, after all, signified the collapse of particular forms of global organization, promote different models of social, cultural, and market integration? Various post-colonial federations were attempted, notably in the Arab world (the United Arab Republic) and in West Africa (the Mali Federation). But none lasted long.[22] Indeed, the contestation so frequently a feature of the end of empire suggests a disintegrative process. After their partition, commercial exchanges and human traffic between India and Pakistan soon withered. So did that between North and South Vietnam. But in destroying the old certainties of imperial connection, decolonization might also be viewed as merely one facet in the steady advance of dollar capitalism, arguably a phenomenon of greater significance in commodity and capital markets than changes of imperial flag. The loss of empire by Britain and France was, in this sense, symptomatic of what in hindsight appears to have been an American century, a key element of which was—and is—the allure of affluent consumerism.[23] One of the reasons why colonial peoples rejected their European rulers was because they wanted more of the prosperity celebrated in western popular culture. Hence, an apparent paradox: thanks to colonial immigration Britain and France became more multi-ethnic places at the same time as they faced mounting anti-colonial pressures. Inward post-war migration from dependent territories suggested that the desire for better living standards trumped everything else, pointing the way towards the economic convergence between metropolitan and formerly colonial societies integral to globalization.

To redress the country's post-war labour shortage, the 1948 British Nationality Act, in force until 1962, allowed colonial and former colonial subjects to settle and work in Britain without restriction. More than 200,000 did so, including approximately 115,000 West Indians and 55,000 from India and Pakistan. Remarkably perhaps, very few responded to the day-to-day discrimination, the poor housing, and institutional racism they confronted by returning to their places of birth.[24] Sex, marriage, even socializing across post-war Britain's new ethnic divides remained limited, low-level racial violence sadly commonplace. Even so, the gradual absorption of empire immigrants, defined by Roy Jenkins, Labour's Home Secretary, in the mid 1960s as 'multiculturalism' continued, although the more expansive sense of British national identity implied by the term was nascent at best. Old imperial habits, particularly the tendency to hierarchize ethnicity and condemn inter-race relationships, gave the lie to official rhetoric proclaiming the emergence of a more tolerant, multi-ethnic and multi-faith Britain.[25] Meanwhile, throughout the same years white Europeans still departed in their thousands—and in the British and Portuguese cases, in their hundreds of thousands—for countries that retained imperial connections to the homeland.[26] The Sterling Area and the Treaty of Rome's annex agreements for francophone Africa also sustained high levels of economic interdependence. Malaya, for instance, stuck to its colonial-era currency board system well into the 1960s. Former members of the French African Community in West and Central Africa maintained close monetary links with France thanks to the linkage of the franc CFA with its metropolitan counterpart.[27] Conversely, the pace of sterling's 1960s decline as a reserve currency only added to the attractions of enhanced access to European markets promised by EEC membership, itself a more realistic alternative than any revival of older empire trade links.[28]

In France, too, inward migration in the immediate aftermath of decolonization was dominated by immigrants from a lost empire.[29] As in Britain, where issues of race and racism became prominent in electoral politics from 1964 onwards, so, too, France's changing immigration patterns provoked ugly statements and some remarkable ideological U-turns.[30] What began as *nostalgérie*, a lament among the former supporters of *Algérie française* for de Gaulle's betrayal of a worthy cause, descended into a racist xenophobia fixated on a North African immigrant 'invasion' of France. Its dangers were supposedly personified by the sexually-predatory criminality of young Algerian men. The argument, crudely expressed in violently homophobic terms that fed on orientalist stereotypes of Arab sexuality, was reducible to this: an emasculated France had become the victim of its loss of imperial will; Algerian immigrants were screwing France and its upstanding citizens. Gratuitously offensive, this theme of racial and sexual inversion in the upside-down post-colonial world in which France found itself became a stock-in-trade of defamatory writings and inflammatory speeches by ultra-rightists, many of whom found succour in Jean-Marie Le Pen's Front National.[31] In this sense, one legacy of France's bitterest colonial fight was a degradation of right-wing politics exemplified by a xenophobia which, for a disenchanted sizeable minority, was more virulent than its colonial antecedents.[32] Little wonder, perhaps, that colonial patterns of segregation and controlled access to housing and public space were recreated in the soulless apartment blocks of the Paris *banlieues*. Their largely immigrant population remained physically and culturally invisible to some of the capital's wealthier residents, a phenomenon one analyst describes as a 'proximity of extremes'. Invisible that is until the November 2005 rioting over quintessentially colonial-style grievances—discriminations in housing, in the employment market, in policing, in access to citizenship.[33]

The polarizing politics of immigration is one indicator that the consequences of decolonization are still playing out in British and French political life.[34] So may we consider the end of empire definitively finished? In

Figure 18. A family waits in the designated area at Orly Airport to return to Algeria after independence in July 1962. It was the reverse traffic of predominantly young male Algerian workers that soon antagonized the French hard right.

much of francophone Africa below the Sahara where relatively little armed conflict preceded self-rule, surreptitious French political, economic, and strategic predominance subsisted well into the 1970s. Its preservation was ensured by Jacques Foccart's powerful coterie of Africa specialists with backdoor access to the Elysée Palace, an influence matched by their access to French Africa's 'big men' in the first generation after formal independence.[35] Hence, an uncomfortable fact: violence tended to secure fuller independence than did negotiation and cosy relationships with favoured client rulers. What John Horne terms 'the rituals of defeat' were usually conducted most fervently in those places where the violence of decolonization was most extreme— military parades and formal commemorations on the one hand, population transfers, and bloody purges against colonial 'collaborators' on the other.

The link between national identity and anti-colonial struggle was—and is—understandably prominent in those societies where the killing, suffering, and loss incurred in the throes of decolonization was greatest.[36] Yet, even in former colonies where the transition to self-government is celebrated as a triumph of non-violent engagement, independent statehood was sometimes matched by imposition of a narrative of heroic resistance, an officially-sanctioned historical memory of national liberation. As Richard Rathbone, historian of modern Ghana, reminds us,

> The modern historiography of Africa has tended to be enraptured, utterly understandably, by the stirring epics of the 'nationalist struggle'. It is almost as if Independence Day constituted the End of History. Published modern West African history is, in many respects, the history of nationalism and successful nationalists... Many Ghanaians remember a different, less triumphal history; they remember instead a history of brutal political competition in the countryside... That story is more concerned with local struggles for power. Those struggles were partly about the resolution of the old question of 'who governs'? But they were also complex struggles about the nature of the post-colonial state.[37]

Rathbone is surely right about the Ghanaian, and several other African, cases. But what about in the former imperial mother-countries: inside France and Britain? How was colonial withdrawal viewed by these domestic audiences? Did they interpret colonial pull-outs as defeats, heroic or otherwise? Or was decolonization looked on more favourably?

Colonial fights, like wars of any sort, were never fair, never demanding of equivalent involvement or sacrifice by all of those in whose name they were fought. This asymmetry, as much evident in levels of emotional commitment as in matters of national mobilization, was particularly stark in wars of decolonization. Take the language employed. What were 'disorders' or 'insurgencies' in western parlance involved life or death choices for those who experienced them in Africa and Asia. Yet some—think Madagascar in the French case, perhaps involvement in the Malaysian–Indonesian Konfrontasi in the British case—passed almost unnoticed 'back home'. We know that the use of diplomatic and legal formulae to mask the reality of wars of decolonization was substantially driven by the absolute French and British requirement to limit foreign oversight. No imperial power welcomed UN scrutiny of their actions or the presence of aid agencies among populations that were displaced by fighting. But this language of obfuscation has tended to persist. It is only in the past twenty years that the Algerian conflict and Mau Mau have acquired the status of 'wars'. Madagascar, Malaya, and other conflicts remain stuck with lesser labels—rebellion or emergency—which, consciously or otherwise, diminish their severity and significance.

Historians, investigative journalists, and leading intellectuals, especially in France, have pointed to extra-judicial killing, systematic torture, mass internment, and other abuses as evidence of just how dirty decolonization's wars could be. Some have gone further, blaming the dismal human rights records of numerous post-colonial states on their former imperial rulers. Others have pinned responsibility on the nature of decolonization itself by suggesting that hasty, violent, or shambolic colonial withdrawals left a power vacuum filled by one-party regimes hostile to democratic inclusion.[38] Whatever their accuracy, the extent to which these accusations have altered French and British public engagement with their recent imperial past remains difficult to assess. The readiness of government and society in both countries to acknowledge the extent of colonial violence indicates a mixed record. In Britain, media interest in such events as the summary execution of Mau Mau suspects, security force rapes of Kikuyu women or the killings at Batang Kali sits uncomfortably with the enduring image of the British imperial soldier as hot, bothered, but restrained.[39] It is to be hoped that recent Foreign and Commonwealth Office releases of some 22,000 decolonization-related documents, apparently 'lost' hitherto, will present the opportunity for a more balanced evaluation of Britain's colonial misdeeds.[40]

In France, by contrast, the media furores and public debates have been more heated. *Le Monde*'s publication on 20 June 2000 of the searing account by former FLN militant Louisette Ighilahriz of her three months of physical, sexual, and psychological torture at the hands of Jacques Massu's 10th

Parachutist Division in Algiers in late 1957 provoked two years of intense controversy over the need to acknowledge the wrongs of the Algerian War. After years in which difficult Algerian memories were either interiorized or swept under capacious official carpets, big questions were at last being asked.[41] Should there be a formal state apology? Should decolonization feature in the school curriculum? Should the victims of the war be memorialized? If so, which victims? Although the soul-searching ran deep, official responses could still be troubling. On 5 December 2002 Jacques Chirac unveiled a national memorial to the Algerian conflict and the concurrent 'Combats' ('wars' was as problematic a word as ever) in Morocco and Tunisia. France's first computerized military monument, the names of some 23,000 soldiers and *harki* auxiliaries who died fighting for France scrolled down vertical LED screens running the length of the memorial columns.

No mention of Algerian victims, but at least a start. Yet, seven months later, on 5 July 2003, another unveiling took place. This one, in Marignane on Marseilles' outer fringe, was less official to be sure. A plaque to four OAS activists carries the inscription 'fighters who fell so that French Algeria

FIGURE 19. Paris monument to Algerian War dead.

might live' (*combattants tombés pour que vive l'Algérie française*). Among those commemorated were Roger Degueldre, leader of the OAS 'delta commandos' who murdered six school inspectors, and Jean-Marie Bastien-Thiry, organizer of the assassination attempts on de Gaulle at Pont-de-Seine and Petit-Clamart. Equally troubling, it took the threat of an academic boycott in 2005 before the Council of State advised President Chirac to withdraw a planned stipulation that French schoolchildren must be taught the 'positive role of the French colonial presence, notably in North Africa'.[42]

One explanation for the intensity of these history wars is that few colonial fights were definitively won or lost at identifiable places and times. The fall of Dien Bien Phu in May 1954, its anniversary celebrated at intervals by the Vietnamese Communist authorities ever since, was the exception, not the rule.

Elsewhere it was harder for people to process victory or defeat as a specific event, as a clean break offering new beginnings, rather than as an inconclusive process that settled nothing.[43] Officials in Kenya reported that Mau Mau was 'all but over' by the end of 1955. Yet emergency rule continued almost five years more. The Malayan Communists, too, were in almost incessant retreat from 1952. Surrender terms were laid down in September 1955. Two years later British aircraft peppered the Malayan jungle, not with bombs but with thirty-four million leaflets offering an amnesty-for-surrender deal to the few hundred guerrillas who remained at large.[44] Even so the 'Emergency' was not finally lifted until 1960.

Adding to the confusion was the fact that the ultimate outcome of a colonial fight could defy the balance of military forces that preceded it. Algeria's FLN emerged triumphant in March 1962. But ALN guerrilla units were wiped out or driven back by French army advances between 1959 and 1961. Even now, over fifty years later, the numbers of Algerian civilians killed by all sides remains something about which France and the FLN regime still in power in Algiers cannot agree.[45] All of this suggests that violent decolonization cannot be read through the prism of direct military confrontation alone. The FLN never ousted the French army. Nevertheless, it won the war by turning the tide of domestic and international opinion in its favour. Such victories were especially dangerous. Grounded in a combination of transnational activism and local terror, they were not militarily total. An undefeated colonial army felt betrayed. Colonial settlers felt unjustifiably abandoned. Both sentiments nurtured reactionary diehards who refused to bend to decisions that, they insisted, had no basis in countervailing facts 'on the ground'. The terrorism of French Algeria's OAS, of Rhodesia's 'bush wars' against Zimbabwean freedom fighters: these were violent refusals to accept the reality of irrevocable decolonization, a reality refuted by their continuing capacity to coerce in the name of white supremacy.

Other nearby conflicts originated, not in the denial of colonial freedom, but in the ossification of internal divisions in the final years of imperial rule. The 1960s closed with a conflict rooted in attempts to redistribute power within the preceding colonial regime. Nigeria's Biafra War began as a secessionist rebellion by the Igbo people of the country's south-east. Faced with pogroms and discrimination in Nigeria's predominantly Muslim northern belt, Igbos, according to their leader Emeka Ojukwu, were the ultimate victims of Britain's decision to weld Nigeria together as a federal, multi-ethnic state.[46] The curtain brought down on British colonial rule in October 1960 did not signify an end to the ethnic, cultural, and economic divisions between North and South entrenched over the previous fifty years. Nor did it alter Britain's abiding concern with wider regional stability and oil investment opportunities.[47] Nigeria's civil war ended in defeat for Biafra, famine across the south, and tens of thousands of civilian deaths, many of them children.[48] It reminds us that decolonization, for all its flag ceremonies and seemingly definite endpoints, left divisive legacies years after the colonial overlords went home.

The Biafra tragedy was exemplary in another way. The involvement of the former imperial power in this, and other developing world conflicts of the 1960s and 1970s, was more than tangential, but less than decisive. Still highly active and, on occasion, bluntly interventionist in sub-Saharan francophone Africa, France nonetheless avoided more fights than it picked. Starting with de Gaulle's 1964 proposal for the neutralization of Vietnam, French and British politicians could rightfully claim some wise initiatives. On both sides of the Channel, imperial world-weariness translated into polite scepticism about the competing modernist visions of America and the Soviet Union for the global 'south'. British and French policy-makers did not anticipate that swathes of Africa and Asia would suddenly flourish thanks to Kennedy's proclamation of a 'decade of development' or Khrushchev's endorsement of 'peaceful co-existence'.[49] The superpower antagonists, plus other ideological enthusiasts for proxy war—Castro's Cuba, Nasser's Egypt, and apartheid South Africa pre-eminent among them—became the principal backers of intra-state violence in the former colonial world.[50]

Perhaps less bruised by decolonization, the British did choose to defend
Malaysian independence against the irredentism of Indonesia's president
Sukarno.[51] But this proved a mercifully short-lived commitment. Indonesian expansionism ground to a halt in autumn 1965 as the army seized
power, massacring untold thousands of Indonesia's leftist opposition in the
process.[52] If Britain and Malaysia had a narrow escape, there was greater
design in Labour's decision to keep out of the other major Southeast Asian
conflagration. Harold Wilson's government spurned Lyndon Johnson's pleas
for greater British engagement in the Vietnam War, a shrewd decision well
worth the cost of vituperative White House condemnation.[53] As we saw in
the last chapter, Wilson's government was careful not to escalate its opposition to Ian Smith's Rhodesian regime to the point of violence and it also
extricated Britain from other imperial commitments east of Suez with relatively little bloodshed.[54] There was no appetite inside the Labour Party for
the maintenance of British bases on the Malaysian peninsula and in
Singapore, particularly after the latter was expelled from the Malaysian
Federation in August 1965. Left-wingers like Richard Crossman, Tony Benn,
and Barbara Castle disparaged the bases as remnants of a discredited
imperial past. More senior Ministers, worried about Britain's worsening
budgetary position, were determined to cut defence spending.[55] Hong
Kong, strategically located and a holder of large credit balances, was retained,
although this meant steering clear of potential clashes with Mao's China,
notably over issues of democratization.[56]

Last flights?

The Hong Kong lease aside, several factors pushed Harold Wilson's government to accelerate the rundown of British imperial defence commitments.[57]
With Britain's balance of payments crisis deepening to the point that sterling came under severe pressure in July 1966, an 'east of Suez' role was unaffordable.[58] Far from staving off a final decision, between April 1967 and
January 1968 Wilson's government brought the timetable for a final withdrawal forward to 1971. Reactions in Canberra, Wellington, and Washington
were predictably hostile. Ostensibly at least, the Minister of Defence Denis
Healey was willing to countenance the redeployment of British forces from
Southeast Asia to northern Australia, although he later admitted that this
proposal 'was all part of the bullshit of negotiations'. In late June 1967 an

exasperated Lyndon Johnson, mired in a widening Vietnam War, even accused Wilson, and the British more generally, of losing their senses.[59] If anything, 'official minds' in Whitehall were thinking with commendable clarity: Britain's decision to draw in its remaining imperial horns was long overdue.

The recent colonial past proved a more dubious guide when formulating British counter-terrorism policies closer to home. Strategies of population control, preventive detention, and internment applied in Malaya, Kenya, and Aden re-appeared, somewhat diluted, in Northern Ireland after 1969.[60] Were such practices transferable, let alone defensible? Their wealth of imperial experience did not prevent Britain's senior intelligence advisers from mis-reading the underlying causes of the Troubles.[61] More recent British actions in Northern Ireland are easier to fit within a pattern of conflict resolution. Indeed, the story of Britain's flight from empire has been dominated by images of voluntary withdrawal, pragmatic leaders choosing to give up on empire before losing it.

One reason why the decisions of leading politicians figure so strongly in histories of British decolonization is that the politicians themselves pro-vided the initial narrative for these events in their press interviews, memoirs and diaries.[62] Adept myth-makers, these policy-makers depicted colonial pull-outs as a mixture of avuncular benevolence and disappointment at the ingratitude of subject peoples.[63] Resultant accounts of individual colonial withdrawals follow a remarkably similar script. Once-implacable anti-colonial opponents, including the strongest of them all, India's Congress movement, are diverted from the road to conflict and coaxed into negotia-tion. While a dose of historical scepticism makes sense before swallowing such recollections, few of these accounts warped the facts beyond recogni-tion. Even British ministers reluctant to give imperial ground frequently did so once they were confronted with the stark reality of limited British resources and the dangers of escalating colonial disorder. Alan Lennox-Boyd's tenure at the Colonial Office between July 1954 and October 1959 coincided with Britain's most testing colonial crises. His gut response to human rights abuses in Kenya, Cyprus, and the Central African Federation was to back the authorities involved, accepting that harsher standards of disciplinary violence pervaded the colonial world. If Lennox-Boyd was no liberal, realism compelled him to accept reforms that diminished settler influence.[64] Colonial policy on his watch could be repressive—in the Kenyan case, sickeningly so—but, elsewhere, expediency prevailed.

This is not to minimize the extent of conflict over alternative strategies. Nor is it to imply that British negotiators retained the initiative as deals were done. Most often, talks were stimulated by some combination of three factors—economic imperatives, the threat or actuality of violence, and the changing strategic orientation of British international power. These three considerations, often itemized as costs or benefits, weighed into policy appreciations. Imperial attachments increasingly figured in the debit column at variance with other, more pressing aspirations including higher rates of economic growth, closer partnership with the USA, and membership of the EEC.[65]

The once critical Colonial Office 'hotline' between the Secretary of State and the Governor *in situ* lost relevance as wider regional pressures constrained governmental choices. What was expedient in Nyasaland, for instance, might spell danger in Southern Rhodesia.[66] The proliferation of political parties, trade unions, civil society organizations, and other lobby groups within individual colonies further complicated governmental efforts to regulate the pace of imperial change. To these changing political calculations we might add two cultural ones, neither of them amenable to precise measurement. The first was declining public engagement with empire affairs. This was itself a by-product of deeper cultural shifts including the growth of mass consumerism and a diminishing deference to authority and tradition in British society. The second was the usually-unexpressed, but widely-held view that it was morally right to call an end to the rigidities of colonialism. Liberal consciences were pricked by highly-publicized cases of brutality—the 1959 Hola massacre and the simultaneous state of emergency in Nyasaland for example. Shining a spotlight on how colonial rule was upheld in time of crisis did not reflect well on what 'being British' or doing things a 'British way' was supposed to mean.[67]

Understanding of decolonization was also bound up with generational clashes in Britain and France. For baby-boomers drawn to the emerging anti-capitalist, hedonistic 'counter-culture' imperial attachments were an unwelcome hangover of a more authoritarian, intolerant Europe, whose power to control and repress was now being challenged by those born during or soon after World War II.[68] The sixties counter-culture that culminated in the worldwide protest movements of 1968 proved less revolutionary than the anti-colonial heroes—Ho Chi Minh, Frantz Fanon and Che Guevara—who provided its pin-ups.[69] Even so, the identification between student radicals, New Left thinkers, and their anti-imperialist heroes confirms how quickly empire connections began to seem not merely old-fashioned, but faintly ridiculous.[70]

Occasionally, imperial nostalgia surfaced. Take, for example, this 1966 press tribute to Britain's career 'colonials', fondly reproduced in the Overseas Service Pensioners Association journal:

> *Many of the district commissioners and the other Colonial officers spent 30 or 40 years on a steamy island or in an arid shrubland village acting as doctor and priest, friend and marriage counsellor, and even father to their charges.*
>
> *They were far from well paid. Today some of them are eking out their pensions in humble guest houses in Cheltenham or Bournemouth. Yet what a rich consolation they have.*
>
> *For they can be certain that they did more for the Colonial peoples in one day than our stay-at-home progressives will accomplish in a lifetime.[71]*

It was not until the 1970s, however, that some ex-colonial officials, returnees, and their descendants made concerted efforts to counteract what they complained were uniformly negative media portrayals and scholarly accounts of imperial Britons. In 1974 Charles Allen, the son of a British civil servant in India, helped produce a hugely popular BBC Radio 4 series and accompanying book, *Plain Tales from the Raj*. Recalling his motives for doing so, he focused on the misrepresentation of those associated with running the British Empire—his father among them. Decried as accomplices in oppression, their hard work was ignored, their good intentions mocked.[72] The hardships of empire service—long family separations, the crushing boredom of remote postings, the poverty of countless 'poor whites' whose lives were anything but privileged; all of this was lost in the rush to condemn empire as not only misconceived but evil.[73]

Such harsh, emotive judgements surely contributed to the widespread belief among former 'colonials' that people 'back home' misunderstood them. The sense of being unappreciated and misconstrued also intensified feelings of longing for lifestyles irrevocably gone. For those born, raised, or simply immersed in Africa's white-settler colonies, nostalgia acquired the hybrid characteristics of the particular locale, its peoples, sights and smells, blended with the metropolitan standards that were more austerely upheld at one remove. *Pied-noir* returnees certainly pined for their lost colonial world. For many, their laments were sharpened by an inability to recapture the wealth and status they had enjoyed as settlers in Algeria.[74] The associated feelings of displacement and loss were surely felt more sharply still by the Algerian loyalist *harki* families forced to flee their homeland in the same post-independence rout. And, unlike their settler returnee equivalents, the *harkis* struggled to make their voices heard. Large numbers were consigned to remote, bleak resettlement centres in southern France. What was supposedly an emergency solution to a short-term housing problem became more or less permanent, providing the physical basis for the long-term marginalization of ex-*harki* communities from mainstream French society.[75]

These reflections suggest rather double-edged conclusions. One is that British and French responses to imminent decolonization caused lasting instability and suffering in some places, while limiting these consequences in others. While, in broad terms, the earlier that imperial authorities reconciled themselves to letting go, the less the resulting destabilization, some shocking exceptions to this general rule give us pause. Hasty, improvised withdrawals, especially if predicated on ethnic or religiously-based partitions of colonial territory, as in the Indian subcontinent and Palestine, triggered violence and intractable regional conflicts. An early and genuine willingness to negotiate was often the critical factor in limiting conflict at the close of empire. But the terms on which withdrawals were arranged, particularly the guarantees for minority groups or otherwise disadvantaged communities, could be equally important in limiting post-colonial disorder.

Ending empire also reverberated more widely, transforming the post-war international system as part of what Odd Arne Westad has dubbed the 'global' Cold War. Former colonies desperate to modernize their economies found the magnetic pull of foreign money and the ideological clutches of foreign backers hard to escape.[76] As the French sociologist Bernard Badie famously remarked, almost everything about the political and economic organization of newly-independent nations bore the mark of colonialism. Territorial borders, trade patterns, the pre-eminence of national and provincial capitals, the 'official' language and the training of senior civil servants, the laws they pledged to uphold, even the structure and content of a schoolchild's day were all, in various ways, colonial constructs. The result was what Badie dubbed an 'imported state'.[77] Determined to overcome these obstacles and reassert their identity, numerous states in Africa and Asia were drawn to the Non-Aligned Movement. In its 1950s heyday the movement's leading lights, including Nehru and Kwame Nkrumah, saw non-alignment as an escape from escalating Cold War friction and the means to lock the Third World into internationalist alternatives.[78] They regarded discrete non-western paths to development in a similar vein.[79]

The Cold War giants alternately wooed these non-aligned states with offers of money and technical expertise or cajoled them with military threats and strategic demands. Those countries with extensive oil or mineral deposits attracted particular interest and rarely retained 'resource sovereignty' over the exploitation of their resources, the argument being that such wealth belonged not to individual societies but to humanity as a whole.[80] Large numbers of former colonial development specialists meanwhile found new employment with UN specialist agencies, the World Bank, the European Community's development arm, and the raft of overseas aid groups that proliferated from the 1960s onwards. Numerous state-backed modernization schemes with massive social and environmental consequences—hydroelectric projects, industrialized logging, and farming monocultures, for instance—acquired greater intensity as a result.[81] By the 1970s the foreign money invested in development was not only greater, it was less European. Colonial-style social engineering also continued long after decolonization, its effects registered most notably in rich world efforts to limit the poor world's population growth.[82]

In the 1960s and 1970s, then, the Cold War migrated south, acquiring a more strongly African and Asian dimension. The contest between liberal capitalism and diverse models of state socialism became a battle increasingly waged in regions adjusting to a post-colonial future. Several former dependencies rejected a zero-sum choice between western-style capitalism and Soviet-style state planning. Kenya and Tanzania, for instance, devised distinctly East African paths of modernization.[83] Elsewhere, however, the hand of foreign involvement was easier to see. From the funds made available for modernization schemes and population control measures to the training provided to police and armed forces, development initiatives illustrated the linkage between forms of decolonization and Cold War rivalries.[84] In 1962, for instance, the Kennedy administration established the Office of Public Safety (OPS) within the US Agency of International Development. Directed by the CIA, its declared aim to 'develop the civilian police component of internal security forces in underdeveloped states' sounded innocuous. Until, that is, the additional OPS purpose of identifying early 'the symptoms of an incipient subversive situation' was added. In this deceptively clinical phrase lurked the basis for recruitment of paramilitary death squads to help keep favoured friends in power. Some of the bitterest conflicts of the 1960s to the 1990s originated in fights for decolonization internationalized into intractable proxy wars characterized by staggering human rights abuses.[85]

In the late twentieth century France and Britain avoided the worst of all this. Should we, then, celebrate the fact that most of the hard work of ending the British and French empires was done by the dawn of the 1960s? The fight or flight dichotomy suggests otherwise. The preceding chapters, substantially about comparison between British and French colonial experience, have, I hope, indicated that for every instance of violence avoided, there were instances of conflict chosen, even positively embraced. Often these choices were made in the light of lessons drawn from other places and other empires. Just as the errors made sometimes caused worst entanglements, so their original commission reflected entangled colonial pasts. Often messy, always interlocked, these histories remind us that Britain and France travelled their difficult roads from empire together.

Glossary

PARTIES, POLITICAL MOVEMENTS, AND ORGANIZATIONS

AEF   *Afrique Equatoriale Française*: the federation of French Equatorial Africa, comprising French Congo, Oubangui-Chari, Gabon, and Chad. The former mandate of French Cameroon, declared a UN trust territory in 1945, was economically tied to the AEF.

AFPFL   **Anti-Fascist People's Freedom League**, Burma.

ALN   *Armée de Libération Nationale*: armed wing of the Algerian FLN.

ANZUS   Australia–New Zealand–US defence treaty, 1951.

AOF   *Afrique Occidentale Française*: the federation of French West Africa, comprising Senegal, Mauritania, French Soudan, Niger, Ivory Coast (Côte d'Ivoire), Guinea, Dahomey, and, from 1948, Upper Volta (Haute-Volta). Federal authorities in Dakar also retained links with Togo, another former mandate, made a UN trust territory in 1945.

CGT   *Confédération Général du Travail*: French trade union confederation.

CMAG   **Chinese Military Advisory Group**, in Vietnam after 1950.

COMININDO **Inter-ministerial committee on Indochina.**

CPP   **Convention People's Party**, founded in the Gold Coast, 1949.

CRO   Commonwealth Relations Office.

DOMs   *Départements d'outre-mer*: French overseas departments, post-1946.

DRV   **Democratic Republic of Vietnam**, established in Hanoi in 1945.

DST   *Direction de la Surveillance du Territoire*, French internal security service.

ENA   *Étoile Nord-Africaine*: North African Star; Algerian nationalist party, founded in 1926.

EOKA   *Ethniki Organosis Kyprion Agoniston*: National Organization of Cypriot Fighters.

FIDES   *Fonds d'Investissement pour le Développement Économique et Social*: Economic and Social Development Fund, set up in 1946.

FLN	*Front de Libération Nationale*: Algerian National Liberation Front founded in 1954.
GPRA	*Gouvernement provisoire de la République algérienne*: Provisional Government of the Algerian Republic.
ICP	Indochinese Communist Party, formed in 1930.
LDH	*La Ligue des Droits de l'Homme*: (Human Rights League), French lobby group established at the height of the Dreyfus Affair in 1898.
KAU	Kenya African Union.
KCA	Kikuyu Central Association.
MCP	Malayan Communist Party.
MDRM	*Mouvement Démocratique de la Rénovation Malgache*: Madagascar nationalist party, founded in 1946.
MNA	*Mouvement National Algérien*: rival to the FLN, led by Messali Hadj.
MPAJA	Malayan Peoples Anti-Japanese Army: largely ethnically Chinese guerrilla force in Malaya in the Second World War.
MRLA	Malayan Races' Liberation Army: armed wing of the Malayan Communist Party.
MRP	*Mouvement Républicain Populaire*: Christian Democrat Party, founded in 1944.
MTLD	*Mouvement pour le Triomphe des Libertés démocratiques*: Algerian nationalist party, forerunner to the FLN.
NATO	North Atlantic Treaty Organization, set up in April 1949.
OAS	*Organisation de l'Armée Secrète*: reactionary counter-terror group.
OS	*Organisation Spéciale*: pre-FLN paramilitary group linked to the MTLD.
PADESM	*Parti des déshérités de Madagascar*: 'Party of the Disinherited of Madagascar'.
PA.NA.MA	*Parti nationaliste malgache*: nationalist party strongest in southern Madagascar.
PCF	*Parti Communiste Français*: French Communist Party, established in 1920.
PLA	People's Liberation Army, national army of the People's Republic of China.
PPA	*Parti Populaire Algérien*: Algerian Popular Party founded in 1937.
PSD	*Parti social démocrate*: [Malagasy] Social Democratic Party.
RDA	*Rassemblement Démocratique Africain*, established in 1946.
RF	Rhodesian Front.

RPF	*Rassemblement du Peuple Français*: Gaullist movement, launched in 1947.
SAA	*Syndicat Agricole Africain*: West African planters' association.
SAS	*Sections Administratives Spécialisées*: army civil affairs specialists in Algeria.
SDECE	*Service de Documentation Extérieure et de Contre-Espionnage*: French overseas intelligence service, broadly equivalent to MI6.
SEAC	**South East Asia Command.**
SEATO	**South East Asia Treaty Organisation**, established 1955.
SFIO	*Section Française de l'Internationale Ouvrière*: unified French Socialist Party, founded in 1905.
TOMs	*Territoires d'outre-mer*: French overseas territories, post-1946.
UDI	**Unilateral Declaration of Independence** (by Southern Rhodesia).
UDMA	*Union démocratique de Manifeste algérien*: Algerian proto-nationalist group led by Ferhat Abbas.
UDSR	*Union Démocratique et Socialiste de la Résistance*: French centre-left party.
UGCC	**United Gold Coast Convention**, founded in 1947.
UMNO	**United Malays National Organization.**
UNSCOP	**UN Special Committee on Palestine.**
VNQDD	**Viet Nam Quoc Dan Dong**: Vietnam National Party, founded in 1927.
VWP	**Dang Lao Dong Viet Nam**: Vietnamese Workers' Party, designation for the Vietnamese Communists from 1951.

ARCHIVES AND PUBLISHED DOCUMENTS

ADA	**Archives Départementales de l'Aude**, Carcassonne
AN	**Archives Nationales**, France
ANOM	**Archives Nationales d'Outre-Mer**, Aix-en-Provence, France
BDEEP	**British Documents on the End of Empire Project**
BLO	**Bodleian Library**, Oxford
CCAC	**Churchill College Archive Centre**, Cambridge
DDF	**Documents Diplomatiques Français**
FRUS	**Foreign Relations of the United States**, Washington, DC: US Government Printing Office, various dates
IOR	**India Office Records**, British Library, London
MAE	**Ministère des Affaires Etrangères**, Paris
MEC	**Middle East Centre**, St Antony's College, Oxford

RHL	Rhodes House Library, Oxford
SHD-DAT	Service Historique de la Défense-Département de l'Armée de Terre, Vincennes
SHM	Service Historique de la Marine, Vincennes, France
TNA	The National Archives, Kew, London
USNA	United States National Archives, College Park, MD

JOURNALS

AHR	*American Historical Review*
CJAS	*Canadian Journal of African Studies*
DH	*Diplomatic History*
DS	*Diplomacy & Statecraft*
EHR	*English Historical Review*
FH	*French History*
FHS	*French Historical Studies*
FPCS	*French, Politics, Culture, and Society*
HJ	*Historical Journal*
IHR	*International History Review*
IJMES	*International Journal of Middle East Studies*
INS	*Intelligence and National Security*
JAH	*Journal of African History*
JICH	*Journal of Imperial and Commonwealth History*
JMH	*Journal of Modern History*
JSEAS	*Journal of South East Asian Studies*
MAS	*Modern Asian Studies*
MES	*Middle Eastern Studies*
PP	*Past & Present*
SWI	*Small Wars and Insurgencies*
OHBE	*Oxford History of the British Empire*

Notes

INTRODUCTION

1. Marie-Sandrine Sgherri, 'La nouvelle bataille de Sétif', *Le Point*, 20 May 2010.
2. '"*Hors-la-loi*": Droit d'inventaire ou droit d'inventer?', *Marianne*, 18 Sept. 2010; '"*Hors-la-loi*"', *Le Nouvel observateur*, 23 Sept. 2010. My thanks to Will Higbee for his insights on the subject.
3. Beatrice Heuser, *The Evolution of Strategy: Thinking War from Antiquity to the Present* (Cambridge University Press, 2010), 18.
4. For details of that colonization, see T. C. W. Blanning, *The French Revolution in Germany: Occupation and Resistance in the Rhineland 1792–1802* (Oxford University Press, 1983); Michael Rowe, *From Reich to State: The Rhineland in the Revolutionary Age, 1780–1830* (Cambridge University Press, 2003); Todd Shepard, *The Invention of Decolonization: The Algerian War and the Remaking of France* (Ithaca, NY: Cornell University Press, 2006), 56.
5. A point made by Christopher Goscha, 'A "total war" of decolonization? Social mobilization and state-building in Communist Vietnam (1949–54)', *War & Society*, 31:2 (2012), 136–62.
6. David French, *The British Way in Counter-Insurgency, 1945–1967* (Oxford University Press, 2011), 47.
7. John Darwin, *The End of the British Empire: The Historical Debate* (Oxford: Blackwell, 1991), 2; Sarah Stockwell, 'Ends of Empire', in Sarah Stockwell, ed., *The British Empire: Themes and Perspectives* (Oxford: Blackwell, 2008), 271. For an emphatic assertion that Britain did not escape such shocks, see Benjamin Grob-Fitzgibbon, *Imperial Endgame: Britain's Dirty Wars and the End of Empire* (Basingstoke: Palgrave-Macmillan, 2011).
8. Odd Arne Westad, *The Global Cold War: Third World Interventions and the Making of our Times* (Cambridge University Press, 2005), 73.
9. John Darwin, 'Decolonization and the end of empire', in Robin Winks, ed., *OHBE, vol. V: Historiography* (Oxford University Press, 1999), 542–4.
10. Mark Philip Bradley, 'Decolonization, the Global South, and the Cold War, 1919–1962', in Melvyn P. Leffler and Odd Arne Westad, eds, *The Cambridge History of the Cold War, i: Origins* (Cambridge University Press, 2010), 464–5.

11. Jennifer Pitts, *A Turn to Empire: The Rise of Imperial Liberalism in Britain and France* (Princeton University Press, 2005), II-III; Jennifer E. Sessions, *By Sword and Plow: France and the Conquest of Algeria* (Ithaca, NY: Cornell University Press, 2011), 58, 64–6; Alice L. Conklin, *A Mission to Civilize: The Republican Idea of Empire in France and West Africa, 1895–1930* (Stanford University Press, 1997).

12. Jeremy Jennings, *Revolution and the Republic: A History of Political Thought in France since the Eighteenth Century* (Oxford University Press, 2011), 494.

13. Ann Laura Stoler and Carole McGranahan, 'Introduction: Reconfiguring imperial terrains', in Stoler, McGranahan and Peter C. Perdue, eds, *Imperial Formations* (Santa Fe, NM: School for Advanced Research Press 2007), 3–42 *passim*; Go, *Patterns of Empire*, 9–12.

14. Claude Liauzu, *Histoire de l'anticolonialisme en France: Du XVIe siècle à nos jours* (Paris: Armand Colin, 2007), especially chs 3, 4, 6.

15. On 'banal imperialism', see: Krishan Kumar, 'Empire, nation, and national identities', in Andrew S. Thompson, ed., *OHBE Companion Volume: Britain's Experience of Empire in the Twentieth Century* (Oxford University Press, 2011), 298–329.

16. Zara Steiner, 'On writing international history: Chaps, maps, and much more', *International Affairs*, 73 (1997), 538.

17. David Anderson, *Histories of the Hanged: The Dirty War in Kenya and the End of Empire* (New York: Norton, 2005), 6.

18. Nicholas Owen, '"Facts are sacred": The Manchester Guardian and colonial violence, 1930–1932', *JMH*, 84:3 (2012), 643–55.

19. A point recently proven in the British colonial case by Huw Bennett's *Fighting the Mau Mau*, chs 3–5; and David French's *The British Way in Counter-Insurgency*, especially chs 4–6.

20. Stephen Jacobson, 'Imperial ambitions in an era of decline', in Alfred W. McCoy, Josep M. Fradera, and Stephen Jacobson, eds, *Endless Empire: Spain's Retreat, Europe's Eclipse, America's Decline* (Madison, WI: University of Wisconsin Press, 2012), 75.

21. French, *The British Way in Counter-Insurgency*, 12–15, 105–32.

22. John Horne, 'Defeat and memory in modern history', in Jenny MacLeod, ed., *Defeat and Memory: Cultural Histories of Military Defeat in the Modern Era* (Basingstoke: Palgrave-Macmillan, 2008), 15.

23. Stockwell, 'Ends of empire', 278–80.

CHAPTER I

1. Historians are fond of quoting Wilson's alarm, most recently Massimiliano Fiore, *Anglo-Italian Relations in the Middle East, 1922–1940* (Farnham: Ashgate, 2010), 2–3.

2. DDF, 1914 (Paris: Imprimerie Nationale, 1999), no. 534, 'Procès-verbal, Séance de la Commission interministérielle des affaires musulmanes', 14 novembre 1914.

3. James F. Searing, 'Conversion to Islam: Military recruitment and generational conflict in a Sereer-Safèn village (Bandia), 1920–38', *JAH*, 44:1 (2003), 80–4.

4. Myron Echenberg, 'Paying the blood tax: Military conscription in French West Africa, 1914–1929', *Revue Canadienne des Études Africaines*, 10:2 (1975), 171–92; 'Les Migrations militaires en Afrique Occidentale Française, 1900–1945', *CJAS*, 14:3 (1980), 429–50. In French West Africa, this method of flight from colonial demands echoed efforts to escape slave recruiters: Bernard Moitt, 'Slavery, flight and redemption in Senegal, 1819–1905', *Slavery and Abolition*, 14:2 (1993), 70–86; Andrew F. Clark, 'Internal migrations and population movements in the Upper Senegal Valley (West Africa), 1890–1920', *CJAS*, 28:3 (1994), 399–420.

5. Alice L. Conklin, *A Mission to Civilize*, 142–50; Joe Lunn, *Memoirs of the Maelstrom: A Senegalese Oral History of the First World War* (Portsmouth, NH: Heinemann, 1999); Anne Summers and R. W. Johnson, 'World War I conscription and social change in Guinea', *JAH*, 19:1 (1978), 25–8.

6. The gratitude expressed in Britain and France for these sacrifices was sullied by racist depictions and discriminatory treatment of colonial soldiers and war workers in Britain and France. See: Tyler Stovall, 'The color line behind the lines: Racial violence in France during the First World War', *AHR*, 103:3 (1998), 739–69; Philippa Levine, 'Battle colors: Race, sex, and colonial soldiery in World War I', *Journal of Women's History* 9:4 (1998), 104–30.

7. Fiore, *Anglo-Italian Relations*, 9–11; Frederick R. Dickinson, *War and National Reinvention: Japan in the Great War, 1914–1919* (Cambridge, MA: Harvard University Press, 1999), 204–37.

8. Zara Steiner, *The Lights that Failed: European International History, 1919–1933* (Oxford University Press, 2005), 17–18, 189–90, 249–50; Patrick Cohrs, *The Unfinished Peace after World War I: America, Britain, and the Stabilisation of Europe, 1919–1932* (Cambridge University Press, 2006), 15–16, 20–67 passim. Even in the United States, internationalist ideas for a global organization with supranational powers to maintain peace were not confined to Woodrow Wilson or the Democratic Party. The Republicans' likely presidential nominee, Theodore Roosevelt, who died of heart failure in Jan. 1919, also had ambitious plans: Stephen Wertheim, 'The League that wasn't: American designs for a legalist-sanctionist League of Nations and the intellectual origins of international organization, 1914–1920', *DH*, 35:5 (2011), 799–832.

9. Susan Pedersen, 'The meaning of the mandates system: An argument', *Geschichte und Gesellschaft* 32 (2006), 560–82; 'Back to the League of Nations', *AHR*, 112:4 (2007), 1099–1117.

10. For the new identity politics in French-ruled Syria, see James L. Gelvin, *Divided Loyalties: Nationalism and Mass Politics in Syria at the Close of Empire* (Berkeley, CA: University of California Press, 1998); Elizabeth Thompson, *Colonial Citizens: Republican Rights, Paternal Privilege, and Gender in French Syria and Lebanon* (New York: Columbia University Press, 2000); Keith Watenpaugh, *Being Modern in the Middle East: Revolution, Nationalism, Colonialism, and the Arab Middle Class*

(Princeton University Press, 2006); Jennifer Dueck, *The Claims of Culture at Empire's End: Syria and Lebanon under French Rule* (Oxford University Press, 2010); Sarah D. Shields, *Fezzes in the River: Identity Politics and European Diplomacy in the Middle East on the Eve of World War II* (Oxford University Press, 2011).

11. Susan Pedersen, 'The impact of League oversight on British policy in Palestine', in Rory Miller, ed., *Britain, Palestine and Empire: The Mandate Years* (Farnham: Ashgate, 2010), 46–65; 'Getting out of Iraq—in 1932: The League of Nations and the road to normative statehood', *AHR*, 115:4 (2010), 975–1000.

12. Barry Eichengreen, *Golden Fetters: The Gold Standard and the Great Depression, 1919–1939* (Oxford University Press, 1992), chs 2–4; Kenneth Mouré, *The Gold Standard Illusion: France, the Bank of France, and the International Gold Standard, 1914–1939* (Oxford University Press, 2002), 40–100 *passim*.

13. Michael Havinden and David Meredith, *Colonialism and Development: Britain and its Tropical Colonies, 1850–1960* (London: Routledge, 1993), 159; Jacques Marseille, *Empire colonial et capitalisme français: Histoire d'un divorce* (Paris: Albin Michel, 1984), 187–207.

14. Robert Boyce, *The Great Interwar Crisis and the Collapse of Globalization* (Basingstoke: Palgrave-Macmillan, 2009), 12–13, chs 5–6.

15. Boyce, *Great Interwar Crisis*, ch. 7; Joe Maiolo, *Cry Havoc: The Arms Race and the Second World War, 1931–1941* (London: John Murray, 2010).

16. Darwin, 'Was there a Fourth British Empire?', in Martin Lynn, ed., *The British Empire in the 1950s: Retreat or Revival?* (Basingstoke: Palgrave-Macmillan, 2006), 21.

17. Two leading economic historians of Southeast Asia stress the variation in hardship, but concur that, for many, it was severe: Anne Booth, 'Four colonies and a kingdom: A comparison of fiscal, trade and exchange rate policies in Southeast Asia in the 1930s', *MAS*, 37:2 (2003), 429–60; Ian Brown, 'Rural distress in Southeast Asia during the world depression of the early 1930s: A preliminary re-examination', *Journal of Asian Studies*, 45:5 (1986), 995–1025.

18. David Arnold, 'Looting, grain riots, and government policy in South India, 1918', *PP*, 84:1 (1979), 111–45.

19. Myron Echenberg, *Black Death, White Medicine: Bubonic Plague and the Politics of Public Health in Colonial Senegal, 1914–1945* (Oxford: James Currey, 2002), 159–74, 184–91.

20. Keith Jeffery, *Field Marshal Sir Henry Wilson: A Political Soldier* (Oxford University Press, 2008), chs 12–13.

21. TNA, CAB 4/7, CID 255B, War Office memo, 27 July 1920; Jon Lawrence, 'Forging a peaceable kingdom: War, violence and the fear of brutalization in post-First World War Britain', *JMH*, 75:3 (2003), 557–9. The pivotal importance of the 'front generation' to post-First World War politics was not solely a British imperial phenomenon: Robert Gerwarth and John Horne, 'The Great War and paramilitarism in Europe, 1917–23', *Contemporary European History*, 19:3 (2010), 267–73; Robert Gerwarth, 'The Central European counter-revolution: Paramilitary violence in

Germany, Austria and Hungary after the Great War', *PP*, 200 (Aug. 2008), 175–209.

22. Michael Rowe, 'Sex, "race" and riot in Liverpool, 1919', *Immigrants and Minorities*, 19:2 (2000), 53–70; Jacqueline Jenkinson, *Black 1919: Riots, Racism and Resistance in Imperial Britain* (Liverpool University Press, 2008); Howard Johnson, 'The anti-Chinese riots of 1918 in Jamaica', *Immigrants and Minorities*, 2:1 (1983), 50–63; W.F. Elkins, 'A source of black nationalism in the Caribbean: The revolt of the B.W.I.R. at Taranto, Italy', *Science and Society* 33:2 (1970), 99–103.

23. Eric D. Weitz, 'From the Vienna to the Paris system: International politics and the entangled histories of human rights, forced deportations, and civilizing missions', *AHR*, 113:5 (2008), 1313–43.

24. Mark Philip Bradley, 'Decolonization, the Global South, and the Cold War', 466; Michael Adas, 'Contested hegemony: The Great War and the Afro-Asian assault on the civilizing mission ideology', *Journal of World History*, 15:1 (2004), 31–63.

25. Mark Mazower, 'An international civilization? Empire, internationalism and the crisis of the mid-twentieth century', *International Affairs* 82 (2006), 533–66; Pedersen, 'The meaning of the mandates system', 560–82.

26. Helen McCarthy, *The British People and the League of Nations: Democracy, Citizenship and Internationalism, c.1918–1945* (Manchester University Press, 2011).

27. C.A. Bayly, 'Empires and Indian Liberals', in Catherine Hall and Keith McClelland, eds, *Race, Nation and Empire: Making Histories, 1750 to the Present* (Manchester University Press, 2010), 88.

28. Erez Manela, *The Wilsonian Moment: Self-Determination and the International Origins of Anticolonial Nationalism* (Oxford University Press, 2007); 'The Wilsonian moment and the rise of anticolonial nationalism: The case of Egypt', *DS*, 12:4 (2001), 99–122.

29. The emergence of explicitly anti-colonial movements was matched by the growth of non-western women's movements in colonial territories. Their primary concern with regional discrimination differed from the feminism of several European and North American women's rights groups, see: Marie Sandell, 'Regional versus international: Women's activism and organisational spaces in the inter-war period', *IHR*, 33:4 (2011), 607–25.

30. Martin Thomas, *Violence and Colonial Order: Police, Workers, and Protest in the European Colonial Empires, 1918–40* (Cambridge University Press, 2012).

31. CCAC, Sir Maurice Hankey papers, HNKY 1/6, 1918 Diary, entry for 3 Oct. 1918.

32. Hankey papers, HNKY 1/6, 1918 Diary, entry for 6 Oct. 1918; Timothy J. Paris, *Britain, the Hashemites and Arab Rule 1920–1925: The Sherifian Solution* (London: Frank Cass, 2003); Martin Thomas, 'Anglo-French imperial relations in the Arab world: Intelligence liaison and nationalist disorder', *DS*, 17:1 (2006), 1–28.

33. Gelvin, *Divided Loyalties*; Gérard D. Khoury, *Une tutelle coloniale: Le Mandat français en Syrie et au Liban* (Paris: Belin, 2006), 27–71.

34. Dan Eldar, 'France in Syria: The abolition of Sharifian government, April–July 1920', *MES*, 29:3 (1993), 487–504.

35. Toby Dodge, *Inventing Iraq: The Failure of Nation Building and a History Denied* (New York: Columbia University Press, 2003); Mary C. Wilson, *King Abdullah, Britain and the Making of Jordan* (Cambridge University Press, 1987).

36. Christopher M. Andrew and A.S. Kanya-Forstner, *France Overseas: The Great War and the Climax of French Imperial Expansion* (London: Thames and Hudson, 1981).

37. Nicholas Owen, 'Critics of Empire in Britain', in Judith Brown and Wm. Roger Louis, eds, *Oxford History of the British Empire*, iv: *The Twentieth Century* (Oxford University Press, 1999), 193-8; R.E. Robinson, 'The moral disarmament of African Empire, 1919-1947', *JICH*, 7:1 (1979), 86-104.

38. Katherine C. Epstein, 'Imperial airs: Leo Amery, air power and empire, 1873-1945', *JICH*, 38:4 (2010), 571-98.

39. CCAC, Leo Amery diaries, AMEL 7/22, 1928 Diary, entry for 26-31 Dec. 1928.

40. Keith Jeffery, *The British Army and the Crisis of Empire, 1918-1922* (Manchester University Press, 1984); Ronald Hyam, *Britain's Declining Empire: The Road to Decolonisation, 1918-1968* (Cambridge University Press, 2006), 32-5.

41. B.J.C. McKercher, *Transition of Power: Britain's Loss of Global Pre-eminence to the United States, 1930-1945* (Cambridge University Press, 1999), 248-77 *passim*.

42. Anne L. Foster, *Projections of Power: The United States and Europe in Colonial Southeast Asia, 1919-1941* (Durham, NC: Duke University Press, 2010); Paul A. Kramer, *The Blood of Government: Race, Empire, the United States and the Philippines* (Chapel Hill, NC: University of North Carolina Press, 2006), chs 3, 5.

43. Keith Nielson, *Britain, Soviet Russia and the Collapse of the Versailles Order, 1919-1939* (Cambridge University Press, 2006), 43, 46-7, 318.

44. John Fisher, 'The Interdepartmental Committee on Eastern Unrest and British responses to Bolshevik and other intrigues against the Empire during the 1920s', *Journal of Asian History*, 34:1 (2000), 1-34.

45. TNA, CAB 4/14, CIP655B, 'The Extension of Soviet Influence in Asia', 15 Dec. 1925.

46. John Ferris, 'The British Empire vs. the hidden hand: British intelligence and strategy and "the CUP-Jew-German-Bolshevik combination", 1918-1924', in Keith Nielson and Greg Kennedy, eds, *The British Way in Warfare: Power and the International System, 1856-1956* (Farnham: Ashgate, 2010), 325-46.

47. Keith Nielson, 'The Foreign Office and the defence of Empire, 1919-1939', in Greg Kennedy, ed., *Imperial Defence: The Old World Order, 1856-1956* (London: Routledge, 2007), 31-2.

48. Keith Jeffery, *MI6: The History of the Secret Intelligence Service 1909-1949* (London: Bloomsbury, 2010), 206-8; David Arnold, 'Police power and the demise of British rule in India, 1930-47', in Anderson and Killingray, *Policing and Decolonisation*, 44.

49. TNA, CAB 4/15, CID 701B, Chiefs of Staff, 'Review of Imperial Defence', 22 June 1926.

50. For naval aspects of British popular imperialism, see: Mary A. Conley, *From Jack Tar to Union Jack: Representing Naval Manhood in the British Empire, 1870–1918* (Manchester University Press, 2009).

51. TNA, CAB 4/11, CID481B, Board of Trade memo, 'French petroleum policy', 11 Feb. 1924.

52. Gary B. Magee and Andrew S. Thompson, *Empire and Globalisation: Networks of People, Goods and Capital in the British World, c.1850–1914* (Cambridge University Press, 2010), chs 2–3.

53. Carl Bridge and Kent Fedorowich, 'Mapping the British world', in Carl Bridge and Kent Fedorowich, eds, *The British World: Culture, Diaspora and Identity* (London: Routledge, 2003), 1–15; James Belich, *Replenishing the Earth: The Settler Revolution and the Rise of the Angloworld* (Oxford University Press, 2009); Darwin, *The Empire Project: The Rise and Fall of the British World System, 1820–1970* (Cambridge University Press, 2009), 12.

54. Hyam, *Britain's Declining Empire*, 70.

55. A.G. Hopkins, 'Rethinking decolonization', *PP*, 200 (Aug. 2008), 213–18; W. David McIntyre, 'The strange death of Dominion status', *JICH*, 27:2 (1999), 193–212. Although still widely understood, the term 'Dominion' fell out of favour and disappeared from official correspondence in the late 1940s.

56. William A. Hoisington Jr., 'In search of a native elite: Casablanca and French urban policy, 1914–24', *The Maghreb Revew*, 12:5–6 (1987), 160–5; Zeynep Çelik, *Urban Forms and Colonial Confrontations: Algiers under French Rule* (Berkeley, CA: University of California Press, 1997).

57. Peter Dunwoodie, *Writing French Algeria* (Oxford: Clarendon Press, 1998), ch. 1; Patricia Lorcin, *Historicizing Colonial Nostalgia: European Women's Narratives of Algeria and Kenya, 1900–Present* (New York: Palgrave-Macmillan, 2012), chs 1, 6.

58. William B. Cohen, *Rulers of Empire: The French Colonial Service in Africa* (Stanford: Hoover Institution Press, 1971), ch. 4.

59. Witness what Laurent Dubois terms the 'republican racism' to emerge in the French Caribbean after what turned out to be temporary slave emancipation in the 1790s: Dubois, *A Colony of Citizens: Revolution and Slave Emancipation in the French Caribbean, 1787–1804* (Chapel Hill, NC: University of North Carolina Press, 2004), 3–4, 166–8.

60. Jean Elizabeth Pederson, ' "Special customs": Paternity suits and citizenship in France and the colonies, 1870–1912', in Julia Clancy-Smith and Frances Gouda, eds, *Domesticating the Empire: Race, Gender, and Family Life in French and Dutch Colonialism* (Charlottesville, VA: University of Virginia Press, 1998), 43–64.

61. For the limits to inter-war assimilation, see: Jonathan K. Gosnell, *The Politics of Frenchness in Colonial Algeria, 1930–1954* (Rochester, NY: University of Rochester Press, 2002).

62. W.B. Cohen, 'The colonized as child: British and French Colonial Rule', *African Historical Studies*, 3:2 (1970), 427–31.

63. James E. Genova, *Colonial Ambivalence, Cultural Authenticity, and the Limits of Mimicry in French-Ruled West Africa, 1914–1956* (New York: Peter Lang, 2004), 94–9.

64. Gary Wilder, *The French Imperial Nation-State: Negritude and Colonial Humanism between the Two World Wars* (University of Chicago Press, 2005), III; Jennifer Boittin, 'Black in France: The language and politics of race in the late Third Republic', *FPCS*, 27:2 (2009), 23–46; Tyler Stovall, 'Aimé Césaire and the making of black Paris', *FPCS*, 27:3 (2009), 44–6.

65. Sophie Quinn-Judge, *Ho Chi Minh: The Missing Years* (London: Hurst, 2003), chs 1, 5.

66. ADA, Albert Sarraut papers, 12J307, Pierre Pasquier report on Yen Bay uprising, 6 June 1930.

67. Alice L. Conklin, ' "Democracy" rediscovered: Civilization through association in French West Africa (1914–1930)', *Cahiers d'Études Africaines*, 145:37 (1997), 59–84.

68. Mahmood Mamdani, *Citizen and Subject: Contemporary Africa and the Legacy of Late Colonialism* (Princeton University Press, 1996), 17–18; also cited in Genova, *Colonial Ambivalence*, 8.

69. Conklin, *A Mission to Civilize*; Genova, *Colonial Ambivalence*.

70. Martin Thomas, 'Fighting "Communist banditry" in French Vietnam: The rhetoric of repression after the Yen Bay uprising, 1930–32', *FHS*, 34:3 (2011), 612–14, 634–9; Hy Van Luong, 'Agrarian unrest from an anthropological perspective: The case of Vietnam', *Comparative Politics*, 17:2 (1985), 153–74.

71. Mark Philip Bradley, 'Becoming "Van Minh": Civilizational discourse and visions of the self in twentieth-century Vietnam', *Journal of World History*, 15:1 (2004), 65–83; Shawn McHale, 'Printing and power: Vietnamese debates over women's place in society, 1918–1934', in K.W. Taylor and J.K. Whitmore, eds, *Essays into Vietnamese Pasts* (Ithaca, NY: Cornell University Press, 1995), 183–92.

72. Wilder, *French Imperial Nation-State*, 202–54.

73. Ronald Chalmers Hood, *Royal Republicans: The French Naval Dynasties Between the World Wars* (Baton Rouge, LA: Louisiana State University Press, 1985).

74. Introduction to Owen White and J.P. Daughton, eds, *In God's Empire: French Missionaries and the Modern World* (New York: Oxford University Press, 2012), 3–20.

75. Odile Goerg, 'The French provinces and "Greater France"', in Tony Chafer and Amanda Sackur, eds, *Promoting the Colonial Idea: Propaganda and Visions of Empire in France* (Basingstoke: Palgrave, 2002), 82–101; John F. Laffey, 'Municipal imperialism in decline: The Lyon chamber of commerce, 1925–1938', *FHS*, 9:3–4 (1975), 329–53.

76. Marianne Boucheret, 'Les Organisations de planteurs de caoutchouc indochinois et l'État au début du XXe siècle à la veille de la Seconde Guerre mondiale', in Hubert Bonin, Catherine Hodeir, and Jean-François Klein, eds, *L'Esprit économique impérial (1830–1970): Groupes de pression et réseaux du patronat colonial en France et dans l'empire* (Paris: Publications de la SFHOM 2008), 716–18.

77. Pierre Brocheux and Daniel Hémery, *Indochina: An Ambiguous Colonization, 1858–1954* (Berkeley, CA: University of California Press, 2009), 189; Y. Gonjo, *Banque colonial ou Banque d'affaires: La Banque de l'Indochine sous la IIIème République* (Paris: CHEFF, 1998).

78. ANOM, Travaux Publiques, 1 TP Carton 167: Rapports de Mission Kair, 1924–5: Routes coloniale 1 et 4; AN, F/14/12432, 'Programme de construction des lignes nouvelles de Chemins de Fer adoptée par les Assemblées Algériennes en 1920.: Rapports de la Commission spéciale', 10 Apr. 1924.

79. Hubert Bonin, 'Les Réseaux bancaires impériaux parisiens', in Bonin et al., *L'Esprit*, 454–5.

80. For contrasting views of colonial party 'insiders' see: C.M. Andrew and A.S. Kanya-Forstner, 'The French "colonial party": Its composition, aims and influence, 1885–1914', *HJ*, 14:1 (1971), 99–128; L. Abrams and D. J. Miller, 'Who were the French colonialists? A reassessment of the *Parti colonial*, 1890–1914', *HJ*, 19:3 (1976), 685–725.

81. ADA, Sarraut Papers, 12J172, 'Le Communisme et les colonies'; CAOM GGM, 6(2)D/55, PCF Section colonial, 'La France du Front Populaire et les peuples coloniaux', 25–29 Dec. 1937.

82. Alice L. Conklin, 'The new "ethnology" and "la situation coloniale" in interwar France', *FPCS*, 20:2 (2002), 29–48.

83. Emmanuelle Sibeud, *Une science impériale pour l'Afrique? La Construction des savoirs africanistes en France 1878–1930* (Paris: EHESS, 2002), 257–72; Wilder, *The French Imperial Nation-State*, 58–61.

84. Hardy's earlier work in Morocco helped shape his ideas: Spencer D. Segalla, 'Georges Hardy and educational ethnology in French Morocco, 1920–26', *French Colonial History*, 4 (2003), 171–90.

85. MAE, série K Afrique 1918–1940, sous-série Affaires musulmanes, vol. 9, K 101–2, 'Les Populations musulmanes de l'Afrique Occidentale et Equatoriale Française et la politique islamique de la France'.

86. Ruth Ginio, 'Colonial minds and African witchcraft: Interpretations of murder as seen in cases from French West Africa in the interwar era', in Martin Thomas, ed., *The French Colonial Mind, i: Mental Maps of Empire and Colonial Encounters* (Lincoln, NE: University of Nebraska Press, 2012), 58–61.

87. Benoît de L'Estoile, 'Rationalizing colonial domination? Anthropology and native policy in French-ruled Africa', in Benoît de L'Estoile, Federico Neiburg and Lygia Sigaud, eds, *Empires, Nations, and Natives: Anthropology and State-Making* (Durham, NC: Duke University Press, 2005), 44–7.

88. Conklin, 'The new "ethnology"', 29–46.

89. Benoît de L'Estoile, 'Rationalizing colonial domination?', 49–54.

90. Helen Tilley and Robert J. Gordon, eds, *Ordering Africa: Anthropology, European Imperialism, and the Politics of Knowledge* (Manchester University Press, 2007), 6–9.

91. Cooper, *Colonialism in Question*, 144.

92. Conklin, '"Democracy" rediscovered', 59–60.

93. Darwin, *The Empire Project*, 8; Mary Dewhurst Lewis, 'Geographies of power: The Tunisian civic order, jurisdictional politics, and imperial rivalry in the Mediterranean, 1881–1935', *JMH*, 80:4 (2008), 791–830.

94. Benjamin N. Lawrence, Emily Lynn Osborn, and Richard L. Roberts, eds, *Intermediaries, Interpreters, and Clerks: African Employees in the Making of Colonial Africa* (Madison, WI: University of Wisconsin Press, 2006), 4–34.

95. Heather J. Sharkey, *Living with Colonialism: Nationalism and Culture in Anglo-Egyptian Sudan* (Berkeley, CA: University of California Press, 2003), 37, 41, 48–9, 52.

96. Sharkey, *Living with Colonialism*, 1.

97. Donald Bloxham and Robert Gerwarth, eds, *Political Violence in Twentieth-Century Europe* (Cambridge University Press, 2011), 15–21; Isobel Hull, *Absolute Destruction: Military Culture and the Practices of War in Imperial Germany* (Ithaca, NY: Cornell University Press, 2005), I; Julia Eichenberg, 'The dark side of independence: Paramilitary violence in Ireland and Poland after the First World War', *Contemporary European History*, 19:3 (2010), 237–48; Michael Silvestri, '"An Irishman is specially suited to be a policeman": Sir Charles Tegart and revolutionary terrorism in Bengal', *History Ireland*, 8:4 (2000), 40–4.

98. The Spanish Moroccan protectorate, a narrow coastal strip of territory opposite Gibraltar, was enshrined in the 1906 Act of Algeciras.

99. MAE, Série M: Maroc, 1917–1940, vol. 89, Direction des affaires indigènes, 'Rapport mensuel, mars 1925'; C. R. Pennell, *A Country with a Government and a Flag: The Rif War in Morocco* (Wisbech: Middle East and North African Studies Press, 1986), 186–91.

100. SHD-DAT, 3H602, Pétain Moroccan inspection mission report, 4 Aug. 1925.

101. TNA, FO 371/11078, W6433/39/28, Marquess of Crewe (Paris) to FO, 6 July 1925.

102. TNA, FO 413/69, W1288/39/28 and W5092/186/28, both Assistant Military Attaché Graham to Marquess of Crewe (Paris), 12 Feb. and 29 May 1925.

103. TNA, FO 371/11083, W9934/4011/28, Consul Ryan (Rabat) to Sir Austen Chamberlain, 13 Oct. 1925.

104. William A. Hoisington Jr, *Lyautey and the French Conquest of Morocco* (Basingstoke: Macmillan, 1995), 196–204.

105. TNA, FO 371/11081, W10017/186/28, Marquess of Crewe to FO, 23 Oct. 1925.

106. SHD-DAT, 3H101/Périodiques M. Pétain, no. 319, Pétain report, 'Bulletin périodique du 30 septembre au 4 octobre 1925'; C. R. Pennell, 'Women and resistance to colonialism in Morocco: The Rif 1916–1926', *JAH*, 28 (1987), 107–18.

107. The best study of the Syrian revolt is Michael Provence, *The Great Syrian Revolt and the Rise of Arab Nationalism* (Austin, TX: University of Texas Press, 2005).

108. N.E. Bou-Nacklie, 'Tumult in Syria's Hama in 1925: The failure of a revolt', *Journal of Contemporary History*, 33:2 (1998), 273–90; James Barr, *A Line in the Sand: The Anglo-French Struggle for the Middle East* (New York: Norton, 2012), 127–9, 136–8.

109. Philip S. Khoury, *Syria and the French Mandate: The Politics of Arab Nationalism, 1920–1945* (London: I. B. Taurus, 1987), 175.

110. Khoury, *Syria*, 163–4.

111. Khoury, *Syria*, 176–7; TNA, AIR 23/91, Major J. Codrington to GHQ Amman, 8 Nov. 1926.

112. Khoury, *Syria*, 178–9. French official reports admitted only 150 civilian deaths.

113. SHD-DAT, 4H67/D2, no. 936/2, Gamelin to Cabinet du Ministre (Guerre), 1 July 1926.

114. Jan Karl Tanenbaum, *General Maurice Sarrail 1856–1929: The French Army and Left-Wing Politics* (Chapel Hill, NC: University of North Carolina Press, 1974), 191–206 *passim*.

115. Michael Provence, 'An investigation into the local origins of the Great Revolt', in Nadine Méouchy, ed., *France, Syrie et Liban 1918–1946* (Damascus: IFEAD, 2002), 378–93; Khoury, *Syria*, 237–8.

116. Key works covering the earlier colonial period include Nicola Cooper, *France in Indochina: Colonial Encounters* (Oxford: Berg, 2001); Daniel Hémery, *Révolutionnaires vietnamiens et pouvoir colonial en Indochine* (Paris: Maspero, 1975); David G. Marr, *Vietnamese Anticolonialism, 1885–1925* (Berkeley, CA: University of California Press, 1971); Mark W. McLeod, *The Vietnamese Response to French Intervention, 1862–74* (New York: Praeger, 1991); Milton E. Osborne, *The French Presence in Cochinchina and Cambodia: Rule and Response (1859–1905)* (Ithaca NY: Cornell University Press, 1969); Hue-Tam Ho Tai, *Radicalism and the Origins of the Vietnamese Revolution* (Cambridge, MA: Harvard University Press, 1992). Among the welter of books on the Indochina War of 1946–54, three distinctive treatments are Christopher Goscha, *Thailand and the Southeast Asian Networks of the Vietnamese Revolution (1885–1954)* (London: Curzon Press, 1999); Hugues Tertrais, *La Piastre et le fusil: Le Coût de la guerre d'Indochine 1945–1954* (Paris: CHEF, 2002); Stein Tønnesson, *Vietnam 1946: How the War Began* (Berkeley, CA: University of California Press, 2010).

117. Pierre Brocheux, 'L'Implantation du mouvement communiste en Indochine française: Le Cas du Nghe-Tinh (1930–1931)', *Revue d'Histoire Moderne et Contemporaine*, 24:1 (1977), 49–74; Martin Bernal, 'The Nghe-Tinh Soviet Movement, 1930–1931', *PP*, 92:1 (1981), 148–68; Tobias Rettig, 'French military policies in the aftermath of the Yên Bay Mutiny, 1930: Old Security Dilemmas Return to the Surface', *South East Asia Research*, 10:3 (2002), 309–31; James C. Scott, *The Moral Economy of the Peasant: Rebellion and Subsistence in Southeast Asia* (New Haven, CT: Yale University Press, 1976), 118–48.

118. David G. Marr, *Vietnamese Tradition on Trial, 1920–1945* (Berkeley, CA: University of California Press, 1981), 15–20; Luong, 'Agrarian Unrest', 165. Luong points out that the majority of the ICP's national leadership came from Confucian scholar families of the mandarin elite in Nghe-An and Ha-Tinh.

119. Irene Nørlund, 'Rice and the colonial lobby: The economic crisis in French Indo-China in the 1920s and 1930s', in Peter Boomgaard and Ian Brown, eds, *Weathering the Storm: The Economies of South East Asia in the 1930s Depression* (Singapore: I.S.E.A.S., 2000), 201–11; Kham Vorapheth, *Commerce et colonisation en Indochine 1860–1945* (Paris: Les Indes savantes, 2004), 371–90.

120. For parallels with another marginalized community treated as inherently rebellious, see Greg Grandin's analysis of state violence against Guatemala's Mayans, *The Last Colonial Massacre: Latin America in the Cold War* (Chicago, IL: University of Chicago Press, 2004), 171–2.

121. Thomas, 'Fighting "Communist banditry"', 615–27.

122. ANOM, Fonds Ministériels Indochine (FM/INDO), Nouveaux Fonds (NF), FM/INDO/NF 2634, Etat-Major 3e Bureau, 'Troupes de l'Indochine, rapport spécial no. 286', n.d., Oct. 1930.

123. Huynh Kim Khánh, *Vietnamese Communism, 1925–1945* (Ithaca, NY: Cornell University Press, 1982), 96; Stephen A. Toth estimates seven to eight executions per year in the *bagne* penal colonies of New Caledonia and French Guiana in the decades prior to Yen Bay, see his *Beyond Papillon: The French Overseas Penal Colonies, 1854–1952* (Lincoln, NE: University of Nebraska Press, 2006), 113.

124. 'Les Treize Assassinés de Yen Bay sont morts en révolutionnaires', *L'Humanité*, 19 June 1930, in Alain Ruscio, *La Question coloniale dans L'Humanité (1904–2004)* (Paris: La Dispute, 2005), 128–31. Earlier beheadings of bandit leaders were not concealed, but celebrated on tourist postcards sold in Hanoi and elsewhere, see Michael G. Vann, 'Of Pirates, Postcards, and Public Beheadings: The Pedagogic Execution in French Colonial Indochina', *Historical Reflections*, 36:2 (2010), 39–58.

125. SHD-DAT, 6N503/D3, EMA Section d'études, 'Note pour le secrétariat général', 20 June 1931. The six French soldiers killed all died during the original Yen Bay mutiny.

126. ADA, Sarraut papers, 12J301, 'La Propagande communiste dans les milieux coloniaux', 27 Apr. 1922; William D. Irvine, *Between Justice and Politics: The Ligue des droits de l'homme, 1898–1945* (Stanford University Press, 2007); 57, 144; Peter Zinoman, *The Colonial Bastille: A History of Imprisonment in Vietnam, 1862–1940* (Berkeley, CA: University of California Press, 2001), 269–70.

127. Norman Ingram, 'Selbstmord or euthanasia? Who killed the Ligue des Droits de l'Homme?', *FH*, 22:3 (2008), 339.

128. Daniel Hémery, 'L'Indochine, les droits humains entre colonisateurs et colonisés: La Ligue des droits de l'homme', *Revue Française d'Histoire d'Outre-Mer*, 88:330–1 (2001), 223–39.

129. Zinoman, *The Colonial Bastille*, 269. Hundreds more received lengthy terms of forced labour.

130. Claude Liauzu, *Histoire de l'anticolonialisme*, 166, 169.

131. Jennings, *Revolution and the Republic*, 492–4, manifesto quotation at 492.

132. Purnima Bose, *Organizing Empire: Individualism, Collective Agency, and India* (Durham, NC: Duke University Press, 2003), 31–7.

133. Susan Kingsley Kent, *Aftershocks: Politics and Trauma in Britain, 1918–1931* (Basingstoke: Palgrave-Macmillan, 2009), 67.

134. Derek Sayer, 'British reaction to the Amritsar massacre, 1919–1920', *PP*, 131 (1991), 130–64; Helen Fein, *Imperial Crime and Punishment: Massacre at Jallianwala Bagh and British Judgement, 1919–20* (Honolulu: University of Hawaii Press, 1986).

135. Robert L. Soloman, 'Saya San and the Burmese rebellion', *MAS*, 3:3 (1969), 209–23. Saya San was a pretender to the Burmese throne.

136. G. H. Bennett, *British Foreign Policy during the Curzon period, 1919–1924* (Basingstoke: Macmillan, 1995), 176.

137. Hyam, *Britain's Declining Empire*, 50–4, quotation at 54.

138. Jacob Metzer, *The Divided Economy of Mandatory Palestine* (Cambridge University Press, 1998), 1–27; Zachary Lochman, *Comrades and Enemies: Arab and Jewish Workers in Palestine, 1906–1948* (Berkeley, CA: University of California Press, 1996), 116–45.

139. Joseph Nevo, 'Palestinian-Arab violent activity during the 1930s', in Michael J. Cohen and Martin Kolinsky, eds, *Britain and the Middle East in the 1930s* (Paris: Armand Colin, 2007), 169–89; Martin Kolinsky, *Law, Order and Riots in Mandatory Palestine, 1928–1935* (Basingstoke: Macmillan, 1994), 40–2.

140. TNA, Ramsey MacDonald Private Office papers, PRO 30/69/276, 'Recent Palestine disturbances', 25 Sept. 1929; CO 638(29), 'Wailing Wall of Jerusalem—Appointment of Commission', 8 Oct. 1929.

141. Mary Ellen Lundsten, 'Wall politics: Zionist and Palestinian strategies in Jerusalem, 1928', *Journal of Palestine Studies*, 8:1 (1978), 3n.2, 7–12, 22–4.

142. Matthew Hughes, 'The Banality of Brutality: British Armed Forces and the Repression of the Arab Revolt in Palestine, 1936–39', *EHR*, 124:507 (2009), 313–54.

143. Barr, *A Line in the Sand*, 162.

144. Matthew Hughes, 'Lawlessness and the law: British armed forces, the legal system and the repression of the Arab Revolt in Palestine, 1936–1939', in Miller, *Britain, Palestine*, 141–56.

145. As Congress President Subhas Chandra Bose noted drily that Indians were expected to fight against Germany and Italy while providing 'a certificate of good conduct' for British and French imperialism. Cited in Nicholas Owen, 'The Cripps Mission of 1942: A Reinterpretation', *JICH*, 30:1 (2002), 63, 68.

146. Ted Swedenburg, *Memories of Revolt: The 1936–1939 Rebellion and the Palestinian National Past* (Fayetteville: University of Arkansas Press, 2003), xxii.

147. Swedenburg, *Memories of Revolt*, 3–12.

148. Yoshua Porath, *The Palestinian Arab National Movement, 1929–1939: From Riots to Rebellion* (London: Frank Cass, 1977); Charles Townshend, 'The defence of Palestine: Insurrection and public security, 1936–1939', *EHR*, 103 (1988), 919–49.

149. Tom Bowden, 'The politics of the Arab rebellion in Palestine, 1936–39', *MES*, 11:2 (1975), 147–74; Yuval Arnon-Ohanna, 'The bands in the Palestinian Arab Revolt, 1936–1939: Structure and organization', *Asian and African Studies*, 15:2 (1981), 229–47.

150. Swedenburg, *Memories of Revolt*, xx–xxi, 35, 94–7.

151. S. Klieman, 'The divisiveness of Palestine: Foreign Office vs. Colonial Office on the issue of partition, 1937', *HJ*, 22 (1979), 423–42; Michael J. Cohen, 'Appeasement in the Middle East: The British White Paper on Palestine, May 1939', *HJ*, 16:3 (1973), 571–96.

152. TNA, WO 106/2018B, COS847(JIC), 'Attitude of the "Arab world" to G.B.', 20 Feb. 1939; CO 831/51/8, 'Secret report on the political situation, Apr. 1939'.

153. TNA, MacDonald papers, PRO 30/69/338, Sir Robert Lindsay Downing Street memo, 10 Sept. 1929; Pedersen, 'Getting out of Iraq', 998–9.

154. Israel Gershoni and James P. Jankowski, *Redefining the Egyptian Nation, 1930–1945* (Cambridge University Press, 1995), 152–7.

155. TNA, FO 1011/170: Egypt 1934–1944 correspondence, Sir Percy Loraine letter to Lt. Colonel P.G. Elgood, 26 Jan. 1937.

156. Michael T. Thornhill, 'Informal Empire, independent Egypt and the accession of King Farouk', *JICH*, 38:2 (2010), 279–302.

157. RHL, Mss. Ind. Ocn. s. 352: Sir Cecil Clementi papers, Malaya papers, box 29/file 1, Letter from I. Hall to Clementi, 12 Mar. 1931.

158. Lynn Hollen Lees, 'Being British in Malaya, 1890–1940', *Journal of British Studies*, 48:1 (2009), 76–101; Anthony C. Milner, *The Invention of Colonial Malaya: Contesting Nationalism and the Expansion of the Public Sphere* (Cambridge University Press, 1995), 282.

159. John Lonsdale, 'Kenya: Home county and African frontier', in Robert Bickers, ed., *Settlers and Expatriates: Britons over the Seas* (Oxford University Press, 2010), 76.

160. Elspeth Joscelin Grant Huxley, *White Man's Country: Lord Delamere and the Making of Kenya*, 2 vols. (London: Chatto & Windus, 1953), 82, cited in Lorcin, *Historicizing Colonial Nostalgia*, 118.

161. RHL, Mss. Afr. s. 1120, Sir Robert Brooke-Popham papers, Kenya correspondence, box III/2, William Ormsby-Gore private letter to Brooke-Popham, 21 Oct. 1936. Regarding the high social status of Kenya's settlers, see C.J. Duder, ' "Men of the officer class": The participants in the 1919 soldier settlement scheme in Kenya', *African Affairs*, 92:366 (1993), 69–87.

162. Brooke-Popham papers, Kenya correspondence, box III/2, Ormsby-Gore to Brooke-Popham, 6 Dec. 1937.

163. John Darwin, 'An undeclared empire: The British in the Middle East, 1918–39', *JICH*, 27:2 (1999), 159–76; Wilder, *French Imperial Nation-State*, introduction and ch. 1.

CHAPTER 2

1. Capitaine Couet, 'De Paris à Dakar à motocyclette', *Le Monde Colonial Illustré*, 190 (avril 1939), 78–9.
2. Julien Maigret, 'Quinzaine impériale de Paris', *Le Monde Colonial Illustré*, 190 (avril 1939), 81–3.
3. Marc Michel, '"Mémoire officielle", discours et pratique coloniale', *Revue Française d'Histoire d'Outre-Mer*, 77 (1990), 145–58; Martin Thomas, 'Economic conditions and the limits to mobilisation in the French Empire, 1936–39', *HJ*, 48:2 (2005), 471–2.
4. Historians George Peden and Zara Steiner argue that the British Empire fell short in this regard: George C. Peden, 'The burden of imperial defence and the continental commitment reconsidered', *HJ*, 27:2 (1984), 405–23; Zara Steiner, *The Triumph of the Dark: European International History, 1933–1939* (Oxford University Press, 2011), 803–4. The term 'imperial nation-state' was coined by Gary Wilder, *The French Imperial Nation-State*.
5. Darwin, *The Empire Project*, 482–3, 491–2; George C. Peden, *Arms, Economics and British Strategy: From Dreadnoughts to Hydrogen Bombs* (Cambridge University Press, 2007), 156–62.
6. Arrested by the Vichy authorities in 1941, Mandel was murdered by the paramilitary *Milice* on 7 July 1944 in reprisal for the killing by Communist resisters of the Vichy Propaganda Minister Philippe Henriot.
7. Bertrand Favreau, *Georges Mandel ou la passion de la République 1885–1944* (Paris: Fayard, 1996), 337–40; Christine Levisse-Touzé, 'La Préparation économique, industrielle et militaire de l'Afrique du Nord à la veille de la guerre', *Revue d'Histoire de la Deuxième Guerre Mondiale*, 142:1 (1986), 1–18.
8. Frederick Cooper, *Decolonization and African Society: The Labor Question in French and British Africa* (Cambridge University Press, 1996), 124–66; David Anderson and David Throup, 'Africans and agricultural production in colonial Kenya: The myth of the war as a watershed', *JAH*, 26 (1985), 327–45. For a lively, positive assessment of empire contributions to Britain's war effort, see Ashley Jackson, *The British Empire and the Second World War* (London: Hambledon, 2006).
9. Siân Nicholas, '"Brushing up your empire": Dominion and colonial propaganda on the BBC's Home Service, 1939–1945', *JICH*, 31:2 (2003), 207–8, 213; Rosaleen Smyth, 'Britain's African colonies and British propaganda during the Second World War', *JICH*, 14:1 (1985), 65–82.
10. TNA, AIR 2/4128, Reports on Anglo-French Staff conference, Singapore, June 1939; AIR 9/112, AFC(J) 25, 26, and 45: June 1939 staff conversations—French delegation papers.

11. Brock Millman, *The Ill-Made Alliance: Anglo-Turkish Relations, 1934–1940* (Montreal: McGill University Press, 1998), 294–300; Elisabeth du Réau, 'Les Balkans dans la stratégie méditerranéenne de la France, avril 1939–mai 1940', *Balkan Studies*, 29:1 (1988), 77–8.

12. SHD-DAT, 7N2837/D2, SHA-2, 'Singapour—La Conférence franco-britannique', n.d. June 1939; DDF, 2nd series, vol. XVII, final report of Singapore talks, 42–55.

13. David Edgerton questions the affordability of British imperial defence commitments in *Warfare State: Britain, 1920–1970* (Cambridge University Press, 2005); and see Phillips O'Brien, 'The Titan refreshed: Imperial overstretch and the British Navy before the First World War', *PP*, 172:1 (2001), 146–69.

14. SHM, TTD 821/Dossier FNEO, 'Conférence anglo-française, Aden, 29 mai au 3 juin 1939'.

15. TNA, Treasury files, T160/987, Reciprocal treatment of imports, 1939–40.

16. Edward Louis Spears' papers, Churchill College, Cambridge, SPRS 1/134/3, 'French volunteer force', Sept. 1940; SPRS 1/137/26, Bank of England, 'Inflation in Syria', 24 Feb. 1942.

17. Edward Louis Spears' papers, Middle East Centre archive, Oxford, box II/6, Note by Major Morton on relations with the Free French, 6 Jan. 1942.

18. Gloria Maguire, *Anglo-American Relations with the Free French* (Basingstoke: Macmillan, 1995), 118–19; Martin Thomas, *The French Empire at War, 1940–45* (Manchester University Press, 1998), 159–64.

19. The indispensable treatment of Free France and its followers is Jean-Louis Crémieux-Brilhac, *La France libre: De l'appel du 18 juin à la libération* (Paris: Gallimard, 1998). De Gaulle's and Pétain's military careers had been entwined since 1914 when the former served as a young Lieutenant in the 33rd Infantry Regiment commanded by, then, Colonel Pétain. The link resumed in 1927 when, after Pétain's appointment as the French Army's chief of staff, de Gaulle became his *aide-de-camp*.

20. Nancy Ellen Lawler, *Soldiers of Misfortune: Ivoirien Tirailleurs of World War II* (Athens, OH: Ohio University Press, 1992). Losses among French African servicemen in the 1940 battle for France are discussed by Myron Echenberg, ' "Morts pour la France": The African soldier in France during the Second World War', *JAH*, 26 (1985), 263–80; Martin S. Alexander, 'Colonial minds confounded: French colonial troops in the battle of France, 1940', in Thomas, *French Colonial Mind*, ii: *Violence, Military Encounters, and Colonialism* (Lincoln, NE.: University of Nebraska Press, 2012), 263–80; 248–82; Raffael Scheck, *Hitler's African Victims: The German Army Massacres of Black French Soldiers in 1940* (Cambridge University Press, 2006).

21. Pieter Lagrou, 'The nationalization of victimhood: Selective violence and national grief in western Europe, 1940–1960', in Richard Bessel and Dirk Schumann, eds, *Life after Death: Approaches to a Cultural and Social History of Europe during the 1940s and 1950s* (Cambridge University Press, 2003), 249.

22. Hanna Diamond, *Fleeing Hitler: France, 1940* (Oxford University Press, 2008); Yves Durand, *La Captivité: Histoire des prisonniers de guerre français, 1939–45* (Paris: FNCPG, 1980).

23. Richard H. Weisberg, *Vichy Law and the Holocaust in France* (London: Routledge, 1997), ch. 6; Lagrou, 'The nationalization of victimhood', 248–9. Nearly 55,000 French Jews were sent to concentration camps during 1942 alone.

24. Lindsey Dodd and Andrew Knapp, '"How many Frenchmen did you kill?", British bombing policy towards France (1940–1945)', *FH*, (2008), 469–92, at 469.

25. Julian Jackson, *The Fall of France: The Nazi Invasion of 1940* (Oxford University Press, 2003), 232–3; Nicholas Atkin, *Pétain* (Harlow: Longman, 1998), 92–4.

26. Alice L. Conklin, Sarah Fishman, and Robert Zaretsky, *France and its Empire since 1870* (Oxford University Press, 2011), 215–17; Stanley Hoffman, 'The Trauma of 1940: A Disaster and its Traces', in Joel Blatt, ed., *The French Defeat of 1940: Reassessments* (Oxford: Berghahn, 1998), 354–63.

27. AN, F60/307: Ministère des Colonies, Vichy: Organisation/administration, 1940–41.

28. Shannon Fogg, *The Politics of Everyday Life in Vichy France: Foreigners, Undesirables, and Strangers* (Cambridge University Press, 2009), 19–55; Kenneth Mouré, 'Food rationing and the black market in France (1940–1944)', *FH*, 24:2 (2010), 262–82.

29. Peter Jackson, 'Recent journeys along the road back to France, 1940', *HJ*, 39:2 (1996), 497; Patrick Finney, *Remembering the Road to World War Two: International History, National Identity, Collective Memory* (London: Routledge, 2011), 150–5.

30. David Wingeate Pike, 'Between the Junes: The French Communists from the Collapse of France to the Invasion of Russia', *Journal of Contemporary History*, 28:3 (1993), 465–85.

31. Olivier Wieviorka, *Une certaine idée de la Résistance: Défense de la France, 1940–1949* (Paris: Editions du Seuil, 1995), 20–3; Rod Kedward, *La Vie en bleu: France and the French since 1900* (London: Penguin, 2005), 272–4.

32. Conklin et al., *France and its Empire*, 228–9; Francine Muel-Dreyfus, *Vichy and the Eternal Feminine* (Durham, NC: Duke University Press, 2001), 97–124.

33. Martin Thomas, 'Resource war, civil war, rights war: Factoring empire into French North Africa's Second World War', *War in History*, 18:2 (2011), 225–48.

34. Martin Thomas, 'After Mers el-Kébir: The armed neutrality of the Vichy French Navy, 1940–1943', *EHR*, 112:447 (1997), 643–7. For Vichy propagandist responses, see: Brett C. Bowles, '"La Tragédie de Mers el-Kébir" and the politics of filmed news in France, 1940–1944', *JMH*, 76:2 (2004), 347–88.

35. TNA, FO 892/65, Note by Spears, 'Weygand, Darlan and the French fleet', 29 Jan. 1941.

36. Jean-Marie Abrail supervised the naval defence of Dunkirk after which he was appointed Governor-General of Algeria. At much the same time, Admiral Jean Decoux, naval commander in the Far East, became Governor of the Indochina

Federation, a post he would hold until Mar. 1945. Jean-Pierre Esteva served as Vichy Resident-Minister in Tunisia and received a life sentence in Mar. 1945 for collaboration. Charles Platon became Vichy's Minister for Colonies. Jean-François Darlan rose furthest, becoming Vichy deputy-premier, then prime minister and commander of Vichy armed forces before his assassination by Gaullist resisters in Algiers on Christmas Eve, 1942.

37. Darwin, *The Empire Project*, 496–7. Akrikaners did, however, enlist in large numbers during the war years, drawn by appeals to their masculinity and martial past. See Albert Grundlingh, 'The King's Afrikaners? Enlistment and ethnic identity in the Union of South Africa's defence force during the Second World War, 1939–1945', *JAH*, 40:3 (1999), 351–65, especially 353–61.

38. Keith Jeffery, 'The Second World War', in Brown and Louis, eds, *OHBE*, iv, 306–28.

39. Margaret Barrett, 'Tug of war: The Free French movement in Australia, 1940–1944', MPhil thesis, University of Sydney, 2012, 1.

40. Kent Fedorowich, 'Doomed from the outset? Internment and civilian exchange in the Far East: The British failure over Hong Kong, 1941–45', *JICH*, 25:1 (1997), 113–40; 'The evacuation of European civilians from Hong Kong and Malaya/Singapore, 1939–1942', in B. Farrell and S. Hunter, eds, *Sixty Years On: The Fall of Singapore Revisited* (Singapore: Eastern Universities, 2002), 122–55.

41. Ian Cowman, 'Main fleet to Singapore? Churchill, the Admiralty and Force Z', *Journal of Strategic Studies*, 18:1 (1995), 79–93; Christopher Bell, 'The "Singapore strategy" and the deterrence of Japan: Winston Churchill, the Admiralty and the dispatch of Force Z', *EHR*, 116:467 (2001), 604–34.

42. Richard Toye, 'An imperial defeat? The presentation and reception of the fall of Singapore', in Brian Farrell, ed., *Churchill and the Lion City: Shaping Modern Singapore* (Singapore: N. U. S., 2011), 108, 111–12, 119–20.

43. Kosmas Tsokhas, 'Dedominionization: The Anglo-Australian experience, 1939–1945', *HJ*, 37:4 (1994), 861–83; Darwin, *The Empire Project*, 502–3.

44. One of Canada's most remarkable contributions was approximately one billion dollars in munitions for which no payment was sought, see: Hector Mackenzie, 'Transatlantic generosity: Canada's "billion dollar gift" to the United Kingdom in the Second World War', *IHR*, 34:2 (2012), 293–314.

45. Darwin, *The Empire Project*, 495, 522–3. The commitment to avoid conscription was diluted by the outcome of a 1942 referendum, popular in English-speaking Canada, which permitted the government to introduce the measure 'if necessary'.

46. Douglas E. Delaney, 'Cooperation in the Anglo-Canadian armies, 1939–1945', in Neilson and Kennedy, *The British Way in Warfare*, 216

47. Delaney, 'Cooperation', 197–217; Paul Dickson, 'Politics of army expansion: General H.D.G. Crerar and the creation of the First Canadian Army, 1941', *Journal of Military History*, 60:2 (1996), 271–9.

48. Nicholas, ' "Brushing Up" ', 210–11.

49. Philip Buckner, ed., *Canada and the British Empire: OHBE Companion Volume* (Oxford University Press, 2008), 107–9; Kent Fedorowich, ' "Cocked hats and small, little garrisons": Britain, Canada and the fall of Hong Kong, 1941', *MAS*, 37:1 (2003), 111–58.

50. Anguished about his captured son, Vincent Massey helped devise British policy-making on British and imperial POWs, see Neville Wylie, *Barbed Wire Diplomacy: Britain, Germany, the Politics of Prisoners of War, 1939–1945* (Oxford University Press, 2010), 1–2, 197, 221–2.

51. The importance of Dominion and, especially, Canadian support for Britain is examined in David Edgerton, *Britain's War Machine: Weapons, Resources and Experts in the Second World War* (London: Allen Lane 2011), 47–85; Buckner, 'Canada and the end of Empire, 1939–1982', 113–27.

52. TNA, WO 193/545, MO5/A, 'India as a war arsenal', signed by 'L. C. R.', n.d., 1940. Aside from its economic and financial contributions, India raised a military force of 2.5 million of whom 24,338 were killed and 79,489 taken prisoner, mostly by the Japanese, see: Pradeep Barua, 'Strategies and doctrines of imperial defence: Britain and India, 1919–45', *JICH*, 25:2 (1997), 253–61.

53. Nicholas Owen, 'The Cripps Mission of 1942', 69–70.

54. Yasmin Khan, 'Sex in an imperial war-zone: Transnational encounters in Second World War India', *History Workshop Journal*, 73:1 (2012), 240.

55. Chandar S. Sundaram, 'Seditious letters and steel helmets: Disaffection among Indian troops in Singapore and Hong Kong, 1940–1, and the formation of the Indian National Army', in K. Roy, ed., *War and Society in Colonial India* 2nd edition (New Delhi: Oxford University Press, 2006), 126–49.

56. Indevar Kamtekar, 'The shiver of 1942', in Roy, *War and Society*, 330–6.

57. Madhusree Mukerjee, *Churchill's Secret War: The British Empire and the Ravaging of India during World War II* (New York: Basic Books, 2010), 76–98.

58. Khan, 'Sex', 242–52.

59. Mark Harrison, *Medicine & Victory: British Military Medicine in the Second World War* (Oxford University Press, 2004), 198.

60. Cited in Martin Francis, 'Men of the Royal Air Force, the cultural memory of the Second World War and the twilight of the British Empire', in Philippa Levine and Susan Grayzel, eds, *Gender, Labour, War, and Empire: Essays on Modern Britain* (Basingstoke: Palgrave-Macmillan, 2009), 186–7. At least 422 men of Caribbean, West African, and Indian subcontinent origin served as aircrew; almost 4,000 as supporting ground-crew. Discrimination seemed less marked in fighter command, whose pilot ranks were always cosmopolitan.

61. Information in this paragraph draws heavily from Jeffery, 'The Second World War', 311–13.

62. Sonya O. Rose, *Which People's War? National Identity and Citizenship in Wartime Britain, 1939–1945* (Oxford University Press, 2003), 247–50.

63. TNA, FO 892/84, Ministry of Information French section advisory committee, intelligence report 39, 17 June 1941; *Journal Officiel* no 197, 17 July 1941; Kenneth Mouré, 'Economic choice in dark times: The Vichy economy', *FPCS*, 25:1 (2007), 108–30.

64. Eric Jennings, *Vichy in the Tropics: Pétain's National Revolution in Madagascar, Guadeloupe, and Indochina, 1940–1944* (Stanford University Press, 2001).

65. Eric Jennings, *Imperial Heights: Dalat and the Making and Undoing of French Indochina* (Berkeley, CA: University of California Press, 2011), 210–13; 'Conservative confluences, "nativist" synergy: Reinscribing Vichy's National Revolution in Indochina, 1940–1945', *FHS*, 27:4 (2004), 601–35.

66. Brocheux and Hémery, *Indochina*, 344–8.

67. TNA, FO 892/172, undated memo on functions of the British mission to the FNC.

68. Mario Rossi, 'United States military authorities and Free France', *Journal of Military History*, 61:1 (1997), 49–64, especially 49–53.

69. TNA, Political Warfare Executive files, FO 892/127, Maurice Dejean memo, 'Washington et Vichy', 4 Feb. 1942.

70. Fredrik Logevall, *Embers of War: The Fall of an Empire and the Making of America's Vietnam* (New York: Random House, 2012), 51–2.

71. MAE, Guerre, 1939–1945, Londres CNF, vol. 299, FFL 2ème bureau, 'Projet d'accord franco-américain', 8 Mar. 1941.

72. Arthur L. Funk, 'Negotiating the "deal with Darlan"', *Journal of Contemporary History*, 8:2 (1973), 81–117; Thomas, *The French Empire at War*, 159–90.

73. MAE, AP288, Maurice Dejean papers, vol. 24, Adrien Tixier to de Gaulle, 1 June 1942.

74. MAE, Dejean papers, vol. 25, Dejean (Beirut) to de Gaulle, 22 Aug. 1942.

75. TNA, FO 892/174, Free French press service, de Gaulle communiqué, 2 Jan. 1943.

76. *Foreign Relations of the United States (FRUS), Conferences at Washington 1941–1942, and Casablanca, 1943*, CCOS meeting, 15 Jan. 1943, p. 573; John Charmley, 'Harold Macmillan and the making of the French Committee of National Liberation', *IHR*, 4:4 (1982), 557.

77. Robert E. Sherwood, ed., *The White House Papers of Harry L. Hopkins*, ii: *Jan. 1942–July 1945* (London: Eyre & Spottiswoode, 1949), 682–3.

78. TNA, WO 204/239, Allied civil affairs memo, 'Dollar-franc rate of exchange', 16 Jan. 1943.

79. SHD-DAT, 2P12/D2, Vichy Secrétariat à la Guerre, bulletin de renseignements 64, 14 Jan. 1943; James J. Dougherty, *The Politics of Wartime Aid: American Economic Assistance to France and French Northwest Africa, 1940–1946* (Westport, CT: Greenwood, 1978), 4–5; Maguire, *Anglo-American Relations*, 120–2. The French Committee of National Liberation (FCNL) negotiated a currency stabilization agreement with the British government that altered franc values throughout the African Empire from 176.6 to 200 per pound in Feb. 1944: TNA, FO 371/40299, E1126/23/89, Spears mission summary 97, 19 Feb. 1944.

80. Jean-Charles Jauffret, ed., *La Guerre d'Algérie par les documents* I (Vincennes: SHAT, 1990);'Manifeste du peuple algérien', 31–8; AN, F60/837, no. 685; Istiqlal executive memo, 'Au sujet des récentes réformes marocaines', 1 Dec. 1944.

81. Jacques Simon, ed., *Messali Hadj par les textes* (Paris: Editions Bouchène, 2000), doc. 17, Interview à *Combat*, 26 July 1946.

82. *Messali Hadj*, doc. 14. Lettre aux membres du Comité de libération, 11 Oct. 1943.

83. SHD-DAT, Fonds privés/Vichy, 1K592/1, Charles-Robert Ageron draft paper, 'Les Mouvements nationalistes dans le Maghreb pendant la deuxième guerre mondiale'; AN, F60/883, no. 1890, General Charles Mast to Georges Bidault, 4 Dec. 1945.

84. SHD-DAT, Fonds privés/Vichy, 1K592/1, Ageron draft paper, 'Les Mouvements nationalistes'.

85. AN, Secrétariat Général du Gouvernement, F⁶⁰/835, Spillman, Directeur du Cabinet, Ministère en A.F.N., to Catroux, 12 Dec. 1944.

86. SHD-DAT, Fonds privés, 1K650/D1, General Jean Richard papers, 'Vue d'ensemble sur la répartition des effectifs mobilisés en Afrique du Nord', n.d. Feb. 1945; Claude d'Abzac-Epezy, 'Épuration, dégagements, exclusions: Les Réductions d'effectifs dans l'armée française (1940–1947)', *Vingtième Siècle*, 59 (1998), 66–9.

87. Gallissot, *La République française et les indigènes*, 156. For fuller details of North African troop recruitment and moral in 1943–5 see: Belkacem Recham, *Les Musulmans algériens dans l'armée française (1919–1945)* (Paris, L'Harmattan, 1996), 236–72.

88. MAE, série Asie-Océanie 1944–1955, sous-série Indochine, vol. 30, 'Notes prises à la conférence de M. le Gouverneur-Général Laurentie sur l'Indochine', n.d. Aug. 1945.

89. TNA, PREM 3/178/2, COS sub-committee, 'Events in Indo-China since 1939', n.d. Mar. 1945.

90. Kiyoko Kurusu Nitz, 'Japanese military policy towards French Indochina during the Second World War: The road to the *Meigo Sakusen* (9 Mar. 1945)', *JSEAS*, 14:2 (1983), 334–8.

91. Martin Thomas, 'Free France, the British Government and the future of French Indo-China, 1940–45', *JSEAS*, 28:1 (1997), 141–4.

92. SHD-DAT, 4Q78/D5, no. 95, 'Perspectives d'évolution du conflit extrême-orient', 5 Aug. 1944.

93. Tønnesson, *Vietnam 1946*, 21–2.

94. Logevall, *Embers*, 84–7.

95. Pierre L. Lamant, 'Le Cambodge et la décolonisation de l'Indochine: Les Caractères particuliers du nationalisme Khmer de 1936 à 1945', in Charles-Robert Ageron, ed., *Les Chemins de la décolonisation* (Paris: CNRS, 1986), 189–99.

96. Ralph B. Smith, 'The Japanese period in Indochina and the *coup* of 9 Mar. 1945', *JSEAS*, 9:2 (1978), 290–1; Sugata Bose, 'Starvation amidst plenty: The making of famine in Bengal, Honan and Tonkin, 1942–45', *MAS*, 24:4 (1990), 699–727.

97. David G. Marr, *Vietnam 1945: The Quest for Power* (Berkeley, CA: University of California Press, 1995), 96–107, quotation at 101.

98. Nicholas, ' "Brushing Up" ', 218–19.

99. Memo by Secretary of State for the Colonies Oliver Stanley, 'Staffing of the Colonial Service in the post-war period', 26 Aug. 1944, in S. R. Ashton and S.E. Stockwell, eds, *BDEEP*, Series A, Volume 1: *Imperial Policy and Colonial Practice, 1925–1945* (London: HMSO, 1996), doc. 6.

100. Joanna Lewis, *Empire State-Building: War and Welfare in Kenya, 1925–52* (Oxford: James Currey, 2000), 79–81; ' "Tropical East Ends" ', 42–66; L. J. Butler, *Industrialization and the British Colonial State: West Africa, 1939–1951* (London: Routledge, 1997), chs 2–4.

101. Memo by Charles Jeffries, 'A plan for the Colonial Office', n.d., Nov. 1942, in Ashton and Stockwell, *BDEEP*, A/1, doc. 4; Charles Jeffries, *Whitehall and the Colonial Service: An Administrative Memoir, 1939–1956* (London: Athlone Press, 1972), 18–19.

102. Catherine R. Schenk, *The Decline of Sterling: Managing the Retreat of an International Currency, 1945–1992* (Cambridge University Press, 2010), 38–9.

103. Anderson and Throup, 'Africans and agricultural production', 336.

104. Sabine Clarke, 'A technocratic imperial state? The Colonial Office and scientific research, 1940–1960', *Twentieth Century British History*, 18:4 (2007), 453–9.

105. Jeffery Cox, 'From the Empire of Christ to the Third World: Religion and the experience of empire in the twentieth century', in Thompson, ed., *Britain's Experience of Empire*, 76–119 *passim*.

106. Anderson and Throup, 'Africans and agricultural production', 333–42.

107. T.N. Harper, 'The politics of disease and disorder in post-war Malaya', *JSEAS*, 21:1 (1990), 89–90.

108. A. J. Stockwell, 'Colonial planning during World War Two: The case of Malaya', *JICH*, 2:3 (1974), 333–51; 'The formation and first years of the United Malays National Organization (U.M.N.O.)', *MAS*, 11:4 (1977), 481–3.

109. Harper, 'The politics of disease', 89.

110. Quoted in Toye, 'An imperial defeat?', 113.

111. Clement Attlee, 'Memorandum on the Indian Situation', 2 Feb. 1942', in B. N. Pandey, ed., *The Indian Nationalist Movement, 1885–1947: Select Documents* (Basingstoke: Macmillan, 1979), 175–8; Nicholas Owen, *The British Left and India: Metropolitan Anti-Imperialism, 1885–1947* (Oxford: Oxford Historical Monographs, 2007), 277–8.

112. Owen, 'The Cripps Mission', 75–9, quotation at 79.

113. Owen, 'The Cripps Mission', 61–83, quotation at 62.

114. Peter Clarke, *The Cripps Version: The Life of Sir Stafford Cripps, 1889–1952* (London: Allen Lane, 2002), 292–322.

115. Nicholas Owen, 'War and Britain's political crisis in India', in Brian Brivati and Harriet Jones, eds, *What Difference Did the War Make?* (Leicester University Press, 1993), 114–20; Bose, 'Starvation', 699–727.

116. For an indictment of British maladministration of India's grain and rice reserves, which were exported to Europe throughout Bengal's famine, see: Mukerjee, *Churchill's Secret*, chs 6–10.

117. Sunil S. Amrith, 'Food and welfare in India, c.1910–1950', *Comparative Studies in Society and History*, 50:4 (2008), 1018–28.

118. IOR, Mss Eur F164/8: Sir Francis Mudie papers, Bengal famine inquiry commission report, 1945.

119. This turn was consistent with a broader transformation of policy-making, see: Kevin Jefferys, 'British politics and social policy during the Second World War', *HJ*, 30:1 (1987), 123–44.

120. Suke Wolton, *Lord Hailey, the Colonial Office and the Politics of Race and Empire in the Second World War* (Basingstoke: Palgrave-Macmillan, 2000); J. M. Lee and M. Petter, *The Colonial Office: War and Development Policy* (London: Ashgate, 1982).

121. Robert D. Pearce, *The Turning Point in Africa: British Colonial Policy, 1938–1948* (London: Routledge, 1982), 158–9; Ina Zweiniger-Barqielowska *Austerity in Britain: Rationing, Controls, and Consumption, 1939–1955* (Oxford University Press, 2002), 45–59, 209–25.

122. Wm. Roger Louis, 'The dissolution of the British Empire', in Brown and Louis, *OHBE*, iv, 331.

123. Richard J. Aldrich, *Intelligence and the War against Japan: Britain, America and the Politics of Secret Service* (Cambridge University Press, 2000), 302–6; Michael H. Hunt, 'The decolonization puzzle in US Policy: Promise versus performance', in David Ryan and Victor Pungong, eds, *The United States and Decolonization* (Basingstoke: Macmillan, 2000), 207–29; Wm. Roger Louis and Ronald Robinson, 'The imperialism of decolonization', *JICH*, 22:3 (1994), 462–511.

124. Quoted in Aldrich, *Intelligence*, 330.

125. Aldrich, *Intelligence*, 330–4; Stockwell, 'The formation', 485–6.

126. The following paragraphs draw from my article 'Divisive decolonization: The Anglo-French withdrawal from Syria and Lebanon, 1944–46', *JICH*, 28:3 (2000), 71–93, at 71–2.

127. AN, René Pleven papers, box 560AP/27, 'Commerce extérieur des premiers mois 1944', n.d., Aug. 1944; 'Situation économique du Sénégal en 1943 et 1944', n.d., 1944.

128. Martin Shipway, *The Road to War: France and Vietnam, 1944–1947* (Oxford: Berghahn, 1996), 90.

129. AN, F60/889, CFLN Secretariat note for de Gaulle, 'Conférence de Brazzaville', 5 Jan. 1944.

130. Shipway, *The Road*, 21–37.

131. Charles-Robert Ageron, 'La Survivance d'un mythe: La Puissance par l'Empire colonial, 1944–1947', *Revue Française d'Histoire d'Outre-Mer*, 72 (1985), 388–97; D. Bruce Marshall, *The French Colonial Myth and Constitution-Making in the Fourth Republic* (New Haven: Yale University Press, 1973).

132. Indispensable studies include Wm. Roger Louis, *The British Empire in the Middle East 1945–1951: Arab Nationalism, the United States and Postwar Imperialism* (Oxford University Press, 1984); Philip S. Khoury, *Syria and the French Mandate:*

The Politics of Arab Nationalism, 1920–1945 (Princeton University Press, 1987); Aviel Roshwald, *Estranged Bedfellows: Britain and France in the Middle East during the Second World War* (Oxford University Press, 1990).

133. Haifa and Jaffa/Tel Aviv were hit, much as they had been by earlier Italian bombing raids between June and Oct. 1940: see Nir Arielli, '"Haifa is still burning": Italian, German and French air raids on Palestine during the Second World War', *MES*, 46:3 (2010), 333–42.

134. MEC, Spears' papers, box III/5, Sir J. Glubb, 'A further note on peace terms', 25 May 1943.

135. Gaullist suspicions are expertly examined by Meir Zamir, 'The "missing dimension": Britain's secret war against France in Syria and Lebanon, 1942–45—Part II', *MES*, 46:6 (2010), 791–812.

136. Charles de Gaulle, *Mémoires de Guerre, iii: Le Salut, 1944–1946* (Paris, 1959), 781–95.

137. Barr, *A Line in the Sand*, 253–97 passim. The French security services were already funding the Stern Gang when two of its members assassinated Lord Moyne, Britain's Minister of State in the Middle East, on 6 Nov. 1944.

138. Shields, *Fezzes in the River*, 20–2, 114–24, 231–5.

139. SHD-DAT, 4H377/D6, Conférence de Chtaura, 22 Feb. 1945.

140. TNA, FO 371/45605, E9747/420/89, Lord Halifax to Bevin, 13 Dec. 1945 and FO minutes; CAB 128/2, JP(45)315, Joint Planning Staff report on Levant evacuation, 16 Dec. 1945.

141. Barr, *A Line in the Sand*, 291.

142. SHD-DAT, 4H360/D1, no. 1591/2S, Commandement Supérieur des Troupes du Levant memo, 1 June 1945; TNA, FO 371/45580, E5800/8/89, War Office Historical Record—Levant 29 May–11 June 1945. Estimates of the numbers killed range from 400 to 700.

143. SHD-DAT, 4H276/D3 EM-1, Instructions to Damascus units, 29 July 1945; TNA, WO 201/1016, Brigadier J.G. Frere reports to GHQ Middle East, 17–30 Sept. 1945.

144. Barr, *A Line in the Sand*, 295–7.

145. Thomas, 'Divisive Decolonization', 89–91.

146. Darwin, *The Empire Project*, 493.

147. Jeffery, 'The Second World War', 327.

148. MAE, série Asie-Océanie 1944–1960, sous-série Indochine, vol. 31, Comité d'Indochine secrétariat notes 21 Apr. 1945.

CHAPTER 3

1. Ronald Hyam, 'The political consequences of Seretse Khama: Britain, the Bangwato and South Africa, 1948–1952', *HJ*, 24:4 (1986), 921–47; Susan Williams, *Colour Bar: The Triumph of Seretse Khama and His Nation* (London: Allen Lane, 2006).

2. John Stuart, 'Empire and Religion in Colonial Botswana: The Seretse Khama controversy, 1948–1956', in Hilary M. Carey, ed., *Empires of Religion* (Basingstoke: Palgrave-Macmillan, 2008), 311–26.

3. Stephen Howe, *Anticolonialism in British Politics: The Left and the End of Empire, 1918–64* (Oxford University Press, 1993), 196–7, also cited in Stuart, 'Empire and Religion', 27.

4. The 1953 marriage of Stafford Cripps' daughter, Peggy to the Ghanaian lawyer Joe Appiah, a high-born Ashante and close friend of Kwame Nkrumah, made the Attlee government's pronouncements about Ruth Williams' choice of partner seem even more hypocritical.

5. Indispensable is Erez Manela, *The Wilsonian Moment*.

6. Westad, *The Global Cold War*, 78, 86.

7. Roger Normand and Sarah Zaidi, *Human Rights at the UN: The Political History of Universal Justice* (Bloomington, IN: Indiana University Press, 2008), 212–20; cited in Simpson, 'The United States and the curious history', 679.

8. Shipway, *The Road to War*, 51–6, 66–74.

9. Simpson, 'The United States and the curious history', 678–81; Mark Mazower, *No Enchanted Palace: The End of Empire and the Ideological Origins of the United Nations* (Princeton University Press, 2009), ch. 4.

10. Stephen Broadberry and Peter Howlett, 'The United Kingdom: "Victory at all costs" ', in Mark Harrison, ed., *The Economics of World War II: Six Great Powers in International Comparison* (Cambridge University Press, 1998), 43–80; Julian Jackson, *France: The Dark Years, 1940–44* (Oxford University Press, 2001).

11. Marr, *Vietnam 1945*, 104; Brocheux and Hémery, *Indochina*, 274, 348. The famine's death toll was hotly contested by the French and their Vietnamese political opponents. Recent histories concur that one million deaths is a 'credible estimate'.

12. Todd Shepard, *The Invention of Decolonization*, 57.

13. Key examples include Irwin M. Wall, *The United States and the Making of Postwar France, 1944–54* (Cambridge University Press, 1991); Richard Kuisel, *Seducing the French: The Dilemma of Americanization* (Berkeley, CA: University of California Press, 1993); William I. Hitchcock, *France Restored: Cold War Diplomacy and the Quest for Leadership in Europe, 1944–1954* (Chapel Hill, NC: University of North Carolina Press, 1998); Michael Creswell, *A Question of Balance: How France and the United States Created Cold War Europe* (Cambridge, MA: Harvard University Press, 2006); Gérard Bossuat, *Les Aides américaines économiques et militaires à la France, 1938–1960* (Paris: CHEFF, 2001); Brian Angus McKenzie, *Remaking France: Americanization, Public Diplomacy, and the Marshall Plan* (New York: Berghahn, 2008); Claire Sanderson, *L'Impossible alliance? France, Grande-Bretagne et défense de l'Europe, 1945–1958* (Paris: Publications de la Sorbonne, 2003). A commendable, recent exception to the rule is Mark Atwood Lawrence, *Assuming the Burden: Europe and the American Commitment to War in Vietnam* (Berkeley, CA: University of California Press, 2007).

14. Giacobbi, a lawyer by training, became the youngest mayor in France when elected to office in his home town of Bastia in 1922. One of the eighty French parliamentarians who refused to vote plenary powers to Marshal Pétain in July 1940, he was stripped of office and later jailed by Corsica's Italian occupiers. Creech-Jones' Methodist upbringing and Independent Labour Party activism underpinned his pacifism, which led to his imprisonment between 1916 and 1919.

15. The limited capacity of Colonial Office reformers to extend African welfare provision is discussed by Joanna Lewis in her *Empire State-Building*, especially 300–5.

16. Pat Thane, 'Family life and "normality" in postwar British culture', in Bessel and Schumann, *Life after Death*, 193–4; Philip Nord, *France's New Deal: From the Thirties to the Postwar Era* (Princeton University Press, 2010), 173–5.

17. Quoted in Hyam, *Britain's Declining Empire*, 142.

18. Darwin, 'Was there a fourth British Empire?' 16, 23–4.

19. Schenk, *The Decline of Sterling*, 38–61.

20. Hopkins, 'Rethinking decolonization', 224–5; Tim Rooth, 'Britain's other dollar problem: Economic relations with Canada, 1945–50', *JICH*, 27:1 (1999), 81–108. The partial exception here was Canada, whose economic connections with the USA grew rapidly after 1945.

21. Darwin, *The Empire Project*, 17.

22. Robert J. Macmahon, *Colonialism and Cold War: The United States and the Struggle for Indonesian Independence* (Ithaca, NY: Cornell University Press, 1981); Ritchie Ovendale, *Britain, the United States and the Transfer of Power in the Middle East, 1945–1962* (Leicester University Press, 1996); Lawrence, *Assuming the Burden*, ch. 1.

23. An argument most often put in relation to Roosevelt's hostility to any resumption of French control in post-war Indochina: Walter LaFeber, 'Roosevelt, Churchill, and Indochina, 1942–45', *AHR*, 80 (1975), 1277–95; Stein Tønnesson, 'Franklin Roosevelt, trusteeship, and Indochina: A reassessment', in Mark Atwood Lawrence and Fredrik Logevall, eds, *First Vietnam War: Colonial Conflict and Cold War Crisis* (Cambridge, MA: Harvard University Press, 2007), 56–73.

24. Mark Atwood Lawrence, 'Explaining the early decisions: The United States and the French War, 1945–1954', in Mark Philip Bradley and Marilyn B. Young, eds, *Making Sense of the Vietnam Wars: Local, National and Transnational Perspectives* (New York: Oxford University Press, 2008), 25–9; more generally: William Roger Louis, *Imperialism at Bay: The United States and the Decolonization of the British Empire* (Oxford: Clarendon Press, 1977).

25. Mary Ann Heiss, 'The evolution of the imperial idea and U.S. national identity', *DH*, 26:4 (2002), 533–8.

26. Victor Pungong, 'The United States and the international trusteeship system', in Ryan and Pungong, *The United States and Decolonization*, 85–95.

27. For background, see: Mary L. Dudziak, *Cold War Civil Rights: Race and the Image of American Democracy* (Princeton University Press, 2000); Thomas Borstelmann, *The Cold War and the Color Line: Race Relations and American Foreign Policy since 1945* (Cambridge, MA: Harvard University Press, 2001); Carol Anderson, *Eyes off the Prize: The United Nations and the African American Struggle for Human Rights, 1944–1955* (Cambridge University Press, 2003); Jason Parker, *Brother's Keeper: The United States, Race, and Empire in the British Caribbean, 1937–1962* (New York: Oxford University Press, 2008), 51–74 *passim*.

28. Louis and Robinson, 'The imperialism of decolonization', 462–511.

29. Simpson, 'The United States and the curious history', 680.

30. Dane Kennedy, 'Essay and reflection: On the American Empire from a British imperial perspective', *IHR*, 29:1 (2007), 83–108.

31. Hunt, 'The decolonization puzzle in US policy', in Ryan and Pungong, *The United States and Decolonization*, 207–14.

32. Amrith, 'Food and welfare', 1026.

33. Harper, 'Disease and disorder', 90–102, 109–13; Stockwell, 'The formation', 485–90.

34. Richard Stubbs, *Hearts and Minds in Guerrilla Warfare: The Malayan Emergency, 1948–1960* (Oxford University Press, 1989), 35–7; A. J. Stockwell, '"A widespread and long-concocted plot to overthrow government in Malaya"? The origins of the Malayan Emergency', *JICH*, 21:3 (1993), 68, 73.

35. Simon Kitson, 'Creating "a nation of resisters"? Improving French self-image, 1944–6', in Monica Riera and Gavin Schaffer, eds, *The Lasting War: Society and Identity in Britain, France and Germany after 1945* (Basingstoke: Palgrave-Macmillan, 2008), 72–9.

36. For background, see: Hilary Footitt, *War and Liberation in France: Living with the Liberators* (Basingstoke: Palgrave-Macmillan, 2004); Patrice Virgili, *Shorn Women: Gender and Punishment in Liberation France* (Oxford: Berg, 2002).

37. The workaday problems and political uncertainties of the post-liberation years are examined by the contributors to Andrew Knapp, ed., *The Uncertain Foundation: France at the Liberation, 1944–1947* (Basingstoke: Palgrave-Macmillan, 2007).

38. Hitchcock, *France Restored*, 14–22; Andrew Shennan, *Rethinking France: Plans for Renewal, 1940–46* (Oxford: Clarendon, 1989), 77–92.

39. Guy Pervillé, 'Le RPF et l'Union Française', in *De Gaulle et le RPF, 1947–1955*, ed. Fondation Charles de Gaulle (Paris, Armand Colin, 1998), 521–3.

40. AN, Fonds MRP, 350AP76, Dossier: 4MRP8/Dr 4, 'Renseignements communiqués par les fédérations sur le R. P. F. Note schématique', 23 Apr. 1947.

41. The fullest accounts of right-wing politics in post-war France are Richard Vinen, *Bourgeois Politics in France, 1945–1951* (Cambridge University Press, 1995); Philip Williams, *Crisis and Compromise: Politics in the Fourth Republic* (Oxford University Press, 1964).

42. Paul Smith, 'Political parties, parliament and women's suffrage in France, 1919–1939', *FH*, 11:3 (1997), 342–50.

43. Christian Bougeard, *René Pleven: Un Français en politique* (Presses Universitaires de Rennes, 1994), 168, 182–91.

44. AN, René Pleven papers, 560AP/27/D1, Commissaire aux Colonies, 'Rapports et notes', 1943–44.

45. Bougeard, *René Pleven*, 90–2, 95, 130–1, 140–5. Pleven spent much of the 1930s working in Britain.

46. AN, René Mayer papers, 363AP32/D1, Marcel Delrieu to René Mayer, 20 Dec. 1950.

47. MAE, série Z: Europe, sous-série Grande-Bretagne, vol. 39, René Massigli to Foreign Ministry, 20 July 1947. Massigli, the Anglophile French Ambassador in London, reported that Attlee's Cabinet was 'stupefied' by the fall of Robert Schuman's government as the Berlin blockade crisis intensified.

48. David Hanley, 'From co-operation to conflict: The French political system and the onset of the Cold War', *French Cultural Studies*, 8:1 (1997), 7–15. Under the Fourth Republic the Chamber of Deputies counted six major party groupings: Socialists (SFIO), Communists (PCF), Christian Democrats (MRP), Radicals, Gaullists (RPF), and the non-Gaullist right (PRL). In practice, the Socialists, Radicals, and Christian Democrats became the new Republic's archetypical parties of government.

49. Jean-Jacques Becker, 'La Scéne intérieure', in Maurice Vaïsse, Pierre Mélandri, and Frédéric Bozo, eds, *La France et l'OTAN 1949–1996* (Vincennes: CEHD, 1996), 103–4.

50. Jennings, *Revolution and the Republic*, 437; Kuisel, *Seducing*, chs 1–3; Charles S. Maier, 'The Marshall Plan and the division of Europe', *Journal of Cold War Studies* 7:1 (2005), 168–74.

51. Jon Cowans, 'French public opinion and the founding of the Fourth Republic', *FHS*, 17:1 (1991), 68–71, 75–91.

52. Successive Fourth Republic governments laid the groundwork for European integration despite the fact that the relationship between French Union territories and a European Community remained unresolved before 1955, see: Seung-Ryeol Kim, 'France's agony between *vocation européenne et mondiale*: The *Union Française* as an obstacle in the French policy of supranational European integration', *Journal of European Integration History*, 8:1 (2002), 61–84.

53. Jean-Pierre Rioux, *The Fourth Republic, 1944–1958* (Cambridge University Press, 1987), 446–9.

54. John Gillingham, *Coal, Steel, and the Rebirth of Europe, 1945–1955: The Germans and French from Ruhr Conflict to Economic Community* (Cambridge University Press, 1991), 137–47, 364–72; Hitchcock, *France Restored*, 4–6, 204–7.

55. Vinen, *Bourgeois Politics in France*, 265–9.

56. Kristen Ross, *Fast Cars, Clean Bodies: Decolonization and the Reordering of French Culture* (Boston: MIT Press, 1996), chs 1–3.

57. Shepard, *Invention of Decolonization*, 40–6.

NOTES TO PAGES 85–88

58. AN, Union Démocratique et Socialiste de la Résistance (UDSR) papers, 412AP/1/D1, 'Tracts et circulaires MLN—UDSR, 1945–46'; AN, 350/AP1/D2, 'Programme du MRP', 8 Nov. 1945.

59. Lagrou, 'The nationalization of victimhood', 243–52; d'Abzac-Epezy, 'Épuration', 62–75.

60. Danièle Zeraffa, 'La Perception de la puissance dans la formation Démocrate Chrétienne', *Revue d'Histoire Moderne et Contemporaine*, 31 (1984): 644–5; Ageron, 'La Survivance', 388–97.

61. Cooper, *Decolonization and African Society*, 184–93; Conklin et al., *France and its Empire*, 250–1.

62. AN, F60/308, Direction du plan de développement économique et sociale, decree, 6 Apr. 1945.

63. SHD-DAT, 4Q119/D8, 'Séances tenues au Comité de Afrique du Nord en octobre 1946'.

64. Steiner, 'On writing international history', 536.

65. The most trenchant recent critic is Martin Shipway, *Decolonization*, 89–90, 127–8.

66. Emmanuelle Saada, 'The absent empire: The colonies in French constitutions', in McCoy, Fradera, and Jacobson, *Endless Empire*, 213–14.

67. Shepard, *Invention of Decolonization*, 40–6.

68. Vincent Auriol, *Journal du Septennat, 1947–1954*, ii: *1948* (Paris: Armand Colin, 1974), entry for 12 Feb. 1948.

69. AN, F[60] 888: Union française, 'Note sur la nécessité d'une constitution de l'Union française'. Laurentie's title was political affairs director.

70. MAE, série Asie-Océanie 1944–1960, sous-série Indochine, vol. 30, no. 3316, Laurentie to Commission d'études et d'information pour l'Indochine', 16 Mar. 1945.

71. AN, F[60] 888: Union française, Commission d'étude de la représentation des territoires d'Outre-Mer à l'Assemblée Constituante, 'Procès-verbal, séance du 11 avril 1945', statement by Laurentie.

72. Gregory Mann and Baz Lecocq, 'Between empire, *umma*, and the Muslim Third World: The French Union and African pilgrims to Mecca, 1946–1958', *Comparative Studies of South Asia, Africa and the Middle East*, 27 (2007), 167–81.

73. The terms of the French Union required Associated States to determine answers to these questions, but did not offer specific solutions. Full members of the Union were, however, expected to place their security forces in the hands of a 'French Union high command' under French direction, see: SHD-T, 4Q119/D8, 'Compte-rendu analytique des séances d'études tenues au Comité de l'Afrique du Nord en octobre 1946'.

74. Richard A. Joseph, 'Settlers, strikers and *sans-travail*: The Douala riots of September 1945', *JAH*, 15:4 (1974): 669–87; Frederick Cooper, 'The Senegalese general strike of 1946 and the labor question in post-war French Africa', *CJAS* 24:2 (1990), 165–215; '"Our strike": Equality, anticolonial politics, and the

1947–48 railway strike in French West Africa', *JAH*, 37:1 (1996), 81–118; Tony Chafer, *The End of Empire in French West Africa: France's Successful Decolonization?* (Oxford: Berg, 2002), 68–70, 121–6.

75. Shipway, 'Thinking like an empire: Governor Henri Laurentie and postwar plans for the late colonial French "empire-state"', in Thomas, *French Colonial Mind*, I, 219–50.

76. Shipway, *Decolonization*, 129–30; Chafer, *The End of Empire*, 61–6.

77. Frederick Cooper, 'Alternatives to nationalism in French Africa, 1945–60', in Jost Düllfer and Marc Frey, eds, *Elites and Decolonization in the Twentieth Century* (Basingstoke: Palgrave-Macmillan 2011), 113–15.

78. Paul Isoart, 'L'Élaboration de la constitution de l'Union française: Les Assemblées constituantes', in Ageron, *Les Chemins*, 27; Christian Bidegaray, 'Le Tabou de l'indépendance dans les débats constituants sur les pays de l'outre-mer français: 1945–1958', in Charles-Robert Ageron and Marc Michel, eds, *L'Afrique noire française: L'Heure des indépendances* (Paris: CNRS Éditions, 1992), 195.

79. USNA, RG 59, 851T.00, FWA, Political 1945–49, box 6326, AMCONGEN, Dakar, to State, 3 Nov. 1945.

80. James I. Lewis, 'The MRP and the genesis of the French Union, 1944–1948', *FH*, 12 (1998): 276–314.

81. MAE, Algérie, vol. 2, 'Statut de l'Algérie', 3 June 1947; James I. Lewis, 'French politics and the Algerian Statute of 1947', *Maghreb Review*, 17 (1992): 147–72; Odile Rudelle, 'Le Vote du statut de l'Algérie', in Serge Berstein and Pierre Milza, eds, *L'Année 1947* (Paris, 2000), 317.

82. Cooper, 'Alternatives to nationalism', 112, 118.

83. Shipway, 'Thinking like an empire', 231–5, 240–4.

84. Catherine Coquery-Vidrovitch, 'Émeutes urbaines, grèves générales et décolonisation en Afrique française', in Ageron, *Les Chemins*, 494–6.

85. Frederick Cooper, 'The dialectics of decolonization: Nationalism and labor movements in postwar French Africa', in Frederick Cooper and Ann Laura Stoler, *Tensions of Empire: Colonial Cultures in a Bourgeois World* (Berkeley, CA: University of California Press, 1997), 406–35.

86. Kim, 'France's agony', 61–84.

87. Frédéric Turpin, 'Le Mouvement Républicain Populaire et la guerre d'Indochine (1944–1954)', *Revue d'Histoire Diplomatique*, 110 (1996): 157–90; 'Le Mouvement Républicain Populaire et l'avenir de l'Algérie (1947–1962)', *Revue d'Histoire Diplomatique*, 113 (1999): 171–203.

88. Pierre Letamendia, *Le Mouvement Républicain Populaire: Histoire d'un grand parti français* (Paris: Beauchesne, 1995), 98–101; Henri Descamps, *La Démocratie Chrétienne et le MRP: De 1946 à 1959* (Paris, 1981), livre 3, 171–223.

89. Neville Kirk, *Labour and the Politics of Empire: Britain and Australia, 1900 to the Present* (Manchester University Press, 2011), 160–6.

90. Rose, *Which People's War?*, 244, citing Cooper, *Decolonization and African Society*, 57.

91. Joseph M. Hodge, 'Colonial experts, developmental and environmental doctrines, and the legacies of late British colonialism', in Christina Folke Ax, Niels Brimnes, Niklas Thode Jensen, and Karen Oslund, eds, *Cultivating the Colonies: Colonial States and their Environmental Legacies* (Athens, OH: Ohio University Press, 2011), 304–5.

92. Jeff D. Grischow, 'Late colonial development in British West Africa: The Gonja development project in the northern territories of the Gold Coast, 1948–57', *CJAS*, 35:2 (2001), 282–3, 287–92.

93. Harper, 'Disease and disorder', 90–5; Paul Kelemen, 'Modernising colonialism: The British Labour Movement and Africa', *JICH*, 34:2 (2006), 223–44; Rahul Nair, 'The construction of a "population problem" in colonial India, 1919–1947', *JICH*, 39:2 (2011), 240–2.

94. Sabine Clarke, ' "The chance to send their first-class men out to the colonies": The making of the Colonial Research Service', in Brett M. Bennett and Joseph M. Hodge, eds, *Science and Empire: Knowledge and Networks of Science Across the British Empire, 1800–1970* (London: Palgrave-Macmillan, 2011) 187–208; Hodge, 'Colonial experts', 300–2.

95. Frederick Cooper, 'Modernizing bureaucrats, "backward Africans", and the development concept', in Frederick Cooper and Randall Packard, eds *International Development and the Social Sciences* (Berkeley, CA: University of California Press, 1998), 64–92.

96. Andrew S. Thompson, introduction to *Britain's Experience of Empire*, 8.

97. Scott Newton, 'J.M. Keynes and the postwar international economic order', *History Compass*, 4:2 (2006), 308–12; 'A "visionary hope" frustrated: J. M. Keynes and the origins of the international monetary order', *DS*, 11:1 (2000): 189–210.

98. Havinden and Meredith, *Colonialism and Development*, 267; also cited in Philip Murphy, *Alan Lennox Boyd: A Biography* (London: I.B. Tauris, 1999), 108.

99. Schenk, *The Decline of Sterling*, 90. During the Korean War boom, Malaya and Singapore's balance of trade with Britain went from a £92 million deficit before the war began in 1949 to a £431 million surplus at the War's peak in 1951.

100. J. S. Hogendorn and K. M. Scott, 'The East African groundnut scheme: Lessons of a large-scale agricultural failure', *African Economic History*, 10:1 (1981), 108; also cited in Timothy H. Parsons, *The Rule of Empires: Those Who Built Them, Those Who Endured Them, and Why They Always Fall* (Oxford University Press, 2010), 335.

101. University of Sussex, Mass Observation Online Archive, file report, 'British Empire and Commonwealth': 'Lincs a Colony Shocks Quizzers', *Daily Mail*, 21 Dec. 1948. Three per cent of respondents thought that the United States was still a British colony; one suggested that Lincolnshire was a British colonial territory.

102. TNA, CAB 129/19, CP(47)191, 'Anglo-French-Belgian Collaboration in Africa', 30 June 1947.

103. Barr, *A Line in the Sand*, part IV.
104. AN, Georges Bidault papers, box 57, Sous-direction du Levant, 'Valise du 15 novembre 1946: Syrie'; MAE, série Y: Syrie-Liban, vol. 36, SDECE intell. report, 27 Sept. 1946.
105. MAE, Nations Unies et Organisations Internationales, vol. 573, Rabat tel. 324, 22 Mar. 1945.
106. AN, Bidault papers, box 112, Residency report, 'Situation politique en Tunisie', 1 Feb. 1946.
107. MAE, Nations Unies et Organisations Internationales, vol. 573, Parodi to Foreign Ministry, 9 July 1947; Foreign Ministry tel. 1202, 17 July 1947; Service d'information memo, 16 Apr. 1951.
108. MAE, série Z: Europe, sous-série Grande-Bretagne, vol. 39, Bevin letter to Robert Schuman and reply, 29 Dec. 1948 and 6 Jan. 1949; Gérard Bossuat, *France, l'aide américaine et la construction européenne 1944–1954* (Paris: CHEFF, 1992), Vol. II.
109. Anne Deighton, 'Entente néo-coloniale?: Ernest Bevin and the proposals for an Anglo-French Third World power, 1945–1949', *DS*, 17:4 (2006), 835–52; Marc Michel, 'La Coopération intercoloniale en Afrique noire, 1942–1950: Néocolonialisme éclairé?', *Relations Internationales*, 34:1 (1983), 155–71; John Kent, *The Internationalization of Colonialism: Britain, France and Black Africa, 1939–1956* (Oxford: Clarendon Press, 1992).
110. Louis, 'The dissolution of the British Empire', in Brown and Louis, *OHBE*, iv, 330.
111. Anne Deighton, 'Britain and the Cold War, 1945–1955', in Leffler and Westad, *Cambridge History of the Cold War*, i, 114.
112. Mass Observation was a left-leaning social survey group founded in 1937 by poet and journalist Charles Madge and the documentary film-maker Humphrey Jennings. It employed panels of volunteers to conduct surveys of public attitudes, principally in London.
113. University of Sussex, Mass Observation Online Archive, 'Interim report by Mass Observation describing peoples' hopes and expectations for the future of the world as they were during the UNO sessions at Westminster, 1946', fo. 403.
114. Todd Shepard, '"History is past politics"? Archives, "tainted evidence", and the return of the state', *AHR*, 115:2 (2010), 479–81.
115. Wm. Roger Louis, 'Public enemy number one: The British Empire in the dock at the United Nations, 1957–71', in Lynn, ed., *The British Empire in the 1950s*, 188.
116. AN, F60/889, 'Programme général de la conférence de Brazzaville (janvier 1944)'.
117. Chafer, *The End of Empire*, 56–7.
118. Shepard, '"History is past politics"?' 480–1, quotation at 481.

CHAPTER 4

1. Stockwell, 'Ends of Empire', 273.
2. Fred Logevall, 'The Indochina Wars and the Cold War, 1945–1975', in Leffler and Westad, *Cambridge History of the Cold War*, ii, 281; Logevall, *Embers*, parts II–VI.
3. An idea best explained in Odd Arne Westad, *The Global Cold War: Third World Interventions and the Making of Our Times* (Cambridge University Press, 2005).
4. Christopher Goscha, *Vietnam: Un état né de la guerre* (Paris: Armand Colin, 2011), 464–7.
5. Mark Philip Bradley, *Imagining Vietnam and America: The Making of Postcolonial Vietnam, 1919–1950* (Chapel Hill, NC: University of North Carolina Press, 2000), 177–89; Mark Atwood Lawrence, 'Universal claims, local uses: Reconceptualizing the Vietnam conflict, 1945–1960', in A. G. Hopkins, ed., *Global History: Interactions Between the Universal and the Local* (Basingstoke: Palgrave-Macmillan, 2006), 229–56.
6. Joya Chatterji, *The Spoils of Partition: Bengal and India, 1947–1967* (Cambridge University Press, 2007), 19–33; 'The fashioning of a frontier: The Radcliffe line and Bengal's border landscape, 1947–52', *MAS*, 33 (1999), 188–9, 199–213.
7. Lucy P. Chester, *Boundaries and Conflict in South Asia: The Radcliffe Boundary Commission and the Partition of Punjab* (Manchester University Press, 2009), 25–40.
8. Chester, *Boundaries*, 41–3; Chatterji, 'The fashioning of a frontier', 193–7.
9. The surgical metaphor is brilliantly deployed by Joya Chatterji in 'The fashioning of a frontier', 185–7; Chester, *Boundaries*, 51–70, 83–8.
10. Stanley Wolpert, *Shameful Flight: The Last Years of the British Empire in India* (New York: Oxford University Press, 2006), 183.
11. Patrick French, *Liberty or Death: India's Journey to Independence and Division* (London: Harper Collins, 1997), 372–5.
12. IOR, Private Office papers, L/PO/12/12, Sir Terence Shone to Sir Archibald Carter, 14 Jan. 1948.
13. Yasmin Khan, *The Great Partition: The Making of India and Pakistan* (New Haven, CT: Yale University Press, 2007), 1–4.
14. David Gilmartin, 'Partition, Pakistan, and South Asian history: In search of a narrative', *Journal of Asian Studies*, 57:4 (1998), 1089–91.
15. Chester, *Boundaries and Conflict*, 128–38, 150–70.
16. Gilmartin, 'Partition, Pakistan', 1068–73. Ian Copland makes the point that Indians were so traumatized by partition violence, and so shocked by Gandhi's assassination, that a mood of reconciliation developed, temporarily burying the horrors of the recent past: 'The further shores of partition: Ethnic cleansing in Rajasthan 1947', *PP*, 160 (Aug. 1998), 238–9.
17. French, *Liberty*, 227–34; R. J. Moore, 'Jinnah and the Pakistan demand', in Mushiral Hasan, ed., *India's Partition: Process, Strategy and Mobilization* (Oxford University Press, 1993), 190–2.

18. Ian Talbot, 'The growth of the Muslim League in the Punjab, 1927–46', in Hasan, *India's Partition*, 238–54.

19. Farzana Shaikh, 'Muslims and political representation in colonial India: The making of Pakistan', in Hasan, *India's Partition*, 83–99.

20. Ayesha Jalal, *The Sole Spokesman: Jinnah, the Muslim League and the Demand for Pakistan* (Cambridge University Press, 1994), 8–9, 182–260 *passim*; Nicholas Owen, *The British Left*, 297.

21. Mithi Mukherjee, 'Transcending identity: Gandhi, nonviolence, and the pursuit of a "different" freedom in modern India', *AHR*, 115:2 (2010), 461–2, 466–71.

22. Owen, 'Critics of empire in Britain', in Brown and Louis, *OHBE, iv* , 200.

23. Sir Harry Haig [Governor United Provinces] to Lord Linlithgow, 4 Dec. 1939, in Pandey, *The Indian Nationalist Movement*, 172–5; Jalal, *The Sole Spokesman*.

24. IOR, L/PO/12/15, Sir A. Henderson meeting with V. P. Menon, 16 Jan. 1947.

25. IOR, MSS EUR, F164/10, Sir Francis Mudie papers, Mudie forecast memorandum on possible political developments, n.d., July 1945.

26. Khan, *The Great Partition*, 15–17.

27. Sumit Sarkar, 'Popular movements and national leadership, 1945–47', *Economic and Political Weekly*, 17:14/16 (1982), 677–89.

28. Khan, *The Great Partition*, 63–8.

29. Gyanendra Pandey, *Remembering Partition: Violence, Nationalism and History in India* (Cambridge University Press, 2001), 45, also cited in Ian Talbot, 'The 1947 violence in the Punjab', in Ian Talbot, ed., *Deadly Embrace: Religion, Politics and Violence in India and Pakistan, 1947–2002* (Oxford University Press, 2007), 1–3.

30. Kavita Daiya, *Violent Belongings: Partition, Gender, and National Culture in Postcolonial India* (Philadelphia: Temple University Press, 2008), especially ch. 3.

31. Catherine Coombs, 'Partition narratives: Displaced trauma and culpability among British civil servants in 1940s Punjab', *MAS*, 45:1 (2011), 207–17.

32. IOR, MSS EUR, Mudie papers, F164/20C: 'Disturbances in East Punjab and contiguous areas during and after Aug. 1947. Part II'.

33. IOR, MSS EUR, Mudie papers, F164/16, West Punjab government instruction to police inspector-generals, 16 Sept. 1947.

34. IOR, MSS EUR, Mudie papers, F164/16, Colonel, Advanced HQ/ME Pakistan, Amritsar, 'Report on East Punjab Situation', 24 Sept. 1947.

35. Vazira Fazila-Yacoobali Zamindar, *The Long Partition and the Making of Modern South Asia: Refugees, Boundaries, Histories* (New Delhi: Penguin, 2008), 22.

36. Copland, 'The further shores', 208–27.

37. Ian Talbot, 'Punjabi refugees' rehabilitation and the Indian state: Discourses, denials and dissonances', *MAS*, 45:1 (2011), 110–12, 125–30.

38. Mahbubar Rahman and Willem van Schendel, ' "I am not a refugee": Rethinking partition migration', *MAS*, 37:3 (2003), 551–75.

39. For differing regional levels of violence, see: Ian Talbot, 'The 1947 violence in the Punjab', Pippa Verdee, 'Partition and the absence of communal violence in Malerkotla', and Yasmin Khan, 'Out of control? Partition violence and the state in Uttar Pradesh', all in Talbot, *Deadly Embrace*, 1–59.

40. IOR, MSS EUR, Mudie papers, F164/18: The Tragedy of Delhi', by D.M. Malik, Chairman, Provincial Muslim League, Delhi. This account, although valuable to the historian, is highly partial.

41. Zamindar, *The Long Partition*, 5–8.

42. Robert Holland, Carl Bridge, and H.V. Brasted, 'Counsels of despair or withdrawals with honour? Partitioning in Ireland, India, Palestine and Cyprus 1920–1960', *Round Table*, 86:342 (1997), 257–68; Radha Kumar, 'The troubled history of partition', *Foreign Affairs*, 76:1 (1997), 23–34.

43. Benny Morris, 'Revisiting the Palestinian exodus of 1948', in Eugene L. Rogan and Avi Shlaim, eds, *The War for Palestine: Rewriting the History of 1948* (Cambridge University Press, 2001), 37–59, and, more searing still: Ilan Pappé, *The Ethnic Cleansing of Palestine* (London: Oneworld, 2006).

44. Penny Sinanoglou, 'British plans for the partition of Palestine, 1929–1938', *HJ*, 52:1 (2009), 131–52.

45. Lucy P. Chester, 'Boundary commissions as tools to safeguard British interests at the end of empire', *Journal of Historical Geography*, 34:3 (2008), 507–10; Chatterji, 'The fashioning', 185–242.

46. John Kent, *British Imperial Strategy and the Origins of the Cold War, 1944–49* (Leicester University Press, 1993), 98, 110.

47. TNA, DEFE 7/957, W.N. Hillier-Fry to Tom Barker, 12 Mar. 1955; Nigel John Ashton, 'The hijacking of a pact: The formation of the Baghdad Pact and the Anglo-American tensions in the Middle East, 1955–1958', *Review of International Studies*, 19:2 (1993), 123–37.

48. TNA, CAB 158/1, JIC(47)4, Joint Intelligence Sub-Committee report, 'Role of the Colonies in War', 30 Jan. 1947; Hyam, *Britain's Declining Empire*, 98, 106–11.

49. TNA, CO 537/3362, Burma Office Information Department memo, n.d. Mar. 1947.

50. Harrison, *Medicine & Victory*, 203.

51. IOR, Mss EUR D545, Sir John Walton collection, D545/17, Report on Burma visit, Nov.–Dec., 1945.

52. TNA, FO 371/62419, UE170/170/53, Economic Department paper, 'Economic effects of loss of India and Burma', 1 Jan. 1947.

53. Some British officials never forgave Aung San for initially aligning with the Japanese to cast off British colonialism. His Burma National Army switched allegiance only in Aug. 1944 when it joined with Burma's Communists to form the AFPFL, see A.J. Stockwell, 'Imperialism and nationalism in South-East Asia', in Louis and Brown, *OHBE*, iv, 482.

54. Hugh Tinker, ed., *Burma: The Struggle for Independence, 1944–1948*, ii: *From General Strike to Independence, 31 Aug. 1946 to 4 Jan. 1948* (London: HMSO: 1984), doc. 83: 'AFPFL and Communists part as friends', *The Burman*, 3 Nov. 1946.

55. IOR, Mss EUR D545, Sir John Walton collection, D545/17, Report on Burma visit, Nov.–Dec., 1945.

56. IOR, Mss EUR MSS EUR F169/1: Sir Hubert Rance papers, file 33/GS47, 'Prosecution of Aung San', Sir Reginald Dorman-Smith to Burma Office, London, 4 June 1946.

57. IOR, Mss Eur MSS EUR F169/2: Rance papers, file 24, Rance to Lord Listowel, 19 Nov. 1947.

58. Tinker, *Burma: The Struggle for Independence*, ii, doc. 105: Sir Hubert Rance to Lord Pethick-Lawrence, 13 Nov. 1946.

59. IOR, Mss EUR, F169/5, Rance papers, file 23/GS47: GOC Burma Command, 'Situation in the immediate future', 28 Mar. 1947.

60. Tinker, *Burma*, ii, doc. 7: Rance to Pethick-Lawrence, 9 Sept. 1946.

61. Tinker, *Burma*, ii, doc. 105 encl.: Sir Raibeart MacDougall, 'Memo on the need to accelerate the programme of constitutional advance for Burma set out in the White Papers of May 1945'.

62. TNA, CO 537/3362, 'Political situation in Burma', n.d., Mar. 1947.

63. TNA, CO 537/3362, F/4795/1371/79, 'Burma—Communist-inspired strikes', 1 Apr. 1948.

64. TNA, CAB 121/684, tels. 691 & 760, reports on army mutinies, 10 & 21 Aug. 1948.

65. TNA, CO 537/3362, XS/14/79(1/47), FO South East Asia Department, 'Future British interests and representation in Burma', 14 Oct. 1947; F8826/17/79, 'Anglo-Burmese Relations', 28 June 1948.

66. Schenk, *The Decline of Sterling*, 65.

67. Louis, 'The dissolution of the British Empire', in Brown and Louis, *OHBE*, iv, 334–9.

68. Hyam, *Britain's Declining Empire*, 120–2.

69. 'Ceylon: New Dominion', by Tom Reid, M.P., *The Listener*, 19 Feb. 1948, p. 285.

70. Michael J. Cohen, 'The Zionist perspective', and Walid Khalidi, 'The Arab perspective', both in Wm. Roger Louis and Robert W. Stookey, eds, *The End of the Palestine Mandate* (London: I. B. Tauris, 1986), 83–5 and 109–10. Division between the Arab League and the Palestinian Higher Arab Committee also weakened their case: Haim Levenberg, *Military Preparations of the Arab Community in Palestine, 1945–1948* (London: Frank Cass, 1993), 9–17, 43–5.

71. Swedenburg, *Memories of Revolt*, 85–93; for similar divisions in the Palestinian women's movement, see: Ellen L. Fleischmann, 'Memory, gender and nationalism: Palestinian women leaders of the Mandate period', *History Workshop Journal*, 47 (1999), 149–55.

72. Hillel Cohen, *Army of Shadows: Palestinian Collaboration with Zionism, 1917–1948* (Berkeley, CA: University of California Press, 2008), 202–13.

73. Cohen, 'Appeasement in the Middle East', 571–96.

74. The repression's ferocity is examined in Hughes, 'The Banality of Brutality', 313–54.

75. TNA, CAB 129/006, CP(46)17, FO memo, 'Revision of the Anglo-Egyptian Treaty of 1936', 18 Jan. 1946; Wilson, *King Abdullah*, 151–67; Avi Shlaim, *The Politics of Partition: King Abdullah, the Zionists and Palestine, 1921–1951* (Oxford University Press, 2004), 126–36.

76. Wm. Roger Louis, 'British imperialism and the end of the Palestine Mandate', in Louis and Stookey, *End*, 2–11.

77. Louis, 'British Imperialism and the end', 19–21.

78. Peter Grose, 'The President versus the diplomats', in Louis and Stookey, *End*, 40–4, 53–6.

79. Barr, *A Line*, 313–17. Zionist lobby groups in France drew equivalent parallels between Jewish freedom fighters and French resisters, winning the support of the country's premier intellectual celebrity couple Simone de Beauvoir and Jean-Paul Sartre.

80. Louis, 'British Imperialism and the End', 4–8; Richard Toye, *Churchill's Empire: The World that Made Him and the World He Made* (Basingstoke: Macmillan, 2010), 251, 277–8.

81. Wm. Roger Louis, *The British Empire in the Middle East: Arab Nationalism, the United States, and Postwar Imperialism, 1945–1951* (Oxford University Press, 1984), 464–77.

82. On 29 Nov. 1947 the UN General Assembly defied British expectations, voting for partition by 33 to 13.

83. Levenberg, *Military Preparations*, 126–32.

84. Zachary Lockman, *Comrades and Enemies: Arab and Jewish Workers in Palestine, 1906–1948* (Berkeley: University of California Press, 1996), 322–35; David De Vries, 'British rule and Arab-Jewish coalescence of interest: The 1946 civil servants' strike in Palestine', *IJMES*, 36:4 (2004), 613–34; David De Vries and Shani Bar-On, 'Politicization of unemployment in British-ruled Palestine', in Matthias Reiss & Matt Perry, eds, *Unemployment and Protest: New Perspectives on Two Centuries of Contention* (Oxford University Press, 2011), 214–19.

85. Cohen, *Army of Shadows*, 212–21, 250–8; Mary C. Wilson, 'King Abdullah and Palestine', *Bulletin of the British Society for Middle Eastern Studies*, 14:1 (1987), 37–41.

86. The potential for deal-making between Israeli leaders and King Abdullah's regime was also critical, see: Avi Shlaim, *The Iron Wall: Israel and the Arab World* (London: Penguin, 2000), 24–5, 28–31.

87. Lockman, *Comrades and Enemies*, 313–14; Louis, 'British imperialism and the end', 19.

88. David Ceserani, 'The British security forces and the Jews in Palestine, 1945–48', in Claus-Christian W. Szejnmann, ed., *Rethinking History, Dictatorship and War: New Approaches and Interpretations* (London: Continuum, 2009) 193, 200.

89. Ceserani, 'The British security forces', 194.

90. French, *The British Way*, 68–9, 146, 148.

91. Ceserani, 'The British security forces', 206–10.

92. For background to the attack, see: Calder Walton, 'British intelligence and the Mandate of Palestine: Threats to British national security immediately after the Second World War', *INS*, 23:4 (2008), 435–62; David Cesarini, 'Remember Cable Street? Wrong battle, mate', *History and Policy*, online journal paper available at http://www.historyandpolicy.org/papers/policy-paper-93.html#S3.

93. Barr, *A Line*, 320–5. The Colonial Office device was assembled by Stern Gang bomb-maker Yaacov Levstein, who, after escaping a Palestine prison in 1943, made contact with a Colonel Alessandri, head of the French security service *Bureau Noir*, and David Knout, a Russian Jewish émigré who founded the French Jewish resistance network, the *Armée Juive*. It was Knout's daughter, Betty, whose stocking malfunctioned. The earlier bombing of the ex-servicemen's Colonies Club was carried out with Stern Gang backing by Robert Misrahi, a student of Jean-Paul Sartre's at the Sorbonne. Midway through a letter-bombing campaign directed against British politicians, both Levstein and Betty Knout were arrested in 1947, but by Belgian, not French, customs officials.

94. Barr, *A Line*, 336–7.

95. Ina Zweiniger-Bargielowska, *Austerity in Britain*, 149, 225–6, 261.

96. David A. Charters, *The British Army and Jewish Insurgency in Palestine, 1945–47* (Basingstoke: Macmillan, 1989); Stuart Cohen, 'Imperial policing against illegal immigration: The Royal Navy and Palestine, 1945–48', *JICH*, 22:2 (1994), 275–93; Steven G. Galpern, *Money, Oil, and Empire in the Middle East: Sterling and Postwar Imperialism, 1944–1971* (Cambridge University Press, 2009), 48–58.

97. See John Julius Norwich, ed., *The Duff Cooper Diaries, 1915–1951* (London: Weidenfeld & Nicolson, 2005), entry for 24 Mar. 1947, p. 434.

98. Jeffery, *MI6*, 689–95.

99. Barr, *A Line*, 341, 347.

100. Levenberg, *Military Preparations*, 85–90; Khalidi, 'The Arab perspective', 126–8.

101. A process most graphically recounted in Pappé, *The Ethnic Cleansing*.

102. Barr, *A Line*, 330–2.

103. *Duff Cooper Diaries*, entries for 19, 23, and 30 July 1947, pp. 444–6.

104. Ellen Jenny Ravndal, 'Exit Britain: British withdrawal from the Palestine Mandate in the early Cold War, 1947–1948', *DS*, 21:3 (2010), 424–5.

105. Barr, *A Line*, 323–4, 329–32, quotation at 324.

106. Dispute over the planning and scale of Israeli security force killings hinges on the incidence of massacre: Benny Morris, 'Operation *Dani* and the Palestinian exodus from Lydda and Ramle in 1948', *Middle East Journal*, 40:1 (1986), 82–109; Alon Kadish and Avraham Sela, 'Myths and historiography of the 1948 Palestine War revisited: The case of Lydda', *Middle East Journal*, 59:4 (2005), 617–34.

107. Ghazi Falah, 'The 1948 Israeli–Palestinian War and Its aftermath: The transformation and de-signification of Palestine's cultural landscape', *Annals of the Association of American Geographers*, 86:2 (1996), 256–85.

108. Morris, 'Revisiting the Palestinian exodus', 37–59; Pappé, *The Ethnic Cleansing*.

109. Ritchie Ovendale, *Britain, the United States, and the End of the Palestine Mandate, 1942–1948* (Woodbridge: Boydell Press, 1989), 306–7.

110. TNA, CAB 158/1, JIC(47)3, 'Provincial autonomy and partition in Palestine', 7 Jan. 1947.

111. Mazower, *No Enchanted Palace*, 150–7.

112. TNA, CO 537/3889, 'Note on position of military forces in Palestine after 15 May 1948'.

113. Worth mentioning here is that Palestine, along with Egypt and, above all, India, was a major holder of sterling balances. These were British wartime debts run up in colonial Treasuries, whose ultimate settlement occurred after British withdrawal, see: Jacob Reuveny, 'The financial liquidation of the Palestine Mandate', *MES*, 27:1 (1991), 113–16, 125–7.

114. DDF, 1947, vol. I, doc. 340, Massigli to Bidault, 19 May 1947.

115. MAE, série Tunisie, 1944–1955, vol. 300, Bureau de centralisation de renseignements d'Algérie intelligence report, 18 May 1948. The French security service in North Africa warned that Maghreb nationalists drew inspiration from the mandate's collapse.

116. MAE, série Asie, Indochine vol. 31, Direction Générale des Etudes et Recherche, note 221/POL, 14 June 1945; Comité de l'Indochine, 'Compte-rendus des nouvelles 21–27 juillet 1945'; Agathe Larcher-Goscha, 'Ambushed by history: Paul Mus and colonial France's "forced re-Entry" into Vietnam (1945–1954)', *Journal of Vietnamese Studies*, 4:1 (2009), 206–39.

117. TNA, WO 208/665, MI2 report, 'FIC—French colonial troops', 10 July 1945; CAB 122/495, JP(45)207, Washington Joint Staff Mission report, 'Liaison with European Allies', 16 Aug. 1945.

118. Goscha, *Vietnam*, 46–50, 66–79.

119. Marr, *Vietnam 1945*, 406–17; Goscha, *Vietnam*, ch. 2.

120. The two indispensable accounts are Stein Tønnesson, *The Vietnamese Revolution of 1945: Roosevelt, Ho Chi Minh, and de Gaulle in a World at War* (Oslo: International Peace Research Institute/Sage, 1991), and Marr, *Vietnam 1945*.

121. Vo Nguyen Giap, 'Mot sang Ba Dinh' in *Mo Ky Nguyen Giap* (Hanoi, 1980), 397, cited in Brocheux and Hémery, *Indochina*, 352.

122. Bradley, *Imagining Vietnam*, 3–4; Tønnesson, *Vietnam 1946*, 2–3, 12–13.

123. Marr, *Vietnam 1945*, 523–8.

124. Brocheux, *Ho Chi Minh*, 103–4; Marr, *Vietnam 1945*, 433–5, 461; R. P. Claude Lange, 'L'Église Catholique au Viêtnam', in Ageron, *Les Chemins*, 181–7; Christopher E. Goscha, 'A rougher side of "popular" resistance: Reflections on the rise and fall of General Nguyen Binh (1910–1951)', in C. E. Goscha and B. de Tréglodé, eds, *Le Viêt Nam depuis 1945: États, marges et constructions du passé* (Paris: Les Indes savantes, 2004), 325–53.

125. Stein Tønnesson, 'Filling the power vacuum: 1945 in French Indochina, the Netherlands East Indies and British Malaya', in Hans Antlöv and Stein Tønnesson, eds, *Imperial Policy and Southeast Asian Nationalism* (London: Curzon Press, 1995), 110–43.

126. Xiaoyuan Liu, 'China and the issue of postwar Indochina in the Second World War', *MAS*, 33:2 (1999), 475–80.

127. Peter M. Dunn, *The First Vietnam War* (London: Hurst, 1985); Peter Dennis, *Troubled Days of Peace: Mountbatten and South East Asia Command* (Manchester University Press, 1987); Timothy Smith, 'Major General Sir Douglas Gracey: Peacekeeper or peace enforcer?' *DS*, 21:2 (2010), 226–39.

128. TNA, FO 959/6, Mountbatten, South Asia Command HQ, to Saigon Consulate, 26 Feb. 1946.

129. Marr, *Vietnam 1945*, 497–9; Goscha, *Vietnam*, 246–7.

130. Brocheux, *Ho Chi Minh*, 106–9; Lin Hua, *Chiang Kai-shek, de Gaulle contre Hô Chi Minh: Viet-nam, 1945–1946* (Paris: L'Harmattan, 1994).

131. The French shelved a planned Operation *Bentré*, predicated on landings in the northern port city of Haiphong and an assault on Hanoi, when Chinese artillery batteries fired on ships preparing to disembark the French invasion force at Haiphong on 6 Mar.: Tønnesson, *Vietnam 1946*, 40–54.

132. Tønnesson, *Vietnam 1946*, 66–71.

133. Christopher E. Goscha, 'Colonial Hanoi and Saigon at war: Social Dynamics of the Viet Minh's 'Underground City', (1945–1954)', *War in History*, 20:2 (2013), 222–50.

134. The Vietminh's *Tu Ve* militia forces also expanded: David G. Marr, 'Creating defense capacity in Vietnam, 1945–1947', in Lawrence and Logevall, *The First Vietnam War*, 90–3.

135. Brocheux, *Ho Chi Minh*, 121. De Gaulle was unimpressed by Bidault's fondness for alcohol, which caused embarrassing gaffes, as when the unfortunate Foreign Minister fell asleep on the General's shoulder during a Nov. 1944 parliamentary debate. See, *The Duff Cooper Diaries*, entry for 25 Nov. 1944.

136. Duiker, *The Communist Road*, 122–3; Jean-Marie d'Hoop, 'Du coup de force japonais au départ du Général de Gaulle', in Gilbert Pilleul, ed., *Le Général de Gaulle et l'Indochine, 1940–1946* (Paris: Plon, 1982), 142–3.

137. MAE, AP288, Maurice Dejean papers, 'Organisation du Vietminh en 1946'.

138. Brocheux, *Ho Chi Minh*, 116–19.

139. US loathing for d'Argenlieu dated from his wartime service as de Gaulle's Governor of New Caledonia, a nickel-rich island in the path of America's Pacific advance against Japan, see Kim Munholland, *Rock of Contention: Free French and Americans at War in New Caledonia, 1940–45* (Oxford: Berghahn, 2004), chs 3–6.

140. Tønnesson, *Vietnam 1946*, 5–6.

141. Martin Thomas, 'French imperial reconstruction and the development of the Indochina War, 1945–1950', in Lawrence and Logevall, *The First Vietnam War*, 130–51.

142. Philippe Devillers, *Paris–Saigon–Hanoi: Les Archives de la guerre, 1944–1947* (Paris: Gallimard, 1988); Shipway, *Road to War*, chs 7–8; Lawrence, *Assuming the Burden*, ch. 4. Dr Van Thinh committed suicide after a Cabinet meeting on 10 Nov. 1946 in which he conceded that the Cochin-China Republic was a sham.

143. Tønnesson, *Vietnam 1946*, 80–1; Brocheux, *Ho Chi Minh*, 120–6.

144. Jacques Valette, 'La Conférence de Fontainebleau (1946)', in Ageron, *Les Chemins*, 247–9; Lawrence, *Assuming the Burden*, 150–4.

145. For details of conditions in Hanoi, see: Goscha, *Vietnam*, 149–58.

146. DDF, 1947, vol. I, docs. 5 and 9.

147. TNA, FO 371/63547, F1969/1969/61, minute by Esler Dening, 7 Feb. 1947.

148. A. S. B. Oliver, 'The Special Commission for South East Asia', *Pacific Affairs*, 21:3 (1948) 285–6.

149. Hyam, *Britain's Declining Empire*, 157–8.

150. TNA, CAB 121/400, JP(47)14, 'Anglo-French treaty—military implication', 7 Feb. 1947.

151. TNA, FO 371/63542, F1035/61/G, Killearn to FO, 26 Jan. 1947, and minutes by Bevin, Attlee, and Duff Cooper, 29–30 Jan. 1947.

152. Buton, 'Le Parti communiste français et le stalinisme', 65.

153. TNA, CAB 121/684: G/Burma/3, annex I to COS(48)122nd Meeting, 3 Sept. 1948.

CHAPTER 5

1. On 4 Oct. 1936 Cable Street in Stepney, East London, witnessed Britain's worst pre-war clashes between Mosley's BUF supporters, members of the local Jewish community, and anti-fascist groups.

2. *BDEEP*, series B, vol. 3: *Malaya, II: The Communist Insurrection, 1948–1953* edited by A. J. Stockwell (London, HMSO, 1995), doc. 146.

3. *BDEEP*, series B, vol. 3: *Malaya, II*, docs. 151, 152 and 246. Lady Gurney, also in the car at the time, escaped serious injury.

4. Malaya's then Governor, Sir Edward Gent introduced emergency measures. Unlawful possession of arms carried the death penalty, security forces could search homes without a warrant, and properties could be sequestered if deemed necessary. The High Commission and Attlee's Cabinet bent to pressure from planters and business interests as attacks increased. Harsher regulations, including a ban on the Malayan Communist Party, followed on 23 July 1948: Stockwell, 'A Widespread and Long-Concocted Plot', 66, 77; *BDEEP*, series B, vol. 3: *Malaya, II*, docs. 150 & 160.

5. Trenchant critics are T. N. Harper, *The End of Empire and the Making of Malaya* (Cambridge University Press, 1999), and Karl Hack, *Defence and Decolonisation in Southeast Asia: Britain, Malaya and Singapore 1941–68* (Richmond: Curzon, 2000); 'British intelligence and counter-insurgency in the era of decolonization: The example of Malaya', *INS*, 14:2 (1999).

6. *BDEEP*, series B, vol. 3: *Malaya, I: The Malayan Union Experiment, 1942–1948*, ch. 3: 'Constitutional conflict: From Malayan Union to Federation, Apr. 1946–Feb. 1948.

7. Misperceptions in this outlook are examined by Anthony Milner: *The Invention of Colonial Malaya: Contesting Nationalism and the Expansion of the Public Sphere* (Cambridge University Press, 1995).

8. Shipway, *Decolonization*, 95–6.
9. Wm. Roger Louis, 'The dissolution of the British Empire in the era of Vietnam', *AHR*, 107:1 (2002), 8.
10. Stockwell, 'The formation', 481–513.
11. Simon C. Smith, *British Relations with the Malay Rulers from Decentralization to Malayan Independence, 1930–1957* (Kuala Lumpur: Oxford University Press, 1995), 66–8. British businesses involved in rubber and tin production were more affected by wartime dislocation, capital shortages, and labour supply problems, see: Nicholas J. White, *Business, Government and the End of Empire: Malaya, 1942–57* (Kuala Lumpur: Oxford University Press, 1996), 72–88, 97–9.
12. *BDEEP*, series B, vol. 3: *Malaya, II*, docs. 146, 148, 153.
13. *BDEEP*, series B, vol. 3: *Malaya, II*, doc. 162.
14. Stockwell, 'A widespread and long-concocted plot', 69, 74, 78–81.
15. Stockwell, 'Imperialism and nationalism', 486.
16. *BDEEP*, series B, vol. 3: *Malaya, II*, doc. 144. The unfortunate Gent died in office, his plane colliding with another as it descended to Northolt Airport on 29 June 1948.
17. TNA, CO 537/5658, CPM(48)15, Cabinet committee on preparations for the meeting of Commonwealth Prime Ministers, 4 Oct. 1948.
18. TNA, CAB 21/1681, JP(50)114(S), 'Comment on the defence of Malaya', 6 Oct. 1950.
19. For the Vietnamese case, see Goscha, 'A "Total War"' 136–62.
20. Christopher Bayly and Timothy Harper, *Forgotten Wars: Freedom and Revolution in South East Asia* (London: Penguin, 2007), 443–9. Few MSS officers could speak Chinese, taking refuge in stereotypical characterization of Chinese actions as inherently inscrutable.
21. French, *The British Way*, 44–5, 65–7, 96–7; Karl Hack, 'Everyone lived in fear: Malaya and the British way of counter-insurgency', *SWI*, 23:4/5 (2012), 671–99.
22. Huw Bennett, '"A very salutary effect": The counter-terror strategy in the early Malayan Emergency, June 1948 to December 1949', *Journal of Strategic Studies*, 32:3 (2009), 417–19, 427–31. For the Palestine parallel: Matthew Hughes, 'Lawlessness', 141–56.
23. Bayly and Harper, *Forgotten Wars*, 449–53.
24. Bennett, 'A very salutary effect', 427–35. Relatives of the men killed at Batang Kali have demanded a fuller investigation and on 8–9 May 2012 the case was reviewed by the British High Court: 'Judicial review into colonial-era massacre opens at high court', *The Guardian*, 7 May 2012.
25. Leong Yee Fong, 'The impact of the Cold War on the development of trade unionism in Malaya (1948–57)', *JSEAS*, 23:1 (1992), 60–73.
26. MAE série Z: Europe, 1944–1960, sous-série: Grande-Bretagne, vol. 95, no. 25/EU, René Massigli to Robert Schuman, 5 Jan. 1950.
27. Nicholas Tarling, 'The UK and the origins of the Colombo Plan', *Commonwealth & Comparative Studies* 24:1 (1986), 3–34.

28. Susan L. Carruthers, *Winning Hearts and Minds: British Governments, the Media and Colonial Counter-Insurgency 1944–1960* (Leicester University Press, 1995), 76–85; Kumar Ramakrishna, *Emergency Propaganda: The Winning of Malayan Hearts and Minds, 1948–1958* (Richmond: Curzon, 2002), 72–86.

29. TNA, CAB 134/497, MAL. C(50)14, 'Outline of future anti-bandit policy', 12 May 1950.

30. Carruthers, *Winning Hearts*, 76–8; French, *The British Way*, 60–1.

31. TNA, CAB 158/6, JIC(49)33, 'Communist influence in the Far East', 29 Apr. 1949; CAB 158/7, JIC(49)48, 'The implications of a Communist success in China', 30 Sept. 1949.

32. Philip Deery, 'The terminology of terrorism: Malaya, 1948–52', *JSEAS*, 34:2 (2003), 236–47; Frank Furedi, 'Creating a breathing space: The political management of colonial emergencies', *JICH*, 21:2 (1993), 94.

33. *BDEEP*, series S, vol. 3: *The Conservative Government and the End of Empire, 1951–1957, II*, doc. 344.

34. *BDEEP*, series B, vol. 3: *Malaya, II*, docs. 258 & 259. Templer also enjoyed influential backing from Field Marshal Montgomery, who was bitterly critical of Malcolm MacDonald's alleged indecisiveness.

35. Kumar Ramakrishna, '"Transmogrifying" Malaya: The impact of Sir Gerald Templer (1952–54)', *JSEAS*, 32:1 (2001), 79–92.

36. Arguments over the Emergency's differing phases are explored in Karl Hack, 'The Malayan Emergency as counter-insurgency paradigm', *Journal of Strategic Studies*, 32:3 (2009), 383–414.

37. *BDEEP*, series B, vol. 3: *Malaya, II*, doc. 206. Appointed on the initiative of Defence Minister Emmanuel Shinwell, Briggs was military commander in Burma at the end of the Second World War.

38. French, *The British Way*, 186–7.

39. Hack, 'The Malayan Emergency', 385–92.

40. French, *The British Way*, 77–80, 119–21. David French estimates that approximately half of Malaya's ethnic Chinese population (1,073,000 out of 2,153,000 according to 1953 census figures) were subjected to forcible resettlement, a figure surpassed in Kenya where sixty-nine per cent (some 1,077,500 of Kenya's roughly 1,555,000 Kikuyu, Meru, or Embu people according to 1948 census figures) were compelled to move to one of the colony's 854 'new villages'.

41. TNA, CAB 21/1681, MAL.C(50)9th Meeting, Malaya Committee minutes of meeting, 25 Sept. 1950; *BDEEP*, series B, vol. 3: *Malaya, II*, docs. 233 and 234.

42. *BDEEP*, series B, vol. 3: *Malaya, II*, doc. 239, joint memo by Gurney and Briggs, 'Federation of Malaya—combined appreciation of the emergency situation', 4 June 1951.

43. Karl Hack, 'Negotiating with the Malayan Communist Party, 1948–89', *JICH*, 39:4 (2011), 608.

44. Karl Hack, '"Screwing down the people": The Malayan Emergency, decolonisation and ethnicity', in Hans Antlöv and Stein Tennesson, eds, *Imperial Policy,*

83–109; Hack, '"Iron claws on Malaya": The historiography of the Malayan Emergency', *JSEAS*, 30:1 (1999), 119.

45. Simon C. Smith, 'General Templer and counter-insurgency in Malaya: Hearts and minds, intelligence and propaganda', *INS*, 16:3 (2001), 60–78.

46. Ramakrishna, *Emergency Propaganda*, 107–11, 151–8, 162–3; Hack, 'Negotiating', 611–12.

47. Karl Hack, '"Iron Claws"', quotation at 123.

48. *BDEEP*, series S, vol. 3: *The Conservative Government and the End of Empire, 1951–1957, II*, edited by David Goldsworthy (London, HMSO, 1994), doc. 341, annex II.

49. Karl Hack, "Iron claws", 104

50. Ramakrishna, 'Transmogrifying' Malaya', 82, 88.

51. *BDEEP*, series B, vol. 3: *Malaya, II*, doc. 301.

52. Tim Harper, 'The British "Malayans"', in Bickers, *Settlers and Expatriates*, 261–4, quotation at 261.

53. *BDEEP*, series B, vol. 3: *Malaya, II*, docs. 270 & 280.

54. *BDEEP*, series B, vol. 3: *Malaya, II*, docs. 283, 298 & 299; Stockwell, 'Imperialism', 487.

55. Hack, 'Negotiating', 612–26. The negotiations, held at Baling in the north state of Kedah on 28–29 Dec. 1955, did not produce a surrender agreement, but they did herald the transfer of internal security responsibilities to Chief Minister Rahman's Malayan Alliance in Jan. 1956.

56. A. J. Stockwell, 'Malaysia: The making of a neo-colony?' *JICH*, 26:2 (1998), 144–5.

57. Hugues Tertrais, 'Le Poids financier de la guerre d'Indochine', in Maurice Vaïsse, ed., *L'Armée française dans la guerre d'Indochine* (Bruxelles, Editions Complexe, 2000), 33–51; 'L'Économie indochinoise dans la guerre (1945–1954)', *Outre-Mers: Revue d'histoire*, 88:330 (2001), 113–29.

58. Mark Philip Bradley, *Vietnam at War* (Oxford University Press, 2009), 43–7.

59. This argument is central to Christopher Goscha's *Vietnam: Un état né de la guerre*.

60. Goscha, *Vietnam*, 161–4.

61. Goscha, 'Colonial Hanoi'.

62. Brocheux and Hémery, *Indochina*, 361–2.

63. Lawrence, *Assuming the Burden*, chs 5–6.

64. Wall, *Making of Postwar France*, 237–8.

65. Lawrence, *Assuming the Burden*, 269.

66. Goscha, *Vietnam*, 378, 393.

67. The pitfalls of regarding Sino-Vietnamese alignment as inevitable are discussed by Christopher E. Goscha, 'Courting diplomatic disaster? The difficult integration of Vietnam into the internationalist Communist movement (1945–1950)', *Journal of Vietnamese Studies*, 1:1/2 (2006), 59–103.

68. Chen Jian, 'China and the first Indo-China War, 1950–54', *China Quarterly*, 133 (Mar., 1993), 86–9.

69. The materiel supplied are detailed in Goscha, *Vietnam*, 113–19.

70. Qiang Zhai, 'Transplanting the Chinese model: Chinese military advisers and the first Vietnam War, 1950–1954', *Journal of Military History*, 57:4 (1993), 689–95.

71. Jian, 'China', 90–2; Goscha, *Vietnam*, 117–18.

72. Jian, 'China', 93.

73. Clayton, *The Wars of French Decolonization*, 53–5; Zhai, 'Transplanting', 700–1. The French defending force was only 260 strong. Few escaped.

74. Frédéric Turpin, 'Cao Bang, autumne 1950: Autoposie d'un désastre', *Revue Historique des Armées*, 3 (2000), 25–34; Logevall, *Embers*, 238–59 *passim*.

75. Bernard Fall, *Street Without Joy: The French Debacle in Indochina* (Mechanicsburg: Stackpole, 1994), 32–3; also cited in Creswell, *A Question of Balance*, 184n.34.

76. Jian, 'China', 92–5; Zhai, 'Transplanting', 702–4.

77. Bougeard, *René Pleven*, 216–17.

78. The Chinese precluded sending troops unless the DRV faced defeat: Eva-Maria Stolberg, 'Vietnam and the Sino-Soviet struggle for ideological supremacy', in Andreas W. Daum, Lloyd C. Gardner, and Wilfried Mausbach, eds, *America, the Vietnam War, and the World* (Cambridge University Press, 2003), 240–2.

79. TNA, CAB 158/11, JIC(50)94, 'Threat to French position in Indochina', 9 Nov. 1950.

80. Alain Ruscio, 'L'Opinion publique et la guerre d'Indochine', *Vingtième Siècle*, 1 (1991), 35–46.

81. David Drake, '*Les Temps Modernes* and the French war in Indochina', *Journal of European Studies*, 28: 109–10 (1998), 25–41.

82. Paul Clay Sorum, *Intellectuals and Decolonization in France* (Chapel Hill, NC: University of North Carolina Press, 1977), 55–6; Jean-Pierre Biondi, *Les Anti-colonialistes (1881–1962)* (Paris: Robert Laffont, 1992), 261–5.

83. Goscha, *Vietnam*, 14–15; Susan Bayly, 'Conceptualizing resistance and revolution in Vietnam: Paul Mus' understanding of colonialism in crisis', *Journal of Vietnamese Studies*, 4:1 (2009), 192–205.

84. Ruscio, *Les Communistes français et la guerre d'Indochine, 1944–54* (Paris: L'Harmattan, 2004); 'French public opinion and the war in Indochina, 1945–1954', in M. Scriven and P. Wagstaff, eds, *War and Society in Twentieth-Century France* (Oxford: Berg, 1992), 117–29.

85. Some Socialists never abandoned the idea of face-to-face negotiations and maintained indirect links with the Vietminh, see Jacques Dalloz, 'Alain Savary, un socialiste face à la guerre d'Indochine', *Vingtième Siècle*, 53:1 (1997), 42–54.

86. For the intelligence dimension, see Alexander Zervoudakis, '*Nihilmirare, nihil contemptare, Omnia intelligere*: Franco-Vietnamese intelligence in Indochina, 1950–1954', INS, 13:1 (1998), 195–229.

87. R. E. M. Irving, *Christian Democracy in France* (London: Allen & Unwin, 1973), 199–200, 205–9.

88. MAE série Z: Europe, sous-série: Grande-Bretagne, 1944–1949, vol. 39, 'Compte-rendu des conversations entre M. Schuman et M. Bevin, Londres', 13 Jan. 1949.

89. Pierre Mendès France, *Oeuvres Complètes*, ii: *Une Politique de l'économie 1943–1954*, (Paris: Gallimard, 1985), 297–303.

90. Jean-Pierre Rioux, 'Varus, Qu'as-tu fait de mes légions?', in Vaïsse, *L'Armée française*, 21–31; Frédéric Turpin, *De Gaulle, les Gaullistes et l'Indochine* (Paris: Les Indes savantes, 2005), 571–2.

91. MAE, Dejean papers, vol. 136, 'Conventions inter-états', Pau, 29 Nov. 1950.

92. MAE, Dejean papers, vol. 136, Haut-Commissariat en Indochine, Conseiller à l'économie et aux finances, 'Rapport d'activité, 1952', 20 Jan. 1953.

93. AN, René Mayer papers, 363AP/28/D1, PM's office memo on defence spending, 7 Aug. 1950.

94. Hugues Tertrais, *La Piastre*, 225–31.

95. Anthony Clayton, *Three Marshals of France: Leadership after Trauma* (London: Brasseys, 1992).

96. Alexander Zervoudakis, ' "Nihil mirare, nihil contemptare, omnia intelligere": Franco-Vietnamese intelligence in Indochina, 1950–1954', *INS*, 13:1 (1998), 195–229.

97. François Guillemot, 'Be men!': Fighting and dying for the state of Vietnam (1951–54)', *War & Society*, 31:2, (2012), 184–92, quotation at 184.

98. Robert Schuman served twice as finance minister, first between June and Dec. 1946, then from Jan. to Nov. 1947; he was prime minister from Nov. 1947 to July 1948, after which he began the first of three spells as foreign minister between 1948 and 1953.

99. Raymond Poidevin, *Robert Schuman, homme d'état, 1886–1963* (Paris: Imprimerie Nationale, 1986), 340–4; Wall, *Making of Postwar France*, 237, 243.

100. AN, 363AP/28, René Mayer papers, Robert Schuman letter to Dean Acheson, 25 Aug. 1951.

101. Marc Michel, 'De Lattre et les débuts de l'américanisation de la guerre d'Indochine', *Revue Française d'Histoire d'Outre-Mer*, 77 (1985), 321–34.

102. USNA, State Department files, Policy Planning Staff records, RG 59/250/D/12/01, Box 15, Record of Washington discussions with General de Lattre, 7 Sept. 1951.

103. MAE, série Asie-Océanie, sous-série: Indochine, vol. 261, Washington tel. 1652, 15 Mar. 1952; Direction Asie-Océanie 'Note pour le Ministre', 23 May 1952.

104. Logevall, *Embers*, 320, 354–5.

105. USNA, State Department files, Policy Planning Staff records, RG 59/250/D/12/01, Box 18, PPS briefing for Secretary of State's conversation with Jean Letourneau, 16 June 1952.

106. Logevall, *Embers*, 322–6.

107. TNA, FO 371/106742, FF1011/1, 'Indochina: Annual review for 1952', 9 Jan. 1953.

108. TNA, FO 371/112774, WF1019/1/54, Paris Embassy report on France for 1953, 30 Jan. 1954.

109. TNA, FO 371/106751, FF10317/43, Churchill minute for Sir William Strang, 1 May 1953.

110. AN, René Mayer papers, 363AP/24/D1, no. 2968/EMCFA, 'Évolution de la situation en Indochine au mois d'avril 1953', 6 May 1953.

111. Goscha, *Vietnam*, 282–315.

112. AN, René Mayer papers, 363AP/24/D2, Jean Letourneau letter to René Mayer, 9 Apr. 1953: summary of SDECE covert funding in Indochina.

113. AN, René Mayer papers, 363AP/24/D2, Général Charles Léchères, 'Compte-rendu de mission en Indochine (30 avril–18 mai 1953)'.

114. AN, René Mayer papers, 363AP/24/D1, 'Note sur les effectifs engagés en Indochine', 'Note sur le développement des armées nationales', 'Du rôle des officiers français dans les armées des États Associés', all undated High Command assessments, 1953.

115. Guillemot, 'Be men!', 194–210.

116. Rioux, *The Fourth Republic*, 211.

117. George Herring, *America's Longest War: The United States and Vietnam 1950–1975* (New York: Knopf, 1986), 26.

118. Duiker, *Communist Road*, 148–9.

119. Jian, 'China', 97–9.

120. Greg Lockhart, *Nation in Arms: The Origins of the People's Army of Vietnam* (London: Allen and Unwin, 1989), 254, n.123.

121. MAE, Dejean papers, vol. 136, Bulletin d'informations, 10 Aug. 1953.

122. Tuang Huang, 'The early South Vietnamese critique of Communism', in Tuong Vu and Wasana Wongsurawat, eds, *Dynamics of the Cold War in Asia: Ideology, Identity, and Culture* (New York: Palgrave-Macmillan, 2009), 18–31.

123. MAE, Dejean papers, vol. 136, Gautier to Minister for Associated States, 19 July 1953; 'Notices sur les groupements politiques et les sectes confessionelles au Viêtnam', 1 Aug. 1953. The Hoa Hao's militant attitude to self-defence was hardly surprising since its spiritual leader Huynh Phu So was killed and dismembered by Vietminh agents before the war began, see Bradley, *Vietnam at War*, 46.

124. MAE, Dejean papers, vol. 138, MAE Direction Asie-Océanie note, 'Négociation de paix en Indochine', 9 Oct. 1953; Dejean (Saigon) to PM, n.d., Nov. 1953.

125. Logevall, *Embers*, parts IV and V captures the mood of rising desperation.

126. MAE, Dejean papers, vol. 138, no. 1599/CAB, Dejean (Saigon) memo for PM's office, 28 Apr. 1954; Thomas Engelbert, 'Vietnamese-Chinese relations in Southern Vietnam during the first Indochina Conflict', *Journal of Vietnamese Studies*, 3:3 (2008), 191–230.

127. Cooper, *France in Indochina*, 184–90. Geneviève de Galard recounted her experiences in *Une femme à Dien Bien Phu* (Paris: Editions des Arènes, 2003). Aside from de Galard's stoicism, *Paris Match* photo montages depicted an increasingly haggard French commander, General Christian de Castries, injured servicemen, and advancing DRV troops stereotypically described as 'yellow hordes'. Vietnamese and North African soldiers in the French garrison's ranks were overlooked.

128. Bertrand de Hartingh, *Entre le peuple et la nation: La République Démocratique du Viêt Nam de 1953 à 1957* (Paris: École française d'Extrême-Orient, 2003), 79–83.

129. MAE, Dejean papers, vol. 138, Lt.-Colonel Cann, 'Aide chinoise au Vietminh', 23 Mar. 1954.

130. Goscha, *Vietnam*, 485–8.

131. Goscha, *Vietnam*, 489.

132. TNA, Anthony Eden private papers, FO 800/790, Churchill message to Eden, 27 Apr. 1954.

133. For contrasting views of the EDC scheme, see: Saki Dockrill, *Britain's Policy for West German Rearmament, 1950–1955* (Cambridge University Press, 1991), chs 6–7; Spencer Mawby, *Containing Germany: Britain and the Arming of the Federal Republic* (Basingstoke: Macmillan, 1999), ch. 4; Renata Dwan, *An Uncommon Community: France and the European Defence Community, 1950–1954* (Oxford University Press, 1996); William I. Hitchcock, *France Restored*; Michael Creswell and Marc Trachtenberg, 'France and the German Question, 1945–1955', *Journal of Cold War Studies*, 5:3 (2003), 5–28; Victor Gavin, 'Power through Europe? The case of the European Defence Community in France (1950–1954)', *FH*, 23:1 (2009), 69–87.

134. TNA, Eden papers, FO 800/790, FR/54/14, Ivone Kirkpatrick minute, 6 Aug. 1954.

135. MAE, Dejean papers, vol. 138, Memo for Bidault, 'Position du Vietminh à la conférence de Genève', 5 June 1954.

136. MAE, Dejean papers, vol. 138, HFA/MA, Commissariat général en Indochine note, 14 June 1954; Pierre Asselin, 'Choosing peace: Hanoi and the Geneva Agreement on Vietnam, 1954–1955', *Journal of Cold War Studies*, 9:2 (2007), 95–104.

137. Laurent Césari, 'Que reste-t-il de l'influence politique française en Indochine (1954–1966)', in Pierre Brocheux, ed., *Du conflit d'Indochine aux conflits indochinois* (Paris: Complexe, 2000), 21–3.

138. Shao Kuo-kang, 'Zhou Enlai's diplomacy and the neutralization of Indochina, 1954–55', *China Quarterly*, 107 (1986), 483–504; Edward Miller, 'Vision, power and agency: The ascent of Ngô Dình Diêm, 1945–1954', *JSEAS*, 35:3 (2004), 433–58.

139. Stephen Tyre, 'The memory of French military defeat at Dien Bien Phu and the defence of French Algeria', in Jenny MacLeod, ed., *Defeat and Memory: Cultural Histories of Military Defeat in the Modern Era* (Basingstoke: Palgrave-Macmillan, 2008), 214–22.

140. TNA, DEFE 11/84, JIC 2005/4, 'South East Asian Defence Organisation', 17 Aug. 1954.

141. TNA, DEFE 11/84, JIC report/2024/54, 19 Aug. 1954.

142. Martin Alexander, 'Seeking France's "lost soldiers": Reflections on the military crisis in Algeria', in Kenneth Mouré and M. S. Alexander, eds, *Crisis and*

Renewal in France, 1918–1962 (Oxford: Berghahn, 2002), 247–8; Jean-Marc Marill, 'L'Héritage indochinois: Adaptation de l'armée française en Algérie (1954–56)', *Revue Historique des Armées* 187:2 (1992), 26–32.

143. Martin S. Alexander and Philip C. F. Bankwitz, 'From *politiques en képi* to military technocrats: De Gaulle and the recovery of the French Army after Indochina and Algeria', in George J. Andreopoulos and Harold E. Selesky, eds, *The Aftermath of Defeat: Societies, Armed Forces, and the Challenge of Recovery* (New Haven, CT: Yale University Press, 1994), 80–5.

144. Tyre, 'The Memory', 225–8; 'The Gaullists, the French Army and Algeria before 1958: Common cause or marriage of convenience', in M. S. Alexander and J. F. V. Keiger, eds, *France and the Algerian War, 154–62: Strategy, Operations and Diplomacy* (London: Frank Cass, 2002), 103–4.

145. Strategic analysts' overly positive assessments of British facility for counter-insurgency are discussed in Richard Popplewell, '"Lacking intelligence": Some reflections on recent approaches to British counter-insurgency, 1900–1960', *INS*, 10:2 (1995), 336–52.

146. TNA, AIR 8/1660, Supply of helicopters to France, 1952–55.

147. MAE, série Asie-Océanie, sous-série: Indochine, vol. 261, 'Indochine', 9 Feb. 1952.

148. *BDEEP*, series B, vol. 3: *Malaya, II*, doc. 301.

149. TNA, WO 32/16218, 'Present situation in Indo-China', 30 Apr. 1953.

150. Irving, *Christian Democracy in France*, 206.

151. Hack, 'The Malayan Emergency', 383–414.

152. French, *The British Way*, 26–7, 116–24.

153. Anderson, *Histories of the Hanged*, 6.

154. These figures are from Brocheux and Hémery, *Indochina*, 372.

CHAPTER 6

1. Nehru letter to John Foster Dulles, 31 Oct. 1956, cited in Sarvepalli Gopal, 'India, the crisis, and the non-aligned nations', in Wm. Roger Louis and Roger Owen, eds, *Suez 1956: The Crisis and its Consequences* (Oxford: Clarendon Press, 1989), 185.

2. Avi Shlaim, 'The protocol of Sèvres, 1956: Anatomy of a war plot', *International Affairs*, 73:3 (1997), 509–29.

3. Colonel Mordechai Bar-On, 'Three days in Sèvres: Oct. 1956', *History Workshop Journal*, 62:1 (2006), 172–4.

4. Bar-On, 'Three days', 180–6.

5. Interactions between the Hungarian uprising, which began on 23 Oct. 1956, and the Suez operation, which started a week later, are explored in Peter G. Boyle, 'The Hungarian revolution and the Suez Crisis', *History* 90:300 (2005), 550–65. Boyle concludes that events in Budapest damaged the USSR far more than the Suez humiliation did the Western powers.

6. Sir Pierson Dixon, UK Ambassador at the United Nations, rued this comparison on 5 Nov. 1956. 'I do not see how we can carry much conviction in our protests against the Russian bombing of Budapest, if we are ourselves bombing Cairo.' Cited in Wm. Roger Louis, 'Public enemy number one', in Lynn, *The British Empire*, 191.

7. David Reynolds, 'Eden the diplomatist, 1931–1956: Suezide of a statesman?' *History*, 74:1 (1989), 64–84. The fullest account of the crisis is Keith Kyle, *Suez* (London: Weidenfeld & Nicolson, 1992). Ronald Hyam argues that Eden misjudged almost everything and was not up to the job of PM, but acted out of character in demonizing Nasser, see *Britain's Declining Empire*, 221–40.

8. Notable early critics were David Carlton, *Anthony Eden: A Biography* (London: Viking, 1981); *Britain and the Suez Crisis* (Oxford: Blackwell, 1981); and, from a pro-Nasserite, Mohamed H. Heikal, *Cutting the Lion's Tail: Suez through Egyptian Eyes* (London: André Deutsch, 1986). Peter Beck's articles reveal the efforts made by Eden and his wife, Lady Avon, to rebuff historians' criticism, plus successive governments' rejection of a public inquiry into collusion: 'Politicians versus historians: Lord Avon's appeasement battle against "lamentably, appeasement-minded" historians', *Twentieth Century British History*, 9:3 (1998), 396–419; ' "The less said about Suez the better": British governments and the politics of Suez's history, 1956–67', *EHR*, CXXIV:508 (2009), 605–40.

9. Peter L. Hahn, *The United States, Great Britain, and Egypt, 1945–1956* (Chapel Hill, NC: University of North Carolina Press, 1991), 224–39.

10. Eden wrote in a Jan. 1957 letter to one of his Cabinet supporters, the Colonial Secretary Alan Lennox-Boyd, that 'I am sure,—more than I ever have been in my life—that we have only to uphold the decision we took in Egypt to be proved a hundred times right.' Quoted in Philip Murphy, *Alan Lennox-Boyd*, 159.

11. Talbot Imlay, 'A success story? The foreign policies of France's Fourth Republic', *Contemporary European History*, 18:4 (2009), 516–17.

12. BLO, Harold Macmillan papers, 1st series diaries, D26, entry for 28 June 1956.

13. BLO, Viscount (Walter) Monckton papers, box 7, 1956 correspondence, notes of Suez committee proceedings, Sept. 1956.

14. A point strongly made by Ronald Hyam in *Britain's Declining Empire*, 227–8.

15. Sue Onslow, ' "Battlelines for Suez": The Abadan Crisis of 1951 and the Formation of the Suez Group', *Contemporary British History*, 17:2 (2003), 1–28.

16. Tony Shaw, *Eden, Suez and the Mass Media: Propaganda and Persuasion during the Suez Crisis* (London, I.B. Tauris, 1996), chs 4–7.

17. BLO, Macmillan papers, D27, fo. 55, entry for 23 Aug. 1956; W. Scott Lucas, *Divided We Stand: Britain, the US and the Suez Crisis* (London: Hodder & Stoughton, 1991) 175–8.

18. Macmillan's spine was stiffened by his son-in-law, Conservative MP (Member of Parliament) and Suez group dynamo Julian Amery: Sue Onslow, 'Unreconstructed nationalists and a minor gunboat operation: Julian Amery, Neil McLean and the Suez Crisis', *Contemporary British History*, 20:1 (2006), 75, 82.

19. A. J. Stockwell, 'Suez 1956 and the moral disarmament of the British Empire', in Simon C. Smith, ed., *Reassessing Suez 1956: New Perspectives on the Crisis and its Aftermath* (Aldershot: Ashgate, 2008), 227–31; Saul Kelly and Anthony Gorst, eds, *Whitehall and the Suez Crisis*; Sue Onslow, *Backbench Debate within the Conservative Party and Its Influence on British Foreign Policy 1948–1957* (Basingstoke: Macmillan, 1997), chs 9–10; 'Unreconstructed nationalists', 73–99.

20. For clashes between Eden's government and the BBC, see Shaw, *Eden, Suez and the Mass Media*, part 2; 'Eden and the BBC during the 1956 Suez Crisis: A myth re-examined', *Twentieth Century British History*, 6:3 (1995), 320–43; Gary D. Rawnsley, 'Overt and covert: The voice of Britain and black radio broadcasting in the Suez Crisis, 1956', *INS*, 11 (1996), 497–522; James R. Vaughan, 'The BBC's external services and the Middle East before the Suez Crisis', *Historical Journal of Film, Radio and Television*, 28:4 (2008), 499–514. The daily Arabic broadcasting declined in influence following Nasser's launch of Radio Cairo's 'Voice of the Arabs' service in 1953.

21. Scott Lucas, 'Conclusion' in Smith, *Reassessing Suez*, 239.

22. Nigel John Ashton, *Eisenhower, Macmillan and the Problem of Nasser* (Basingstoke: Palgrave-Macmillan, 1996); Glen Balfour-Paul, *The End of Empire in the Middle East: Britain's Relinquishment of Power in Her Last Three Arab Dependencies* (Cambridge University Press, 1991).

23. Wm. Roger Louis, 'The tragedy of the Anglo-Egyptian settlement of 1954', in Louis and Owen, *Suez 1956*, 48–71. Eden was also instrumental in sealing alliances with Middle Eastern partners, although this fed his misapprehension that Britain could remain a regional arbiter without the USA: Kevin Ruane, 'SEATO, MEDO, and the Baghdad Pact: Anthony Eden, British foreign policy and the collective defence of Southeast Asia and the Middle East, 1952–1955', *DS*, 16:1 (2005), 171–3, 180–93.

24. John Kent, *British Imperial Strategy*, 133–4; *BDEEP*, series B, vol. 4: John Kent, ed., *Egypt and the Defence of the Middle East*, part II, docs. 180, 186–7, 193, 196–8, 202.

25. Hyam, *Britain's Declining Empire*, 221–6.

26. TNA, DEFE 10/324, Working Party on Middle East redeployment, 'Outline of the current state of affairs', 12 Mar. 1952; Michael Mason, 'The decisive volley: The battle of Ismailia and the decline of British influence in Egypt, January–July, 1952', *JICH*, 19:1 (1991), 45–64.

27. Darwin, *The Empire Project*, 598–9; Michael Thornhill, 'Britain, the United States and the rise of an Egyptian leader: The politics and diplomacy of Nasser's consolidation of Power, 1952–4', *EHR*, 119:483 (2004), 892–921.

28. Daniel Le Couriard, 'Les Socialistes et les débuts de la guerre d'Indochine (1946–1947)', *Revue d'Histoire Moderne et Contemporaine*, 31 (1984), 339–48; Gérard Bossuat, 'Guy Mollet: La Puissance française autrement', *Relations Internationales*, 57:1 (1989), 26–7.

29. Redha Malek, *L'Algérie à Evian: Histoire des négociations secrètes, 1956–1962* (Paris: Editions du Seuil, 1995), 24–6; Mohammed Harbi, *Le F.L.N.: Mirage et réalité:*

Des origines à la prise du pouvoir (1945–1962) (Paris: Editions J.A., 1985), 197. These talks, conducted with FLN executive members Mohammed Yazid and Mohammed Khider, included meetings in Belgrade (July) and Rome (Sept.). The Algerians were rightly sceptical that the Socialists could carry the government and armed forces with them.

30. Martin Thomas, *The French North African Crisis: Colonial Breakdown and Anglo-French Relations, 1945–1962* (Basingstoke: Macmillan, 2000), 104–5, 129.

31. François Bédarida and Jean-Pierre Rioux, eds, *Pierre Mendès France et le mendé-sisme: L'Expérience gouvernementale et sa posterité (1954–1955)* (Paris: Fayard 1985); J. Chêne, E. Aberdam, and H. Morsel, eds, *Pierre Mendès France: La Morale en politique* (Grenoble: Presses Universitaires de Grenoble, 1990).

32. Denis Lefebvre, *Guy Mollet: Le Mal Aimé* (Paris: Plon, 1992), 177–8.

33. Thomas, *French North African Crisis*, 109–20.

34. Bertjan Verbeek, *Decision-Making in Great Britain during the Suez Crisis: Small Groups and a Persistent Leader* (Aldershot: Ashgate, 2003), 17–30.

35. Christopher Brady, 'The Cabinet system and management of the Suez Crisis', *Contemporary British History*, 11:2 (1997), 77–84; Charles Cogan, 'De la politique du mensonge', in Maurice Vaïsse, ed., *La France et l'opération de Suez de 1956* (Paris: ADDIM, 1997), 130–1.

36. Sharkey, *Living with Colonialism*, 71–3, 91, quotation at 71.

37. Janice Boddy, *Civilizing Women: British Crusades in Colonial Sudan* (Princeton University Press, 2007), 284–310 *passim*, quotation at 310.

38. W. Travis Hanes III, *Imperial Diplomacy in the Era of Decolonization: The Sudan and Anglo-Egyptian Relations, 1945–1956* (Westport, CT: Greenwood Press, 1995), chs 4–6.

39. Wm. Roger Louis, 'The dissolution of the British Empire', in Brown and Louis, *OHBE*, iv, 340–1.

40. TNA, Macmillan Private Office papers, FO 800/678, Ivone Kirkpatrick minute, 23 Nov. 1955.

41. TNA, FO 371/118676, J1023/6G, Selwyn Lloyd memo, 'Communism and Africa', 21 Apr. 1956.

42. Nasser confided to Tito and Nehru in July 1956 talks on the Yugoslavian island of Brioni that Soviet arms supplies were useful diplomatic levers. The 'Brioni Declaration' also affirmed the non-aligned nations' support for Algerian independence, see: Heikal, *Cutting the Lion's Tail*, 98–9, 112–13; DDF, 1956, II, no. 59 n. 2.

43. Project *Alpha* was a counterpoise to Egypt's Nov. 1955 arms deal with Czechoslovakia, see Shimon Shamir, 'The collapse of Project Alpha', in Louis and Owen, *Suez 1956*, 78–99. The Aswan Dam project promised Egypt hydroelectric power and extensive cotton irrigation. By the time the Americans withdrew financial support for it on 19 July, Nasser had secured alternative Soviet funding: Douglas Little, 'The Cold War in the Middle East: Suez Crisis to Camp David Accords', in Leffler and Westad, *Cambridge History of the Cold War*, ii, 306–7.

44. To British annoyance, the French became principal supplier to the Israeli air-force, having provided surplus weaponry, including Mosquito fighter-bombers, during the 1948 war, see: Zach Levey, 'French–Israeli Relations, 1950–1956: The strategic dimension', in Smith, *Reassessing Suez*, 87–106.

45. Harold Dooley, 'Great Britain's "last battle" in the Middle East: Notes on Cabinet planning during the Suez Crisis of 1956', *IHR*, 11:3 (1989), 487–90; Kyle, *Suez*, 91–6; Onslow, 'Unreconstructed', 77.

46. TNA, Eden papers, FO 800/726, Prime Minister's telegram to Eisenhower, no. 3568, 5 Aug. 1956.

47. MAE, série Europe 1944–1960, sous-série Grande-Bretagne, vol. 138, London tel. 3006, Chauvel to Christian Pineau, 27 July 1956.

48. TNA, Eden papers, FO 800/726, Prime Minister's telegrams to Eisenhower, nos. 3568, 4061, 5181, 5 Aug., 6 Sept., and 5 Nov. 1956.

49. Hugh Gaitskell, *The Diary of Hugh Gaitskell, 1945–1956*, ed. Philip M. Williams (London: Jonathan Cape, 1983), entry for 30 July 1956, 558–9, Bevan quotation at 549.

50. James Jankowski, *Nasser's Egypt, Arab Nationalism, and the United Arab Republic* (Boulder, CO: Lynne Rienner, 2002), 1–2, 11–18, chs 3–4. Labour backbencher Richard Crossman may have done so. He held informal discussions with Nasser and Colonel Anwar Sadat in Cairo in late Dec. 1953. Nasser, in Crossman's account, was unwilling as yet to contemplate using force against Britain: *The Backbench Diaries of Richard Crossman*, ed. Janet Morgan (London: Book Club, 1981) 287.

51. What resistance historian Rod Kedward terms its 'ambivalent legacy' became more complex as French practices in Algeria became dirtier and a small minority of French men and women turned, instead, to supporting FLN 'resistance' networks, see Kedward, *La Vie en bleu*, 336–48. Equally revealing is Martin Evans, *The Memory of Resistance: French Opposition to the Algerian War, 1954–1962* (Oxford: Berg, 1997).

52. Amery and Mclean's involvement with MI6 deputy-chief George Young, their clandestine work against Nasser, and Amery's contacts with Bourgès-Maunoury, and Mollet are reconstructed by Sue Onslow, 'Unreconstructed Nationalists', 75–95. In the weeks leading up to the Suez operation, Amery offered a back-channel to the French ministers, who were worried about faltering British resolve.

53. Georgette Elgey, 'Le Gouvernement Guy Mollet et l'intervention', and Charles-Robert Ageron, 'L'Opération de Suez et la guerre d'Algérie', in Vaïsse, *La France et l'opération*, 27–8, 43–9; DDF, 1956, II, nos. 109 and 112.

54. SHD-DAT, 1H1374/D2, 'Situation des effectifs stationnées en AFN, 1 janvier 1956'.

55. TNA, FO 371/113797, Algiers Consulate to FO African Dept., 10 Jan. 1956.

56. Martin Thomas 'Order before reform: The spread of French military operations in Algeria, 1954–1958', in David Killingray and David Omissi, eds, *Guardians of*

Empire: The Armed Forces of the Colonial Powers, c. 1700–1964 (Manchester University Press, 1999), 198–220.

57. Philip M. Williams, *Crisis and Compromise*, 48–9.

58. 'Dictatorship of the Populace', *New York Times*, 7 Feb. 1956.

59. Samuel Kalman, '*Le Combat par tous les moyens*: Colonial violence and the extreme right in 1930s Oran', *FHS*, 34:1 (2011), 125–53.

60. Martin Evans, *Algeria: France's Undeclared War* (Oxford University Press, 2012), ch. 6.

61. Henri Lerner, *Catroux* (Paris: Albin Michel, 1990), 325–6; DDF, 1955, II, docs. 157, 172, 199.

62. Shepard, *Invention of Decolonization*, 47–54, 75–7; Stephen Tyre, 'From *Algérie française* to *France musulmane*: Jacques Soustelle and the myths and realities of 'integration', 1955–1962', *FH*, 20:3 (2006), 276–96.

63. Daniël Joly, *The French Communist Party and the Algerian War* (Basingstoke: Palgrave-Macmillan, 1991), 93–9.

64. TNA, FO 371/118676, J1023/16, FO minute by I.C. Alexander, 5 May 1956.

65. 'Testimony of Georges Mattéi', in Martin Alexander, Martin Evans, and J.F.V. Keiger, eds, *The Algerian War and the French Army: Experiences, Images, Testimonies* (Basingstoke: Palgrave-Macmillan, 2002), 250.

66. Danièle Joly, 'France's military involvement in Algeria: The PCF and the *oppositionels*', in Scriven and Wagstaff, *War and Society*, 141–5; Evans, *Algeria*, ch. 6.

67. Raphaëlle Branche, *L'Embuscade de Palestro: Algérie 1956* (Paris: Armand Colin, 2010), 7–9, chs 1–4, *France Dimanche* image, p. 54. One of the captured men died in an army rescue operation; two others were never found.

68. Roger Faligot and Pascal Krop, *La Piscine: Les Services secrets français 1944–1984* (Paris: Seuil, 1985), 139–44.

69. MAE, série Europe 1944–1960, sous-série Grande-Bretagne, vol. 142 'Compte-rendu de la visite en Algérie des Parlementaires britanniques, 15–22 octobre 1956'.

70. *The Diary of Hugh Gaitskell, 1945–1956*, letters to Eden and replies, 3–10 Aug. 1956, pp. 570–5.

71. MAE, Europe 1944–1960, sous-série Grande-Bretagne, vol. 139, London tel. 1598/DP, Jean Chauvel to Christian Pineau, 3 Sept. 1956.

72. Maurice Vaïsse, 'France and the Suez Crisis', in Louis and Owen, *Suez 1956*, 137. Pineau rewrote his part in events, using the fact that his Foreign Ministry was ignored by Bourgès-Maunoury's defence planners to suggest that he doubted the wisdom of intervention, see Pineau, *Suez 1956* (Paris: Robert Laffont, 1976).

73. Faligot and Krop, *La Piscine*, 148; Douglas Porch, *The French Secret Services: From the Dreyfus Affair to the Gulf War* (London: Macmillan, 1996), 366–72.

74. TNA, Macmillan private office papers, FO 800/672, WF1051/33. Gladwyn Jebb conversation with Ambassador Jean Chauvel, 7 June 1955.

75. Cited in Levey, 'French–Israeli Relations', 102; see also Lucas, *Divided We Stand*, 158–60.

76. SHD-DAT, 9U4/D15, 'Situation militaire au Moyen-Orient en date du 26 septembre 1956'.

77. William I. Hitchcock, 'Crisis and modernization in the Fourth French Republic: From Suez to Rome', in Mouré and Alexander, *Crisis and Renewal*, 232.

78. Lord Gladwyn, *Memoirs of Lord Gladwyn* (London: Weidenfeld & Nicolson, 1972), 282; Shlaim, 'The Protocol', 514–15.

79. MAE, série Europe 1944–1960, sous-série Grande-Bretagne, vol. 139, Pineau radio broadcast, 14 Sept. 1956.

80. Dalloz, 'Alain Savary', 42–54.

81. Omar Carlier, *Alain Savary, politique d'honneur* (Paris: Presses de Sciences Po., 2002), ch. 9.

82. TNA, FO 371/119558, JN10317/15, A.C.E. Malcolm to FO African Dept., 24 Oct. 1956; DDF, 1956, I, nos. 187, 236, 253.

83. Evans, *Algeria*, 186–7.

84. Pierre Dubois, 'L'Aéronautique navale et les opérations d'Algérie, 1954–1962', *Revue Historique des Armées*, 187 (1992), 113.

85. Mohamed Fathi Al Dib, Nasser's liaison officer to the FLN, notes that the President sanctioned arms shipments to ALN fighters soon after the Algerian rebellion began in Nov. 1954. An Egyptian naval officer, Azzat Soliman, was appointed to find suitable vessels and the first materiel arrived in western Algeria in Dec. At least ten successful deliveries were made before the *Athos* (originally a British-registered ship) was impounded. The Egyptians also trained ALN guerrillas in Spanish Morocco, activity monitored by the SDECE. Mohamed Fathi Al Dib, *Abdel Nasser et la Révolution algérienne* (Paris: L'Harmattan, 1985), 41–3, 175–6; Malek, *L'Algérie à Evian*, 23–9.

86. USNA, RG 59, 751S.00, Ambassador Dillon to John Foster Dulles, 23 Oct. 1956.

87. MAE, série Amérique, sous-série: États-Unis, 1952–1963, vol. 342, Washington tel. 6589, 23 Oct. 1956.

88. This paragraph draws on my *French North African Crisis*, 114. The key information about who approved what came from Savary's disgruntled *chef de cabinet* Jean Chazel in conversation with US Ambassador Dillon in Paris on 24 Oct.: NARA, RG 59, 751S.00 box 3378, Memo of conversation. Also useful is Lefebvre, *Guy Mollet*, 228–32.

89. TNA, FO 371/131663, JR1016/26, copy of US State Dept research branch report, 'The leadership of the Algerian Liberation Front', 22 May 1958; Harbi, *Le F.L.N.: Mirage et Réalité*, 184–92.

90. Peter G. Boyle, ed., *The Eden-Eisenhower Correspondence, 1955–1957* (Chapel Hill, NC: University of North Carolina Press, 2005), 149, 163, 167–8; Hahn, *The United States*, 212–13.

91. Cited in Darwin, *The Empire Project*, 603.

92. Diane B. Kunz, 'The importance of having money: The economic diplomacy of the Suez Crisis', in Louis and Owen, *Suez 1956*, 215–16; for an insider's summary of the US position, see (former Assistant Secretary of State) Robert Bowie's 'Eisenhower, Dulles, and the Suez Crisis', in the same volume, 189–214.

93. Hahn, *The United States*, 231–5.

94. Steven G. Galpern, *Money,* 178–92.

95. Kunz, 'The Importance of Having Money', 217–31; *The Economic Diplomacy of the Suez Crisis* (Chapel Hill, NC: University of North Carolina Press, 1991), 29, 50, 116–52.

96. Martin Lynn, introduction to *The British Empire in the 1950s*, 8.

97. Thompson, introduction to *Britain's Experience of Empire*, 8.

98. Wm. Roger Louis, 'American anti-colonialism and the dissolution of the British Empire', *International Affairs*, 61:3 (1985), 414.

99. MAE, série Europe 1944–1960, sous-série Grande-Bretagne, vol. 139, London tel. 5253, 28 Nov. 1956.

100. Louis, 'Public enemy', 190.

101. Stockwell, 'Suez 1956', 231–42; Robert Holland, *Britain and the Revolt in Cyprus, 1954–1959* (Oxford: Clarendon Press, 1998), 144–7, 157–71.

102. For the remarkable extent of Amery's plotting, see Sue Onslow, 'Julian Amery and the Suez Crisis', in Smith, *Suez Reassessed*, 71–5.

103. Sabine Jansen, ed., *Les Grands Discours parlémentaires de la Quatrième République de Pierre Mendès France à Charles de Gaulle* (Paris: Armand Colin, 2006), 234–40.

104. MAE, série Europe 1944–1960, sous-série Grande-Bretagne, vol. 139, Direction générale politique circular to overseas posts, 31 Oct. 1956.

105. This minor diplomatic offensive was prompted by Hervé Alphand, French representative to the UN, who signalled the likely damage to French interests in the US and among UN member states: DDF, 1956, III, nos. 74 and 77.

106. TNA, FO 371/130625, WF1011/1, annual review for France, 21 Jan. 1957; Maurice Vaïsse, 'Aux origines du mémorandum de septembre 1958', *Relations Internationales*, 58 (1989), 254.

107. Maurice Vaïsse, 'Post-Suez France', in Louis and Owen, *Suez 1956*, 339.

108. Vaïsse, 'Post-Suez France', 336–40. 'Europe will be your revenge', Adenauer was reputed to have told Mollet on 6 Nov. 1956, the very day Operation *Musketeer* was halted.

109. TNA, DEFE 7/1127, General Keightley report, 'Operations in Egypt, November to December 1956', 10 June 1957; SHD-DAT, 9U4/D51, no. 281/GH1, 'Rapport du Général Brohon', 27 Nov. 1956.

110. TNA, FO 800/727, Selwyn Lloyd papers, tel. DTG 010900/Z.

111. TNA, FO 800/727, Lloyd papers, tel. 2363, 1 Nov. 1956.

112. Crossman, *The Backbench Diaries of Richard Crossman*, 551–2.

113. SHD-DAT, 9U4/D53, 'Amiral Barjot projet pour Général Keightley', n.d., Nov. 1956; André Beaufre, *The Suez Expedition, 1956* (London: Faber and Faber, 1969), 108–21.

114. TNA, FO 800/727, Lloyd papers, Paris Embassy telegram 2570, 9 Nov. 1956. Ironically, Mollet accepted this request: telegram 414, Isaacson to FO, 10 Nov. 1956.

115. NARA, RG 59, 751S.00, box 3378, Consul Lewis Clark to State Dept., 9 Oct. 1956; Jacques Massu, *La Vraie Bataille d'Alger* (Paris: Plon, 1971).

116. SHD-DAT, 9U4/D52, Barjot report, 'Conclusions à tirer de l'opération EGYPTE', 31 Dec. 1956.

117. Dunn, *The First Vietnam War*; Timothy O. Smith, *Britain and the Origins of the Vietnam War: UK Policy in Indochina, 1943–1950* (Basingstoke: Palgrave-Macmillan, 2007).

118. Nicholas J. White, 'Decolonisation in the 1950s: The version according to British business', in Lynn, *The British Empire*, 102.

119. I differ slightly here from Matthew Connelly's key argument that the FLN transformed the war's stakes—and ultimately won it—by taking its arguments to an international audience: Matthew Connelly, *A Diplomatic Revolution: Algeria's Fight for Independence and the Origins of the Post-Cold War Era* (Oxford University Press, 2002), 278–81.

120. Sohail H. Hashmi, 'Zero plus zero plus zero': Pakistan, the Baghdad Pact, and the Suez Crisis', *IHR*, 33:3 (2011), 525–44. The Baghdad Pact, a collective security treaty between Britain, Pakistan, Turkey, Iran, and Iraq, was under a year old when the Suez nationalization occurred.

121. Louis, 'Public Enemy', 192–3. Wm. Roger Louis contends that Britain's hypocritical rhetoric about self-determination stirred UN criticism. France, like Portugal, was at least blatantly 'colonialist', although the French, too, were exasperated by General Assembly attacks, see my 'France accused: French North Africa before the United Nations, 1952–1962', *Contemporary European History*, 10:1 (2001), 91–121.

122. MAE, série Europe 1944–1960, sous-série Grande-Bretagne, vol. 138, Cairo tels. 724 and 727, Dorget to Foreign Ministry, 3 Aug. 1956.

123. MAE, série Europe 1944–1960, sous-série Grande-Bretagne, vol. 138, General Marcel Pénette, Washington Military Attaché, to Ministry of National Defence, 8 Aug. 1956.

124. Quoted in Peter Hennessey and Mark Laity, 'Suez—what the papers say', *Contemporary Record*, 1 (Apr. 1987), 8.

CHAPTER 7

1. TNA, FO 371/21605, C15366/141/17, Consul Helm-Smith (Tananarive) to FO, 4 Nov. 1938.

2. Jean-François Zorn, 'When French Protestants replaced British Missionaries in the Pacific and Indian Oceans, or, How to avoid the colonial trap', in White and Daughton, *In God's Empire*, ch. 10.

3. Gwyn Campbell, 'The Menalamba Revolt and brigandry in imperial Madagascar, 1820–1897', *International Journal of African Historical Studies* 24:2 (1991), 259–61, 288–91. The revolt was so-called because of the 'Mena' (red) daub on their clothing (lamba).

4. Gwyn Campbell, 'Crisis of faith and colonial conquest: The impact of famine and disease in late nineteenth-century Madagascar', *Cahier d'Études africaines*, 32:127 (1992), 409–53; 'Missionaries, *Fanompoana* and the Menalamba Revolt in late nineteenth-century Madagascar', *Journal of Southern African Studies*, 15:1 (1988), 54–73; Stephen Ellis, 'The political elite of Imerina and the revolt of the Menalamba: The creation of a colonial myth in Madagascar, 1895–1898', *JAH*, 21 (1980), 221–33. The Anglican Church, largely staffed by the London Missionary Society, was declared the state church of Imerina in 1869.

5. Yves G. Paillard, 'Domination coloniale et récupération des traditions autochtones: Le Cas de Madagascar de 1896 à 1914', *Revue d'Histoire Moderne et Contemporaine*, 38 :1 (1991), 82–104.

6. Gwyn Campbell, 'Unfree labour and the significance of abolition in Madagascar, c.1825–97', in Gwyn Campbell, ed., *Abolition and its Aftermath in Indian Ocean Africa and Asia* (London: Routledge, 2005), 5, 66–82.

7. Gwyn Campbell, 'Madagascar and the slave trade, 1810–1895', *JAH*, 22:2 (1981), 207–27. Madagascar's slaving was variously sustained in the nineteenth century by Mauritius-based British traders, Zanzibar-based Omani traders, and Creole traders from various Indian Ocean settlements.

8. Solofo Randrianja, *Société et luttes anticoloniales à Madagascar (1896 à 1946)* (Paris: Karthala, 2001), chs 3–4.

9. TNA, FO 371/21605, C15366/141/17, Helm-Smith to Foreign Office, 4 Nov. 1938.

10. Francis Koerner, *Madagascar: Colonisation française et nationalisme malgache*, 191–4, 307–12; Jennings, *Vichy in the Tropics*, 31–78.

11. Jacques Tronchon, *L'Insurrection malgache de 1947* (Paris: Karthala, 1986), 23–4.

12. G. Wesley Johnson, 'African political activity in French West Africa, 1900–1945', in Michael Crowder and J. Ajayi, eds, *History of West Africa* (Harlow: Longman, 1987), 542.

13. Lucile Rabearimanana, 'Les Malgaches et l'idée d'indépendance de 1945 à 1956', in Ageron, *Chemins*, 263; Martin Shipway, 'Madagascar on the Eve of Insurrection, 1944–7: The Impasse of a Liberal Colonial Policy,' *JICH*, 24:1 (1996)', 81–2.

14. ANOM, 3D34: Mission Merat report, 20 July 1949. The Free French administration established a new 'native affairs' service, or 'direction des affaires Malgaches', on 27 Dec. 1943.

15. Liliana Mosca, 'À l'origine de la répression de 1947 à Madagascar: Raisons nationales ou logique internationale?', *Africa: Rivista trimestrale di studi e documentazione dell'Istituto Italiano per l'Africa e l'Oriente*, 62:2 (2007), 258–9.

16. Virginia Thompson and Richard Adloff, *The Malagasy Republic: Madagascar Today* (Stanford University Press, 1965), 54–5.

17. AN, BB[18] 3776[2], sous-dossier: émeutes de Madagascar, mars 1947, no. 344/RC, Le Procureur général près la Cour d'appel de Madagascar et dépendances, Tananarive, à Monsieur le Garde des sceaux, 19 Apr. 1947; Rabearimanana, 'Les Malgaches', 267.

18. AN, BB[18] 3776[2], sous-dossier: Émeutes de Madagascar, mars 1947, no. 344/RC, 19 Apr. 1947.

19. Tronchon, *L'Insurrection malgache*, 40–53.

20. Tronchon, *L'Insurrection malgache*, 56–63. There was some vengefulness in the repression, the Tristani camp of the *tirailleurs sénégalais* having been attacked on the rebellion's first night.

21. AN, BB[18] 3776[2], de Coppet speech to Representative Assembly, Antsirabe, 19 Apr. 1947.

22. AN, BB[18] 3776[2], sous-dossier: émeutes de Madagascar, mars 1947, Raseta letter to Vincent Auriol, 15 Apr. 1947.

23. Thompson and Adloff, *The Malagasy Republic*, 65.

24. The fallacy of reducing the rebellion to the work of a single umbrella movement is a central argument of Jacques Tronchon's *L'Insurrection malgache*, 11, 22–36.

25. AN, BB[18] 3776[2]: Troubles de Madagascar, arrestations de parlementaires, Ravoahanguy—Rabemanandjara, 15 Apr. 1947; Tronchon, *L'Insurrection malgache*, 'Statuts du MDRM', 249–51.

26. Jennifer Cole, *Forget Colonialism: Sacrifice and the Art of Memory in Madagascar* (Berkeley, CA: University of California Press, 2001), 229.

27. Solofo Randrianja, 'Aux origines du M.D.R.M. 1939–1946', in Francis Arzalier and Jean Suret-Canale, eds, *Madagascar 1947: La Tragédie oubliée* (Paris: Temps des Cérises, 1999), 65–79.

28. Douglas Little, 'Cold War and colonialism in Africa: The United States, France, and the Madagascar Revolt of 1947', *Pacific Historical Review*, 59:4 (1990), 529, 535–8.

29. ANOM, 6(2)D123, sous-dossier: HCRF Madagascar, no. 476/DISCF, R. Baron, Chef de la Sûreté Générale Tananarive, 17 Jan. 1947; no. 704/DISCF, 'Renseignements', 23 Jan. 1947.

30. Rabearimanana, 'Les Malgaches', 265; Raymond Delval, 'L'Histoire du PADESM (Parti des déshérités de Madagascar), ou, Quelques faits oubliés de l'histoire malgache', in Ageron, *Chemins*, 276–7.

31. Delval, 'L'Histoire du PADESM', 277–8.

32. ANOM, 6(2)D176, 'Renseignements sur le PADESM, rivalités avec le MDRM, 1946–56'; Shipway, 'Madagascar', 91–4.

33. Gérard Bossuat, 'Le Plan Marshall dans la modernisation de la France', in Serge Berstein and Pierre Milza, eds, *L'Année 1947* (Paris: Presses de Sciences Po., 2000), 58–61.

34. Olivier Dard, 'Théoriciens et praticiens de l'économie: Un changement de paradigm', in Berstein and Milza, *L'Année 1947*, 78–93 *passim*.

35. René Gallissot, *La République française et les indigènes: Algérie colonisée, Algérie algérienne (1870–1962)* (Paris: Éditions de l'Atelier, 2006), 162–5.

36. ANOM, Affaires Politiques, C2116/D2, EMGDN, 'Note sur le Statut de l'Algérie', n.d., May 1947; Odile Rudelle, 'Le Vote du statut de l'Algérie', in

Berstein and Milza, *L'Année 1947*, 313–14; Lewis, 'French Politics and the Algerian Statute', 147–72.

37. The Sétif uprising is discussed in ch. 11.

38. Christine Sellin, 'Paul Ramadier et l'Indochine en 1947', in Serge Berstein, ed., *Paul Ramadier: La République et la Socialisme* (Paris: Complexe, 1990), 377–85; B.D. Graham, *Choice and Democratic Order: The French Socialist Party, 1937–1950* (Cambridge University Press, 1994), 369–72; Martin Thomas, 'The colonial policies of the Mouvement Républicain Populaire, 1944–1954: From reform to reaction', *EHR*, 118:476 (2003), 380–411.

39. AN, Fonds MRP, 350AP7, Dossier: 1MRP6/Dr. 2, Secrétariat Général 'Note sur l'organisation du M.R.P.', n.d.; Henri Descamps, *La Démocratie Chrétienne et le MRP: De 1946 à 1959*, book 3, 171–223; Letamendia, *Le Mouvement Républicain Populaire*, 151–251.

40. Serge Berstein, 'De Gaulle, l'état, la république', in Fondation Charles de Gaulle, actes du colloque, *De Gaulle et le Rassemblement du peuple français (1947–1955)* (Paris: Armand Colin, 1998), 386–8.

41. Frédéric Turpin, 'Le RPF et la guerre d'Indochine (1947–1954)', in Fondation Charles de Gaulle, *De Gaulle et le Rassemblement du peuple français*, 530–1.

42. Lewis, 'The MRP', 298–302.

43. Irwin M. Wall, *French Communism in the Era of Stalin* (Westport, CT: Greenwood Press, 1984), ch. 3.

44. Marc Michel, 'L'Empire colonial dans les débats parlémentaires', in Berstein and Milza, *L'Année 1947*, 191–201.

45. AN, UDSR papers, 412AP/1, 'Réflexions sur l'UDSR', 8 July 1946; Philip M. Williams, *Crisis and Compromise*, 174–5.

46. Dalloz *L'Humanité* on Indochina

47. Jean-Jacques Becker, 'L'Anti-communisme de l'SFIO', in Berstein, ed., *Paul Ramadier*, 199–201.

48. Bruce D. Graham, 'Le Choix atlantique ou troisième force internationale?' in Berstein, *Paul Ramadier*, 160; Bruno Béthouart, 'Le MRP, un nouveau partenaire', in Serge Berstein, Frédéric Cépède, Gilles Morin and Antoine Prost, eds, *Le Parti Socialiste entre Résistance et République* (Paris: Publications de la Sorbonne, 2000), 257–8.

49. AN, BB[18] 3776[2], sous-dossier: émeutes de Madagascar, mars 1947, de Coppet tel., 12 Apr. 1947.

50. AN, BB[18] 3776[2], de Coppet tel. to Ministry of Overseas France, 13 Apr. 1947.

51. Thompson and Adloff, *The Malagasy Republic*, 64–7. Only 75 Deputies attended the first National Assembly debate on the Madagascar Revolt.

52. Jacqueline Lévi-Valensi, ed., *Camus at Combat: Writing, 1944–1947* (Princeton University Press, 2006), 290.

53. AN, BB[18] 3776[2]: Troubles de Madagascar, 'Procès de Tananarive'.

54. Thompson and Adloff, *The Malagasy Republic*, 54; Christian Bidégaray, 'Le Tabou de l'indépendance dans les débats constituants: 1945–1958', in Ageron and Michel, *L'Afrique noire*, 194.

55. Yves Beigbeder, *Judging War Crimes and Torture: French Justice and International Criminal Tribunals and Commissions (1940–2005)* (Leiden: Brill Academic, 2006), 83–4; Jacques Tronchon, 'La Nuit la plus longue…du 29 au 30 mars 1947', in Arzalier and Suret-Canale, eds, *Madagascar 1947*, 118–26.

56. Beigbeder, *Judging War Crimes*, 87–8; Tronchon, *L'Insurrection malgache*, 329–33.

57. Beigbeder, *Judging War Crimes*, 87–8.

58. Mairéad Ni Bhriain, 'Intellectual discourse and the trial of the Malagasy deputies', in Antoine Masson and Kevin O'Connor, eds, *Representations of Justice* (Brussels: Peter Lang, 2007), 64–5.

59. Beigbeder, *Judging War Crimes*, 85–8. This prosecutor exceeded his authority here as the three men were originally charged, not with murder (to which a death sentence could apply) but with organizing sedition, a political crime for which the death penalty was abolished in 1848.

60. Thompson and Adloff, *The Malagasy Republic*, 67.

61. AN, BB[18] 3776[2], no. 226, Minister for Overseas France to Prime Minister's office, 5 Mar. 1948.

62. Sorum, *Intellectuals and Decolonization*, 42, 57. The former deputies were not permitted to return to Madagascar before independence in 1960, however.

63. ANOM, 3D32, Mission Demaille, 1947–48, no. 2/DC, Inspecteur des Colonies Demaille to Ministre de la France d'Outre-Mer, Tamatave, 12 Oct. 1947.

64. ANOM, 3D32, Mission Demaille, 'Rapport concernant le problème de la récupération des stocks de café des campagnes antérieures dans les districts touchés par la rébellion', 28 Oct. 1947.

65. TNA, FO 371/73721, J908/1019/69, Consular report on the Madagascar rebellion, 26 Jan. 1949.

66. Tronchon, *L'Insurrection malgache*, dossier 7: 'Témoignages d'Européens sur l'insurrection', 268–75. Rural settlers' fear of sudden attack was a perennial aspect of colonial rule, but levels of colonial repression in response to it increased markedly after World War I: see Ann Laura Stoler, 'Sexual affronts and racial frontiers: European identities and the cultural politics of exclusion in colonial Southeast Asia', *Comparative Studies in Society and History*, 34:3 (1992), 514–51; David Anderson, 'Sexual threat and settler society: Black perils in Kenya, c.1907–1930', *JICH*, 38:1 (2010), 47–74; Martin Thomas, 'Eradicating "Communist banditry" in French Vietnam: The rhetoric of repression after the Yen Bay Uprising, 1930–32', *FHS*, 34:3 (2011), 611–48.

67. ANOM, 6(2)D123, no. 97/S/D1, R. Baron, Chef de la Sûreté, 'Renseignements', 22 Jan. 1948.

68. Tronchon, *L'Insurrection malgache*, 48–53.

69. ANOM, 3D32, Mission Demaille, 'Rapport concernant le rétablissement de la confiance franco-malgache', Tananarive, 4 June 1948.

70. Jennifer Cole and Karen Middleton, 'Rethinking ancestors and colonial power in Madagascar', *Africa*, 71:1 (2001), 10–11; Cole, 'Narratives and moral projects: Generational memories of the Malagasy 1947 rebellion', *Ethos*, 31:1 (2003), 104, 111.

71. AN, BB[18] 3776[2], no. 31035, Ministère de la France d'Outre-Mer, Services judiciaires, Ministre de la France d'Outre-Mer a Monsieur le Garde des Sceaux, 27 June 1952. In total, Madagascar's civil courts sentenced 3,629 people for involvement in the uprising. Of these, 128 received the death penalty, 283 received life terms, and 3,218 received lesser terms of imprisonment, often with forced labour.

72. Thompson and Adloff, *The Malagasy Republic*, 56, 66. Numbers of summary killings are unverified.

73. Cooper, *Decolonization*, 187–8.

74. Thompson and Adloff, *The Malagasy Republic*, 60–3.

75. Rabearimanana, 'Les Malgaches et l'idée d'indépendance', 268–70.

76. Beigbeder, *Judging War Crimes*, 83–4.

77. Cooper, *Decolonization*, 225–6.

78. ANOM, 3D32: Mission Demaille, 1947–48, 'Rapport concernant le rétablissement de la confiance franco-malgache', Tananarive, 4 June 1948.

79. Little, 'Cold War and colonialism', 542; Tronchon, *L'Insurrection malgache*, dossier 8: 'Témoignages sur les tortures', 276–87.

80. Beigbeder, *Judging War Crimes*, 83.

81. ANOM, 3D32, Mission Demaille, comments by Pierre de Chevigné, 4 June 1948.

82. Thompson and Adloff, *The Malagasy Republic*, 62.

83. Lucile Rabearimanana, 'Femmes Merina et vie politique à Madagascar durant la décolonisation', in Chantal Chanson-Jabeur and Odile Goerg, eds, *'Mama Africa'* (Paris: L'Harmattan, 2006), 320–7.

84. ANOM, 3D34: Mission Merat, 1949, Report on Nosy Lava penitentiary, 20 May 1949. The *bagne* was the colloquial term for a penal colony, i.e. any prison system with forced labour, particularly the French Guyana penal colony, infamous for its appalling conditions.

85. Ibid. 271–4; Delval, 'L'Histoire du PADESM', 287.

86. Lucile Rabearimanana, 'Les Tananariviens face à la proclamation de l'indépendance de Madagascar', in Ageron and Michel, eds, *L'Afrique noire*, 577–9.

87. SHD-DAT, 14H48/D2, 'Plan de mobilisation en cas de troubles graves des T. O. M.', 26 Aug. 1958.

88. Octave Mannoni, 'Psychologie de la révolte malgache', *Esprit*, 166 (Apr. 1950), 581–95.

89. Cole, 'Narratives', 110–16.

90. Mosca, 'À l'origine de la répression', 262–72.

91. Lorcin, *Historicizing Colonial Nostalgia*, 146–7.

CHAPTER 8

1. The parallels between the Madagascar insurrection and the Mau Mau are succinctly described—and rejected—by Martin Shipway, *Decolonisation and Its Impact*, 144–7.

2. David French, *The British Way*, chs 4–5.

3. Lynn, introduction' to *The British Empire in the 1950s*, 2–5.

4. Philip Murphy, *Party Politics and Decolonization: The Conservative Party and British Colonial Policy in Tropical Africa, 1951–1964* (Oxford: Clarendon, 1995), 50; Ronald Hyam, 'The geopolitical origins of the Central African Federation: Britain, Rhodesia and South Africa, 1948–1953', *HJ*, 30:1 (1987), 145–8.

5. John Darwin calls the federation 'a bizarre construct of grand imperial strategy and settler sub-imperialism', Darwin, 'The Central African Emergency, 1959', *JICH*, 21:3 (1993), 219.

6. Murphy, *Party Politics*, 58–9, 73–7. The three conglomerates were British South Africa (BSA), the Rhodesian Selection Trust, and Rhodesian Anglo-American Limited.

7. Philip Murphy, 'Intelligence and decolonization: The life and death of the federal intelligence and security bureau, 1954–63', *JICH*, 29:2 (2001), 104–12; Darwin, 'Central African Emergency', 219.

8. L. J. Butler, *Copper Empire: Mining and the Colonial State in Northern Rhodesia, c.1930–1964* (Basingstoke: Palgrave-Macmillan, 2007), 201–5.

9. Hyam, 'The geopolitical origins', 156–7.

10. Philip Murphy, ' "Government by blackmail": The origins of the Central African Federation reconsidered', in Lynn, *The British Empire*, 53–73; ' "An intricate and distasteful subject": British planning for the use of force against the European settlers of Central Africa, 1952–1965', *EHR*, CXXI:492 (2006), 750.

11. L. J. Butler, 'Britain, the United States, and the demise of the Central African Federation, 1959–63', *JICH*, 28:3 (2000), 131–4; Darwin, 'Central African Emergency', 217.

12. Murphy, *Party Politics*, 61–8, 86–7, 231–2; Racial discrimination was embedded in Southern Rhodesian law and 'insolent' African behaviour, particularly in the workplace, was liable to punishment. Allison K. Shutt, ' "The natives are getting out of hand": Legislating manners, insolence and contemptuous behaviour in Southern Rhodesia, c.1910–1963', *Journal of Southern African Studies*, 33:3 (2007), 653–72.

13. BLO, Barbara Castle papers, MS Castle 243, ANC/2/4, Northern Rhodesian ANC President H. M. Nkumbula and Secretary-General Kenneth Kaunda to Lusaka Governor, 24 Jan. 1958.

14. These official concerns about communist infiltration had ebbed and flowed since the Second World War, see: TNA, CO 537/4307, MI5 memo, 'Communist influence in the African Continent', 10 Mar. 1949; J1017/18/G, FO Research Department memo 'A survey of Communism in Africa', 30 Aug. 1950; Philip Murphy, 'Creating a Commonwealth intelligence culture: The view from Central Africa, 1945–1965', *INS*, 17:3 (2002), 131–62.

15. TNA, CO 1015/2056, Sir Arthur Benson, Government House, Lusaka, letter to W (Bill) L. Gorell Barnes, Colonial Office, 22 Sept. 1957.

16. BLO, Castle papers, MS Castle 243, John Hatch, Labour Party Commonwealth Officer, to Castle, 25 Oct. 1956; fos. 52–4: 'Memo on the industrial dispute in

Northern Rhodesia', n.d., Nov. 1956; TNA, CO 1015/2056, Sir Arthur Benson, 'Emergency Powers bill', 5 Oct. 1957; CA(57)38, Colonial Policy Committee, 'Powers of colonial governors', n.d., Dec. 1957.

17. BLO, Castle papers, MS Castle 244, 'African National Congress, Northern Rhodesia, 'Comments on the proposals for constitutional change', n.d., May 1958.
18. Darwin, 'Central African Emergency', 220–1.
19. Megan Vaughan, 'Suicide in late colonial Africa: The evidence of inquests from Nyasaland', *AHR*, 115:2 (2010), 387.
20. Butler, 'Britain, the United States', 133–4.
21. Darwin, *The Empire Project*, 619–21.
22. Darwin, 'Central African Emergency', 219–21.
23. TNA, CO 1015/2056, Sir Arthur Benson letter to 'Bill', W.L. Gorell Barnes, 2 Mar. 1959.
24. The restrictions enacted in Northern Rhodesia hinged on a ban imposed on ANC activities, see: Castle papers, MS Castle 244, Kenneth Kaunda letter to Commander T.S.L. Fox-Pitt, 20 Mar. 1959.
25. TNA, CO 1015/2056, tel. 546/15/01, Sir Arthur Benson to Lennox-Boyd, 4 Mar. 1959.
26. TNA, CO 1015/2056, Benson letter to Gorell Barnes, 2 Mar. 1959.
27. TNA, CO 1015/2056, tel. CAA546/15/01, Lennox-Boyd to Benson, 5 Mar. 1959. Macmillan chided the Colonial Secretary at a private dinner on 14 Dec. 1958 for making an 'injudicious speech' on Cyprus policy to a Conservative Party meeting that was leaked to the press: Macmillan Diaries, 2nd ser., d. 34, fo.4, entry for 14 Dec. 1958.
28. A view also propounded in Darwin, 'Central African Emergency', 227.
29. Hyam, *Britain's Declining Empire*, 263.
30. Castle papers, MS Castle 245, fos. 130–3 and 153–5, Barbara Castle articles, 'The died detainee', *New Statesman*, 14 Feb. 1959; 'Eleven dead men', *New Statesman*, 16 May 1959.
31. BLO, Macmillan papers, Diaries, 2nd ser., d. 35, fos. 16–17, entry for 5 Mar. 1959.
32. BLO, Macmillan papers, Diaries, 2nd ser., d. 35, fos. 24–34, entries for 11 and 17 Mar. 1959.
33. BLO, Macmillan papers, Diaries, 2nd ser., d. 35, fos. 20–4, 74–6, entries for 9 and 10 Mar., 10 and 24 Apr. 1959.
34. BLO, Macmillan papers, Diaries, 2nd ser., d. 35, fo. 120, entry for 4 June 1959.
35. BLO, Macmillan papers, Diaries, 2nd ser., d. 36, fos. 18–27, entries for 16, 17 and 22 June 1959.
36. BLO, Macmillan papers, Diaries, 2nd ser., d. 36, fos. 63 and 76, entries for 13 and 18 July 1959. Macmillan's fear was that Attorney-General Sir Reginald Manningham-Buller would force the 'highly-strung' Lennox-Boyd to resign, destroying the Cabinet's residual unity in the process.

37. BLO, Macmillan papers, Diaries, 2nd ser., d. 35, fo. 120, 4 June 1959.

38. BLO, Macmillan papers, Diaries, 2nd ser., d. 37, fos.70–8, entries for 16 and 24 Nov. 1959.

39. Hyam, *Britain's Declining Empire*, 282–5; Butler, 'Britain, the United States', 132–5.

40. Murphy, "Government by blackmail", 54, 60.

41. Murphy, 'Intelligence and decolonization', 124.

42. Alice Ritscherle, 'Disturbing the people's peace: Patriotism and "respectable" racism in British responses to Rhodesian independence', in Levine and Grayzel, *Gender*, 199.

43. Ranajit Guha, 'Not at home in empire', *Critical Inquiry*, 23:3 (1997), 487–9.

44. Will Jackson, *Madness and Marginality: The Lives of Kenya's White Insane* (Manchester University Press, 2012), ch. 1.

45. David M. Hughes, *Whiteness in Zimbabwe: Race, Landscape and the Problem of Belonging* (New York: Palgrave-Macmillan, 2010), 2; cited in Jackson, *Madness*, ch. 1 n. 56.

46. Anderson, *Histories of the Hanged*, 1, 55–7, quotation at p. 1.

47. Hyam, *Britain's Declining Empire*, 103. Baring joined the Indian civil service but cemented his reputation with wartime postings to Southern Rhodesia as governor in 1942, thence to South Africa as high commissioner in 1944.

48. David A. Percox, 'Mau Mau and the arming of the state', in E. S. Atieno Odhiambo and John Lonsdale, eds, *Mau Mau and Nationhood* (Oxford: James Currey 2003), 121–54.

49. Georgia Sinclair, *At the End of the Line: Colonial Policing and the Imperial Endgame, 1945–80* (Manchester University Press, 2006), 154–60.

50. David Throup, 'Crime, politics and the police in colonial Kenya, 1939–63', in Anderson and Killingray, *Police and Decolonization*, 140–8.

51. David M. Anderson, 'British abuse and torture in Kenya's counter-insurgency, 1952–1960', *SWI*, 23:4/5 (2012), 700–19.

52. Anderson, *Histories of the Hanged*, 18–19. Membership of the Kikuyu Cultural Association was approaching 4,000 by the time Kenyatta left for London.

53. Bruce Berman and John Lonsdale, 'Custom, modernity, and the search for *Kihooto*: Kenyatta, Malinowski and the making of *Facing Mount Kenya*', in Helen Tilley and Robert J. Gordon, eds, *Ordering Africa: Anthropology, European Imperialism, and the Politics of Knowledge* (Manchester University Press, 2007), 174–5, 180.

54. Carol Polsgrove, *Ending British Rule in Africa: Writers in a Common Cause* (Manchester University Press 2009), 6–12, 25–30.

55. Berman and Lonsdale, 'Custom', 181, 185–7.

56. John Lonsdale, 'Authority, gender and violence: The War within Mau Mau's fight for land and freedom', in Atieno Odhiambo and Lonsdale, *Mau Mau*, 46–53, quotation at 53.

57. For the Red Cross case, see: Fabian Klose, 'The colonial testing ground: The International Committee of the Red Cross and the violent end of empire', *Humanity*, 2:1 (2011), 107–26.

58. Lorcin, *Historicizing Colonial Nostalgia*, 43.

59. Anderson, *Histories of the Hanged*, 93–7.

60. Lonsdale, 'Kenya: Home county and African frontier', 80, 101–5. Lonsdale refers to over thirty farmhouse assaults in the first six months of 1953. For the strictures of inter-racial hierarchy, see Dane Kennedy, *Islands of White: Settler Society and Culture in Kenya and Southern Rhodesia, 1890–1939* (Durham, NC: Duke University Press, 1987); and for the social opprobrium heaped on so-called 'poor whites' who fell short of settler society's standards, see: Will Jackson, 'Bad blood, psychopathy and politics of transgression in Kenya colony, 1939–1959', *JICH*, 39:1 (2011), 73–94.

61. Jackson, *Madness*, ch. 2.

62. Jackson, *Madness*, ch. 2.

63. Bruce Berman, *Control and Crisis in Colonial Kenya: The Dialectic of Domination* (London: James Currey, 1990), 262–4, 282–8.

64. Settler critics underestimated the Governor's conservatism. Mitchell favoured collaboration with traditional Kenyan elites rather than significantly greater involvement of educated Africans, including party political representatives, in Kenya's Executive Council, see: Murphy, *Party Politics*, 17–18.

65. John Lonsdale, 'KAU's cultures: Imaginations of community and constructions of leadership in Kenya after the Second World War', *Journal of African Cultural Studies*, 13:1 (2000), 109–22.

66. Berman, *Control and Crisis*, 322–5.

67. John Lonsdale, 'Mau Maus of the mind: Making Mau Mau and remaking Kenya', *JAH*, 31:3 (1990), 393–421.

68. Daniel Branch, *Defeating Mau Mau, Creating Kenya: Counterinsurgency, Civil War, and Decolonization* (Cambridge University Press, 2009), 36–9.

69. Anderson, *Histories of the Hanged*, 11–12, 28–30, 39–43.

70. Hyam, *Britain's Declining Empire*, 189–90.

71. Branch, *Defeating Mau Mau*, 2–3, 24, 40–52; Caroline Elkins, 'Detention, rehabilitation and the destruction of Kikuyu society', in Atieno Odhiambo and Lonsdale, *Mau Mau*, 191–226.

72. Branch, *Defeating Mau Mau*, 16–18.

73. The legislation enabling these evictions passed into law in 1940, but its enforcement was delayed by the Second World War, see David M. Anderson and David W. Throup, 'Africans and Agricultural Production', 327–46. For the agronomic background: Richard Waller, '"Clean" and "dirty": Cattle disease and control policy in colonial Kenya', *JAH*, 45:1 (2004), 69–78.

74. The disruption of Kikuyu village society emerges from the oral evidence compiled in former aid worker Greet Kershaw's *Mau Mau from Below* (Oxford: James Currey, 1997). Further explanations of the post-war crisis in Kikuyu agriculture are Tabitha Kanogo, *Squatters and the Roots of Mau Mau* (London: James Currey, 1987), especially chs 4–5; and David Throup, *Economic and Social Origins of Mau Mau, 1945–1953* (Oxford: James Currey, 1987); Lonsdale, 'Authority', 56–9;

Anderson, *Histories of the Hanged*, 24–9; Christopher Youé, 'Black squatters on white farms: Segregation and agrarian change in Kenya, South Africa and Rhodesia, 1902–1963', *IHR*, 24:3 (2002), 558–602.

75. Elkins, 'Detention', 201; Bruce Berman and John Lonsdale, *Unhappy Valley: Conflict in Kenya and Africa: Book Two: Violence and Ethnicity* (Oxford: James Currey, 1992), ch. 12.

76. Joanna Lewis, '"Daddy wouldn't buy me a Mau Mau": The British popular press and the demoralization of empire', in Atieno Odhiambo and Lonsdale, *Mau Mau*, 232–47.

77. *Kazi ya Mau Mau!* Nairobi Government booklet, 1953.

78. MAE, Série K: Afrique-Levant, Sous-série: Possessions britanniques, 1944–1952, file 9, A. Beaulieux, 'A. S. Kenya African Union', 8 July 1948. Ronald Hyam describes Kenyatta as 'probably the most misunderstood nationalist leader in the history of British Africa', see: *Britain's Declining Empire*, 190.

79. MAE, Série K: Afrique-Levant, Sous-série: Possessions britanniques, Kenya, Administration de la colonie, répression du mouvement Mau Mau, 1953–1959, no. 12/AL, 'Le Procès de JOMO KENYATTA', 13 Jan. 1953. Although a key witness was found to have lied in court, Kenyatta was eventually sentenced to seven years' hard labour.

80. Anderson, *Histories of the Hanged*, 124–35; Branch, *Defeating Mau Mau*, 56–9.

81. Anderson, *Histories of the Hanged*, 151–80 *passim*.

82. MAE, Série K: Afrique-Levant, Sous-série: Possessions britannique, 1944–1952, file 9, 'A.S. de la situation au Kenya au cours de la première quinzaine de mai'.

83. Anderson, *Histories of the Hanged*, 230–2.

84. Perversely, the Nairobi government cited the consolidation of Mau Mau bands into larger groups as evidence that they faced greater security force pressure. MAE, Série Afrique-Levant, Sous-série: Nord-Est Africain britannique, 1953–1959, file 3, Morand to Direction Afrique-Levant, 30 Apr. 1953.

85. David M. Anderson, 'The Battle of Dandora swamp: Reconstructing the Mau Mau land freedom army, October 1954', in Atieno Odhiambo and Lonsdale, *Mau Mau*, 157–63, 170–1.

86. Anderson, *Histories of the Hanged*, 235–44.

87. Ibid. no. 132/AL, Morand to Foreign Minister, 30 Apr. 1953.

88. MAE, Série Afrique-Levant, Sous-série: Nord-Est Africain britannique, 1953–1959, file 3: Kenya, no. 171/AL, Morand to Direction Afrique-Levant, 16 juin 1953.

89. Ibid. no. 241/AL, Morand to Direction Afrique-Levant, 17 Sept. 1953. 'A. S. La Situation au Kenya au cours des mois de juillet et d'août'.

90. Prisoners' strategies of resistance to interrogation are examined in Derek R. Peterson, 'The intellectual lives of Mau Mau detainees, *JAH*, 49:1 (2008), 73–91.

91. MAE, Série Afrique-Levant, Sous-série: Nord-Est Afrique britannique, 1953–1959, file 3: Kenya Information Service Swahili pamphlet, 'Mau Mau'; no. 257/AL, Morand memo, 28 Sept. 1953.

92. Ibid. no. 333/AL, Morand, 'A.S. Situation au Kenya', 20 Nov. 1953.

442 NOTES TO PAGES 228–232

93. Ibid. nos. 47 & 61, Morand to Direction Afrique-Levant, 18 & 23 Feb. 1954.
94. TNA, CO 822/796. 'Operation Anvil, Outline Plan', Nairobi, 22 Feb. 1954.
95. TNA, CO 1066/16: Operation 'Anvil', Operation 'Scaramouche' and camp visits, 1954–55.
96. French, *The British Way*, 30, 106, 110–11, 124.
97. MAE, Série Afrique-Levant, Sous-série: Nord-Est Afrique britannique, 1953–1959, file 3: Kenya, no. 44/AL, Morand, 'A.S. La Situation au Kenya', 28 Jan. 1955.
98. BLO, Barbara Castle papers, MS Castle 245, 'Justice in Kenya', *The New Statesman and Nation*, 17 Dec. 1955; Anderson, *Histories of the Hanged*, 7–8.
99. MAE, Nord-Est Afrique britannique, 1953–1959, file 3, Nairobi consulate, 'Exécutions pour crimes et délits pendant l'état d'urgence', s.d., janvier 1955.
100. Anderson, *Histories of the Hanged*, 36–7.
101. Caroline Elkins, *Imperial Reckoning: The Untold Story of Britain's Gulag in Kenya* (New York: Henry Holt, 2005). Cambridge historian Ronald Hyam considers the 'gulag' label overblown and misleading, suggesting a policy of elimination where none existed; see *Britain's Declining Empire*, 192 n. 111. His point is a fair one, although Kenya's detention camp system evolved into a massive programme whose punishments, brain-washing, and social engineering were redolent of Soviet practices.
102. Murphy, *Alan Lennox-Boyd*, 150–1. The Colonial Secretary Lennox-Boyd inspected the Manyani camp during an East African tour in Oct. 1954 and praised camp authorities for working to improve it.
103. For the war's gender dynamics, see Tabitha Kanogo, 'Kikuyu women and the politics of protest: Mau Mau', in Sharon MacDonald, Pat Holden and Shirley Ardener, eds, *Images of Women in Peace and War: Cross-Cultural and Historical Perspectives* (London: Macmillan, 1987), 78–99; Luise White, 'Separating the men from the boys: Constructions of gender, sexuality, and terrorism in central Kenya, 1939–1959', *International Journal of African Historical Studies*, 23:1 (1990), 1–25; A. M. White, 'Fanon and the African woman combatant', in Alfred Nhema and Paul Tiyambe Zeleza, eds, *The Roots of African Conflicts: The Causes and Costs* (Oxford: James Currey, 2008), 136–55.
104. Elkins, 'Detention', 205.
105. BLO, Macmillan papers, Diaries, 2nd ser., d. 36, fo. 18, entry for 16 June 1959.
106. Sloan Mahone, 'The psychology of rebellion: Colonial medical responses to dissent in British East Africa', *JAH*, 47:2 (2006), 241–58.
107. Lewis, *Empire State-Building*, 287–9, 342–3.
108. Jackson, *Madness*, ch. 6, pre cue for n. 6.
109. Elkins, 'Detention', 198–202, Anderson, *Histories of the Hanged*, 46–7.
110. Berman, *Control and Crisis*, 359–63.
111. Peterson, 'The intellectual lives', 73–91.
112. Two individuals, John Cowan, prisons officer in charge of the Mwea camps in Central Province, and Terence Gavaghan, a local District Officer, enforced the

'dilution technique' the most rigorously, see: Elkins, *Imperial Reckoning*, 317–30; Elkins, 'Detention', 213–15.

113. Anderson, *Histories of the Hanged*, 4; Murphy, *Alan Lennox-Boyd*, 149.

114. Toye, *Churchill's Empire*, 294–5, 299; Murphy, *Alan Lennox-Boyd*, 152–5.

115. Spruyt, *Ending Empire*, 128–30.

116. Murphy, *Alan Lennox-Boyd*, 152–3.

117. Daniel Branch, *Kenya: Between Hope and Despair, 1963–2010* (New Haven, CT: Yale University Press, 2011), ch. 1.

118. This is a key conclusion of Daniel Branch's *Defeating Mau Mau*, 208–12.

119. Darwin, 'Central African Emergency', 218.

CHAPTER 9

1. Norman Etherington, 'The missionary experience in British and French empires', in White and Daughton, *In God's Empire*, 279.

2. Elizabeth Schmidt, 'Top down or bottom up? Nationalist mobilization reconsidered, with special reference to Guinea', *AHR*, 110 (Oct., 2005), 975–1014. And for a different view, Mairi MacDonald, 'A vocation for independence: Guinean nationalism in the 1950s', in Chafer and Keese, eds, *Francophone Africa at Fifty* (Manchester University Press, forthcoming).

3. Eric Silla, *People Are Not the Same: Leprosy and Identity in Twentieth-Century Mali* (Portsmouth, NH: Heinemann, 1998), 117, 129–34.

4. A conclusion in tune with Sarah Stockwell, 'Ends of Empire', 275, and Ebere Nwaubani, *The United States and Decolonization in West Africa, 1950–1960* (Rochester, NY: University of Rochester Press, 2001), 16–17.

5. Yves Person, 'French West Africa and decolonization', in Prosser Gifford and Wm. Roger Louis, eds, *The Transfer of Power in Africa: Decolonization, 1940–1960*, (New Haven: Yale University Press, 1982), 141–2.

6. Holland, *European Decolonization*, 158.

7. Conklin, *A Mission to Civilize*, 23–37.

8. Municipal councils were set up in Senegal between 1872 and 1879, see H. O. Idowu, 'The establishment of elective institutions in Senegal, 1869–1880', *JAH*, 9:2 (1968), 261–77. On 1 Oct. 1916 male adult *originaires* (original inhabitants) of the four communes were granted French citizenship without forfeiting their customary rights as practising Muslims.

9. Catherine Coquery-Vidrovitch, 'Nationalité et citoyenneté en Afrique occidentale française: Originaires et citoyens dans le Sénégal colonial', *JAH*, 42:2 (2001), 285–305.

10. USNA, RG 59, 851 T.00, French Africa, Political 1945–1949, box 6328, US Consulate Brazzaville memcon., 'Postwar prospects in French Equatorial Africa', 14 July 1945.

11. This and subsequent paragraphs draw heavily on Catherine Coquery-Vidrovitch, 'L'Impact des intérêts coloniaux: S. C. O. A. et C. F. A. O. dans l'Ouest Africain, 1910–1965', *JAH*, 16:4 (1975), 595–621.

12. Richard A. Joseph, 'Settlers, strikers and *sans-travail*: The Douala riots of September 1945', *JAH*, 15:4 (1974), 669.

13. Timothy C. Weiskel, 'Independence and the *longue durée*: The Ivory Coast "miracle" reconsidered', in Gifford and Louis, *Decolonization*, 358–63.

14. John Kent, 'United States reactions to empire, colonialism, and Cold War in black Africa, 1949–57', *JICH*, 33:2 (2005), 198–209.

15. USNA, RG 59, 851T.00, French West Africa, Political 1945–49, box 6327, AMCONGEN, Dakar, 'Long range economic and social planning in French West Africa', 5 Dec. 1945.

16. USNA, RG 59, 851T.00, French West Africa, Political 1950–54, box 5008, AMCONGEN, Dakar, 'Tentative proposals for development of Africa by ECA funds', 29 June 1950.

17. J.-C. Berthélemy, 'L'Économie de l'Afrique occidentale française et du Togo, 1946–1960', *Revue Française de l'Histoire d'Outre-Mer*, 67:248, (1980), 301.

18. Tony Chafer, 'Education and political socialisation of a national-colonial political elite in French West Africa, 1936–47', *JICH*, 35:3 (2007), 441, 448–9.

19. Murphy, *Party Politics*, 107–12, 117–19. Sir Edward Spears and Duncan Sandys were among those with interests in British West African mining consortia. Beyond West Africa, several more either sat on the board or held investments with Tanganyika Concessions Limited, a company also linked to the vast Belgian Congo conglomerate, the *Union Minière du Haut Katanga*.

20. Polsgrove, *Ending British Rule*, 75–6.

21. Irwin, 'A wind of change?', 914–16. As Irwin explains, the pre-eminent importance of defeating apartheid goes a long way to explaining the pan-Africanist view.

22. Frederick Cooper, 'Alternatives to nationalism in French Africa, 1945–1960', in Jost Dülffer and Marc Frey, eds, *Elites and Decolonization in the Twentieth Century* (Basingstoke: Palgrave-Macmillan, 2011), 110–24.

23. Catherine Atlan, 'Demain la balkanisation? Les Députés africains et le vote de la Loi-cadre (1956)', in Becker, *AOF*, 358–75.

24. Cooper, 'Alternatives to nationalism', 110–33.

25. Frederick Cooper, 'Possibility and constraint: African independence in colonial perspective', *JAH*, 49 (2008), 167–8.

26. Cooper, 'Possibility', 171–5.

27. Cooper, 'Alternatives to nationalism', 114–16.

28. Alexander Keese, 'A culture of panic: "Communist" scapegoats and decolonization in French West Africa and French Polynesia (1945–1957)', *French Colonial History*, 9 (2008), 136–8.

29. Elizabeth Schmidt, 'Cold War in Guinea: The Rassemblement Démocratique Africain and the struggle over Communism, 1950–1958', *JAH*, 48:1 (2007), 99, 102–3.

30. Schmidt, 'Cold War', 100–1; *Cold War and Decolonization in Guinea, 1946–1958* (Athens, OH: Ohio University Press, 2007), 13–15, 25–7.

31. Chafer, 'Education', 449–50. The Socialist Minister for Overseas France, Marius Moutet, was particularly hostile to the RDA, viewing it through the prism of Socialist rivalry with the French Communists.

32. Schmidt, 'Cold War in Guinea', 100; Mairi S. MacDonald, 'A "frontal attack on irrational elements": Sékou Touré and the management of elites in Guinea', in Düllfer and Frey, Elites, 195–8.

33. Frederick Cooper, 'Alternatives to empire: France and Africa after World War II', in Douglas Howland and Luise White, eds, The State of Sovereignty: Territories, Laws, Populations (Bloomington, IN: Indiana University Press, 2009), 98–105.

34. BDEEP, series B, vol. 7: Nigeria, Part I: Managing Political Reform, 1943–1953 (London: HMSO, 2001), ed. Martin Lynn, docs. 11–15.

35. For contrasting verdicts on Nigeria's 'chiefly politics', see Olufemi Vaughan, 'Chieftaincy politics and communal identity in western Nigeria, 1893–1951', JAH, 44:2 (2003), 285–91; Peter K. Tibenderana, 'The irony of indirect rule in the Sokoto Emirate, Nigeria, 1903–1944', African Studies Review, 31:1 (1988), 67–92.

36. 'Nigeria—conquerors and conquered', W. Ormsby Gore, M.P., The Listener, 4 Dec. 1929.

37. BDEEP, series B, vol. 7: Nigeria, Part I, docs. 31, 32; John Flint, 'Scandal at the Bristol Hotel: Some thoughts on racial discrimination in Britain and West Africa and its relationship to the planning of decolonisation, 1939–1947', JICH, 12:1 (1983), 74–93.

38. Carolyn A. Brown, We were all slaves: African Miners, Culture, and Resistance at the Enugu Government Colliery (Portsmouth, NH: Heinemann, 2003), 282–317.

39. BDEEP, series B, vol. 7: Nigeria, Part I, docs. 80–84; Carolyn A. Brown, 'Becoming "men", becoming "workers": Race, gender, and workplace struggle in the Nigerian coal industry, 1937–1949', in Peter Alexander and Rick Halpern, eds, Racializing Class, Classifying Race: Labour and Difference in Britain, the USA and Africa (London: Macmillan, 2000), 168–9, 186–8.

40. Graham Furniss, 'On engendering liberal values in the Nigerian colonial state: The idea behind the Gaskiya Corporation', JICH, 39:1 (2011), 96–8, 109–14.

41. BDEEP, series B, vol. 7: Nigeria, Part I, doc. 30.

42. Phia Steyn, 'Oil exploration in colonial Nigeria, c.1903–58', JICH, 37:2 (2009), 261–6.

43. BDEEP, series B, vol. 7: Nigeria, Part I, docs. 52, 54, 69, 74.

44. Martin Lynn, '"We cannot let the North down": British policy and Nigeria in the 1950s', in Lynn, The British Empire, 144–60.

45. Martin Lynn, 'The Nigerian self-government crisis of 1953 and the Colonial Office', JICH, 34:2 (2006), 246–8.

46. John Flint, 'Managing nationalism: The Colonial Office and Nnamdi Azikiwe', JICH, 27:1 (1999), 143–58.

47. Lynn, '"We cannot"', quotation at 154.

48. BDEEP, series B, vol. 7: Nigeria, Part I, doc. 49.

49. Lynn, ' "We cannot" ', 154–8.
50. Lynn, 'The Nigerian self-government crisis', 251–3.
51. *BDEEP*, series B, vol. 7: *Nigeria, Part I*, doc. 187.
52. Lynn, 'The Nigerian self-government crisis', 253–4.
53. *BDEEP*, series B, vol. 7: *Nigeria, Part I*, doc. 205.
54. *BDEEP*, series B, vol. 7: *Nigeria, Part I*, docs. 190–192, 198, 202.
55. *BDEEP*, series B, vol. 7: *Nigeria, Part I*, doc. 210.
56. *BDEEP*, series B, vol. 7: *Nigeria, Part II: Moving to Independence, 193–1960*, docs. 238, 241; Lynn, 'The Nigerian self-government crisis', 255–7.
57. Lynn, ' "We cannot" ', 154–60.
58. The classic elaboration of this argument is J.M. Lee, ' "Forward thinking" and war: The Colonial Office during the 1940s', *JICH*, 6:1 (1977), 64–78.
59. Richard Crook, 'Decolonization, the colonial state and chieftaincy in Ghana', *African Affairs*, 85:338 (1986), 90. For contrasting views of indirect rule's application to Gold Coast chieftaincy politics, see Roger S. Gocking, 'Indirect rule in the Gold Coast: Competition for office and the invention of tradition', *CJAS*, 28:3 (1994), 421–5, 438–42. For convincing evidence that such prodding cut both ways, see Sean Stilwell, 'Constructing colonial power: Tradition, legitimacy and government in Kano, 1903–63', *JICH*, 39:2 (2011), 195–7, 204–14.
60. Roger S. Gocking, 'British justice and the native tribunals of the southern Gold Coast Colony', *JAH*, 34:1 (1993), 110–12.
61. John Flint, 'Planned decolonization and its failure in British Africa', *African Affairs*, 82:328 (1983), 389–411; Robert Pearce, 'The Colonial Office and planned decolonization in Africa', *African Affairs*, 83:330 (1984), 77–93. For the view that self-government did not mean decolonization: Crook, 'Decolonization, the colonial state', 75–86.
62. Richard Rathbone, 'A murder in the Gold Coast: Law and politics in the 1940s', *JAH*, 30 (1989), 445–56.
63. Rathbone, 'A murder', 456–61.
64. Francis K. Danquah, 'Sustaining a West African cocoa economy: Agricultural science and the swollen shoot contagion in Ghana, 1936–1965', *African Economic History*, 31:1 (2003), 44–8.
65. Danquah, 'Sustaining', 49–57. Ironically, once elected to office in 1951 Nkrumah endorsed further cutting out to stem the spread of swollen shoot.
66. David Killingray, 'Soldiers, ex-servicemen, and politics in the Gold Coast, 1939–50', *Journal of Modern African Studies*, 21:3 (1983), 531–3.
67. Richard Rathbone, 'Police intelligence in Ghana in the late 1940s and 1950s', in Robert Holland, ed., *Emergencies and Disorder in the European Empires after 1945* (London: Cass, 1994), 107–9.
68. *BDEEP*, series B, vol. I: *Ghana, Part I: 1941–1952* (London: HMSO, 1992), edited by Richard Rathbone, docs. 21, 23, 25; Richard Rathbone, 'Political intelligence', 84.
69. Danquah, 'Sustaining', 52.

70. *BDEEP*, series B, vol. I: *Ghana, Part I: 1941–1952*, xlii–xlviii, docs. 32–37, 64–67, 85.
71. *BDEEP*, series B, vol. I: *Ghana, Part I: 1941–1952*, doc. 78.
72. Rathbone, 'Political intelligence', 84–91.
73. *BDEEP*, series B, vol. I: *Ghana, Part I: 1941–1952*, docs. 44, 88–89.
74. Richard Crook, 'Decolonization, the colonial state', 95–9, 103–5.
75. Jean Marie Allman, ' "Hewers of wood, carriers of water": Islam, class, and politics on the eve of Ghana's independence', *African Studies Review*, 34:2 (1991), 1–2, 6–11.
76. *BDEEP*, series B, vol. I: *Ghana, Part II: 1952–1957*, docs. 157, 158, 160.
77. Richard Rathbone, 'Kwame Nkrumah and the chiefs: The fate of "natural rulers" under nationalist governments', *Transactions of the Royal Historical Society*, 6th Ser.: 10 (2000), 48, 57–60; Jean Marie Allman, 'The youngmen and the porcupine: Class, nationalism and Asante's struggle for self-determination, 1954–57', *JAH*, 31:2 (1990), 263–79.
78. Kate Skinner, 'Reading, writing and rallies: The politics of "freedom" in southern British Togoland, 1953–1956', *JAH*, 48:1 (2007), 125–32.
79. Rathbone, 'Kwame Nkrumah', 51–5, 61; *Nkrumah and the Chiefs: The Politics of Chieftaincy in Ghana, 1951–1960* (Oxford: James Currey, 2000), 89–103.
80. Philippe Dewitte, 'La CGT et les syndicats d'Afrique occidentale française (1945–1957)', *Le Mouvement Social*, 117 (1981), 4–5, 10–11.
81. Ibid. 98–9; regarding ex-servicemen's politics, see Gregory Mann, *Native Sons: West African Veterans and France in the Twentieth Century* (Durham, NC: Duke University Press, 2006), 108–45.
82. Coquery-Vidrovitch, *Africa, Endurance and Change South of the Sahara*, 265–8.
83. Cooper, *Decolonization*, 241–7.
84. Ibid. 278–86; Timothy Oberst, 'Transport workers, strikes and the "imperial response": Africa and the post World War II conjuncture', *African Studies Review*, 31:1 (1988), 117–33; Jean Suret-Canale, 'L'Indépendance de la Guinée: Le Rôle des forces intérieures', in Ageron and Michel, *L'Afrique noire française*, 131–2.
85. Frederick Cooper: 'The Senegalese general strike', 165–215; ' "Our strike" ', *JAH*, 37:1 (1996), 81–118.
86. Cooper, *Decolonization and African Society*, 282. Equivalent benefits for African workers in the private sector were not conceded until 1956.
87. Chafer, *End of Empire*, chap. 2. The essential qualification for subject voting rights was a French education or military service.
88. Cooper, 'The dialectics of decolonization', 425.
89. Chafer, *End of Empire*, 105–9.
90. Schmidt, *Cold War*, 35–43, 49–63; Klaas van Walraven, 'Decolonization by referendum: The anomaly of Niger and the fall of Sawaba, 1958–1959', *JAH*, 50:2 (2009), 273.
91. Alexander Keese, ' "*Quelques satisfactions d'amour-propre*": African elite integration, the *loi-cadre*, and involuntary decolonisation of French tropical Africa', *Itinerario* 26 (2003), 37–38.

92. Person, 'French West Africa and decolonization', 151; Hargreaves, *Decolonization in Africa*, 141–2.

93. Chafer, *End of Empire*, ch. 3. René Pleven was leader of the UDSR.

94. Schmidt, 'Cold War', 102–19; *Mobilizing the Masses: Gender, Ethnicity, and Class in the Nationalist Movement in Guinea, 1939–1958* (Portsmouth, NH: Heinemann, 2005).

95. For the *négritude* pioneer Martiniquan poet, Aimé Césaire's divorce from French Communism during the years of RDA realignment, see: Thomas A. Hale and Kora Véron, 'Aimé Césaire's break from the Parti Communiste Français: *Nouveaux élans, nouveaux défis*', *FPCS*, 27:3 (2009), 47–62.

96. Benjamin Stora, *Nationalistes Algériens et Révolutionnaires Français au temps du Front Populaire* (Paris: Editions L'Harmattan, 1987); T. -A. Schweitzer, 'Le Parti communiste français, le Comintern et l'Algérie dans les années 1930', *Le Mouvement Social*, 78 (1972), 115–36.

97. These ambiguities are discussed in G. Wesley Johnson, 'Les Élites au Sénégal pendant la période d'indépendance', in Ageron and Michel, *L'Afrique noire française*, 26–36.

98. Schmidt, 'Cold War', 103–19.

99. Tony Chafer, 'Students and nationalism: The role of students in the nationalist movement in Afrique Occidentale Française (AOF), 1946–60', in Charles Becker, Saliou Mbaye, and Ibrahima Thioub, eds, *AOF: réalités et heritages: Sociétés ouest-africaines et ordre colonial, 1895–1960* 2 vols, (Dakar: Direction des Archives du Sénégal, 1997), 395–6, 402–3.

100. AN, UDSR papers, 412AP/34, Jean Gunsett letter to Joseph Perrin (Senator for Côte d'Ivoire), 7 June 1956.

101. Thierno Bah, 'Les Étudiants de l'Afrique noire et la marche à l'indépendance', in Ageron and Michel, *L'Afrique noire française*, 41–56.

102. Gregory Mann, 'Fetishizing religion: Allah Koura and French 'Islamic Policy' in late colonial French Soudan (Mali)', *JAH*, 44:2 (2003), 263–5, 280–1.

103. Robert Launay and Benjamin F. Soares, 'The formation of an "Islamic sphere" in French colonial West Africa', *Economy and Society*, 28 (1999), 497; also cited in Mann, 'Fetishizing religion', 265.

104. Elizabeth A. Foster, 'A mission in transition: Race, politics, and the decolonization of the Catholic Church in Senegal', in White and Daughton, *In God's Empire*, 271–3.

105. J. G. Vaillant, *Black, French and African: A Life of Léopold Sédar Senghor* (Cambridge, MA: Harvard University Press, 1990). Kwame Nkrumah disparaged 'Negritude', dismissing it as elitist and inauthentic.

106. Person, 'French West Africa', 161.

107. Cooper, *Decolonization and African Society*, 424–5.

108. Chafer, *End of Empire*, ch. 6.

109. Martin Shipway, 'Gaston Defferre's *loi-cadre* and its application, 1956–57: Last chance for a French African "empire-state"?' in Tony Chafer and Alexander Keese, eds, *Francophone Africa at Fifty* (Manchester University Press, forthcoming).

110. SHD-DAT, 14H48/D5, no. 02859, Direction des Affaires Militaires, 'Organisation militaire des T.O.M. en vue du maintien et rétablissement de l'ordre', 27 June 1956; no. 3116, 3eme Bureau, 'Action psychologique et sécurité intérieure', n.d., June 1956.
111. Cooper, 'Alternatives to empire', 107–9.
112. Cooper, Possibility', 175.
113. An argument developed by Fred Cooper in both 'Possibility', 169–77, and 'Alternatives to empire', 110–24.

CHAPTER 10

1. BLO, Macmillan Diaries, 2nd ser., d. 37, fo.64, entry for 10 Nov. 1959.
2. BLO, Macmillan Diaries, 2nd ser., d. 37, fo.55–7, entry for 30 Oct. 1959.
3. The prime minister was physically sick with worry immediately before he delivered the speech.
4. British newspaper readers were introduced to Macmillan as electoral super-hero by cartoonist Vicky (Victor Weisz) in an *Evening Standard* cartoon on 6 Nov. 1959. As Ronald Hyam notes, since the mid 1950s Macmillan had employed a different elemental metaphor—the tidal-wave—to describe the unstoppable force of African nationalism: *Britain's Declining Empire*, 242–3.
5. Hyam, *Britain's Declining Empire*, 258–60.
6. For more complex readings of the speech and its context, see L.J. Butler and Sarah Stockwell, eds, *Wind of Change* (Basingstoke: Palgrave-Macmillan, 2013).
7. Schmidt, *Cold War*, ch. 6; also cited in Cooper, 'Possibility', 168.
8. TNA, WO 216/913, GOC Ghana letters to Sir Francis Festing, 7 Mar. and 26 Aug. 1959.
9. TNA, FO 371/137966, J1075/21, 22, 23 and 27: Sir Harold Caccia Washington dispatches, and record of tripartite talks on Africa, 16–21 Apr. 1959.
10. Cooper, 'Alternatives to empire', 125.
11. Chipman, *French Power in Africa* (Oxford: Blackwell, 1989), 106–7.
12. Cooper, 'Alternatives to empire', 124–7.
13. Schmidt, 'Top down or bottom up?' 975–1014.
14. Van Walraven, 'Decolonization by referendum', 271–9. Niger was the only AOF territory other than Guinea in which significant numbers were affiliated to a radical nationalist party, Sawaba, built on the wreckage of the earlier Parti Progressiste Nigérien that had fallen victim to French repression of RDA-affiliated groups in the early 1950s.
15. Cooper, 'Alternatives to empire', 124–9.
16. Alexander Keese, 'First lessons in neo-colonialism: The personalisation of relations between African politicians and French officials in sub-Saharan Africa, 1956–66', *JICH*, 35:4 (2007), 593–613.
17. Hyam, *Britain's Declining Empire*, 265–6.

18. For a brilliant survey of these policy reviews, see Hyam, *Britain's Declining Empire*, 250–7.

19. Macmillan Diaries, 2nd ser., d. 34, fo.48, entry for 22 Jan. 1959; Deborah Posel, *The Making of Apartheid, 1948–1961: Conflict and Compromise* (Oxford: Clarendon Press, 1991), 227–55; Ronald Hyam, 'The parting of the ways: Britain and South Africa's departure from the Commonwealth, 1951–1961', *JICH*, 26:2 (1998), 157–75.

20. Hyam, *Britain's Declining Empire*, 271–2; Robert Holland, *Britain and the Revolt*, 133, 223.

21. Andrekos Varnava, 'Reinterpreting Macmillan's Cyprus policy, 1957–1960' *Cyprus Review*, 22:1 (2010), 91.

22. Holland, *Britain and the Revolt*, 129–30, 153.

23. Carruthers, *Winning Hearts*, 239–41.

24. For background: David Goldsworthy, 'Britain and the international critics of colonialism, 1951–1956', *Journal of Commonwealth and Comparative Politics*, 29:1 (1991), 1–24.

25. René Girault, 'La France en accusation à l'ONU, ou les pouvoirs d'une organisation internationale', *Relations Internationales*, 76:3 (1993), 411–22; Martin Thomas, 'France accused', *Contemporary European History*, 10:1 (2001), 91–121; Suha Bölükbasi, 'The Cyprus dispute and the United Nations: Peaceful non-settlement between 1954 and 1996', *IJMES*, 30:3 (1998), 411–15; Edward Johnson, 'Britain and the Cyprus problem at the United Nations, 1954–58', *JICH*, 28:3 (2000), 114–27; Holland, *Britain and the Revolt*, 41–5, 218–19.

26. Holland, *Britain and the Revolt*, 46; Martin Thomas, 'Defending a lost cause? France and the United States' vision of imperial rule in French North Africa, 1946–1956', *DH*, 26:2 (2002), 228–39.

27. Owen, 'Critics of empire in Britain', in Brown and Louis, *OHBE*, iv: *The Twentieth Century*, 204–7.

28. Josiah Brownell, 'The taint of communism: The Movement for Colonial Freedom, the Labour Party, and the Communist Party of Great Britain, 1954–70', *Canadian Journal of History*, 42:2 (2007), 235–58.

29. Robert Skinner, *The Foundations of Anti-Apartheid: Liberal Humanitarians and Transnational Activists in Britain and the United States, c.1919–64* (Basingstoke: Palgrave-Macmillan, 2010), chs 5–6.

30. French, *The British Way*, 106–9, 176–8; Holland, *Britain and the Revolt*, 135–41.

31. Hyam, *Britain's Declining Empire*, 152–3.

32. Holland, *Britain and the Revolt*, 18–19. Organized through the Cypriot Orthodox Church, voting was not conducted in secret and Turkish Cypriots, understandably, did not take part. Even so, the 96.5 per cent vote in favour of *Enosis* was striking.

33. Bölükbasi, 'The Cyprus dispute', 413.

34. Holland, *Britain and the Revolt*, 98.

35. For background to the Emergency, see Robert Holland, 'Never, Never Land: British colonial policy and the roots of violence in Cyprus, 1950–54', in

Holland, *Emergencies*, 148–76; and, in the same collection, for initial security responses to EOKA, see David M. Anderson, 'Policing and communal conflict: The Cyprus Emergency, 1954–60', 177–89.

36. Holland, *Britain and the Revolt*, 74–82. Riots in Nicosia on 17 Sept. 1955 culminated in the destruction of the city's British Institute. They were preceded by Turkish violence against Greeks in Istanbul and Izmir, a scary portent of what might occur if the Cyprus problem were not contained.

37. Murphy, *Alan Lennox-Boyd*, 117–19. As Robert Holland notes, 'the British were never to be quite clear where Makarios' religion ended and his politics began'. For instance, while staying in Athens in July 1952, the Archbishop joined soon-to-be EOKA leader Colonel George Grivas in swearing a 'holy sacred oath' to strive for *Enosis*. See Holland, *Britain and the Revolt*, 25, 28–9.

38. Holland, *Britain and the Revolt*, 84.

39. Holland, *Britain and the Revolt*, 99–105. On 14 Dec. 1955 132 AKEL members were arrested and sent to detention camps.

40. Holland, *Britain and the Revolt*, 115–19. When Lennox-Boyd got wind of *La Bastille*, he insisted that Seychelles Governor, Sir William Addis, house Makarios in his more felicitously-named country residence, *Sans Souci* (*Without a Care*).

41. RHL, MSS., 'British Rule in Cyprus—a personal reminiscence', n.d., p.22.

42. A useful reading of the conflicting international pressures over Cyprus at the time is: Evanthis Hatzivassiliou, 'Blocking Enosis: Britain and the Cyprus question, March–December 1956', *JICH*, 19:2 (1991), 247–63.

43. TNA, AIR 8/1926, JP(57)81, COS memo, 'Military policy for Cyprus', 3 July 1957; Chief of Air Staff brief, 10 July 1957. RAF planners were particularly critical of partition, warning that bases would have to be re-supplied through hostile Greek Cypriot territory.

44. Evanthis Hatzivassiliou, *Britain and the International Status of Cyprus, 1955–59* (Minneapolis, MN: University of Minnesota Press, 1997), 128–35.

45. Rauf Denktash obituary, *The Economist*, 21 Jan. 2012.

46. Varnava, 'Reinterpreting', 92–3.

47. Holland, *Britain and the Revolt*, 243–5, 253–6. The massacre of eight Greek Cypriot detainees dumped by a Police detachment outside the Turkish village of Guenyeli on 12 June 1958 provided shocking proof both of worsening cross-communal hatreds and of security-force irresponsibility.

48. Holland, *Britain and the Revolt*, 204–6.

49. BLO, Macmillan Diaries, 2nd ser., d. 29, fos.88–9, entry for 7 July 1957.

50. Holland, *Britain and the Revolt*, 236–61 passim.

51. BLO, Macmillan Diaries, 2nd ser., d. 29, fos.88–97, entries for 7, 10 and 11 July 1957.

52. Holland, *Britain and the Revolt*, 274–6.

53. TNA, DEFE 5/85, COS(58)243, 'Release of military manpower from police duties in colonial territories', 30 Oct. 1958.

54. TNA, DEFE 5/87, COS(58)272, British Defence Co-ordination Committee report, 'Cyprus', 1 Dec. 1958.

55. Holland, *Britain and the Revolt*, 295–7.
56. The argument that the Cyprus settlement was primarily a Greco-Turkish government achievement is made in Varnava, 'Reinterpreting', 95–100.
57. Lynn, '"We cannot let the North down"', 155–60.
58. James R. Brennan, 'Youth, the TANU Youth League and managed vigilantism in Dar es Salaam, Tanzania, 1925–73', *Africa*, 76:2 (2006), 227–32. TANU's highly-effective youth wing devoted greater effort to intimidating internal opponents than to fighting the colonial authorities.
59. John Darwin, *The Historical Debate*, 74–9.
60. Catherine R. Schenk, *Britain and the Sterling Area: From Devaluation to Convertibility in the 1950s* (London: Routledge, 1994), 20–5; Schenk, *The Decline of Sterling*, 84–7.
61. Sarah Stockwell, 'Instilling the "sterling tradition": Decolonization and the creation of a central bank in Ghana', *JICH*, 26:2 (1998), 100–1, 109–15.
62. MAE série Z: Europe, 1944–1960, sous-série: Grande-Bretagne, vol. 95, no. 5122, René Massigli to Foreign Ministry, 12 Dec. 1952.
63. MAE série Z: Europe, 1944–1960, sous-série: Grande-Bretagne, vol. 95, Massigli memo, 'Problème de la convertibilité', 13 Dec. 1952.
64. Darwin, *The Empire Project*, 582–3.
65. Schenk, *The Decline of Sterling*, 88–9.
66. Catherine Hodeir, *Stratégies d'Empire: Le Grand Patronat colonial face à la décolonisation* (Paris: Belin, 2003), 281–301.
67. Schenk, *The Decline of Sterling*, 89–93.
68. Robert F. Dewey, Jr, *British National Identity and Opposition to Membership of Europe, 1961–63: The Anti-Marketeers* (Manchester University Press, 2009), 30–8, 177–91.
69. Ibid. 60–8.
70. 'The Commonwealth and Europe', Harold Macmillan, M.P., *The Listener*, 27 Sept. 1962.
71. White, 'Decolonisation in the 1950s', 100–22.
72. Schenk, *The Decline of Sterling*, 92–3; Gerald Krozewski, *Money and the End of Empire: British Economic Policy and the Colonies, 1947–1958* (Basingstoke: Palgrave, 2001), 131–7.
73. White, 'Decolonisation in the 1950s', 102–5.
74. White, 'Decolonisation in the 1950s', 106–17.
75. TNA, DEFE 7/1296, Ministerial Committee on Strategic Export Policy first meeting', 8 June 1956.
76. TNA, DEFE 13/274, SE(O)CP(56)23, MOD Strategic Exports Committee, 'Export of arms to the Middle East', 13 Nov. 1956. Also in Nov. 1956 the existing ban on British arms supplies to Egypt and Syria was extended to include Saudi Arabia and Yemen.
77. TNA, DEFE 13/214, Supply of Arms to the Middle East, Apr. 1958. Sometimes this caution backfired. US refusal to finance the sale of state-of-the-art British

HunterVI aircraft to Iraq's monarchical regime in early 1958 exposed the limitations of British influence.

78. TNA, DEFE 7/1295, memo by Sir Frank Lee, Board of Trade Permanent Secretary,'Commercial prospects in the Middle East', 20 Apr. 1959; FO tel. 2508 to Washington Embassy, 29 May 1959.

79. TNA, DEFE 5/91, COS(59)122, annex, 'The Middle East and Africa', 30 Apr. 1959.

80. TNA, DEFE 5/92, COS(59)146, annex, COS committee memo, 'Long-term deployment of the Army', 24 June 1959.

81. TNA, DEFE 5/92, COS(59)162, COS comments on Africa committee report, 'Africa—the next ten years', 6 July 1959.

82. TNA, DEFE 7/1013, C.-in-C. Mediterranean to GHQ Middle East, 'US and UK Planning in Libya, 7 Aug. 1958; D(28)4, MOD Defence Committee brief, 'Libya garrison', n.d.

83. Spencer Mawby, 'Britain's last imperial frontier: The Aden Protectorates, 1952–59', *JICH*, 29:2 (2001), 75–100.

84. Nigel John Ashton, 'A microcosm of decline: British loss of nerve and military intervention in Jordan and Kuwait, 1958 and 1961', *HJ*, 40:4 (1997), 1072–83; Clive Jones, ' "Among ministers, mavericks and mandarins": Britain, covert action and the Yemen civil war, 1962–64', *MES*, 40:1 (2004), 99–122.

85. TNA, DEFE 5/91, COS(59)122, annex, 'The Middle East and Africa', 30 Apr. 1959.

86. The notion of a mid twentieth-century British Middle Eastern 'moment' was refined by Elizabeth Monroe in, *Britain's Moment in the Middle East, 1914–1956* (London: Cox and Wyman, 1963).

87. Stuart Ward, ' "No nation could be broker": The satire boom and the demise of Britain's world role', in ed., *British Culture and the End of Empire* (Manchester University Press, 2001), 91–109.

88. A conclusion borne out by Louis and Robinson, 'Imperialism of Decolonization'.

89. TNA, DEFE 4/132, COS(PAR)(60), annex:'Military strategy for circumstances short of global war', 21 June 1960.

90. TNA, PREM 11/3336, PM/61/3, Minutes by de Zulueta and Foreign Secretary, 5 and 10 Jan. 1961.

91. TNA, PREM 11/3336, De Zulueta note, 'Discussions with the French about European minorities in Africa', 13 Jan. 1961; Rambouillet talks transcript, 28 Jan. 1961.

92. Cooper, 'Possibility', 169.

93. Murphy, *Party Politics*, 216–18, quotation at p. 217.

94. Murphy, *Party Politics*, 238.

95. BLO, Castle papers, MS Castle 16, fos.8–9, 11 Dec. 1963.

96. BLO, Castle papers, MS Castle 16, fos.11–13, 11 Dec. 1963.

97. Andrew S. Thompson, introduction to *Britain's Experience of Empire in the Twentieth Century*, 17.

98. Linda Colley, 'Europe, not empire: Britain's foreign policy challenge', *The Guardian*, 6 Jan. 2012.

CHAPTER 11

1. Martin Evans, *Algeria*, 131–2.
2. Jean-Charles Jauffret, ed., *La Guerre d'Algérie par les documents*, ii, 359–61.
3. Evans, *Algeria*, 118–23; Mohammed Harbi, *Le FLN: Mirage et réalité* (Paris: Editions Jeune Afrique, 1981), 96–100. The nine were Hocine Aït Ahmed, Ahmed Ben Bella, Mohammed Boudiaf, Rabah Bitat, Mostefa Ben Boulaïd, Larbi Ben M'hidi, Mourad Didouche, Mohammed Khider, and Belkacem Krim. The leadership remained broadly collective, but was prone to factional splits; Boudiaf played the leading organizational role. Force of circumstance and the rising influence of guerrilla (ALN) leaders also altered its complexion: Ben Boulaïd Ben M'hidi, and Didouche died at the hands of the French army; Ben Bella, Bitat, Boudiaf, and Khider spent most of the war in jail.
4. Gilbert Meynier, *Histoire intérieure du F.L.N., 1954–1962* (Paris: Fayard, 2002), 121–3.
5. ANOM, Marcel Edmond Naegelen, Cabinet files, 9cab/48, menées anti-nationales, atteintes à la sûreté de l'Etat, MTLD, 1947–51; 9cab/58: Renseignements RG, 1948–51.
6. Meynier, *Histoire intérieure*, 129–48; Evans, *Algeria*, 127–9.
7. MAE, série: Afrique-Levant 1944–1959, sous-série: Algérie 1944–1952, vol. 6, Algiers prefect, 'Note sur l'activité subversive du PPA-MTLD, Département d'Alger', n. d. 1950; Meynier, *Histoire Intérieure*, 87; Harbi, *Le F.L.N.: Mirage et réalité*, 70–6.
8. AN, René Mayer papers, 363AP32/D3, no. 3266, Governor-General Roger Léonard to Interior Ministry, 3 Jan. 1955.
9. Jean-Charles Jauffret, 'The origins of the Algerian War: The reaction of France and its army to the emergencies of 8 May 1945 and 1 Nov. 1954', *JICH*, 21:3 (1993), 24–8.
10. Jean-Louis Planche, *Sétif 1945* (Paris: Perrin, 2006), 135–51; Jean-Pierre Peyroulou, *Guelma, 1945: Une subversion française dans l'Algérie coloniale* (Paris: La Découverte, 2009); Martin Thomas, 'Colonial violence in Algeria and the distorted logic of state retribution: The Sétif Uprising of 1945', *Journal of Military History* 75:1 (2011), 523–56.
11. AN, René Mayer papers, 363AP32/D3, no. 497/CC, Léonard to Interior Minister, 22 Jan. 1955.
12. Denis Roland, 'Jacques Soustelle, de l'ethnologie à la politique', *Guerres Mondiales et Conflits Contemporains*, 180 (Oct. 1995), 171–85; Jacques Soustelle, 'L'État actuel des travaux concernant l'histoire ancienne du Mexique', *Revue Historique*, 213:1 (1955), 39–46; Aleksandar Bošković, 'In the age of the fifth sun: Jacques Soustelle's studies of Aztec religion', *Anthropos*, 87:4/6 (1992), 533–7.

13. Bernard Ullmann, *Jacques Soustelle: Le Mal Aimé* (Paris: Plon, 1995), 186–90; Geoffrey Adams, *The Call of Conscience: French Protestant Responses to the Algerian War, 1954–1962* (Waterloo: Wilfrid Laurier University Press, 1998), 27–8;

14. Cited in Alistair Horne, *A Savage War of Peace: Algeria, 1954–1962* (New York: NYRB Classics, 2006), 108, and in Chipman, *French Power in Africa*, 78.

15. Evans, *Algeria*, 131–3; Shepard, *Invention*, 69–70.

16. AN, René Mayer papers, 363AP32/D1, Constantine Conseil Général motion delivered by Dr Abdelkader Bendjelloul, n.d., Sept. 1954.

17. Cited in Shepard, *Invention*, 64.

18. Stephen Tyre, 'From *Algerie française*, *FH*, 20:3 (2006), 276–96.

19. Xavier Yacono, 'Les Pertes algériennes de 1954 à 1962', *Revue de l'Occident Musulman et de la Méditerranée*, 34 (1983), 119–34.

20. Guy Pervillé, 'La Guerre d'Algérie: Combien de morts?' in Harbi and Stora, *La Guerre d'Algérie*, 476–85.

21. Martha Crenshaw Hutchinson, *Revolutionary Terrorism: The FLN in Algeria, 154–1962* (Stanford, CA: Hoover Institution Press, 1978).

22. Jacques Frémeaux, 'Usage et obsolescence des Français d'Algérie', in Jean-Charles Jauffret, ed., *Des hommes et des femmes en guerre d'Algérie* (Paris: Autrement, 2003), 49.

23. Rémi Kauffer, 'OAS: La Guerre franco-française d'Algérie', in Harbi and Stora, *La Guerre d'Algérie*, 470.

24. Emma Kuby, 'A war of words over an image of war: The Fox-Movietone scandal and the portrayal of French violence in Algeria, 1955–1956', *FPCS*, 30:1 (2012), 46–57. Faure's hapless government alleged that the gendarme was bribed by employees of Fox Movietone News, whose French cameraman Georges Chassagne captured the original incident.

25. Tramor Quéméneur, 'La Détention ou l'illégalité: Trois parcours de refus d'obéissance dans la guerre d'Algérie', in Jauffret, *Des hommes et des femmes*, 431–42; 'Testimony of Georges Mattéi', in Martin S. Alexander, Martin Evans, and J.F.V. Keiger, eds, *The Algerian War and the French Army: Experiences, Images, Testimonies* (Basingstoke: Palgrave-Macmillan, 2002), 249–53.

26. Lazreg, *Torture*, 123–30.

27. Todd Shepard, ' "Something notably erotic": Politics, "Arab men", and sexual revolution in postdecolonization France, 1962–1974', *Journal of Modern History*, 84:1 (2012), 87–8.

28. Raphaëlle Branche and Jim House, 'Silences on state violence during the Algerian War of independence: France and Algeria, 1962–2007', in Efrat Ben-Ze'ev, Ruth Ginio, and Jay Winter, eds, *Shadows of War: A Social History of Silence in the Twentieth Century* (Cambridge University Press, 2010), 119–20.

29. Marnia Lazreg, *The Eloquence of Silence: Algerian Women in Question* (London: Routledge, 1994), chs 3, 6–7.

30. Neil MacMaster, *Burning the Veil: The Algerian War and the 'Emancipation' of Algerian Women, 1954–62* (Manchester University Press, 2009), 209–16.

31. Natalya Vince, 'Transgressing boundaries: Gender, race, religion, and *"Françaises musulmanes"* during the Algerian War of independence', *FHS*, 33:3 (2010), 459–63; Cherifa Bouatta, 'Feminine militancy: *Moudjahidates* during and after the Algerian War', in Valentine M. Moghadam ed., *Gender and National Identity: Women and Politics in Muslim Societies* (London: Zed Books, 1994), 19–26. The fullest collection of *moudjahida* accounts was compiled by former fighter-turned-historian Djamila Amrane: *Des femmes dans la guerre d'Algérie: Entretiens* (Paris: Karthala, 1994).

32. Lazreg, *Torture*, 157–67.

33. Raphaëlle Branche, *La Torture et l'armée pendant la guerre d'Algérie* (Paris: Gallimard, 2001), 303–6; 'Des viols pendant la guerre d'Algérie', *Vingtième Siècle*, 75 (2002), 123–32; 'La Sexualité des appelés en Algérie', in Jauffret, *Des hommes et des femmes*, 412–13. Branche is scrupulous in identifying instances of sexual violence, making clear how commonplace it became.

34. MacMaster, *Burning the Veil*, 316–22, 334–41.

35. Natalya Vince, 'To be a *moudjahida* in independent Algeria: Itineraries and memories of women veterans of the Algerian War', PhD thesis, University of London, 2009, 33–4.

36. MacMaster, *Burning the Veil*, chs 7–9; Lazreg, *Torture*, 146–52.

37. Diane Sambrone, 'La Politique d'émancipation du gouvernement français à l'égard des femmes algériennes pendant la guerre d'Algérie', in Jauffret, *Des hommes et des femmes*, 228–42; Vince, 'Transgressing boundaries', 446–9, 464–7.

38. Martin Evans, *The Memory of Resistance: French Opposition to the Algerian War (1954–1962)* (Oxford: Berg, 1997), 39–44; Marie-Pierre Ulloa, *Francis Jeanson: A Dissident Intellectual from the French Resistance to the Algerian War* (Stanford University Press, 2007).

39. Shepard, *Invention*, 66–7.

40. Shepard, *Invention*, 75–7.

41. Annie Cohen-Solal, 'Camus, Sartre and the Algerian War', *Journal of European Studies*, 28:1 (1998), 43–50.

42. Shepard, *Invention*, 63–4, 68; James D. Le Sueur, *Uncivil War: Intellectuals and Identity Politics During the Decolonization of Algeria* (Philadelphia: University of Pennsylvania Press, 2001), ch. 4.

43. Le Sueur, *Uncivil War*, 86–90, 96–117; David Carroll, 'Camus's Algeria: Birthrights, colonial injustice, the fiction of a French-Algerian people', *Modern Language Notes*, 112 (1997), 517–49.

44. Jennings, *Revolution and the Republic*, 494–500.

45. Shepard, *Invention*, 61–2, 71–2.

46. Le Sueur, *Uncivil War*, 249–53.

47. Le Sueur, *Uncivil War*, 224–5.

48. Jane E. Goodman and Paul A. Silverstein, eds, 'Introduction', in *Bourdieu in Algeria: Colonial Politics, Ethnographic Practices, Theoretical Developments* (Lincoln, NE: University of Nebraska Press, 2009), 10–22.

49. Jacques Marseille, 'L'Investissement public en Algérie après la Deuxième Guerre Mondiale', *Revue Française d'Histoire d'Outre-Mer*, 70:260 (1983), 180–9; Nathalie Ruz, 'La Force du "Cartierisme"', in Jean-Pierre Rioux, ed., *La Guerre d'Algérie et les Français* (Paris: Fayard, 1990), 328–33.

50. SHD-DAT, 1H1106/D1, 'Tableaux de l'économie algérienne, 1960'.

51. For the long history of internment camps in Algeria, see Sylvie Thénault, *Violence ordinaire dans l'Algérie coloniale: Camps, internements, assignations à résidence* (Paris: Odile Jacob, 2011); Michel Cornaton, *Les Camps de regroupement de la guerre d'Algérie* (Paris: L'Harmattan, 1998).

52. On ideas of 'good' and 'bad' French colonists, see Jennifer E. Sessions, *By Sword and Plow*, 232–4; Benjamin Stora, 'The "southern" world of the *pieds noirs*: References to and representations of Europeans in colonial Algeria', in Caroline Elkins and Susan Pedersen, eds, *Settler Colonialism in the Twentieth Century* (London: Routledge, 2005), 226, 231. Stora suggests that fewer than three per cent of Algerian settlers exceeded the average standard of living in France.

53. Jean-Jacques Jordi, 'L'Inconscience ou le peril', in Jean-Jacques Jordi and Guy Pervillé, eds, *Alger, 1940–1962: Une ville en guerres* (Paris: Autrement, 1999), 96–9.

54. Stathis Kalyvas, *The Logic of Violence in Civil War* (Cambridge University Press, 2006), 183–91.

55. Guy Pervillé, 'Une capital convoitée', in Jean-Jacques Jordi and Guy Pervillé, eds, *Alger, 1940–1962: Une ville en guerres* (Paris: Autrement, 1999), 127–8.

56. Lorcin, *Historicizing Colonial Nostalgia*, 146.

57. Stora, 'The "southern" world', 236–8.

58. Patricia M. E. Lorcin, 'Introduction', to Lorcin, ed., *Algeria & France: Identity, Memory, Nostalgia* (Syracuse, NY: Syracuse University Press, 2006), xxiii.

59. Émilie Elongbil Ewane, 'Hébergement et répression: Le Centre de la Part-Dieu', in Raphaëlle Branche and Sylvie Thénault, *La France en guerre, 1954–1962: Expériences métropolitaines de la guerre d'indépendance algérienne* (Paris: Autrement, 2008), 419–25; Jim House and Andrew Thompson, 'Immigration and housing during and after decolonisation: Britain and France, 1945–1974', in Andrew Thompson, ed., *Writing Imperial Histories* (Manchester University Press, 2013), ch. 10.

60. Neil MacMaster, *Colonial Migrants and Racism: Algerians in France, 1900–62* (Basingstoke: Macmillan, 1997), 193.

61. Jacques Valette, *La Guerre d'Algérie des Messalistes, 1954–1962* (Paris: L'Harmattan, 2001).

62. Linda Amiri, *La Bataille de France: La Guerre d'Algérie en France* (Paris: Robert Laffont, 2004); Valette, *La guerre d'Algérie des Messalistes*; Ali Haroun, *La 7ᵉ Wilaya: La Guerre du FLN en France 1954–1962* (Paris: Seuil, 1986).

63. Emmanuel Blanchard, 'Contrôler, enfermer, éloigner: La Répression policière et administrative des algériens de métropole (1946–1962)', in Branche and Thénault, *La France en guerre*, 318–31; Blanchard, *La Police Parisienne et les Algériens (1944–1962)* (Paris: Nouveau Monde, 2011), 127–41, 166–73, 313–58.

64. For the juridical foundations of the clearest example, apartheid South Africa, see: Posel, *The Making of Apartheid*; Ivan Evans, 'Racial violence and the origins of segregation in South Africa', in Caroline Elkins and Susan Pedersen, eds, *Settler Colonialism in the Twentieth Century* (London: Routledge, 2005), 183–202.

65. Caroline Elkins, 'Race, citizenship, and governance: Settler tyranny and the end of Empire', in Elkins and Pedersen, *Settler Colonialism*, 203–22.

66. Philip Murphy makes this point about leading Southern Rhodesians of the Central African Federation: see, 'Government by blackmail', 54–64; also cited in Stockwell, 'Ends of Empire', 276.

67. Political scientist Hendrik Spruyt highlights the correlation between settler influence, the incidence of colonial violence and partition schemes, *Ending Empire: Contested Sovereignty and Territorial Partition* (Ithaca, NY: Cornell University Press, 2005), 27, 36–8.

68. Jackson, *Madness*.

69. Philippe Bourdrel, *La Dernière Chance de l'Algérie française: Du gouvernement socialiste au retour de De Gaulle, 1956–1958* (Paris: Albin Michel, 1996), 21–8.

70. Evans, *Algeria*, 148–9.

71. This argument is pivotal to Evans, *Algeria*.

72. Thomas, *The French North African Crisis*, 103–5.

73. SHD-DAT, 1H1379/D1, EMA-1, 'Plan d'urgence 1ère partie', 18 Mar. 1956; Marill, 'L'Héritage indochinois', 31–2.

74. SHD-DAT, 1H1374/D3, EMA summary, 'Situation des trois armées en Algérie, 1956'.

75. Alain Monchabion, 'Un positionnement syndical original: L'Union des grandes écoles', in Branche and Thénault, *La France en guerre*, 165–6.

76. Thomas, 'Order before reform', in Killingray and Omissi, *Guardians of Empire*, 198–221.

77. Fredrik Logevall, *Choosing War: The Lost Chance for Peace and the Escalation of War in Vietnam* (Berkeley, CA: University of California Press, 1999), chs 9–12; Brian VanDeMark, *Into the Quagmire: Lyndon Johnson and the Escalation of the Vietnam War* (Oxford University Press, 1991).

78. Evans, *Algeria*, 126–7.

79. Some 1.2 million Algerian Muslims fell under the initial 'state of siege' restrictions: USNA, RG 59, 751S.00, box 3375, Algiers Consulate to State Department, 13 Apr. 1955.

80. SHD-DAT, 1H1374/D2, EMA-3, 'Algérie—organisation territoriale', 5 Feb. 1955; Service Historique de l'Armée de l'Air, carton Z23344, Robert Lacoste, 'Directive générale', 19 May 1956.

81. AN, René Mayer papers, 363AP32/D1, Pierre-Charles Dupuch to Soustelle, 11 July 1955.

82. Benjamin Stora, 'Le Massacre du 20 août 1955: Récit historique, bilan historiographique', *Historical Reflections*, 36:2 (2010), 97–107.

83. Charles-Robert Ageron, 'L'Insurrection du 20 août 1955 dans le nord Constantinois: De la résistance armée à la guerre au peuple', in Charles-Robert Ageron, ed., *La Guerre d'Algérie et les Algériens, 1954–1962* (Paris: Armand Colin, 1997), 27–50; Evans, *Algeria*, 140–1.

84. Thomas, 'Colonial Violence in Algeria', 523–56; Peyroulou, *Guelma, 1945*; Planche, *Sétif.*

85. A rare exception is a dossier of Algerian depositions detailing security force and vigilante violence: ANOM, Gouvernement Général de l'Algérie (GGA), Cabinet Chataigneau, 8cab/166, Commissaire Divisionnaire Bergé to Directeur Général de la Sécurité Générale, 20 Jan. 1946.

86. Lazreg, *Torture*, 111–15.

87. These definitions draw on Charles Tilly, 'Contentious choices', *Theory and Society*, 33:3/4 (2004), 473.

88. There are parallels with the way that Guatemalan government and military defended violence against the country's Mayan population: Greg Grandin, *The Last Colonial Massacre*, 188–90.

89. James McDougall, 'Savage wars? Codes of violence in Algeria, 1830s–1990s', *Third World Quarterly*, 26:1 (2005), 119. For careful analysis of 'logical' communal violence in another settler society, see: Branch, *Defeating Mau Mau*, 49–60.

90. Joshua Cole, 'Massacres and their historians: Recent histories of state violence in France and Algeria in the twentieth century', *FPCS*, 28:1 (2010), 110–16.

91. TNA, FO 371/118302, Baghdad, Cairo, and Washington tels., 25, 27, and 30 Aug. 1955.

92. TNA, FO 371/118302, Bonn consulate to FO, 23 Aug. 1955.

93. M. S. Alexander and P. C. F. Bankwitz, 'From *politiques en képi* to military technocrats: De Gaulle and the recovery of the French Army after Indochina and Algeria,' in G. Andreopoulos and H. Selesky eds, *The Aftermath of Defeat: Societies, Armed Forces and the Challenge of Recovery* (New Haven, CT: Yale University Press, 1994), 83–7.

94. TNA, FO 493/174, MA/Paris/322, Report by Brigadier A.C.F. Jackson, 17 Nov. 1955.

95. TNA, Macmillan Private Office papers, FO 800/672, memcon. with Julius Holmes, 6 Oct. 1955.

96. AN, René Mayer papers, 363AP32/D1, Pierre-Charles Dupuch to Bône Mayor, 15 Oct. 1955.

97. AN, René Mayer papers, 363AP32/D1, no. 105/PR, Dupuch to René Mayer, 15 Oct. 1955.

98. AN, René Mayer papers, 363AP32/D4, sous-dossier 'Maurice Papon', 1949–57; L. Mazzuca, Chair of Sétif Radical Party, to René Mayer, 14 Nov. 1951.

99. Vann Kelly, 'A prefect's road from Bordeaux, through Algeria, and beyond, August 1944–October 1961', in Richard J. Golsan, ed., *Memory and Justice on Trial: The Papon Affair* (London: Routledge, 2000), 50–6.

100. AN, René Mayer papers, 363AP32/D4, no. 4510, Papon 'Directive concernant l'action politique', 4 Sept. 1956; SHD-DAT, 1H2404/D1, no. 825/RM10, Bureau psychologique, 23 Feb. 1957.

101. Danièle Joly, *The French Communist Party*, 93–9, 137–9; 'France's military involvement in Algeria: The PCF and the *oppositionnels*', in Scriven and Wagstaff, *War and Society*, 130–4.

102. AN, MRP papers, 350AP/85/D5, Jean Fonteneau to Georges Le Brun Keris, 6 June 1956.

103. AN, MRP papers, 350AP/85/D5, Pierre Pflimlin, 'Déclaration sur l'Algérie faite au Comité nationale du MRP', 8 July 1956.

104. Vote rigging peaked during Marcel-Edmond Naegelen's 1948 to 1951 governorship. A tough Socialist deputy from Alsace, he led the clampdown against the MTLD and gerrymandered Algeria's electoral districts, insisting that the local population 'expected' political guidance from their administrators. Letamendia, *Le Mouvement Républicaine Populaire*, 355; USNA, RG 59, 751S.00, box 3700, Algiers Consulate to State Department, 2 Mar. 1950.

105. TNA, FO 371/113795, JF1019/6 and FO 371/119357, JF1019/33, Algiers Consular reports to FO, 26 Apr. 1955 and 26 Jan. 1956.

106. Raphaëlle Branche, *L'Embuscade de Palestro: Algérie 1956* (Paris: Armand Colin, 2010).

107. Evans, *The Memory of Resistance*, 141.

108. Jean-François Sirinelli, 'Les Intellectuels dans la mêlée', in Rioux, *La Guerre d'Algérie*, 118–20.

109. Evans, *Algeria*, 199; Marc Sadoun, 'Les Socialistes entre principes, pouvoir et mémoire', in Rioux, *La Guerre d'Algérie*, 229–30. André Philip parted company with the Socialists in 1958, later aligning with de Gaulle. Alain Savary resigned as Minister of State for Moroccan and Tunisian Affairs in Nov. 1956. Michel Rocard published a report criticizing Algeria's rural resettlement camps. Other leading Socialists who contested Mollet's decisions included Daniel Mayer, Marceau Pivert, and Gaston Defferre.

110. Danielle Tartakowsky, 'Les Manifestations de rue', in Rioux, *La Guerre d'Algérie*, 132–3.

111. Evans, *The Memory of Resistance*, 77–81; Mohammed Khane, '*Le Monde*'s coverage of the army and civil liberties during the Algerian War, 1954–58', in Alexander, Evans, and Keiger, *The Algerian War and the French Army*, 174–92.

112. Donald Reid, 'Review article: *The Question* of Henri Alleg', *IHR*, 29:3 (2007), 573–86. Harold Macmillan's Private Office received a sack of letters from outraged constituents after *The Manchester Guardian* serialized Alleg's harrowing story in Mar. 1958: Conservative Party Archive, Bodleian Library, Oxford, CC04/7/167.

113. Anthony Nutting, 'Nationalism in the Middle East: The tragedy of Algeria', *New York Herald Tribune*, 15 May 1957.

114. Egyptian aid is detailed in Fathi Al Dib, *Abdel Nasser* (Paris: L'Harmattan, 1985), 41–3, 175–204.

115. MAE, série Europe 1944–1960, sous-série Grande-Bretagne, vol. 142, Jean Chauvel to Christian Pineau (transcript of in-flight conversation), 28 Sept. 1956.

116. MAE, série Europe 1944–1960, sous-série Grande-Bretagne, vol. 142, 'Compte-rendu de la visite en Algérie des Parlementaires britanniques, 15–22 Oct. 1956'.

117. 'Mémoire du PPA signé de Mohammed Khider', 3 Sept. 1953, in Mohammed Harbi, *Les Archives de la révolution algérienne* (Paris: Editions Jeune Afrique, 1981), doc. 2.

118. AN, René Mayer papers, 363AP32/D4, Maurice Papon, 'Le Problème tunisien: Réflexions sur la méthode', 6 Dec. 1952.

119. MAE, série Afrique-Levant, sous-série: Algérie, vol. 4, Cairo tel. 451, 21 Mar. 1952.

120. 'Rapport d'Aït Ahmed, Bureau politique du PPA, au Comité central élargi', in Harbi, *Les Archives*, doc. 1.

121. Harbi, *Le FLN: Mirage et réalité*, 143; Proclamation du FLN, 1 Nov. 1954, in Harbi, *Les Archives*, 102.

122. Heinz-Gerhard Haupt and Klaus Weinhauer, 'Terrorism and the state', in Bloxham and Gerwarth, *Political Violence*, 194–5; Connelly, *Diplomatic Revolution*, 96–7.

123. Jacques Frémeaux, 'La Guerre d'Algérie et les relations internationales', *Relations Internationales*, 105:1 (2001), 60–5.

124. TNA, FO 371/125933, JR10345/4, Congressional Record, 2 July 1957. Kennedy chaired the Africa sub-committee of the Senate foreign relations committee.

125. Robert J. Bookmiller, 'The Algerian war of words: Broadcasting and revolution, 1954–1962', *Maghreb Review*, 14:3–4 (1989), 196–213; Charles-Robert Ageron, 'Un aspect de la guerre d'Algérie: La Propagande Radiophonique du FLN et des états arabes', in Ageron, *La Guerre d'Algérie*, 245–59.

126. SHD-DAT, 1H1101/D1, Inspection des Forces Armées, AFN, 2ème Division, 'Action de la rébellion à l'extérieur de l'Algérie', 28 Sept. 1957.

127. Fabian Klose, '"Source of embarrassment": Human rights, state of emergency, and wars of decolonization', in Stefan-Ludwig Hoffmann, ed., *Human Rights in the Twentieth Century* (Cambridge University Press, 2011), 237–57.

128. Matthew Connelly, 'Rethinking the Cold War and decolonization: The grand strategy of the Algerian war of independence', *IJMES*, 33:2 (2001), 223–41.

129. Sylvie Thénault, *Une drôle de justice: Les Magistrats dans la guerre d'Algérie* (Paris: La Découverte, 2001), part II.

130. MacMaster, *Burning the Veil*, 318.

131. MAE, série Europe, sous-série Grande-Bretagne, vol. 143, Ministry secretariat note, 13 Feb. 1958. The MPs singled out the unreliability of confessions extracted under torture.

132. Lazreg, *Torture*, 161–3. Djamila Boupacha suffered broken ribs, multiple cigarette burns, and was raped with a beer bottle. As we saw in the Preface,

another *fidayate,* Louisette Ighilahriz's account of her experiences in an Algiers torture centre triggered a media storm when published in France in 2001.

133. Judith Surkis, 'Ethics and violence: Simone de Beauvoir, Djamila Boupacha, and the Algerian War', *FPCS,* 28:2 (2010), 38–55.

134. Vince, 'Transgressing boundaries', When Boupacha was freed from prison in the weeks following the Algerian ceasefire on 26 Apr. 1962 she was reluctant to return to Algeria, lamenting that women would be confined to a life of domesticity in an FLN-run state: see MacMaster, *Burning the Veil,* 381.

135. Christopher E. Goscha, 'Hanoi and Saigon at War: The making of the Viet Minh's underground cities (1945–54)', *War in History,* (2012), Jim House, 'L'Impossible Contrôle d'une ville coloniale: Casablanca, décembre 1952', *Genèses,* 1:86 (2012), 78–103.

136. Robert Malley, *The Call from Algeria: Third Worldism, Revolution, and the Turn to Islam* (Berkeley, CA: University of California Press, 1996), 84–8, 122–30.

137. Re-named in commemoration of its young revolutionary heroine, rue Hassiba Ben Bouali is now a major Algiers thoroughfare.

138. Christopher Cradock & M. L. R. Smith,' "No fixed values":A reinterpretation of the influence of the theory of *Guerre révolutionnaire* and the Battle of Algiers, 1956–1957', *Journal of Cold War Studies,* 9:4 (2007), 68–105.

139. This paragraph draws on Martin Evans' excellent account of the battle in *Algeria,* 201–21.

140. SHD-DAT, 1H1104/D4, 'Regroupement des populations', 22 Mar. 1958.

141. TNA, FO 371/125949, JR10217/3, Paris Chancery to FO, 30 July 1957.

142. TNA, FO 371/131674, JR10317/1, Jebb to FO, 27 Dec. 1957; Evans, *Algeria,* 200–1, 212.

143. Raphaëlle Branche, 'La Commission de sauvegarde pendant la guerre d'Algérie: Chronique d'un échec annoncé', *Vingtième Siècle,* 61:1 (1999), 14–29.

144. Jean-Charles Jauffret, 'The war culture of French combatants in the Algerian conflict', in Alexander, Evans, and Keiger, *The Algerian War and the French Army,* 104.

145. Roland Barthes, 'La Grammaire africaine', in *Mythologies* (Paris: Editions du Seuil, 1957), 230; Huw Bennett, 'Soldiers in the court room: The British Army's part in the Kenya Emergency under the legal spotlight', *JICH,* 39:5 (2011), 717–30.

146. Jean-Charles Jauffret, 'Pour une typologie des hommes du contingent en guerre d'Algérie', in Jauffret, *Des hommes et des femmes,* 386–7.

CHAPTER 12

1. TNA, FO 371/125945, JR1201/3, Colonel A. J. Wilson, Algeria inspection, 8–16 Jan. 1957.

2. Paul Villatoux, 'Le Colonel Lacheroy théoricien de l'action psychologique', in Jean-Charles Jauffret, ed., *Des hommes et des femmes,* 494–507.

3. Brigadier J. A. H. Mitchell, 'Personality notes' on Algiers corps commanders: TNA, FO 371/131685, JR1193/19, 'Report on visit to 10e Région militaire, 16–31 Oct. 1958'.

4. TNA, FO 371/125945, JR1201/3, Wilson, Algeria inspection report, 8–16 Jan. 1957.

5. TNA, FO 371/125945, JR1201/16, encl.: Jackson report to FO, 12 Aug. 1957.

6. TNA, FO 371/131663, JR1016/12A, 'Present military situation', 27 Feb. 1958.

7. SHD-DAT, 1H1104/D4, no. 2200/DN, Secrétariat permanent de la Défense nationale en Algérie (DNA), 'Organisation des services de surveillance et de fermature des frontières', 15 Oct. 1957.

8. TNA, FO 371/131668, JR1018/11, 'Frontier barrier between Algeria and Tunisia', 28 Apr. 1958.

9. SHD-DAT, 1H1101/D1, DNA, 'Quelques noms et quelques chiffres concernant la rébellion Algérienne', 21 Oct. 1958.

10. TNA, FO 371/131685, JR1193/7, War Office report, 'Military operations in Algeria', based on Wilson's inspection tour, 10–18 July 1958, pp. 3–4.

11. TNA, FO 371/131685, JR1193/7, War Office report, *op cit*, pp. 4–5, 13–15. Wilson misunderstood the actions of ALN civilian auxiliaries, notably in Eastern Algeria, see: Daho Djerbal, 'Mounadiline et moussebiline, les forces auxiliaires de l'ALN du nord-Constantinois', in Jauffret, *Des hommes et des femmes*, 292–6.

12. TNA, FO 371/131685, JR1193, Roderick Sarell to Brigadier Mitchell, 19 Sept. 1958; author's interview with Sarell, Newbury, Berkshire, 13 Mar. 2000.

13. The exception was the Army's Fifth Bureau, responsible for psychological warfare, whose mission was to induce Algerian civilians to side with France, see SHD-DAT, 1H2404/D2,' RM10, 5ème Bureau memo, 'Activités et problèmes du 5ème Bureau pour la période avril–juin 1958', 7 July 1958.

14. Neil MacMaster, 'The 'silent native': *Attentisme*, being compromised, and banal terror during the Algerian War of independence, 1954–62', in Thomas, *French Colonial Mind: Violence*, 283–303.

15. Odile Rudelle, *Mai 1958, de Gaulle et la République* (Paris: Plon, 1988), 103–10; Jean Charlot, *Le Gaullisme d'opposition, 1946–1958* (Paris: Fayard, 1983), 347–60.

16. Jean-Pierre Bat, 'Jacques Foccart, *eminence grise* for African affairs', in Chafer and Keese, *Francophone Africa*.

17. Martin Thomas, 'Policing Algeria's borders, 1956–1960: Arms supplies, frontier defences and the Sakiet affair', *War & Society*, 13:1 (1995), 81–99; Geoffrey Barei, 'The Sakiet Sidi Youssef incident of 1958 in Tunisia and the Anglo-American "good offices" mission', *Journal of North African Studies*, 17:2 (2012), 355–71.

18. Irwin M. Wall, *France, the United States, and the Algerian War* (Berkeley, CA: University of California Press, 2001), 99–133; Connelly, *Diplomatic Revolution*, 160–7.

19. Alexander Keese, *Living with Ambiguity: Integrating an African Elite in French and Portuguese Africa, 1930–61* (Stuttgart: Franz Steiner Verlag, 2007), 100–1, 124–5, 280.

20. Miles Kahler, *Decolonization in Britain and France: The Domestic Consequences of International Relations* (Princeton University Press, 1984), 91–7.
21. MacMaster, *Burning the Veil*, 118–23.
22. MacMaster, *Burning the Veil*, 114–15.
23. MacMaster, *Burning the Veil*, 116–44.
24. Author's interview with Roderick Sarell, 13 Mar. 2000.
25. BLO, Macmillan papers, Diaries, 2nd ser., d. 31, fo. 111, entry for 16 May 1958.
26. Claude d'Abzac-Epezy, 'La Société militaire, de l'ingérence à l'ignorance', in Rioux, *La guerre d'Algérie*, 245–9.
27. Evans, *Algeria*, 232–5; Macmillan papers, Diaries, 2nd ser., d. 31, fo. 135, entry for 31 May 1958: For Macmillan, 'Everything turns on the Socialists, whom Mollet is trying to lead into acquiescence.'
28. Jansen, *Les Grands Discours parlémentaires*, 271–5.
29. AN, MRP papers, 350AP/85/D5, MRP2, MRP Secretariat, 'La Situation du MRP à Alger', n.d., May 1960. In May 1960 the Algiers section established a rival 'Algerian MRP' to push for integration.
30. AN, MRP papers, 350AP/76/D4, MRP8, Confédération Française des Travailleurs Chrétiens pamphlet, 'Devant les événements de mai 1958: Pour quoi?'
31. AN, MRP papers, 350AP/85/D5, Algiers federation to MRP Congress, 8 May 1961; 'Testament de la section d'Alger', 16 May 1962; 'Appel du Congrès National', 16 May 1962.
32. Mohammed Harbi and Gilbert Meynier, *Le F.L.N.: Documents et Histoire, 1954–1962* (Paris: Fayard, 2004), 358–60; Meynier, *Histoire intérieure*, 352–5.
33. MAE, série Europe 1944–1960, sous-série Grande-Bretagne, vol. 143, Jean Chauvel to Foreign Ministry, 18 Sept. 1958.
34. TNA, FO 371/131672, JR1024/8, JR1024/9, JR1024/20, JR1024/27: tels. on GPRA recognition, Sept.–Oct. 1958.
35. Evans, *Algeria*, 244; DDF, vol. II, 1958, doc. 285n.1.
36. Michèle Cointet, *De Gaulle et l'Algérie française, 1958–1962* (Paris: Perrin 1995), 64–6.
37. SHD-DAT, 1H2035/D1, EMI-3, 'Le Barrage avant de la frontier tunisienne', n.d., Mar. 1960.
38. Thomas, 'Policing Algeria's borders', 81–99.
39. Bar-On, 'Three days in Sèvres', 173.
40. SHD-DAT, Z23344, General Martial Valin, 'Aspects de la situation militaire en Algérie', Jan. 1959; Yoav Gortzak, 'Using indigenous forces in counterinsurgency operations: The French in Algeria, 1954–1962', *Journal of Strategic Studies*, 32:2 (2009), 307–33.
41. SHD-DAT, 1H2036/D1, General Olié to Challe, 3 Jan. 1960.
42. Harbi and Meynier, *Le F.L.N.: Documents et Histoire*, 530–9; Meynier, *Histoire intérieure*, 448.
43. Charles de Gaulle, *Memoirs of Hope* (London: Weidenfeld & Nicolson, 1971), 60–2; Cointet, *De Gaulle et l'Algérie française*, 38–9.

44. Government controls on Algeria's internal market were also tightened to break the FLN's grip over the rural economy, see: SHD-DAT, 1H1104/D6, Delegate-General's office, 'Organisation de la lutte économique et financière contre la rébellion', 28 Oct. 1959.

45. SHD-DAT, 1H2467/D1bis, 'Discours prononcé par de Gaulle à Constantine', 3 Oct. 1958.

46. ANOM, Marius Moutet papers, PA 28, C28/D170, 'Rapport sur le programme arrêté par les députés d'Algérie et du Sahara', 8 Dec. 1958.

47. SHD-DAT, 1H1106/D3, Statistique générale de l'Algérie, 'Plan de Constantine', 1960.

48. Daniel Lefeuvre, 'L'Échec du Plan de Constantine', in Rioux, *La Guerre d'Algérie*, 320.

49. Charles-Robert Ageron, 'Complots et purges dans l'armée de libération algérienne (1958–1961)', *Vingtième Siècle*, 59:1 (1998), 15–27; Evans, *Algeria*, 261–8.

50. Evans, *Algeria*, 271.

51. Alexander and Bankwitz, 'From *politiques en képi*', 91–2.

52. Evans, *Algeria*, 271–2.

53. Alexander, 'Seeking France's "lost soldiers" : Reflections on the Military Crisis in Algeria', in Kenneth Mouré and M. S. Alexander, eds, *Crisis and Renewal in France, 1918–1962* (Oxford: Berghahn, 2002), 250.

54. SHD-DAT, 1H2734, Corps d'Armée d'Alger (CAA), 3ème bureau, 'Évolution de la rébellion sur le territoire du CAA, Oct.–Dec. 1960', 27 Dec. 1960.

55. TNA, FO 371/138606, JR1193/3, Meeting with Colonel Alain de Boisseau, 18 Apr. 1959; FO 371/147328, 'Calendar of events: Algeria, 1959'; PREM 11/3200, 'Algeria', 2 Mar. 1960.

56. TNA, FO 371/147365, JR1193/5, Inter-service liaison mission report to FO, 17 Oct. 1960; FO 371/155514, 'Calendar of events for Algeria, 1960'.

57. Philip Hemming, 'Macmillan and the end of the British Empire in Africa', in Richard Aldous and Sabine Lee, eds, *Harold Macmillan and Britain's World Role* (Basingstoke: Macmillan, 1996), 111.

58. TNA, FO 371/143694, WUN11922/27, Admiralty Directorate of Plans, 'French Mediterranean fleet withdrawal', 4 Mar. 1959; FO 371/154573, WUN1196/5, France and NATO', 19 Jan. 1960.

59. TNA, DEFE 13/178, Harold Watkinson note for PM, 14 Apr. 1961; Mervyn O'Driscoll, 'Explosive challenge: Diplomatic triangles, the United Nations, and the problem of French nuclear testing, 1959–1960', *Journal of Cold War Studies*, 11:1 (2009), 28–56.

60. French, *The British Way*, 201–18. French notes that the British Army was a more assiduous institutional learner than the Colonial Office about the limits of counter-insurgency.

61. TNA, DEFE 7/2234, JP(61)149, 'British strategy in the sixties', 19 Dec. 1961; Watkinson note to Treasury Chief Secretary, both 19 Dec. 1961.

62. See Jeffrey A. Lefebvre, 'Kennedy's Algerian dilemma: Containment, alliance politics and the "rebel dialogue" ', *MES*, 35:2 (1999), 61–82.

63. TNA, FO 371/169107, Paris despatch no 1, 3 Jan. 1963; Shepherd, *Iain MacLeod*, 158–9, 193–5.

64. Shepard, ' "Something notably erotic" ', 89.

65. Shepard, *Invention*, 90–8.

66. Shepard, *Invention*, 82–3, 97–100, 114–15.

67. TNA, FO 371/147347, FO monthly report on Algeria, 8 April–8 May 1960; Jeffery S. Ahlman, 'The Algerian question in Nkrumah's Ghana, 1958–1960: Debating violence and nonviolence in African decolonization', *Africa Today*, 57:2 (2010), 80–2.

68. Evans, *Algeria*, 299. The internment camp regime was gradually wound down during 1961.

69. AN, MRP papers, 350AP/85/D5, Jean Franceschi to MRP President, 29 Apr. 1961.

70. Evans, *Memory of Resistance*, 188–93; Claire Guyot, 'Entre morale et politique: Le Centre catholique des intellectuels français face à la décolonisation', *Vingtième Siècle*, 63 (1999), 75–86.

71. TNA, PREM 11/3337, Dixon to Foreign Office, 14 July 1961.

72. Jean-François Sirinelli, 'Guerre d'Algérie, guerre des pétitions? Quelques jalons', *Revue Historique*, 291:1 (1988), 73–100.

73. Philip Dine, 'French culture and the Algerian War: Mobilizing icons', *Journal of European Studies*, 28:1 (1998), 51–68. As Dine notes, photo-journalism and gestures like the 1958 decision by ten Algerian footballers to quit the French league to form an Algerian 'national' team in Tunis probably did more than intellectual argument to persuade the French public of the war's injustice.

74. Jim House and Neil MacMaster, *Paris 1961: Algerians, State Terror, and Memory* (Oxford University Press, 2006), 137–8, 216–26.

75. House and MacMaster, *Paris 1961*, 99–100. Under the curfew terms all Algerians residing in the Paris Prefecture were prohibited from leaving their homes between 8.30 p.m. and 5.30 a.m. Their cafés were required to shut by 7 p.m. and use of motor vehicles during the curfew period was banned.

76. Kelly, 'A prefect's road', 62–4.

77. House and MacMaster, *Paris 1961*, 105–11; Neil MacMaster, 'Identifying "terrorists" in Paris: A police experiment with IBM machines during the Algerian War', *FPCS*, 28:3 (2010), 23–45.

78. House and MacMaster, *Paris 1961*, 161–7.

79. House and MacMaster, *Paris 1961*, 139–3, 149–57, 216–41.

80. SHD-DAT, 1H2467/D1bis, Bureau du moral, 'Subversion O.A.S. dans l'armée', 31 Mar. 1962.

81. Evans, *Algeria*, 309–15; House and MacMaster, *Paris 1961*, 247–52.

82. Cited in Shepard, *Invention*, 105.

83. The 'official line' of an honourable peace was repeated in instructions issued by Armed Forces Minister Pierre Messmer to French commanders in the week

before the cease-fire: SHD-DAT, 1H2467/D6, no. 106/MA/CAB/INF/CS, 'Les Termes probables de la négociation', 8 Mar. 1962.

84. TNA, PREM 11/3641, Salan letter to Macmillan, 3 Mar. 1962.
85. Evans, *Algeria*, 303–4; Berny Sebe, 'In the shadow of the Algerian War: The United States and the Common Organisation of Saharan Regions/ *Organisation commune des régions sahariennes* (OCRS), 1957–62', *JICH*, 38:2 (2010), 303–22.
86. Olivier Dard, 'Réalités et limites de l'internationalisation de l'anti-anticoloni-alisme de la guerre d'Algérie au début des années 70', in Olivier Dard and Daniel Lefeuvre, eds, *L'Europe face à son passé colonial* (Paris: Riveneuve editions, 2008), 254–61.
87. Martin Thomas, 'A path not taken? British perspectives on French colonial violence after 1945', in L. J. Butler and Sarah Stockwell, eds, *Wind of Change* (Basingstoke: Palgrave-Macmillan, 2013).
88. TNA, DEFE 7/2200, Joint Planning Staff brief, 8 Dec. 1959.
89. Murphy, '"An intricate and distasteful subject"', 752–69.
90. The full story is recounted by Matthew Hughes, 'Fighting for white rule in Africa: The Central African Federation, Katanga, and the Congo Crisis, 1958–1965', *IHR*, 25 (2003), 592–615.
91. Murphy, '"An intricate and distasteful subject"', 755–7.
92. For a positive assessment of the range of British strategic options at the time of Rhodesia's Unilateral Declaration of Independence, see Carl Watts, 'Killing kith and kin: The viability of British military intervention in Rhodesia, 1964–5', *Twentieth Century British History* 16 (2005), 382–415.
93. Murphy, '"An intricate and distasteful subject"', 756–7.
94. A point convincingly made by Philip Murphy in '"An intricate and distasteful subject"', 746–9, 776.
95. John W. Young, *The Labour Governments, 1964–1970*, ii: *International Policy* (Manchester University Press, 2003), 173–8.
96. John W. Young, 'The Wilson Government and the debate over arms sales to South Africa', *Contemporary British History*, 12:3 (1998), 62–86; Tim Bale, '"A deplorable episode"? South African arms sales and the statecraft of British social democracy', *Labour History Review*, 62:1 (1997), 22–40.
97. Alice Ritscherle, 'Disturbing the people's peace: Patriotism and "respectable" racism in British responses to Rhodesian independence', in Levine and Grayzel, *Gender*, 197–8.
98. Donal Lowry, 'Rhodesia 1890–1980: "The lost Dominion"', in Bickers, *Settlers*, 112–14.
99. Ritscherle, 'Disturbing', 200.
100. Young, *The Labour Governments*, Vol. II, 174–6.
101. Lowry, 'Rhodesia 1890–1980', 116–22. Smith was a wartime fighter pilot. In 1969 Rhodesia's settlers numbered 228,296 among a black population approaching five million.

102. Mark Stuart, 'A Party in three pieces: The Conservative split over Rhodesian oil sanctions, 1965', *Contemporary British History*, 16:1 (2002), 51–88.

103. Ritscherle, 'Disturbing', 201–2, 209.

104. Francis, 'Men of the Royal Air Force', 180–4, quotation at 180. Battle of Britain hero Douglas Bader became an outspoken *News of the World* columnist, a staunch defender of white minority rule.

105. Josiah Brownell, ' "A sordid tussle on the Strand": Rhodesia House during the UDI rebellion (1965–80)', *JICH*, 38:3 (2010), 472–91.

106. Lowry, 'Rhodesia', 123–8, 134–5, 146; Ritscherle, 'Disturbing', 203; Josiah Brownell, 'The hole in Rhodesia's bucket: White emigration and the end of settler rule', *JSAS*, 34:3 (2008), 591–610.

107. *The Guardian*, 12 Oct. 1965, quoted in Ritscherle, 'Disturbing', 211.

108. Joanna Warson, 'A transnational decolonisation: Britain, France and the Rhodesian problem, 1965–1969', in Chafer and Keese, *Francophone Africa*. British oil companies BP and Shell also breached sanctions restrictions: see Young, *The Labour Governments*, Vol. II, 181.

109. Harold Wilson, *The Labour Government, 1964–1970: A Personal Record* (London: Weidenfeld & Nicolson, 1971), 303.

110. Wilson, *The Labour Government*, 305–6.

111. Wilson, *The Labour Government*, 307–18.

112. Young, *The Labour Governments*, Vol. II, 64–80, 102–9, 155–9, 200–10; Matthew Jones, 'A decision delayed: Britain's withdrawal from South East Asia reconsidered', *EHR*, 67:472 (2002), 569–95.

113. *The Times*, 7 Mar. 1968; Young, *The Labour Governments*, Vol. II, 185.

114. Jacob Abadi, 'Great Britain and the Maghreb in the epoch of pan-Arabism and Cold War', *Cold War History*, 2:2 (2002), 142.

115. Shepard, *Invention*, 76, citing Alain Peyrefitte, *C'était de Gaulle*, i: *La France redevient la France* (Paris: Fayard, 1994), 54.

116. Dominique Pestre, 'Scientists in time of war: World War II, the Cold War, and science in the United States and France', *FPCS*, 24:1 (2006), 27–39, at 33 & 36.

117. Andrea Smith, 'Coerced or free? Considering post-colonial returns', in Richard Bessel and Claudia B. Haake, eds, *Removing Peoples: Forced Removal in the Modern World* (Oxford University Press, 2009), 395–414.

CHAPTER 13

1. These opening paragraphs rely on M. Kathryn Edwards, 'Traître au colonialisme? The Georges Boudarel affair and the memory of the Indochina War', *French Colonial History*, 11 (2010), 193–209.

2. On the derivation of 'crimes against humanity' see Geoffrey Robertson, *Crimes Against Humanity: The Search for Global Justice* (London: Penguin, 2006), chs 2–3, 5–7.

3. Bousquet was Interior Ministry secretary general responsible for the Vichy Police. He helped direct the round-up of Jews in France who were then sent to Nazi death camps. Paul Touvier served in Vichy's paramilitary *Milice*. He ordered the execution of seven Jewish hostages on 29 June 1944 in reprisal for the Resistance's assassination of Vichy Propaganda Minister Philippe Henriot. Papon was secretary general in the Gironde Prefecture. He authorized the detention of over 1,500 Jews, including large numbers of children, and then handed them over to the Germans to be sent to the gas chambers. As we have seen, his wartime record proved no bar to his later career in Algeria and Paris. Bousquet was assassinated just before his trial; Touvier was eventually convicted in 1994 and Papon in 1998: Richard J. Golsan, ed., *Memory, the Holocaust, and French Justice: The Bousquet and Touvier Affairs* (London: University Press of New England, 1996); 'Memory's *bombes à retardement*: Maurice Papon, crimes against humanity and 17 Oct. 1961', *Journal of European Studies*, 28 (1998), 158–72; 'Maurice Papon and crimes against humanities in France'; and Christopher Flood, 'Extreme right-wing perspectives on the Touvier and Papon trials', in Golsan, *Memory and Justice*, 1–33 and 73–95.

4. Geoff Eley, 'Imperial imaginary, colonial effect: Writing the colony and the metropole together', in Catherine Hall and Keith McClelland, *Race, Nation and Empire* (Manchester University Press, 2010), 220–8; Ann Laura Stoler and Frederick Cooper, 'Between metropole and colony: Rethinking a research agenda', in Cooper and Stoler, *Tensions of Empire*, 1–56; Robert Aldrich and Stuart Ward, 'Ends of empire: Decolonizing the nation in British and French historiography', in Stefan Berger and Chris Lorenz, *Nationalising the Past: Historians as Nation Builders in Modern Europe* (Basingstoke: Palgrave-Macmillan, 2010), 259–81; and Catherine Hall and Sonya O. Rose, eds, *At Home with the Empire: Metropolitan Culture and the Imperial World* (Cambridge University Press, 2006).

5. Understandably, this viewpoint was popular among post-colonial nationalist regimes, although it could result in historical distortion. An extreme case, Robert Mugabe's Zimbabwe, is thoughtfully discussed by Terence Ranger, 'Nationalist historiography, patriotic history and the history of the nation: The struggle over the past in Zimbabwe', *JSAS*, 30:2 (2004), 215–34.

6. Darwin, 'Decolonization', in Winks, ed., *OHBE*, v:, 552; also cited in Elkins, 'Race, citizenship, and governance', 203.

7. TNA, CO 1027/172, Information Department, 'French colonial publicity in the USA', 31 Dec. 1958.

8. John Lewis Gaddis, 'Grand strategies in the Cold War', in Leffler and Westad, *Cambridge History of the Cold War*, ii, 12.

9. Hopkins, 'Rethinking decolonization', 216.

10. Ahlman, 'The Algerian question in Nkrumah's Ghana', 76–80; Plummer, *In Search of Power*, 69–85, 101.

11. Roland Burke, *Decolonization and the Evolution of International Human Rights* (Philadelphia: University of Pennsylvania Press, 2010), chs 1–2; Meredith Terretta, '"We

had been fooled into thinking that the UN watches over the entire world": Human rights, UN trust territories, and Africa's decolonization', *Human Rights Quarterly*, 34:2 (2012), 330–1.

12. Jim Tomlinson, 'The decline of the Empire and the economic decline of Britain', *Twentieth Century British History*, 14:3 (2003), 203–12; Marseille, *Empire colonial*, 356–60.

13. I do not wish to imply, though, that the 'fight or flight' model can explain everything. For instance, missionaries and the work of colonial religious conversion cries out for reassessment. Indeed, the religious legacy of empire in Africa and Asia is arguably stronger than any other administrative or cultural 'hangover'. Africa's fast-growing Anglican movement and the rude health of West African and Vietnamese religious observance point to an imperial offshoot whose vigorous growth cannot be tied to local trajectories of fight or flight. On this point, see Norman Etherington, 'The missionary experience in British and French empires', in White and Daughton, *In God's Empire*, 282–3.

14. An observation first made by political scientist Tony Smith, 'The French colonial consensus and people's war, 1946–58', *Journal of Contemporary History*, 9 (1974): 217–47.

15. TNA, FO 371/119350, JF1015/8, D.J. Mill-Irving to African Department, 28 Jan. 1956.

16. See Stuart Ward's thoughtful review of Wendy Webster's, *Englishness and Empire, 1939–1965* (Oxford University Press, 2005): 'Echoes of empire', *History Workshop Journal*, 61 (2006), 273–5.

17. Murphy, '"An intricate and distasteful subject"', 746–9. The fertile Mitidja plain south of Algiers was the heartland of settler agriculture.

18. Gavin Nardocchio-Jones, 'From Mau Mau to Middlesex? The fate of Europeans in independent Kenya', *Comparative Studies of South Asia, Africa and the Middle East*, 26:3 (2006), 492–5, 497–504.

19. The gap between Britain's retrospective image of orderliness and widespread violence has been highlighted by Ronald Hyam, *Britain's Declining Empire*, 398–9, and Caroline Elkins, 'The reassertion of the British Empire in Southeast Asia', *Journal of Interdisciplinary History*, 39:3 (2009), 368–71.

20. Ian Talbot, 'The end of the European colonial empires and forced migration: Comparative case studies', Panikos Panayi and Pippa Virdee, eds, *Refugees and the End of Empire: Imperial Collapse and Forced Migration in the Twentieth Century* (Basingstoke: Palgrave-Macmillan, 2011), 28–50.

21. Elizabeth Buettner, 'From somebodies to nobodies: Britons coming home from India', in Martin Daunton and Bernhard Rieger, eds, *Meanings of Modernity: Britain from the Late Victorian Era to the Second World War* (Oxford: Berg, 2001), 221–40.

22. Sponsored by Gamal Nasser, Egypt and Syria formed the United Arab Republic in Jan. 1958. Syrian secession in Sept. 1961 spelt the UAR's demise. Federation between Senegal and French Sudan (present-day Mali) was also short-lived,

lasting from Apr. 1959 until Aug. 1960. See: Jankowski, *Nasser's Egypt*, 115–36, 161–78; Monique Lakroum, 'Sénégal-Soudan (Mali): Deux états pour un empire', in Coquery-Vidrovitch and Goerg, *L'Afrique occidentale au temps des français*, 188–9.

23. The limitations of American supremacy are examined in A. G. Hopkins, 'Capitalism, nationalism and the new American Empire', *JICH*, 35:1 (2007), 95–117; Dane Kennedy, 'Essay and reflection: On the American Empire from a British imperial perspective', *IHR*, 29:1 (2007), 83–108; Louisa Rice, 'Cowboys and Communists: Cultural diplomacy, decolonization and the Cold War in French West Africa', *Journal of Colonialism and Colonial History*, 11:3 (2010).

24. Sonya O. Rose, 'Who are we now? Writing the post-war "nation", 1948–2001', in Hall and McClelland, *Race, Nation and Empire* (Manchester University Press, 2010), 164. For living conditions and women's experiences, see Wendy Webster, *Imagining Home: Gender, Race And National Identity, 1945–1964* (London: Routledge, 1998), ch. 3.

25. Elizabeth Buettner, ' "Would you let your daughter marry a Negro?": Race and sex in 1950s Britain', in Levine and Grayzel, *Gender*, 221–32.

26. Marjory Harper & Stephen Constantine, *Migration and Empire: OHBE Companion Volume* (Oxford University Press, 2010), 338–40; Hopkins, 'Rethinking decolonization', 221–2.

27. Chafer, *The End of Empire*, 12.

28. Schenk, *The Decline of Sterling*, 117, 425.

29. Max Silverman, *Deconstructing the Nation: Immigration, Racism and Citizenship in Modern France* (London: Routledge, 1992), 42–57.

30. Infamous landmarks here were the 1964 election victory of Conservative anti-immigration candidate Peter Griffiths in the West Midlands seat of Smethwick and on 20 Apr. 1968 Conservative MP for Wolverhampton South-West Enoch Powell's 'Rivers of Blood' speech, an invective warning of the dangers of continuing Commonwealth immigration to Britain. See: Amy Whipple, 'Revisiting the "rivers of blood" controversy: Letters to Enoch Powell', *Journal of British Studies*, 48:3 (2009), 717–35; Peter Brooke, 'India, post-imperialism and the origins of Enoch Powell's "rivers of blood" speech', *HJ*, 50:3 (2007), 669–87.

31. Shepard, ' "Something notably erotic" ', 92–107. There were colonial antecedants to allegations of criminality endemic among Algerian male immigrants, see: Emmanuel Blanchard, 'Le Mauvais Genre des Algériens: Des hommes sans femme face au virilisme policier dans le Paris d'après-guerre', *Clio: Histoire, Femmes et Sociétés*, 27:2 (2008), 209–22.

32. Jim Wolfreys, 'Neither right nor left? Towards an integrated analysis of the Front National', in Nicholas Atkin and Frank Tallett, eds, *The Right in France: From Revolution to Le Pen* (London: I. B. Tauris, 2003), 263, 270–2.

33. Etienne Balibar, 'Uprisings in the "*Banlieues*",' *Constellations*, 14 (2007), 48; cited in Ann Laura Stoler, 'Colonial Aphasia: Race and Disabled Histories in France', *Public Culture*, 23:1 (2010), 127.

34. For differing views of this process in Britain, see John M. MacKenzie, 'The persistence of empire in metropolitan culture', in Stuart Ward, ed., *British Culture and the End of Empire* (Manchester University Press, 2001), 21–34; Stephen J. Howe, 'Internal decolonization? British policies since Thatcher as postcolonial trauma', *Twentieth Century British History*, 14:3 (2003), 288–91.

35. Bruno Charbonneau, 'Dreams of empire: France, Europe and the new interventionism in Africa', *Modern and Contemporary France*, 16:3 (2008), 279–95; Jean-Pierre Bat, 'Jacques Foccart'.

36. John Horne, 'Defeat and memory in modern history', in MacLeod, *Defeat and Memory*, 11–14.

37. Richard Rathbone, 'Kwame Nkrumah and the chiefs', 47.

38. Henry F. Carey, 'The postcolonial state and the protection of human rights', *Comparative Studies of South Asia, Africa and the Middle East*, 22:1&2 (2002), 59–61, 67–9.

39. French, *The British Way*, 166–73.

40. The background to these 'lost' documents is described in David M. Anderson, 'Mau Mau in the High Court and the "lost" British Empire archives: Colonial conspiracy or bureaucratic bungle?', *JICH*, 39:5 (2011), 699–716, and Huw Bennett, 'Soldiers in the Court Room'. See also Mandy Banton, 'Destroy? "Migrate"? Conceal? British strategies for the disposal of sensitive records of colonial administrations at independence', *JICH*, 40:2 (2012), 323–37.

41. Benjamin Stora, *La Gangrène et l'oubli: La Mémoire de la guerre d'Algérie* (Paris: La Découverte, 1991), chs 16, 17.

42. Daniel Lefeuvre, 'La France face à son passé colonial: Un double enjeu', in Dard and Lefeuvre, *L'Europe face à son passé colonial*, 366–9.

43. Horne, 'Defeat and Memory', 19–24.

44. French, *The British Way*, 194–6; Kumar Ramakrishna, 'Content, credibility and context: Propaganda, government surrender policy and the Malayan Communist mass surrender of 1958', *INS*, 14:4 (1999), 242–66.

45. Raphaëlle Branche, 'Cinquante ans après la guerre d'Algérie, il est temps de parler!' <http://www.lemonde.fr/idees/article/2012/07/05/cinquante-ans-apres-la-guerre-d-algerie-il-est-temps-de-parler_1729180_3232> accessed 28 June, 2013.

46. Emeka Ojukwu obituary, *The Economist*, 3 Dec. 2011; Young, *The Labour Governments*, Vol. II, 196–200.

47. Chibuike Uche, 'Oil, British interests and the Nigerian Civil War', *JAH*, 49:1 (2008), 111–35.

48. Christie Achebe, 'Igbo women in the Nigerian-Biafran War, 1967–1970', *Journal of Black Studies*, 43:2 (2012), 785–811. Estimates of fatalities range from a low of 50,000 to a figure of one million, see Young, *The Labour Governments*, Vol. II, 193.

49. Michael E. Latham, 'The Cold War in the Third World, 1963–1975', in Leffler and Westad, eds, *Cambridge History of the Cold War*, Vol. II, 260–7; Latham,

Modernization as Ideology: American Social Science and 'Nation Building' in the Kennedy Era (Chapel Hill, NC: University of North Carolina Press, 2000); Roy Allison, *The Soviet Union and the Strategy of Non-Alignment in the Third World* (Cambridge University Press, 1988), ch. 1.

50. Piero Gleijeses, *Conflicting Missions: Havana, Washington, and Africa, 1959–1976* (Chapel Hill, NC: University of North Carolina Press, 2002), chs 2, 4, 10; Robert Scott Jaster, *The Defence of White Power: South African Foreign Policy Under Pressure* (Basingstoke: Macmillan, 1988); Chen Jian, *Mao's China and the Cold War* (Chapel Hill, NC: University of North Carolina Press, 2001), chs 3, 9; Stephen F. Jackson, 'China's Third World foreign policy: The case of Angola and Mozambique, 1961–93', *China Quarterly*, 143, (June, 1995), 387–422.

51. Matthew Jones, *Conflict and Confrontation in South East Asia, 1961–1965: Britain, the United States, Indonesia and the Creation of Malaysia* (Cambridge University Press, 2001), chs 8–10.

52. Louis, 'The Dissolution of the British Empire in the era of Vietnam', 15–16.

53. Rhiannon Vickers, 'Harold Wilson, the British Labour Party, and the war in Vietnam', *Journal of Cold War Studies*, 10:2 (2008), 41–70; Fredrik Logevall, *Choosing War*, 339–40, 373.

54. Saki Dockrill, *Britain's Retreat from East of Suez: The Choice between Europe and the World?* (Basingstoke: Palgrave-Macmillan, 2002), 114–18, chs 6–9.

55. Matthew Jones, 'A decision delayed: Britain's withdrawal from South East Asia reconsidered, 1961–68', *EHR*, 67:472 (2002), 569–95.

56. Chi-Kwan Mark, 'Lack of means or loss of will? The United Kingdom and the decolonization of Hong Kong, 1957–1967', *IHR*, 31:1 (2009), 70–1.

57. The East of Suez retreat was never total. In autumn 2011 nineteen warships, two submarines and sixty-eight military aircraft, plus 4,000 service personnel from Britain, Australia, New Zealand, Malaysia, and Singapore took part in joint military exercises marking the fortieth anniversary of the 'Five Power Defence Arrangements' (FPDA) concluded on 1 Nov. 1971. A strategic sticking plaster applied by the British to cover their East of Suez withdrawal, the FPDA has proved remarkably durable and now focuses on piracy, humanitarian and disaster relief alongside rising Chinese sea power. See 'Banyan: Echoes of Dreamland', *The Economist*, 5 Nov. 2011, p. 76, <http://www.economist.com/node/21536609> accessed 28 June 2013.

58. Dockrill, *Britain's Retreat*, 114–18.

59. Andrea Benvenuti, 'The British are "taking to the boat": Australian attempts to forestall Britain's military disengagement from Southeast Asia, 1965–1966', *DS*, 20:1 (2009), 86–106, quotation at p. 90.

60. Martin Conway and Robert Gerwarth, 'Revolution and counter-revolution', in Bloxham and Gerwarth, *Political Violence*, 166.

61. Eunan O'Halpin, '"A poor thing but our own": The Joint Intelligence Committee and Ireland, 1965–72', *INS*, 23:5 (2008), 658–80.

62. Rose, 'Who are we now?' 154–5.

63. John Darwin, 'British decolonization after 1945: A pattern or a puzzle', *JICH*, 12:2 (188), 188, 206; also cited in Elizabeth Buettner, *Empire Families: Britons and Late Imperial India* (Oxford University Press, 2004), 264–5.

64. Murphy, *Alan Lennox-Boyd*, 102–4, 118–21, 152–5.

65. Darwin, 'Was there a fourth British Empire?' 27–8.

66. Murphy, *Party Politics*, 19–22.

67. David French, 'Nasty not nice: British counter-insurgency doctrine and practice, 1945–1967', *SWI*, 23:4/5 (2012), 744–61.

68. James Mark, Nigel Townson, and Polymaris Voglis, 'Inspirations', in Robert Gildea, James Mark and Anette Warring, eds, *Europe's 1968: Voices of Revolt* (Oxford University Press, 2013), 87–100.

69. Jeremi Suri, 'The rise and fall of an international counterculture, 1960–1975', *AHR*, 114:1 (2009), 48–9; Julian Jackson, 'The mystery of May 1968', *FHS*, 33:4 (2010), 625–53; Michael Scott Christofferson, 'The French "sixties"', *FPCS*, 26:3 (2008), 126–40.

70. Guiliano Garavini, 'The colonies strike back: The impact of the Third World on western Europe, 1968–1975', *Contemporary European History*, 16:3 (2007), 299–319.

71. Cited in Elizabeth Buettner, '"We don't grow coffee and bananas in Clapham Junction you know!" Imperial Britons back home', in Bickers, *Settlers*, 322–3.

72. Simon J. Potter, 'Empire, cultures and identities in nineteenth and twentieth century Britain', *History Compass*, 5 (2007), 57.

73. Buettner, *Empire Families*, 2–3, 252–3, and on complex expatriate identities: Mrinalini Sinha, 'Britishness, clubbability, and the colonial public sphere: The genealogy of an imperial institution in colonial India', *Journal of British Studies*, 40:4 (2001), 489–521; Lynn Hollen Lees, 'Being British', 76–101.

74. Patricia M. E. Lorcin, 'Historiographies of Algiers', in Zeynep Çelik, Julia Clancy-Smith, and Frances Terpak, eds, *Walls of Algiers: Narratives of the City through Text and Image* (Seattle: University of Washington Press, 2009), 241–2.

75. Claire Eldridge, '"We've never had a voice": Memory construction and the children of the *harkis* (1962–1991)', *FH*, (2009), 88–107.

76. Simpson, 'The United States and the curious history', 678–85. For the Algerian case, see Jeffrey James Byrne, 'Our own special brand of socialism: Algeria and the contest of modernities in the 1960s', *DH*, 33:3 (2009), 427–47.

77. Westad, *The Global Cold War*, 90; Aaron Windel, 'British colonial education in Africa: Policy and practice in the era of trusteeship', *History Compass*, 7:1 (2009), 17.

78. Westad, *The Global Cold War*, 97–104.

79. Subir Sinha, 'Lineages of the developmentalist state: Transnationality and village India, 1900–1965', *Comparative Studies in Society and History*, 50:1 (2008), 57–61.

80. Rob Nixon, *Slow Violence and the Environmentalism of the Poor* (Cambridge, MA: Harvard University Press, 2011), especially the introduction and chs 1–2.

81. Joseph M. Hodge, 'Colonial experts, 308–13; Gregory A. Barton, 'Environmentalism, development and British policy in the Middle East 1945–65', *JICH*, 38:4 (2010), 619–39.

82. Matthew Connelly, 'Population control is history: Perspectives on the international campaign to limit population growth', *Comparative Studies in Society and History*, 45:1 (2003), 125–8.

83. Daniel Speich, 'The Kenyan style of "African Socialism": Developmental knowledge claims and the explanatory limits of the Cold War', *DH*, 33:3 (2009), 456–66.

84. Brad Simpson, 'Indonesia's "accelerated modernization" and the global discourse of development, 1960–1975', *DH*, 33:3 (2009), 467–8, 482–6; Jeremy Kuzmarov, 'Modernizing repression: Police training, political violence, and nation-building in the "American century"', *DH*, 33:2 (2009), 197–209.

85. Kuzmarov, 'Modernizing repression', 201–18.

Select Bibliography

BOOKS AND ARTICLES

Abadi, Jacob, 'Great Britain and the Maghreb in the epoch of pan-Arabism and Cold War', *Cold War History*, 2:2 (2002), 125–60.

d'Abzac-Epezy, Claude, 'Épuration, dégagements, exclusions: Les Réductions d'effectifs dans l'armée française (1940–1947)', *Vingtième Siècle*, 59:1 (1998), 62–75.

Achebe, Christie, 'Igbo women in the Nigerian-Biafran War, 1967–1970', *Journal of Black Studies*, 43:2 (2012), 785–811.

Adams, Geoffrey, *The Call of Conscience: French Protestant Responses to the Algerian War, 1954–1962* (Waterloo: Wilfrid Laurier University Press, 1998).

Adas, Michael, 'Contested hegemony: The Great War and the Afro-Asian assault on the civilizing mission ideology', *Journal of World History*, 15:1 (2004), 31–63.

Ageron, Charles-Robert, 'La Survivance d'un mythe: La Puissance par l'Empire colonial, 1944–1947', *Revue Française d'Histoire d'Outre-Mer*, 72 (1985), 388–97.

——ed., *Les Chemins de la décolonisation* (Paris: CNRS, 1986).

——ed., *La Guerre d'Algérie et les Algériens, 1954–1962* (Paris: Armand Colin, 1997).

——and Marc Michel, eds, *L'Afrique noire française: L'Heure des indépendances* (Paris: CNRS Éditions, 1992).

Ahlman, Jeffery S., 'The Algerian question in Nkrumah's Ghana, 1958–1960: Debating violence and nonviolence in African decolonization', *Africa Today*, 57:2 (2010), 67–84.

Aldrich, Richard J., *Intelligence and the War against Japan: Britain, America and the Politics of Secret Service* (Cambridge University Press, 2000).

Aldrich, Robert, and Stuart Ward, 'Ends of Empire: Decolonizing the nation in British and French historiography', in Stefan Berger and Chris Lorenz, eds, *Nationalising the Past: Historians as Nation Builders in Modern Europe* (Basingstoke: Palgrave-Macmillan, 2010), 259–81.

Alexander, Martin, Martin Evans, and J. F. V. Keiger, eds, *The Algerian War and the French Army: Experiences, Images, Testimonies* (Basingstoke: Palgrave-Macmillan, 2002).

——and J. F. V. Keiger, eds, *France and the Algerian War: Strategy, Operations and Diplomacy* (London: Frank Cass, 2002).

Alexander, Peter, and Rick Halpern, eds, *Racializing Class, Classifying Race: Labour and Difference in Britain, the USA and Africa* (London: Macmillan, 2000).

Allison, Roy, *The Soviet Union and the Strategy of Non-Alignment in the Third World* (Cambridge University Press, 1988).

Allman, Jean Marie, '"Hewers of wood, carriers of water": Islam, class, and politics on the eve of Ghana's independence', *African Studies Review*, 34:2 (1991), 1–26.

—— *The Quills of the Porcupine: Asante Nationalism in an Emergent Ghana* (Madison, WI: University of Wisconsin Press, 1993).

——'The youngmen and the porcupine: Class, nationalism and Asante's struggle for self-determination, 1954–57', *JAH*, 31:2 (1990), 263–79.

Amiri, Linda, *La Bataille de France: La Guerre d'Algérie en France* (Paris: Robert Laffont, 2004).

Amrane, Djamila, *Des femmes dans la guerre d'Algérie: Entretiens* (Paris: Karthala, 1994).

Amrith, Sunil S., 'Food and welfare in India, c.1910–1950', *Comparative Studies in Society and History*, 50:4 (2008), 1010–35.

Amsden, Alice H., *Escape from Empire: The Developing World's Journey through Heaven and Hell* (Boston: MIT Press, 2007).

Anderson, Carol, *Eyes off the Prize: The United Nations and the African American Struggle for Human Rights, 1944–1955* (Cambridge University Press, 2003).

Anderson, David M., 'British abuse and torture in Kenya's counter-insurgency, 1952–1960', *SWI*, 23:4/5 (2012), 700–19.

—— *Histories of the Hanged: The Dirty War in Kenya and the End of Empire* (New York: Norton, 2005).

——'Mau Mau in the High Court and the "lost" British Empire archives: Colonial conspiracy or bureaucratic bungle?' *JICH*, 39:5 (2011), 699–716.

——'Punishment, race and the "raw native": Settler society and Kenya's flogging scandals, 1895–1930', *Journal of Southern African Studies*, 37:3 (2011), 479–98.

——'Sexual threat and settler society: Black perils in Kenya, c.1907–1930', *JICH*, 38:1 (2010), 47–74.

—— and David Throup, 'Africans and agricultural production in colonial Kenya: The myth of the war as a watershed', *JAH* 26 (1985), 327–45.

—— and David Killingray, eds, *Policing and Decolonisation: Politics, Nationalism and the Police, 1917–65* (Manchester University Press, 1992).

Andreopoulos, George J., and Harold E. Selesky, eds, *The Aftermath of Defeat: Societies, Armed Forces, and the Challenge of Recovery* (New Haven, CT: Yale University Press, 1994).

Antlöv, Hans, and Stein Tønnesson, eds, *Imperial Policy and Southeast Asian Nationalism* (London: Curzon Press, 1995).

Arzalier, Francis, and Jean Suret-Canale, eds, *Madagascar 1947: La Tragédie oubliée* (Paris: Temps des Cérises, 1999).

Arielli, Nir, '"Haifa is still burning": Italian, German and French air raids on Palestine during the Second World War', *MES*, 46:3 (2010), 331–47.

Arnold, David, 'Looting, grain riots, and government policy in South India, 1918', *PP*, 84:1 (1979), 111–45.

Arnon-Ohanna,Yuval,'The bands in the Palestinian Arab Revolt, 1936–1939: Structure and organization', *Asian and African Studies*, 15:2 (1981), 229–47.

Ash, Catherine B., 'Forced labour in colonial West Africa', *History Compass*, 4:3 (2006), 402–6.

Ashton, Nigel John, *Eisenhower, Macmillan and the Problem of Nasser* (Basingstoke: Palgrave Macmillan, 1996).

——'The hijacking of a pact: The formation of the Baghdad Pact and the Anglo-American tensions in the Middle East, 1955–1958', *Review of International Studies*, 19:2 (1993), 123–37.

——'A microcosm of decline: British loss of nerve and military intervention in Jordan and Kuwait, 1958 and 1961', *HJ*, 40:4 (1997), 1069–83.

Asselin, Pierre, 'Choosing peace: Hanoi and the Geneva agreement on Vietnam, 1954–1955', *Journal of Cold War Studies*, 9:2 (2007), 95–126.

Atkin, Nicholas, and Frank Tallett, eds, *The Right in France: From Revolution to Le Pen* (London: I. B. Tauris, 2003).

Auriol,Vincent, *Journal du Septennat, 1947–1954*, 7 vols (Paris: Armand Colin, 1971 et seq.)

Aussaresses, Général Paul, *Services spéciaux: Algérie, 1955–1957* (Paris: Perrin, 2001).

Bale, Tim, ' "A deplorable episode"? South African arms sales and the statecraft of British social democracy', *Labour History Review*, 62:1 (1997), 22–40.

Balfour-Paul, Glen, *The End of Empire in the Middle East: Britain's Relinquishment of Power in Her Last Three Arab Dependencies* (Cambridge University Press, 1991).

Banton, Mandy,'Destroy? "Migrate"? Conceal? British strategies for the disposal of sensitive records of colonial administrations at independence', *JICH*, 40:2 (2012), 323–37.

Bar-On, Colonel Mordechai,'Three days in Sèvres: October 1956', *History Workshop Journal*, 62:1 (2006), 172–86.

Barei, Geoffrey, 'The Sakiet Sidi Youssef incident of 1958 in Tunisia and the Anglo-American "Good Offices" Mission', *Journal of North African Studies*, 17:2 (2012), 355–71.

Barr, James, *A Line in the Sand: The Anglo-French Struggle for the Middle East* (New York: Norton, 2012).

Barton, Gregory A., 'Environmentalism, development and British policy in the Middle East 1945–65', *JICH*, 38:4 (2010), 619–39.

Barua, Pradeep, 'Strategies and doctrines of imperial defence: Britain and India, 1919–45', *JICH*, 25:2 (1997), 240–66.

Bayly, Susan,'Conceptualizing resistance and revolution in Vietnam: Paul Mus' understanding of colonialism in crisis', *Journal of Vietnamese Studies*, 4:1 (2009), 192–205.

Beck, Peter,' "The less said about Suez the better": British governments and the politics of Suez's history, 1956–67', *EHR* CXXIV:508 (2009), 605–40.

——'Politicians versus historians: Lord Avon's appeasement battle against "lamentably, appeasement-minded" historians', *Twentieth Century British History*, 9:3 (1998), 396–419.

Becker, Charles, Saliou Mbaye, and Ibrahima Thioub, eds, *AOF: réalités et heritages: Sociétés ouest-africaines et ordre colonial, 1895–1960*, 2 vols, (Dakar: Direction des Archives du Sénégal, 1997)

Beigbeder, Yves, *Judging War Crimes and Torture: French Justice and International Criminal Tribunals and Commissions (1940–2005)* (Leiden: Brill Academic, 2006).

Belich, James, *Replenishing the Earth: The Settler Revolution and the Rise of the Anglo-world* (Oxford University Press, 2009).

Bell, Christopher, 'The "Singapore strategy" and the deterrence of Japan: Winston Churchill, the Admiralty and the dispatch of Force Z', *EHR*, 116:467 (2001), 604–34.

Ben-Ze'ev, Efrat, Ruth Ginio, and Jay Winter eds, *Shadows of War: A Social History of Silence in the Twentieth Century* (Cambridge University Press, 2010).

Bennett, Brett M., and Joseph M. Hodge, eds, *Science and Empire: Knowledge and Networks of Science Across the British Empire, 1800–1970* (London: Palgrave-Macmillan, 2011).

Bennett, G.H., *British Foreign Policy during the Curzon period, 1919–1924* (Basingstoke: Macmillan, 1995).

Bennett, Huw, *Fighting the Mau Mau: The British Army and Counter-Insurgency in the Kenya Emergency* (Cambridge University Press, 2012).

——'Soldiers in the court room: The British Army's part in the Kenya Emergency under the legal spotlight', *JICH*, 39:5 (2011), 717–30.

——'"A very salutary effect": The counter-terror strategy in the early Malayan Emergency, June 1948 to December 1949', *Journal of Strategic Studies*, 32:3 (2009), 415–44.

Benvenuti, Andrea, 'The British are "taking to the boat": Australian attempts to forestall Britain's military disengagement from Southeast Asia, 1965–1966', *DS* 20:1 (2009), 86–106.

Berman, Bruce, *Control and Crisis in Colonial Kenya: The Dialectic of Domination* (London: James Currey, 1990).

——and John Lonsdale, *Unhappy Valley: Conflict in Kenya and Africa: Book Two: Violence and Ethnicity* (Oxford: James Currey, 1992).

Bernal, Martin, 'The Nghe-Tinh Soviet Movement, 1930–1931', *PP*, 92:1 (1981), 148–68.

Bernard, Stéphane, *The Franco-Moroccan Conflict, 1943–1956* (New Haven, CT: Yale University Press, 1968).

Berstein, Serge, *Paul Ramadier: La République et le socialisme* (Paris: Editions Complexe, 1990).

——and Pierre Birnbaum and Jean-Pierre Rioux, eds, *De Gaulle et les élites* (Paris: Fondation Charles de Gaulle, 2008).

——and Frédéric Cépède, Gilles Morin, and Antoine Prost, eds, *Le Parti socialiste entre Résistance et République* (Paris: Publications de la Sorbonne, 2000).

——and Pierre Milza, eds, *L'Année 1947* (Paris: Presses de Sciences Po., 2000).

Blanchard, Emmanuel, 'Le Mauvais Genre des Algériens: Des hommes sans femme face au virilisme policier dans le Paris d'après-guerre', *Clio: Histoire, Femmes et Sociétés* 27:2 (2008): 209–22.

—— *La Police parisienne et les Algériens (1944–1962)* (Paris: Nouveau Monde éditions, 2011).

Blanning, T. C. W., *The French Revolution in Germany: Occupation and Resistance in the Rhineland 1792–1802* (Oxford University Press, 1983).

Bloxham, Donald, and Robert Gerwarth, eds, *Political Violence in Twentieth-Century Europe* (Cambridge University Press, 2011).

Boittin, Jennifer, 'Black in France: The language and politics of race in the late Third Republic', *FPCS*, 27:2 (2009), 23–46.

Bölükbasi, Suha, 'The Cyprus dispute and the United Nations: Peaceful non-settlement between 1954 and 1996', *IJMES*, 30:3 (1998), 411–34.

Bonin, Hubert, Catherine Hodeir, and Jean-François Klein, eds, *L'Esprit économique impérial (1830–1970): Groupes de pression et réseaux du patronat colonial en France et dans l'empire* (Paris: Publications de la SFHOM 2008).

Bookmiller, Robert J., 'The Algerian war of words: Broadcasting and revolution, 1954–1962', *Maghreb Review*, 14:3–4 (1989), 196–213.

Boomgaard, Peter, and Ian Brown, eds, *Weathering the Storm: The Economies of South East Asia in the 1930s Depression* (Singapore: I.S.E.A.S., 2000).

Booth, Anne, 'Four colonies and a kingdom: A comparison of fiscal, trade and exchange rate policies in Southeast Asia in the 1930s', *MAS*, 37:2 (2003), 429–60.

—— 'Night watchman, extractive, or development states? Some evidence from late colonial Southeast Asia', *Economic History Review*, 60:2 (2007), 241–66.

Borstelmann, Thomas, *The Cold War and the Color Line: Race Relations and American Foreign Policy since 1945* (Cambridge, MA: Harvard University Press, 2001).

Bose, Purnima, *Organizing Empire: Individualism, Collective Agency, and India* (Durham, NC: Duke University Press, 2003).

Bose, Sugata, 'Starvation amidst plenty: The making of famine in Bengal, Honan and Tonkin, 1942–45', *MAS*, 24:4 (1990), 699–727.

Bošković, Aleksandar, 'In the age of the fifth sun: Jacques Soustelle's studies of Aztec religion', *Anthropos*, 87:4/6 (1992), 533–7.

Bossuat, Gérard, *Les Aides américaines économiques et militaires à la France, 1938–1960* (Paris: Comité pour l'histoire économique et financière de la France, 2001.

—— *France, l'aide américaine et la construction européenne 1944–1954* (Paris: CHEFF, 1992).

Bou-Nacklie, N. E., 'Tumult in Syria's Hama in 1925: The failure of a revolt', *Journal of Contemporary History*, 33:2 (1998), 273–90.

Bourdrel, Philippe, *La Dernière Chance de l'Algérie française: Du gouvernement socialiste au retour de De Gaulle, 1956–1958* (Paris: Albin Michel, 1996).

Bowden, Tom, 'The politics of the Arab rebellion in Palestine, 1936–39', *MES*, 11:2 (1975), 147–74.

Bowles, Brett C., 'La Tragédie de Mers el-Kébir' and the politics of filmed news in France, 1940–1944', *JMH*, 76:2 (2004), 347–88.

Boyce, Robert, *The Great Interwar Crisis: And the Collapse of Globalization* (Basingstoke: Palgrave-Macmillan, 2009).

Boyle, Peter G. ed., *The Eden-Eisenhower Correspondence, 1955–1957* (Chapel Hill, NC: University of North Carolina Press, 2005).

Bradley, Mark Philip, 'Becoming "Van Minh": Civilizational discourse and visions of the self in twentieth-century Vietnam', *Journal of World History*, 15:1 (2004), 65–83.

—— *Imagining Vietnam and America: The Making of Postcolonial Vietnam, 1919–1950* (Chapel Hill, NC: University of North Carolina Press, 2000).

—— and Marilyn B. Young, eds, *Making Sense of the Vietnam Wars: Local, National and Transnational Perspectives* (New York: Oxford University Press, 2008).

Branch, Daniel, *Defeating Mau Mau, Creating Kenya: Counterinsurgency, Civil War, and Decolonization* (Cambridge University Press, 2009).

—— *Kenya: Between Hope and Despair, 1963–2010* (New Haven, CT: Yale University Press, 2011.

Branche, Raphaëlle, *La Guerre d'Algérie: Une histoire apaisée?* (Paris: Seuil, 2005).

—— *La Torture et l'armée pendant la guerre d'Algérie* (Paris: Gallimard, 2001).

—— 'Des viols pendant la guerre d'Algérie', *Vingtième Siècle*, 75 (juillet–septembre 2002), 123–32.

—— and Sylvie Thénault, eds, *La France en guerre, 1954–1962: Expériences métropolitaines de la guerre d'indépendance algérienne* (Paris: Autrement, 2008).

—— and Fabrice Virgili, eds, *Rape in Wartime* (Basingstoke: Palgrave-Macmillan, 2012).

Brennan, James R., 'Youth, the TANU Youth League and managed vigilantism in Dar es Salaam, Tanzania, 1925–73', *Africa*, 76:2 (2006), 221–46.

Bridge, Carl, and Kent Fedorowich eds, *The British World: Culture, Diaspora and Identity* (London: Routledge, 2003).

Brivati, Brian, and Harriet Jones, eds, *What Difference Did the War Make?* (Leicester: Leicester University Press, 1993).

Brocheux, Pierre, 'L'Implantation du mouvement communiste en Indochine française: Le Cas du Nghe-Tinh (1930–1931)', *Revue d'Histoire Moderne et Contemporaine*, 24:1 (1977), 49–74.

—— and Daniel Hémery, *Indochina: An Ambiguous Colonization, 1858–1954* (Berkeley, CA: University of California Press, 2009).

—— ed., *Du conflit d'Indochine aux conflits indochinois* (Paris: Editions Complexe, 2000).

Brooke, Peter, 'India, Post-imperialism and the origins of Enoch Powell's "rivers of blood" speech', *HJ*, 50:3 (2007), 669–87.

Brower, Benjamin Claude, *A Desert Named Peace: The Violence of France's Empire in the Algerian Sahara, 1844–1902* (New York: Columbia University Press, 2009).

Brown, Carolyn A., *We Were All slaves: African Miners, Culture, and Resistance at the Enugu Government Colliery* (Portsmouth, NH: Heinemann, 2003).

Brown, Ian, 'Rural distress in Southeast Asia during the world depression of the early 1930s: A preliminary re-examination', *Journal of Asian Studies*, 45:5 (1986), 995–1025.

Brownell, Josiah, ' "A sordid tussle on the Strand": Rhodesia House during the UDI Rebellion (1965–80)', *JICH*, 38:3 (2010), 471–99.

——'The taint of communism: The Movement for Colonial Freedom, the Labour Party, and the Communist Party of Great Britain, 1954–70', *Canadian Journal of History*, 42:2 (2007), 235–58.

Buckner, Philip ed., *Canada and the British Empire: Oxford History of the British Empire Companion Volume* (Oxford University Press, 2008).

Buettner, Elizabeth, *Empire Families: Britons and Late Imperial India* (Oxford University Press, 2004).

——'Problematic Spaces, problematic races: Defining "Europeans" in late Colonial India', *Women's History Review*, 9:2 (2000), 277–98.

Burke, Roland, *Decolonization and the Evolution of International Human Rights* (Philadelphia: University of Pennsylvania Press, 2010).

Burrin, Philippe, *Living with Defeat: France under the German Occupation, 1940–44* (London: Hodder Arnold, 1996).

Burton, Andrew, 'Townsmen in the making: Social engineering and citizenship in Dar es Salaam, *c.*1945–1960', *International Journal of African Historical Studies*, 36:2 (2003), 331–65.

Burton, Richard D. E., *Blood in the City: Violence and Revelation in Paris, 1789–1945* (Ithaca, NY: Cornell University Press, 2001).

Butler, L. J., 'Britain, the United States, and the demise of the Central African Federation, 1959–63', *JICH*, 28:3 (2000), 131–51.

——*Copper Empire: Mining and the Colonial State in Northern Rhodesia, c.1930–1964* (Basingstoke: Palgrave-Macmillan, 2007).

——*Industrialization and the British Colonial State: West Africa, 1939–1951* (London: Routledge, 1997).

Byrne, Jeffrey James, 'Our own special brand of socialism: Algeria and the contest of modernities in the 1960s', *DH*, 33:3 (2009), 427–47.

Campbell, Gwyn, ed., *Abolition and its Aftermath in Indian Ocean Africa and Asia* (London: Routledge, 2005).

——'Crisis of faith and colonial conquest: The impact of famine and disease in late nineteenth-century Madagascar', *Cahier d'Études Africains*, 32:127 (1992), 409–53.

——'Madagascar and the slave trade, 1810–1895', *JAH*, 22:2 (1981), 207–27.

——'The Menalamba Revolt and brigandry in imperial Madagascar, 1820–1897', *International Journal of African Historical Studies* 24:2 (1991), 259–91.

——'Missionaries, *Fanompoana* and the Menalamba Revolt in late nineteenth century Madagascar', *Journal of Southern African Studies*, 15:1 (1988), 54–73.

Carey, Henry F., 'The postcolonial state and the protection of human rights', *Comparative Studies of South Asia, Africa and the Middle East*, 22:1&2 (2002) 59–75.

Carey, Hilary M., ed., *Empires of Religion* (Basingstoke: Palgrave-Macmillan, 2008).

Carlier, Omar, *Alain Savary, politique d'honneur* (Paris: Presses de Sciences Po., 2002).

Carlton, David, *Anthony Eden: A Biography* (London: Viking, 1981).

—— *Britain and the Suez Crisis* (Oxford: Blackwell, 1981).

Carroll, David, 'Camus's Algeria: Birthrights, colonial injustice, the fiction of a French-Algerian people', *Modern Language Notes*, 112 (1997), 517–49.

Carruthers, Susan L., *Winning Hearts and Minds: British Governments, the Media and Colonial Counter-Insurgency 1944–1960* (London: Leicester University Press, 1995).

Çelik, Zeynep, *Urban Forms and Colonial Confrontations: Algiers under French Rule* (Berkeley, CA: University of California Press, 1997).

Chafer, Tony, *The End of Empire in French West Africa: France's Successful Decolonization?* (Oxford: Berg, 2002).

—— And Alexander Keese, eds, *Francophone Africa at Fifty* (Manchester University Press, 2013).

—— And Amanda Sackur, eds, *Promoting the Colonial Idea: Propaganda and Visions of Empire in France* (Basingstoke: Palgrave, 2002).

Chalmers Hood, Ronald, *Royal Republicans: The French Naval Dynasties Between the World Wars* (Baton Rouge, LA: Louisiana State University Press, 1985).

Chanson-Jabeur, Chantal, and Odile Goerg, eds, *'Mama Africa': Hommage à Catherine Coquery-Vidrovitch* (Paris: L'Harmattan, 2006).

Charlot, Jean, *Le Gaullisme d'opposition, 1946–1958* (Paris: Fayard, 1983).

Charmley, John, 'Harold Macmillan and the making of the French Committee of National Liberation', *IHR*, 4:4 (1982), 553–67.

Charters, David A., *The British Army and Jewish Insurgency in Palestine, 1945–47* (Basingstoke: Macmillan, 1989).

Chatterji, Joya, *The Spoils of Partition: Bengal and India, 1947–1967* (Cambridge University Press, 2007).

—— 'The fashioning of a frontier: The Radcliffe Line and Bengal's border landscape, 1947–52', *MAS*, 33 (1999), 185–242.

Chester, Lucy P., *Borders and Conflict in South Asia: The Radcliffe Boundary Commission and the Partition of Punjab* (Manchester University Press, 2009).

—— 'Boundary commissions as tools to safeguard British interests at the end of Empire', *Journal of Historical Geography*, 34:3 (2008), 494–515.

Chipman, John, *French Power in Africa* (Oxford: Blackwell, 1989).

Clark, Andrew F., 'Internal migrations and population movements in the Upper Senegal Valley (West Africa), 1890–1920', *CJAS*, 28:3 (1994), 399–420.

Clarke, Peter, *The Cripps Version: The Life of Sir Stafford Cripps, 1889–1952* (London: Allen Lane, 2002).

—— *The Last Thousand Days of the British Empire: Churchill, Roosevelt, and the Birth of the Pax Americana* (London: Allen Lane, 2007.

Clarke, Sabine, 'A Technocratic Imperial State? The Colonial Office and Scientific Research, 1940–1960', *Twentieth Century British History*, 18:4 (2007), 453–80.

Clavin, Patricia, and Jens-Wilhelm Wessels, 'Transnationalism and the League of Nations: Understanding the work of its economic and financial organisation', *Contemporary European History*, 14:4 (2005), 465–92.

Cohen, Gerard Daniel, *In War's Wake: Europe's Displaced Persons in the Postwar Order* New York: (Oxford University Press, 2012).

Cohen, Hillel, *Army of Shadows: Palestinian Collaboration with Zionism, 1917–1948* (Berkeley, CA: University of California Press, 2008).

Cohen, Michael J., 'Appeasement in the Middle East: The British white paper on Palestine, May 1939', *HJ*, 16:3 (1973), 571–96.

——and Martin Kolinsky, eds, *Britain and the Middle East in the 1930s: Security Problems* (Basingstoke: Macmillan, 1990).

Cohen, Stuart, 'Imperial policing against illegal immigration: The Royal Navy and Palestine, 1945–48', *JICH*, 22:2 (1994), 275–93.

Cohen, William B., 'The colonized as child: British and French Colonial Rule', *African Historical Studies*, 3:2 (1970), 427–31.

——*Rulers of Empire: The French Colonial Service in Africa* (Stanford: Hoover Institution Press, 1971).

Cohen-Solal, Annie, 'Camus, Sartre and the Algerian War', *Journal of European Studies*, 28:1 (1998), 43–50.

Cohrs, Patrick, *The Unfinished Peace after World War I: America, Britain, and the Stabilisation of Europe, 1919–1932* (Cambridge University Press, 2006).

Cointet, Michèle, *De Gaulle et l'Algérie française, 1958–1962* (Paris: Perrin 1995).

Cole, Jennifer, *Forget Colonialism: Sacrifice and the Art of Memory in Madagascar* (Berkeley, CA: University of California Press, 2001).

——'Narratives and moral projects: Generational memories of the Malagasy 1947 Rebellion', *Ethos*, 31:1 (2003), 95–126.

Cole, Joshua, 'Massacres and their historians: Recent histories of state violence in France and Algeria in the twentieth century', *FPCS*, 28:1 (2010), 106–26.

Conklin, Alice L., '"Democracy" rediscovered:. Civilization through association in French West Africa (1914–1930)', *Cahiers d'Études Africaines*, 145:37 (1997), 59–84.

——'Histories of colonialism: Recent studies of the modern French Empire', *FHS*, 30:2 (2007), 306–32.

——'The new "ethnology" and "la situation coloniale" in interwar France', *French Politics, Culture and Society*, 20:2 (2002), 29–48;.

——*A Mission to Civilize: The Republican Idea of Empire in France and West Africa, 1895–1930* (Stanford University Press, 1997).

Conley, Mary A., *From Jack Tar to Union Jack: Representing Naval Manhood in the British Empire, 1870–1918* (Manchester University Press, 2009).

Connelly, Matthew, *A Diplomatic Revolution: Algeria's Fight for Independence and the Origins of the Post-Cold War Era* (New York: Oxford University Press, 2002).

——'Population control is history: New perspectives on the international campaign to limit population growth', *Comparative Studies in Society and History*, 45:1 (2003), 122–47.

——'Rethinking the Cold War and decolonization: The grand strategy of the Algerian war of independence', *IJMES*, 33:2 (2001), 221–45.

——'Taking off the Cold War lens: Visions of North–South conflict during the Algerian war for independence', *AHR*, 105:3 (2000), 739–69.

Coombs, Catherine, 'Partition narratives: Displaced trauma and culpability among British civil servants in 1940s Punjab', *MAS*, 45:1 (2011), 201–24.

Cooper, Duff, *The Duff Cooper Diaries, 1915–1951*, ed. John Julius Norwich (London: Weidenfeld & Nicolson, 2005).

Cooper, Frederick, *Decolonization and African Society: The Labor Question in French and British Africa* (Cambridge University Press, 1996).

——'"Our Strike": Equality, anticolonial politics, and the 1947–48 railway strike in French West Africa', *JAH*, 37:1 (1996), 81–118.

——'Possibility and constraint: African independence in colonial perspective', *JAH*, 49 (2008), 167–96.

——'The Senegalese general strike of 1946 and the labor question in post-war French Africa', *CJAS* 24:2 (1990), 165–215.

——and Randall Packard, eds, *International Development and the Social Sciences: Essays on the History and Politics of Knowledge* (Berkeley, CA: University of California Press, 1998).

——and Ann Laura Stoler, eds, *Tensions of Empire: Colonial Cultures in a Bourgeois World* (Berkeley, CA: University of California Press, 1997).

Cooper, Nicola, *France in Indochina: Colonial Encounters* (Oxford: Berg, 2001).

Copland, Ian, 'The further shores of partition: Ethnic cleansing in Rajasthan 1947', *PP*, 160 (August 1998), 203–39.

Cornaton, Michel, *Les Camps de regroupement de la guerre d'Algérie* (Paris: L'Harmattan, 1998).

Cowans, Jon, 'French public opinion and the founding of the Fourth Republic', *FHS*, 17:1 (1991), 62–95.

Cowman, Ian, 'Main fleet to Singapore? Churchill, the Admiralty and Force Z', *Journal of Strategic Studies*, 18:1 (1995), 79–93.

Crémieux-Brilhac, Jean-Louis, *La France libre: De l'appel du 18 juin à la libération* (Paris: Gallimard, 1998).

Creswell, Michael, *A Question of Balance: How France and the United States Created Cold War Europe* (Cambridge, MA: Harvard University Press, 2006).

——and Marc Trachtenberg, 'France and the German question, 1945–1955', *Journal of Cold War Studies*, 5:3 (2003), 5–28.

Crook, Richard, 'Decolonization, the colonial state and chieftaincy in Ghana', *African Affairs*, 85:338 (1986), 75–107.

Crossman, Richard, *The Backbench Diaries of Richard Crossman*, Janet Morgan, ed. (London: Book Club, 1981).

Crowder, Michael, and J. Ajayi, eds, *History of West Africa* (Harlow: Longman, 1987).

Daiya, Kavita, *Violent Belongings: Partition, Gender, and National Culture in Postcolonial India* (Philadelphia: Temple University Press, 2008).

Dalloz, Jacques, 'Alain Savary, un socialiste face à la guerre d'Indochine', *Vingtième Siècle*, 53:1 (1997), 42–54.

Danquah, Francis K., 'Sustaining a West African cocoa economy: Agricultural science and the swollen shoot contagion in Ghana, 1936–1965', *African Economic History*, 31:1 (2003), 43–74.

Darwin, John, 'The Central African Emergency, 1959', *JICH*, 21:3 (1993), 217–34.

—— *The Empire Project: The Rise and Fall of the British World System, 1820–1970* (Cambridge University Press, 2009).

—— *The End of the British Empire: The Historical Debate* (Oxford: Blackwell, 1991).

——'An undeclared Empire: The British in the Middle East, 1918–39', *JICH*, 27:2 (1999), 159–76.

——'What was the late colonial state?' *Itinerario*, 23:3–4 (1999), 73–82.

Daunton, Martin, and Bernhard Rieger, eds, *Meanings of Modernity: Britain from the Late Victorian Era to the Second World War* (Oxford: Berg, 2001).

De Vries, David, 'British rule and Arab-Jewish coalescence of interest: The 1946 civil servants' strike in Palestine', *IJMES*, 36:4 (2004), 613–38.

Deery, Philip, 'The terminology of terrorism: Malaya, 1948–52', *JSEAS*, 34:2 (2003), 231–47.

Deighton, Anne, 'Entente néo-coloniale?: Ernest Bevin and the proposals for an Anglo-French Third World power, 1945–1949', *DS*, 17:4 (2006), 835–52.

Dennis, Peter, *Troubled Days of Peace: Mountbatten and South East Asia Command* (Manchester University Press, 1987).

Descamps, Henri, *La Démocratie chrétienne et le MRP de 1946 à 1959* (Paris: Pichon et Durand-Auzias, 1981).

Dewey, Jr, Robert F., *British National Identity and Opposition to Membership of Europe, 1961–63: The Anti-Marketeers* (Manchester University Press, 2009).

Diamond, Hanna, *Fleeing Hitler: France, 1940* (Oxford University Press, 2008).

Dickinson, Frederick R., *War and National Reinvention: Japan in the Great War, 1914–1919* (Cambridge, MA: Harvard University Press, 1999).

Dickson, Paul, 'The politics of army expansion: General H. D. G. Crerar and the creation of the First Canadian Army, 1941', *Journal of Military History*, 60:2 (1996), 271–98.

Dine, Philip, 'French culture and the Algerian War: Mobilizing icons', *Journal of European Studies*, 28:1 (1998), 51–68.

—— *Images of the Algerian War: French Fiction and Film, 1954–1992* (Oxford: Clarendon Press, 1994).

Dockrill, Saki, *Britain's Policy for West German Rearmament, 1950–1955* (Cambridge University Press, 1991).

—— *Britain's Retreat from East of Suez: The Choice between Europe and the World?* (Basingstoke: Palgrave-Macmillan, 2002).

Dodd, Lindsey, and Andrew Knapp, '"How many Frenchmen did you kill?", British bombing policy towards France (1940–1945)', *FH*, 22:4 (2008), 469–92.

Dodge, Toby, *Inventing Iraq: The Failure of Nation Building and a History Denied* (New York: Columbia University Press, 2003).

Dougherty, James J., *The Politics of Wartime Aid: American Economic Assistance to France and French Northwest Africa, 1940–1946* (Westport, CT: Greenwood, 1978).

Drake, David, '*Les Temps Modernes* and the French War in Indochina', *Journal of European Studies*, 28: 109–10 (1998), 25–41.

Drayton, Richard, 'Where does the world historian write from? Objectivity, moral conscience and the past and present of imperialism', *Journal of Contemporary History*, 46:3 (2011), 671–85.

Drew, Allison, *We are no longer in France: Communists in Colonial Algeria* (Manchester University Press, 2014).

Duder, C. J., '"Men of the officer class": The participants in the 1919 soldier settlement scheme in Kenya', *African Affairs*, 92:366 (1993), 69–87.

Dudziak, Mary L., *Cold War Civil Rights: Race and the Image of American Democracy* (Princeton University Press, 2000).

Dueck, Jennifer, *The Claims of Culture at Empire's End: Syria and Lebanon under French Rule* (Oxford University Press, 2010).

Dunn, Peter M., *The First Vietnam War* (London: Hurst, 1985).

Durand, Yves, *La Captivité: Histoire des prisonniers de guerre français, 1939–45* (Paris: FNCPG, 1980).

Dwan, Renata, *An Uncommon Community: France and the European Defence Community, 1950–1954* (Oxford University Press, 1996).

Echenberg, Myron, *Black Death, White Medicine: Bubonic Plague and the Politics of Public Health in Colonial Senegal, 1914–1945* (Oxford: James Currey, 2002).

——'Les Migrations militaires en Afrique Occidentale Française, 1900–1945', *CJAS*, 14:3 (1980), 429–50.

——'Paying the blood tax: Military conscription in French West Africa, 1914–1929', *Revue Canadienne des Etudes Africaines*, 10:2 (1975), 171–92.

Edgerton, David, *Warfare State: Britain, 1920–1970* (Cambridge University Press, 2005).

—— *Britain's War Machine: Weapons, Resources and Experts in the Second World War* (London: Allen Lane 2011).

Eichenberg, Julia, 'The dark side of independence: Paramilitary violence in Ireland and Poland after the First World War', *Contemporary European History*, 19:3 (2010), 237–48.

Eichengreen, Barry, *Golden Fetters: The Gold Standard and the Great Depression, 1919–1939* (Oxford University Press, 1992).

Eldar, Dan, 'France in Syria: The abolition of Sharifian government, April–July 1920', *MES*, 29:3 (1993), 487–504.

Elkins, Caroline, *Imperial Reckoning: The Untold Story of Britain's Gulag in Kenya* (New York: Henry Holt, 2005).

——'The reassertion of the British Empire in Southeast Asia', *Journal of Interdisciplinary History*, 39:3 (2009), 361–85.

Elkins, W. F., 'A source of black nationalism in the Caribbean: The revolt of the B. W. I.R. at Taranto, Italy', *Science and Society* 33:2 (1970), 99–103.

Ellis, Stephen, 'The political elite of Imerina and the revolt of the Menalamba: The creation of a colonial myth in Madagascar, 1895–1898', *JAH*, 21 (1980), 219–34.

Epstein, Katherine C., 'Imperial airs: Leo Amery, air power and empire, 1873–1945', *JICH*, 38:4 (2010), 571–98.

Evans, Martin, *Algeria: France's Undeclared War* (Oxford University Press, 2012).

—— *The Memory of Resistance: French Opposition to the Algerian War, 1954–1962* (Oxford: Berg, 1997).

Falah, Ghazi, 'The 1948 Israeli–Palestinian War and its aftermath: The transformation and de-signification of Palestine's cultural landscape', *Annals of the Association of American Geographers*, 86:2 (1996), 256–85.

Farrell, Brian, ed., *Churchill and the Lion City: Shaping Modern Singapore* (Singapore: N.U.S., 2011).

Fathi Al Dib, Mohamed, *Abdel Nasser et la Révolution algérienne* (Paris: L'Harmattan, 1985).

Fedorowich Kent, '"Cocked hats and small, little garrisons": Britain, Canada and the fall of Hong Kong, 1941', *MAS*, 37:1 (2003), 111–58.

——'Doomed from the outset? Internment and civilian exchange in the Far East: The British failure over Hong Kong, 1941–45', *JICH*, 25:1 (1997), 113–40.

Feichtinger, Moritz, Stephan Malinowski, and Chase Richards, 'Transformative invasions: Western post-9/11 counterinsurgency and the lessons of colonialism', *Humanity*, 3:1 (2012), 35–63.

Fein, Helen, *Imperial Crime and Punishment: Massacre at Jallianwala Bagh and British Judgement, 1919–20* (Honolulu: University of Hawaii Press, 1986).

Fiore, Massimiliano, *Anglo-Italian Relations in the Middle East, 1922–1940* (Farnham: Ashgate, 2010).

Fisher, John, 'The Interdepartmental Committee on Eastern Unrest and British responses to Bolshevik and other intrigues against the Empire during the 1920s', *Journal of Asian History*, 34:1 (2000), 1–34.

——'Syria and Mesopotamia in British Middle Eastern policy in 1919', *MES*, 34:2 (1998), 129–70.

Fleischmann, Ellen L., 'Memory, gender and nationalism: Palestinian women leaders of the Mandate period', *History Workshop Journal*, 47 (1999), 141–58.

Flint, John, 'Managing nationalism: The Colonial Office and Nnamdi Azikiwe', *JICH*, 27:1 (1999), 143–58.

——'Planned decolonization and its failure in British Africa', *African Affairs*, 82:328 (1983), 389–411.

——'Scandal at the Bristol Hotel: Some thoughts on racial discrimination in Britain and West Africa and its relationship to the planning of decolonisation, 1939–1947', *JICH*, 12:1 (1983), 74–93.

Fogg, Shannon L., *The Politics of Everyday Life in Vichy France: Foreigners, Undesirables, and Strangers* (Cambridge University Press, 2009).

Fondation Charles de Gaulle, actes du colloque, *De Gaulle et le Rassemblement du peuple français (1947–1955)* (Paris: Armand Colin, 1998).

Fong, Leong Yee, 'The impact of the Cold War on the development of trade unionism in Malaya (1948–57)', *JSEAS*, 23:1 (1992), 60–73.

Footitt, Hilary, *War and Liberation in France: Living with the Liberators* (Basingstoke: Palgrave-Macmillan, 2004).

Foster, Anne L., *Projections of Power: The United States and Europe in Colonial Southeast Asia, 1919–1941* (Durham, NC: Duke University Press, 2010).

Frémeaux, Jacques, 'La Guerre d'Algérie et les relations internationales', *Relations Internationales*, 105:1 (2001), 59–76.

French, David, *The British Way in Counter-Insurgency, 1945–1967* (Oxford University Press, 2011).

——'Nasty not Nice: British Counter-Insurgency Doctrine and Practice, 1945–1967', *SWI*, 23:4/5 (2012), 744–61.

French, Patrick, *Liberty or Death: India's Journey to Independence and Division* (London: Harper Collins, 1997).

Funk, Arthur L., 'Negotiating the "deal with Darlan"', *Journal of Contemporary History*, 8:2 (1973), 81–117.

Furedi, Frank, 'Creating a breathing space: The political management of colonial emergencies', *JICH*, 21:2 (1993), 89–106.

Furniss, Graham, 'On engendering liberal values in the Nigerian colonial state: The idea behind the Gaskiya Corporation', *JICH*, 39:1 (2011), 95–119.

Gaitskell, Hugh, *The Diary of Hugh Gaitskell, 1945–1956*, ed. Philip M. Williams (London: Jonathan Cape, 1983).

Gallissot, René, *La République française et les indigènes: Algérie colonisée, Algérie algérienne (1870–1962)* (Paris: Éditions de l'Atelier, 2006).

Galpern, Steven G. *Money, Oil, and Empire in the Middle East: Sterling and Postwar Imperialism, 1944–1971* (Cambridge University Press, 2009).

de Gaulle, Charles, *Memoirs of Hope*, tr. Terence Kilmartin (London: Weidenfeld & Nicolson, 1971).

Gavin, Victor, 'Power through Europe? The case of the European Defence Community in France (1950–1954)', *FH*, 23:1 (2009), 69–87.

Gelvin, James L., *Divided Loyalties: Nationalism and Mass Politics in Syria at the Close of Empire* (Berkeley, CA: University of California Press, 1998).

Gershoni, Israel, and James P. Jankowski, *Redefining the Egyptian Nation, 1930–1945* (Cambridge University Press, 1995).

Gerwarth, Robert, 'The Central European counter-revolution: Paramilitary violence in Germany, Austria and Hungary after the Great War', *PP*, 200 (August 2008), 175–209.

——and John Horne, 'The Great War and paramilitarism in Europe, 1917–23', *Contemporary European History*, 19:3 (2010), 267–73.

Gildea, Robert, James Mark, and Anette Warring, eds, *Europe's 1968: Voices of Revolt* (Oxford University Press, 2013).

Gillingham, John, *Coal, Steel, and the Rebirth of Europe, 1945–1955: The Germans and French from Ruhr Conflict to Economic Community* (Cambridge University Press, 1991).

Gilmartin, David, 'Partition, Pakistan, and South Asian history: In search of a narrative', *Journal of Asian Studies*, 57:4 (1998), 1068–95.

Girault, René, 'La France en accusation à l'ONU, ou, Les Pouvoirs d'une organisation internationale', *Relations Internationales*, 76:3 (1993), 411–22.

Gleijeses, Piero, *Conflicting Missions: Havana, Washington, and Africa, 1959–1976* (Chapel Hill, NC: University of North Carolina Press, 2002).

Go, Julian, *Patterns of Empire: The British and American Empires, 1688 to the Present* (Cambridge University Press, 2011).

Gocking, Roger S., 'British justice and the native tribunals of the Southern Gold Coast Colony', *JAH*, 34:1 (1993), 93–113.

——'Indirect rule in the Gold Coast: Competition for office and the invention of tradition', *CJAS*, 28:3 (1994), 421–46.

Goldsworthy, David, 'Britain and the international critics of colonialism, 1951–1956', *Journal of Commonwealth and Comparative Politics*, 29:1 (1991), 1–24.

Golsan, Richard J., *Memory and Justice on Trial: The Papon Affair* (London: Routledge, 2000).

——*Memory, the Holocaust, and French Justice: The Bousquet and Touvier Affairs* (London: University Press of New England, 1996).

——'Memory's *bombes à retardement*: Maurice Papon, Crimes against Humanity and 17 October 1961', *Journal of European Studies*, 28 (1998), 158–72.

Gonjo, Y., *Banque colonial ou banque d'affaires: La Banque de l'Indochine sous la IIIème République* (Paris: CHEFF, 1998).

Goodman, Jane E., and Paul A. Silverstein eds, *Bourdieu in Algeria: Colonial Politics, Ethnographic Practices, Theoretical Developments* (Lincoln, NE: University of Nebraska Press, 2009).

Goscha, Christopher E, *Thailand and the Southeast Asian Networks of the Vietnamese Revolution (1885–1954)* (London: Curzon Press, 1999).

——'A "total war" of decolonization? Social mobilization and state-building in Communist Vietnam (1949–54)', *War & Society*, 31:2, (2012), 136–62.

——*Vietnam: Un état né de la guerre* (Paris: Armand Colin, 2011).

——and B. de Tréglodé, eds, *Le Viêt Nam depuis 1945: États, marges et constructions du passé* (Paris: Les Indes savantes, 2004).

Graham, B. D., *Choice and Democratic Order: The French Socialist Party, 1937–1950* (Cambridge University Press, 1994).

Grandin, Greg, *The Last Colonial Massacre: Latin America in the Cold War* (Chicago, IL: University of Chicago Press, 2004).

Grischow, Jeff D., 'Late colonial development in British West Africa: The Gonja development project in the northern territories of the Gold Coast, 1948–57', *CJAS*, 35:2 (2001), 282–312.

Grob-Fitzgibbon, Benjamin, *Imperial Endgame: Britain's Dirty Wars and the End of Empire* (Basingstoke: Palgrave-Macmillan, 2011).

Grundlingh, Albert, 'The King's Afrikaners? Enlistment and ethnic identity in the Union of South Africa's defence force during the Second World War, 1939–1945', *JAH*, 40:3 (1999), 351–65.

Guillemot, François, '"Be men!": Fighting and dying for the state of Vietnam (1951–54)', *War & Society*, 31:2 (2012), 184–210.

Hack, Karl, 'Between terror and talking, the place of "negotiation" in colonial conflict', *JICH*, 39:4 (2011), 539–49.

——'British intelligence and counter-insurgency in the era of decolonization: The example of Malaya', *INS*, 14:2 (1999), 124–55.

——*Defence and Decolonisation in Southeast Asia: Britain, Malaya and Singapore 1941–68* (Richmond: Curzon, 2000).

——'"Iron claws on Malaya": The historiography of the Malayan Emergency', *JSEAS*, 30:1 (1999), 99–125.

——'The Malayan Emergency as counter-insurgency paradigm', *Journal of Strategic Studies*, 32:3 (2009), 383–414.

——'Negotiating with the Malayan Communist Party, 1948–89', *JICH*, 39:4 (2011), 607–32.

Hall, Catherine, and Keith McClelland, eds, *Race, Nation and Empire: Making Histories, 1750 to the Present* (Manchester University Press, 2010).

——and Sonya O. Rose, eds, *At Home with the Empire: Metropolitan Culture and the Imperial World* (Cambridge University Press, 2006).

Hanagan, Michael, 'Charles Tilly and violent France', *FHS*, 33:2 (2010), 283–97.

Hanley, David, 'From co-operation to conflict: The French political system and the onset of the Cold War', *French Cultural Studies*, 8:1 (1997), 3–15.

Harbi, Mohammed, *Les Archives de la révolution algérienne* (Paris: Editions Jeune Afrique, 1981).

——*Le F. L. N.: Mirage et réalité des origines à la prise du pouvoir (1945–1962)* 2nd edn, (Paris: Editions Jeune Afrique, 1985.)

Harbi, Mohammed, and Gilbert Meynier, *Le F. L.N.: Documents et Histoire, 1954–1962* (Paris: Fayard, 2004).

Haroun, Ali, *La 7ᵉ Wilaya: La Guerre du FLN en France, 1954–1962* (Paris: Seuil, 1986).

Harper, Marjory, and Stephen Constantine, *Migration and Empire: OHBE Companion Volume* (Oxford University Press, 2010).

Harper, T. N., *The End of Empire and the Making of Malaya* (Cambridge University Press, 1999).

——'The politics of disease and disorder in post-war Malaya', *JSEAS*, 21:1 (1990), 88–113.

Harrison, Mark, *Medicine & Victory: British Military Medicine in the Second World War* (Oxford University Press, 2004).

——ed., *The Economics of World War II: Six Great Powers in Comparison* (Cambridge University Press, 1998).

Hartingh, Bertrand de, *Entre le peuple et la nation: La République Démocratique du Viêt Nam de 1953 à 1957* (Paris: École française d'Extrême-Orient, 2003).

Hartley, Anthony, *Gaullism: The Rise and Fall of a Political Movement* (London: Routledge, 1972).

Hasan, Mushiral ed., *India's Partition: Process, Strategy and Mobilization* (Oxford University Press, 1993).

Hashmi, Sohail H., '"Zero plus zero plus zero": Pakistan, the Baghdad Pact, and the Suez Crisis', *IHR*, 33:3 (2011), 525–44.

Hatzivassiliou, Evanthis, 'Blocking Enosis: Britain and the Cyprus question, March–December 1956', *JICH*, 19:2 (1991), 247–63.

—— *Britain and the International Status of Cyprus, 1955–59* (Minneapolis, MN: University of Minnesota Press, 1997).

Havinden, Michael, and David Meredith, *Colonialism and Development: Britain and its Tropical Colonies, 1850–1960* (London: Routledge, 1993).

Heikal, Mohamed H., *Cutting the Lion's Tail: Suez through Egyptian Eyes* (London: André Deutsch, 1986).

Heiss, Mary Ann, 'The evolution of the imperial idea and U.S. national identity', *DH*, 26:4 (2002), 511–40.

Hémery, Daniel, 'L'Indochine, les droits humains entre colonisateurs et colonisés: La Ligue des droits de l'homme', *Revue Française d'Histoire d'Outre-Mer*, 88:330–1 (2001), 223–39.

—— *Révolutionnaires vietnamiens et pouvoir colonial en Indochine* (Paris: Maspero, 1975).

Hitchcock, William I., *France Restored: Cold War Diplomacy and the Quest for Leadership in Europe, 1944–1954* (Chapel Hill, NC: University of North Carolina Press, 1998).

Hodeir, Catherine, *Stratégies d'empire: Le Grand Patronat colonial face à la décolonisation* (Paris: Belin, 2003).

Hodge, Joseph M., 'Colonial experts, developmental and environmental doctrines, and the legacies of late British colonialism', in Christina Folke Ax, Niels Brimnes, Niklas Thode Jensen, and Karen Oslund, eds, *Cultivating the Colonies: Colonial States and their Environmental Legacies* (Athens, OH: Ohio University Press, 2011), 300–25.

Hoffman, Katherine E., 'Purity and contamination: Language ideologies in French colonial native policy in Morocco', *Comparative Studies in Society and History*, 50:3 (2008), 724–52.

Hoisington Jr, William A., 'In search of a native elite: Casablanca and French urban policy, 1914–24', *The Maghreb Revew*, 12:5–6 (1987), 160–5.

—— *Lyautey and the French Conquest of Morocco* (Basingstoke: Macmillan, 1995).

Holbrook, Wendell P., 'British propaganda and the mobilization of the Gold Coast war effort, 1939–1945', *JAH*, 26:4 (1985), 347–61.

Holland, Robert, *Blue-Water Empire: The British in the Mediterranean since 1800* (London: Allen Lane, 2012).

—— *Britain and the Revolt in Cyprus, 1954–1959* (Oxford: Clarendon Press, 1998).

—— and Carl Bridge and H.V. Brasted, 'Counsels of despair or withdrawals with honour? Partitioning in Ireland, India, Palestine and Cyprus 1920–1960', *Round Table*, 86:342 (1997), 257–68.

——ed., *Emergencies and Disorder in the European Empires after 1945* (London: Frank Cass, 1994).

Hopkins, A. G., 'Capitalism, nationalism and the new American Empire', *JICH*, 35:1 (2007), 95–117.

——'Rethinking decolonization', *PP*, 200 (August 2008), 211–47.

——ed., *Global History: Interactions Between the Universal and the Local* (Basingstoke: Palgrave-Macmillan, 2006).

Horne, Alistair, *A Savage War of Peace: Algeria, 1954–1962* (New York: NYRB Classics, 2006)

House, Jim, 'L'Impossible Contrôle d'une ville coloniale: Casablanca, décembre 1952', *Genèses*, 1:86 (2012), 78–103.

House, Jim, and Neil MacMaster, *Paris 1961: Algerians, State Terror, and Memory* (Oxford University Press, 2006).

Howe, Stephen, *Anticolonialism in British Politics: The Left and the End of Empire, 1918–64* (Oxford University Press, 1993).

——'Internal decolonization? British policies since Thatcher as post-colonial trauma', *Twentieth Century British History*, 14:3 (2003), 286–304.

Howland, Douglas, and Luise White, eds, *The State of Sovereignty: Territories, Laws, Populations* (Bloomington, IN: Indiana University Press, 2009).

Hua, Lin, *Chiang Kai-Shek, de Gaulle contre Hô Chi Minh: Viet-nam, 1945–1946* (Paris: L'Harmattan, 1994).

Hughes, Matthew, 'The Banality of brutality: British armed forces and the repression of the Arab Revolt in Palestine, 1936–39', *EHR*, 124:507 (2009), 313–54.

——'Fighting for white rule in Africa: The Central African Federation, Katanga, and the Congo Crisis, 1958–1965', *IHR*, 25 (2003), 592–615.

——'From law and order to pacification: Britain's suppression of the Arab Revolt in Palestine, 1936–39', *Journal of Palestine Studies*, 39:2 (2010), 6–22.

Hull, Isobel, *Absolute Destruction: Military Culture and the Practices of War in Imperial Germany* (Ithaca, NY: Cornell University Press, 2005).

Hutchinson, Martha Crenshaw, *Revolutionary Terrorism: The FLN in Algeria, 154–1962* (Stanford, CA: Hoover Institution Press, 1978).

Hyam, Ronald, *Britain's Declining Empire: The Road to Decolonisation, 1918–1968* (Cambridge University Press, 2006).

——'The geopolitical origins of the Central African Federation: Britain, Rhodesia and South Africa, 1948–1953', *HJ* 30:1 (1987), 145–72.

——'The parting of the ways: Britain and South Africa's departure from the Commonwealth, 1951–1961', *JICH*, 26:2 (1998), 157–75.

——'The political consequences of Seretse Khama: Britain, the Bangwato and South Africa, 1948–1952', *HJ*, 24:4 (1986), 921–47.

Ighilahriz, Louisette, *Algérienne* (Paris: Fayard, 2001).

Imlay, Talbot, 'A success story? The foreign policies of France's Fourth Republic', *Contemporary European History*, 18:4 (2009), 499–519.

Ingram, Norman, 'Selbstmord or euthanasia? Who killed the Ligue des Droits de l'Homme?', *FH*, 22:3 (2008), 337–57.

Irvine, William D., *Between Justice and Politics: The Ligue des droits de l'homme, 1898–1945* (Stanford University Press, 2007).

Irwin, Ryan M., 'A wind of change? White redoubt and the postcolonial moment, 1960–1963', *DH*, 33:5 (2009), 897–925.

Jackson, Ashley, *The British Empire and the Second World War* (London: Hambledon, 2006).

Jackson, Julian, *The Fall of France: The Nazi Invasion of 1940* (Oxford University Press, 2003).

——France: The Dark Years, 1940–44 (Oxford University Press, 2001).

Jackson, Stephen F., 'China's Third World foreign policy: The case of Angola and Mozambique, 1961–93', *China Quarterly*, 143, (June, 1995), 387–422.

Jackson, Will, 'Bad blood, psychopathy and politics of transgression in Kenya Colony, 1939–1959', *JICH*, 39:1 (2011), 73–94.

Jalal, Ayesha, *The Sole Spokesman: Jinnah, the Muslim League and the Demand for Pakistan* (Cambridge University Press, 1994).

Jankowski, James, *Nasser's Egypt, Arab Nationalism, and the United Arab Republic* (Boulder, CO: Lynne Rienner, 2002).

Jansen, Sabine, ed., *Les Grands Discours parlémentaires de la Quatrième République de Pierre Mendès France à Charles de Gaulle* (Paris: Armand Colin, 2006).

Jaster, Robert Scott, *The Defence of White Power: South African Foreign Policy Under Pressure* (Basingstoke: Palgrave-Macmillan, 1988).

Jauffret, Jean-Charles, ed., *La Guerre d'Algérie par les documents*, ii: *Les Portes de la guerre: Des occasions manquées à l'insurrection, 1946–1954* (Vincennes: S.H.AT., 1998).

——Des hommes et des femmes en guerre d'Algérie (Paris: Autrement, 2003).

——'The origins of the Algerian War: The reaction of France and its army to the emergencies of 8 May 1945 and 1 November 1954', *JICH*, 21:3 (1993), 17–29.

Jeffery, Keith, *The British Army and the Crisis of Empire, 1918–1922* (Manchester University Press, 1984).

——Field Marshal Sir Henry Wilson: A Political Soldier (Oxford University Press, 2008).

——MI6: The History of the Secret Intelligence Service 1909–1949 (London: Bloomsbury, 2010).

Jefferys, Kevin, 'British politics and social policy during the Second World War', *HJ* 30:1 (1987), 123–44.

Jeffries, Charles, *Whitehall and the Colonial Service: An Administrative Memoir, 1939–1956* (London: Athlone Press, 1972).

Jenkinson, Jacqueline, *Black 1919: Riots, Racism and Resistance in Imperial Britain* (Liverpool University Press, 2008).

Jennings, Eric T., 'Conservative confluences, "nativist" synergy: Reinscribing Vichy's National Revolution in Indochina, 1940–1945', *FHS*, 27:4 (2004), 601–35.

—— *Imperial Heights: Dalat and the Making and Undoing of French Indochina* (Berkeley, CA: University of California Press, 2011).

—— *Vichy in the Tropics: Pétain's national Revolution in Madagascar, Guadeloupe, and Indochina, 1940–1944* (Stanford University Press, 2001).

Jennings, Jeremy, *Revolution and the Republic: A History of Political Thought in France since the Eighteenth Century* (Oxford University Press, 2011).

Jian, Chen, 'China and the First Indo-China War, 1950–54', *China Quarterly*, 133 (March, 1993), 85–110.

—— Johnson, Edward, 'Britain and the Cyprus Problem at the United Nations, 1954–58', *JICH*, 28:3 (2000), 113–30.

—— *Mao's China and the Cold War* (Chapel Hill, NC: University of North Carolina Press, 2001).

Johnson, Howard, 'The anti-Chinese riots of 1918 in Jamaica', *Immigrants and Minorities*, 2:1 (1983), 50–63.

Joly, Danièle, *The French Communist Party and the Algerian War* (Basingstoke: Palgrave-Macmillan, 1991).

Jones, Clive, '"Among ministers, mavericks and mandarins": Britain, covert action and the Yemen civil war, 1962–64', *MES*, 40:1 (2004), 99–126.

Jones, Matthew, *Conflict and Confrontation in South East Asia, 1961–1965: Britain, the United States, Indonesia and the Creation of Malaysia* (Cambridge University Press, 2001).

—— 'A decision delayed: Britain's withdrawal from South East Asia reconsidered, 1961–68', *EHR*, 67:472 (2002), 569–95.

Jordi, Jean-Jacques, and Guy Pervillé, eds, *Alger, 1940–1962: Une ville en guerres* (Paris: Autrement, 1999).

Kadish, Alon, and Avraham Sela, 'Myths and historiography of the 1948 Palestine War revisited: The case of Lydda', *Middle East Journal*, 59:4 (2005), 617–34.

Kahler, Miles, *Decolonization in Britain and France: The Domestic Consequences of International Relations* (Princeton University Press, 1984).

Kalman, Samuel, '*Le Combat par tous les moyens*: Colonial violence and the extreme right in 1930s Oran', *FHS*, 34:1 (2011), 125–53.

Kalyvas, Stathis, *The Logic of Violence in Civil War* (Cambridge University Press, 2006).

Kanogo, Tabitha, *Squatters and the Roots of Mau Mau* (London: James Currey, 1987).

Kedward, Rod, *La Vie en bleu: France and the French since 1900* (London: Allen Lane, 2005).

Keese, Alexander, 'A culture of panic: "Communist" scapegoats and decolonization in French West Africa and French Polynesia (1945–1957)', *French Colonial History*, 9 (2008), 131–45.

—— 'First lessons in neo-colonialism: The personalisation of relations between African politicians and French officials in sub-Saharan Africa, 1956–66', *JICH*, 35:4 (2007), 593–613.

—— *Living with Ambiguity: Integrating an African Elite in French and Portuguese Africa, 1930–61* (Stuttgart: Franz Steiner, 2007).

Keese, Alexander, ' "Quelques satisfactions d'amour-propre": African elite integration, the *loi-cadre*, and involuntary decolonisation of French tropical Africa', *Itinerario* 26 (2003), 33–57.

Keiger, J. F. V., *Raymond Poincaré* (Cambridge University Press, 1997).

Kelemen, Paul, 'Modernising colonialism: The British Labour Movement and Africa', *JICH*, 34:2 (2006), 223–44.

——'The British Labour Party and the economics of decolonization: The debate over Kenya', *Journal of Colonialism and Colonial History* 8:1 (2008), 1–33.

Kelly, George Armstrong, *Lost Soldiers: The French Army and Empire in Crisis, 1947–1962* (Cambridge, MA: MIT Press, 1965).

Kennedy, Dane, 'Essay and reflection: On the American Empire from a British imperial perspective', *IHR*, 29:1 (2007), 83–108.

——*Islands of White: Settler Society and Culture in Kenya and Southern Rhodesia, 1890–1939* (Durham, NC: Duke University Press, 1987).

Kennedy, Greg, ed., *Imperial Defence: The Old World Order, 1856–1956* (London: Routledge, 2007).

Kent, John, *America, the UN and Decolonisation: Cold War Conflict in the Congo* (London: Routledge, 2011).

——*British Imperial Strategy and the Origins of the Cold War, 1944–49* (Leicester University Press, 1993).

——*The Internationalization of Colonialism: Britain, France and Black Africa, 1939–1956* (Oxford: Clarendon Press, 1992).

Kent, Susan Kingsley, *Aftershocks: Politics and Trauma in Britain, 1918–1931* (Basingstoke: Palgrave-Macmillan, 2009).

Kershaw, Greet, *Mau Mau from Below* (Oxford: James Currey, 1997).

Khan, Yasmin, *The Great Partition: The Making of India and Pakistan* (New Haven, CT: Yale University Press, 2007).

——'Sex in an imperial war-zone: Transnational encounters in Second World War India', *History Workshop Journal*, 73:1 (2012), 240–58.

Khánh, Huynh Kim, *Vietnamese Communism, 1925–1945* (Ithaca, NY: Cornell University Press, 1982).

Khoury, Gérard D., *Une tutelle coloniale: Le Mandat français en Syrie et au Liban* (Paris: Belin, 2006).

Khoury, Philip S., 'Factionalism among Syrian nationalists during the French Mandate', *IJMES*, 13 (1981), 441–69.

——*Syria and the French Mandate: The Politics of Arab Nationalism, 1920–1945* (London: I. B. Taurus, 1987).

Killingray, David, 'Soldiers, ex-servicemen, and politics in the Gold Coast, 1939–50', *Journal of Modern African Studies*, 21:3 (1983), 523–34.

——and David Omissi, eds, *Guardians of Empire: The Armed Forces of the Colonial Powers, c. 1700–1964* (Manchester University Press, 1999).

Kim, Seung-Ryeol, 'France's agony between *vocation européenne et mondiale*: The *Union française* as an obstacle in the French policy of supranational European integration', *Journal of European Integration History*, 8:1 (2002), 61–84.

Kirk, Neville, *Labour and the Politics of Empire: Britain and Australia, 1900 to the Present* (Manchester University Press, 2011).

Klieman, S., 'The divisiveness of Palestine: Foreign Office vs. Colonial Office on the issue of partition, 1937', *HJ*, 22 (1979), 423–42.

Klose, Fabian, 'The colonial testing ground: The International Committee of the Red Cross and the violent end of empire', *Humanity*, 2:1 (2011), 107–26.

Knapp, Andrew, ed., *The Uncertain Foundation: France at the Liberation, 1944–1947* (Basingstoke: Palgrave-Macmillan, 2007).

Kolinsky, Martin, *Law, Order and Riots in Mandatory Palestine, 1928–1935* (Basingstoke: Macmillan, 1994).

Kramer, Paul A., *The Blood of Government: Race, Empire, the United States and the Philippines* (Chapel Hill, NC: University of North Carolina Press, 2006).

Krozewski, Gerald, *Money and the End of Empire: British Economic Policy and the Colonies, 1947–1958* (Basingstoke: Palgrave, 2001).

Kuby, Emma, 'A war of words over an image of war: The Fox-Movietone scandal and the portrayal of French violence in Algeria, 1955–1956', *FPCS*, 30:1 (2012), 46–67.

Kuisel, Richard, *Seducing the French: The Dilemma of Americanization* (Berkeley, CA: University of California Press, 1993).

Kumar, Radha, 'The troubled history of partition', *Foreign Affairs*, 76:1 (1997), 23–34.

Kuzmarov, Jeremy, 'Modernizing repression: Police training, political violence, and nation-building in the "American century"', *DH*, 33:2 (2009), 191–221.

LaFeber, Walter, 'Roosevelt, Churchill, and Indochina, 1942–45', *AHR*, 80 (1975), 1277–95.

Laffey, John F., 'Municipal imperialism in decline: The Lyon chamber of commerce, 1925–1938', *FHS*, 9:3–4 (1975), 329–53.

Latham, Michael E., *Modernization as Ideology: American Social Science and 'Nation Building' in the Kennedy Era* (Chapel Hill, NC: University of North Carolina Press, 2000).

Larcher-Goscha, Agathe, 'Ambushed by history: Paul Mus and colonial France's "forced re-Entry" into Vietnam (1945–1954)', *Journal of Vietnamese Studies*, 4:1 (2009), 206–39.

Lawler, Nancy Ellen, *Soldiers of Misfortune: Ivoirien Tirailleurs of World War II* (Athens, OH: Ohio University Press, 1992).

Lawrence, Benjamin N., Emily Lynn Osborn, and Richard L. Roberts, eds, *Intermediaries, Interpreters, and Clerks: African Employees in the Making of Colonial Africa* (Madison, WI: University of Wisconsin Press, 2006).

Lawrence, Jon, 'Forging a peaceable kingdom: War, violence and the fear of brutalization in post-First World War Britain', *JMH*, 75:3 (2003), 557–89.

Lawrence, Mark Atwood, and Fredrik Logevall, eds, *The First Vietnam War: Colonial Conflict and Cold War Crisis* (Cambridge, MA: Harvard University Press, 2007).

Lazreg, Marnia, *The Eloquence of Silence: Algerian Women in Question* (London: Routledge, 1994).

—— *Torture and the Twilight of Empire: From Algiers to Baghdad* (Princeton University Press, 2008).

L'Estoile, Benoît de, Federico Neiburg, and Lygia Sigaud, eds, *Empires, Nations, and Natives: Anthropology and State-Making* (Durham, NC: Duke University Press, 2005).

Le Sueur, James D., *Uncivil War: Intellectuals and Identity Politics During the Decolonization of Algeria* (Philadelphia: University of Pennsylvania Press, 2001).

Lee, Christopher J., ed., *Making a World After Empire: The Bandung Moment and its Political Afterlives* (Athens, OH: Ohio University Press, 2010).

Lee, J. M., '"Forward thinking" and war: The Colonial Office during the 1940s', *JICH* 6:1 (1977), 64–78.

——and M. Petter, *The Colonial Office: War and Development Policy* (London: Ashgate, 1982).

Lees, Lynn Hollen, 'Being British in Malaya, 1890–1940', *Journal of British Studies*, 48:1 (2009), 76–101.

Leffler, Melvyn P., and Odd Arne Westad, eds, *Cambridge History of the Cold War*, 3 vols (Cambridge University Press, 2010).

Lerner, Henri, *Catroux* (Paris: Albin Michel, 1990).

Lessard, Micheline, '"Cet ignoble trafic": The kidnapping and sale of Vietnamese women and children in French colonial Indochina, 1873–1935', *French Colonial History*, 10 (2009), 1–34.

Letamendia, Pierre, *Le Mouvement Républicain Populaire: Histoire d'un grand parti français* (Paris: Beauchesne, 1995).

Levenberg, Haim, *Military Preparations of the Arab Community in Palestine, 1945–1948* (London: Frank Cass, 1993).

Lévi-Valensi, Jacqueline, ed., *Camus at Combat: Writings, 1944–1947* (Princeton University Press, 2006).

Levine, Philippa, 'Battle colors: Race, sex, and colonial soldiery in World War I', *Journal of Women's History* 9:4 (1998), 104–30.

——and Susan Grayzel eds, *Gender, Labour, War and Empire: Essays on Modern Britain* (Basingstoke: Palgrave-Macmillan, 2008).

Levisse-Touzé, Christine, 'La Préparation économique, industrielle et militaire de l'Afrique du Nord à la veille de la guerre', *Revue d'Histoire de la Deuxième Guerre Mondiale*, 142:1 (1986), 1–18.

Lewis, James I., 'French politics and the Algerian Statute of 1947', *Maghreb Review*, 17:1 (1992), 147–72.

——'The MRP and the genesis of the French Union, 1944–1948', *FH*, 12:2 (1998), 276–314.

Lewis, Joanna, *Empire State-Building: War and Welfare in Kenya, 1925–52* (Oxford: James Currey, 2000).

——'"Tropical East Ends" and the Second World War: Some contradictions in Colonial Office welfare initiatives', *JICH* 28:2 (2000), 42–66.

Lewis, Mary Dewhurst, 'Geographies of power: The Tunisian civic order, jurisdictional politics, and imperial rivalry in the Mediterranean, 1881–1935', *JMH*, 80:4 (2008), 791–830.

Liauzu, Claude, *Histoire de l'anticolonialisme en France: Du XVIe siècle à nos jours* (Paris: Armand Colin, 2007).

Little, Douglas, 'Cold War and colonialism in Africa: The United States, France, and the Madagascar Revolt of 1947', *Pacific Historical Review*, 59:4 (1990), 527–52.

Liu, Xiaoyuan, 'China and the issue of postwar Indochina in the Second World War', *MAS*, 33:2 (1999), 445–82.

Lochman, Zachary, *Comrades and Enemies: Arab and Jewish Workers in Palestine, 1906–1948* (Berkeley, CA: University of California Press, 1996).

Lockhart, Greg, *Nation in Arms: The Origins of the People's Army of Vietnam* (London: Allen and Unwin, 1989).

Logevall, Fredrik, *Choosing War: The Lost Chance for Peace and the Escalation of War in Vietnam* (Berkeley, CA: University of California Press, 1999).

——*Embers of War: The Fall of an Empire and the Making of America's Vietnam* (New York: Random House, 2012).

Lonsdale John, 'KAU's Cultures: Imaginations of community and constructions of leadership in Kenya after the Second World War', *Journal of African Cultural Studies*, 13:1 (2000), 107–24.

——'Mau Maus of the mind: Making Mau Mau and remaking Kenya', *JAH*, 31:3 (1990), 393–421.

Lorcin, Patricia M. E., *Historicizing Colonial Nostalgia: European Women's Narratives of Algeria and Kenya, 1900–Present* (New York: Palgrave-Macmillan, 2012).

Louis, Wm. Roger, *The British Empire in the Middle East: Arab Nationalism, the United States, and Postwar Imperialism, 1945–1951* (Oxford University Press, 1984).

——'The dissolution of the British Empire in the era of Vietnam', *AHR*, 107:1 (2002), 1–25.

——*Imperialism at Bay: The United States and the Decolonization of the British Empire* (Oxford: Clarendon Press, 1977).

——and Roger Owen, eds, *Suez 1956: The Crisis and its Consequences* (Oxford: Clarendon Press, 1989).

——and Ronald Robinson, 'The imperialism of decolonization', *JICH*, 22:3 (1994), 462–511.

——and Robert W. Stookey eds, *The End of the Palestine Mandate* (London: I. B. Tauris, 1986).

Lucas, W. Scott, *Divided We Stand: Britain, the US and the Suez Crisis* (London: Hodder & Soughton, 1991).

Lundsten, Mary Ellen, 'Wall politics: Zionist and Palestinian strategies in Jerusalem, 1928', *Journal of Palestine Studies*, 8:1 (1978), 3–24.

Lunn, Joe, *Memoirs of the Maelstrom: A Senegalese Oral History of the First World War* (Portsmouth, NH: Heinemann, 1999).

Luong, Hy Van, 'Agrarian unrest from an anthropological perspective: The case of Vietnam', *Comparative Politics*, 17:2 (1985), 153–74.

Lynn, Martin, 'The Nigerian self-government crisis of 1953 and the Colonial Office', *JICH*, 34:2 (2006), 245–61.

——ed., *The British Empire in the 1950s: Retreat or Revival?* (Basingstoke: Palgrave-Macmillan, 2006).

McCarthy, Helen, *The British People and the League of Nations: Democracy, Citizenship and Internationalism, c.1918–1945* (Manchester University Press, 2011).

McCoy, Alfred W., Josep M. Fradera, and Stephen Jacobson, eds, *Endless Empire: Spain's Retreat, Europe's Eclipse, America's Decline*, (Madison, WI: University of Wisconsin Press, 2012).

MacDonald, Sharon, Pat Holden, and Shirley Ardener, eds, *Images of Women in Peace and War: Cross-Cultural and Historical Perspectives* (London: Macmillan, 1987).

McIntyre, W. David, 'The strange death of Dominion status', *JICH*, 27:2 (1999), 193–212.

McKenzie, Brian Angus, *Remaking France: Americanization, Public Diplomacy, and the Marshall Plan* (New York: Berghahn, 2008).

Mackenzie, Hector, 'Transatlantic generosity: Canada's "billion dollar gift" to the United Kingdom in the Second World War', *IHR*, 34:2 (2012), 293–314.

McKercher, B. J .C., *Transition of Power: Britain's Loss of Global Pre-eminence to the United States, 1930–1945* (Cambridge University Press, 1999).

MacLeod, Jenny, ed., *Defeat and Memory: Cultural Histories of Military Defeat in the Modern Era* (Basingstoke: Palgrave-Macmillan, 2008).

McLeod, Mark W., *The Vietnamese Response to French Intervention, 1862–74* (New York: Praeger, 1991).

Macmahon, Robert J., *Colonialism and Cold War: The United States and the Struggle for Indonesian Independence* (Ithaca, NY: Cornell University Press, 1981).

MacMaster, Neil, *Burning the Veil: The Algerian War and the 'Emancipation' of Algerian Women, 1954–62* (Manchester University Press, 2009).

—— *Colonial Migrants and Racism: Algerians in France, 1900–62* (Basingstoke: Macmillan, 1997.

Magee, Gary B., and Andrew S. Thompson, *Empire and Globalisation: Networks of People, Goods and Capital in the British World, c.1850–1914* (Cambridge University Press, 2010).

Maguire, Gloria, *Anglo-American Relations with the Free French* (Basingstoke: Macmillan, 1995).

Mahone, Sloan, 'The psychology of rebellion: Colonial medical responses to dissent in British East Africa', *JAH*, 47:2 (2006), 241–58.

Maier, Charles S., 'The Marshall Plan and the division of Europe', *Journal of Cold War Studies* 7:1 (2005), 168–74.

Maiolo, Joe, *Cry Havoc: The Arms Race and the Second World War, 1931–1941* (London: John Murray, 2010).

Malley, Robert, *The Call from Algeria: Third Worldism, Revolution, and the Turn to Islam* (Berkeley, CA: University of California Press, 1996).

Mann, Gregory, 'What was the *indigénat?* The "empire of law" in French West Africa', *JAH*, 50 (2009), 331–53.

—— and Baz Lecocq, 'Between empire, *umma*, and the Muslim Third World: The French Union and African pilgrims to Mecca, 1946–1958', *Comparative Studies of South Asia, Africa and the Middle East*, 27 (2007), 167–81.

Manela, Erez, 'The Wilsonian moment and the rise of anticolonial nationalism: The case of Egypt', *DS*, 12:4 (2001), 99–122.

—— *The Wilsonian Moment: Self-Determination and the International Origins of Anti-colonial Nationalism* (Oxford University Press, 2007).

Marill, Jean-Marc, 'L'Héritage indochinois: Adaptation de l'armée française en Algérie (1954–56)', *Revue Historique des Armées* 187:2 (1992), 26–32.

Mark, Chi-Kwan, 'Lack of means or loss of will? The United Kingdom and the decolonization of Hong Kong, 1957–1967', *IHR*, 31:1 (2009), 45–71.

Markides, Diana, 'Britain's "New Look" Policy for Cyprus and the Makarios-Harding Talks, January 1955–March 1956', *JICH* 23:3 (1995), 479–502.

Marr, David G., *Vietnamese Anticolonialism, 1885–1925* (Berkeley, CA: University of California Press, 1971).

Marseille, Jacques, *Empire colonial et capitalisme français: Histoire d'un divorce* (Paris: Albin Michel, 1984).

—— 'L'Investissement public en Algérie après la deuxième guerre mondiale', *Revue Française d'Histoire d'Outre-Mer*, 70:260 (1983), 179–97.

Masson, Antoine, and Kevin O'Connor, eds, *Representations of Justice* (Brussels: Peter Lang, 2007).

Maul, Daniel, '"Help Them Move the ILO Way": The International Labor Organization and the modernization discourse in the era of decolonization and the Cold War', *DH*, 33:3 (2009), 387–404.

Mawby, Spencer, 'Britain's last imperial frontier: The Aden Protectorates, 1952–59', *JICH*, 29:2 (2001), 75–100.

—— *Containing Germany: Britain and the Arming of the Federal Republic* (Basingstoke: Macmillan, 1999).

Mazower, Mark, 'An international civilization? Empire, internationalism and the crisis of the mid-twentieth century', *International Affairs*, 82 (2006), 533–66.

—— *No Enchanted Palace: The End of Empire and the Ideological Origins of the United Nations* (Princeton University Press, 2009).

Metzer, Jacob, *The Divided Economy of Mandatory Palestine* (Cambridge University Press, 1998).

Meynier, Gilbert, *Histoire Intérieure du F.L.N., 1954–1962* (Paris: Fayard, 2002).

Michel, Marc, *L'Appel à l'Afrique: Contributions et réactions à l'effort de guerre en AOF (1914–1919)* (Paris: Publications de la Sorbonne, 1982).

Miller, Edward, 'Vision, power and agency: The ascent of Ngô Dình Diêm, 1945–1954', *JSEAS* 35:3 (2004), 433–58.

Miller, Rory, ed., *Britain, Palestine and Empire: The Mandate Years* (Farnham: Ashgate, 2010).

Milner, Anthony, *The Invention of Colonial Malaya: Contesting Nationalism and the Expansion of the Public Sphere* (Cambridge University Press, 1995).

Moghadam, Valentine M., ed., *Gender and National Identity: Women and Politics in Muslim Societies* (London: Zed Books, 1994).

Moitt, Bernard, 'Slavery, flight and redemption in Senegal, 1819–1905', *Slavery and Abolition*, 14:2 (1993), 70–86.

Monroe, Elizabeth, *Britain's Moment in the Middle East, 1914–1956* (London: Cox and Wyman, 1963).

Mosca, Liliana, 'À l'origine de la répression de 1947 à Madagascar: Raisons nationales ou logique internationale?', *Africa: Rivista trimestrale di studi e documentazione dell'Istituto italiano per l'Africa e l'Oriente*, 62:2 (2007), 257–78.

Motadel, David, 'Islam and the European Empires', *HJ*, 55:3 (2012), 831–56.

Mouré, Kenneth, *The Gold Standard Illusion: France, the Bank of France, and the International Gold Standard, 1914–1939* (Oxford University Press, 2002).

——and Martin S. Alexander, eds, *Crisis and Renewal in France, 1918–1962* (Oxford: Berghahn, 2002).

Moyn, Samuel, *The Last Utopia: Human Rights in History* (Cambridge, MA: Harvard University Press, 2010).

Mukerjee, Madhusree, *Churchill's Secret War: The British Empire and the Ravaging of India during World War II* (New York: Basic Books, 2010).

——'Transcending identity: Gandhi, nonviolence, and the pursuit of a "different" freedom in modern India', *AHR*, 115:2 (2010), 453–73.

Munholland, Kim, *Rock of Contention: Free French and Americans at War in New Caledonia, 1940–45* (Oxford: Berghahn, 2004).

Murphy, Philip, *Alan Lennox-Boyd: A Biography* (London: I.B. Tauris, 1999).

——'Creating a Commonwealth intelligence culture: The view From Central Africa, 1945–1965', *INS*, 17:3 (2002), 131–62.

——'Intelligence and decolonization: The life and death of the Federal Intelligence and Security Bureau, 1954–63', *JICH*, 29:2 (2001), 101–30.

——' "An intricate and distasteful subject": British planning for the use of force against the European settlers of Central Africa, 1952–1965', *EHR* CXXI:492 (2006), 746–77.

——*Party Politics and Decolonization: The Conservative Party and British Colonial Policy in Tropical Africa, 1951–1964* (Oxford: Clarendon Press, 1995).

Nair, Rahul, 'The construction of a "population problem" in colonial India, 1919–1947', *JICH*, 39:2 (2011), 227–47.

Nardocchio-Jones, Gavin, 'From Mau Mau to Middlesex? The fate of Europeans in independent Kenya', *Comparative Studies of South Asia, Africa and the Middle East*, 26:3 (2006), 491–505.

Neilson, Keith, *Britain, Soviet Russia and the Collapse of the Versailles Order, 1919–1939* (Cambridge University Press, 2006).

——and Greg Kennedy, eds, *The British Way in Warfare: Power and the International System, 1856–1956* (Farnham: Ashgate, 2010).

Newton, Scott, 'J. M. Keynes and the postwar international economic order', *History Compass*, 4:2 (2006), 308–13.

——'A "visionary hope" frustrated: J. M. Keynes and the origins of the international monetary order', *DS*, 11:1 (2000): 189–210.

Nhema, Alfred, and Paul Tiyambe Zeleza, eds, *The Roots of African Conflicts: The Causes and Costs* (Oxford: James Currey, 2008).

Nicholas, Siân, '"Brushing up your empire": Dominion and colonial propaganda on the BBC's Home Service, 1939–1945', *JICH*, 31:2 (2003), 207–30.

Nitz, Kiyoko Kurusu, 'Japanese military policy towards French Indochina during the Second World War: The road to the *Meigo Sakusen* (9 March 1945)', *JSEAS*, 14:2 (1983), 328–53.

Nixon, Rob, *Slow Violence and the Environmentalism of the Poor* (Cambridge, MA: Harvard University Press, 2011).

Nord, Philip, *France's New Deal: From the Thirties to the Postwar Era* (Princeton University Press, 2010).

Normand, Roger, and Sarah Zaidi, *Human Rights at the UN: The Political History of Universal Justice* (Bloomington, IN: Indiana University Press, 2008).

Nugent, Paul, *Smugglers, Secessionists, and Loyal Citizens on the Togo-Ghana Frontier* (Athens, OH: Ohio University Press, 2002).

Nwaubani, Ebere, *The United States and Decolonization in West Africa, 1950–1960* (Rochester, NY: University of Rochester Press, 2001).

O'Brien, Phillips, 'The Titan refreshed: Imperial overstretch and the British Navy before the First World War', *PP*, 172:1 (2001), 146–69.

O'Halpin, Eunan, '"A poor thing but our own": The Joint Intelligence Committee and Ireland, 1965–72', *INS*, 23:5 (2008): 658–80.

Odhiambo, E. S. Atieno, and John Lonsdale, eds, *Mau Mau and Nationhood* (Oxford: James Currey 2003).

Osborne, Milton E., *The French Presence in Cochinchina and Cambodia: Rule and Response (1859–1905)* (Ithaca NY: Cornell University Press, 1969).

Ovendale, Ritchie, *Britain, the United States, and the End of the Palestine Mandate, 1942–1948* (Woodbridge: Boydell Press, 1989).

——*Britain, the United States and the Transfer of Power in the Middle East, 1945–1962* (Leicester University Press, 1996).

Owen, Nicholas, *The British Left and India: Metropolitan Anti-Imperialism, 1885–1947* (Oxford: Oxford Historical Monographs, 2007).

——'The Cripps mission of 1942: A reinterpretation', *JICH*, 30:1 (2002), 61–98.

——'"Facts are sacred": The Manchester Guardian and colonial violence, 1930–1932', *JMH*, 84:3 (2012), 643–78.

Paillard, Yves G., 'Domination coloniale et récupération des traditions autochtones: Le Cas de Madagascar de 1896 à 1914', *Revue d'Histoire Moderne et Contemporaine*, 38:1 (1991), 73–104.

Panayi, Panikos, and Pippa Virdee, eds, *Refugees and the End of Empire: Imperial Collapse and Forced Migration in the Twentieth Century* (Basingstoke: Palgrave-Macmillan, 2011).

Pandey, B. N., ed., *The Indian Nationalist Movement, 1885–1947: Select Documents* (Basingstoke: Macmillan, 1979).

Pandey, Gyanendra, *Remembering Partition: Violence, Nationalism and History in India* (Cambridge University Press, 2001).

Pappé, Ilan, *The Ethnic Cleansing of Palestine* (London: Oneworld, 2006).

Paris, Timothy J., *Britain, the Hashemites and Arab Rule 1920–1925: The Sherifian Solution* (London: Frank Cass, 2003).

Parker, Jason, *Brother's Keeper: The United States, Race, and Empire in the British Caribbean, 1937–1962* (New York: Oxford University Press, 2008).

Parsons, Timothy H., *The Rule of Empires: Those Who Built Them, Those Who Endured Them, and Why They Always Fall* (Oxford University Press, 2010).

Paxton, Robert O., *Vichy France: Old Guard and New Order, 1940–1944* (London: Barrie & Jenkins, 1972).

Pearce, Robert D., 'The Colonial Office and planned decolonization in Africa', *African Affairs*, 83:330 (1984), 77–93.

—— *The Turning Point in Africa: British Colonial Policy, 1938–1948* (London: Routledge, 1982).

Peden, George C., *Arms, Economics and British Strategy: From Dreadnoughts to Hydrogen Bombs* (Cambridge University Press, 2007).

——'The burden of imperial defence and the continental commitment reconsidered', *HJ*, 27:2 (1984), 405–23.

Pedersen, Susan, 'Back to the League of Nations', *AHR*, 112:4 (2007), 1099–117.

——'Getting out of Iraq—in 1932: The League of Nations and the road to normative statehood', *AHR*, 115:4 (2010), 975–1000.

——'The meaning of the mandates system: An argument', *Geschichte und Gesellschaft* 32 (2006), 560–82.

Pennell, C. R., *A Country with a Government and a Flag: The Rif War in Morocco* (Wisbech: Middle East and North African Studies Press, 1986).

——'Women and resistance to colonialism in Morocco: The Rif 1916–1926', *JAH*, 28 (1987), 107–18.

Pestre, Dominique, 'Scientists in time of war: World War II, the Cold War, and science in the United States and France', *FPCS*, 24:1 (2006), 27–39.

Peterson, Derek R., 'The intellectual lives of Mau Mau detainees', *JAH*, 49:1 (2008), 73–91.

Peyrefitte, Alain, *C'était de Gaulle*, ii: *La France redevient la France* (Paris: Fayard, 1994).

Peyroulou, Jean-Pierre, *Guelma, 1945: Une subversion française dans l'Algérie coloniale* (Paris: Editions la Découverte, 2009).

Phimister, Ian, and Brian Raftopoulos, '"Kana sora ratswa ngaritswe": African nationalists and black workers—the 1948 general strike in colonial Zimbabwe', *Journal of Historical Sociology*, 13:3 (2000), 289–324.

Pilleul, Gilbert, ed., *Le Général de Gaulle et l'Indochine, 1940–1946* (Paris: Plon, 1982).

Pitts, Jennifer, *A Turn to Empire: The Rise of Imperial Liberalism in Britain and France* (Princeton University Press, 2005).

Planche, Jean-Louis, *Sétif 1945: Histoire d'un massacre annoncé* (Paris: Perrin, 2006).

Plummer, Brenda Gayle, *In Search of Power: African Americans in the era of Decolonization, 1956–1974* (Cambridge University Press, 2013).

Polsgrove, Carol, *Ending British Rule in Africa: Writers in a Common Cause* (Manchester University Press 2009).

Popplewell, Richard, '"Lacking Intelligence": Some reflections on recent approaches to British counter-insurgency, 1900–1960', *INS*, 10:2 (1995), 336–52.

Porath, Yoshua, *The Palestinian Arab National Movement, 1929–1939: From Riots to Rebellion* (London: Frank Cass, 1977).

Posel, Deborah, *The Making of Apartheid, 1948–1961: Conflict and Compromise* (Oxford: Clarendon Press, 1991).

Potter, Simon J., 'Empire, cultures and identities in nineteenth and twentieth century Britain', *History Compass*, 5 (2007), 51–71.

Provence, Michael, *The Great Syrian Revolt and the Rise of Arab Nationalism* (Austin, TX: University of Texas Press, 2005).

Rahman, Mahbubar, and Willem van Schendel, '"I am not a refugee": Rethinking partition migration', *MAS*, 37:3 (2003), 551–84.

Ramakrishna, Kumar, 'Content, credibility and context: Propaganda, government surrender policy and the Malayan Communist mass surrender of 1958', *INS*, 14:4 (1999), 242–66.

——*Emergency Propaganda: The Winning of Malayan Hearts and Minds, 1948–1958* (Richmond: Curzon, 2002).

——'"Transmogrifying" Malaya: The impact of Sir Gerald Templer (1952–54)', *JSEAS*, 32:1 (2001), 79–92.

Ranger, Terence, 'Nationalist historiography, patriotic history and the history of the nation: The struggle over the past in Zimbabwe', *Journal of Southern African Studies*, 30:2 (2004), 215–34.

Rathbone, Richard, 'Kwame Nkrumah and the chiefs: The fate of "natural rulers" under nationalist governments', *Transactions of the Royal Historical Society*, 6th Ser.: 10 (2000), 45–63.

——'A murder in the Gold Coast: Law and politics in the 1940s', *JAH*, 30 (1989), 445–61.

——*Nkrumah and the Chiefs: The Politics of Chieftaincy in Ghana, 1951–1960* (Oxford: James Currey, 2000).

Ravndal, Ellen Jenny, 'Exit Britain: British withdrawal from the Palestine Mandate in the early Cold War, 1947–1948', *DS*, 21:3 (2010), 416–33.

Recham, Belkacem, *Les Musulmans algériens dans l'armée française (1919–1945)* (Paris, L'Harmattan, 1996).

Réau, Elisabeth du, 'Les Balkans dans la stratégie méditerranéenne de la France, avril 1939–mai 1940', *Balkan Studies*, 29:1 (1988), 71–88.

Reiss, Matthias, and Matt Perry, eds, *Unemployment and Protest: New Perspectives on Two Centuries of Contention* (Oxford University Press, 2011).

Rettig, Tobias, 'French military policies in the aftermath of the Yên Bay Mutiny, 1930: Old Security Dilemmas Return to the Surface', *South East Asia Research*, 10:3 (2002), 309–31.

Reuveny, Jacob, 'The financial liquidation of the Palestine Mandate', *MES*, 27:1 (1991), 112–30.

Rice, Louisa, 'Cowboys and Communists: Cultural diplomacy, decolonization and the Cold War in French West Africa', *Journal of Colonialism and Colonial History*, 11:3 (2010).

Riera, Monica, and Gavin Schaffer, eds, *The Lasting War: Society and Identity in Britain, France and Germany after 1945* (Basingstoke: Palgrave-Macmillan, 2008).

Rioux, Jean-Pierre, *The Fourth Republic, 1944–1958*, English translation (Cambridge University Press, 1987).

—— *La Guerre d'Algérie et les Français* (Paris: Fayard, 1990).

Robertson, Geoffrey, *Crimes Against Humanity: The Search for Global Justice*, new edition (London: Penguin, 2006).

Robinson, R. E., 'The moral disarmament of African Empire, 1919–1947', *JICH*, 7:1 (1979), 86–104.

Rogan, Eugene L., and Avi Schlaim, eds, *The War for Palestine: Rewriting the History of 1948* (Cambridge University Press, 2001).

Roland, Denis, 'Jacques Soustelle, de l'ethnologie à la politique', *Guerres Mondiales et Conflits Contemporains*, 180 (October 1995), 171–85.

Rooth, Tim, 'Britain's other dollar problem: Economic relations with Canada, 1945–50', *JICH*, 27:1 (1999), 81–108.

Rose, Sonya O., *Which People's War? National Identity and Citizenship in Wartime Britain, 1939–1945* (Oxford University Press, 2003).

Ross, Kristen, *Fast Cars, Clean Bodies: Decolonization and the Reordering of French Culture* (Boston: MIT Press, 1996).

Rossi, Mario, 'United States military authorities and Free France', *Journal of Military History*, 61:1 (1997), 49–64.

Rowe, Michael, *From Reich to State: The Rhineland in the Revolutionary Age, 1780–1830* (Cambridge University Press, 2003).

—— 'Sex, "race" and riot in Liverpool, 1919', *Immigrants and Minorities*, 19:2 (2000), 53–70.

Roy, K., ed., *War and Society in Colonial India*, 2nd edn (New Delhi: Oxford University Press, 2006).

Ruane, Kevin, 'SEATO, MEDO, and the Baghdad Pact: Anthony Eden, British foreign policy and the collective defence of Southeast Asia and the Middle East, 1952–1955', *DS*, 16:1 (2005), 169–99.

Rudelle, Odile, *Mai 1958, de Gaulle et la République* (Paris: Plon, 1988).

Ruscio, Alain, *La Question coloniale dans L'Humanité (1904–2004)* (Paris: La Dispute, 2005).

Sandell, Marie 'Regional versus international: Women's activism and organisational spaces in the inter-war period', *IHR*, 33:4 (2011), 607–25.

Sanderson, Claire, *L'Impossible Alliance? France, Grande-Bretagne et défense de l'Europe, 1945–1958* (Paris: Publications de la Sorbonne, 2003).

Sarkar, Sumit, 'Popular movements and national leadership, 1945–47', *Economic and Political Weekly*, 17:14/16, (1982), 677–89.

Sayer, Derek, 'British reaction to the Amritsar massacre, 1919–1920', *PP*, 131 (1991), 130–64.

Scheck, Raffael, *Hitler's African Victims: The German Army Massacres of Black French Soldiers in 1940* (Cambridge University Press, 2006).

Schenk, Catherine R., *Britain and the Sterling Area: From Devaluation to Convertibility in the 1950s* (London: Routledge, 1994).

—— *The Decline of Sterling: Managing the Retreat of an International Currency, 1945–1992* (Cambridge University Press, 2010).

Schmidt, Elizabeth, *Cold War and Decolonization in Guinea, 1946–1958* (Athens, OH: Ohio University Press, 2007).

—— 'Cold War in Guinea: The Rassemblement Démocratique Africain and the struggle over Communism, 1950–1958', *JAH*, 48:1 (2007), 95–121.

—— *Mobilizing the Masses: Gender, Ethnicity, and Class in the Nationalist Movement in Guinea, 1939–1958* (Portsmouth, NH: Heinemann, 2005).

—— 'Top down or bottom up? Nationalist mobilization reconsidered, with special reference to Guinea', *AHR* 110 (October, 2005), 975–1014.

Schmidt, Heike, *Colonialism and Violence in Zimbabwe: A History of Suffering* (Oxford: James Currey, 2013).

Scott, James C., *The Moral Economy of the Peasant: Rebellion and Subsistence in Southeast Asia* (New Haven, CT: Yale University Press, 1976).

Scriven, Michael, and Peter Wagstaff, eds, *War and Society in Twentieth-Century France* (Oxford: Berg, 1992).

Searing, James F., 'Conversion to Islam: Military recruitment and generational conflict in a Sereer-Safèn village (Bandia), 1920–38', *JAH*, 44:1 (2003), 73–94.

Sebe, Berny, 'In the shadow of the Algerian War: The United States and the Common Organisation of Saharan Regions/Organisation commune des régions sahariennes (OCRS), 1957–62', *JICH*, 38:2 (2010), 303–22.

Seeley, Janet, 'Social welfare in a Kenyan town: Policy and practice, 1902–1985', *African Affairs*, 86:345 (1987), 541–66.

Segalla, Spencer D., 'Georges Hardy and educational ethnology in French Morocco, 1920–26', *French Colonial History*, 4 (2003), 171–90.

Seidman, Michael, 'The pre-May 1968 sexual revolution', *Contemporary French Civilization*, 25:1 (2001), 25–41.

Sessions, Jennifer E., *By Sword and Plow: France and the Conquest of Algeria* (Ithaca, NY: Cornell University Press, 2011).

Shao, Kuo-kang, 'Zhou Enlai's diplomacy and the neutralization of Indochina, 1954–55', *China Quarterly*, 107 (1986), 483–504.

Sharkey, Heather J., *Living with Colonialism: Nationalism and Culture in Anglo-Egyptian Sudan* (Berkeley, CA: University of California Press, 2003).

Shepard, Todd, '"History Is past politics"? Archives, "tainted evidence", and the return of the state', *AHR*, 115:2 (2010), 474–83.

Shepard, Todd, *The Invention of Decolonization: The Algerian War and the Remaking of France* (Ithaca, NY: Cornell University Press, 2006).

——'"Something notably erotic": Politics, "Arab men", and sexual revolution in postdecolonization France, 1962–1974', *JMH*, 84:1 (2012), 80–115.

Sherwood, Robert E., ed., *The White House Papers of Harry L. Hopkins: January 1942– July 1945* (London: Eyre & Spottiswoode, 1949).

Shields, Sarah D., *Fezzes in the River: Identity Politics and European Diplomacy in the Middle East on the Eve of World War II* (Oxford University Press, 2011).

Shipway, Martin, *The Road to War: France and Vietnam, 1944–1947* (Oxford: Berghahn, 1996).

Shlaim, Avi, *The Iron Wall: Israel and the Arab World* (London: Penguin, 2000).

Shutt, Allison K., 'The natives are getting out of hand': Legislating manners, insolence and contemptuous behaviour in Southern Rhodesia, c.1910–1963', *Journal of Southern African Studies*, 33:3 (2007), 653–72.

Sibeud, Emmanuelle, *Une science impériale pour l'Afrique? La Construction des savoirs africanistes en France 1878–1930* (Paris: EHESS, 2002).

Silverman, Max, *Deconstructing the Nation: Immigration, Racism and Citizenship in Modern France* (London: Routledge, 1992).

Silvestri, Michael, '"An Irishman is specially suited to be a policeman": Sir Charles Tegart and revolutionary terrorism in Bengal', *History Ireland*, 8:4 (2000), 40–4.

Simpson, Brad, 'Indonesia's "accelerated modernization" and the global discourse of development, 1960–1975', *DH*, 33:3 (2009), 467–86.

——'The United States and the curious history of self-determination', *DH*, 36:4 (2012), 675–94.

Sinanoglou, Penny, 'British plans for the partition of Palestine, 1929–1938', *HJ*, 52:1 (2009), 131–52.

Sinclair, Georgina, *At the End of the Line: Colonial Policing and the Imperial Endgame, 1945–80* (Manchester University Press, 2006).

Sinha, Mrinalini, 'Britishness, clubbability, and the colonial public sphere: The genealogy of an imperial institution in colonial India', *Journal of British Studies*, 40:4 (2001), 489–521.

Sinha, Subir, 'Lineages of the developmentalist state: Transnationality and village India, 1900–1965', *Comparative Studies in Society and History*, 50:1 (2008), 57–90.

Sirinelli, Jean-François, 'Guerre d'Algérie, guerre des pétitions? Quelques jalons', *Revue Historique*, 291:1 (1988), 73–100.

Skinner, Kate, 'Reading, writing and rallies: The politics of "freedom" in southern British Togoland, 1953–1956', *JAH*, 48:1 (2007), 123–47.

Skinner, Robert, *The Foundations of Anti-Apartheid: Liberal Humanitarians and Transnational Activists in Britain and the United States, c.1919–64* (Basingstoke: Palgrave-Macmillan, 2010).

Smith, Paul, 'Political parties, parliament and women's suffrage in France, 1919–1939', *FH*, 11:3 (1997), 338–58.

Smith, Ralph B., 'The Japanese period in Indochina and the *coup* of 9 March 1945', *JSEAS*, 9:2 (1978), 268–301.

Smith, Simon C., *British Relations with the Malay Rulers from Decentralization to Malayan Independence, 1930–1957* (Singapore: Oxford University Press, 1995).

——'General Templer and counter-insurgency in Malaya: Hearts and minds, intelligence and propaganda', *INS*, 16:1 (2001), 60–78.

Smith, Timothy O., *Britain and the Origins of the Vietnam War: UK Policy in Indochina, 1943–1950* (Basingstoke: Palgrave-Macmillan, 2007).

——'Major General Sir Douglas Gracey: Peacekeeper or peace enforcer?' *DS*, 21:2 (2010), 226–39.

Smith, Tony, 'The French colonial consensus and people's war, 1946–58', *Journal of Contemporary History*, 9 (1974): 217–47.

Smyth, Rosaleen, 'Britain's African colonies and British propaganda during the Second World War', *JICH*, 14:1 (1985), 65–82.

Soloman, Robert L., 'Saya San and the Burmese rebellion', *MAS* 3:3 (1969), 209–23.

Sorum, Paul Clay, *Intellectuals and Decolonization in France* (Chapel Hill, NC: University of North Carolina Press, 1977).

Soustelle, Jacques, 'L'État actuel des travaux concernant l'histoire ancienne du Mexique', *Revue Historique*, 213:1 (1955), 39–46.

Speich, Daniel, 'The Kenyan style of "African socialism": Developmental knowledge claims and the explanatory limits of the Cold War', *DH*, 33:3 (2009), 449–66.

Spruyt, Hendrik, *Ending Empire: Contested Sovereignty and Territorial Partition* (Ithaca, NY: Cornell University Press, 2005).

Steiner, Zara, *The Lights that Failed: European International History, 1919–1933* (Oxford University Press, 2005).

——'On writing international history: Chaps, maps, and much more', *International Affairs*, 73 (1997), 531–46.

—— *The Triumph of the Dark: European International History, 1933–1939* (Oxford University Press, 2011), 803–4.

Steyn, Phia, 'Oil exploration in colonial Nigeria, c.1903–58', *JICH*, 37:2 (2009), 249–74.

Stilwell, Sean, 'Constructing colonial power: Tradition, legitimacy and government in Kano, 1903–63', *JICH*, 39:2 (2011), 195–225.

Stockwell, A. J., '"A widespread and long-concocted plot to overthrow government in Malaya"? The origins of the Malayan Emergency', *JICH*, 21:3 (1993), 66–88.

——'Colonial planning during World War Two: The case of Malaya', *JICH*, 2:3 (1974), 333–51.

——'The formation and first years of the United Malays National Organization (UMNO)', *MAS*, 11:4 (1977), 481–513.

——'Malaysia: The making of a neo-colony?' *JICH*, 26:2 (1998), 138–56.

Stockwell, Sarah E., ed., *The British Empire: Themes and Perspectives* (Oxford: Black-well, 2008).

——'Instilling the "sterling tradition": Decolonization and the creation of a central bank in Ghana', *JICH*, 26:2 (1998), 100–19.

Stoler, Ann Laura, 'Colonial Aphasia: Race and Disabled Histories in France', *Public Culture*, 23:1 (2010), 121–56.

——'Sexual affronts and racial frontiers: European identities and the cultural politics of exclusion in colonial Southeast Asia', *Comparative Studies in Society and History*, 34:3 (1992), 514–51.

——Carole McGranahan, and Peter C. Perdue, eds, *Imperial Formations* (Santa Fe, NM: School for Advanced Research Press 2007).

Stora, Benjamin, *La Gangrène et l'oubli: La Mémoire de la guerre d'Algérie* (Paris: La Découverte, 1991).

——'Le Massacre du 20 août 1955: Récit historique, bilan historiographique', *Historical Reflections*, 36:2 (2010), 97–107.

Stovall, Tyler, 'Aimé Césaire and the making of black Paris', *FPCS*, 27:3 (2009), 44–6.

——'The color line behind the lines: Racial violence in France during the First World War', *AHR*, 103:3 (1998), 739–69.

Stuart, Mark, 'A Party in three pieces: The Conservative split over Rhodesian oil sanctions, 1965', *Contemporary British History*, 16:1 (2002), 51–88.

Surkis, Judith, 'Ethics and violence: Simone de Beauvoir, Djamila Boupacha, and the Algerian War', *FPCS*, 28:2 (2010), 38–55.

Summers, Anne, and R. W. Johnson, 'World War I conscription and social change in Guinea', *JAH*, 19:1 (1978), 25–38.

Sutherland, Nina, 'Trois continents, une guerre, un empire: Francophone Narratives of War and Occupation in the French Empire', *French Cultural Studies*, 22:3 (2011), 187–96.

Swedenburg, Ted, *Memories of Revolt: The 1936–1939 Rebellion and the Palestinian National Past* (Fayetteville: University of Arkansas Press, 2003).

Szejnmann, Claus-Christian W., *Rethinking History, Dictatorship and War: New Approaches and Interpretations* (London: Continuum, 2009).

Tai, Hue-Tam Ho, *Radicalism and the Origins of the Vietnamese Revolution* (Cambridge, MA: Harvard University Press, 1992).

Talbot, Ian, 'Punjabi refugees' rehabilitation and the Indian state: Discourses, denials and dissonances', *MAS*, 45:1 (2011), 109–30.

——ed., *Deadly Embrace: Religion, Politics and Violence in India and Pakistan, 1947–2002* (Oxford University Press, 2007).

Tanenbaum, Jan Karl, *General Maurice Sarrail 1856–1929: The French Army and Left-Wing Politics* (Chapel Hill, NC: University of North Carolina Press, 1974).

Tarling, Nicholas, 'The United Kingdom and the origins of the Colombo Plan', *Commonwealth & Comparative Studies* 24:1 (1986), 3–34.

Taylor, K. W., and J. K. Whitmore, eds, *Essays into Vietnamese Pasts* (Ithaca, NY: Cornell University Press, 1995).

Terretta, Meredith, '"We had been fooled into thinking that the UN watches over the entire world": Human rights, UN Trust Territories, and Africa's decolonization', *Human Rights Quarterly*, 34:2 (2012), 329–60.

Tertrais, Hugues, 'L'Économie indochinoise dans la guerre (1945–1954)', *Outre-Mers: Revue d'histoire*, 88:330 (2001), 113–29.

—— *La Piastre et le fusil: Le Coût de la guerre d'Indochine 1945–1954* (Paris: CHEF, 2002).

Thénault, Sylvie, *Violence ordinaire dans l'Algérie coloniale: Camps, internements, assignations à résidence* (Paris: Odile Jacob, 2011).

Thomas, Martin, 'After Mers el-Kébir: The armed neutrality of the Vichy French Navy, 1940–1943', *EHR*, 112:447 (1997), 643–70.

—— 'Anglo-French imperial relations in the Arab world: Intelligence liaison and nationalist disorder', *DS*, 17:1, (2006), 1–28.

—— 'The colonial policies of the Mouvement Républicain Populaire, 1944–1954: From reform to reaction', *EHR*, 118:476 (2003), 380–411.

—— 'Colonial violence in Algeria and the distorted logic of state retribution: The Sétif uprising of 1945', *Journal of Military History* 75:1 (2011), 523–56.

—— 'Defending a lost cause? France and the United States' vision of imperial rule in French North Africa, 1946–1956', *DH*, 26:2 (2002), 215–47.

—— 'The discarded leader: General Henri Giraud and the foundation of the French Committee of National Liberation', *FH*, 10:1 (1996), 86–111.

—— 'Economic conditions and the limits to mobilisation in the French Empire, 1936–39', *HJ*, 48:2 (2005), 471–98.

—— 'France accused: French North Africa before the United Nations, 1952–1962', *Contemporary European History*, 10:1 (2001), 91–121.

—— 'Free France, the British Government and the future of French Indo-China, 1940–45', *JSEAS*, 28:1 (1997), 137–60.

—— *The French Colonial Mind, i: Mental Maps of Empire and Colonial Encounters*, 2 vols (Lincoln, NE: University of Nebraska Press, 2012).

—— *The French Colonial Mind, ii: Violence, Military Encounters, and Colonialism* (Lincoln, NE.: University of Nebraska Press, 2012).

—— *The French Empire at War, 1940–45* (Manchester University Press, 1998).

—— *The French North African Crisis: Colonial Breakdown and Anglo-French Relations, 1945–1962* (Basingstoke: Macmillan, 2000).

—— 'Fighting "Communist banditry" in French Vietnam: The rhetoric of repression after the Yen Bay uprising, 1930–32', *FHS*, 34:3 (2011), 611–48.

—— 'Policing Algeria's borders, 1956–1960: Arms supplies, frontier defences and the Sakiet affair', *War & Society*, 13:1 (1995), 81–99.

—— 'Resource war, civil war, rights war: Factoring empire into French North Africa's Second World War', *War in History*, 18:2 (2011), 225–48.

Thompson, Andrew S., ed., *OHBE Companion Volume: Britain's Experience of Empire in the Twentieth Century*, (Oxford University Press, 2011).

—— ed., *Writing Imperial Histories* (Manchester University Press, 2013).

Thompson, Elizabeth, *Colonial Citizens: Republican Rights, Paternal Privilege, and Gender in French Syria and Lebanon* (New York: Columbia University Press, 2000).

Thompson, Virginia, and Richard Adloff, *The Malagasy Republic: Madagascar Today* (Stanford University Press, 1965).

Thornhill, Michael, 'Britain, the United States and the rise of an Egyptian leader: The politics and diplomacy of Nasser's consolidation of power, 1952–4', *EHR*, 119:483 (2004), 892–921.

——'Informal Empire, independent Egypt and the accession of King Farouk', *JICH*, 38:2 (2010), 279–302.

Throup, David W., *Economic and Social Origins of Mau Mau, 1945–1953* (Oxford: James Currey, 1987).

Tibenderana, Peter K., 'The irony of indirect rule in the Sokoto Emirate, Nigeria, 1903–1944', *African Studies Review*, 31:1 (1988), 67–92.

Tilley, Helen, and Robert J. Gordon, eds, *Ordering Africa: Anthropology, European Imperialism, and the Politics of Knowledge* (Manchester University Press, 2007).

Tomlinson, Jim, 'The decline of the Empire and the economic decline of Britain', *Twentieth Century British History*, 14:3 (2003), 201–21.

Tønnesson, Stein, *Vietnam 1946: How the War Began* (Berkeley, CA: University of California Press, 2010).

——*The Vietnamese Revolution of 1945: Roosevelt, Ho Chi Minh, an de Gaulle in a World at War* (Oslo: International Peace Research Institute/Sage, 1991).

Townshend, Charles, 'The defence of Palestine: Insurrection and public security, 1936–1939', *EHR*, 103 (1988), 919–49.

Tsokhas, Kosmas, 'Dedominionization: The Anglo-Australian experience, 1939–1945', *HJ*, 37:4 (1994), 861–83.

Turpin, Frédéric, 'Cao Bang, autumne 1950: Autoposie d'un désastre', *Revue Historique des Armées*, 3 (2000), 25–34.

——'Le Mouvement républicain populaire et l'avenir de l'Algérie (1947–1962)', *Revue d'Histoire Diplomatique*, 113 (1999): 171–203.

——'Le Mouvement républicain populaire et la guerre d'Indochine (1944–1954)', *Revue d'Histoire Diplomatique*, 110 (1996): 157–90.

Tyre, Stephen, 'From *Algerie française* to *France musulmane*: Jacques Soustelle and the myths and realities of "integration", 1955–1962', *FH*, 20:3 (2006), 276–96.

Uche, Chibuike, 'Oil, British interests and the Nigerian civil war', *JAH*, 49:1 (2008), 111–35.

Ullmann, Bernard, *Jacques Soustelle: Le Mal Aimé* (Paris: Plon, 1995).

Ulloa, Marie-Pierre, *Francis Jeanson: A Dissident Intellectual from the French Resistance to the Algerian War* (Stanford University Press, 2007).

Vaillant, Derek W., 'La Police de l'air: Amateur radio and the politics of aural surveillance in France, 1921–1940', *FPCS*, 28:1 (2010), 1–24.

Vaïsse, Maurice, ed., *L'Armée française dans la guerre d'Indochine* (Bruxelles, Éditions Complexe, 2000).

——ed., *La France et l'opération de Suez de 1956* (Paris: ADDIM, 1997).

——and Pierre Mélandri and Frédéric Bozo, eds, *La France et l'OTAN 1949–1996* (Vincennes: CEHD, 1996).

Valette, Jacques, *La Guerre d'Algérie des Messalistes, 1954–1962* (Paris: L'Harmattan, 2001).

VanDeMark, Brian, *Into the Quagmire: Lyndon Johnson and the Escalation of the Vietnam War* (Oxford University Press, 1991).

Van Goethem, Geert, 'Labor's second front: The foreign policy of the American and British trade union movements during the Second World War', *DH*, 34:4 (2010), 663–80.

Vann, Michael G., 'Of pirates, postcards, and public beheadings: The pedagogic execution in French colonial Indochina', *Historical Reflections*, 36:2 (2010), 39–58.

Varnava, Andrekos, 'Reinterpreting Macmillan's Cyprus policy, 1957–1960' *Cyprus Review*, 22:1 (2010), 79–106.

Vaughan, Megan, 'Suicide in late colonial Africa: The evidence of inquests from Nyasaland', *AHR*, 115:2 (2010), 385–404.

Vaughan, Olufemi, 'Chieftaincy politics and communal identity in western Nigeria, 1893–1951', *JAH*, 44:2 (2003), 285–91.

Vince, Natalya, 'To be a *moudjahida* in independent Algeria: Itineraries and memories of women veterans of the Algerian War', PhD thesis, University of London, 2009.

——'Transgressing boundaries: Gender, race, religion, and "*Françaises musulmanes*" during the Algerian War of Independence', *FHS*, 33:3 (2010), 445–74.

Vinen, Richard, *Bourgeois Politics in France, 1945–1951* (Cambridge University Press, 1995).

Virgili, Patrice, *Shorn Women: Gender and Punishment in Liberation France* (Oxford: Berg, 2002).

Vorapheth, Kham, *Commerce et colonisation en Indochine 1860–1945* (Paris: Les Indes Savantes, 2004).

Vu, Tuong, and Wasana Wongsurawat, eds, *Dynamics of the Cold War in Asia: Ideology, Identity, and Culture* (New York: Palgrave-Macmillan, 2009).

Wall, Irwin M., *French Communism in the Era of Stalin* Westport, (CT: Greenwood Press, 1984).

——*The United States and the Making of Postwar France, 1945–1954* (Cambridge University Press, 1991).

Waller, Richard, '"Clean" and "dirty": Cattle disease and control policy in colonial Kenya', *JAH*, 45:1 (2004), 45–80.

Walraven, Klaas van, 'Decolonization by referendum: The anomaly of Niger and the fall of Sawaba, 1958–1959', *JAH*, 50:2 (2009), 269–92.

Walton, Calder, 'British intelligence and the Mandate of Palestine: Threats to British national security immediately after the Second World War', *INS*, 23:4 (2008), 435–62.

Ward, Stuart, 'Echoes of Empire', review of Wendy Webster, *Englishness and Empire, 1939–1965* (Oxford University Press, 2005), in *History Workshop Journal*, 61 (2006), 264–78.

——ed., *British Culture and the End of Empire* (Manchester University Press, 2001).

Watenpaugh, Keith, *Being Modern in the Middle East: Revolution, Nationalism, Colonialism, and the Arab Middle Class* (Princeton University Press, 2006).

Watts, Carl, 'Killing kith and kin: The viability of British military intervention in Rhodesia, 1964–5', *Twentieth Century British History* 16 (2005), 382–415.

Webster, Wendy, *Englishness and Empire, 1939–1965* (Oxford University Press, 2005).

——*Imagining Home: Gender, Race And National Identity, 1945–1964* (London: Routledge, 1998).

Weisbrode, Kenneth, 'International administration between the Wars: A reappraisal', *DS*, 20:1 (2009), 30–49.

Weitz, Eric D., 'From the Vienna to the Paris system: International politics and the entangled histories of human rights, forced deportations, and civilizing missions', *AHR*, 113:5 (2008), 1313–43.

Wertheim, Stephen, 'The League that wasn't: American designs for a legalist-sanctionist League of Nations and the intellectual origins of international organization, 1914–1920', *DH*, 35:5 (2011), 797–836.

Westad, Odd Arne, *The Global Cold War: Third World Interventions and the Making of Our Times* (Cambridge University Press, 2005).

Whipple, Amy, 'Revisiting the "rivers of blood" controversy: Letters to Enoch Powell', *Journal of British Studies*, 48:3 (2009), 717–35.

White, Luise, 'Separating the men from the boys: Constructions of gender, sexuality, and terrorism in central Kenya, 1939–1959', *International Journal of African Historical Studies*, 23:1 (1990), 1–25.

White, Nicholas J., 'Reconstructing Europe through rejuvenating empire: The British, French, and Dutch experiences compared', *PP* 210:supplement 6 (2011), 211–36.

White, Owen, and J. P. Daughton, eds, *In God's Empire: French Missionaries and the Modern World* (New York: Oxford University Press, 2012).

Wilder, Gary, *The French Imperial Nation-State: Negritude and Colonial Humanism between the Two World Wars* (University of Chicago Press, 2005).

Williams, Philip M., *Crisis and Compromise: Politics in the Fourth Republic* (London: Longman, 1964).

Williams, Susan, *Colour Bar: The Triumph of Seretse Khama and His Nation* (London: Allen Lane, 2006).

Wilson, Mary C., 'King Abdullah and Palestine', *Bulletin of the British Society for MES*, 14:1 (1987), 37–41.

——*King Abdullah, Britain and the Making of Jordan* (Cambridge University Press, 1987).

Wilson, Harold, *The Labour Government, 1964–1970: A Personal Record* (London: Weidenfeld & Nicolson, 1971).

Windel, Aaron, 'British colonial education in Africa: Policy and practice in the era of trusteeship', *History Compass*, 7:1 (2009), 1–21.

Wingate Pike, David, 'Between the Junes: The French Communists from the collapse of France to the invasion of Russia', *Journal of Contemporary History*, 28:3 (1993), 465–85.

Wolpert, Stanley, *Shameful Flight: The Last Years of the British Empire in India* (New York: Oxford University Press, 2006).

Wolton, Suke, *Lord Hailey, the Colonial Office and the Politics of Race and Empire in the Second World War* (Basingstoke: Palgrave-Macmillan, 2000).

Wylie, Neville, *Barbed Wire Diplomacy: Britain, Germany, the Politcs of Prisoners of War, 1939–1945* (Oxford University Press, 2010).

Yacono, Xavier, 'Les Pertes algériennes de 1954 à 1962', *Revue de l'Occident Musulman et de la Méditerranée*, 34 (1983), 119–34.

Youé, Christopher, 'Black squatters on white farms: Segregation and agrarian change in Kenya, South Africa and Rhodesia, 1902–1963', *IHR*, 24:3 (2002), 558–602.

Young, John W., *The Labour Governments, 1964–1970*, ii: *International Policy* (Manchester University Press, 2003).

——'The Wilson government and the debate over arms sales to South Africa', *Contemporary British History*, 12:3 (1998), 62–86.

Zamindar, Vazira Fazila-Yacoobali, *The Long Partition and the Making of Modern South Asia: Refugees, Boundaries, Histories* (New Delhi: Penguin, 2008).

Zamir, Meir, 'The "missing dimension": Britain's secret war against France in Syria and Lebanon, 1942–45—Part II', *MES*, 46:6 (2010), 791–899.

Zervoudakis, Alexander, '*Nihil mirare, nihil contemptare, Omnia intelligere*: Franco-Vietnamese intelligence in Indochina, 1950–1954', *INS* 13:1 (1998), 195–229.

Zhai, Qiang, 'Transplanting the Chinese model: Chinese military advisers and the first Vietnam War, 1950–1954', *Journal of Military History*, 57:4 (1993), 689–715.

Zinoman, Peter, *The Colonial Bastille: A History of Imprisonment in Vietnam, 1862–1940* (Berkeley, CA: University of California Press, 2001).

Zoubir, Yahia, 'US and Soviet policies towards France's struggle with anticolonial nationalism in North Africa', *Canadian Journal of History*, 30:4 (1995), 439–66.

——'The United States, the Soviet Union and decolonization of the Maghreb, 1945–62', *MES*, 31:1 (1995), 58–84.

Zweiniger-Barqielowska, Ina, *Austerity in Britain: Rationing, Controls, and Consumption, 1939–1955* (Oxford University Press, 2002).

Picture Acknowledgements

© British cartoon archive/Mirrorpix: **13**; © Getty Images: **1, 2, 5, 8, 9, 17, 18**; © Imperial War Museums (HU 89852): **3**; © Martin Thomas: **4, 14, 15, 16, 19**; © Middle East Centre Archive, St Antony's College, Oxford. GB165-0504 Palestine Pamphlets Collection 3/15 Palestine Partition Commission Report: **6**; © Musee des Troupes de marine/French National Archives: **11**; © Pictorial Press Ltd/Alamy: **10**; © Popperfoto/Getty Images: **7**

The publisher and author apologize for any errors or omissions in the above list. If contacted they will be pleased to rectify these at the earliest opportunity.

Index